Business Networks in Clusters and Industrial Districts

During the 1980s the Marshallian concept of industrial district (ID) became widely popular due to the resurgence of interest in the reasons that make the agglomeration of specialized industries a territorial phenomenon worth being analyzed. The analysis of clusters and IDs has often been limited, considering only the local dimension of the created business networks. The external links of these systems have been systematically under-evaluated.

This book offers a deep insight into the evolution of these systems and the internal-external mechanism of knowledge circulation and learning. This means that the access to external knowledge (information or R&D cooperative research) or to productive networks (global supply chains) is studied in order to describe how external knowledge is absorbed and how local clusters or districts become global systems. It provides a unified approach: showing that existing capabilities expand when locally embedded knowledge is combined with accessible external knowledge. In this view, external knowledge linkages reduce the danger of cognitive 'lock-in' and 'over-embeddedness', which may become important obstacles to local learning and innovation when technological trajectories and global economic conditions change.

Bringing together a selection of essays from international experts, this book will be of interest to researchers and students of management and regional studies, industrial districts, international business and to policy makers.

Fiorenza Belussi is Associate Professor of Strategic Management and Organization at the University of Padua, Italy.

Alessia Sammarra is Assistant Professor of Strategic Management and Organization at the Faculty of Economics, University of L'Aquila, Italy.

Regions and Cities

Series editors: Ron Martin, University of Cambridge, UK; Gernot Grabher, University of Bonn, Germany; Maryann Feldman, University of Georgia, USA; Gillian Bristow, University of Cardiff, UK.

Regions and Cities is an international, interdisciplinary series that provides authoritative analyses of the new significance of regions and cities for economic, social and cultural development, and public policy experimentation. The series seeks to combine theoretical and empirical insights with constructive policy debate and critically engages with formative processes and policies in regional and urban studies.

Business Networks in Clusters and Industrial Districts

The governance of the global value chain

Edited by Fiorenza Belussi and Alessia Sammarra

Routledge
Taylor & Francis Group

LONDON AND NEW YORK

First published 2010
by Routledge
2 Park Square, Milton Park, Abingdon, Oxon, OX14 4RN

Simultaneously published in the USA and Canada
by Routledge
270 Madison Avenue, New York, NY 10016

Routledge is an imprint of the Taylor & Francis Group, an informa business

Typeset in Times New Roman by
Pindar NZ, Auckland, New Zealand
Printed and bound in Great Britain by
MPG Books Group, UK

British Library Cataloguing in Publication Data
A catalogue record for this book is available from the British Library

Library of Congress Cataloging in Publication Data
Business networks in clusters and industrial districts: the governance of
the global value chain/edited by Fiorenza Belussi and Alessia Sammarra.
   p. cm.
 Includes bibliographical references and index.
 1. Business networks. 2. Industrial clusters. 3. Industrial districts. 4.
International organization. I. Belussi, Fiorenza. II. Sammarra, Alessia.
 HD69.S8B8673 2009
 658'.046—dc22   2008054418

ISBN10: 0-415-45784-X (hbk)
ISBN10: 0-203-87555-9 (ebk)

ISBN13: 978-0-415-45784-2 (hbk)
ISBN13: 978-0-203-87555-1 (ebk)

Contents

Figures and tables

Figures

Tables

Contributors

Tine Aage has submitted her PhD dissertation at DRUID Academy, Copenhagen Business School, Copenhagen, Denmark. She is a consultant at the regional innovation centre, Sjaelland, Denmark.

Bjørn T. Asheim is Full Professor in Economic Geography at the Department of Social and Economic Geography, University of Lund, Sweden, and co-founder of the new Centre of Excellence CIRCLE (Centre for Innovation, Research and Competence in the Learning Economy), P.O. Box 117, SE-221 00 Lund, Sweden.

Lorenzo Bacci is Senior Researcher at IRPET, in Florence, Istituto Regionale per la Programmazione Economica della Toscana, via Giuseppe La Farina, 27, 50132 Firenze, Italy.

Fiorenza Belussi, PhD SPRU, Sussex University, is Associate Professor in Economics and Management at the University of Padua, Via del Santo 33, 35123 Padua, Italy. She has been visiting at the Copenhagen Business School, Freiburg University, San Paolo University, and at the Boston University.

Najoua Boufaden is Research Assistant at ADIS, Université Paris Sud, Jean Monnet Faculty, Université Paris Sud XI. 54, Bd Desgranges. 92331 Sceaux Cedex, France.

Annalisa Caloffi is Research Fellow at the Department of Economics, University of Florence, via delle Pandette, 9, 50124 Firenze, Italy.

Cristina Chaminade is Associate Professor CIRCLE (Centre for Innovation, Research and Competence in the Learning Economy), University of Lund, P.O. Box 117, SE-221 00 Lund.

Lars Coenen is PhD in Social and Economic Geography at Lund University, is Assistant Professor at CIRCLE (Centre for Innovation Research and Competence in the Learning Economy), Lund University, P.O. Box 117, SE-221 00 Lund, Sweden.

Dirk Fornahl is Scientific Director of the BAW Institute for Regional Economic Research, Wilhelm-Herbst-Str. 5, 28359 Bremen, Germany.

Renato Garcia is Associate Professor in Industrial Economics at the Polytechnic School at University of São Paulo, Brazil Departamento de Engenharia de Produção Escola Politécnica da Universidade de São Paulo Av.Prof. Almeida Prado, travessa 2, n.128, Ed. Biênio, 2o. Andar 05508–900 São Paulo-SP-Brazil.

Sandrine Labory is Lecturer in Applied Economics at the University of Ferrara, Faculty of Economics, via Voltapaletto, 11, 44100 Ferrara, Italy.

Mauro Lombardi is Associate Professor of Political Economy at the University of Florence, Dipartimento di Scienze Economiche, via delle Pandette, 9, 50127 Firenze, Italy.

Sofiène Lourimi is Research Assistant at ADIS, Université Paris Sud, Jean Monnet Faculty, Université Paris Sud XI, 54, Bd Desgranges. 92331 Sceaux Cedex, France.

Simona Montagnana, PhD in Economics of Production and Development at the Faculty of Economics in Varese, University of Insubria, via Monte Generoso 71, 21100 Varese, Italy. She is a researcher at IReR (Istituto Regionale di Ricerca della Lombardia).

Jerker Moodysson is PhD in Social and Economic Geography at Lund University, is Assistant Professor at CIRCLE (Centre for Innovation Research and Competence in the Learning Economy), Lund University, P.O. Box 117, SE-221 00 Lund, Sweden.

Alessia Sammarra, PhD at the University of Rome, is Assistant Professor in Economics and Management at the University of L'Aquila, P.zza Del Santuario 19, 67040 Roio Poggio (AQ), Italy and collaborates with the University Luiss Guido Carli, Rome, Italy. She has been visiting at University of Illinois at Urbana-Champaign (US).

Gabriela Scur, PhD Industrial Engineering/Professor Assistant. Email: gabriela.sul@gmail.com.

Silvia Rita Sedita, PhD in Economics and Management of Small Firms and Local Systems at the University of Florence, Italy, is Research Assistant at the University of Padua, Via del Santo 33, 35123 Padua, Italy. She has been visiting at Copenhagen Business School and at the University of Tokyo.

André Torre is Full Professor in Economic Geography at INRA-AgroParisTech Joint Research Unit, Versailles-Grignon Research Centre, France.

Chung Anh Tran is a PhD student at the Universität Karlsruhe (KIT), Institute for Economic Policy Research (IWW), Postfach 69 80 D-76128 Karlsruhe, Germany.

Jan Vang is associate professor in globalization at the Copenhagen Institute of Technology, Aalborg University, Department of Business Studies, Fibigerstræde 4 DK 9220 Aalborg, Denmark.

Preface

*Fiorenza Belussi (Padua University) and
Alessia Sammarra (L'Aquila University)*

After several decades and despite an incredible number of books and articles, industrial districts and clusters (IDs&Cs) still capture the interest of scholars and policy makers. The reason for such enduring fascination is that when a wide consensus was finally reached on the importance of geographical proximity, agglomeration and local spillovers, IDs&Cs had already evolved into complex systems with mobile boundaries (Biggiero 1999; Belussi, Gottardi and Rullani 2003; Gertler and Wolfe 2006). This transformation undermines the traditional perspectives (Becattini 1987; Porter 1998), and forces us to critically rethink the reasons clusters and districts exist, extend, exhaust or expand (Maskell and Kebir 2006).

Our intent is to go back to the origin of the discussion, which started with Marshall, when he highlighted the reasons that make the agglomeration of specialized industries a territorial phenomenon worth analyzing. In the current literature, the analysis of spatial clustering has often resulted in an overproduction of concepts, where the cluster/district categories sometimes overlap, and are not mutually exclusive, or where typologies are poorly described.

For instance, in the Anglo-Saxon tradition, the terms industrial district (ID) and cluster have often been used interchangeably, while in the Italian context the Marshallian concept of ID has been utilized in a more spatially bound meaning (districts are limited areas of a high concentration of similar firms operating in the same sector), and as a new socio-economic unit of analysis, which looks at the economic benefits stemming from closed and cooperative social interactions between a population of firms and inhabitants (Becattini 1987). This book presents some interesting 'Italianate' cases of industrial districts (Markusen 1996), but also offers examples of weak territorialization and clustering that remain far from the 'pure' model of the industrial district.

While the Marshallian ID refers to the creation of a specific local system, which has a subjective identity, *ad hoc* created institutions, and an evolutionary pattern, a Porterian 'cluster' is much more indistinct: its identification depends strongly on the research assumptions. In fact, a Porterian 'cluster' does not have a minimum threshold of agglomeration.

To shift from the cluster concept to the district notion we need three necessary conditions: (1) agglomeration (density of similar, or interrelated, firms in a restricted area); (2) interaction with the local institutions and among the individual firms; and (3) social embeddedness (high levels of identity, trust and cooperation). The first condition may or may not be related to a specific cluster, depending on the functional or territorial definition of a cluster. The second condition is linked to the relationships with local formal institutions (R&D centres, universities, etc.). This second condition is often applied to the cluster approach. The third necessary condition is linked with the Marshallian ID approach: a communitarian view of the economic and social system under examination, where embeddedness and density define a unique and historically path-dependent territorial system (Belussi and Sedita 2009).

While the traditional literature firmly supported the importance of endogenous development processes (Becattini and Rullani 1996; Paniccia 2002), focusing on the internal structure and dynamics of IDs&Cs (Krugman 1995), the most recent contributions have begun to question this view, emphasizing the need to reconsider the role of external linkages (Gallaud and Torre 2005).

This book offers some fresh insights into the internal-external mechanism of knowledge circulation and learning 'at the boundary'. The territorial density of firms and actors offers a way of analyzing the mechanism of local interactions, and local knowledge circulation. By contrast, access to external knowledge is provided by establishing translocal business networks, and R&D cooperative research. Thus, IDs&Cs evolution is both related to the working of endogenous forces and to the localized absorption of external knowledge. Firms and IDs&Cs differ greatly in their absorption capability. This is why, in the course of our analysis, this volume offers an in-depth consideration of the network literature and international business studies (Cooke 2002; Asheim and Isaksen 2000; Maskell and Malmberg 1999; Håkansson and Snehota 1995; Guerrieri and Pietrobelli 2001). Therefore, we have tried both to explore the endogenous forces which create spatial agglomerations and the exogenous elements that are at work relocating activities (and firms): long-distance subcontracting chains, foreign direct investment (FDI), and R&D long-distance collaborations, giving rise to manufacturing outsourcing and knowledge offshoring (Doz, Olk and Smith Ring 2000; Pyndt and Pedersen 2005). This has a tremendous significance when we analyze the IDs&Cs relocation issue, and the entering of districts into different types of value chains (related to distribution) and inter-district collaborations (related to the type of activities: knowledge-intensive or labour-intensive) that are exchanged among the firms within the various local systems.

Two conceptual approaches have contributed to a step forward in this direction. The first is the global value chain approach (Gereffi and Korzeniewicz 1994), which has been fruitfully applied to the analysis of IDs&Cs' growth trajectories in both developing and developed countries (Bell and Albu 1999, Giuliani, *et al.* 2005a and 2005b; Sammarra and Belussi 2006; Schmitz 2004). This approach is aimed mainly at explaining the IDs&Cs development outcome depending on the positioning and control that local firms acquire in global value chains (Gereffi, *et al.* 2005).

The second approach is focused on the process of innovation and knowledge generation in IDs&Cs (Bathelt, *et al.* 2004; Boschma and ter Wal 2007; Breschi and

Lissoni 2001; Belussi, Sammarra and Sedita 2008; Biggiero and Sammarra 2008). The central idea in this stream of studies is that IDs&Cs can better expand and upgrade existing capabilities when locally embedded knowledge is combined with accessible external knowledge. In this view, external knowledge linkages reduce the danger of cognitive 'lock-in' and 'over-embeddedness', which may become important obstacles to local learning and innovation, especially when technological trajectories and global economic conditions change.

What is new in this book is to merge these approaches in order to provide a more comprehensive and articulated understanding of the transformations of IDs&Cs in permeable systems, which continuously redefine their boundaries. In order to do so, the contributions collected offer different and complementary perspectives on the ways district and cluster firms redefine their business networks in a global context through long-distance subcontracting chains, creation of FDI initiatives, and R&D long-distance collaborations.

The book builds on a conceptual framework that explores the reorganization of business networks in IDs&Cs along two dimensions. The two important flows under observation are: (1) the inflows/outflows of material resources and manufacturing activities; and (2) the inflows/outflows of knowledge.

With reference to the first dimension, the wealth of experiences presented in this book shows that increasing global competition has generally resulted in the massive outflow of production activities from Western IDs&Cs through relocation. This is clearly documented in the contributions devoted to the analysis of three Italian industrial districts: the Montebelluna sportswear district (Chapter 5), the Vibrata Valley clothing district (Chapter 6), and the Verona footwear district (Chapter 4). However, as argued in the conceptual framework illustrated in Chapter 1, the effect of relocation on the industrial district's long-term sustainability differs depending on the possibility of using the international fragmentation of the district value chain as a means of fostering different forms of upgrading. In order to discriminate between the possible outcomes, Chapter 1 proposes a taxonomy of relocation strategies. In this regard, the theoretical implication that emerges from the reading of this book is that, whereas the analysis of global value chains has a significant capacity for explaining the possibilities of upgrading for the enterprises within them, its transposition to the cluster level needs to be carefully calibrated. Any cluster may indeed comprise different global and local value chains, with complex direct and indirect effects on the development of the cluster which cannot be deterministically defined.

Outflows of manufacturing activities from Western IDs&Cs can potentially favour the formation of embryonic clusters in foreign countries. In this respect, Fiorenza Belussi (Chapter 9) and Simona Montagnana (Chapter 10) illustrate the experience of agglomeration of footwear firms in the region of Timisoara, in Romania.

Although the outflow of production activities characterize the evolution of most Western industrial districts, the study conducted by Fiorenza Belussi and Silvia Sedita in the Arzignano leather-tanning district (Chapter 7) accounts for an opposite trend. This chapter provides an interesting example of 'inverse relocation', which involves 'transferring cheap labour' into Western IDs&Cs as an alternative to the relocation of manufacturing activities to low-labour-cost countries though international subcontracting and/or FDI.

The second dimension explored in the book concerns the inflow and outflow of knowledge. Chapter 2 by Fiorenza Belussi and Silvia Sedita provides a conceptual elaboration on the learning processes that occurs in IDs&Cs based on the interaction between localized and distance learning. To capture the intertwined processes of knowledge generation and acquisition from local and external contexts the concept of 'learning at the boundaries' is introduced and discussed. The importance of this learning model is especially evident in high-tech industries, such as biotechnology, pharmaceuticals, telecommunication and aerospace, characterized by the complexity of the knowledge base required to foster innovation. The structure of these industries seems to conceal globalization and spatial agglomeration through a small worldwide pattern of connections: spatial agglomeration and interaction in local clusters is connected globally through the participation of local firms in distant inter-organizational networks thanks to various forms of formal and informal R&D collaborations. This dual geography emerges as a central theme also from the empirical studies collected in this book. In Chapter 16, concentrating on four regions in Germany, Fornahl and Tran explore the balance between local and external linkages and cooperative knowledge generation in the biotechnology industry. In Chapter 17, Moodysson, Coenen and Asheim investigate different forms of knowledge flows among actors in the Medicon Valley cluster by breaking down a number of innovation processes into concrete activities that are analyzed with regard to the spatial distribution of collaborators involved.

This book aims to make a special contribution in revealing the process of external knowledge acquisition in the context of IDs&Cs. Indeed, while the mechanisms that enact and foster local learning processes have received extensive attention in the traditional IDs&Cs literature, external learning mechanisms still deserve further theoretical and empirical investigation. In order to fulfil this aim, one of the efforts made in this book is to identify the different modes of external knowledge acquisition. In this regard, Bell and Albu (1999) argue that a relevant analytical dimension that can be proficiently used to classify different mechanisms of external knowledge acquisition concerns the distinction between active and passive mechanisms. Indeed, as the authors noted, 'knowledge may be acquired from external sources, either relatively passively as a by-product from various kinds of interactions with the outside world or from a range of more deliberate and active search efforts' (1999, p. 1724). The wealth of experience presented in this book confirms this view, providing quite differentiated examples of IDs&Cs where these different approaches prevail, leading to differentiated upgrading and evolutionary outcomes.

In addition to the active/passive perspective stressed by Bell and Albu (1999), this book identifies the degree of selectivity that characterizes the process of knowledge acquisition as another relevant analytical dimension. Recent empirical research from different industrial settings rejects the widely and tacitly accepted assumption that knowledge diffuses easily and evenly across cluster firms on the basis of social and geographical proximity (Boschma and ter Wal 2007; Biggiero and Sammarra 2008). In their study of the Barletta footwear cluster, Boschma and ter Wal (2007) found that only a limited number of cluster firms were connected non-locally. This example emphasizes a selective view of external knowledge acquisition where only some local firms – often the leading enterprises – play the role of 'knowledge gatekeepers', who search for and absorb non-local knowledge, and transmit it into the cluster (Aage and Belussi 2008). In addition to this selective model, Chapter 3 illustrates several ways in which IDs&Cs absorb external information and knowledge, which range from the centralistic models based on the pivotal role of few knowledge gatekeepers to the direct peer model, where many actors and firms process external information.

One of the central ideas that emerges from the conceptual and empirical contributions collected in the book is that internal and external knowledge acquisition are not independent. Although they represent two distinct phenomena, they nurture each other through a self-reinforcing process (Sammarra and Belussi 2006). This argument is clearly exemplified by the polar cases of two Italian industrial districts illustrated in the book: the Montebelluna sportsystem and the Vibrata Valley. The longitudinal study of the Vibrata Valley (Chapter 6) shows that external linkages cannot ensure long-term local competitiveness when the district lacks endogenous drivers of growth and development. The underdevelopment of the local knowledge base hinders the absorption and recombination of external knowledge. By contrast, the Montebelluna experience (Chapter 5) shows that district firms were able to capture external knowledge, understand its potential and exploit it because their own know-how and technical capabilities allowed for a constructive reception of such knowledge.

The permeability between the internal and external contexts affects the competitiveness and sustainability of IDs&Cs. The degree of permeability does not depend exclusively on the strategy enacted by local firms. Local institutions are indeed crucial actors that can favour the inflow of tangible resources (e.g. capital and investments) as well as the acquisition of external knowledge. In this regard, Najoua Boufaden, Sofiène Lourimi and André Torre (Chapter 15) illustrate the role played by institutions in the implementation and functioning of two clusters in the Greater Paris Region, one dedicated to biotechnologies, the other to optics-photonics.

The variety of IDs&Cs from different world regions presented in this book offers an important contribution to improving current understanding of the role played by local policies on cluster development within different business and institutional contexts. With reference to Bangalore's software innovation system and cluster, Chapter 18 by Jan Vang and Cristina Chaminade is concerned with examining the importance of local innovation systems for the transition of cluster firms in developing countries that strive to move from competing on costs to competing on innovations, and it discusses the related policy consequences. Special attention is paid to policies supporting the innovative potential of the indigenous small and medium-sized firms (SMEs) in this transition process. Moving from India to China, Chapter 14 by Annalisa Caloffi focuses on the different policy levers for cluster development and discusses their relevance within some industrial clusters in Guangdong province.

The structure of the book and a brief outline of each chapter is as follows.

Chapter 1 by Fiorenza Belussi and Alessia Sammarra discusses the effect of globalization on the evolution of IDs&Cs in the light of two conceptual approaches. The first refers to the global value chain perspective and focuses on relocation processes that incorporate district firms into global commodity chains. The second integrates the local development literature with the study of multinational enterprises in order to highlight the fundamental role that multinationals entering into IDs&Cs can play for local development outcomes and upgrading.

In Chapter 2, Fiorenza Belussi and Silvia Sedita propose a conceptual contribution on the learning processes at work in modern IDs&Cs. The authors discuss a new approach based on the interaction between localized and distance learning fostered through informal and formal channels of knowledge transfer. On the one hand, communities of practice characterize a spontaneous and non-deliberate form of social interaction, while, on the other hand, business networks configure themselves as effective mechanisms through which firms access complementary capabilities, both to reduce the production costs and to augment the innovative capacity.

Chapter 3 by Tine Aage offers a stimulating analysis on the way in which industrial districts absorb external information and knowledge. The central gatekeeper strategy implies that the external information is driven by leading firms, which diffuse the external information to other firms and agents in the district. Besides this centralistic strategy, the author discusses other models, such as the direct peer model, where many actors and firms process external information, or mixed models, where firms match information deriving from secondary internal sources (local leader firms) and originally collected external information.

In Chapter 4 Fiorenza Belussi brings a new important approach to the study of industrial districts, introducing the concept of organizational proximity. Her work mainly describes the pattern of evolution of the Verona industrial district (ID), specialized in men's (and boys') walking shoes of middle quality, located in the east part of the Veneto region, in Verona, where relocation processes have occurred through the creation of organizational international linkages. From a spatial point of view, the Verona footwear local system, formed by 412 firms and 4520 employees (2002 estimates), is more a cluster than a traditional Italian district, because it is not localized in a continuous territorial concentration but it is indeed articulated in three main local poles, within the same province (Bussolengo, a municipality near Lake Garda, Verona, the capital of the province, and the Val D'Alpone Valley, on the eastern border of the province, towards Vicenza). The district is still populated by SMEs, which statistically represent the majority of firms, but clearly the role of medium-sized firms is now relevant. The Verona ID is not an evolutionary system. Its production specialization has been quite stable and the district firms are not strongly innovative, nor have large dynamic groups emerged in the last decades with a few remarkable exceptions (such as PDG, a firm that supplies many shoe components and machinery). In Verona many firms are highly decentralized but there is the presence of some informal groups. Many local firms nowadays limit themselves to work upstream (marketing, selling, buying raw materials, designing the product and the collection), and downstream (logistics and shipments).

This process has implied the building of extra-district supply chains where firms benefit from organizational proximity (Verona firm technicians fly to Timişoara every two weeks, and organize direct inspections in the subcontracting factory, or provide assistance, and systematically control Romanian subcontractors). Face to face exchange of information, knowledge spillovers, and learning, are now delocalized as well. Firm controllers work typically two weeks in Timişoara, then they take a week off, and often they work two weeks in the Verona firm, to organize quality control.

Chapter 5 by Fiorenza Belussi illustrates the evolution of a famous industrial district located in the north-east area of Italy, known as the Montebelluna 'sport-system district'. This, in contrast to previous cases analyzed, is considered one the most innovative districts in Italy because it is made up of dynamic firms, which have introduced important radical innovations, and it is marked by the presence of some international companies, established in the 1990s through FDI. The author argues that static external economies, like those based on proximity (e.g. 'industrial atmosphere', labour market specialization, presence of ancillary sectors, etc.) cannot be advocated to explain the historical evolutionary path of the district, while new knowledge generation, absorption of external knowledge, innovativeness and firm strategy appear to be the explanatory determinants.

Chapter 6 by Alessia Sammarra provides an in-depth analysis of the phenomenon of industrial districts' crisis. The empirical context is the Vibrata Valley clothing district, located in the northernmost part of Abruzzo, in central Italy. The longitudinal analysis shows that the Vibrata Valley has developed as a 'satellite district' with a strong subcontracting vocation and dependence on external national commissioning firms. This imprinting has been maintained over time and still represents the main structural and cultural weakness of the district. Only a small number of local firms were able to pursue product upgrading by improving quality and moving into more sophisticated product lines. Most local companies have tried to face new competitive challenges by reproducing the same strategic perspective followed in the past that is focusing on low-cost advantages and price competitiveness. This evidence illustrates that 'satellite districts' in advanced as well as in developing countries do not offer favourable conditions for a full process of local upgrading.

In Chapter 7 Fiorenza Belussi and Silvia Sedita offer an alternative way to approach the relocalization of Western IDs towards developing countries, which consists of 'moving labour' as an alternative to the transfer of the production to low-labour-cost countries. The resulting new configuration of the organization of production is here called 'inverse' relocation. The empirical context is the leather tanning Arzignano district, specialized in high-volume production of bovine leather and calfskin, for the footwear, furnishing and automotive industries. The case presented induces some reflections on the alternative ways open for territorial development, which avoids the de-industrialization issue, and pushes local firms to invest more in locally based research and in the training of professionals.

Chapter 8 by Lorenzo Bacci, Mauro Lombardi and Sandrine Labory deals with the evolution of external linkages among firms in the Tuscan leather industry. This implies the study of the 'connective geometry' between the productive agents, on the basis of specific indicators of the structure of their relationships. Particular attention is paid to leaders, that is, companies that hold one or more (generally a portfolio of) important fashion brand names (Dior, Chanel, Gucci, Prada, and so on) that have organized large subcontractors and networks in Tuscany. The main results of the research are twofold. First, the transformations and reconfigurations of the relationships tend to favour the hierarchization of relationships among the various district firms. Second, the problems of international delocalization or relocation of production appear less incisive for this high-value industry positioned in a high-quality niche.

Chapter 9 by Fiorenza Belussi presents the footwear cluster of Timişoara, which is, in fact, localized over an extended area of three counties: Arad, Timis and Bihor. The cluster took off after 1989, thanks to the entry of foreign investments attracted by the particularly low labour costs, devolved to the acquisition of many state companies near economic collapse, or to greenfield FDI. The footwear sector in the area is just a part of a more heterogeneous manufacturing cluster extending over an entire region. In this chapter it is argued that the cluster of Timişoara is a satellite cluster rather than a Marshallian district, because it lacks endogenous entrepreneurs and local innovation.

On the same line of reasoning Chapter 10, by Simona Montagnana, contributes to the study of clustering of 'satellite IDs'. By investigating the footwear industry of Timişoara it assesses whether technological and knowledge transfer from foreign to domestic firms has occurred. The analysis explores two related issues: on the one hand, it considers linkages that foreign firms, in particular Italian ones, have established with domestic firms, and investigates their effects on local development; on the other hand, it aims at assessing the possible dependence of domestic firms on foreign (mainly Italian) customers. The result of this research suggests that the internationalization process of small ID Italian firms has not reproduced the whole district '*filière*' (value supply chain), but only a part: the most labour-intensive. At the same time it has not replicated the typical district social model. The inter-firm local networks are only focused on reducing labour costs. Vertical relationships among firms appear not greatly cooperative and last for only short periods. Moreover, the ties between Italian and domestic firms are scarce, weak and rarely based on trust. Flows of technology and knowledge are unidirectional: from the foreign (Italian) firms to the local subcontracting firms. The latter are not involved in any strategic process. The study emphasizes that none of the local subcontracting firms seems to have undergone a satisfactory catching up process, or to have achieved a significant degree of autonomy.

In Chapter 11 Belussi and Sedita address the issue of how globalization has contributed to increase the symbiotic division of labour among IDs&Cs specialized in the same industry. This issue is empirically illustrated through a qualitative analysis of three horticultural districts: two of them, the less advanced, are placed in Italy (Pistoia, and Saonara), the other (Boskoop) is part of the larger horticultural

Dutch cluster. Despite the lack of natural resources and unfavourable climate, the high labour and energy costs, the Dutch horticulture cluster has acquired a leading position in the global value chain. The application of science and the role of local institutions are explanatory factors for this successful evolutionary path. The Italian districts analyzed, which enjoy better endowed resources, are now strongly dependent on the entire Dutch cluster.

In Chapter 12 Fiorenza Belussi and Bjørn Asheim develop a theoretical reflection on the influence that entry FDI (by acquisition) produces on the knowledge governance of IDs. They compare two interesting IDs: Jæren in Norway and Montebelluna in Italy. In both cases the internationalization process was characterized by inflows of FDI and outflows of investment focused on the acquisition and absorption of external strategic knowledge and by the creation of a multinational structure by district firms. However, how can we evaluate the entry of multinationals in the district analyzed? The authors discuss why multinational companies (MNCs) enter these districts and how the entry of multinationals changed the model of knowledge governance within the districts, influencing the mechanism of knowledge spillovers that typically characterized the model of the IDs.

Chapter 13 by Renato Garcia and Gabriela Scur discusses the pattern of knowledge generation and diffusion and the learning processes of the two most important industrial districts in the Brazilian ceramic tile industry. The first, Criciuma, is located in the state of Santa Catarina, in the south of Brazil; while the former is around Santa Gertrudes, a city in the state of São Paulo. In both cases, it is possible to note the importance of the local community and the presence of institutions that foster the productive and innovative efforts put in place by the local producers. These efforts are particularly important because of increasing competition in the global market generated by Chinese imports of tiles. These two districts, which cover a very important share of the Brazilian market, are technologically dependent on the Italian leader firms of the Sassuolo district which sell them the new machinery, new designs and new components.

Annalisa Caloffi, in Chapter 14, summarizes the main results of her empirical study focused on the specialized manufacturing towns in the Guangdong province of China, which represent a new modality of top-down agglomerated economies, helping us to deepen our understanding of the variety of factors supporting China's industrial growth. There is not just, of course, cheap labour, land availability and the existence of a large internal market, but also state, regional and local policies attracting foreign direct investments and multinational firms able to manage global value chains. Recent investigations have also pointed out the role of native local entrepreneurship. An important point discussed is the role of innovation policies in affecting the different paths of clusters upgrading. Caloffi concludes her analysis by discussing the challenges to the Italian industrial districts created by China's rapid growth.

In Chapter 15 Najoua Boufaden, Sofiène Lourimi and André Torre develop an analysis of the 'Ile-de-France' high-tech clusters of biotech and optics-photonics, localized around Paris. They show the constantly increasing role of institutions, both local, national and at a European level, in the setting and growth of clusters.

This growing institutional implication has a double dimension. First, the growth of high-tech clusters is not at all a spontaneous mechanism related to the proper working of market forces. Public support of the development of the French 'pôles de compétitivités' is becoming central to the French national industrial policy. Second, high-tech clusters require several local intermediate institutions (technical networks, technical centres, incubators, cluster development institutions, and regional capital ventures). Their role in economic development has a growing importance, especially concerning technological transfer between local firms and other cluster animators (public firms, laboratories and universities). Nevertheless, this institutional environment might be fuzzy and in part redundant.

In Chapter 16 Dirk Fornahl and Anh Tran analyze four biotech clusters within the German BioRegio contest (Munich, Jena, Rhineland and Rhine-Neckar-Triangle). The main focus of their work is to understand the modalities of localized and distance learning. They provide some empirical evidence through the mapping of geographic networks of the co-inventors based in the four selected biotech clusters, during the period 1995–2007. They show that all four clusters have a mixture of local, national and international linkages, but the consistency differs over time and place. Jena and Rhine-Neckar start with a high share of local linkages which decreased over time, giving place to national and international linkages, while the Rhineland has more national linkages and its periphery already started with more international linkages. Munich, in contrast, shows a surprising small number of international connections. The multinational companies play an important role in the bridging of geographic space with many linkages, often involving US firms. Since Munich has no such firms, there is a low degree of international connectivity.

Chapter 17 shifts the focus towards the biotechnology industry in Denmark and Sweden. The biotechnology cluster under observation is the Medicon Valley cluster, located in the bi-national Øresund region (which spans greater Copenhagen, in Denmark, and Scania, in southern Sweden, including the university town Lund, and Sweden's third biggest city Malmö). Medicon Valley can be considered a potential mega centre. The life science sector in Scania has long traditions through the presence of Astra (subsequently merged with Zeneca to become AstraZeneca) and Pharmacia (subsequently merged with Upjohn to become Pharmacia & Upjohn, and later acquired by Pfizer). Today there are about 130 DBFs (of which approximately 70 per cent are located on the Danish side of Medicon Valley), 70 pharmaceutical companies, and 130 medtech companies. Also local university research, which represents the earliest stages of the biotech value chain, is an important source of innovation. The authors, Jerker Moodysson, Lars Coenen and Bjørn Asheim, address their analysis to the pattern of localization of inventive activity and knowledge circulation. They conclude by affirming that learning activities in biotech clusters appear to be both a local and a global phenomenon.

Chapter 18 by Jan Vang and Cristina Chaminade analyzes the cluster/district of Bangalore in India, a developing country. The evolution of this local system shows that it is not true that IDs&Cs may be able to develop only by entering the global value chain and absorbing the lowest technological activities. In fact, some local innovation systems, based in developing countries, are now hosting indigenous firms which have moved up the value chain (traditional upgrading), innovating their product niche strategy, and/or using the new competences acquired in the initial phases for diversified upgrading. The authors' work allows us to understand how a 'satellite' local system and 'a low-cost provider' evolves into an innovative 'machine', and how this transition process can be supported by intelligent public policies. The authors investigate how the local system of innovation develops to support the needs of the indigenous firms, and especially the SMEs, in this transition process.

References

Aage T. and Belussi F. (2008), 'From fashion to design: creative networks in industrial districts', *Industry and Innovation*, 15(5): 475–91.

Asheim B. and Isaksen A. (2000), 'Localised knowledge, interactive learning and innovation: Between regional networks and global corporations'. In I. E. Vatne and M. Taylor (eds.), *The Networked Firm in a Global World: Small Firms in New Environments*, Aldersot: Ashgate.

Bathelt H., Malmberg A. and Maskell P. (2004), 'Clusters and knowledge: local buzz, global pipelines and the process of knowledge creation', *Progress in Human Geography*, 28(1): 31–56.

Becattini G. (1987), 'L'unità di Indagine', in G. Becattini (ed.), *Mercato e forze locali: il distretto industriale*, Bologna: Il Mulino.

Becattini G. and Rullani E. (1996), 'Local systems and global connections: the role of knowledge', in F. Cossentino, F. Pyke and W. Sengenberger (eds.), *Local and Regional Response to Global Pressure: the Case of Italy and Its Industrial Districts*, Geneva: Ilo.

Bell M. and Albu M. (1999), 'Knowledge systems and technological dynamics in industrial clusters in developing countries', *World Development*, 27(9): 1715–34.

Belussi F., Gottardi G. and Rullani E. (eds.) (2003), *The Technological Evolution of Industrial Districts*, Boston: Kluwer.

Belussi F., Sammarra A. and Sedita S. R. (2008), 'Managing long distance and localized learning in the Emilia Romagna Life Science Cluster', *European Planning Studies*, 16: 665–92.

Belussi F. and Sedita S. (2009), 'Life cycle vs. multiple path dependency in industrial districts', *European Planning Studies*, forthcoming.

Biggiero L. (1999) 'Markets, hierarchies, networks, districts: a cybernetic approach', *Human Systems Management*, 18: 71–86.

Biggiero, L. and Sammarra A. (2008), 'Does geographical proximity enhance knowledge exchange? The case of the aerospace industrial cluster of central Italy', *International Journal of Technology Transfer & Commercialization*, forthcoming.

Boschma, R. A. and ter Wal A. L. J. (2007), 'Knowledge networks and innovative performance in an industrial district: the case of a footwear district in the south of Italy', *Industry and Innovation*, 14: 177–99.

Breschi, S. and Lissoni F. (2001) 'Knowledge spillovers and local innovation systems', *Industrial and Corporate Change*, 10: 975–1005.

Cooke P. (2002), *Knowledge Economies: Clusters, Learning and Cooperative Advantage*, London: Routledge.

Doz Y, Olk P. and Smith Ring P. (2000), 'Formation processes of R&D consortia: which path to take? Where does it lead?', *Strategic Management Journal*, 21: 239–66.

Gallaud D. and Torre A. (2005), 'Geographiacal proximity and circulation of knowledge through inter-firm cooperation', *Scienze Regionali*, 4(2): 5–25.

Gereffi G. and Korzeniewicz M. (eds.) (1994), *Commodity Chains and Global Capitalism*, Westport: Praeger.

Gereffi G., Humphrey J. and Sturgeon T. (2005): 'The governance of global value chains', *Review of International Political Economy*, 12: 78–104.

Gertler M. and Wolfe D. (2006): 'Spaces of knowledge flows: clusters in a global context', in B. Asheim, P. Cooke and R. Martin (eds.), *Clusters and Regional Development: Critical Reflections and Explorations. London and New York*, Routledge: 218–35.

Giuliani E., Pietrobelli C. and Rabellotti R. (2005), 'Upgrading in global value chains: lessons from Latin American clusters', *World Development*, 33(4): 549–73.

Giuliani E., Rabellotti R. and van Dijk M. P. (eds.) (2005), *Cluster Facing Competition: The Importance of External Linkages*, Aldershot: Ashgate.

Guerrieri P. and Pietrobelli C. (2001) 'Models of industrial clusters' evolution and changes in technological regimes', in P. Guerrieri, S. Iammarino and C. Pietrobelli (eds.), *The Global Challenge to Industrial Districts: Small and Medium-sized Enterprises in Italy and Taiwan*, Cheltenham: Edward Elgar.

Håkansson H. and Snehota I. (1995), *Developing Relationships in Business Networks*, London: Routledge.

Krugman P. (1995), *Development, Geography, and Economic Theory*, Cambridge, Mass: MIT Press.

Markusen A. (1996) 'Sticky places in slippery space: a typology of industrial districts', *Economic Geography*, 72: 293–313.

Maskell P. and Kebir L. (2006), The Theory of the Cluster – what it takes and what it implies', in B. Asheim, P. Cooke and R. Martin, *Clusters and Regional Development*, Routledge, pp. 30–49.

Maskell P. and Malmberg A. (1999), 'The competitiveness of firms and regions: "ubiquitification" and the importance of localised learning', *European Urban and Regional Studies*, 6: 9–25.

Paniccia I. (2002), *Industrial Districts*, Cheltenham: Edward Elgar.

Porter M. (1998), *On Competition*, Boston: Harvard Business School Press.

Pyndt J. and Pedersen T. (2005), *Managing Global Offshoring Strategies: A Case Study Approach*, Copenhagen: Copenhagen Business School Press.

Sammarra A. and Belussi F. (2006) 'Evolution and relocation in fashion-led Italian districts: evidence from two case-studies', *Entrepreneurship & Regional Development*, 18: 543–62.

Sammarra A. and Biggiero L. (2008) 'Heterogeneity and specificity of inter-firm knowledge flows in innovation networks', *Journal of Management Studies*, 45(4): 800–29.

Schmitz H. (2004), *Local Enterprises in the Global Economy: Issues of Governance and Upgrading*, Cheltenham: Elgar.

Part I

The business model of industrial districts and clusters between the knowledge-based view and the global chain perspective

1 The international fragmentation of the industrial districts and clusters (IDs&Cs) value chain between relocation and global integration

Fiorenza Belussi (University of Padua) and Alessia Sammarra (University of L'Aquila)

1.1 Introduction

The aim of this introductory chapter is to trace the evolution of localized production systems specialized in specific economic activities (such as industrial districts, clusters, local high-tech milieus, etc.), within the context of the increasing globalization of the economy.

One of the most fruitful streams of research in this direction is the one combining the two main paradigms in development literature: the industrial districts and the global commodity chain perspectives (Bair and Gereffi 2001). Two special issues of World Development (Humphrey 1995; Nadvi and Schmitz 1999) extensively focused on the topic of industrial districts in developing countries. The specific aim of these special issues was to verify whether the industrial district model, originally formulated on the successful experiences of geographically bounded and sectorally specialized clusters of small and medium-sized enterprises in the so called Third Italy, could provide an effective development model in other world regions, especially in emerging countries. The strongest research findings that have emerged from this stream of studies are twofold (Bair and Gereffi 2001). First, the initial formulation of the industrial districts model was found to be too narrow and culture-bound to capture the variety and heterogeneity of developing country experiences. In this respect, this stream of research has come to a conclusion not dissimilar from the one that emerged from the most recent studies on industrial districts in developed countries, and from Italy as well. Indeed, the recent literature has extensively documented the empirical variety of industrial districts, emphasizing that, although representing a specific form of economic agglomeration, industrial districts are characterized by a multiplicity of possible typologies and evolutionary patterns of growth, innovation and learning (Markusen 1996; Belussi and Gottardi 2000; Paniccia 2002; Belussi, *et al.* 2003; Sammarra 2003; Belussi 2006). The second important finding was the need to focus on the connection between local producers and global buyers (Humphrey and Schmitz 2002). From this viewpoint, growth trajectories and local development outcomes of industrial districts and clusters are, to some extent, dependent on the external links that incorporate district firms into global commodity chains. These types of chains are now common in specialized local systems and influence the local contexts, both depressing or upgrading local firms and IDs&Cs (Gereffi, Humphrey and Sturgeon 2005).

Another relevant stream of research concerned with understanding the effect of globalization on IDs&Cs is the one combining the local development literature with the study of multinational enterprises (Biggiero 2002; Biggiero and Sammarra 2003; Birkinshaw and Sölvell 2000; Sammarra 2003). While early formulations of the industrial district model have almost exclusively focused on the role of locally owned SMEs and local institutions, recent studies have emphasized the fundamental role that multinationals entering into industrial districts can play for local development outcomes and for industrial districts upgrading. IDs&Cs can provide proximity benefits, and are attractive areas for foreign direct investment inflows, and this process can further generate a catalyst effect (Andersson, Forsgren and Holm 2002; Heise, McDonald and T selmann 2002; Malmberg and Sölvell 1997). Some researchers have hypothesized that the entry of knowledgeable actors such as multinational enterprises (MNEs) in IDs&Cs has given rise to a significant process of technological transfer between MNE subsidiaries and local firms (Gordon 1996; Dunning 1996, 1998 and 2000; Enright 1998). Guerrieri and Pietrobelli (2001), and Ernst, *et al.* (2001), have empirically studied the rapid take-off of Far East IDs&Cs along the lines of the learning processes linked to the subcontracting chains. Quite opposite to that, other authors have asserted that in the cases analyzed by them this has never occurred (Lipsey 2002; Veugelers and Cassiman 2001; Bair and Gereffi 2001). Despite the differentiated outcomes reported in the literature, the most important indication that has emerged from this stream of studies is that the multinational and the industrial district models are not in opposition. Indeed, instead of eliminating regionalization, the multinationals' expansion is co-evolving with, and is sometimes reinforcing, clustering processes.

Building on both theoretical perspectives, this chapter illustrates how different channels of internationalization are modifying industrial districts, in some cases strengthening, and in others weakening their competitiveness, with respect to new global challenges. Two distinct (although not alternative) forms of internationalization are discussed (Sammarra 2003). The first form – defined as active internationalization – occurs when the opening up process is enacted by local enterprises which relocate or expand some activities of their value chain abroad. In IDs&Cs, the offshoring of manufacturing activities through long-distance subcontracting chains, or newly created FDI based in low-labour-cost countries, represents the most important change that occurred in the 1990s in Western countries' IDs&Cs. From this perspective the evolution of IDs&Cs imitates the behaviour of global companies that occurred in the 1960s (Dunning 1981, 1993). The second form – called passive internationalization – takes place when foreign enterprises enter the district through FDI and/or other modes of entry. The focus on such processes allows us to explore the endogenous centrifugal elements that are at work, producing a relocation of activities (and firms) and the exogenous centripetal forces, which further intensify spatial agglomerations.

1.2 IDs&Cs facing international fragmentation and the global value chain

1.2.1 International fragmentation

The fragmentation of the production process is nowadays a major theme in research in international economics (Gereffi and Korzeniewicz 1994; Arndt and Kierzkowski 2001), business (Maskell, *et al.* 2007), geography (Dicken 2003, 2007; Dicken, *et al.* 2001; Coe and Bunnell 2003), and sociology (Kenney and Florida 1994). In the beginning, this literature was stimulated by the notion of globalization. This represented not a precise idea, but a way of rethinking the traditional perspective that sees the world economy as a single market, unimpeded by national boundaries, where we observe a convergence of consumer preferences, capital markets, ways of firms sourcing materials and components on the basis of a complex assessment of costs, logistics, national policies, and other factors, and where new knowledge that is produced and used at local level tends to migrate on an international scale (Badracco 1991).

Productive fragmentation is clearly related to the growth of international trade and intermediate product exchanges. Fenestra (2003) has explicitly connected the fragmentation of production with the increasing integration of global commerce. Trade benefits now arise because of the entry of new countries bearing low labour costs, and this allows for firms to decrease – often at a surprising level – their total production costs. This tends to link and to integrate the economies of developed and developing countries (Gereffi and Korzeniewicz 1994).

Arnd and Kierzkowski (2001) utilize the concept of fragmentation in order to describe a model of international division of labour which allows for several producers, localized in different countries, to organize their production in common, with the support of business networks through which raw materials, parts and components are re-worked and assembled. Managers are in charge to directly coordinate the various production stages, which cross the boundaries of countries and continents, either through trade, or with coordinated lines of traffic of passive perfectioning (TPP), in some cases with the direct responsibility of the final firm producer for the transportation, logistics, insurance and quality control.

The 'slicing up' of the whole (or aggregated) value chain represents a major change in the new post-Fordist paradigm of production. This tendency has been acknowledged even by the quite orthodox economist Krugman (1995), and is widely discussed by researchers specializing in business studies, who have creatively used the seminal contribution of Porter (1985), developing new insights on the theory of structural change and the emergence of novel organizational principles of business strategy (Robertson and Langlois 1995; Belussi 1993; Langlois 2001).

The recent trend of internationalization of sectors and activities through firms outsourcing has been explored mainly through descriptive case studies or surveys.

Recently, *Business Week* (Engardio, *et al.* 2003) has evaluated the displacement of jobs in Western economies based, during the 1960s and 1970s, on the restructuring of textile and clothing sectors, footwear products and consumer electronic components, and during the 1980s on simple service activities related to the treatment of standard procedures, such as credit card bill management, airline reservations, call-centre activities and relatively standardized software products. The recent advancements in information and communication technologies (ICTs) (*Economist* 2004) will tend to increase the phases that firms can manage through offshoring and outsourcing, including services and high-value activities based in low-cost countries, and, in particular, in China and India. Fragmentation and integration are particularly visible if we consider the role of multinationals. International production systems have emerged, thanks to the role played by MNEs, which

> locate different parts of the production process, including various services functions, across the globe [...] The organization and distribution of production activities and other functions is what is commonly known as the global value chain. It extends from technology sourcing and development, production, to distribution and marketing (Unctad 2002: 121–3).

Since the beginning, these changes have revealed the paradox of globalization: the dramatic expansion of productive capacity has not necessarily increased the level of development of many countries (Kaplinsky 2000). This has been viewed by Kaplinsky, *et al.* (2002), as a possible 'immiserizing growth' model. However, there are counterintuitive examples in the East Asian countries' experience that show how initial outsourcing processes from large MNEs, producing final products, have transferred technology and new capabilities to local firms in developing countries. This has occurred in Taiwan, Singapore, South Korea, and other places. While systematic comparisons are rare, the works of Hobday (1995), Lall (2001), Saxenian and Hsu (2001), and Unido (2002) for Asia, and the study of Cassiolato (1992) for South America, have stressed the learning effects that have occurred during those periods in developing countries, with the unintended consequence, for the MNEs, that many local firms and suppliers have shifted from the position of original equipment manufacture (OEM), to own-design manufacture (ODM), and from ODM to own-brand manufacture (OBM), challenging the competitiveness of the old incumbents.

The success of the Taiwanese computer industry provides (in Acer) a brilliant example of a firm that started from a position of inferiority, within a hierarchical subcontracting chain, but rapidly experienced a fast process of product and process upgrading, being able to acquire new capabilities in design and marketing, and moving up to higher chain functions. As argued by Humphrey and Schmitz (2004), this clearly requires strategic intention, but the question as to why such strategic intention is more common in East Asia than in other parts of the developing world remains unanswered. The chain approach, even if combined with the cluster approach, is ultimately not sufficient to explain these differences. Institutional factors and implicit innovation policies (trade regulations, tax and monetary policies) are proposed as possible explanatory variables. During the 1980s and 1990s, East Asian countries did not suffer much from the kind of disabling policies that have characterized many countries in Africa and South America, driving industrial managers into speculation activities rather than strategic upgrading efforts.

1.2.2 The global value chain approach

Various definitions have emerged in the literature to indicate the process of governance of production chains, such as supply chains, international production networks, and global commodity chains (Gereffi and Kaplinsky 2001). These structures represent an intermediate form of market coordination, located between the 'regime' of pure anonymous market transactions, and the model of 'fit by authority': the vertically integrated firm. The global commodity chain approach is a theoretical specification of the network firm paradigm (Thorelli 1986; Thompson, *et al.* 1991; Powell 1990; Davidow and Malone 1992; Belussi and Arcangeli 1998; Todeva 2006).

A commodity chain is defined as the whole range of discrete, though interrelated, activities involved in the design, production and marketing of a product (Gereffi and Korzeniewicz 1994; Gereffi 1999). In global industries (Gereffi, Humphrey and Sturgeon 2005), different activities of the same commodity chain are increasingly spread across national boundaries, requiring international integration and coordination. Therefore, *global commodity chains* indicate those cases characterized by extensive international fragmentation and coordination of activities. Thus, a global commodity chain is a governance structure of production, where a set of activities is organized by several separate firms, ruled by a leading organization. A global commodity chain is also defined as 'a set of transnational interorganizational linkages that constitute the production, the distribution and consumption of a commodity' (Korzeniewicz 1992: 314). Hopkins and Wallerstein (1994: 17) define a commodity chain as 'a network of labor and production processes whose end result is a finished commodity'. They emphasize the interrelations and interdependencies between firms and industries, implying that a change in one dimension will affect all other dimensions as well. The focus is on the geographical and organizational fragmentation of the production, and on the industrial coordination or governance of the organizationally and geographically dispersed chain activities, exerted by a powerful actor, which is responsible for planning, financing and integrating the various productive phases. Humphrey and Schmitz (2000) propose to replace the original definition of 'global commodity chain' with the more general term of 'global value chain' in order to focus the analysis 'on the question of who adds value where along the chain' (p. 10) and avoid the risk of restricting the scope of analysis to standardized products. Following this suggestion, in the rest of this chapter, we will adopt the definition of 'global value chain' (GVC) to refer to this theoretical approach.

A critical distinction in the GVC approach is between buyer-driven and producer-driven chains. As explained by Gereffi (1999: 41), producer-driven chains are those in which large (usually multinational) manufacturers play the central role in coordinating backward and forward linkages along the value chain. The producer-driven chains characterize those technology-intensive industries, such as automobiles, aerospace, semiconductors and heavy machinery, where final assembling firms must develop a particular ability in dealing with architectural knowledge (Henderson and Clark 1990). On the contrary, buyer-driven chains have emerged within large retailers and distributors, where brand producers have segmented the markets, playing a pivotal role in setting up decentralized production networks. Buyer-led chains are typical within labour-intensive industries or consumer goods (garments, footwear, toys, houseware and consumer electronics). These firms operate in a regime of oligopoly, characterized by high entry barriers. The most profitable segments of the value chain are downstream, and they are related to the direct contact with the consumer (selling and post-selling services). In producer-driven commodity chains, the highest profits are usually in the hands of the industrial firms playing the role of final assemblers. Profits derive from their technological leadership, and from the huge scale economies resulting from the high volumes of goods manufactured. In buyer-driven chains, the key players are the retailers, which sell simpler branded goods, manufactured based on orders. They compete by concentrating their investments in areas like branding, advertising, marketing and sales, where entry barriers are high.

A central claim of Gereffi, the main proponent of the GVC approach, is that these two governance structures are not to be understood as mutually exclusive, but as a contrasting pole 'in a spectrum of industrial organizational possibilities' (Gereffi, 1994: 99). What he is not analyzing is the continuous integration of production into modern retailing nets (see the cases of the most successful international clothing-footwear firms: Benetton during the 1970s and Zara during the 1980s, or the extraordinary success of IKEA in the furniture business during the 1990s), which in fact renders the two forms as quite undistinguishable.

The GVC approach offers a useful perspective to study the influence of globalization and internationalization on the evolution of IDs&Cs because it sheds light on the possible effect that the incorporation of district firms into global value chains offers for local development outcomes. In order to examine this issue, Humphrey and Schmitz (2002) conceptualize a process of upgrading, distinguishing four types. The 'simplest' forms are process and product upgrading, which consist respectively of: (1) transforming input into output more efficiently by reorganizing the production system or introducing superior technology, and (2) moving into more sophisticated product lines in terms of increased unit values. The 'more complex' forms of upgrading are functional and intersectoral upgrading. The former implies acquiring new superior functions in the value chain, such as R&D, design and/or marketing, and abandoning existing low-value added activities. The latter means applying the competence acquired in a particular function to move into a new sector. For instance, in Taiwan, competence in producing TVs was used to make monitors and then to move into the computer sector (Guerrieri and Pietrobelli 2004).

One central claim in the GVC approach is that the incorporation of IDs&Cs in global chains often favours local firms upgrading, especially in less developed countries. With respect to East Asia, Gereffi (1999) found that the incorporation into GVC led by foreign leaders, particularly foreign buyers, has almost automatically promoted process, product and functional upgrading among small local producers. However, other scholars studying Latin American clusters arrived at a less optimistic view. Humphrey and Schmitz (2002) found that the most frequent modalities were product and process upgrading. However, even this positive shift might be not sufficient to influence the international ranking of the position of the individual ID&C, and the profitability chances of local firms. Often, local upgrading of products and processes in an ID&C are dictated by external foreign firms. Thus, local firms belonging to a developing country ID&C lack original capability in product design and in the ability to sell their products in the international market channels. The case of Sinos footwear valley in the south of Brazil, described by Humphrey and Schmitz (2007), shows that despite a certain level of local upgrading in products, in the early 1990s the district suffered from a long-standing crisis caused by Chinese producers, who undercut Brazilian products in the US market. Thus, Brazilian firms lost their market, and were unable to rapidly substitute it with the entry into new distributive chains, or to target their internal market because they lacked the necessary sophisticated design capabilities. In their study of the footwear cluster of Sinos Valley in Brazil, Navas-Alemán and Bazan (2005) found similar results. Their study focused on the implementation of quality, labour and environmental standards among local firms promoted by value chain leaders, and its implications for local firms upgrading. They found that the standards were implemented differently according to the type of governance prevalent in the value chain (US and European directed network versus domestic and Latin American value chain) and the type of standards at stake. Specifically, they found that in US and European directed value chains, local compliance tended to be higher, although only standards that mattered for global leaders were promoted, such as quality process standards and the prohibition of child labour. Other standards, such as environmental standards, or other core labour standards, were not implemented and monitored in an equal way. Therefore, while the insertion in US and European led global chains helped local firms to adopt standards that were important for global buyers' competitiveness – also contributing positively to foster the local firms' process and product upgrading – the effect on other crucial forms of upgrading and on the incentives to adopt the socially most needed standards, was not equally positive.

One possible explanation raised to interpret the differentiated outcome that the insertion in GVC generates on local development outcomes lies in the different type of governance structures that characterize the value chain. In this regard, Humphrey and Schmitz (2000) distinguish three types of governance: (1) network, (2) quasi-hierarchy, and (3) hierarchy. Network governance occurs when power differences among firms are not accentuated and firms share their competencies within the chain. Quasi-hierarchy characterizes the coordination patterns between legally independent firms having unequal power, with a leader in the chain defining the rules to which the rest of the actors have to comply. Hierarchy is the governance model that is applied when actors in the chain are owned by the leading firms. They argue that different types of governance can offer less or more favourable conditions for transferring information, knowledge and capabilities among the various actors involved in the chain. Consistent with this view, Pietrobelli and Rabellotti (2005) found that, in quasi-hierarchical value chains, the chain leaders favoured local firms' product and process upgrading, while functional upgrading was almost always inhibited. This evidence was supported by the empirical examination of 40 SME clusters in Latin America with different sectoral specializations, ranging from traditional manufacturing industries, such as footwear and clothing, to electronics and automotive sectors.

While the empirical evidence offers support to this view, two possible limitations implied in this approach should be acknowledged. A first point of criticism, addressed also by Palpacuer (2000), is the issue of power exerted by the leading firms over the other agents of the chain. What the particular power consists of, and how it is gained, is not much discussed in the GCV approach. In fact, subcontractors and assemblers can apply simultaneously different strategies, depending on the scale of activity and resources involved, as the Swedish school IMP have emphasized, well beyond any dyadic relationship (Ford, *et al.* 1998; Ford 2002) as appears indeed in the framework of cases examined by Gereffi. The level of subcontractor autonomy appears to us as just one of the multifaceted characteristics of any business relation which renders any simplification very problematic. Dependency is a matter of choice and a matter of circumstances (Axelsson and Easton 1992).

A second point on which the GVC approach is theoretically weak is the poorly regarded importance of the local context. The GVC approach lacks focus on the role of institutions, and of the different territories in which the industry is embedded. In other words, the GVC is an under-socialized theory, where the variety models of capitalism (Hall and Soskice 2001) are not taken into account, and where the specific knowledge base perspective is excluded by the range of possibilities open to local networks to spontaneously activate a process of change. It is important to observe that actors within each GVC may behave differently, not because they are inserted in more or less hierarchical structures, but because they are the product of different institutional environments (Whitley 1996). Indeed, what is going on in the local context, and the capabilities accumulated by the firms during their development, are a decisive strategic tool that can be applied by firms. Let us take the case studied by Rabellotti (2004) of the effect of globalization on the firms of the Riviera del Brenta district. While the paper stresses the functional downgrading of the district firms which have entered the value chains led by the international top high-fashion companies (Prada, HTM), in a kind of pessimistic vein, local shoe producers in recent years have adopted a dual strategy of working for the top brand (accepting their diktat on fashion design, strict productive requirements, and timing), but, at the same time, they have maintained significant autonomy, exploring the market with their own products. Many firms are now better endowed with top fashion design capabilities, and they have activated a process of learning in design. The district, as a whole, has not begun a process of irreversible decline (Tassetto 2008). Hierarchical chains in dynamic districts do not perform at the same level as hierarchical chains in weak or immature clusters, because they belong to different resources-endowed contexts, in terms of entrepreneurships, technological capabilities, and possibilities to explore new markets, etc.

While these remarks underline the need to avoid any deterministic application of the GVC framework, this theoretical approach has the merit of having significantly contributed to the study of clusters by pointing at their connection with external actors and their positioning in a global context. In this regard, the GVC framework can be also applied in order to understand the linkages that are activated among the IDs&Cs themselves, in terms of the international division of labour and knowledge interactions. First, the key point that this novel approach underlines is that, in analyzing the dynamics and structure of global industries, we find different typologies of IDs&Cs that emerge within a process of the 'symbiotic division' of labour. Some IDs&Cs become specialized in the value-added activities of research and product conceptualization (e.g. the Dutch district of Booskoop in Holland, and Sassulo or Montebelluna in Italy), while others are dealing with the most labour-intensive tasks of manufacturing (see the Italian cases of Saonara, Pistoia and Kenia presented in Chapter 4, or the case of Timişoara presented in Chapters 11 and 12, and the case of the Brazilian tile districts discussed in Chapter 15). The governance type of chain links (Bair and Gereffi 2001; Giuliani, *et al.* 2005) of local firms is indeed bounded by the knowledge base of the individual ID&C. One of the main consequences of globalization on an ID&C is the hierarchization occurring between a technological leading ID&C and other local systems, which structurally depend on the knowledge creation process of leaders.

1.3 Internationalization strategies and upgrading outcomes in Western IDs&Cs

In several Western IDs&Cs, complex forms of upgrading have been successfully pursued, such as in the case of intersectoral upgrading in Silicon Valley that has now given rise to a biotech cluster (Pisano 2006), or in the case of the European high-tech clusters that are often localized in urban research-intensive contexts, such as the biotech cluster in Munich (Lechner and Dowling 1999) or in Paris (see Chapters 10 and 16). However, for several Western IDs&Cs, globalization is threatening local development and competitiveness, emphasizing the need for proactive strategies that help them to react to a changing global scenario through a profound restructuring of the local value chains.

Generally, local firms in Western IDs&Cs specialized in traditional manufacturing sectors have built their competitiveness by focusing on specific manufacturing phases of the value chain. Constraints in financial, technological and managerial resources, typical of SMEs, have been compensated for through the development of distinctive technical capabilities and/or the exploitation of cost advantages deriving from specialization. Current changes in the global industries structure have progressively undermined these factors of competitive advantage, threatening the positioning in the global value chains of a large number of industrial districts in advanced countries.

The most relevant reaction to the new threats imposed by increased global competition was the enactment of massive relocation processes. The empirical evidence shows that in Western IDs&Cs, low-value-added and labour-intensive activities are outsourced abroad through international subcontracting chains (Schmitz 2004), or through a new process of district internationalization based on 'small multinationals' (district FDI). These two channels of active internationalization have been extensively pursued both by large firms and SMEs, including family firms, which were traditionally thought to be less prone to international growth (Belussi, *et al.* 2008). However, the effect of relocation on the long-term sustainability of the industrial district model may differ, depending on the possibility of using international fragmentation of the district value chain as a means to foster cluster firms' upgrading.

Often, relocation is a means to achieve *process upgrading*. In this case, district firms use FDI and/or international subcontracting to take advantage of differences in labour wages and factor prices across countries, thereby obtaining efficiency improvements by setting up an international production network (Jones and Kierzkowski 2000). This form has been defined as '*replicative relocation*' (Sammarra 2005; Sammarra and Belussi 2006), meaning that relocating firms are not strengthening their strategic position in the global value chain, since they are trying to face new competitive challenges by reproducing a strategic orientation focused on low cost advantages and price competitiveness. However, this form of upgrading alone is not sufficient to reinforce the competitiveness of industrial districts in advanced countries, as illustrated by Sammarra (see Chapter 6) with reference to the Val Vibrata clothing district in Italy. Replicative relocation produces an increase in the competitive pressure on local subcontractors, who are gradually substituted by foreign suppliers. In this case, relocation can seriously become a destructive process with the risk of leading, in the medium term, to a dismantling of the local production system, as emerging economies are gradually displacing industrialized countries as producers of inexpensive products for the low-price segments of the worldwide market.

Relocation becomes a means for more complex and profitable forms of upgrading when district firms transfer low-added-value activities abroad while they focus on high-value operations, keeping within district boundaries those phases which are either capital or knowledge intensive. This form has been defined as '*selective relocation*' (Sammarra 2005; Sammarra and Belussi 2006), meaning that the outflow of low-value-added activities of the district value chain are compensated for through a gradual process of functional upgrading. Such a restructuring process requires proactive strategies, since district firms need to build on new sources of competitive advantage based on the acquisition or internal development of resources and capabilities, which allow them to control strategic activities of the global chain, or to move into a new sector. In the Montebelluna sports district, local firms have massively transferred labour-intensive manufacturing activities to the Eastern European countries, although they remain rooted in the district, where they have invested in core activities of the sportswear global value chain such as prototyping, R&D, design, marketing and distribution (Sammarra and Belussi

2006). As illustrated in Chapter 5, the Montebelluna district has followed a model of 'selective relocation' where the gradual dismissal of local subcontracting firms was absorbed and compensated for by the process of district functional upgrading, and by establishing high barriers to low-cost imitators and competitors from developing countries.

According to many researchers (Leoncini and Montresor 2008; Camuffo 2003), in the last few decades in the best performing Italian IDs&Cs, complex forms of upgrading were successfully pursued and implemented thanks to the adoption of less decentralized modes of coordination in a frame of positive dynamism towards internationalization, the construction of brand image (e.g. Della Valle in the footwear district of Marche, or Geox in Montebelluna), and the enlargement of investment into retailing nets. These proactive strategies were not available to all district firms, since only the major local companies, endowed with sufficient resources, were able to invest significantly in functional upgrading. However, in several cases, the leading firms' strategies have had positive consequences for the whole local system, as exemplified by the Veneto eyewear district (Gambarotto and Solari 2005), the Montebelluna sportswear district (Chapter 5), and the packaging district (Boari and Lipparini 1999).The role played by major leading companies was, thus, crucial in the reshaping process of the district value chain. In general, the leading firms have decided to outsource locally for most of the quality and small series productions, while they outsource internationally for standardized low-cost items. District leading firms are now operating as large buyer centres through the internal governance of international subcontracting chains. Outsourcing of manufacturing activities was compensated for by the entry of local leading firms into global distribution networks (as in the case of the Belluno eyeglasses district), and a process of formation of district grouping firms or moderate hierarchies, which have replaced the original destructured network relationships (Boari and Lipparini 1999). Relational models based on reciprocal dependence among small co-located firms were abandoned, and more decided hierarchies emerged (Corò and Grandinetti 1999).

In several successful experiences of district upgrading, the reshaping of the local value chain has been driven by the strategic behaviour enacted by local leading firms which were able to change the traditional business model of typical district firms, organized mainly on a local base. The establishment of external linkages involved a wide spectrum of activities of the value chain, ranging from the sourcing of raw materials to manufacturing and retailing. This led to the emergence of a new 'open network' business model that extends the firms' value chain beyond the district borders.

Unfortunately, this radical transformation of the traditional district model has not always occurred. While most IDs&Cs were able to expand their standardized manufacturing activities abroad through massive relocation, only in some cases were cluster firms able to adopt the role of global leader in the chain, combining a relocation strategy with functional and intersectoral upgrading. There is, indeed, a great deal of heterogeneity in terms of upgrading outcomes across Western IDs&Cs.

One structural factor which helps in explaining these differentiated outcomes is district internal variety (Sammarra and Belussi 2006). Internal variety concerns organizational differentiation in terms of size, ownership, organizational model, economic specialization, strategies and capabilities (Rabellotti and Schmitz 1999; Lazerson and Lorenzoni 1999). Internal variety is a relevant structural property, which can significantly affect district upgrading potential. For instance, the presence of medium-sized as well as large firms can represent an important structural condition, helping industrial districts to activate functional and sectoral upgrading. Indeed, for larger firms it is generally easier to acquire superior functions in the value chain by developing internal R&D activities, which are increasingly important to permit more radical innovations or to creating their own sales networks, which allow for a consolidation of the local firms' position in foreign and internal markets, bypassing international wholesalers.

While the internationalization of both production and retail is a key factor in upgrading and obtaining a larger share of value in global chains, there is growing awareness that cognitive openness is a precondition for district firms to survive (Bathelt, *et al.* 2004; Breschi and Lissoni 2001; Boschma and ter Wal 2007; Giuliani 2005; Vang and Chaminade 2007). The establishment of external knowledge linkages (national and/or global) through R&D alliances and other forms of external exploration and innovation reduces the danger of cognitive 'lock-in' and 'over-embeddedness', which may become important obstacles to local learning and innovation, especially when technological trajectories and global economic conditions change.

In the past, in the absence of really severe technological breakthroughs, many Western IDs&Cs were quite self-sufficient in their capability of generating the necessary knowledge for adopting or adapting incremental innovation in process and product technologies. Firms in IDs&Cs were flexible agents, endowed with a special capability of developing new combinatory sets, starting from the pool and the locally accumulated stock of existing knowledge (Becattini and Rullani 1996; Maggioni and Bramanti 2002). However, the globalization process is exerting pressures towards a new model of open innovation (Chesbrough 2003), and firms in IDs&Cs must explore and examine those new distant knowledge sources that are not ubiquitous (Maskell 1999). While local knowledge linkages still remain effective to enact 'knowledge-using-and-replicating mechanisms' which favour the transmission of existing knowledge, external linkages and knowledge sources are fundamental 'knowledge-changing mechanisms' which expand and upgrade the cluster's existing capabilities (Bell and Albu 1999). The importance of external knowledge linkages is especially crucial in high-tech IDs&Cs, where technological alliances with external MNEs, large university departments with a good reputation, or private and public research centres are critical in order to access heterogeneous and geographically distributed knowledge and capabilities (Moodysson and Jonsson 2007; Braunerhhjelm and Feldman 2006; Belussi, Sammarra and Sedita 2008).

1.4 MNEs' investments in IDs&Cs

While most parts of industrial districts in advanced countries are experiencing internationalization through outflow processes of activities relocated abroad, other districts are also going through other forms of internationalization, driven by the inward investments of MNEs.

Among the Italian districts, two exemplar cases of such forms of 'passive internationalization' are the biomedical district located in the province of Modena (Biggiero 2002; Biggiero and Sammarra 2003; Sammarra 2003; Belussi and Sammarra 2005), and the Montebelluna sports district (Chapter 5; Sammarra and Belussi 2006). In the biomedical district, the MNEs' entry has occurred through the acquisition of firms founded by local entrepreneurs in two eras of big inward foreign investments: the periods of 1987–88 and 1994–95. At present, the district hosts some of the most important multinationals in the worldwide biomedical industry, such as Gambro, B. Braun-Carex, Mallinkrodt, Baxter, and Fresenius. The Montebelluna district is also characterized by the presence of leading multinational companies in the sports industry (e.g. Rossignol, Lange, HTM, and Nike), which settled in the district in the 1990s through the acquisition of local companies.

To date, in both cases, the empirical evidence shows that the MNEs' entry has contributed to fostering local development and upgrading, helping district firms to overcome the constraints of their local dimension. Multinationals' entry benefited the district with new financial resources and with direct access to the world market demands. Further, MNEs' investments into the districts have produced positive externalities in terms of higher reputation and visibility that the local system has acquired worldwide, generating indirect advantages also for the local firms, which were not directly incorporated into the multinational global networks through proprietary linkages. As illustrated by Biggiero and Sammarra (2003), Sammarra (2003) and Biggiero (2002), for the biomedical district located in the province of Modena (Italy), the ability to attract FDI, especially from large MNEs with a high visibility, may signal at the international level that the cluster has developed distinctive local capabilities, and this may result in a foreign investment snowball effect benefiting the entire cluster.

Industrial districts can gain several potential advantages from MNEs' entry. MNEs may provide access to assets, skills and routines that may usefully complement the location-bound knowledge of cluster firms. Through collaboration or direct competition with local producers (subcontractors of the MNE and final firms), multinational companies can generate different kinds of knowledge spillovers. Voluntary or involuntary knowledge transfers include:

1 managerial and technical competencies through internal training which contribute to the local labour market upgrading;
2 knowledge and information on the evolution of international markets;
3 innovative managerial models, such as new organizational arrangements and procedures, and management techniques.

The incorporation of local firms into the hierarchal governance chain of MNEs can facilitate district firms in upgrading. Indeed, while global buyers or foreign providers may not be likely to transfer managerial and technological capabilities to local subcontractors that would elevate them from the status of suppliers to potential competitors (Bair and Gereffi 2001), MNEs are generally prone to facilitate knowledge transfer within their own network of foreign subsidiaries, fostering their functional upgrading through the transfer of product, process and management skills and innovations between the units of their transnational network (Biggiero 2002). However, as already mentioned, knowledge transfer is not necessarily a voluntary or selective process. Spatial contiguity facilitates mimetic processes. Therefore, knowledge spillovers can also benefit local independent firms, which are not part of the multinational network.

Advantages deriving from inward FDI are not unidirectional. On one hand, MNEs can directly or indirectly contribute to transmitting knowledge to host regions through knowledge spillovers. On the other hand, there may be reverse knowledge flows, where knowledge is transferred from the industrial district to the MNE's headquarters in the home country, or to its affiliates in other host countries. Studies on MNEs argue that an increasing amount of FDI can be explained by the quest for new knowledge, which is available in specific foreign locations (Cantwell 1989; Cantwell and Iammarino 2000). FDI by MNEs increasingly takes the form of knowledge-seeking investment, whereby the MNE attempts to augment its knowledge base through obtaining access to foreign pools of knowledge by becoming a participant in various localized knowledge clusters simultaneously (Rugman and Verbeke 2001). Indeed, being directly present where knowledge is generated is a more effective way to absorb it, in comparison with cross-border transfers, because its informal and tacit component, which is often very important, can be acquired only through face-to-face contacts and workers' mobility (Jaffe, *et al.* 1993; Kogut and Zander 1992; Shan and Song 1997). An MNE's entry into a local cluster also allows it to benefit from a local market of skilled and experienced employees, and can therefore reduce its search and recruitment costs.

IDs&Cs' capacity to attract the multinational enterprises' knowledge-seeking investments depends on local innovativeness and accumulated capabilities. MNEs appear especially prone to performing R&D investments in foreign locations with a strong technological activity, and this leads to a further strengthening of indigenous R&D activities, thus illustrating the co-evolution of domestic firms and foreign subsidiaries in host country clusters. In Italy, for instance, both the biomedical district of Mirandola, and the Montebelluna sports system, were able over time to develop a local reservoir of a highly specialized technical know-how, developing worldwide distinctive manufacturing capabilities, which have attracted the foreign investments of some of the most important multinationals which decided to invest in the district to access the local capabilities and contextual knowledge by purchasing local firms. This evidence suggests that the processes of local knowledge creation and external knowledge absorption co-evolve over time, and nurture each other according to a mutually reinforcing mechanism.

Highly dynamic local clusters usually benefit from the presence of inward FDI;

in contrast, such virtuous cycles of co-evolution between indigenous and foreign cluster participants are much more uncertain in the case of weak or immature clusters, in which foreign firms typically limit the scope and depth of their cluster ties.

1.5 Conclusion

Globalization is modifying the traditional territorial forms, changing inner ties, and strengthening the need for local systems to open up to the outside. Increasing internationalization of markets, production and research drives IDs&Cs to pass beyond the local borders, recommending collaboration over an extended geographical scale.

Outward flows through relocation and inward investments channelled by MNEs are modifying the traditional structure of IDs&Cs. The effect on local development is not unidirectional. Relocation strengthens IDs&Cs' long-term compositeness when local firms match internationalization strategies with functional and sectoral upgrading. Another important mechanism, which can facilitate ID&C upgrading, is related to the entry of foreign multinationals, which can potentially create an in–out flow of knowledge from a specific industrial district to the global environment. High-tech IDs&Cs co-evolve, developing numerous external linkages and R&D-focused alliances.

The various IDs&Cs operating in low-tech and high-tech sectors are quite heterogeneous, since local firms depend strongly on local institutions, local capabilities, external GVC, and other external linkages. The capacity to deal with extra-district operators is diverse. Also diverse is the ability to absorb knowledge on the basis of external relations. The different set of capabilities owned by each single ID&C shapes the way it positions itself in the global supply chain. Depending on the capabilities (both developed internally and acquired externally) owned by the individual ID&C (and the individual firms), they might appear as global leaders or followers, even within the same sector. Relocation activities from IDs&Cs impact on the establishment of a GVC. However, within the same ID&C, various models can coexist, and the upgrading opportunities are not just bounded by the type of GVC firms feed into. The final result in terms of evolutionary growth possibilities in developing countries is a balance between upgrading capabilities depending on knowledge absorption through a GVC, and local dynamic capabilities related to knowledge creation, learning and strategic improvements of local conditions. In Western IDs&Cs, it can be hypothesized that cost-reduction offshoring processes will be gradually substituted by knowledge-seeking external linkages. This clearly will also change the direction and the scope of existing GVCs.

References

Amighini A. and Rabellotti R. (2004), 'How do Italian footwear industrial districts face globalisation?' Working paper.

Anderson U., Fosgren M. and Holm U. (2002), 'The strategic impact of external networks: Subsidiary performance and competence development in the multinational corporation',

Strategic Management Journal, 23: 979–6.

Arndt, S. and Kierzkowski, H. (eds.) (2001), *Fragmentation: New Production Patterns in the World Economy*, Oxford: Oxford Univ. Press.

Axelsson B. and Easton G. (eds.) (1992), *Industrial Networks*, London: Routledge.

Badracco J. (1991), *The Knowledge Link: How Firms Compete through Strategic Alliances*, Boston: Harvard Press.

Bair J. and Gereffi G. (2001), 'Local clusters in global chains: the causes and consequences of export dynamism in Torreon's blue jeans industry', *World Development*, 29(11): 1885–1903.

Becattini G. and Rullani E. (1996), 'Local systems and global connections: the role of knowledge', in F. Cossentino, F. Pyke and W. Sengenberger (eds.), *Local and Regional Response to Global Pressure: The Case of Italy and its Industrial Districts,* Geneva: ILO.

Bathelt H., Malmberg A. and Maskell P. (2004), 'Clusters and knowledge: local buzz, global pipelines and the process of knowledge creation', *Progress in Human Geography*, 28: 31–56.

Bell M. and Albu M. (1999), 'Knowledge systems and technological dynamics in industrial clusters in developing countries', *World Development*, 27(9): 1715–34.

Belussi F. (1993), 'The transformation of the 1980s: the growth of network companies, or the return of flexibility in large business?', *International Journal of Technology Management*, 9: 188–9.

——. (2005), 'On the theory of spatial clustering: the emergence of various forms of agglomeration', in F. Belussi and A. Sammarra (eds.), *Industrial Districts, Relocation, and the Governance of the Global Value Chain*, Padova: Cleup.

——. (2006), 'In search of a theory of spatial clustering: agglomeration vs active clustering', in B. Asheim, P. Cooke and R. Martin (eds.), *Clusters in Regional Development*, Routledge: London.

Belussi F. and Arcangeli F. (1998), 'A typology of networks: flexible and evolutionary firms', *Research Policy*, 27: 415–28.

Belussi F. and Gottardi G. (eds.) (2000), *Evolutionary Patterns of Local Industrial Systems*, Aldershot: Ashgate.

Belussi F., Gottardi G. and Rullani E. (eds.) (2003), *The Technological Evolution of Industrial Districts*, Boston: Kluwer

Belussi F., Sammarra A. and Sedita S. (2008), 'Managing long distance and localised learning in the Emilia Romagna life science cluster', *European Regional Studies*, 16(5): 665–92.

Biggiero L. (2002), 'The location of multinationals in industrial districts: knowledge transfer in biomedicals', *Journal of Technology Transfer*, 27: 111–22.

Biggiero L. and Sammarra A. (2003), 'The biomedical valley: structural, relational and cognitive aspects', in F. Belussi, G. Gottardi and E. Rullani (eds.), *The Technological Evolution of Industrial Districts*, Boston: Kluwer, pp. 367–88.

Birkinshaw J. and Sölvell O. (2000), 'Leading-edge multinationals and leading-edge clusters', *International Studies of Management and Organization*, 33(2): 3–9.

Boari C. and Lipparini A. (1999), 'Networks within industrial districts: organizing knowledge creation and transfer by means of moderate hierarchies', *Journal of Management and Governance*, 3: 339–60.

Boschma R. A. and ter Wal A. L. J. (2007), 'Knowledge networks and innovative performance in an industrial district: the case of a footwear district in the South of Italy', *Industry and Innovation*, 14: 177–99.

Braunerhhjelm P. and Feldman M. (2006), *Cluster Genesis: Technology-Based Industrial Development*, Oxford: Oxford Univ. Press.

Breschi S. and Lissoni F. (2001), 'Knowledge spillovers and local innovation systems', *Industrial and Corporate Change*, 10: 975–1005.

Camuffo A. (2003), 'Transforming industrial districts: large firms and small business networks in the Italian Eyewear industry', *Industry and Innovation*, 10(4): 377–401.

Cantwell J. A. (1989), *Technological Innovation and Multinational Corporations*, Oxford: Basil Blackwell.

Cantwell J. and Iammarino S. (2000), 'Multinational corporations and the location of technological innovations in the UK regions', *Regional Studies*, 34: 317–22.

Cassiolato J. (1992), 'The user-producer connection in high-tech: a case study banking of automation in Brazil', in H. Schmitz and J. Cassiolato (eds.), *Hi Tech for Industrial Development*, London: Routledge.

Chesbrough H. W. (2003), *Open Innovation: The New Imperative for Creating and Profiting from Technology*, Boston: Harvard Business School Press.

Coe N. and Bunnell T. (2003), 'Spatializing knowledge communities: towards a conceptualisation of transnational innovation networks', *Global Networks*, 3(4): 437–56.

Corò G. and Grandinetti R. (1999), 'Evolutionary pattern of Italian industrial districts', *Human System Management*, 18: 117–29.

Davidow W. and Malone M. (1992), *The Virtual Corporation: Structuring and Revitalizing the Corporation for the 21st Century*, New York: Harper Collins.

Dicken P. (2003), *Global Shift: Mapping the Changing Contours of the World Economy*, London: Sage.

——. (2007), *Global Shift: Reshaping the Global Economic Map*, London: Sage.

Dicken P., Kelly P., Olds K. and Yeung H.W. (2001), 'Chains and networks, territories and scales: towards a relational framework for analyzing the global economy', *Global Networks*, 1(2): 99–123.

Dunning J. (1981), *International Production and Multinational Enterprise*, London: Allen & Unwin.

——. (1993), *Multinational Enterprise and the Global Economy*, Massachusetts: Addison-Wesley, Readings.

——. (1996), 'The geographical sources of the competitiveness of firms: some results of a new survey', *Transnational Corporations*, 5: 1–30.

——. (1998), 'Globalisation, Technological Change and the Spatial Organization of Economic Activity', in A. Chandler, P Hagstrom, O Sölvell (eds.) (1998) *The Dynamic Firm: The Rold of Technology, Strategy, and Regions*, Oxford: Oxford University Press.

——. (2000), 'The eclectic paradigm as an envelope for economic and business theories of MNE activity', *International Business Review*, 9(2): 163–90.

Economist, The (2004), 'A word of work – a survey of outsourcing', 13 November: 1–16.

Engardio P., Bernstein A. and Kriplani M. (2003), 'Is your job next?', *Business Week*, February, 3: 50–60.

Enright M. (1998), 'Regional Clusters and Firm Strategy', in A. Chandler, P Hagstrom, O Sölvell (eds.) (1998), *The Dynamic Firm: The Role of Technology, Strategy, and Regions*, Oxford: Oxford University Press.

Fenestra R. (2003), *Advanced International Trade: Theory and Evidence*, Princeton: Princeton Univ. Press.

Ford D. (ed.) (2002), *Understanding Marketing and Purchasing*, London: Thomson.

Ford D., Gadde L-E, Håkansson H., Lundgren A., Snehota I., Turnbull P. and Wilson D. (1998), *Managing Business Relationships*. Chichester: Wiley.

Gambarotto F. and Solari S. (2005) 'How do local institutions contribute to fostering competitiveness of industrial clusters? The upgrading process in the Italian eyewear system', in E. Giuliani, R. Rabellotti and M. P. van Dijk (eds.), *Cluster Facing Competition: The Importance of External Linkages*, Aldershot: Ashgate, pp. 177–93.

Gereffi G. (1999), 'International trade and industrial upgrading in the apparel commodity chain', *Journal of International Economics*, 48: 37–70.

Gereffi G. and Kaplinky R. (2001), 'The value of value chain: spreading the gains from globalisation', *IDS Bulletin*, 32(3).

Gereffi G. and Korzeniewicz M. (eds.) (1994), *Commodity Chains and Global Capitalism*, Westport: Praeger.

Gereffi G., Humphrey J. and Sturgeon T. (2005), 'The governance of global value chains', *Review of International Political Economy*, 12: 78–104.

Giuliani E. (2005), 'Technological learning in a Chilean wine cluster and its linkages with the national system of innovation, in E. Giuliani, R. Rabellotti and M. P. van Dijk (eds.), *Cluster Facing Competition: The Importance of External Linkages*, Aldershot: Ashgate, pp. 155–76.

Giuliani E. and Bell M. (2005), 'The micro-determinants of meso-level learning and innovation: evidence from a Chilean cluster', *Research Policy*, 34: 47–68.

Giuliani E., Pietrobelli C. and Rabellotti R. (2005), 'Upgrading in global value chains: lessons from Latin American clusters', *World Development*, 33(4): 549–73.

Gordon R. (1996), 'Industrial districts and the globalisation of innovation: regions and networks in the new economic space', in X. Vence-Desa and S. Metcalfe (eds.), *Wealth From Diversity*, Dordrecht: Kluwer.

Guerrieri P. and Pietrobelli C. (2001), 'Models of Industrial Clusters' Evolution and Changes in Technological Regimes', in P. Guerrieri, S. Iammarino and C. Pietrobelli (2001), *The Global Challenge to Industrial Districts: Small and Medium-Sized Enterprises in Italy and Taiwan*, Cheltenham: Edward Elgar.

——. (2004), 'Industrial districts evolution and technological regimes: Italy and Taiwan', *Technovation*, 24(11): 899–914.

Guerrieri P., Iammarino S. and Pietrobelli C. (2001), *The Global Challenge to Industrial Districts: Small and Medium-Sized Enterprises in Italy and Taiwan*, Cheltenham: Edward Elgar.

Hall P. and Soskice D. (2001), *Varieties of Capitalism: The Institutional Foundations of Comparative Advantage*, Oxford: Oxford University Press.

Hanson G., Mataloni R. and Slaughter M. (2001), 'Expansion strategies of US multinational firms', *Brooking Trade Forum 2001*.

Henderson R. and Clark K. (1990), 'Architectural innovation: the reconfiguration of existing product technologies and the failure of established firms', *Administrative Science Quarterly*, 35: 9–30.

Hobday M. (1995), *Innovation in East Asia: the Challenge to Japan*, Aldershot: Edward Elgar.

Hopkins T. and Wallerstein I. (1994), 'Commodity chain in the capitalistic world-economy prior to 1800', in G. Gereffi and M. Korzeniewicz (eds.) (1994), *Commodity Chains and Global Capitalism*, Westport: Praeger.

Humphrey, J. (1995), 'Special issue on industrial organization and manufacturing competitiveness in developing countries', *World Development*, 23(1).

Humphrey J. and Schmitz H. (2000), Governance and Upgrading: Linking Industrial Cluster and Global Value Chain Research', *IDS Working Paper*, 120, Brighton: Institute of Developmental Studies, University of Sussex.

——. (2002), 'How does insertion in global value chains affect upgrading industrial clusters?', *Regional Studies*, 36(9): 1017–27.

——. (2004), 'Governance in global value chains', in H. Schmitz (ed.), *Local Enterprises in the Global Economy*. Cheltenham: Edward Elgar, pp. 95–109.

——. (2007), 'How does insertion in global value chains affect upgrading in industrial clusters?', *Regional Studies*, 36(9): 1017–27.

Jaffe A., Trajtenberg, M. and Henderson, R. (1993) 'Geographic localization and knowledge spillovers as evidenced by patent citations', *Quarterly Journal of Economics*, 108: 577–98.

Johanson, J. and Vahlne J. (1977), 'The internationalisation process of the firm: a model of knowledge development and increasing foreign market commitment', *Journal of International Business Studies*, 8(1): 23–32.

Jones R. and Kierzkowski H. (2000), 'A framework for fragmentation', in S. Arndt and H. Kierzkowski (eds.), *Fragmentation in International Trade,* Oxford: Oxford University Press.

Kaplinsky R. (2000), 'Globalisation and unequalisation: what can be learned from value chain analysis?', *Journal of Development Studies*, 37(2), 117–46.

Kaplinsky R., Morris R. and Readman J. (2002), 'The globalisation of product markets and immiserising growth: lesson from the South African Furniture industry', *World Development*, 30(7), 1159–77.

Kenney M. and Florida R. (1994), 'Japanese maquiladoras: production organisation and global commodity chains', *World Development*, 22: 2744.

Kogut B. and Zander U. (1992), 'Knowledge of the firm, combinative capabilities, and the replication of technology', *Organization Science*, 3: 383–97.

Korzeniewicz M. (1992), 'Global commodity networks and the leather footwear industry: emerging forms of economics organisation in a postmodern world', *Sociological Perspectives*, 35(2): 313–27.

Krugman P. (1995), 'Growing world trade: causes and consequences', *Brooking Papers on Economic Activity*, 1: 327–42.

Lall S. (2001), *Competitiveness, Technology and Skills*, Aldershot: Edward Elgar.

Langlois R. (2001), 'The vanishing hand: the changing dynamics of industrial capitalism', SSRN working paper.

Lazerson M. H. and Lorenzoni G. (1999), 'The firms feed industrial districts: a return to the Italian source', *Industrial and Corporate Change*, 8: 235–66.

Lechner C. and Dowling, M. (1999), 'The evolution of industrial districts and regional networks. The case of the biotechnology region of Munich/Martinsried', *Journal of Management and Governance*, 3: 309–38.

Leoncini R. and Montresor S. (eds.) (2008), *Dynamic Capabilities between Firm Organization and Local Systems of Production*, London: Routledge.

Lipsey R. (2002), 'Home and host country effects of FDI'. Available online at http://ideas.repec.org/p/nbr/nberwo/9293

Maggioni M. and Bramanti A. (2002), 'Local and Global Networks in the Economics of SMEs – is Proximity the Only Thing that Matters?' in R. McNaughton and M. Green, (eds.) *Global Competition and Local Networks*, London: Gower.

Malmberg A. and Sölvell O. (1997), 'Localised innovation processes and the sustainable competitive advantage of firms: a conceptual model', in M. Taylor and S. Conti (eds.), *Interdependent and Uneven Development: Global and Local Perspectives*, Aldershot: Ashgate.

Markusen A. (1996), 'Sticky places in slippery space: a typology of industrial districts',

Economic Geography, 72: 293–313.

Maskell P. (1999), 'Future challenges and institutional preconditions for regional development policy of economic globalisation', paper presented at workshop 'Information processes and path-dependent evolution: local systems' response to changes in context, Padua University, 27 November.

Maskell P., Pedersen T., Petersen B. and Dick-Nielsen J. (2007), 'Learning paths to offshore outsourcing: from cost reduction to knowledge seeking', *Industry and Innovation*, 14(3): 239–57.

McDonald F., Tüselmann H., Heisr A. and Williams D. (2003), 'Employment in host regions and foreign direct investment', *Environment and Planning C: Government and Policy*, 21: 687–701.

Moodysson J. and Jonsson O. (2007), Knowledge collaboration and proximity, *European Urban and Regional Studies*, 14(2): 115–31.

Nadvi K. and Schmitz H. (1999), 'Special issue on industrial clusters in developing countries', *World Development*, 27(9).

Navas-Alemán L. and Bazan L. (2005), 'Making value chain governance work for implementation of quality. Labor and environmental standards: Upgrading challenges in the footwear industry', in E. Giuliani, R. Rabellotti and M. P. van Dijk (eds.), *Cluster Facing Competition: The Importance of External Linkages*, Aldershot: Ashgate, pp. 39–60.

Palpacuer F. (2000), 'Competence-based strategies and global production networks', *Competition and Change*, 4(4): 354–400.

Paniccia I. (2002), *Industrial districts: Evolution and Competitiveness in Italian Firms*, Cheltenham: Edward Elgar.

Pietrobelli C. and Rabellotti R. (2005) 'Upgrading in global value chains: lessons from Latin American clusters', in E. Giuliani, R. Rabellotti and M. P. van Dijk (eds.), *Cluster Facing Competition: The Importance of External Linkages*, Aldershot: Ashgate, pp. 13–37.

Pisano G. (2006), *Science Business: The Promise, the Reality, and the Future of Biotech*, Harvard, MA: Harvard Business School.

Porter M. (1985), *Competitive Advantage*, New York: The Free Press.

Powell W. (1990), 'Neither market nor hierarchy: network forms of organization', *Research in Organisational Behaviour*, 12: 295–336.

Rabellotti R. (2004), 'How globalisation affects Italian industrial districts: the case of Brenta'. In H. Schmitz (ed.), *Local Enterprises in the Global Economy: Issues of Governance and Upgrading*, Cheltenham: Edward Elgar.

Rabellotti R. and Schmitz H. (1999), 'The internal heterogeneity of industrial districts in Italy, Brazil and Mexico', *Regional Studies*, 33(2): 97–108.

Robertson P. and Langlois R. (1995), 'Innovation, networks, and vertical integration', *Research Policy*, 24: 543–62.

Rugman A. M. and Verbeke A. (2001) 'Subsidiary specific advantages in multinational enterprises', *Strategic Management Journal*, 22(3): 237–50.

Sammarra A. (2003), 'Lo sviluppo dei distretti industriali', *Percorsi tra globalizzazione e localizzazione*, Roma: Carocci.

——. (2005), 'Relocation and the international fragmentation of industrial districs value chain: matching local and global perspectives', in F. Belussi and A. Sammarra (eds.), *Industrial Districts, Relocation, and the Governance of the Global Value Chain*, Padova: Cleup, pp. 61–70.

Sammarra A. and Belussi F. (2006), 'Evolution and relocation in fashion-led Italian distrcts: evidence from two case-studies', *Entrepreneurship and Regional Development*, forthcoming.

Saxenian A. and Hsu J. (2001), 'The Silicon Valley-Hsinchu connection: technical communities and industrial upgrading', *Industrial and Corporate Change*, 10(4): 893–920.

Schmitz H. (ed.) (2004), *Local Enterprises in the Global Economy: Issues of Governance and Upgrading*, Cheltenham: Edward Elgar.

Shan W. and Song J. (1997), 'Foreign direct investment and the sourcing of technological advantage: evidence from the biotechnology industry', *Journal of International Business Studies*, 28(2): 267–84.

Tassetto F. (2008), 'L'evoluzione recente del distretto calzaturiero della Riviera del Brenta', unpublished thesis, Faculty of Science Policy, University of Padua.

Thompson G., Frances J., Levacic R. and Mitchel J. (eds.) (1991), *Markets, Hierarchies and Networks*, London: Sage.

Thorelli H. B. (1986), 'Networks: between market and hierarchies', *Strategic Management Journal*, 7: 37–51.

Todeva E. (2006), *Business Networks*, Oxford: Routledge.

Unctad (2002), *World Investment Report: Transitional Corporations and Export Competitiveness*, New York and Geneva: United Nation Conference on Trade and Development Publications.

Unido (2002), *Industrial Development Report, 2002/2003, Competing through Innovation and Learning*, Vienna: Unido.

Vang J. and Chaminade C. (2007), Cultural clusters, global-local linkages and spillovers: theoretical and empirical insights from an exploratory study of Toronto's film cluster', *Industry and Innovation*, 14: 401–20.

Vernon R. (1966), 'International investment and international trade in the product cycle', *Quarterly Journal of Economics*, 80: 190–207.

Veugelers R. and Cassiman B. (2001), 'Foreign subsidiaries as a channel of international technology diffusion', IESE Research Paper, Barcelona: University of Navarra. Available online at http://ideas.repec.org/e/pre105.html

Whitley R. (1996), 'Business systems and global commodity chains: competing or complementary forms of economic organisation?', *Competition & Change*, 1: 411–25.

2 Localized and distance learning in industrial districts

Fiorenza Belussi and Silvia Rita Sedita
(Padua University)

2.1 Introduction

More than 100 years after Alfred Marshall conceptualized the model of industrial district (ID), the interest in the spatial agglomeration of specialized industries has remained surprisingly unchanged.

The echo of Marshall's description of the ways in which a localized cluster composed of a bunch of small and medium-sized firms can reach an adequate competitive strength, benefiting from a vast array of external economies, can be found in various disciplines, such as industrial economics, business studies, economic geography, sociology, urban planning, social network analysis, and political science.

Summing up this vast array of contributions, we can identify six important elements which are involved in the formation of localized external economies: (1) the pooling of skilled workers in the local labour market; (2) the presence of ancillary industries and specific infrastructures; (3) the use of highly specialized machinery related to firm specialization; (4) the existence of constructive cooperation among local firms (promoted by a vertically extended inter-firm division of labour); (5) the transparency of competition (related to the significant number of existing rivals at local level); and finally, and more importantly, (6) the existence of a special 'industrial atmosphere' in which firms are immersed, that stimulates the transfer of knowledge, the introduction of novelties, and the rapid adoption of 'good ideas'. These characteristics are the keynotes of the industrial district model, and, in this first approximation, they are the result of a long-lasting localization, giving rise to an 'organic whole': a localized and strongly specialized local industrial system characterized by the presence of embedded social networks. Obviously, this short description does not account for the variety of the districtualization processes that occurred in many countries and regions during different historical periods,[1] nor does it discuss the different terminology adopted in the various disciplines to denote the phenomenon of territorial specialization based on specific industrial district typologies, which have been named alternatively cluster, local industrial system, local milieus, and so on and so forth.

It is important to observe that in the original Marshallian version, the ID concept possessed some descriptive features (being industrial districts formed by a local community of workers, businessmen, and representatives of local civic and social associations) that were lost in the subsequent development of the theory of industrial organization, interested only in the conceptualization of positive locational economies, collapsing the ID to a 'pure' economic model of scale economies driven by agglomeration. Accordingly, the rich substratum of dense social relationships, business networks, and flows of information and knowledge related to the interactions of local actors, implied by a realistic representation of the ID, remained obscured.

Since then the literature counts many tentative ways of dealing with the issue of localized economies. The socio-economic approach of Marshall was given new life both by American business scholars (Porter 1998; Harrison 1992) and economic geographers (Saxenian, Scott, Storper, Feldman), and by several contemporary researchers in Italy (Becattini 1990; Belussi and Gottardi 2000) and in Europe (Maskell and Kebir 2005).

Many contributions illustrated and discussed in detail in Section 2.2 that attempted to reintroduce the Marshallian analysis referred to the 'social' aspects of the ID model, but they failed to incorporate the most advanced theories and methodologies derived from economic sociology and from social network research, limiting the level of analysis to a purely descriptive and suggestive approach. Several important lines of investigations were omitted. How do ID entrepreneurs grasp the 'knowledge in the air'? How is knowledge disseminated among local competing enterprises? Is it a matter of labour mobility, direct observation through the competitor's windows, or other factors? And more importantly, are IDs net importers of outside-created new technology or do they possess an autonomous capability of generating novelties and innovations? How has the model of localized learning discussed above, related to a kind of closed system (well alive during Marshallian times), transformed itself into a more complex system (typical of the post-Fordist era), where 'learning at the boundaries' dominates, which is a composite mix of related varieties of localized and distance learning?

In this perspective our contribution, mainly conceptual, tries to develop a more rigorous analysis.

It starts from the traditional Marshallian view, containing in essence a modern theory of localized learning, but it adds the more recent theories on communities of practice (CoPs), described as loci of situated learning and 'learning at the boundaries' (Lave and Wenger 1991; Brown and Duguid 1991), which lead us to reflect on their functional role within the ID learning mechanism as providers of problem-solving knowledge and sometimes innovations, whose origin is also embedded in the firms' absorbing capability of external-to-the-district innovations. Furthermore, our analysis aims to illustrate and contrast the coexistence, within the ID model, of a 'spontaneous' mechanism of 'knowledge sharing' among the various local agents with the more deliberate form of 'knowledge creation and transfer', which is organized through business networks, either local or international. The latter normally takes place in vertical production networks, strategically determined by the need of access to lower production costs, or to innovative inputs (through manufacturing outsourcing and/or knowledge offshoring) or in the building of new relationships with local or external knowledgeable institutions. In this article we maintain that radical innovations find a fertile environment in these forms of non-spontaneous networks, while incremental innovations are often the result of spontaneous forms of social interactions or the by-product of local and distance inter-firm relationships. We assume that:

1 local learning through communities of practice within the industrial district is conducive to incremental innovation;
2 local learning through R&D institutions may give rise to radical innovations;
3 distance learning through communities of practice extending outside the district is conducive to incremental innovation;
4 distance learning through firms networks may be conducive to both radical (e.g. R&D networks) or incremental learning (e.g. international subcontracting); and that finally
5 boundary learning (which is the 'blending' of all this local and distant learning), will lead to sustained multiple innovations within an open system model of radical and incremental innovations.

The chapter proceeds as follows: in Section 2.2 there is a comprehensive summary of the evolution of the literature related to the concept of ID. We review both the oldest contributions on localized learning mechanism and the newest ones, which provide a fresh view on the distance learning mechanisms. In Section 2.3 a theoretical framework is developed, explaining the role of localized and distance learning, under the unifying approach illustrated by the 'learning at the boundaries' concept. Finally, Section 2.4 provides some concluding remarks on the implications of our theoretical analysis, which has been driven by an interdisciplinary approach to the understanding of the learning process within IDs.

2.2 From localized learning to distance learning in IDs

2.2.1 The Marshallian heritage

The concept of the ID can be traced back to the *Principles of Economics*, where Marshall describes how an agglomeration (cluster) of small and medium-sized firms fosters the development of external economies, the old terminology used by Marshall prior to Young's discovery of the increasing returns mechanism, allowing the ID to enjoy the same economies of scale (and the consequent division of labour) that normally benefit giant companies:

> external economies [. . .] can often be secured by the concentration of many small businesses of a similar character in particular localities: or, as is commonly said, by the localization of industry. (Marshall 1920: IV.IX.25)

The benefits given by the specialized deployment of local resources are at the basis of this seminal process of concentration of industrial activities, which creates a local pool of skilled workers, allowing the possibility of sharing investments in new and expensive machinery, and the creation of an 'industrial atmosphere' that enhances knowledge spillovers:

> The mysteries of the trade become no mysteries; but are as it were in the air, and children learn many of them unconsciously.
>
> (Marshall 1920: IV.X.7)

The type of knowledge circulating in the Marshallian district is mainly tacit, rooted in practice, and technical. The degree of codification is very low, and the experience of more skilled workers is passed on to the new generations, by word of mouth. The Marshallian view had been abandoned for 50 years, until it came back to life, thanks to the work of Becattini, who finds evidence of the Marshallian theories in his study on Tuscany. Becattini defines an ID as a

> socio-territorial entity which is characterised by the active presence of both a community of people and a population of firms in one naturally and histori-cally bounded area. In the district, unlike in other environments, such as the manufacturing towns, community and firms tend to merge.
>
> (Becattini 1990: 38)

In his neo-Marshallian perspective, Becattini looks at the ID as a local agglomera-tion of small and medium-sized enterprises, all involved in the same productive process, but where everyone is specialized in a particular phase. Everyone is in-dependent of each other, but participates in a local network of geographic, social and productive relationships. As a result, an integrated industrial area arises, which produces economies that are external to the single firm, but internal to the localized 'thickening' of intra-inter industrial and social relationships. Thus, the ID is the extreme synthesis of the social-economic interactions between the mechanism of light industrialization and the embeddedness of a specific local production system into a social community.

This new social perspective of industrial organization is characterized by the introduction of the concept of the community as fundamental to the definition of an industrial district, which now goes beyond the idea of a cluster of localized firms. Becattini introduces an important variation to the Marshallian view, trying to specify the vague concept of 'knowledge in the air'. A necessary condition for the existence of the ID is the presence of social interactions, and the sense of belonging to a local community, which, in turn, becomes a crucial element of the key role of the community/district identity (created by a system of shared values, institutions and rules). The ID becomes a living metaphor of an institutional arrangement, which mixes the neoclassical view of self-interested agents (local firms) with a more sociological perspective, which describes how actors are motivated in their actions by social obligations, as theoretically assumed at a more general level by Lyons and Mehta, (1997) and by Hollingsworth (2000). This calls for the introduction in the framework of analysis of the idea of communities, associations, and various forms of social and business networks (Smith-Doerr and Powell 2003). The economic coordination that in the neoclassical paradigm appears to be organized by impersonal calculative transactions is transformed in the ID model as an 'embedded' transaction, influenced by social ties, different variation of self-built trust, reputation, solidarity, norms, habits and co-evolved rules of conduct. Geographical proximity allows the growth of reciprocal trust between the actors of the district, derived from repeated exchanges and from the sense of belonging to the same community (Becattini 1990; Dei Ottati 1994).[2] The presence of frequent and eradicated relationships characterizes in the ID what has elsewhere been called social capital (Jacobs 1961; Bourdieu 1985; Coleman 1988; Putnam 1993).[3]

The main consequence derived from a 'social' theory of the ID is that it represents a configuration of an institutional arrangement that reduces transaction costs among local actors and improves cooperation among local actors (business firms and institutions).

2.2.2 Industrial districts as localized networks and communities of practices

During the end of the 1980s this 'social' approach to the theory of the ID became widespread. In particular, many studies underlined the emergence of business networks in IDs, both as a pervasive effect of the existing local social connectedness (Brusco 1982; You and Wilkinson 1994), and as a novel organizational form, which retains some characteristics of the functioning of the market (flexibility) together with an amelioration of the costs of the hierarchy (internal coordination costs), as discussed, among others, by Powell (1990), Belussi and Arcangeli (1998) and Kogut (2000). Business networks were viewed as relational forms of governance with more or less dispersed authority where separate resources are deployed conjointly in a cooperative modality (Thorelli 1986; Storper and Harrison 1991). The network perspective becomes a common practice among scientists under the rubric of regional agglomeration or regional learning systems (Scott 1988; Harrison 1992; Amin and Robins 1990; Camagni 1991; Saxenian 1994; Lazerson 1995; You 1995; Antonelli 1994; Gordon 1996; Asheim 1996; Enright 1998; Staber 1998, 2001; Pilotti 2000; Castilla, *et al.* 2000; Acs 2000; Jarrillo 1988). This literature has highlighted that firms located in industrial districts are able to produce a better economic performance, as compared with inefficient giant firms, and that Toyotistic systems of production, based on subcontracting nets, supersede the Fordist model of organization (Harrison 1994). Localized networks of firms, as argued by Piore and Sable (1984), often proved to be a better organizational form to deal with flexible demand and to transfer knowledge as compared with the large firm model. The work of Bellandi (1992) has stressed the role of the so-called 'decentralized capabilities' occurring at international level in IDs. Others have compared the Italianate model of IDs with other types of localized networks (Markusen 1996). Other researchers, in a similar vein, have related the vitality of the decentralized firm model of Silicon Valley with the declining stability of Boston Route 128, an area where large corporations are located (Dorfman 1983; Saxenian 1994). They have argued that although firms in both cases are co-located in two specialized districts, and firms can benefit from a high geographical proximity, the two local systems show divergent dynamics. The different performance and adaptability to changes exhibited by firms located in Silicon Valley can be explained by a sort of 'district effect', related, among others, to the following aspects: the presence of small specialized firms (sources of variability for the local system), the role of social networks in providing seed capital to firms (positive cooperation among financial institutions and firms), the rapid diffusion of knowledge due to the frequency of informal contacts (quick knowledge contagion). Networks of innovators were also detected by Lissoni and Pagani (2003) in the textile machine production district of Brescia.

The literature developed on the issue of industrial networks has been rich in relation to the themes tackled, with many empirical cases (Staber 2001). However, most of the studies of district networks are more descriptive than analytical. The new toolkits of social network analysis (Smith-Doerr and Powell 2003), consisting of detailed descriptions of networks structures, have not yet been largely applied. The large-scale network of the Ohta machine-tools industrial district in Tokyo described by Nakano and White (2006) represents a first attempt to use the social network analysis in depth to illustrate the relational structure of the ID production network. What is missing (Staber 2001) is a systematic analysis of the conditions under which certain network structures in IDs lead to innovation. Emergent relevant issues, which have scarcely been taken into consideration, are: if the location of new knowledge in the network is at the centre or at the periphery (or within specific actors-nodes); the topology of networks; and the properties of the networks (density, intensity of relations, centrality of actors-main nodes). The logic-in-use seems to be that the presence of a network indicates cooperation and that cooperation brings innovation, but as we know this chain of causation is profoundly misleading. Subcontracting relations do not always generate new knowledge. Institutional factors constrain or favour cooperation and/or innovation, as has been claimed extensively by Todeva in her long literature review (2006). Social embeddedness can produce cumulative advantage, but it can also turn out to 'lock in' effects. Ties that bind can also become ties that blind (Grabher 1993); embeddedness may produce too much conformity (Sorensen and Audia 2000), or pathological ossification (Loasby 1998). In a study on the garment industry in New York, Uzzi (1997) found that performance is not just correlated with the number of firm ties (social capital hypothesis) but with an intermediate number of ties; thus, firm success requires neither over-embeddedness nor under-embeddedness.

The variety of growth patterns observed among IDs and clusters calls for a new theoretical framework able to analyze with more accuracy the interaction between the social and the economic sphere, considering the conditions of emergence and existence of IDs, and detecting the potential evolutionary trajectory, where the behaviour of agents-nodes (learning) is in a first theorization associated with specific ID structures and with the specific characteristics of nodes. There is a lack of large-scale testing on causality relationships between the various variables taken into consideration in explaining economic and innovative performance, also within the business studies tradition (Håkansson and Snehota 1995; Håkansson and Ford 2000). A necessary precondition is to deepen our knowledge of the different social networks that exist within a given ID.

In the old Marshallian framework, belonging to a communitarian social network was just defined in relation to the agent's perception of identity, depending on the historical setting, but in modern IDs, as discussed by Saxenian (1994), Belussi and Pilotti (2002), Bellandi (1992), Giuliani (2005), Giuliani and Bell (2005), Håkanson (2005), Iammarino and McCann (2006), communities are formed by specific segments of labour markets, technicians, entrepreneurs and profession-als, which form cognitive subsets. As a matter of fact, these sub-communities are communities of practice. Therefore, a link can be established between the literature on contemporary IDs and the CoPs approach (Brown and Duguid 1991; Lave and Wenger 1991; Wenger 1999, 2000). The knitted structure of interactions between entrepreneurs, workers and institutions, due to the sharing of work and non-work activities, are in IDs generated by geographical and social proximity. As has been argued in the sociological literature, communities of practice are able to generate knowledge and nurture the local community (see Brown and Duguid 1991; Swann, Scarbrough and Robertson 2002).

Lave and Wenger (1991) first introduced the concept of CoP in 1991, underlining the importance of sharing practice in the process of learning in large corporations. They describe a CoP as

> an activity system about which participants share understanding concerning what they are doing and what that means in their lives and for their community. Thus, they are united in both action and in the meaning that that action has, both for themselves and for the larger collective.
>
> (Lave and Wenger 1991: 98)

These communities are organisms constituted by groups of professionals, informally bound together, driven by a common purpose, to share their distinctive capabilities to solve organizational problems. They could be, for instance, engineers engaged in deep-water drilling, or consultants specialized in strategic marketing, or 'reps' offering technical support (see the case of Xerox in Orr 1990). One of the most important features that characterize their existence is their organic, spontaneous and informal nature. The members' attitude of giving their own contribution to the problem solving process is reinforced by the self-selected membership mechanism of participation.

The CoP's main purpose is to develop members' capabilities and build exchange knowledge, which becomes useful, for example, to drive strategies and generate new lines of business, but also to support incremental innovations, the latter often emerging from 'local adaptations of work practices within communities, in response to new problems' (Swan, Scarbrough and Robertson 2002: 477).

A defining feature of a CoP lies in the process of 'self-perpetuating' (Wenger 2000), as opposed to other forms of aggregation, such as a functional group, a network, a team, or a project team. The last one, for example, is normally formed by a group of workers built to accomplish a specific task,[4] and exists until the project has been completed. Instead a CoP, as Wenger and Snyder (2000) explain, has the property of lasting for a long time, allowing the sedimentation of a social capital. This tacit and common based knowledge lifts over time the potentiality of the community and its ability to solve problems (Lesser and Everest 2001).

CoPs are an important locus where the process of learning in a social perspective activates, involving the mutual engagement of all the members, although the latter are difficult to detect empirically (Handley, *et al.* 2006). Learning is the result of the interplay between competences defined in a social community, and personal experiences. Therefore, a community of practice can be viewed as a social container of the heterogeneous competences that frame a learning system.

In IDs, these communities play the role of key small social networks. Professionals and skilled workers upgrade their knowledge and interpret the novelties that appear on the market, applying peer evaluation during the selection of new knowledge, and fostering a mechanism of social validation. It can be hypothesized that such communities of practice are more developed in old and mature IDs, while they are absent in newly developed IDs localized in NICs or in Eastern countries, where satellite forms of districts, formed only by dependent subcontractors[5] (see Markusen 1996), typically operate.

This transition from a 'communitarian district', where individuals just perceive themselves as members of a community to which they are attached by a general sense of belonging, to an 'ID endowed with working CoPs', is only tentatively suggested here, because the analysis of the role of local communities of practice represents a quite new field of research. For instance the existence of working CoPs in IDs has been detached in the Riviera del Brenta district in Italy (an ID specialized in high-quality/fashion shoe-making; see Belussi 2000) where there is an active community of designers, who elected a local bar as a meeting point to informally share new ideas and tendencies of the market. It is also useful to mention the work of Lissoni and Pagani (2003), who 'counted' the number of networks in a local cluster, namely the hosiery machinery in Brescia, with the goal of detecting the patterns of local relationships and their effect on the introduction of incremental innovations. They associate these relationships with the concept of epistemic communities (Haas 1992; Thomson 2005), but we believe that the concept of communities of practice fits better. If we refer to IDs, tacit knowledge transfer is more crucial; it is particularly the case of those operating in fashion, music and more generally in industries where creativity is a fundamental element of competitive advantage. One of the main features distinguishing the two communities lies, in fact, in the types of knowledge produced (Amin and Cohendet 1999 and 2004; Cohendet 2005). Epistemic communities are viewed as related to the production of knowledge that is mainly explicit (but not codified, because it sticks inside the community as explained by Baumard 1999), due to the presence of a codebook (displaced or not – Haas 1992, Cowan, David and Foray 1999).

Communities of practice, on the contrary, are related to exchanges of practices and know-how, which are mainly assumed to take a tacit form, and to be socially localized (Brown and Duguid 1991, Lave and Wenger 1991).

In this vein Benner (2003) contributes to the theoretical debate on localized learning, showing how communities of practice in Silicon Valley, supported by local institutions, play a significant role in spurring individual and collective learning processes in the region. He uses the case study of an association of women in Internet design and development occupations (Silicon Valley Webgirls), which works as a facilitator for cross-firm learning communities. Besides, also some studies on industrial districts at European level have proved the existence of communities of practice, such as in the case of the vibrant community of engineering professionals in the electronics industrial district of Madrid (Rama, *et al.* 2003), and of the Danish NorCom telecom district (Reinau 2007).

2.2.3 Industrial districts as tools of localized learning

In the ample literature produced in the last two decades on the subject, an important analytical passage occurred when researchers started to address their attention more precisely to the characteristics of the ID model linked to the enforcement of innovation capabilities of firms. On this issue we can find some illustrative evidence coming from some ID case studies, concerning both IDs specialized in high-tech sectors and IDs belonging to low-tech sectors. According to these studies the following factors were stressed (Belussi and Gottardi 2000):

- the influence of territorial and social proximity in knowledge transmission;
- the importance of proximity (and of informal situations) for the activation of flows of tacit knowledge among the local agents;
- the importance of non-R&D-based innovations;
- the crucial role of accumulation of practical knowledge and its localized nature;
- the role played by the associative local institutions (collective actors) as meta-organizers in the diffusion and creation of knowledge.

The articulation of tacit knowledge finds its privileged locus in the narration of firms' histories, in the retrieval of workers' experiences and in its oral transmission, in the various moments of 'situated' learning favoured by the existence of multiple relationships (also external to the working place) that agents build with local partners with whom they share some common culture, interests and lifestyles. Co-localized firms in IDs naturally benefit from this embeddedness, and from the existence of strong ties – the 'strong tie' end of Granovetter's (1973) paradigmatic dichotomy – with the most knowledgeable actors. This allows a substantial reduction in the costs of access to knowledge. While tacit knowledge is commonly perceived as sticky (Von Hippel 1998), and difficult to articulate, in the IDs' rich relational tissue, the local community works as a transfer mechanism. In a global world where the access to resources (and codified knowledge) is practically ubiquitous (Maskell 1999), the only strategy pursued by firms to differentiate themselves from their rivals is to use complex monitoring strategies to disentangle knowledge sources (such as cluster-specific architectural knowledge, see Pinch, *et al.* 2003) or knowledge sources that can be available only to a restricted club of members, and/or embedded in a local codebook (Cowan and Foray 1997). Local capabilities in dynamic contexts, nurtured by localized forms of tacit knowledge, are among the most relevant drivers of the competitiveness of IDs (Maskell and Malmberg 1999; Storper 1997; Amin 1993). While ICT can help with codifiable knowledge, the crucial tacit dimension remains elusive and localized. Obviously, we need caution when dealing with the equation posed by Gertler (2003) that 'tacit equals local and codifiable equals global'. Organizational proximity (Torre and Rallet 2005), and not geographical proximity, is often at the basis of tacit knowledge transfer among geographically distant agents, such as in the case of meetings among the multinational headquarters and its units, or of managers travelling among clients and subcontractors, or of participants in a trade fair or exhibition.

The recognition of the importance of the geography of knowledge spillovers appears to be another perspective through which to discuss the concept of localized learning. It has been found, for instance, that in US patent citations by other scientists a marked territorial dimension was followed. Patents registered by distant agents tended to be cited less frequently than patents registered by spatially proximate inventors (Jaffe, *et al.* 1993; Audretsch 1998; Audretsch and Feldman 1996; Caniëls and Romijn 2005). However, the importance of knowledge spillovers has probably been exaggerated, and much of what has been linked to knowledge spillovers, such as the labour mobility of experts or scientists from university to firms, is in reality an aspect related to the functioning of the labour market, although in specific cases connoted by the existence of a significant agglomeration of similar firms (Zucker, Darby and Armstrong 1998).

There is a general consensus on the idea that IDs are characterized by a strong propensity towards incremental innovations, favoured by the interaction between agents and by the incentive of imitation (Belussi and Pilotti 2002; Belussi and Gottardi 2000; Antonelli 1995).

On the one hand, the local context fuels the generation of incremental innovations, and, on the other hand, the visibility of innovation fuels the adoption by followers. Innovators, who cannot prevent knowledge from leaking outside their organization, are challenged to find out new solutions (in terms of new products or new production processes) for bypassing imitators. This may generate a recursive process of local learning, based on exploration and exploitation activities (Nelson and Winter 1982; Nelson 1992; March 1991).

Cainelli and De Liso (2004) in their empirical investigation on the evaluation of the 'district effect' and 'innovation effect' in the economic performance[6] of firms, operating in traditional sectors, pinpoint the relevance of the combination of both knowledge spillovers (involuntary, through informal mechanisms), and formal innovation activities (mostly product innovation). The results of this study support the thesis of the innovativeness of IDs, generated both by intentional and non-intentional activities.

In particular, in 2001, an influential article redirected attention towards the mechanism of localized learning related to the clusterization of local systems (thus overlapping with the ID concept) (Maskell 2001), which emphasized the role of the cluster/ID as a specific local innovation system (different from other categories such as regional or national innovation systems). The ID model was thus taken up by the international literature as an extraordinary and powerful device, where learning activities and new knowledge can be developed at territorial level along both the vertical and the horizontal dimension. As regards the former, the attention was focused on the line that connects some business partners, possessing dissimilar but complementary capabilities that carry out transactions along the productive *filière*. It was maintained that frequent and close interactions between the same members of the local production network benefit by the reduction of transaction costs (including research and information costs) and of bargaining and decision costs (due to the existence of trust, social capital, and reputation), and from learning by interaction. As regards the latter, it was maintained that the existence of local rivals, which share similar capabilities and conduct similar activities, enforces the reciprocal observation of business models and novelties introduced in the production cycle; thus, on one hand, it stimulates imitation but, on the other hand, it provides the right incentive to variation, triggering parallel experimentations and knowledge explorations. The self-reproduction of the local system, in other words, relies significantly on learning by monitoring.

2.2.4 Industrial districts as tools of distance learning

The transition from neo-Marshallian districts (mainly closed local networks) to global districts (evolutionary post-Marshallian) has been recently emphasized by the literature (Amin and Thrift 1992), where attention is focused on the network connections that run through and across different spatial configurations. In the context of globalization, innovation inputs are unlikely to be locally confined. Globalization has also reduced the importance of traditional localized production factors (Simmie and Sennen 1999; Kleeble, *et al.* 1999). Key inputs appear to be inter-firm international research collaborations, and the use of international scientific and professional competencies. Linkages with customers and clients in international markets are therefore crucial to the commercial success of innovative new products. Clearly we are not talking here of a 'death of distance' (Cairncross 2001), but we focus our attention on the combination of close and distant interactions that occurs in IDs. The coined expression 'distance learning' brings us into a kind of intermediate position, and far from other stringent territorial metaphors like the idea of over-spatially bounded systems or, in contrast, of the under-spatially bounded knowledge flows typical of global systems *à la* Manuel Castells (1996).

The emergence of stable nets of external subcontractors and strategic suppliers stresses the new openness of IDs. Corò and Grandinetti (1999) have studied through an empirical analysis the evolutionary patterns of 19 Italian industrial districts, discovering that:

the district is relating with an increasing number of outside actors, resources and competences and, as a consequence, it is undergoing a transformation from being a rather confined system of relationships into something rather different

(Corò and Grandinetti 1999: 119)

The novel features that characterize the dynamics of modern IDs and clusters are the new forms of distance learning, related to the use of external-to-the-district informal and formal channels of absorption/creation of knowledge flows. International networks of firms and constellations of external communities of practice are at work to activate a process of exploration, selection, activation and nurturing of knowledge outside the boundaries of the district.

In order to be competitive, and above all to introduce complex innovations, IDs must be able to develop strategic relations with service providers outside the district, covering the fields where their internal competences are weak (often: information technology, quality management, marketing communication and so forth). This 'opening' process, obviously, occurs at different levels, and it is parallel to the tendency of Western companies to increase the share of their foreign R&D (Gerybadze and Reger 1999).

ID gatekeepers work as external knowledge absorbers through searching, transcoding and transferring. Researchers that have related the innovative capability of local firms to the use of external sources of knowledge for innovation have found a significant presence of national and international agents like universities, centres of research, and consultant agencies. We are referring here to the cases described in the works of Morrison on the low-tech districts in Italy (2004), and of Powell, Koput and Smith-Doerr (1996) on the biotech district of Boston. While in some cases external gatekeepers provide a unique access to a determined knowledge source, in others they contribute to the building of knowledge-creating relationships. In biotech clusters, if spatial concentration appears to be linked to large companies, forefront institutions, leading universities, and localized human capital, such as star scientists (Zucker, *et al.* 1998), global alliances are diffusely built in the field of R&D collaboration and for licensing (Moodysson, Coenen and Asheim 2006). Empirical research on knowledge and firms dynamics demonstrates a dual local-global logic of localization and knowledge flows around nodes of excellence interconnected by global networks (Feldman 2004; Coenen, Moodysson and Asheim 2004; Cooke 2004).

Saxenian (1999, 2005) has demonstrated the increasing role of skilled immigrants in the development of Silicon Valley. They are also at the basis of the development of the software district of Bangalore, in India, which has been developed by the repatriation of emigrants. Transnational social networks which subsequently become business networks are not to be interpreted simply as brain drain or access to cheap offshore production, but they ensure the building of a mutually beneficial connection of transnational technical communities, which favour the circulation of people, capital, technologies and ideas (Coe and Bunnell 2003). Similarly, Andersen and Lorenzen (2007) reported the case of some Danish entrepreneurs that came back from Boston to start up a new firm in Medicon Valley (near Copenhagen). In many Far East countries high-tech districts developed thanks to the transfer of knowledge facilitated by the localization of global multinationals or international suppliers, which slowly upgraded the local firms' capabilities. It is important to recall here the interesting evolution of the Hsinchu area in Taiwan, supported by the relocalization of Taiwanese-American companies which moved their base to Taiwan in order to tap into a huge reservoir of capital in the island, as is narrated by Hsu (2003).

Distance learning is directly linked to the firm's 'absorptive capacity' (Cohen and Levinthal 1990). With this term Aage (2001) addresses the ID's capability of achieving external knowledge, which is re-processed inside the system, as an 'internalization' of the competences acquired. Her study of the clothing ID, in Jutland (Denmark), shows the relevance of external information sources for increasing internal innovative capabilities; she refers particularly to the role played by shows and fairs, relations with suppliers, and trend studios (Aage 2004). Her results might appear to stress the devaluation of district embeddedness. But this is not the case. It does not signal the end of the dense internal networking, but it provides empirical evidence of the presence of multi-scale linkages for knowledge acquisition and transfer.

The recent cognitive 'openness' of IDs, also in low-tech sectors, is partially due to the use of ICT (Chiarvesio, Di Maria and Grandinetti 2005). However, electronic knowledge exchanges do not substitute face-to-face communications (Belussi 2005; Ciarli and Rabellotti 2006). Knowledge flows are easier as a result of the increasing adoption of international-shared languages and ICT infrastructures. Consequently, the access to multiple knowledge sources is made possible, favouring economies of variety, and enhancing heterogeneity. The process of achieving new knowledge, and consequently bridging it into the ID, has been studied in the literature by some developmental economists (Humphrey and Schmitz 2002) and proved empirically by recent analyses of external linkages and distant R&D/technology collaborations (Giuliani, et al. 2005; Morrison 2004). The productive relationships with foreign partners, including external suppliers, customers, research and market institutes, has improved the local capabilities of ID firms, building global supply chains, as is well illustrated in Gereffi, et al. (2005) and Bair and Gereffi (2001).

Recently, Bathelt, Malmberg and Maskell (2004) have deepened the duality that characterizes the process of local learning, introducing the concept of global pipelines. They juxtapose the local 'buzz' phenomenon with the 'global pipelines' building process. Even if the use of this metaphor has not created a large consensus (see, for instance, Cooke 2005), it is clear that the introduction of these two concepts responds to the need to limit the impact of the local learning perspective, and to use a much more realistic analytical frame, where the role of knowledge flows deriving from long-distance relationships is taken in account.

The following table (Table 2.1) summarizes the contributions found in the literature, and briefly overviewed in this section, which have tried to investigate the two main forms of learning occurring in spatially limited industrial settings: localized and distance learning.

Our contribution attempts to merge the two types of learning within an integrated theoretical framework, informing on the drivers of the innovative capacities of firms located in IDs. The following section illustrates our theoretical propositions.

2.3 Learning in IDs: combining localized and distance learning

In this new analytical perspective developed in our paper, the ID learning process, which leads to an innovative output, can be broken down into its main determinants:

Table 2.1 From localized learning to distance learning in IDs: a survey of the literature

Prevalent type of learning	Main contributions		Key concepts
Localized learning	**The Marshallian heritage**	Marshall (1920)	Elements involved with the formation of 'districtualization' giving rise to localized external economies: 1 Pooling of skilled workers 2 Ancillary industries and specific infrastructures 3 Firm specialization 4 Constructive cooperation 5 'Industrial atmosphere' which favours knowledge transmission
	The modern view	Becattini (1979, 1990) Dei Ottati (1994)	ID as an institutional arrangement that reduces transaction costs among local actors and improves cooperation; important role assigned to the concept of local community
		Porter (1998) Saxenian (1994) Scott (2006) Storper (1997) Feldman (2005) Bellandi (1992)	The discovering of IDs as local innovation systems
		Maskell (2001) Camagni (1991) Asheim (1996);	Localized learning Untraded interdependencies

(continued)

Prevalent type of learning	Main contributions	Key concepts
	Antonelli (1994, 2000) Saxenian (1994) Storper (1995)	
	Storper and Harrison (1991) Markusen (1996) Izushi (1997) Paniccia (1988) Robertson and Langlois (1995)	IDs as local systems working through a decentralized governance
	Lazerson (1995) Lissoni and Pagani (2003) Lazzeretti and Storai (2003) Scott (2006)	
	Brusco (1982) You and Wilkinson (1994) Giuliani (2005) Iammarino and McCann (2006) Håkanson (2005)	IDs as tools of social connectedness
Distance learning	**The global perspective**	Amin and Thrift (1992) Scott (1992)	Local nodes in global networks The world economy as a mosaic of regions consisting of localized networks of transactions embedded in global networks
	IDs as open evolving systems	Corò and Grandinetti (1999) Belussi and Gottardi (2000) Belussi and Pilotti (2002) Moodysson, Coenen and Asheim (2006) Feldman (2004) Cooke (2002a and 2002b, 2004) Saxenian (1999, 2005) Coe and Bunnell (2003) Andersen and Lorenzen (2005) Hsu (2003) Bathelt, Malmberg and Maskell (2004)	Local systems with absorbing capability of external knowledge

Prevalent type of learning	Main contributions	Key concepts
	Humphrey and Schmitz (2002) Boschma and ter Wal (2005) Scott (2006) Bell and Abu (1999)	
	Oinas (2002)	Local systems as interconnected places

- informal ties between individuals at the local/global level – inter-personal level;
- business ties between firms at the local/global level – inter-organizational level.

Innovations in IDs are, in fact, internally supported by firms' strategies, and by their proactive efforts (R&D, engineering departments, focused working groups), but they are also the result of firm interactions, both by means of communities of practices (including local professionals and constellations of CoPs) and business networks (including suppliers, customers, universities and institutions,[7] operating at the local level or situated outside the district). In some cases business networks are wholly internationalized, as in the case of the global supply chains reported by Gereffi, *et al.* (2005) and Bair and Gereffi (2001). In many situations, informal interpersonal ties compensate for the structural shortcomings of formal inter-organizational arrangements (Grabher and Ibert 2006).

The result is a model of 'open innovation' (Chesbrough 2003; Langlois and Robertson 1992; Langlois 2003), rooted in a learning-at-the-boundaries mechanism, which is able to activate simultaneously local and external-to-the-district actors. As Cooke (2006) notes, not all of the openness is geographically proximate, because distant networks play a strategic part, and cognitive and relational proximities (both at the interpersonal and inter-organizational level) come into play (see also Boschma 2005), building, as a consequence, a multi-spatial (geographically hybrid) knowledge domain. Learning in modern IDs involves a two-way mechanism: learning occurs when different communities of practices (local and distant) match and integrate their knowledge, or in a rather radical way, through a deliberate effort of building innovation-oriented alliances, networks and collaborations, which overcome the district boundaries.

The essential reference here is Powell, *et al.* (1996).

> Rather than using external relations as a temporary mechanism to compensate for capabilities a firm has not yet mastered, firms use collaborations to

expand their competencies. Firms opt for sustaining the ability to learn, via interdependence, over independence by means of vertical integration' … at the core of this relationship is a vital need to access relevant knowledge: knowledge of a sort that is sophisticated and widely dispersed and not easily produced or captured inside the boundaries of a firm. … [M]uch of the relevant knowledge is neither located inside an organization nor readily available to purchase. … When the sources of knowledge are disparate and the pathways of technological development uncharted, we would expect the emergence of networks of learning.

(Powell, *et al.* 1996: 143)

Scattered examples of district firms that have 'learnt at the boundaries' can be found in Italy in the district of Montebelluna and Mirandola (Belussi and Sammarra 2005). We refer to the innovation of the 'breathing sole' by Geox Group, a districtual firm, located in Montebelluna, with an output of 180 million euro. The innovation was conceptualized through a firm network, involving the internal lab, the Polytechnic of Milan, and the University of Tokyo. Very similar is the case of RanD, in the medical district of Mirandola (in the province of Modena), which cultivates R&D connections with the district of Minneapolis (the largest global biomedical district in the world), and with the US firm Medtronic located there.

It is relevant to underline that learning in IDs is not just building one pipeline, but it is related to the capability to blend together:

1 the work of different communities of practice (whose borders are more ample than the district ones), which functions for the incremental and radical upgrading of the knowledge existing in the district; and
2 the deliberate strategic activity of forming global firms' networks, which offshores knowledge and operates for incremental and radical knowledge upgrading.

Pipelines, without the work of communities of practice, are sterile; communities of practice, without strong R&D investments through external linkages, are weak in the process of new knowledge building.

There are many sources of localized and distance learning. We therefore distinguish between informal and business networks (Håkansson and Johanson 1988; Ibarra, *et al.* 2005). This segmentation variable is clearly inspired by the work of Powell and Grodal (2005), where they emphasize that networks can be characterized (among other features) by formal (purposive, strategic alliances between two parties) or informal ties (based on shared experience). This approach has also been recently adopted by Bell (2005), in his empirical contribution on the evaluation of the innovativeness of a cluster of Canadian mutual fund companies, where he investigates the relative importance of formal and informal networks.

The geography of ties informs on the geographical proximity of the members of the network, and the density of ties. We can therefore hypothesize that local ties tend to be strong, while external ties can be weak if temporary, or strong if they involve stable inter-firm networks. Following our theoretical discussion, and the social network theory, we assume the existence of the following heuristic pattern. Incremental innovations are more likely to occur along strong local ties, which require frequent and repeated interactions and, as the cognitive distance between agents is often too small (Nooteboom 1992, 2006a and 2006b; Loasby 2000), they are conducive to a small amount of new information. The type of learning derived from CoPs' interactions is somewhat innovative, but still conservative (Porac, Thomas and Baden-Fuller 1989), and thus not conducive to radical innovation (Amin and Roberts 2006).

Radical innovations are more likely to take place along distant weak ties, which have the character of being spatially scattered and infrequent. If the cognitive distance between agents is large enough, novel information and knowledge support the creation of Schumpeterian 'novel combinations' (see Granovetter 1973; Powell and Grodal 2005; Nooteboom 1992; Amin and Roberts 2006). Distance learning is based on the role of district boundary spanners, which engage multiple relationships with both local and distant actors.

Local and distance business interactions can have mainly two orders of explanation:

1 *the search for capabilities, which the firm lacks (or which are less costly to buy/organize outside);*
2 *the need to form alliances through which to build entirely new competences, and discovering new knowledge and innovations.*

Already Richardson (1972), in his seminal article, highlighted the motivations for firms to enter business networks: in order to reach complementary but dissimilar competencies they lack, and that need to fit the specific organizational productive demand, and which cannot be bought on the market ready-made. In the IDs, this has implied an evolutionary process which has shifted the firm searching from local to global referring to: (1) the search for specialized producers, and for critical competences; (2) the scanning of the market for cheaper producers, either geographically co-located or more and more dispersed in low-wages countries. In a period of fragmented but integrated global production processes, the construction of global supply chains (Gereffi, *et al.* 2005) has gained ground, both as buyer-driven chains (ruled by retailers and large commercial buyers) or producer-driven chains (MNCs). International inter-firm alliances (Nooteboom 2006b) are boosted either by strategy (collusion, eliminating a competitor), or efficiency (scale and scope), market positioning (fast market entry), or, finally, access to complementary competence (mostly for innovation purposes). The combination of localized and distance learning, due to informal and/or formal collaborations, gives rise to a set of collective competences (Oinas 1999, 2002) that are used in a vast range of organizational activities (R&D, production, sourcing, logistics and so on), favouring incremental and/or radical innovation processes. Stemming from the hypothesis that learning activities are situated (Lave and Wenger 1991), they can alternatively take place in localized business structures, such as the district local supply chains (including local institutions and research centres), or in local communities of practice, as well as in global supply chains (including external institutions and research centres) and constellation of communities (Ward 2000). Learning opportunities allows firms to explore their technological 'related variety' (Boschma and Iammarino 2007), building a firm-specific technological trajectory.

2.4 Conclusions

The unit of analysis of theoretical survey presented is the industrial district, a model of organization of the production that, if ingrained in the Italian production fabric, appears as a diffuse industrial model also in other countries. This chapter has supported the introduction of a new approach to district learning process, based on the interaction between localized and distance learning. It has sought to deepen the theoretical understanding of the learning processes for innovation occurring in industrial districts, through informal and formal channels of knowledge transfer. On the one hand, communities of practice characterize a spontaneous and non-deliberate form of social interaction, while, on the other hand, business networks configure themselves as effective mechanisms through which firms access complementary capabilities, both to reduce the production costs and to augment innovative capacity.

We distinguish between incremental and radical innovations. It can be argued that the district form is suitable to deal both with (1) the upgrading of knowledge, and with incremental innovations (due to the existence of various interacting local CoPs and of interactions between weak – in terms of knowledge and innovative capabilities – actors of the local supply chain), and (2) with double loop learning (Argyris 1976), radical learning, and innovation oriented projects (due to the existence of constellation of CoPs and global supply chains), which can take either the forms of deliberate (local and distant) R&D collaborations with other strong – in terms of knowledge and innovative capabilities – firms or institutions.

Our work, mainly conceptual, appears to us an insightful avenue for future studies, in which the process of localized and distance learning (through CoPs and business networks) could be supported by more empirical evidence.

Moreover, it can be argued that distant learning through external knowledge linkages and international constellations of CoPs in industrial districts could be fuelled and cultivated by political and social institutions as a way to absorb new knowledge and therefore to enforce the growth of local diffused capabilities. Besides, external linkages could be enhanced by local policy makers by investing in virtual interaction platforms (such as websites, blogs and forums), and by sponsoring the active participation of local knowledge workers in international trade fairs and exhibitions, or by attracting scientists trained in leading US or European institutions.

Notes

1 For a discussion see Markusen (1996), Robertson and Langlois (1995), and Paniccia (1998). Interestingly, some authors have also suggested the existence of hybrid forms (Coe 2001). A description of Japanese IDs can be found in Izushi (1997). The ID concept and the theoretical and empirical contributions on the issue are absolutely not confined by the Italian boundaries, being not a restricted phenomenon, but, on the contrary, a diffuse mode (as has also been pinpointed by Scott 1992).

2 This local system clearly differs from the Perroux type mechanism (1955) of local growth, where the sources of efficiency are uniquely based on the external effects derived by the external introduction from outside of growing 'motor' firms.

3 For a comparison with Bourdieu and Putnam's concepts of social capital see M. Siisiäinen (2000).

4 We recall here the team involved in the enhancing of the 'knowledge creating company' described by Nonaka and Takeuchi (1995), and implied in the Japanese concept of 'ba'. The Japanese philosopher Nishida has proposed this concept originally, and (later) Shimizu, and it is close to the English word 'place'. It refers to organizational contexts within which individuals interact at a specific time and place over a certain time period, a kind of shared space for emerging relationships, as has been described by Pilotti (2000).

5 The idea behind this is that social networks need times to develop, cooperative behaviour among firms are path-dependent, and favourable environmental conditions are necessary. So, the 'cloning' of IDs, away from the places where they were spontaneously formed, is not possible, and the pure delocalisation of activities or the transfer of subcontracting activities towards low-cost countries is not reproducing the original socio-economic formula.

6 Five regression models are estimated, measuring the performance, in terms of change in real value added between 1992 and 1995, of a sample of 1218 firms operating in traditional sectors in two different years: 1992 and 1995. Data come from three statistical sources: Community Innovation Survey (CIS), Italian Structural Business Statistics (SCI – Sistema dei Conti delle Imprese) and Italian Business Register (ASIA – Archivio Statistico delle Imprese Attive).

7 We refer here to the Triple Helix model proposed by Etzkowitz and Leydesdorff (1997), who have deeply stressed the importance of spatially based interactions between universities, firms and government in the process of evolution of innovation systems.

References

Aage T. (2001), 'External relations and industrial districts', paper presented at the DRUID Nelson and Winter Summer Conference. URL: http://www.druid.dk/conference/nw/paper1/aage.pdf

——. (2004), 'Efficient information acquisition by industrial districts. Intensity, speed, and direction of external information sources. The case of the industrial district of clothing in Jutland', paper presented at the DRUID Summer Conference, Elsinore, Denmark. URL: www.druid.dk.

Acs Z. (ed.) (2000), *Regional Innovation, Knowledge and Global Change*, London: Pinter.

Amin A. (1993), *The Difficult Transition from Informal to Marshallian District*, mimeo, University of Newcastle upon Tyne.

Amin A. and Cohendet P. (1999), 'Learning and adaptation in decentralised business networks', *Environ. Planning* D: Society and Space, 17: 87–104.

——. (2004). *The Architecture of Knowledge: Communities, Competences and Firms.* Oxford: Oxford University Press.

Amin A. and Roberts J. (2006), 'Communities of Practice? Varieties of situated learning', paper presented at the DIME Conference on Communities of Practice, Durham, 27–8 October.

Amin A. and Robins K. (1990), 'Industrial districts and regional development: limits and possibilities', in F. Pyke, G. Becattini and W. Sengenberger (eds.) *Industrial Districts and Inter-Firm Cooperation in Italy*, Geneva: ILO.

Amin A. and Thrift N. (1992), 'Neo-Marshallian nodes in global networks', *Internat. J. of Urban and Regional Res.*, 16: 571–87.

Andersen K. and Lorenzen M. (2007). 'The stretching of weak ties, clusters, pipelines, and the creation of small worlds', paper presented at the Winter Druid Conference, December.

Antonelli C. (1994), 'Technological districts, localised spillovers and productivity growth. The Italian evidence on technological externalities in core regions', *Internat. Rev. of Appl. Econom.*, 14: 18–30.

——. (1995), *The Economics of Localized Technological Change and Industrial Dynamics*, Boston: Kluwer Academic Publishers.

——. (2000), 'Collective knowledge, communication and innovation: the evidence of technological districts', *Regional Studies*, 34.

Argote, L. and Ingram P. (2000), 'Knowledge transfer: a basis for competitive advantage in firms, *Organ. Behav. Hum. Decis. Processes*, 82(1): 150–69.

Argyris C. (1976), *Increasing Leadership Effectiveness*, New York: Wiley.

Asheim B. (1996), 'Industrial districts as "learning regions": a condition for prosperity', *European Planning Stud.*, 4: 379–400.

Audretsch D. (1998), 'Agglomeration and the location of innovative activity', *Oxford Rev. of Econom. Policy*, 14(2): 18–29.

Audretsch D. and Feldman M. (1996), 'R&D spillovers and the geography of innovation and production', *Amer. Econom. Rev.*, 86(3): 630–52.

Bair J. and Gereffi G. (2001), 'Local clusters in global chains: the causes and consequences of export dynamism in Torreon's blue jeans industry', *World Dev.*, 29(11): 1885–1903.

Bathelt, H., Malmberg A. and Maskell P. (2004), 'Clusters and knowledge: local buzz, global pipelines and the process of knowledge creation', *Prog. Hum. Geog.* 28(1): 31–56.

Baumard, P. (1999), *Tacit Knowledge in Organisations*, London: Sage.

Becattini, G. (1990), 'The industrial district as a socio-economic notion', in F. Pyke, G. Becattini and W. Sengerberger (eds.) *Industrial Districts and Inter-firm Cooperation in Italy*, Geneva: International Institute for Labour Studies.

Bell G. (2005), 'Clusters, networks, and firm innovativeness', *Strategic Management J.*, 26: 287–95.

Bell M. and Abu M. (1999), 'Knowledge systems and technological dynamism in industrial clusters in developing countries', *World Dev.* 27: 1715–34.

Bellandi M. (1992), 'The incentives to decentralised industrial creativity in local systems of small firms', *Revue d'Economie Industrielle*, 59: 99–110.

Belussi F. (2005), 'Are industrial districts formed by networks without technologies? The diffusion of Internet applications in three Italian clusters', *Eur. Urban and Regional Stud.*, 12(3): 247–68.

Belussi, F. (ed.) (2000), *Tacchi a spillo. Il distretto calzaturiero della Riviera del Brenta come forma organizzata di capitale sociale*, Padua: Cleup.

Belussi, F. and Arcangeli F. (1998), 'A typology of networks: flexible and evolutionary firms', *Res. Policy*, 27: 415–28.

Belussi F. and Gottardi G. (eds.) (2000), *Evolutionary Patterns of Local Industrial Systems*, Aldershot: Ashgate.

Belussi F. and Pilotti L. (2002), 'Knowledge creation, learning and innovation in Italian industrial districts', *Geografiska Annaler*, 84B(2): 125–39.

Belussi F. and Sammarra A. (eds.) (2005), *Industrial Districts, Relocations, and Governance of the Global Value Chain*, Padua: Cleup.

Benner C. (2003), 'Learning communities in a learning region: the soft infrastructure of cross-firm learning networks in Silicon Valley', *Environ. and Planning A*, 35: 1809–30.

Boschma R. (2005), 'Proximity and innovation: a critical assessment, *Regional Stud.,* 39: 61–74.

Boschma R. and Iammarino S. (2007), 'Related variety and regional growth in Italy', paper presented at DRUID Summer Conference, Copenhagen, 18–20 June.

Boschma R and ter Wal A. L. (2005), 'Knowledge networks and innovative performance in an industrial district: the case of a footwear district in the south of Italy', *Indust. and Innovation*, forthcoming.

Bourdieu P. (1985). 'The forms of capital', in J. C. Richardson (ed.), *Handbook of Theory and Research for the Sociology of Education*, Connecticut: Greenwood Press.

Brown J. S. and Duguid P. (1991), 'Organizational learning and communities-of-practice: towards a unified view of working, learning, and innovation', *Organ. Sci.* 2(1): 40–57.

Brusco S. (1982), 'The Emilian Model: productive decentralisation and social integration', *Cambridge J. of Econom.*, 6: 167–84.

Cainelli G. and De Liso N. (2004), 'Can a Marshallian district be innovative? The case of Italy', in G. Cainelli and R. Zoboli (eds.), *The Evolution of Industrial Districts*, Heidelberg: Physica Verlag.

Cairncross F. (2001), *The Death of Distance: How the Communication Revolution will Change our Life*, London: Texere.

Camagni R. (1991), *Innovation Networks: Spatial Perspectives*, London: Belhaven Press.

Caniëls M. and Romijn H. (2005), 'What drives innovativeness in industrial clusters? Transcending the debate', *Cambridge J. of Econom.*, 29: 497–515.

Castells M. (1996). *The Rise of the Network Society*. London: Blackwell.

Castilla E., Hwang H., Granovetter E. and Granovetter M. (2000), 'Social networks in Silicon Valley', in C. Lee, W. Miller, M. Handcock and H. Rowen (eds.), *The Silicon Valley Edge*, Stanford: Stanford University Press.

Chesbrough H. W. (2003), *Open Innovation: The New Imperative for Creating and Profiting from Technology*. Harvard Business School Press.

Chiarvesio M., Di Maria E. and Grandinetti R. (2005), *Le ICT a supporto dell'innovazione aziendale. Filiere e distretti industriali nella provincia di Pordenone*, Milan: Franco Angeli.

Ciarli T. and Rabellotti R. (2006), 'ICTs in industrial districts: an empirical analysis on adoption, use and impact', *Indust. and Innovation* 14(3): 277–303.

Coe N. (2001): 'A hybrid agglomeration? The development of a satellite-Marshallian industrial district in Vancouver's film industry', *Urban Stud.*, 38(10): 1753–75.

Coe N. and Bunnell T. (2003), 'Spatializing knowledge communities: towards a conceptualization of transnational innovation networks', *Global Networks*, 3(4): 437–56.

Coenen L., Moodysson J. and Asheim B. (2004), 'Nodes, networks and proximity: on knowledge dynamics of the Medicon Valley biotech cluster', *Eur. Planning Stud.*, 12(7): 1003–18.

Cohen, W. M. and Levinthal D. A. (1990), 'Absorptive capacity: a new perspective on learning and innovation', *Admin. Sci. Quart.* 35(1): 128–52.

Cohendet P. (2005), 'On knowing communities'. Presented at 'Advancing Knowledge and the Knowledge Economy' conference, National Academies, Washington, DC.

Coleman J. (1988), 'Social capital in the creation of human capital', *Amer. J. Sociol.* 94: 95–120.

Cooke P. (2002a), 'Regional innovation systems: general findings and some new evidence from the biotechnology clusters', *J. of Tech. Transfer*, 27: 133–45.

Cooke P. (2002b), *Knowledge Economies: Clusters, Learning, and Cooperative Advantages*, London and New York: Routledge.

——. (2004), 'Globalisation of bioscience: knowledge capabilities and economic geography', paper presented at the Annual Association of American Geographers, Philadelphia, 14–19 March.

——. (2005), 'Regionally asymmetric knowledge capabilities and open innovation, exploring "globalisation 2" – a new model of industry organisation', *Res. Policy*, 34: 1128–49.

——. (2006), 'Between implicit and explicit knowledge: translational proximities and innovation', paper presented at the DIME Conference on Communities of Practice, Durham, 27–8 October.

Cooke P. and Huggins R. (2002), 'High technology clustering in Cambridge', in A. Amin, S. Goglio and F. Sforzi (eds.), *The Institutions of Local Development*, London: IGU.

Corò G. and Grandinetti R. (1999), 'Evolutionary patterns of Italian industrial districts', *Hum. Syst. Manage.*, 18(2): 117–29.

Cowan R. and Foray D. (1997), 'The economics of codification and diffusion of knowledge', *Ind. Corp. Change*, 6(3): 595–622.

Cowan R., David P. A. and Foray D. (1999), 'The explicit economics of knowledge codification', *Ind. Corp. Change*, 9(2): 211–53.

Dei Ottati G. (1994), 'The industrial district. Transaction problems and the "community market"', *Cambridge J. of Econom.*, 18(2): 529–46.

Dorfman N. (1983), 'Route 128: the development of a regional high-technology economy', *Res. Policy*, 12: 299–316.

Enright M. (1998), 'Regional clusters and firm strategy', in A. Chandler, P. Hagstrom and O. Sölvell (eds.), *The Dynamic Firm: The Role of Technology, Strategy, and Regions*, Oxford: Oxford University Press, 1998.

Etzkowitz H. and Leydesdorff L. (1997), *Universities and the Global Knowledge Economy*, London: Pinter.

Feldman M. (2004), 'Knowledge externalities and the anchor hypothesis: the locational dynamics of the US biotech industry', paper presented at the Annual Meeting of the Association of American Geographers, Philadelphia, 14–17 March.

——. (2005) 'The locational dynamic of the US biotech industry: knowledge externalities and the anchor hypothesis', in Quadrio Curzio and Fortis (eds.) *Research and Technological Innovation*, Berlin: Phisica Verlag, Springer.

Gereffi, G., Humphrey J. and Sturgeon T. (2005), 'The governance of global value chains', *Rev. Int. Polit. Econ.*, 12(1): 78–104.

Gertler M. (2003), 'Tacit knowledge and the economic geography of context, or The undefinable tacitness of being (there)', *J. of Econom. Geography*, 3: 75–99.

Gerybadze A. and Reger G. (1999), 'Globalisation of R&D: recent changes in management of innovation in transnational corporations', *Res. Policy*, 28(2–3): 251–74.

Giuliani E. (2005), 'The structure of cluster knowledge networks: uneven and selective, not pervasive and collective', DRUID Working Paper No. 05–11. URL: http://www.druid.dk/wp/pdf_files/05–11.pdf

Giuliani E. and Bell M. (2005), 'The micro-determinants of meso-level learning and innovation: evidence from a Chilean wine cluster', *Res. Policy*, 34(1): 47–68.

Giuliani E., Rabellotti R. and van Dijk M. P. (eds.) (2005), *Cluster Facing Competition: the Importance of External Linkages*, Aldershot: Ashgate.

Gordon R. (1996), 'Industrial districts and the globalisation of innovation: regions and networks in the new economic space', in X. Vence-Desa and S. Metcalfe (eds.), *Wealth from Diversity*, Dordrecht: Kluwer.

Grabher G. (1993), 'The weakness of strong ties. The lock-in of regional development in the Ruhr area', in G. Grabher (ed.), *The Embedded Firm: On the Socio-economics of Industrial Networks*, London: Routledge.

Grabher G. and Ibert O. (2006), 'Bad company? The ambiguity of personal knowledge networks', *J. of Econom. Geography*, 6, S. 251–71.

Granovetter M. S. (1973), 'The strength of weak ties', *Amer. J. Sociol.*, 78: 1360–80.

Haas P. M. (1992), 'Introduction: epistemic communities and international policy coordination', *Internat. Organ.* 46(1).

Håkanson L. (2005), 'Epistemic communities and cluster dynamics: on the role of knowledge in industrial districts', *Indust. and Innovation*, 12(4): 433–63.

Håkansson H. and Ford D. (2000), 'How should companies interact in business networks?' *Small Bus. Econ.*, 16: 293–302.

Håkansson H. and Johanson J. (1988), 'Formal and informal cooperation strategies in international industrial networks', in F. J. Contractor and P. Lorange (eds.), *Cooperative Strategies in International Business*, Lexington Books.

Håkansson H. and Snehota I. (1995), *Developing relationships in Business Networks*, London: Routledge.

Handley K., Sturdy A., Fincham R. and Clark T. (2006), 'Within and beyond communities of practice: making sense of learning through participation, identity and practice', *Journal of Management Studies*, 43(3): 641–53.

Harrison B. (1992), 'Industrial districts: old wine in new bottles', *Regional Stud.*, 26: 469–83.

——. (1994), *Lean and Mean: The Changing Landscape of Corporate Power in the Age of Flexibility*, London and New York: The Guildford Press.

Hollingsworth R. (2000), 'Doing institutional analysis: implication for the study of innovation', ICE-Working Paper no. 9, Austin Academy of Science.

Hsu J. (2003), 'The evolving institutional embeddedness of late-industrial district in Taiwan', *Economische en Sociale Geografie*, 95(2): 218–32.

Humphrey J. and Schmitz H. (2002), 'How does insertion in global value chains affect upgrading in industrial clusters', *Regional Stud.*, 36(9): 1017–27.

Iammarino S. and McCann P. (2006), 'The structure and evolution of industrial clusters: transactions, technology and spillovers', *Res. Policy*, 35(7): 1018–36.

Ibarra, H., Kilduff M. and Tsai W. (2005), 'Zooming in and out: connecting individuals and collectivities at the frontiers of organizational network research', *Organ. Sci.*, 16(4): 359–71.

Izushi H. (1997), 'Conflict between two industrial networks: technological adaptation and inter-firm relationships in the ceramics industry in Seto, Japan', *Regional Studies*, 31(2): 117–29.

Jacobs J. (1961), *Death and Life of Great American Cities.* New York: Random House.

Jaffe A., Trajtenberg M. and Henderson R. (1993), 'Geographic localisation of knowledge spillovers as evidenced by patent citations', *The Quarterly J. of Econom.*, 108(3): 577–98.

Jarrillo C. (1988), 'On strategic network', *Strategic Management J.*, 9: 31–41.

Kleeble D., Lawson C., More B. and Wilkinson F. (1999), 'Collective learning processes, networking and institutional thickness in the Cambridge region', *Regional Stud.*, 33(4): 319–12.

Kogout B. (2000), 'The network as knowledge: generative rules and the emergence of structure', *Strategic Management J.*, 21: 405–25.

Langlois R. N. (2003), 'The vanishing hand: the changing dynamics of industrial capitalism', *Ind. Corp. Change*, 12(2): 351–85.

Langlois R. N. and Robertson P. L. (1992), 'Networks and innovation in a modular system: lessons from the microcomputer and stereo component industries', *Res. Policy*, 21(4): 297–313.

Lave J. and Wenger E. (1991), *Situated Learning. Legitimate Peripheral Participation.* Cambridge: Cambridge University Press.

Lazerson M. (1995), 'A new Phoenix? Modern putting-out in the Modena knitwear industry', *Admin. Sci. Quart.*, 40: 34–59.

Lazzeretti L. and Storai D. (2003), 'An ecology based interpretation of district "complexification": the Prato district evolution from 1946–1993', in F. Belussi, G. Gottardi and E. Rullani (eds.), *The Technological Evolution of Industrial Districts*, Boston: Kluwer.

Lesser E. and Everest K. (2001), 'Using communities of practices to manage intellectual capital', *Ivey Bus. J.* (March–April): 37–41.

Lissoni F. and Pagani M. (2003), 'How many networks in a local cluster? Textile machine production and innovation in Brescia', T. Brenner and D. Fornahl (eds.), *Cooperation, Networks, and Institutions in Regional Innovation Systems*, Cheltenham: Edward Elgar.

Loasby B. (1998), 'Industrial districts as knowledge communities', in M. Bellet and C. L'Harmet (eds.), *Industry, Space and Competition*, Cheltenham: Edward Elgar.

——. (2000), 'Organisations as interpretative systems', paper presented at the DRUID Summer Conference, Rebild, Denmark. URL: http://www.druid.dk/summer2000/Gallery/nyloasby.pdf.

Lyons B. and Mehta J. (1997), 'Contracts, opportunism and trust: self interest and social orientation', *Cambridge Journal of Economics*, 21(2): 239–57.

McDermott R. (1999), 'Learning across teams: how to build communities of practice in team-based organizations', *Knowledge Manage. Rev.*, 8 (May–June): 32–6.

March J. (1991), 'Exploration and exploitation in organisational learning', *Organ. Sci.* 2: 71–87.

Markusen A. (1996), 'Sticky places in slippery space: a typology of industrial districts', *Econom. Geography*, 72: 293–313.

Marshall A. (1920), *Principles of Economics*, 8th edition, Philadelphia: Porcupine Press.

Maskell P. (1999), 'Globalisation and industrial competitiveness: the process and the consequences of "ubiquification"', in E. Maleki and P. Oinas (eds.), *Making Connections: Technological Learning and Regional Economic Exchange*, Aldershot: Ashgate.

——. (2001), 'Towards a knowledge-based theory of the geographical cluster', *Ind. Corp. Change*, 10(4): 921–43.

Maskell P. and Kebir L. (2005), 'What qualifies as a cluster theory?', DRUID Working Papers 05–9, DRUID, Copenhagen Business School, Department of Industrial Economics and Strategy/Aalborg University, Department of Business Studies. URL: http://www.druid.dk/wp/pdf_files/05–9.pdf

Maskell P. and Malmberg A. (1999), 'Localised learning and industrial competitiveness', *Cambridge J. Econ.*, 23: 167–85.

Moodysson J, Coenen L. and Asheim B. (2006), 'Explaining spatial patterns of innovation:

analytical and synthetic modes of knowledge creation in Medicon Valley Life Science Cluster', *Environmental and Planning*, forthcoming.

Morrison A. (2004), 'Gatekeepers of knowledge within industrial districts: who they are, how they interact', Cespri WP: 163.

Nakano T. and White D. R. (2006), 'The large-scale network of a Tokyo industrial district: small-world, scale-free, or depth hierarchy?', Working Papers Series, Center on Organizational Innovation, Columbia University. URL: http://www.coi.columbia.edu/pdf/nakano_white_lsn.pdf.

Nelson R. (1992), 'The roles of firms in technical advance: a perspective from evolutionary theory', in G. Dosi, R. Giannettini, P. Toninelli (eds.), *Technology and Enterprises in an Historical Perspective*. Oxford: Oxford University Press.

Nelson R. and Winter S. (1982), *An Evolutionary Theory of Economic Change*, Cambridge: Harvard University Press.

Nonaka I. and Takeuchi H. (1995), *The Knowledge Creating Company*. New York: Oxford University Press.

Nooteboom B. (1992), 'Towards a dynamic theory of transactions', *J. Evol. Econ.*, 2(4): 281–99.

——. (2006a), 'Cognitive distance in and between COPS and firms: where do exploitation and exploration take place, and how are they connected?', CentER Discussion Paper Series No. 2007–04. URL: http://ssrn.com/abstract=962330

——. (2006b), 'Learning and innovation in inter-organizational relationships and networks', CentER Discussion Paper Series No. 2006–39. URL: http://ssrn.com/abstract=903754.

Oinas P. (1999), 'Activity-specificity in organizational learning: implications for analysing the role of proximity', *GeoJournal*, 49: 363–72.

——. (2002), 'Competition and collaboration in interconnected places: towards a research agenda', *Geografiska Annaler*, 84B: 65–76.

Orr J. (1990), 'Sharing knowledge, celebrating identity: war stories and community memory in a service culture', in D. S. Middleton and D. Edwards (eds.), *Collective Remembering: Memory in Society*, Beverly Hills, CA: Sage Publications.

Paniccia I. (1998), 'One, a hundred, thousands of industrial districts: organizational variety in local networks of small and medium-sized enterprises', *Organ. Stud.*, 19: 667–99.

Perroux F. (1955), 'Note sur la notion de pôle de croissance', *Economie Appliquée*. 1(2): 307–20.

Pilotti L. (2000), 'Networking, strategic positioning and creative knowledge in industrial districts', *Hum. Syst. Manage.*, 19: 121–33.

Pinch S., Henry N., Jenkins M. and Tallman S. (2003), 'From "industrial districts" to "knowledge clusters": a model of knowledge dissemination and competitive advantage in industrial agglomerations', *J. of Econom. Geography*, 3: 373–88.

Piore M. J. and Sabel C. F. (1984), *The Second Industrial Divide*, New York: Basic Books.

Porac J. F., Thomas H. and Baden-Fuller C. (1989), 'Competitive groups as cognitive communities: the case of Scottish knitwear manufacturers', *J. Manage. Stud.*, 26(4): 397–416.

Porter M. (1998), *On Competition*, Boston: Harvard Business School Press.

Powell W. (1990), 'Neither market nor hierarchy: network forms of organisation', *Res. in Organ. Behaviour*, 12: 295–336.

Powell W. and Grodal S. (2005), 'Networks of innovators', in J. Fagerberg, D. Mowery and R. Nelson (eds.), *The Oxford Handbook of Innovation*, New York: Oxford University Press, pp. 56–85.

Powell W. W., Koput K. W. and Smith-Doerr L. (1996), 'Interorganisational collaboration and the locus of innovation: networks of learning in biotechnology', *Admin. Sci. Quart.*, 41 (March): 116–45.

Putnam R. (1993), *Making Democracy Work: Civic Traditions in Modern Italy*, Princeton: Princeton University Press.

Rama R., Ferguson D. and Melero A. (2003), 'Subcontracting networks in industrial districts: the electronics industries of Madrid', *Regional Stud.*, 37(1): 71–88.

Reinau K. (2007), 'Local clusters in globalized world', paper presented at the Druid winter conference.

Richardson G. (1972), 'The organisation of industry', *Econ. J.*, 82: 883–96.

Robertson P. and Langlois N. (1995), 'Innovation, networks, and vertical integration', *Res. Policy*, 24: 543–62.

Saxenian A. (1994), *Regional Advantage: Culture and Competition in Silicon Valley and Route 128*, Cambridge, MA: Harvard University Press.

——. (1999), *Silicon Valley New Immigrant Entrepreneurs*, San Francisco: Public Policy Institute.

——. (2005), 'From brain drain to brain circulation: transnational communities and regional upgrading in India and China', *Stud. in Comparative Development*, 40(2): 35–61.

Scott A. (1988), *New Industrial Spaces: Flexible Production Organisations and Regional Development in North America and Western Europe*, London: Pion.

——. (1992), 'The role of large producers in industrial districts: a case study of high technology systems houses in southern California', *Regional Stud.*, 26(3): 265–75.

——. (2006), 'Entrepreneurship, innovation and industrial development: geography and the creative field revisited', *Small Bus. Econom.*, 26(1): 1–24.

Siisiäinen M. (2000), 'Two concepts of social capital: Bourdieu vs. Putnam', paper presented at ISTR Fourth International Conference: 'The Third Sector: For What and for Whom?' Trinity College, Dublin, Ireland, URL: http://www.jhu.edu/~istr/conferences/dublin/workingpapers/siisiainen.pdf.

Simmie J. and Sennen J. (1999), 'Innovative clusters: global or local linkages?', *National Inst. Econom. Rev.*, 170: 87–98.

Smith-Doerr L. and Powell W. (2003), 'Networks and economic life', in N. Smeser and R. Swdberg (eds.), *Handbook of Economic Sociology*, Princeton: Russell Sage Foundation and Princeton University Press.

Sorensen O. and Audia P. (2000). 'The social structure of entrepreneurial activity: geographic concentration of footwear production in the United States, 1940–89', *Amer. J. of Sociology*, 106: 424–62.

Staber U. (1998), 'Inter-firm co-operation and competition in industrial districts', *Organ. Stud.*, 4: 701–24.

——. (2001), 'The Structure of Networks in Industrial Districts', *Internat. J. of Urban and Regional Res.*, 25: 537–2.

Storper M. (1995), 'The resurgence of regional economies ten years later: the region as a nexus of untraded interdependencies', *Eur. Urban and Regional Stud.*, 2(3).

——. (1997), *The regional world: territorial development in a global economy*, New York: Guilford Press.

Storper M. and Harrison B. (1991), 'Flexibility, hierarchy and regional development: the changing structure of industrial production systems and their forms of governance in the 1990s', *Res. Policy*, 20: 407–22.

Swann J., Scarborough H. and Robertson M. (2002), 'The Construction of "Communities of Practice" in the Management of Innovation', *Management Learning*, 33(4): 477–96.

Thomson M. (2005), 'Structural and epistemic parameters in communities of practice', *Organ. Sci.*, 16: 151–64.

Thorelli H. (1986), 'Networks: between markets and hierarchies', *Strategic Manage. J.* 7: 37–51.

Todeva E. (2006), *Business Networks*, London: Routledge.

Torre A. and Rallet A. (2005), 'Proximity and localization', *Regional Stud.*, 39(1): 47–59.

Uzzi B. (1997), 'Social structure and competition in interfirm networks', *Admin. Science Quart.*, 42: 35–67.

Von Hippel E. (1998), 'Economics of product development by users: the impact of "sticky" local information', *Manage. Sci.*, 44(5): 629–44.

Ward A. (2000), 'Getting strategic value from constellations of communities', *Strategy and Leadership.* 28(2): 4–9.

Wenger E. C. (1999), 'Learning as social participation', *Knowledge Manage. Rev.*, 6 (January–February): 30–3.

——. (2000), 'Communities of practice and social learning systems', *Organ.* 7(2): 225–46.

Wenger E. C., Snyder W. M. (2000), 'Communities of practice: the organisational frontier', *Harvard Bus. Rev.*, (January–February): 139–45.

You J. (1995), 'Small firms in economic theory', *Cambridge J. of Econ.*, 19: 441–62.

You J. and Wilkinson F. (1994), 'Competition and cooperation: towards understanding industrial districts', *Rev. of Political Econom.*, 6: 259–78.

Zucker L., Darby M. and Armstrong J. (1998), 'Geographically localised knowledge spillovers or markets?', *Econom. Enquiry*, 26: 65–86.

3 Boundary-spanning strategies of industrial districts

The impact of absorptive capacity

Tine Aage (Region Zealand-Sor, Copenhagen)

3.1 Introduction

It is common knowledge that learning in organizations such as firms, and in different types of clusters, is based on a recombination of existing knowledge and new information. In the literature, determinants for different strategies of organizational information acquisition have been identified, which has not been the case for organizational forms like industrial districts. This chapter discusses the main explanations for different information acquisition strategies, and for the absorption of external information in industrial districts.

3.2 Industrial districts from a knowledge-based perspective: the missing link

Industrial districts, as well as other types of clusters, have enjoyed a fair deal of attention, both in relation to theoretical and empirical research. A central part of the literature within this field is concerned with the advantages of firms located within industrial districts. According to the literature, these advantages derive nearly exclusively from the *internal* characteristics and dynamics found in industrial districts (Becattini 1990; Marshall 1920; Storper 1995).

The internal characteristics, which have been identified over the years, have mostly been related to the two main analytical traditions based on the transaction cost approach, and the external economies of industrial districts, respectively (Antonelli 2000). The transaction cost approach underlines the reduction of costs related to the coordination of goods and services among the firms in the industrial districts. The reduced costs are, according to the literature, the result of a market characterized by proximity between agents and firms, where the development of institutions, like confidence and trust, supports the coordination mechanisms. The identified benefits of external economies are likewise a result of the proximity between agents and firms, which include: a shared labour market, specialized services and production inputs, as well as the presence of a pool of knowledge available to the agents in the district (Marshall 1920). Increasing returns based on these external economies are often explained by the access of firms and agents to knowledge and capabilities related more to the district than the single firm or agent

(Marshall 1920). In the literature, both the reduction of transaction costs, and the external economies of industrial districts, support the dynamics and knowledge creation unfolding in industrial districts (Antonelli 2000).

The focus on the internal characteristics and dynamics of industrial districts to ensure competitive advantages does not follow the general development in the literature on organizations. In this literature, the acquisition of external information is crucial to the ability of firms to respond to external changes in technologies and markets and to stay competitive (Nonaka 1991, 1994; Tecce and Pisano 1994). This rich literature includes the organizational structures of firms, and strategies, to support the ability of organizations to acquire external information. External information acquisition by industrial districts has not enjoyed the same attention. A literature review[1] on the acquisition of external information by industrial districts, and other types of clusters, has revealed that even though some researchers point to the importance of external information acquisition of industrial districts, this is not included in their analytical framework, nor is it related to commodity chain research (Dicken 2003, 2003; Wolfe 2003). Still more recently, awareness has been gained of the importance of external information acquisition and absorption. This implies that the absorption of external information has importance for knowledge creation and learning inside industrial districts. Seldom has this awareness been included in the analytical framework. Empirical research has been conducted on local–global dynamics around nodes of excellence interconnected by global networks, and the role of MNCs. Some authors have stressed the importance of including the boundary-spanning strategies to the analytical framework of external information acquisition of industrial districts. In these studies there is a tendency to focus on the gatekeeper strategy as the only boundary-spanning mechanism used by the industrial districts to acquire external information (Giuliani 2002; Morrison 2004). This research often implies that the external information in industrial districts is acquired and absorbed by a few central leading firms, which diffuse the external information to other firms and agents in the district. The gatekeeper and the direct peer strategy are examined as two central strategies to acquire and absorb external information from a knowledge-based perspective. In this research, the two strategies are studied in relation to, respectively, the position of firms in districts as leader or non-leader firms in industrial districts, and the knowledge characteristics of the firms and the distinction between knowledge and information. This chapter also focuses on how industrial districts acquire external information from sources outside the industrial district, and on what can explain differentiated strategies to acquire external information. In this work it is suggested that external information acquisition in industrial districts is primarily determined by the firm's relations inside the industrial district, and by the derived internal knowledge creation mechanisms. The chapter likewise argues that the need for external information, and the emergence of boundary-spanning strategies, varies across the knowledge creation dimensions of industrial districts, based on the different types of firms' relations.

3.3 Absorptive capacities and the related sub-process of external information acquisition from an industrial district perspective

Absorptive capacity is a concept developed to estimate the ability of an organization to learn by many sources, including external information (Cohen and Levinthal 1989, 1990). The sub-processes of acquisition, implementation and commercialization of the external information, in combination with the internal accumulation of knowledge of the organization, constitute absorptive capacity. It is the characteristics of the prior knowledge base that have an important impact on the absorptive capacity of an organization. The prior knowledge base is the result of the ongoing activities, and of the knowledge creation mechanisms of the organization. Prior knowledge of the organization increases the ability of the firm to recognize the value of new external information, and activates the learning process from external information to built-in organizational knowledge, giving rise to creativity and problem solving skills through the recombination of new and old knowledge. Knowledge accumulation, over time, also enhances the ability of the firm to identify and evaluate (technical) future opportunities. In this way, the accumulation of knowledge permits the firm to predict more accurately the nature and commercial potentialities of technological advances, and to hold future absorptive capacity for the organization, within a certain field of activities.

Low investments in development of prior related knowledge put firms at the risk of neglecting new developments, or they risk absorbing the 'wrong' external information. The structure of the firm knowledge pool also influences the ability to absorb external information. The firm knowledge pool determines the cognitive distance (and communication impedance) between the organization and the potential external information sources existing in the environment. The structure of the knowledge pool is here related to the degree of specialization of knowledge. Specialized knowledge emerges inside organizations to enhance internal communication. Within the organization, specialized knowledge is based on idiosyncratic activities and routines, and its development goes in synchrony with the development of a local language. On the one hand, a very specialized language will often hamper the communication with external information sources, due to communication impedances. On the other hand, organizations with a broader and more general knowledge pool will share, more easily, languages and symbols with external information sources, supporting the process of external information acquisition (Cohen and Levinthal 1989, 1990). The problems with the creation of a local specialized language, and of symbols favouring internal communication, but hampering the ability to acquire external information, are widely recognized (Tushman and Katz 1980; Loasby 2000). Firms seem to be facing a dilemma. They are urged to specialize their knowledge in order to be effective and competitive, but at the same time this specialization hampers their ability to acquire external information, due to the cognitive distance between the 'internal to the firm' knowledge base, and the external information sources. The cognitive distance can be related to what has been called 'semantic noise', which includes difficulties in communicating.

The greater the mismatch between language and cognitive orientation, the greater will be the problems with external information acquisition. The problems include the time-consuming codification process needed to transfer the knowledge, misperception, and misunderstanding of the content of the information (Tushman and Katz 1989, 1990). The knowledge creation mechanisms determine how long it takes to implement the external information into the pool of prior knowledge, on which depends further absorption of external information into the organization. The sub-process of external information acquisition enjoys special attention, as it is this process which is most directly involved in the boundary spanning between the industrial district and the external information sources located outside the district. In the work of Zahra and George (2002), the ability of an organization to acquire external information is measured in relation to three variables: intensity, speed and direction. Intensity is based on the amount of external information the organization acquires, and speed is determined by how fast the new external information is processed into the accumulated knowledge, which constitutes the prior knowledge of the organization.

Finally, the direction is related to the ability of the organization to acquire the right type of external information to be integrated in the firm's knowledge pool. The direction and orientation enables the organization to focus on common aims, and select useful external information, avoiding costly external information overload (Bathelt, *et al.* 2004; Loasby 2000). The existing literature on external information acquisition has focused on an individual type of agency, mostly represented by firms or subdivisions in firms, disregarding the organizational form of industrial districts. In the work of Lawson (1999), this gap is covered, and Lawson argues that industrial districts, in many ways, can be approached as an organizational form such as firms. In his work on industrial districts, a plurality of collective organizations and agents exist: the firms, in which we find a great deal of agents' interactions, and the social system, characterized by frequent interactions between agents across firms and organizations based in the district. Interactions among agents in productive systems, like the industrial district, lead to the development of social systems with associated rules and practices (Lawson 1999: 156). With this definition, Lawson introduces a central characteristic of the industrial district, which includes the ability to indirectly 'direct' the behaviour of the firms and other agents located inside the districts. Successful firms, or other types of leadership, can likewise create a diffuse orientation and establish a type of indirect leadership. Collective historical references support this thesis (Miner and Haunschild 1995).

3.4 Boundary-spanning strategies

In the literature, the acquisition of external information occurs between the boundaries of the provider and the receiver of external information. Tushman and Katz (1980) have stressed the existence of two prototypes of boundary-spanning strategies that meet the process of external information acquisition: the gatekeeper strategy and the direct peer strategy. The two strategies relate to the degree of communication impedance between the provider and the receiver of external information (Table 3.1).

According to Tushman and Katz (1980), different types of communication structures derive from the activities that the organizations undertake. In their empirical work they show that different boundary-spanning strategies, represented by the direct peer and gatekeeper strategies, can be used to handle the different characteristics of external information acquisition from outside to meet the different organizational needs of organizational activities.

In their work they operate with universal or general activities on one side, and local or specialized activities on the other side. The universal activities are exemplified with research, which build on knowledge known and language shared by persons outside and inside the organization. Universal or general activities will often result in a general cognitive structure inside the organization, which imply low communication impedance between the organization and external information sources. They also argue that organizations conducting more universal and general activities will make use of the direct peer strategy. The reasons are that costs of transforming the external information into understandable organizational knowledge are quite low, due to cognitive proximity between the environment and the organization, just like the direct peer strategy prevents that information undergoing misinterpretation as it is transferred through a third person (Tushman and Katz 1980).

The gatekeeper strategy is argued to be most suitable for organizations (or units responsible for conducting specific tasks within an organization), which deal with local defined and specialized activities. This is mostly due to the relatively high cost of accessing the external information sources, and the transformation of external information into the more specialized local language. The gatekeeper strategy requires that a key person from the firm undertakes the costly external information acquisition from external sources, transforms it, and diffuses it to the other members of the organization or the unit (Cohen and Levinthal 1990; Tushman and Katz 1980). From an industrial district perspective, the gatekeeper strategy will imply that few firms will undertake the external information acquisition, and diffuse the external information to other firms in the district. The direct peer strategy when considered in terms of the industrial district perspective presupposes that each of the firms undertake external information acquisition. This implies that the direct peer strategy will acquire relatively more external information than the gatekeeper strategy, measured in number of firms acquiring external information. Figure 3.1 shows how the different boundary-spanning strategies in the vertical

Table 3.1 Boundary-spanning strategies and the level of communication impedances

	Level of cognitive problems and communication impedances
Direct peer	Low
Gatekeeper	High

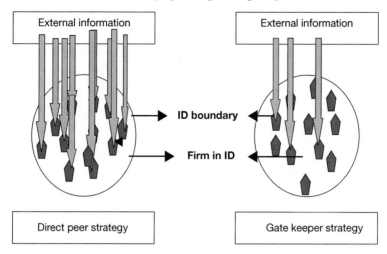

Figure. 3.1 Boundary-spanning strategies: direct peer and gatekeeper strategy.
Source: Aage (forthcoming).

and horizontal dimensions theoretically unfold. The figure shows that due to the direct peer strategy, the horizontal dimension receives relatively more external information, because all the firms and other agents are highly dependent on access to external information sources. The vertical dimension acquires relatively less external information, as shown by the numbers of external information sources. Within the horizontal and vertical dimensions, external information is diffused among different firms and agents. Different diffusion mechanisms are dominant in the two dimensions due to the different relations among firms producing similar and complementary activities, or competitors and collaborators. The high degree of variation and a large pool of shared knowledge explain the ability to process the external information faster in the horizontal dimension, than within the vertical.

3.5 Absorptive capacity in the horizontal and vertical dimension of industrial districts

The knowledge creation mechanism found in industrial districts in general supports a high absorptive capacity (Bathelt, *et al.* 2004).

The knowledge variation and spillover effects constitute a fast learning curve, which secures a fast processing of external information into place-specific and contextual knowledge. The contextual knowledge pool established within the industrial district supports the further absorptive capacity of the district.

The shared pool of knowledge enables firms to avoid the trade-off between holding a specialized or general pool of knowledge, favouring either internal or external communication, as identified by Cohen and Levinthal. Single firms and agents conduct their activities within the unique boundaries of their firms (or other organizations), but at the same time they access the broader pool of knowledge of the district. In this way, the firms are able to enjoy the benefits of specialization without hampering their ability to acquire external information – a central competitive advantage in a knowledge-based economy.

Even though some benefits apply to districts in general, the absorptive capacity and information acquisition will differ in the other two dimensions. The main characteristics of these two types of dimensions are presented in Table 3.2.

With respect to the uniqueness of the single industrial district two ideal types of dimensions can be identified, based on the combination of the nature of activities dominating in each of the dimensions, the horizontal and the vertical. These two dimensions derive from the seminal work of Richardson (1972), for whom the activities of the firm are the key variable for understanding the organizational form of firm coordination in the market. Coordination of activities and capabilities, within the same phases of production, implies the coordination of possible similar capabilities. The coordination of activities in different phases of production implies the coordination of complementary and different activities and capabilities.

In this way, the coordination of similar and dissimilar activities gives rise to different knowledge creation and learning mechanisms. In the industrial district model, following the work of Maskell (2001), this process can be represented by the two ideal types of the vertical and horizontal dimensions. Both dimensions will be traceable in the same industrial district, but often, inside each individual industrial district, one will dominate over the other.

3.5.1 The horizontal dimension of industrial districts

According to Maskell (2001), the horizontal dimension of industrial districts is based on firms conducting similar activities. These firms are often competitors, as they produce nearly the same product. The horizontal dimension is characterized by the Marshallian district type, where: (1) small similar firms are competing in the same market niche; (2) there is a large market for specialized skills; and (3) there is a collective pool of already existing knowledge, which diffuses rapidly due to the fact that there is *knowledge in the air*. The nature of the horizontal dimension

Table 3.2 Characteristics of the horizontal and vertical dimensions of industrial districts

	Horizontal dimension	*Vertical dimension*
Activities	Similar	Complementary
Firm relations	Competitors	Input – output
Coordination	Observation	Cooperation
Knowledge creation mechanisms	Variation	Specialization
Institutions	Rules and reputation	Trust/rules and reputation
Knowledge base	Same	Uneven

provides excellent opportunities to learn through the process of variation. In this way, the firms take advantage of the location in a live laboratory, where different interpretations of the same information give rise to a large number of solutions to the same problems.

Furthermore, the existence of this 'laboratory' enables them to test the efficacy of different solutions, and to enhance the success of evaluating and selecting the best (for the market) interpretation (Becattini and Rullani 1996). Besides the basic elements of knowledge creation, related to the concept of variation, as well as monitoring, comparison, and imitation of different solutions, the process of learning in the horizontal line is dominated by 'watching, discussing and comparing dissimilar solutions – often emerging from everyday practices' (Maskell 2001: 927). As the firms produce nearly the same products, and conduct nearly the same activities, they tend to have, therefore, similar capabilities. It is, thus, easy for the firms to do reverse engineering, and to decode (Maskell 2001) the actions of their competitors (in every field of firm competitiveness, from business strategies to product development). The role of imitative strategies as an information diffusion mechanism (Belussi and Pilotti 2002) is central in the horizontal dimension.

According to Richardson, the coordination of similar activities at firm level is often conducted within one organization, under the direction of a central leadership. The presence of similar activities directed and interpreted under the command of several entrepreneurs, or managers, constitutes an explanation of the competitive advantages found in industrial districts, due to the high degree of variation. Despite the individual differences existing among entrepreneurs and managers, in the horizontal dimension, there is a 'central mechanism' at work, an orientation mechanism of the activities conducted, and a focusing mechanism of knowledge creation, animated by the indirect authority of district institutions, which guide the behaviour of the agents (Lawson 1999; Lorentzen and Foss 2002).

3.5.2 The vertical dimension of industrial districts

Firms conducting complementary activities, in forward and backward input–output relations, constitute the vertical dimension of industrial districts. The vertical dimension is characterized primarily by its pool of specialized inputs and services, and firms are often related to each other through cooperation. Coordination in the vertical dimension is dominated by close cooperation among firms, to adjust quantities and qualities. An important institution in relation to cooperation is trust, which eases and lowers the cost of the transaction (Maskell 2001). While knowledge creation and learning, in the vertical dimension, are primarily activated in the context of firms subcontracting relations, the knowledge creation and learning processes taking place in the horizontal dimension have attracted less attention (Dicken and Malmberg 2001).The shared capabilities, as a result of conducting the same activities, leave the individual firms in the industrial district with a relatively good ability to evaluate other firms' products or interpretations of the market needs, and to compare them to their own chosen strategies. The possibility of these observations and evaluations cuts short the process of market-driven innovations, and enhances the success rate of products introduced onto the market. The different knowledge creation and learning mechanisms represented in the two dimensions likewise contribute in different ways to increase the knowledge pool (Table 3.2). The knowledge pool represents the collective contribution of knowledge from the firms and agents in the two dimensions. The knowledge pool can be accessed by the agents in the two dimensions, through the collective knowledge creation and learning mechanisms unfolding in the district. The knowledge pool of the vertical dimension is described as uneven. This implies that the contribution of the single firm and agent to the common knowledge pool of the vertical dimension is different. This also means that the pool of knowledge is more specialized, and sometimes inaccessible, as it contains differentiated inputs. Moreover, access to the knowledge pool is more difficult for the single agent, as a cognitive distance between the total knowledge pool and the single agent exists. The knowledge pool emerging in the horizontal dimension has been labelled in Table 3.2 as the 'same'. This implies that the firms and agents in the dimension contribute with the same knowledge to the knowledge pool. This results in a more general pool of knowledge, where the cognitive distance between the single agent and the common pool is relatively small. The different characteristics of the two knowledge pools also support the recent research results on access to the collective pool of knowledge. The knowledge pool in the vertical dimension only enables a limited access to knowledge in the air (Giuliani 2005), while the access to knowledge in the air 'is more likely to take place in the horizontal dimension' (Saxenian 1994; Belussi and Sedita 2005). Finally, the two dimensions contribute differently to the character of production factors available to the firms. Within the vertical dimension of the district, idiosyncratic production factors outside the firm, but inside the district, are available. The idiosyncratic production factors are an outcome of the knowledge creation mechanism of cooperation and coordination of complementary knowledge. In the horizontal dimension, the production factors of the horizontal dimension will be close to equal, because they conduct the same activity. These firms must therefore search for production factors located outside the industrial district, to access idiosyncratic production factors, leaving them with a competitive advantage. The differences in the knowledge bases – the access to idiosyncratic inputs, and the mode of coordination of the two dimensions – has an impact on the ability of firms to look for external knowledge (external to the district), and if they want to remain alive, and competitive, they need to do so.

3.6 External information acquisition in industrial districts

Above, the varied absorptive capacities and the ability to accumulate knowledge, among different knowledge dimensions of industrial districts, were presented. The *need* for external information likewise differed among firms, as a result of the different location of idiosyncratic production factors constituting a competitive advantage, respectively, along the horizontal and the vertical knowledge creation dimension. The differentiated absorptive capacity and the need for external information by the two knowledge creation dimensions call for a more differentiated approach to external information acquisition, and boundary-spanning strategies, than the single focus on the traditional gatekeeper model account for. The absorptive capacity in (respectively) the horizontal and vertical dimensions will be discussed, in relation to the variables of intensity, speed and direction, which constitute the ability of external information acquisition of industrial districts.

3.6.1 External information acquisition on the horizontal dimension

Several characteristics of the knowledge creation and learning mechanisms can be identified in the horizontal dimension, which give to the district firm superior information acquisition capabilities. The co-location of firms conducting the same activities within the same industrial sector creates the basis for a high intensity of external information, within a specialized field. The intensified external information is a result of both a high utilization of the external information, and a high number of external relations, as all the firms in the same district seek external information within the same activities. The speed of learning is supposed to be high, due to the scan, search, selection and variation process in the structure. The firms in these types of districts (Marshallian district) use each of the other firms as a laboratory, creating various solutions, where the fuel is competition. One could say that they compete to possess the best interpretative system as they move from acquiring external information towards the commercialization of the final product. The district internal mechanisms help the distribution of the external information within the district. Access to the general pool of knowledge, experiences with previous developments within the district, and the presence of lead firms, give firms good opportunities for meeting the right direction and for selecting the right type of external information (Barney 1986). The pool of agents and firms possess nearly the same knowledge, skills and competencies; likewise, they constitute a highly critical base, which is both able to evaluate not-yet-realized possibilities, and to select useful and new external information.

3.6.2 External information acquisition on the vertical dimension

In the vertical dimension, the knowledge creation and learning mechanisms are structured by input–output relations, as a result of the need for complementary knowledge. This means that the degree of specialization of the common knowledge pool to which the single agent has access is relatively less than within the horizontal dimension. As information is often acquired from the firms with whom they collaborate with, and which are located inside the district, the intensity of external information will likewise be relatively lower than along the horizontal dimension. Along the vertical dimension (upstream and downstream) there is a relatively small number of agents holding the same knowledge; firms have only a few contacts, and this lowers the capabilities of absorption and acquisition of external information. This reduces the speed by which the district, as a whole, if the vertical relation is dominant, is able to acquire external information, or to be orientated in an ongoing fashion. In general, it may be concluded that absorptive capabilities (and external information acquisition capabilities) are often higher in the horizontal as opposed to vertical dimension of industrial districts.

3.7 Boundary-spanning strategies of the two dimensions

According to Zahra and George (2002), successful capabilities of external information acquisition correspond to a high input of external information. The assumption that all firms need a high degree of external relations is too narrow, as the information needs of firms vary, just as the cost aspect is not included in the definition of the successful capabilities of acquiring external information. The costs of external information acquisition have to be included in the evaluation of the ability to acquire external information, like any other production factor. Instead of approaching the issue from the perspective of the acquisition of capabilities being high or low, it is more useful to examine the match between the intensity (measured by the amount of external information sources) and the needs of the organization. Considering the costs, the match between the need and the amount of information acquired should be the primary focus for the measurement of the efficiency of external information acquisition. To meet the different needs for external information and the different abilities to process the external information into the firm pool of knowledge, different strategies for the acquisition process should be available.

The higher the ability of processing external information sources and the location of idiosyncratic competitive production factors outside the industrial district, the higher is the call for the use of the direct peer strategy of the horizontal dimension. This strategy implies that the dimension will be supplied with a high amount of external information. On the other hand, the lower the capability of processing the external information into the prior knowledge pool and the relatively lower need of external information, due to the location of idiosyncratic production factors inside the district, call for the use of the gatekeeper strategy of the vertical dimension. The gatekeeper strategy implies a relatively lower amount of external information, as only few firms will undertake the acquisition process. The centralistic strategy likewise minimizes the costs if there are knowledge barriers, or high communication impedances. The efficient match between knowledge creation dimensions and boundary-spanning strategies are presented in Table 3.3. Theoretically, it is possible to argue for a more mixed approach to information acquisition and boundary-spanning strategies, among different types of industrial districts. Here, the direct peer and gatekeeper strategies have been suggested as two ideal types.

3.8 Discussion and conclusions

This article suggests that the external information acquisition of industrial districts is more complex than often assumed. In this chapter, the centralistic gatekeeper strategy vs. the more decentralized direct peer strategy has been discussed. The two strategies efficiently meet the differentiated capabilities and needs of different types of firms in the industrial district, just like they match different costs due to

Table 3.3 Efficient boundary-spanning strategies by the horizontal and vertical dimension of industrial districts

		Dimension of industrial districts	
		Horizontal	*Vertical*
Strategy	Gatekeeper	Low efficiency	High efficiency
	Direct peer	High efficiency	Low efficiency

the cognitive distance and communication impedances between the district and the external information sources.

Reasons for the traditional focus on the centralistic gatekeeper model could be that the analytical framework to access external information acquisition of industrial districts still focuses on cost minimization. Another reason could be that most studies of industrial districts address only the vertical relations (Dicken and Malmberg 2001). In this work, it is argued that a match exists in industrial districts between the gatekeeper strategies and the prevalence of vertical relations, and direct peer strategies, which are more related to the horizontal dimension of competitiveness, and we need to include both strategies to amplify the forms of external knowledge access.

Notes

1 Based on an extensive literature review of the research on external information acquisition by industrial districts. For selection criteria and journals included see Aage (2006).

References

Aage T. (2006), PHD Thesis, Institute of Industrial Economics and Strategy, CBS Copenhagen.

Antonelli C. (2000), 'Collective knowledge communication and innovation: the evidence of technological districts', *Regional Studies*, 34(6): 35–47.

Bathelt H., Malmberg A. and Maskell P. (2004), 'Clusters and knowledge: local buzz, global pipelines and the process of knowledge creation', *Progress in Human Geography*, 28(1): 31–56.

Becattini G. (1990), 'The Marshallian industrial district as a socio-economic concept', in F. Pyke, G. Becattini and W. Sengenberger (eds.) *Industrial Districts and inter-firm Co-operation in Italy*, Geneva: International Institute for Labour Studies.

Becattini G. and Rullani, E. (1996), 'Local systems and global connections: the role of knowledge', in F. Pyke and W. Sengenberger (eds.), *Local and Regional Response to Global Pressure*, Geneva: ILO.

Belussi F. and Pilotti L. (2002), 'The development of an explorative analytical model of knowledge creation, learning and innovation within the Italian industrial districts',

Geografiska Annaler, 84: 19–33.

Belussi F. and Sedita S. R. (2005), '"Learning at the boundaries" in industrial districts through communities of practice and networks', in F. Belussi and A. Sammarra (eds.), *Industrial Districts, Relocation, and the Governance of the Global Value Chain*. CLEUP.

Cohen W. M. and Levinthal D. A. (1989), 'Innovation and learning: the two faces of R&D', *Economic Journal*, 99: 569–96.

———. (1990), 'Absorptive capacity: a new perspective on learning and innovation', *Administrative Science Quarterly*, 35: 128–52.

Dicken P. (2003), *Global Shift: Mapping the Changing Contours of the World Economy*, London: Sage.

Dicken P. and Malmberg, A. (2001), 'Firms in territories: a relational perspective', *Economic Geography*, 77(4): 345–63.

Foss N. J. (1996), 'Introduction. The emerging competence perspective', in N. J. Foss and C. Knudsen (eds.), *Towards a Competence Theory of the Firm*, London: Routledge.

Giuliani E. (2002), 'Cluster absorptive capability: an evolutionary approach for industrial clusters in developing countries', Conference Paper DRUID Summer 2002, Copenhagen.

———. (2003), 'Knowledge in the air and its uneven distribution: a story of a Chilean wine cluster', Conference Paper for DRUID Winter 2003, Aalborg.

———. (2005), 'The structure of cluster knowledge networks: uneven and selective, not pervasive and collective', Conference Paper for DRUID Summer Conference on 'Dynamics of Industry and Innovation: Organizations, Networks and Systems', Copenhagen.

Lawson C. (1999), 'Towards a competence theory of the region', *Cambridge Journal of Economics*, 23: 151–66.

Loasby B. (1998), 'Industrial districts as knowledge communities', in M, Bellet and C. L'Harmet (eds.), *Industry, Space and Competition*, Cheltenham: Edward Elgar.

———. (2000), 'Organisations as interpretative systems', Conference Paper from DRUID Summer 2000, Aalborg.

Lorenzen M. and Foss N. (2002), 'Cognitive coordination, institutions, and clusters: an explorative discussion', in T. Brenner (ed.), *The Influence of Cooperations, Networks and Institutions on Regional Innovation Systems*. Cheltenham: Edward Elgar.

Maskell P. (2001), 'Towards a knowledge-based theory of the geographical cluster', *Industrial and Corporate Change*, 10(4): 921–43.

Marshall A. (1920), *Principles of Economics*, 8th edition, reprinted 1982, London: MacMillan & Co Ltd.

Miner A. S. and Haunschild P. R. (1995), 'Population level learning', *Research in Organisational Behaviour*, 17: 115–66.

Morrison, A. (2004): 'Do leading firms feed industrial districts? Evidence from an Italian furniture cluster', Conference paper for DRUID Winter 2004, Aalborg.

Nonaka I. (1991), 'The knowledge-creating company', *Harvard Business Review*, Nov.–Dec: 96–104.

———. (1994), 'A dynamic theory of organizational knowledge', *Organization Science*, 5(1): 14–37.

Oinas P. (2002), 'Competition and collaboration in interconnected places: towards a research agenda', *Geografiske Annaler*, 84(2): 65–76.

Richardson G. (1972), 'The organisation of industry', *The Economic Journal*, 82(2): 883–96.

Saxenian A. (1994), *Regional Advantage*, Harvard, MA: Harvard University Press.

Storper M. (1995), 'The resurgence of regional economies ten years later: the region as a nexus of untraded interdependencies, *European Urban and Regional Studies*, 2(3).

Teece D. and Pisano G. (1994) 'The Dynamic Capabilities of Firms: an Introduction', *Industrial and Corporate Change* 3(3) 537–6.

Tushman M. L. and Katz R. (1980), 'External communication and project performance: an investigation into the role of gatekeepers', *Management Science*, 26(11): 1071–85.

Wolfe D. A. (2003), 'Clusters from the inside and out: lessons from the Canadian study of cluster development', Conference Paper for Druid Summer 2003, Copenhagen.

Zahra S. A. and George G. (2002), 'Absorptive capacity: a review, reconceptualization, and extension', *Academy of Management Review*, 27(2): 185–203.

Part II

Industrial districts in the global value chains

Marshallian and evolutionary districts

4 From proximity advantages to organizational advantages through the global extension of an industrial district

The case of the footwear district of Verona

Fiorenza Belussi (Padua University)

4.1 Introduction[1]

This chapter describes the pattern of evolution of the Verona industrial district (ID), specializing in men's (and boys') walking shoes of medium quality, located in the east of the Veneto region, in Northern Italy. From a spatial point of view, the Verona district is more a cluster than a traditional Italian district,[2] because it is articulated in three main local poles, internal to the same province (Bussolengo, near Lake Garda; Verona; and the territory between the D'Alpone Valley and the area of San Bonifacio and Cologna Veneta, at the western border of the province, in the direction of Vicenza). In 2002, the district was composed of 324 companies,[3] and 4038 employees (our interpretations of the Chamber of Commerce data). This nearly corresponds with the total make-up of the footwear sector of the province, which in 2002 was comprised 412 firms and 4520 employees. The total turnover of the district was estimated at about 1000 million euro, of which 60 per cent was exported abroad.[4] The Verona district is one of the most important footwear districts in Italy,[5] together with Montebelluna and the Riviera del Brenta (a local system specializing in women's shoes covering the high market segment, as discussed by Rabellotti 2004, and Belussi 2000).

4.2 The historical development of the district

The Verona district belongs to a very well developed region of Northern Italy. Verona, in particular, represents an important node for outflows towards the north of Europe. The area is also characterized by a significant density of firms: there is a manufacturing firm (establishment) for every 50 inhabitants. In the province of Verona the levels of unemployment are particularly low: around 3.5 per cent (Veneto Lavoro 2002). This area benefits from an income per capita, related to a standard purchasing power, which is 30 per cent higher than the average European level (Veneto Lavoro 2002). The socio-economic context is characterized by a traditional farmer culture (where the values of the entrepreneurship scores high), and by diffused values of solidarity and cooperation deriving from the local Catholic culture.

The footwear sector in the province of Verona has a very long craft-shop tradition, developed to serve the needs of a population devoted to agriculture. So, the production of shoes in the area began with the 'sgalmara' product (a kind of wooden sabot). Raw materials utilized included the leather exterior.

During the first years of the 1910s, local craft-shops started to produce women's sabots made of velour. During the 1930s small factories with 10–20 employees which specialized in the footwear sector opened up (Figure 4.1). The district 'anchors firms' were firms that do not exist anymore, such as Trevisani, Specchiarle, Piccoli and Leonardi (Zanfei 1978). Then came some large entrepreneurial initiatives, like Maria Pia Calzaturificio[6] established in Bussolengo (and closed during the 1980s), or the firm 3A Antonini,[7] localized in Verona. Another large firm active in Verona during the 1930s was a maker of military shoes, Calzaturificio Rossi. During those times it reached a total of 600 employees, but in 1961 it was shut down.

Since the beginning, the local area specialized only in very simple products: working shoes and sandals. The highest growth of the district occurred in the period of the great start-up of the Italian district model: between the 1950s and 1960s. In that period, the Verona area increased the level of employment in the shoe industry from 2900 to 8833 employees.

The Verona area was a buyer-driven pole. Most of the local firms developed their production in relation to the German market, and the requirements of foreign traders who used to come to Verona from the north of Europe to find cheap products of medium quality.

The maximum expansion of the district was reached during the 1970s, when it reached levels of about 600 firms and 9000 employees (Table 4.1). Between 1971 and 2002 it was observed that there was a brusque employment contraction of about 4000 units, and a severe contraction of the number of existing firms.

In the course of its development of more than 50 years, the localization of the sector has kept its territorial shape of being 'three-polarized'. In the province of Verona, the more stable pole has been the one of San Giovanni Ilarione, where local firms, such as Frau, Luisa and Valbrunella, scarcely look to international subcontracting, and have maintained their competitive position in the market niche of low-priced women's walking shoes. Their peripheral localization, in an isolated mountain valley in a rural environment, also allowed an efficient management of labour mobility and flexibility.[8] On the contrary, in Verona and in Bussolengo, a clear contraction of footwear activities occurred during that time.

The Verona district decline is a result of incipient relocation (Chamber of Commerce and the local university, 1999) of production towards eastern countries (and particularly Romania) or other low-labour costs countries (such as Argentina). In the Verona pole, the shrinking of activities affected the two major firms of the area: 3A Antonini and Canguro.[9]

Nowadays, the district is characterized by a good number of small family firms, and a few important medium-sized companies of 150–200 employees (Monterosa, 3A Antonini, Frau, and Olip).

Table 4.1 The district evolution 1971–2002

	Establishments/firms		Employees	
	1971	2002	1971	2002
First district pole Verona	187	24	2176	354
Second district pole Bussolengo	200	235	4228	2655
Third district pole d'Alpone Valley	35	65	1049	1029
Verona district	422	324	7453	4038
Total province	609	412	8833	4520

Source: Interpretation of Chamber of Commerce archive and Istat 1971 census data.

During the 1990s, a shakeout process affected the firms in the district. Only half of the existing firms remained active. Actually, we have estimated that the employment level did not exceed 4500 units. After the relocation process, several local subcontractors (tomaifici) closed down, and those still in existence operate only on the shortest batches and on the preparation of collections. The district produces about 40–5 million pairs yearly.

The Verona productive pole is not an evolutionary system. The productive typology of the district has remained unchanged for more than 50 years: casual shoes of medium quality and price, such as moccasins, sandals, espadrilles, indigo shoes, etc., are produced in large batches. This segment is particularly exposed to the international competition of newly industrialized countries (NICs), and China (Onida, *et al.* 1992). Local firms are not strongly innovative, nor have large dynamic groups emerged in the last few decades. Many medium-sized local firms are quite dynamic in terms of exports and relocation strategy, but, apart from the local leading firm, 3A Antonini, they do not invest heavily in brand strategies, product upgrading, R&D activity, patents, proprietary outlets, and ICTs.

This district is a typical case of a Marshallian district. Local firms are relatively small and technologically passive with few remarkable exceptions.[10] All things considered, this district has moderate innovation capabilities (Belussi and Pilotti 2002).

4.3 From a local to a global value chain: building new forms of organizational proximity

The international literature has studied the process of formation of buyer-driven supply chains or producer-driven supply chains as alternative modalities, involving traditional simple manufactured goods, like textiles and footwear, or more complex items, like cars, computers or machinery (Gereffi, *et al.* 2005). Many contributions have, then, speculated on the impact that these different chains have

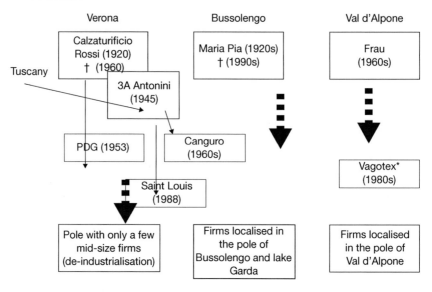

Figure 4.1 'Anchor' firms for the footwear district in Verona – origins of the three poles: years of foundation and new firm start-ups.

Notes
† The firm is non-existent. If available, we reported the date of closure.
* This firm has not been considered in our database because it is a textile firm; however, it now produces advanced fabrics and components for the footwear industry too.

played on the upgrading of firms localized in clusters in developing countries. The authoritative conclusion is that clusters are limited in their development by the existence of powerful global value chains (Bair and Gereffi 2001). Thus, the model of industrial districts has been found to be scarcely useful in explaining the pattern of transformation of firms in their tentative upgrading in product, process and functions. The case presented here shows, indeed, that the model of the Italian district is more complex and heterogeneous than initially supposed, and that, in some cases, small and medium districtual firms have transformed themselves into a mixed form of buyer-driven/producer global chains. In the case presented here, the district of Verona has undertaken these changes only in the latest stage of its evolutionary path.

The growth path of the Verona district can be illustrated by the following stages:

1 the 'embryonic' development between the two world wars up to 1944, where the technical competences and capabilities started to be explored in the area by some craft-workers;
2 the 'rapid take-off' of the 1950s and 1960s based on a drastic change to a type of development based on industrial and large firms, allowing them to meet the German demand;

3   the 'maturity stage' of the 1970s with the initial crisis of the largest organizations (with the exception of 3A Antonini); in this period, district firms experimented with a significant process of 'productive decentralization' where many activities (cutting, upper sewing, and assembling) were delegated to local subcontractors;

4   the 'slow decline' linked to the relocation phase of the 1980s and 1990s, where the district shifted from local outsourcing to 'distance' international subcontracting. Instead of building temporary and ubiquitous nets, district firms have selected a modality of relocation that allows the reproduction of some benefits of proximity, through the building of stable organizational links.

This last stage of the district has implied:

•   a new direction of the subcontracting nets towards long-distance nets;
•   the creation of joint ventures and FDI abroad;
•   a better development of logistic functions;
•   a higher use of ICTs;
•   a migration of knowledge embodied in technicians to control the phases of the production realized abroad;
•   the selection of a specific relocalization pattern that gives rise to new forms of agglomeration.

The Verona district is specialized in the production of simple low-cost walking shoes for men and boys. While the Rivera del Brenta produces a typical high-fashion product, the Verona shoes have the reputation of being tailored without any stylistic content. They are strong, simple and standardized, as required by a non-demanding market such as the German area. Products are only a little more sophisticated than those manufactured in the NIC countries. When the Verona producers moved some phases of production abroad they already had firmly in their hands their final clients or distributive channels. All the final firms were able to manufacture a finished good to a standard design, but some already had the capacity to produce an original collection,[11] and some were working for well-known brands (such as the British Clarks, Dr Scholls' shoes, etc.). There are also many medium-sized firms with quite well-known Italian brands.[12]

It has been calculated that in Verona there are about 50 main final firms (Chamber of Commerce and the local university, 1999). All operate with foreign distributors and many of them are large exporters. There is, then, a significant fringe of small firms that work for the Italian market and for a few independent shops. Their profits are rather uncertain, tied to the economic situation of their clients: they often wait 90–120 days to receive the payments for their goods shipped. Some firms are pure commercial entities, and work on spot opportunities. The group of specialized suppliers is wide (sole makers, punch makers, mould makers, and sellers of leather, components and accessories, etc.). In the Verona district there are a very small number of independent shoe designers: each season, firms tend to reproduce very similar models.

Small and medium-sized firms work with quite modern technologies. Most machines are essentially power-assisted hand tools, and this explains why labour costs are still so important in determining the final costs. Assembly is still the phase which requires more skilled labour.

The overall process of change in the footwear industry has often been described as 'intensification' of work organization, in order to increase labour productivity. In the last few years, new technologies of rapid prototyping have started to be developed.[13]

The application of ICT technologies has allowed a better management of the decentralized system of production, and a more global system involving international supply chains. During this time, the technical optimal size for each operation has decreased, so that it can justify nowadays, on average, a dimension of 15–40 employees. Increasing returns seem now connected to design, marketing, brand and retailing. A model of the footwear filière is reported in Figure 4.2. This is an extreme synthetic schema, because there are more than 100 different operations involved in the construction of a shoe, depending on the model. As a general statement, we can see that all operations linked to the upper production and to assembling can be subcontracted by the final firms. Many firms nowadays limit themselves to work upstream (marketing, selling, buying raw materials, designing the collection), and downstream (logistics, shipments, and distribution or retailing).

In the most dynamic firms, nearly all manufacturing activities take place in foreign countries. However, firms from Verona use temporary forms of proximity. Technicians fly into Timişoara every two weeks, and organize direct inspections in the subcontracting factories, or provide assistance. Face-to-face exchanges of information and knowledge are now delocalized abroad.

4.4 Results from a survey

4.4.1 Some methodological notes

The information presented in our work derives from 30 in-depth interviews with firms, a sample extracted from the list of the existing firm population (CERVED data), and from seven qualitative interviews with local actors. We have interviewed the major local firms, and the main district local agents/actors, such as the local chamber of commerce, the local trade unions, the entrepreneurial associations, and the president of Fo.ca.ver., a consortium that organizes training activities. Data on firms and local actors were collected in the period April to August 2003. The subjects interviewed (a face-to-face interview of two to three hours' duration) were the entrepreneur or a top-ranking manager in the case of the largest firms, and the person responsible for the local institution. For the completion of information collection, follow-up telephone interviews were often necessary.

The district firm population can be divided into three segments:
- final firms (calzaturifici);
- specialized firms producing special parts and components; and

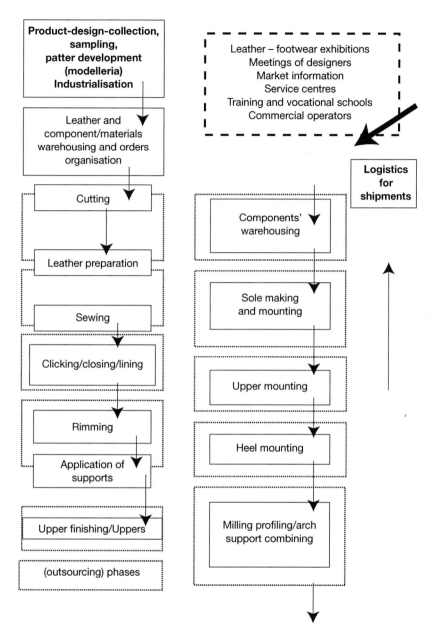

Figure 4.2 The productive footwear filière.

- subcontractors of capacity (they are not responsible for designing and selling of the production; they are made-to-order firms, and receive all raw materials from the commissioning firm).

4.4.2 Some firm characteristics

We interviewed a total number of 30 firms or establishments. In the sample selected there is a representative mix of the composite nature of the district:

- large and small producers;
- producers of the middle–low market segment;
- firms with intense relocation and no internationalized firms;
- final firms and intermediate producers and component producers;
- final firms and component producers.

As shown in Table 4.2, the 30 firms selected have produced a total turnover of 421.8 million euro in 2001, of which about 44 per cent is exported. The firms interviewed declared a total number of 1407 employees in the same year (we count here only the district local employment, excluding the FDI related units).

We interviewed 21 final firms and nine producers of intermediate products/phases/services. Sixteen final firms produce products/services manufactured according to the firms' market assessments, while five produce products/services manufactured according to customers' specifications (they make up only 10 per cent of the total turnover declared by final firms). These final producers lack market autonomy because they work as subcontractors for other final producers (however, sometimes they also produce their own collection). Some large firms work for consolidated brand names, such as the British Clarks, but they are trying to become more 'independent' from their commissioning firms. The majority of the sample

Table 4.2 The district firm population

	Sample			District		
	1999	*2000*	*2001*	*1999**	*2000**	*2001**
Number of establishments	30	30	30	450	400	324
Number of persons employed	1361	1391	1407	5500	5000	4038
Total turnover Million Euro	384.116	407.165	421.808	800.000	900.000	1000.000

Note
* Our estimate.

turnover is produced by 16 final firms of medium size (50–249 employees), which is also the category with more working units (1103).

The sample of small firms (one to nine employees) is well represented, despite difficulties encountered in interviewing 'factotum' entrepreneurs. All firms interviewed are not affiliated to multinationals. A significant part of our sample (33.3 per cent) is formed by firms which belong to a group. Nine out of 10 have complete control over the group. They cover 63 per cent of the total employment of the sample. Group firms have plants abroad: they control 26 establishments.

This shows that even relatively small organizations in the district have access to the benefit of the global economy.

Interviewed firms are family business firms. Only in half of the sample are external managers involved in the organization.

Interviewed entrepreneurs have a low level of formal education. More than half of the sample (16 entrepreneurs) possess only a compulsory certificate, while 11 entrepreneurs have a diploma from secondary school. Only three entrepreneurs possess a university degree.

The degree of qualification of the workforce is reported in Table 4.3. This indicator does not support the view of Verona as a knowledge-intensive district, such as, for instance, it is in Montebelluna (where 43 per cent of the workforce possess a university qualification or hold a diploma).

Local firms employ a mainly Italian workforce. Immigrant workers are mainly involved in the non-qualified tasks of warehousing, as porters, and with simple assembly tasks.

Table 4.3 Distribution of employees by qualification and employment size classes

| | *Qualification and status* | *Employment size classes* | | | | |
		1–9	*10–19*	*20–49*	*50–249*	*Total*
All employees	Employees with university qualifications	4		0	107	111
	Employees holding diplomas	5	1	31	267	304
	Qualified employees	20	28	6	328	382
	Employees with intermediate qualification	19	19	85	407	530
	Employees without qualifications	0	0	11	69	80
	Total	48	48	133	1178	1407

4.4.2.1 Final firms

Final firms, on average, work with 6.7 subcontractors. Relationships are typically long term (see Table 4.4), also for Central and Eastern European Countries (CEECs), and international subcontractors. Among the group of 21 final firms interviewed, only four firms do not resort to subcontracting. Eleven firms declared utilizing CEEC subcontractors, three firms international subcontractors (excluding CEECs), and the remaining four firms use only subcontractors localized in the district. Eight firms use both foreign and local subcontractors.

Products or tasks are supplied according to the commissioning firm's strict technical specifications. Verona firms are involved in routine standardized network relations. In the case of international subcontractors, firms' external technicians supervise the production abroad.

The 'migration' of knowledge is attached to those temporary relations of proximity. Often machinery and plants are also transferred from the commissioning firm to foreign subcontractors.

4.4.2.2 Subcontractors

Local firms producing mainly intermediate products are, here, defined as subcontractors (producers of specialized components are also included in this category). Local subcontractors are composed of autonomous and dependent firms. The dominant group here (in terms of output produced) is that of firms working on the basis

Table 4.4 Distribution of final firms by length of interaction with subcontractors/suppliers and location of subcontractors/suppliers

	Type of subcontractors/suppliers by location			
Length of relationship	Local	National	CEECs	International (excluding CEECs)
	Absolute value	Absolute value	Absolute value	Absolute value
1 year or less*	1	0	1	0
2–3 years**	5		7	0
More than 3 years***	6	1	3	3
Total	12	1	11	3

Notes
* number of firms saying that the largest percentage of the relationships with local subcontractors lasts one year or less;
** number of firms saying that the largest percentage of the relationships with local subcontractors lasts two to three years;
*** number of firms saying that the largest percentage of the relationships with local subcontractors lasts more than three years.

of their own specific design (Table 4.5). Local subcontractors exhibit a relatively strong market position because typically they work for more than one customer (Table 4.6). They are controlled by their clients in terms of prices, quality control and standards, delivering systems, and time scheduling.

Table 4.5 Distribution of firms (establishments) producing mainly intermediate products/ services by type of production

	Number of subcontractors/ intermediate firms		Turnover Percentage value Million euro	Share of output
Type of production	*a.v.*	*p.v.*		
Standard products/services				
Products/services manufactured according to commissioning firms' specifications	5		1030	2.4
Products/services manufactured according to the firms' own specifications/design	4		41,840	97.6
Total	9	100	42,870	100

Table 4.6 Distribution of client firms by the number of subcontractors/intermediate firms in the last three years (1999–2001)

Number of client firms	2001		2000		1999	
	a.v.	*p.v.*	*a.v.*	*p.v.*	*a.v.*	*p.v.*
One	1	11.1	1	11.1	1	11.1
2–3	2	22.2	2	22.2	1	11.12
4–5	2	22.2	1	11.1	2	22.2
6–10	1	11.1	2	22.2	2	22.2
More than 10	3	33.3	3	33.3	3	33.3
Total	9	100.0	9	100.0	9	100.0
Total number of clients	191		195		198	
Average number of clients by client firms	21.2		21.7		22.0	

4.4.3 Innovation activity

Within the footwear industry there are no extremely high technological opportunities. New technologies are developed in the automation of machinery, and technical development is in the hands of external producers.[14] Footwear firms typically focus their efforts on immediate productive tasks. They do not normally possess specialized human resources to develop internal applied research.

In the Verona district, R&D activity is performed only by seven firms (out of 30), which occupy 18 employees. This corresponds to about 1 per cent of the total sample turnover. The largest firms of the district are the R&D performers (including 3A Antonini, Olip, Calz, Frau, Maxi, and Maritan). Patenting activity has been found only among the three largest firms (3A Antonini, Olip, and Frau).

4.4.3.1 Innovation diffusion

In the majority of our sample (20 firms) firms did not adopt any technological product innovation. In nine firms, technological product innovation was generated internally (Table 4.7).

The adoption of commercial innovations was seen in only seven firms, and only two (3A Antonini and Olip) have adopted new commercial outlets.

4.4.3.2 Sources of firm knowledge

In this empirical survey we also investigated the importance of the various sources of knowledge for the firm (Table 4.8). Interviewed evaluation could vary from 1 – not relevant, to 5 – most relevant. In the sample, the most important 'internal' source of knowledge is 'Knowledge gained from continuous improvement of production processes' (1.7), and not R&D (1.5). The more important 'external' source is related to the district knowledge; 'Knowledge derived from interactions with clients and/or suppliers' (3.0). At international level the most important sources (2.9) appear to be related to the 'Knowledge gained from publicly available information (e.g. trade fairs, publications)'.

'District' knowledge receives higher marks than national or international knowledge, confirming the existence of a Marshallian district. However, district firms are also efficient absorbers of international knowledge sources linked to trade fairs, publications, etc.

4.4.3.3 Horizontal cooperation

Among our sample the existence of agreements with other companies is not greatly diffused. Verona firms cooperate mainly on training issues (this involves 12 firms, about 40 per cent of the sample). Agreements are more frequent among larger firms.

Table 4. 7 Innovativeness of the firms (establishments) in the sample by employment size-classes in the last three years (1999–2001)

	Employment size-classes				
	1–9	*10–19*	*20–49*	*50–249*	*Total*
Adoption of product innovation					
No innovation	10	4	3	3	20
Generated by the firm	1		1	7	9
Generated within the district					
Generated in the country					
Generated abroad				1	1
Adoption of process innovation					
No innovation	10	4	3	1	18
Generated by the firm	1		1	7	9
Generated within the district				3	3
Generated in the country					
Generated abroad					
Adoption of innovation in the organization of production					
No innovation	10	4	4	5	23
Generated within the firm	1			5	6
Generated within the district				1	1
Generated in the country					
Generated abroad					
Adoption of innovation in the organization of sales and distribution					
No innovation	10	4	4	5	23
Generated by the firm	1			5	6
Generated within the district				1	1
Generated in the country					
Generated abroad					

4.4.3.4 Firm's rivalry

Who are the main competitors of the Verona footwear firms? Interviewed en-trepreneurs perceived that the main competitors are located in the district. The competitors of the largest firms are both local and foreign firms, which benefit from low labour costs in developing countries. The bigger the firms the larger is the radius of action of their potential competitors.

Table 4.8 Ranking of the most relevant sources of technical knowledge (average values*)

| Sources of knowledge | Rank (average values) | | | | Employment size-classes |
	Internal to firms	District	National	International	50–249
Knowledge gained through in-house R&D	1.5	–	–	–	1.9
Knowledge gained from continuous improvement of production processes	2.6	–	–	–	3.9
Knowledge derived from parent or subsidiary companies	1.3	–	–	–	1.2
Knowledge developed through company's internal education and training programmes	1.8	–	–	–	2.8
Other	1.1	–	–	–	1.0
Knowledge embedded in experts hired on the labour market	–	1.7	1.5	1.5	
Knowledge derived from interactions with clients and/or suppliers	–	3.0	2.2	2.0	
Knowledge derived from cooperation with other companies	–	1.9	1.5	1.4	
Knowledge derived from imitation of products	–	2.3	2.2	1.7	
Knowledge embedded in technologies, licences, and components, acquired from outside (technological innovation)	–	2.4	2.5	1.9	
Knowledge gained from interactions with public institutions (e.g. universities, public research centres, local government, etc.)	–	1.5	1.4	1.1	
Knowledge gained from interactions with semi-public institutions (e.g. chambers of commerce, industry associations, trade unions, etc.)	–	1.5	1.3	1.1	

	Rank (average values)				Employment size-classes
Sources of knowledge	Internal to firms	District	National	International	50–249
Knowledge gained from publicly available information (e.g. trade fairs, publications)	–	1.9	1.7	2.9	
Others	–	1.1	1.1	1.0	

Note
* Evaluations could vary from 1 (not relevant) to 5 (most relevant).

4.4.4 The globalization of the district

4.4.4.1 Export flows

Export flows estimated, in 2001, were 185,975 million euro, corresponding to 42.4 per cent of the total sales of the firms (Table 4.9). In our sample, 17 firms from 21 final producers are exporting firms. Among the non-exporters, we find Calzaturificio Frau (150 employees), which produces casual comfort shoes for the national market. The entrepreneur wants to preserve, as much as possible, the original idea of the 'Made in Italy' concept. It uses exclusively local or national subcontractors.

Export flows are in the hands of the largest district firms: those with more than 50 employees.

The EU market is the largest exporting area (72.9 per cent of total exports). In particular, Germany and France are the most important foreign markets. Preferred routes of exports are intermediaries and traders.

Table 4.9 Exports and imports of firms by employment size classes in the last three years (1999–2001)

	Years	Employment size classes				
		1–9	10–19	20–49	50–249	Total
Export Million Euro	2001	0.8	1.0	77.013	107.162	185.975
	2000	0.7	1.0	79.118	99.197	180.016
	1999	4.3	1.0	79.821	93.562	178.683

Note
* Data refer to 17 cases (none absent).

There are no inward investments in the Verona district, and the large multinational buyers, such as Puma, Nike and Adidas, are more connected with Montebelluna. However, in the Verona district Nike deals with one of its biggest international subcontractors.

4.4.4.2 International subcontracting strategies

On average, each firm in the district is engaged in subcontracting with at least eight to 10 firms, four or five of them from CEEC countries. Flows related to the governance of the global supply chains mainly involve subcontractors located in CEEC countries, and above all, in Romania. In the district, all firms with more than 50 employees have developed global sub-contracting chains in eastern countries (Table 4.10). Smaller firms typically use only local subcontractors. In 2001, 12 district firms have established international global chains in CECC countries, using 85 subcontractors. The main motivation for using subcontracting in CEEC countries is the low cost of labour. Only eight firms import finished items, including Olip, Girza and Calzaturificio Maxi. Often, the finishing of the product occurs in Verona, because firms label their product as 'Made in Italy'. The stages of the value chain involving high-value activity related to design, marketing and communication, prototyping and R&D activity are kept in the district.

CEEC subcontractors are on average large in size, being firms with more than 250 employees. The subcontractors are changed frequently, usually because they do not respect client standards, or because they produce work of low quality. CEEC subcontractors were selected by asking customers or distributors; business associations played a minor role. Contracting companies influence CEEC subcontractors in all possible relevant areas: prices, choices of machinery (sometimes they transfer their own old machinery to CEEC subcontractors); on-site inspections connected to the control of quality standards and procedures; production planning, and delivery systems. In practice, the level of autonomy of CEEC subcontractors is very low,

Table 4.10 Number of CEEC subcontractors by employment size classes of subcontracting client firm in the last three years (2001)

	Employment size classes							
	1–19		*20–49*		*50–249*		*Total*	
	Firms	*CEECS Sub.*	*Firms*	*CEECS Sub.*	*Firms*	*CEECS Sub.*	*Firms*	*CEECS Sub.*
Relocating firms	1	5	2	7	9	73	12	85
Non-relocating firms	14		2		2		18	

not to say non-existent. The comparison between CEEC and district subcontractors is pitiful: they are unable to rapidly adjust themselves to changes in product and volumes, and they lack the required technical capability because the local labour force is not sufficiently well trained. The only big advantage in the use of CEEC subcontractors is related to costs. CEEC subcontractors are often managed (or owned) by former Italian entrepreneurs (from Marche or Veneto).

4.4.4.3 Foreign direct investment

While in the literature on internationalization FDI and other forms of contractual alliances are perceived as alternative modalities of globalization (Casson 1990; Horstmann and Markusen 1996), Verona firms have explored the opportunity of building international subcontracting chains not excluding the recourse to FDI (Table 4.11). FDI strategies involve a significant segment of our sample (nine companies). Firms investing aboard through FDI are the largest companies of the district. FDIs are developed in order to better control quality standards, production efficiency, and logistics. Outward processing through FDI has also motivated entry into new markets, and the expansion of sales. But this is still a minor explanation of the FDI. Firms that are engaged in CEECs' FDI have usually opted for greenfield investments. The preferred country selected for FDI initiatives is Romania.

FDI strategies, in contrast with Montebelluna, do not involve licensing and commercial distribution strategies. As shown in Table 4.12, seven firms involved in international subcontracting have also activated FDI. Often, the two options are not alternative strategies but, on the contrary, complementary decisions.

4.4.4.4 The impact of relocation and FDI strategies on the district

The strategies of relocation through international subcontracting and FDI have inevitably transformed the Verona district. In the last 30 years local employment has halved, but this is not a sign of a clear decline, because the biggest local firms

Table 4.11 Firms with FDI in CEECs by type of investment and employment size classes: modalities

Types of FDI in CEECs	*Employment size classes (2001)*			
	1–19	*20–49*	*50–249*	*Total*
Firms with FDI	0	1	8	9
Number of FDI	0	1	10	11
Greenfield (new) investment	–	1	8	9
Acquisition of an existing local company	–	0	1	1
Joint equity venture	–	0	1	1
Firms without FDI	15	3	3	21

Table 4.12 Firms with FDI and international subcontracting chains in CEECs by type of investment and employment size classes

FDI and international subcontracting in CEECs	Employment size classes (2001)			
	1–19	*20–49*	*50–249*	*Total*
No FDI & IS	14	2	1	17
Only IS	1	1	3	5
Only FDI	0	0	1	1
Dual strategy	0	1	6	7

transformed themselves into small MNCs. In the district, buyer-driven chains and producer-driven chains have fused into a new model of internationalization, which uses a dual modality of combining more or less risky strategies.

Local leader firms have shrunk, because they only concentrate on services and knowledge-intensive operations: marketing, logistics, projecting and general firm functions. For the leading companies, such as 3A Antonini, Olip or Diamant, the relocation process has been an opportunity to increase sales and international competitiveness.

The relocation process in Verona has created a new demand for qualified workers and 'global chain controllers'. Thus, the district will have to prepare in future with new professional employees.

4.5 Some conclusions on the evolutionary path of the Verona district

The Verona district represents a case of evolution (Sammarra 2003; Varaldo and Ferrucci 1997; Varaldo 1988) of a satellite district into a canonical Marshallian district. In its origins it was supported by the existence of craft-shop diffused abilities. During the 1960s the decisive triggering factor was the presence of German buyers. The crisis during the 1970s of some large established organizations generated a typical Italian district, made up of small and medium-sized organizations. The sole large firm that survived in the last 50 years is 3A Antonini. In the course of the Verona district history we observed a continuous firm reshuffling.

But firm heterogeneity is still present. Despite the firms' average specialization in medium-quality shoes, Rotta is involved in high-quality items. Diamant works for Nike. Olip is scaling up its market niche.

In Verona there are now several brand producers. Most of Dr Scholl's and Clarks' shoes are subcontracted here to new producers. 3A Antonini played a significant role in building the Italian fashion industry of the 1980s, introducing the Lumberjack brand. A new firm has recently created the Logan brand.

The international competition is actually very high: Verona must defend in Europe its 45 million pairs produced annually against the newly entered China, which now produces about 7 billion shoes (Anci 2002; Bercellesi 2003) each year.[15]

The globalization of the district has not replicated the district abroad, but has created a second 'layer' district, localized in a very dispersed area around Timişoara, Arad and Oradea, where standardized manufacturing activities have been relocated (some large establishments are also in Bucharest). All raw materials and semi-components still come from the headquarters of firms in Verona. Will Timişoara have the chance to become an 'Italianate' district in future? Probably the answer is no: in a globalized world, the low labour costs existing in China will operate as a centrifugal force. This new type of division of labour, stemming from the use of FDI and global supply chains, has given rise to a twin 'infant district' in Timişoara, but the replication has been 'imperfect'. Temporary proximity has created some organizational links, useful for the activation of global flows, and firm linkages, but the chances for Timişoara to create a system endowed with endogenous genuine local entrepreneurial capabilities are scarce.

Notes

1 This chapter is mainly based on a comprehensive survey organized within the project Industrial Districts WEST-EAST Relocation policies organized by the Tagliacarne Institute of Rome. See 'The Verona Footwear district' written by F. Belussi and M. Bosa (Assosport Treviso).

2 The Verona district is localized in a province characterized by the presence of a multitude of manufacturing sectors. Considering the methodological criteria of the Italian law L. 917 – see for instance Anastasia and Corò (1993), and Anastasia, Corò and Crestanello (1995) – of the three footwear poles, only the D'Alpone Valley, with the municipality of San Giovanni Ilarione, appears to possess the parameters of being a highly specialized area in footwear activities. Verona and Bussolengo are, in fact, composite multi-sector areas including several commercial firms.

3 The largest firms of the Verona district are now 3A Antonini, Olip, Effegi, Freemod, Calzaturificio Frau, and Monterosa, whose sales are in excess of 60 million euro.

4 In 2002, the volume of the three IDs localized in the Veneto region (Montebelluna, Riviera del Brenta and Verona) reached 26.9 per cent of the national export flows in footwear, of which 799.2 million lire can be attributed to the Montebelluna district, 643.8 million to the Riviera del Brenta district, and 605 million to the Verona district.

5 In 2001, in Italy, the footwear industry represented a quite significant economic sector: 111,650 employees; 8670 million euro of output, and 7230 million euro of exports (see: www.ueitalia2003.it; Thomas 2001). Intensive commercial flows of outward processing trade (OPT), linked to the globalization of sub-contracting chains have recently characterized the sector (Amighini and Rabellotti 2006).

6 Pietro Vessanelli was the founder of the Maria Pia Calzaturificio, which started production as a subcontractor (upper maker 'giunteria'). At the end of the 1970s the Maria Pia Calzaturificio was the first Italian producer with 55 million lire of sales and 726 employees (Zanfei 1981).

7 Ilvo Antonini came from Illasi during the 1930s. He had acquired some professional experience in Tuscany. After the Second World War, Alvaro Antonini, with the money of another brother – Gaetano – allowed Ilvo to open up a factory in Verona. In the mid-1950s the firm moved to Borgo Roma (it already had 180 employees), and then to

ZAI, in a newly created industrial estate, where four establishments were created. The 3A Antonini group immediately became a large industrial firm.

8 One entrepreneur interviewed, Renzo D'Arcano, commented, 'Can we be still competitive in a world where every big firm delocalizes?' The answer given is clear: 'We have a good trade-off between price and quality, and this is our real advantage. We don't spend so much money in advertisements but we focus resources on research and development of the product. Our supply chain is short, just inside the district, so it is easier to control it and organize efficiently.'

9 Canguro was founded in 1966, by a former worker of Antonini. It specialized in the production of 'Clark' shoes. At the end of the 1970s the firm had 428 employees, while in 2002 it declared only 28 labour units. This debacle occurring during the 1980s was related to the inability to manage the international subcontracting chains in China and Taiwan.

10 The Verona district has greatly benefited from the presence of two innovative component suppliers: PDG and Vagotex, textile producers localized in Colognola ai Colli. PDG is partner of a large group (Despa, De Gara Montichiari, De Gara Firenze, and De Gara Strà). Vagotext has experimented in the last few years with the introduction of new components in the market (such as carbonfit – an anti-bacterial cork sole – or new types of linings). PDG has introduced numerous incremental novelties in machinery and materials (such as fabric material for security, protection and anti-perspiration, antistatic lining, thermo-adhesive textiles, technical closings, thermo-regulative fabric, composite fibres, strip cuts – to cut insoles coming from strips of cellulose materials of various thicknesses automatically, new fabrics, and new thermo-regulating materials, like Outlast, which has been developed by NASA). PDG and Vagotext are searching worldwide for external innovations worthy of being applied by firms in the sector. Some R&D activities are organized by the local footwear consortium Fo.ca.ver., sponsored by the Veneto region, to produce rapid models and moulds for prototyping.

11 3a Antonini' Cal., Effegi Style, Olip, Calz Monterosa, Girza, Stilman Footwear, Calz. Maxi, Montexport, Canguro, Calz. Frau, Calz. Thema, Calz. Sartori, Saint Luis, Calz Larika, Calz. 2 Zeta, Calz Niki, Calz. European, Calz Rosetta, Calz. Valbrunella, Calz. Boomerang Calz. Fraven, Calz System, Calz. Dogi, Claz. Carrillon, Calz. Jumbo, Calz Exportac, Diamant, Relaxshoes, The Best, Calz. 3 Nogarine, Galmond, and Calz. Luisport.

12 Lumberjack (3a Antonini), Defense (Girza), Frau (Frau), Maxi and Cangrande (Calzaturificio Maxi), Maritan, Moyid, Marco Ferretti, Carmine D'Urso (Maritan), Mistic and Lauranna (Lauranna), Polsa and Paolo Sartori (Sartori), Zen Age (Saint Luis), Rotta (Rotta), and Diamant (Diamant).

13 See www.cnr.it/cnr/news.

14 In Vigevano (Lombardy), there is an industrial district specializing in footwear technology. This was an old footwear district, where, during the 1950s and 1960s, local firms diversified their production towards mechanical activity (Bravo and Merlo 2002). The entrepreneurs gained their first technical experience in mechanical repairing of footwear machinery, developing a process of learning by using.

15 The real point is the absence of reciprocity: while the WTO agreement has opened up the European market, Italian products pay a 38 per cent tariff and China only 8 per cent. See also www.fotoshoes.com.

References

Amighini A. and Rabellotti R. (2006), How do Italian footwear industrial districts face globalization? *European Planning Studies*, 14(4): 485–502.

Anastasia B. and Corò G. (1993), *I distretti industriali in Veneto,* Nuova dimensione, Ediciclo, Portogruaro.

Anastasia B., Corò G., and Crestanello P. (1995), 'Problemi di individuazione dei distretti industriali: esperienze regionali e rapporti con le politiche', *Oltre il Ponte*, 52.

Anci (2002), L'industria calzaturiera italiana 2001, Relazione economico statistica, Milano: Anci.

Bair J. and Gereffi G. (2001), 'Local clusters in global chains: the causes and consequences of export dynamism in Torreon's blue jeans industry, *World Development*, 29(11): 1885–1903.

Belussi F. (ed.) (2000), *Tacchi a spillo. Il distretto calzaturiero della Riviera del Brenta come forma organizzata di capitale sociale*, Padova: Cleup.

Belussi F. and Pilotti L. (2002), 'Knowledge creation, learning and innovation in Italian industrial districts', *Geografiska Annaler*, 84: 19–33.

Bercellesi M. (2003), 'Cina, partner o concorrente?', *Tecnica Calzaturiera*, October.

Bravo G. and Merlo E. (2002), 'Sviluppo e crisi del distretto di Vigevano', in G. Provasi (a cura di), *Le istituzioni dello sviluppo*, Roma: Donzelli.

Casson M. (1990), *Multinational Corporations*, Edward Elgar: London.

Cerved Data, Chamber of Commerce, various years.

Chamber of Commerce and the Verona University (1999), Romania chiama Verona, mimeo, Verona.

Gereffi G., Humphrey J. and Sturgeon T. (2005), 'The governance of global value chains', *Review of International Political Economy*, 12(1): 78–104.

Horstmann I. and Markusen J. R. (1996), 'Exploring new markets: direct investment, contractual relations and the multinational enterprise', *International Economic Review*, 37(1): 1–19.

Lavoro V. (2002), *Il mercato del lavoro nel Veneto*, Milan: Angeli.

Onida F., *et al.* (1992), *I distretti industriali: crisi o evoluzione?*, Milano: Egea.

Rabellotti R. (2004), 'How globalisation affects Italian industrial districts: the case of Brenta', in H. Schmitz (ed.), *Local Enterprises in the Global Economy*, London: Edward Elgar.

Sammarra A. (2003), *Lo sviluppo dei distretti industriali*. Percorsi tra globalizzazione e localizzazione, Roma: Carocci.

Thomas A. (2001), 'Cenni sull'evoluzione del settore calzaturiero', *Novus Campus*, 1.

Varaldo R. (1988), *Il sistema delle imprese calzaturiere*, Torino: Giappichelli.

Varaldo R. and Ferrucci L. (eds.) (1997), *I distretti industriali tra logiche di sistema e logiche di impresa*, Milano: Angeli.

Zanfei A. (1981), Quale modernizzazione per un settore tradizionale. Il calzaturiero nella provincia di Verona, ricerca coordinata da F. Belussi, Ires Veneto, Litografia Villotta.

5 The evolution of a technologically dynamic district

The case of Montebelluna

Fiorenza Belussi (University of Padua)

5.1 Introduction

This chapter[1] describes the pattern of evolution of a famous industrial district located in the north-east of Northern Italy. The Montebelluna district, located in the province of Treviso, is the world leader in technical sports shoes, ski and trekking boots, motorcycle boots and bicycle shoes. The district is marked by the presence of some international companies, established in the 1990s through the acquisition of local firms.

The Montebelluna district is considered one of the most innovative in Italy because it is made up of dynamic evolutionary firms which have introduced important radical innovations in the past, which have given rise to the international dominance of the district in the technologies for the production of ski boots. Related to that, the district has achieved widespread success in its international market outlets (Belussi and Pilotti 2002). The district specializes[2] in sports shoes and in sports garments, but it produces numerous other technical products, so it has been defined as 'the sport-system district' (Club dei distretti industriali 2003).

The district was formed in 2004 by about 400 firms (300 producers of footwear and 100 producers of clothing) that employ around 8000 workers. Montebelluna represents a model of an evolutionary district, because, over time, its industrial structure has evolved, and there are now dominant Schumpeterian players in the district. Even if the role of SMEs is still relevant, numerous informal and formal groups have also been created.

In Section 5.2, an overview of the district is presented. Section 5.3 deals with the analysis of its historical formation. In Section 5.4 the results of our empirical survey are presented. Section 5.5 presents an assessment of the evolutionary pattern of the district in the context of globalization.

5.2 An evolutionary district

The Montebelluna district is situated within an industrial local economy strongly characterized by the presence of SMEs.[3] In the province of Treviso, 46 per cent of the working population is active in manufacturing. The GNP per capita in the province is 30 per cent higher than the European average (Veneto Lavoro 2002).

In the Treviso area there is a firm (establishment) for every nine inhabitants. It is important to stress that the local entrepreneurial culture has helped the contextual climate for the dynamics of entrepreneurship. Until the 1960s, the Veneto area was a territory plagued by emigration. But the market opportunity, opened by the development of the large European market, completely changed the historical profile of the area. These opportunities were explored by the Veneto entrepreneurs, who have modest origins, and are typically ex-blue collar worker employees.

The whole district is composed of the following municipalities, which include both the 'historical part of the district'[4] and the 'fringe area'[5] of adjacent external municipalities, where in the 1980s many new modern plants were established, by the newly created firms, or by the older district firms which expanded their activity.

Today about 400 companies (Figure 5.1) and 8000 employees form the district (6000 units in footwear and 2000 in clothing).[6] The district is still characterized by a significant number of SMEs, family-owned firms, and a few important local larger companies, deriving from the original nucleus of the first founders, which were created at the end of the last century and during the first decades of the nineteenth century (Tecnica, Caberlotto, Calzaturificio Alpina, Dolomite, Munari, and Nordica). Many of them, after three generations, are still in the marketplace. Between the two wars, the growth of the district was gradual but not insignificant. The real take-off of the district occurred during the 1960s, in the great period of growth of the Italian economy, the so called 'economic miracle', helped by the constitution of the European market, and by wide application of new technologies, largely spread by European (German) and American companies. The growth of the market allows for a deeper international specialization, and the district could benefit from the stable growth of international demand for mountain and ski boots. The number of firms grew dramatically during the 1970s, thanks to the innovative products (plastic ski boots) that the local district's firms were able to introduce into the market. During the 1980s, too, the continuous vitality of the district (and the creation of new market niches) expanded the stock of the district firms.

A few large verticalized firms, and an elevated number of small and medium-sized enterprises, composed the Montebelluna district after the beginning of the 1980s. Thanks to a high degree of division of labour, small craft firms could afford to enter the market as subcontractors, and large local firms were continuously using outsourcing practices: decentralising tasks, activities, and the buying of intermediate or ready-made products.

After 1989, the local population of firms started to steadily shrink. In 1989 the number of district firms reached its peak of 800 units, and later it declined to 600 (at the beginning of the 1990s) and then to about 300 (in 2000). The decline in the number of firms is not a sign of economic backwardness, but derives from the combined effect of two processes: firm concentration, and relocation of activities in low-labour-cost countries.

However, all the economic indicators show that in the last few years a continuous pattern of growth, in terms of firm sales and exports flows, has occurred. An obvious indicator of the performance of the district is the total output realized in Montebelluna. Despite the declining number of local firms and employment, data on production and output are still positive, showing a general trend of expansion. Including clothing (but not Benetton), the output of the Montebelluna district has grown from 1992 billion lire in 1999, to 2834 billion lire in 2001 (Osem 2001).

Clearly, in the last decade, the number of local subcontracting firms declined – the decline (Figure 5.2) is mainly concentrated in the firm population segment of the so-called 'tomaifici' (producers of uppers). In the meantime, large groups emerged in the district, and in 1989 the Benetton group entered the district with the acquisition of Nordica, one of the largest leading local firms.

In 2000, the final footwear firms were employing 5661 employees, and indirect activities (subcontracting firms and specialized suppliers) were responsible for 3471 employees, so the total employment of the footwear district was 8782 units (Osem 2001).

Despite the presence of large firms, in 2000, 5109 employees, corresponding to 58 per cent of the total district workforce, were occupied in small firms (with fewer than 100 employees). Therefore, Montebelluna can still be considered a district, but the role of dominant players has increased.

It has been calculated that between 1997 and 2001, the sportswear district's working population decreased by about 1000 workers. Those who lost their jobs were people working in subcontracting firms (mainly 'tomaifici'), that have lost their commissioning work, because of the transfer of subcontracting to Eastern countries. But often, the relocation of activities to those countries has also required a relocation of the Montebelluna subcontractors.

Firms have 'migrated' together with their suppliers and trusted collaborators. Many small owners of subcontracting firms, which suddenly lost their 'outsourced' orders, have opened up new workshops in Romania, or work there as super-controllers of the quality of local subcontractors (our interviews). Therefore, many former subcontractors now work as controllers of large global supply chains activated by the major local companies. In addition, we have to consider that this district is located within an area of full employment, with one of the lowest unemployment rates in Italy. The district is still rich in manufacturing activities, specialized suppliers, designers and other activities connected with the filière of the sport-system; it has not become a 'hollow system', which only governs external, delocalized and a-spatial production activities (the American model). Geographical proximity of producers still plays a role, and so does organizational proximity, because many relationships with subcontractors, face-to-face exchanges of information, and cooperative firm interactions, now occur in a new dimension of temporary proximity.

It is important to observe that for 8000 employees working in Montebelluna, in footwear/plastic and clothing-textile activities, in the external belt of subcontracting activities – decentralized mainly in Eastern countries – there are about 60,000 workers, whose 'command' is in the hands of Montebelluna firms, as has been estimated recently by the director of the 'boot museum', Aldo Durante (our interview), an expert on the history of the Montebelluna district. It is, in fact, striking for an external observer, but, in 2006, the Treviso association of entrepreneurs defined Timişoara as the eighth province of the Veneto region.

Official data of export trends in the province of Treviso show that in 2001 local firms exported about 430,292,000 euro worth of goods to Romania (ISTAT 2002). These data register all operations of supplying components for Romanian subcontracting firms, and correspond to about 35 per cent of the total output produced in the Montebelluna district in the shoe and sport clothing segment.

5.3 The historical development of the district

The district's original specialization was the mountain boot (made in leather). The anchor firms of the district – still active today – were founded at the end of the nineteenth century and the beginning of the twentieth: Tecnica (1890), Dolomite (1897), Alpina and Munari (1908), and, then, Pivetta and Vendramin (1919), and Nordica (1926).

Montebelluna began manufacturing country shoes and various sorts of horse boots (as is documented in the local museum of boots) from the fifteenth century. In the same period in which Luigi Voltan in Stra (1898) set up the first automated factory for elegant shoes, in Montebelluna the production of boots came about with the birth of Tecnica (1890).

Montebelluna represents a paradigmatic case of co-evolution of local institutions and the local economy. During the 1980s we register the formation of the most important district institutions: the museum of Montebelluna, which has also played a role as a catalytic organizer of entrepreneurs' cooperation in many projects (training, information and knowledge diffusion); the centre 'Tecnologia Design', responsible for the application of cad-cam technologies and for rapid prototypation. Then, recently, an important role has been played by the Chamber of Commerce that in Italy is a public institution, whose government is left to the members of the productive associations (entrepreneurs and trade unions). This institution has promoted the participation of local entrepreneurs in fairs, and it has organized an Observatory on Fashion Trends.

The presence of a strong economic community is traceable, above all, in the periods in which the district suffered from economic difficulties and firms' crises. At those times, local entrepreneurs intervened directly to avoid local bankruptcies and to help each other (a famous case is the one regarding the saving of Lotto). A few years ago the local bank, Cassa Marche, founded a private university (technically ruled by Padua and Venice University, to continue the Veneto dictum of *divide et impera* – divide and rule). After 600 years, the university was back in Treviso.

The upgrading of technical knowledge in Montebelluna dates back to 1937 when Vitaliano Bramani (from Turin) invented the Vibram sole, made of rubber, a waterproof material, particularly suited to walking in the mountains. This innovation was promptly adopted in Montebelluna. After the Second Word War, during the 1960s, the entrepreneurs of Montebelluna started to introduce several modifications to the ski boot, in order to improve its robustness and stability. In particular, they introduced a steel plate on the sole and a new system of blockage. In 1962, a local firm launched onto the market a boot with a metal lever, a technological improvement that replaced the traditional shoelaces: an innovation immediately imitated by all others firms of the district. In the 1960s the firms of the district introduced a new method of sole vulcanization, which links the sole with the upper, and subsequently PVC injection, which represents an even better system for linking the two components. During the 1960s, the local producers sponsored a process of standardization of components and ski binding. This became necessary in order to coordinate the vast networks of subcontractors and technical parts producers. During 1967, the entrepreneurs of Montebelluna made numerous attempts to shift their production from leather to plastic. A failed experiment produced the first model of leather boot covered with a thin plastic skin.

The real big technological revolution, with the creation of a new technological system, occurred thanks to the improvement of the international patent registered by technician Bob Lange. In the US in 1957, Bob Lange proposed the first plastic ski boot, soon to be known as 'plastiques fantastiques' by some appreciative French ski racers. This innovation attracted the attention of the entrepreneurs of Montebelluna, who showed it in Colorado, at an important US winter sport exhibition.

His invention was perfected in Montebelluna by Nordica, which replaced the Lange fusion with the injection method, using some expertise from a firm situated in Padua (Lorenzin). After a while, Lange himself opened a factory in Italy near Montebelluna in order to have access to the modified technology and to the suppliers of technology, already well developed in the vicinity. The 1960s and 1970s saw them main growth of the firms in the district, and the production of ski boots increased from 180,000 in 1963 to 1,000,000 in 1970 and to 4,100,000 in 1979. Many of the historical firms adopted the new technology (Nordica, Dolomite, Munari, San Giorgio, and Tecnica); many others which did not believe in these novelties (or which did not have the necessary funds to reorganize the productive cycle) started to diversify into new products (sports shoes, leisure shoes, etc.). This radical change also produced a new district division of labour between the final firms, the subcontractors for the more simple tasks, and the producers of technology (specialized suppliers).

At the end of the 1970s, the number of district firms specialized in footwear production grew to 511 (with 9710 employees in ski boot production and 12,000 as a whole in the sport-system sector).

The second relevant diversification was the introduction of the after-ski boot in plastic material. The first model was the Moon Boot by Tecnica (1970), which was inspired by the astronauts that in that year flew to the moon. In a few years the production of after-ski items took off. At the end of the 1970s, Montebelluna was producing about 7.5–8.0 million pairs of this new product.

The third diversification was quite parallel, and was in the field of sports shoes, such as jogging, ice and roller skates, basketball, football, motocross, dancing, cycling, tennis, and leisure shoes.

The overproduction of the 1980s created a typical firm shake-out, with the exit of some important producers from the district, but new products (with the fourth productive diversification) made up for the decline in demand for the more traditional production.

In the subsequent period, during the 1990s, new products like trekking, snow-boarding, in-line skates, football shoes, and sport shoes for walking (city shoes), which saw the birth of two emerging local champions, Geox and Stonefly, were able to stabilize the district's total output. From 1979 to 1996 the number of district firms increased from 511 to 526, and the local employment moved from 7316 employees to 7647 (these data cover only direct employment in footwear firms).

Since the end of the 1970s, Montebelluna has been recognized worldwide as the world centre for sports shoes, and even *Newsweek* in February 1979 dedicated an article to it, defining Montebelluna as the capital of the 'snow industry'. This district can be described not only as a classical example of a canonical (Marshallian) industrial district, where production is fractionated in a myriad of small and medium-sized firms, but where activities are organized on the basis of a district division of labour, which is based on final firms (branded and non-branded final producers), and subcontracting (leather cutting firms, machinery producers, model makers, designers, upper producers, boot assembling firms, die makers, sole producers, injection specialists, mould firms, producers of levers, shoe laces, etc.). Between the beginning of the 1980s and the end of the 1990s, Montebelluna became an area of extraordinary international concentration of competencies and production capabilities: a globally specialized area which directly or indirectly produced a large share of the total world output of a distinct range of products. As reported by local sources (Osem 2001), at present 80 per cent of motorcycle shoes produced in the world, 75 per cent of all ski boots, 65 per cent of after-ski boots, 50 per cent of technical mountain shoes, and 25 per cent of in-line skates are manufactured in Montebelluna.

In the mid-1990s the Montebelluna district was already very open to international markets. About 70–80 per cent of ski boot production was exported. And at the end of the 1990s, considering all the diversified range of products, half of its total production (1100 billion lire)[7] was exported to EU countries (such as Germany, France, Spain and the UK) and into the US and Japan. Many large local companies had opened commercial offices abroad, and an intense exchange of external relationships, and commercial and productive contacts characterized the daily work of local firms (Aage 2002). After the important year of 1989, East European countries provided a unique opportunity to develop global supply chains, based on the simple phases in manufacturing, such as shoe assembly.

There are some elements related to the specificity of the formation of the stock of knowledge in the Montebelluna district that must be highlighted:

1 the localization of the producers of machinery (interestingly, Oima was previously producing in China, but has now come back to Montebelluna – this is a clear case of failing delocalization);
2 the presence of designers (pattern makers), fashion experts and (now) the Fashion Observatory;
3 the presence of specialized suppliers (Nike tried to use cheaper suppliers in Eastern European countries but it reversed its decision, because the quality in Montebelluna was far superior).

Trigger events were necessary to use the accumulated local knowledge:

- in the 1970s: ski boot improvements of the Lange patent through development of injection machinery – Nordica played an important role;
- in the 1980s: application of local technical knowledge to new products (creation of differentiated market niches), so the ski boot district became the sport-system district – important roles were played by many leader firms, such as Lotto;
- in the 1990s: new niches were created: the city-sport shoes – important roles were played by Geox and Stonefly.

5.4 Results from a survey

5.4.1 Some methodological notes

The information detailed in this chapter derives from 30 in-depth interviews with managers and entrepreneurs and from 10 qualitative interviews with local actors. The sample has been constructed using the CERVED archive of the Chamber of Commerce of Treviso. We have interviewed the major local firms (including the MNCs which entered the ID during the 1990s). Data were collected in the period April–June 2003. The subjects interviewed (a face-to-face interview of about two to three hours' duration) were the entrepreneur or a top-ranking manager in the case of larger firms, and the person responsible for the local institution. For the completion of information collection, follow-up telephone interviews were often necessary.

We interviewed a total of 30 district firms (establishments). In the sample selected there is a representative mix of the composite nature of the district firms:

- large and small producers;
- clothing and footwear firms;
- ski boot producers and producers of sports shoes;
- producers of the high and middle–low market segments;
- local and multinational firms;
- firms with intense relocation and no internationalized firms;
- final firms and firm producers, mainly intermediate producers, and component producers;
- final firms and machinery producers.

5.4.2 Firms' characteristics

As shown in Table 5.1, the 30 firms selected have produced (in 2001) a total turnover of 1.5 trillion euro, of which about 60 per cent is exported (0.9 trillion). The sum of firms' output is larger that the total district sales estimated by the foundation Museo dello Scarpone, because we included export-to-export output. ID firms

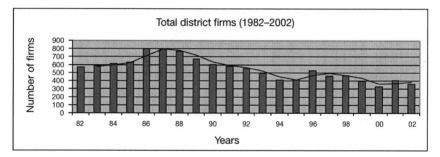

Figure 5.1 Evolution of the population of district firms (1982–2002).
    Source: Merlo (2003) and CERVED. (Textile firms are excluded from this analysis).

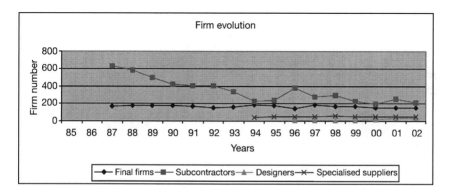

Figure 5.2 Evolution of the population of district firms by typology (1982–2002).
    Source: Merlo (2003) and CERVED.

interviewed, in 2001, had a total workforce of 3636 employees (we count here only the district local employment excluding the FDI related units).

The majority of the sample turnover (Table 5.2) is produced in 16 firms of medium size (50–249 employees), which is also the category with more working units (1699). In the sample there is only one very large firm with more than 500 employees (the Nordica spa, now owned by Tecnica).

Our sample covers an ample variety of the firm population of the district. Twenty-five firms are local (Nordica, acquired in the past by Benetton, is now owned by the largest local districtual firm: Tecnica),[8] while five are owned by external capital. Multinational companies[9] and external companies own relatively small firms in the district (or subsidiaries), so, in terms of employees, independent firms constitute the larger, and more important, segment (2537 employees out of 3636). The existence of independent district companies is the guarantee of district autonomy. They are completely free to choose their productive and commercial strategies, and they are more akin to the district destiny. Twenty-five firms can be categorized as final producers, and five are intermediate producers, or producers

Table 5.1 Overall picture of the firms in the sample compared to the whole district

	Sample			District		
	1999	2000	2001	1999	2000	2001
Number of establishments (sport system only)	30	30	30	491	460	464
Number of persons employed (sport system only)	3257	3538	3636	8596*	8897*	8943*
Turnover (sport system production only) (Million euro)	1280	1384	1527**	1,206,856,998	1,426,916,622	1,492,663,369
Turnover per person (sport system production only)	420,117	391,073	393,103	140,397	160,382	166,909
Total Value of Investment in capital goods (1000 euro)	24,275	25,093	29,486	Not available	Not available	Not available

Source: Foundation 'Museo dello Scarpone'.

Notes

* data collected are not homogeneous, and often include FDI employment

** data collected through the aggregation of firm's output. They include also export-to-export output.

Table 5.2 Distribution of firms (establishments) in the sample by type of products and employment size classes

		Employment size-classes						
		Total	1–9	10–19	20–49	50–249	250–499	500+
Firms producing mainly intermediate products/services	Number of establishments	5	0	0	2	3	0	0
	Number of persons employed	364	0	0	66	298	0	0
	Turnover 000 euro	69,740	0	0	8400	61,340		
	Total Value of investment in capital goods* (000 euro)	4045			150	3895		
Firms producing mainly final products/services	Number of establishments	25	0	2	6	13	3	1
	Number of persons employed	3272	0	31	179	1401	1161	500
	Turnover 000 euro	1,457,807	0	7350	53,431	894,475	355,551	1,470,000
	Total Value of investment in capital goods (000 euro)	25,441,869	0	100	1,290,063	17,736,519	6,114,287	200
Total	Total number of establishments	30	0	2	8	16	3	1
	Total number of persons employed	3,636	0	31	245	1,699	1,161	500
	Total turnover (million euro)	1,527,547	0	7,350	61,831	955,815	355,551	147

of machinery for the boot sector.[10] Two final producers are firms which produce a complete product, but they lack any market independence, and they work as subcontractors for other final producers. The other 23 companies enjoy a complete level of autonomy.

Our sample covers the more prestigious international brands, such as Tecnica, Nordica, Rollerblade, Sidi, Rossignol, Roces, Risport, Lotto, Diadora, Dolomite, Dal Bello, Scarpa, HTM, Lange, SIDI, Asolo, Geox, and Stonefly.

The local founders of our firms are mainly second or third-generation entrepreneurs, coming from family businesses (16 interviewed); six were technicians in a large district firm, and four have, in the past, worked in a multinational. Two entrepreneurs come from the university, and only one entrepreneur has previous working experience in a small firm. Small firms have been acknowledged as good incubators for entrepreneurship, but in old districts, such as Montebelluna, the reproduction of capable entrepreneurs is more a mechanism of old anchor firms.

Interviewed firms (Table 5.3) are mainly part of multi-plant organizations: seven firms are pluri-localized in the district (with 10 or more establishments), and 13 firms own many establishments outside the district and abroad (31 establishments). Firms with establishments located outside the districts (13 out of 30), in terms of the number of employees, cover the most significant part of our sample employees (62.7 per cent). They are mid-size firms (175.5 employees per firm), while some local independent units are smaller (79.7).

Among the 25 final firms analyzed, not one is involved in the production of standardized products. Twenty-two firms manufacture their items according to their own firms' market assessments, and three firms make their products according to customers' specifications.

The level of formal education among the interviewed entrepreneurs is low: only 12 entrepreneurs hold university or secondary school diplomas. However, in the district, the qualifications of the firm's workforce are quite high: 16 per cent of the workforce possess a university qualification, 27 per cent hold a diploma, about 19 per cent are definable as qualified employees, and 28 per cent of employees possess an intermediate qualification. In fact, the percentage of non-qualified

Table 5.3 Distribution of firms and establishments*

	Only one establishment		More than one establishment but located only in the district*		More than one establishment but located outside the district*		Total	
	Firms	*Estab.*	*Firms*	*Estab.*	*Firms*	*Estab.*	*Firms*	*Establishments*
Firms	10	10	7	17	13	44	30	71

Note
* including the firm interviewed.

manufacturing workers is small (only about 10 per cent of the total labour force of the interviewed firms). This indicator can be considered a rough estimation of the importance of human capital in the district. These elevated levels of workforce qualifications are not at all common in footwear districts. Table 5.4 supports the view of Montebelluna as a knowledge-intensive district.

The Montebelluna district, after the intense process of re-localization of the 1990s, has transformed itself into a high-tech area, which performs the most strategic and crucial phases of the production process of planning, marketing, product design, technology development, and prototyping. From our interviews it emerged that local firms employ a mainly Italian workforce. Immigrant workers were found only in the larger firms sampled. In each firm this grouping did not exceed the number of five to eight units, and they were involved in non-qualified tasks (warehousing, porters and simple assembly).

5.4.2.1 Final firms

The Montebelluna district is characterized by high production decentralization and inter-firm division of labour.

On average, each final firm works with 15 subcontractors (Table 5.5). Relationships are typically long term, for CEECs and for international subcontractors. Small firms (1–49 employees) work typically with six or seven subcontractors,

Table 5.4 Distribution of employees by qualification and employment size classes

Qualification and status		Employment size classes					Total	
		1–19	20–49	50–249	250–449	500+	a.v	p.v.
All employees	Employees with university qualifications		12	174	108	300	594	16.3
	Employees with diplomas	14	57	531	281	100	983	27.0
	Qualified employees	4	63	357	234	50	708	19.5
	Employees with intermediate qualification	13	76	435	438	50	1012	27.8
	Employees without qualifications		37	202	100		339	9.4
		31	245	1699	1161	500	3636	100

Table 5.5 Distribution of client firms by the number of subcontractors in the last three years (1999–2001)

Number of client firms	2001 a.v.	2000 a.v.	1999 a.v.
1	1	1	1
2–3	4	5	5
4–5	3	2	2
6–10	7	7	7
More than 10	9	9	9
Total	24	24	24
Total subcontractors	374	363	358
Average number of subcontractors for each firm	15.6	15.1	14.9

while mid-size firms involve one to 20. Quality control methods used are frequently random visits to the subcontractor workshops and the introduction of specific standards. In the case of CEEC subcontractors, the commissioning firm sends internal technicians into the subcontracting firm to supervise production. Districtual knowledge migrates through the international movements of machinery, plants, standard specification and above all human capital. International subcontracting chains can work only if they are 'sustained' by the knowledge possessed by the district technicians.

5.4.2.2 Subcontractors

In our survey, we interviewed seven component producers and two final firms working mainly on clients' specific designs. Their market position is strong: they work for local foreign clients and for international markets. They typically possess a large number of clients (Table 5.6), and are involved in very stable relationships. Their clients, with the exception of a moderate control on time scheduling and prices, weakly control them.

5.4.3 Innovation activity

The strong international success of the Montebelluna district is explained by the intense innovation activity that is taking place in local firms. Twenty-two firms out of 30 performed R&D: in 2001, firms invested a total value of 27 million euro, involving 329 technicians in R&D activities.[11] This corresponds to about 2 per cent of the total sample turnover. The sole large firm without R&D is in fact performing R&D in its headquarters in Paris, and also several small firms are linked with an R&D laboratory; only very small firms (with fewer than 19 employees) do not

Table 5.6 Distribution of subcontractors/intermediate firms by the number of client firms in the last three years (1999–2001)

Number of client firms	2001		2000		1999	
	a.v.	*p.v.*	*a.v.*	*p.v.*	*a.v.*	*p.v.*
1	1		1		1	
2–3	1		1		1	
4–5	0		0		0	
6–10	0		0		0	
More than 10	5		5		5	
Total	7	100	7	100	7	100

typically perform R&D activities, or rarely register a patent. District firms have registered 127 international technological patents in the same year.

This confirms that Montebelluna is not a canonical Marshallian district anymore, but a high-tech evolutionary district.

5.4.3.1 Innovation diffusion

As expected, the propensity to innovate in the sampled firms is very high (Table 5.7). Twenty-four firms introduced product innovation in the last three years (1999–2001), and in 22 cases they were internally generated.

A significant number of district firms are also active in the introduction of organizational innovations (11 firms) and commercial innovations (16 firms).

5.4.3.2 Sources of firm knowledge

The most important source of knowledge for firms is R&D gained through in-house activities (3.9), and knowledge gained from continuous (3.3) improvement of production processes (Table 5.8). For large firms, internal R&D is even more crucial. External sources (such as interaction with international clients, participation at international fairs, and the utilization of national consultants) are not considered by district firms to be relevant.

The two other cited sources of local knowledge are interactions with clients and suppliers (2.5), and knowledge embedded in experts (1.8).

5.4.3.3 Horizontal cooperation

During 1999–2001, 11 firms (about 30 per cent of the sample) developed joint agreements with other companies. Formal agreements (nine cases) supersede informal agreements (two cases). Agreements are focused on innovation (joint development of new products and processes). Agreements are more frequent

Table 5.7 Innovativeness of the firms (establishments) in the sample by employment size classes in the last three years (1999–2001)

	Employment size-classes					
	1–19	*20–49*	*50–249*	*250–449*	*500+*	*Total*
Adoption of product innovation						
No innovation	1	2	3	0	0	6
Generated by the firm	1	6	11	3	1	22
Generated within the district			1			1
Generated in the country			1			1
Generated abroad						0
Adoption of process innovation						
No innovation	2	2	5	0	0	9
Generated by the firm		2	8	3	1	14
Generated within the district		1	2			3
Generated in the country		2	1			3
Generated abroad		1				1
Adoption of innovation in the organization of production						
No innovation	1	1	9	0	1	11
Generated within the firm		1	3	2		6
Generated within the district	1	1	1	1		4
Generated in the country		4	3			7
Generated abroad		1				1
Adoption of innovation in the organization of sales and distribution						
No innovation	2	2	9	2	1	16
Generated by the firm		2	4			6
Generated within the district		1		1		2
Generated in the country		2	2			4
Generated abroad		1	1			2

Table 5.8 Ranking of the most relevant sources of technical knowledge (average values*)

Sources of knowledge	Rank (average values)				Employment size classes 250–499
	Internal to firms	District	National	International	
Knowledge gained through in-house R&D	3.9	–	–	–	5.0
Knowledge gained from continuous improvement of production processes	3.3	–	–	–	1.0
Knowledge derived from parent or subsidiary companies	2.0	–	–	–	3.7
Knowledge developed through company's internal education and training programmes	2.0	–	–	–	2.7
Other	1.0	–	–	–	1.0
Knowledge embedded in experts hired on the labour market		1.8	1.3	1.3	
Knowledge derived from interactions with clients and/or suppliers		2.5	1.7	2.9	
Knowledge derived from cooperation with other companies		1.4	1.2	1.2	
Knowledge derived from imitation of products		1.5	1.2	1.3	
Knowledge embedded in technologies, licences, and components, acquired from outside (technological innovation)		1.4	1.4	1.5	
Knowledge gained from interactions with public institutions (e.g. universities, public research centres, local government, etc.)		1.4	1.5	1.6	

(*continued*)

| Sources of knowledge | Rank (average values) | | | Employment size classes 250–499 |
	Internal to firms	District	National	International	
Knowledge gained from interactions with semi-public institutions (e.g. chambers of commerce, industry associations, trade unions, etc.)		1.7	1.3	1.1	
Knowledge gained from publicly available information (e.g. trade fairs, publications)		1.5	2.0	2.4	
Others		1.1	1.0	1.0	

Note
* Evaluations could vary from 1 (not relevant) to 5 (most relevant).

among independent firms and among larger firms. Training activities are organized by local actors (by Montebelluna Museo dello Scarpone; and by the centre 'Tecnologia design').

5.4.3.4 Firm's rivalry

The principal competitors of Montebelluna firms are those located in the district (3.6), and foreign firms located abroad (3.3), but not multinational subsidiaries located in the district (1.7).

5.4.4 The globalization of the district

5.4.4.1 Export flows

In our sample, 29 firms are exporters, with the exception of a subcontractor of a final firm (which is a high exporter). Export flows are largely in the hands of final firms. Independent firms cover the largest segment of exports (760 million euro). The EU market represents the largest area of export flows (58 per cent of total exports). The rest of the world covers 33 per cent, and CEECs cover 7 per cent.

Import flows are connected with the rest of the world and with CEECs, particularly Romania. Large firms are more able to place their products at a more global scale, while small firms target, principally, the EU market.

Table 5.9 Exports and imports of firms by employment size classes in the last three years (1999–2001) values

	Years	Employment size classes					Total
		1–19	20–49	50–249	250–449	500+	
Export	2001	2,000,000	46,442,267	6,224,225,000	180,760,955	50,000,000	901,628,222
*	2000	2,000,000	45,011,168	574,919,000	174,543,379	40,000,000	836,473,547
	1999	2,000,000	32,292,104	429,011,000	174,831,730	30,000,000	668,134,834
Import	2001		7,053,552	9,205,100			99,104,552
	2000		5,001,773	78,479,000			83,480,773
	1999		2,551,247	27,458,000			30,009,247

Notes
* data refer to 24 firms (five absent cases; one firm had no direct export flows)
* data refer only to eight firms (11 unreported cases; in 11 cases no import flows were given).

5.4.4.2 International subcontracting strategies

Subcontracting and raw material sourcing are related to the acquisition of inter-mediate inputs, final products (which are full-package orders), or services (Table 5.10). At the time of our interviews, in 2003, local outsourcing (measured in values and not in quantities) represented one-third of intermediate products, and one-quarter of final products. CEEC countries were dominant in intermediate products, while a significant share of final products was acquired in non-CEEC countries (such as China[12] and the Far East).

If each district firm is, on average, engaged in subcontracting with about 10–12 firms, half of them are located in CEEC countries (Table 5.11). Small firms deal on average with three or four subcontractors, mid-size firms with 10–13, and large firms also with 25–30.

In 2002, out of a total number of 133 CEEC subcontractors, 82 were located in Romania (62 per cent), 16 in Hungary (12 per cent), five in the Czech Republic, and two in Slovenia. The size of CEEC subcontractors is generally large: 44.4 per cent of them (59 firms) have more than 250 employees. Also, small districtual firms use very large CEEC subcontractors. CEEC subcontractor firms are typically price takers with no power of bargaining. The price is imposed by the final firm and it is calculated for piecework (or for minutes worked). The contracting company provides all the necessary materials (and sometimes the necessary machinery).

Table 5.10 The geographical distribution of subcontracting and raw material sourcing

	District	Italy	CEECs	Non-CEECs	Total
Raw materials	16.6	63.7	0.0	19.7	100.0
Intermediate products	35.6	0.5	56.9	7.0	100.0
Final products	24.9	0.0	36.5	38.6	100.0
Services	57.8	32.8	0.0	9.4	100.0

Table 5. 11 Number of CEEC subcontractors by employment size classes of district firms in the last three years (1999–2001), average number by firm

Years	Employment size classes					
	1–19	20–49	50–249	250–449	500+	Total
2001	4	1.5	4.6	13.3	30	6.5 (131)
2000	4	1.3	5.4	10.0	30	6.5 (129)
1999	4	1.7	4.6	10.0	30	6.1 (122)

Note
Data refer to 20 firms.

Table 5.12 Most used modes of entry in foreign markets by employment size classes: modalities

Modes of entry	Employment size classes					
	1–19	20–49	50–249	250–449	500+	Total
Commercial FDI						
Wholly owned subsidiary		2	10	3	1	16
Joint equity venture		3	3			6
Foreign minority holdings		1	4			5
Licensing	1	1	5	1		8
Franchising						0
Management contracts		1				1
Turnkey projects						0
Contractual joint ventures			2	1		3
Other						
Total (firms)	1	8	24	5	1	39 (19)
Industrial FDI						
Greenfield (new) investment		2	7		1	10
Acquisition of an existing local company					1	1
Joint equity venture with an existing local company					1	1
Other (e.g. cooperation agreements, merger)		1				1
Total (firms)		*3*	*7*		*3*	*13 (10)*

Site inspections are common, as well as the daily presence of technicians coming from the final district firm. CEEC subcontractors have been selected by asking customers or distributors, and following the example of their neighbours.

5.4.4.3 Foreign direct investment

The internationalization of firms in the Montebelluna district is in part an efficiency-seeking investment (motivated by the search for low-labour costs), but also a market-seeking investment.

Local district firms have, in fact, developed new commercial strategies for entering foreign markets. Nineteen firms from our sample undertook a commercial FDI, while 10 set up a manufacturing FDI. In Table 5.12 we can count 39 commercial initiatives, and most of them involve the establishment of a subsidiary in a foreign country.

The destinations of the investment were the following countries: the US, Canada and North Europe (and particularly the UK, which is considered a bridge for the US market), and the Far East. Industrial FDI corresponds to 13 initiatives: most of them are greenfield investments. Six initiatives are based in Romania.

The processes of relocation that occurred in the last decade have transformed the district radically. The local shoe sector lost about 1500–2000 employees who have been re-employed locally in other sectors. Many district firms now operate only on the high-value phases of the global chain: marketing, logistics, general firm functions, projecting, low series production, high-quality series production, and prototypes.

Considering the firms, which have utilized the FDI strategy, only in three cases have they reduced their internal employment (while half of the sample has reduced local subcontracting). In fact, they have increased their productivity and market power, so internal employment has been reshuffled towards other internal activities.

Montebelluna firms influence their FDI subsidiaries in relation to prices and technology. On the other hand, subsidiaries enjoy a moderate autonomy on the entry decisions in CEEC countries. However, firms already engaged in FDI initiatives (mostly *greenfield*) tend to be quite 'mobile' and often revise their previous decision for selecting a new 'relocation'. We can speak about a 'continual geographical remodelling' of the production filière, as discussed by Ansoff (1965) and Normann and Ramirez (1994).

5.5 Some conclusions regarding the evolutionary pattern of the Montebelluna district

The analysis of the Montebelluna district has shown that canonical Marshallian districts can change over time. Two triggering factors sustain this transformation: the entry of Schumpeterian innovators, and the emergence of leading firms. The district changed radically during the 1990s, because many firms relocated their activities to East European countries. While the international literature has studied

Table 5.13 Firms with FDI and international subcontracting chains in CEECs by type of investment and employment size classes

FDI and international subcontracting in CEECs	Employment size classes (2001)					
	1–19	*20–49*	*50–249*	*250–499*	*500+*	*Total*
No FDI & IS	1	3	2	0	0	6
Only IS	1	3	7	3	0	14
Only FDI	0	1	3	0	0	4
Dual strategy	0	1	4	0	1	6

the influence of external global supply chains on districts, in our case, the district endogenously produced its global chains and successfully organized a relocation process. Not all district firms in those years relocated, of course, but only the mid–largest ones (Grandinetti 1993; Grandinetti and Rullani 1992, 1996). The relocation of subcontracting required the existence of high volumes and quality that was not too high a level. The Montebelluna case did not follow a complete relocation, but a model of 'equilibrated delocalization' (some activities are still maintained in the district, such as projecting and prototyping, marketing, R&D, high-quality subcontracting, and several manufacturing activities focused on low series and high quality).

Notes

1 This chapter is partially based on the work written by F. Belussi and F. Callegari within the project West-East ID, coordinated by the Institute Tagliacarne of Rome. It was part of the funded project under the 5th Framework Programme.
2 Footwear, code NACE 19.30, sportswear code NACE 18.24.3, and sports tools and accessories, code NACE 36.40.
3 See, for instance, Anastasia and Corò (1993), and Anastasia, Corò and Crestanello (1995). The area, which characterizes the district of the production of the sports items, is relatively small (about 553 square kilometres), and corresponds to a circle with a radius of about 13 kilometres (around 8 miles). The area has 159,362 inhabitants.
4 Caerano, Cornuda, Crocetta, Pederobba, Montebelluna, Maser, Nervesa, Trevignano, Volpago, and Giavera del Montello.
5 Altivole, Arcade, Asolo, Castelcucco, Castello di Godego, Cavaso del Tomba, Fonte, Monfumo, Povegliano, Riese Pio X, and Vedelago.
6 Recent estimates (Club dei distretti industriali 2003), speak of about 428 firms (2003 data) and 8600 employees (2003 data).
7 Data provided by the Chamber of Commerce of Treviso.
8 Benetton entered the district of Montebelluna acquiring one of the largest firms, but it was not able to meet its business model, based on an exclusive brand name and specialized chain stores, with the prevailing sportswear demand, that requires technical complexity of items, and multi-brand large stores. In 2003, due to large losses, Nordica was sold to a local district entrepreneur.
9 Incidentally, we must note that we also interviewed a firm in the past acquired by Nike, the largest international MNC of the sportswear sector (14,000 direct workers employed), that, with its headquarters in Oregon, at Beaverton, USA, organizes an international supply chain of about 500,000 workers (employed in autonomous subcontracting firms in developing countries). In 2004, the firm (now Novation spa) was sold by Nike to a private investment entity founded by the Aksìa Group.
10 Note that 'intermediate firm' is a residual category, and we included here those firms which did not produce final products for the mass market (such as shoes, boots, and sports tools).
11 In four cases we were not able to calculate the exact amount of R&D expenditure.
12 For instance, a large quantity of jogging shoes or trekking shoes.

References

Aage T. (2002), 'Absorptive capacity of firms in industrial district', paper presented at Siena, 8–11 November, Eape Conference.

Anastasia B. and Corò G. (1993), *I distretti industriali in Veneto,* Nuova dimensione, Ediciclo, Portogruaro.

——. (1996), *Evoluzione di un'economia regionale*, Nuova Dimensione, Portogruaro.

Anastasia B., Corò G., and Crestanello P. (1995), 'Problemi di individuazione dei distretti industriali: esperienze regionali e rapporti con le politiche', *Oltre il Ponte*, no. 52.

Ansoff H. I. (1965), *Corporate Strategy*, New York: McGraw-Hill.

Asheim B. (1996), 'Industrial districts as learning regions. Conditions for prosperity', *European Planning Studies*, 4: 379–400.

Asheim B. and Isaksen A. (2002), 'Regional innovation systems: the integration of local "sticky" knowledge with global "ubiquitous knowledge"', *Journal of Technology Transfer*, 27: 77–86.

Baccarani C. and Golinelli G. (1993), 'Tratti del divenire dei distretti industriali', *Quaderno dell'Istituto Tagliacarne*, 8: 15–46.

Belussi F. and Gottardi G. (eds.) (2000), *Evolutionary Patterns of Local Industrial Systems*, Aldershot: Ashgate.

Belussi F. and Pilotti L. (2002), 'Knowledge creation, learning and innovation in Italian industrial districts', *Geografiska Annaler*, 84: 19–33.

Belussi F., Gottardi G. and Rullani E. (eds.) (2003), *The Technological Evolution of Industrial Districts*, forthcoming, Boston: Kluwer.

Centro Estero Veneto (2003), *Indagine sulla presenza imprenditoriale veneta in Romania*, paper, Venezia.

Club dei distretti industriali (2003), *Guide to the Italian Industrial districts – 2004*, Fondazione del Museo dello scarpone, Montebelluna, Treviso.

Corò G. (2000), 'La delocalizzazione: minaccia, necessità o opportunità?', in I. Diamanti and D. Marini (eds.), *Nord Est 2000, Rapporto sulla società e l'economia, Fondazione Nord Est*, Venice.

Corò G. and Grandinetti R. (1999), 'Evolutionary patterns of Italian industrial districts', *Human Systems Management*, 2.

Corò G. and Rullani E. (1998), 'Percorsi locali di internazionalizzazione. Competenze e auto-organizzazione nei distretti industriali del nordest', Franco Angeli: Milano.

Crestanello P. and Dalla Libera E. (2003), 'The delocalisation of production abroad: the case of the fashion industry of Vicenza', paper presented at the Conference on 'Clusters, Industrial Districts and Firms', Modena, September 2003.

Durante A. (1997), 'Montebelluna fa giocare il mondo, Fondazione Museo dello scarpone', Montebelluna.

Durante A. and Durante V. (a cura di), *Rapporto OSEM*, ediz. 2001 e 2002, Fondazione Museo dello Scarpone, Montebelluna.

Grandinetti R. (1993), 'L'internazionalizzzione "sommersa" delle piccole imprese', *Rivista Italian di Economia e Statistica*, 47: 3–4, 119–42.

Grandinetti R. and Rullani E. (1992), 'Internazionalizzazione e piccole imprese: elogio della varietà', *Piccola Impresa/Small Business*, 3.

——. (1996), *Impresa transnazionale ed economia globale*, Nis, Roma.

IPI (2002), L'esperienza italiana dei distretti industriali, Ministero delle attività produttive, Roma.

ISTAT – Istituto Nazionale di Statistica (2002), *Statistiche sul Commercio Estero*, Roma.

Lipparini A. (1997), *Architetture e assetti relazionali per l'organizzazione delle attività della catena del valore alla scala internazionale*, in G. Lorenzoni (a cura di), *Architetture reticolari e processi di internazionalizzazione*, Bologna: Il Mulino, pp. 159–94.

Litvak I. (1990), 'Instant international: strategic reality for small high technology firms in Canada', *Multinational Business*, Summer, 2: 1–12.

Lorenzen M. and Mahnke V. (2002), 'Global strategies and acquisition of local knowledge: how MNCs enter regional clusters', DUID Working Paper 8: 1–24.

Lorenzoni G. (1997), *Architetture reticolari e processi di internazionalizzazione*, Bologna: Il Mulino.

Maccarini M., *et al.* (2002), 'Growth paths of the Italian SMEs and their local clusters: the internationalisation strategy', paper presented at the international conference "Business policies and strategies in a global market". A framework for SMEs: case studies, Turin, 14 November.

Madsen T. and Servais P. (1997), 'The internationalisation of born global: an evolutionary process?' *International Business Review*, 6(6): 561–83.

Maskell P. and Malmberg A. (1999), 'Localised learning and industrial competitiveness', *Cambridge Journal of Economics*, 23: 167–85.

Merlo D. (2003), 'Nati-mortalità delle imprese del distretto della calzatura sportiva di Montebelluna', Facoltà di Statistica, Padua University, unpublished manuscript.

Normann R. and Ramirez R. (1994), *Designing interactive strategy: From value chain to calue constellation*, NewYork: Wiley.

Osem (Osservatorio Socio Economico Montelliano) (2001), Rapporto Osem 2001, Veneto Banca, Treviso.

Piva C. (2002), 'I processi di globalizzazione dei distretti industriali, il caso di Montebelluna', unpublished thesis, Padua University.

Quadrio Curzio A. and Fortis M. (2000), *Il made in Italy oltre il 2000*, Bologna: Il Mulino.

Schiattarella R. (1999), 'La delocalizzzione internazionale: problemi di definizione e de-limitazione. Un'analisi per il settore del Made in Italy', *Economia e Politica Industriale*, 103.

Veneto Lavoro (2002), *Il mercato del lavoro nel Veneto*, Milano: Angeli.

6 A 'low road' to competitiveness in the global apparel industry

The case of the Vibrata Valley district

Alessia Sammarra (University of L'Aquila)

6.1 Introduction

The textile-clothing industry plays a fundamental role in the economy of both developed and developing countries. In the European Union the sector is largely composed by small and medium-sized enterprises (SMEs) frequently concentrated in a number of regions and geographically concentrated industrial districts and clusters (Hanzl-Weiß, 2004). For instance, in Italy, out of 199 industrial districts localized in the country, 69 (that is, 35 per cent) are primarily specialized in textile-clothing (Istat 1996).

In recent decades, the global structure of the clothing sector has undergone a deep process of modernization and transformation (Box 6.1). Among the major trends of change, two aspects deserve particular attention. The first one concerns the turnover in power relation between industry and distribution. While, in the past, the textile-clothing industry was largely dominated by vertical relationships with a highly fragmented distribution system, today distribution is increasingly being controlled by a small number of big players (especially in the low to middle-priced market segments), which are in a position to impose the rules of the game to the upstream part of the apparel value chain. The second, although not in relevance, driver of change is related to the ongoing process of globalization and liberalization which exposes firms in developed countries to increasing competition from a large number of low-labour-cost countries (especially from Asia).

The combination of these two factors has favoured an increasing level of international fragmentation of the global apparel value chain. Starting from sourcing of raw materials via design and production to distribution and marketing, the apparel value chain is organized as a collection of specialized activities and each activity is located where it can contribute the most to the value of the end product. Design and other finishing activities in the production of clothing items are qualified-work, labour-intensive phases which are usually concentrated in countries with a long tradition and a strong image of quality and creativity. The assembly stage of the clothing chain is still a low-qualified, labour-intensive phase and it is the stage that is most likely to be farmed out to lower-cost firms. Further, international transport of fabrics and semi-finished garments is relatively easy and inexpensive because they are high value-added products in relation to weight. These technical characteristics explain the increasing recourse to outward processing trade (OPT) and the rising trend of relocation undertaken by the US and Western European clothing industry in developing countries.

Box 6.1 Major trends of change in the European textile-clothing (T/C) industry

Increased import penetration	Europe is the largest importer of both textiles (40 per cent of world imports) and clothing (more than 45 per cent). Over the period 1990 to 1999, the degree of import penetration grew from 12 per cent to 23 per cent for textiles, and from 30 per cent to 46 per cent for clothing. The EU ranks second for export in the T/C industry after China. Over the period 1990 to 1998, Europe's share in total clothing world exports decreased from 10.5 per cent to 8.8 per cent. In textiles, Europe's share has instead increased from 14.5 per cent to 15.2 per cent in 1998.
Decreased employment	Over the period 1980 to 1995, Europe has lost as much as 47 per cent of employees in textiles and 40 per cent in clothing.
Productive fragmentation vs. economic concentration	Most firms are small and medium-sized, the average company having 19 employees in 1999. However, a considerable percentage of turnover is generated by a restricted number of big companies. For instance, in Italy, the share of the top five companies is 12 per cent for textiles and 25 per cent for clothing.
Differential in labour costs and productivity	The T/C industry is generally labour intensive: labour costs are estimated at 60 per cent of total production costs for clothing and 40 per cent for textiles. Labour cost comparisons for the clothing industry illustrate the large wage gap between EU western countries where they range from US$4.5 in Portugal to US$23 in Denmark in comparison with EU eastern countries where they amount to about US$2.77 in Poland or US$1.04 in Romania; with North Africa countries (e.g. US$1.36 in Morocco) and Asian countries (e.g. US$0.22 in Vietnam and US$0.43 in China). This competitive disadvantage is partly offset by high levels of labour productivity which are much higher in the EU than in Asia but lower than in the US, Japan or Switzerland.

Increased importance of distribution	In the past, the European T/C industry was characterized by a powerful industry and a weak and fragmented distribution system composed by SMEs retailers. Nowadays distribution is increasingly being controlled by a limited number of big players which are in the position to put the upstream part of the T/C industry under considerable pressure as far as terms of payment and delivery are concerned. The system has thus changed from being 'industry driven' to 'distribution driven'.
Increased rate of marketing and advertising (M&A)	In recent years, the European clothing and distribution sector have witnessed an increase in M&A which have involved a growing number of medium-sized companies. One of the main objectives of this activity has been to increase the profitability of investments in brands and distribution networks.
Increased internationalization and relocation	As a result of globalization and the conclusion of preferential trade agreements, the European T/C industry has witnessed an increasing trend towards the internationalization and relocation of production, and an ever more complex diversification of sources of supply. Up to now, EU manufacturers have typically preferred Eastern European and North African countries over the Asian ones due to their geographical proximity and their higher quality standards.

Source: Author's own based on Stengg (2001).

The emergence of powerful global leaders (retailers and top fashion companies), and the increasing international fragmentation of the clothing value chain, are putting into question the long-term sustainability of several European clothing districts. This has eroded the competitive advantage associated to the traditional vocation of efficient and flexible subcontracting areas. Indeed, these profound transformations have severely challenged the traditional sources of competitiveness of both individual firms and industrial districts in developed countries.

Using a case study design, this chapter investigates such a process of change, focusing on the evolutionary trend of the Vibrata Valley clothing district (VVD), located in the northernmost part of Abruzzo, in Central Italy.[1] Through an in-depth analysis, this study shows that local firms have not been able over time to emancipate themselves from their original role of subcontractors by developing internal branding and design capabilities. This evolutionary path does not encourage optimistic expectations with respect to the district's future in the global economy. Indeed, it is increasingly clear that the Italian and European clothing industry, in order to maintain its competitive edge, has to continuously improve production technology and distribution methods and design new innovative products. Only the development of intangible resources (knowledge, design, information, logistics) can prevent a competitive decline, enabling industrial districts specialized in traditional manufacturing industries to redefine their position within global commodity chains. Unfortunately, at present, these success factors required are exactly the key weaknesses of the VV clothing ID.

The chapter is structured as follows. The next section illustrates the research methodology. The historical formation and evolution of the district is presented in Section 6.3. Section 6.4 is devoted to analyzing the main structural characteristics of the district with respect to the economic, institutional and cognitive dimensions, while Section 6.5 illustrates the international orientation of district firms. In Section 6.6 findings gathered from fieldwork are discussed in light of the recent scientific debate about industrial districts' evolution and globalization processes. Conclusions are discussed in Section 6.7.

6.2 Research methodology

This study applies a case study design (Yin 1989). This methodology was selected to provide a 'thick description' of the industrial district's change dynamics.

The case study integrates qualitative and quantitative data collection methods. The author collected documents and conducted 10 in-depth semi-structured open-ended interviews with key informants and local institutional actors. Further, a survey was carried out through face-to-face interviews on the basis of a semi-structured detailed questionnaire.

The questionnaire's sections covered a number of relevant areas of investigation such as: (1) company background and internal organization; (2) innovative activity and sources of knowledge; (3) linkages with local and external subcontractors/client firms; (4) horizontal linkages with district firms and institutions; (5) internationalization. Two specialized interviewers (including the author) carried out the survey and the questions were addressed to the owner or general manager of the firm. If this was not possible, we interviewed the person in charge of powers and duties. Fieldwork was conducted during spring and fall 2003.

Table 6.1 Sample vs. district: a comparison

	Sample	*District**
No. of firms	30	484
No. of establishments	36	514
No. of persons employed	1590	5603
Average size of firms (in no. of employees)	53	12

Source: *ISTAT (2001).

A stratified sample of 30 firms was selected in order to represent all the different phases of the district production chain. However, given the theoretical focus on globalization and relocation processes, the sampling strategy was aimed at selecting theoretical rather than probability samples. The comparison between district and sample data (Table 6.1) shows that the firm average size in the sample is overestimated with respect to the whole district. Indeed, the district make-up is for overwhelmingly composed by micro and small enterprises, which is also typical of most of the Italian IDs, whose productive make-up is still characterized by a strong fragmentation.

6.3 Historical formation and evolution

The Vibrata Valley district (VVD) is located in the province of Teramo, in the northernmost part of the Italian region of Abruzzo. It covers an area of 627.56 sq km and comprises 20 municipalities.[2] The heart of the district is S. Egidio alla Vibrata, where about 60 per cent of clothing firms are localized.[3] A number of authors have previously identified this area as an industrial district (Viesti 2000; Paniccia 2002).

The formation of the VV clothing district is rooted in ancient traditions. The textile craftsmanship was related to the processing of hemp, which was grown in the area of Teramo until the late 1960s. Following the Second World War, some clothing firms were established in the area, mostly specialized in the manufacturing of shirts. Already By 1951 employment in the textile/clothing sector was already estimated at around 1200 units, climbing to 2000 in 1961 (Viesti 2000).

The real take-off of the district started in the 1970s and was marked by a strong increase in firms' birth rate, which has led to the formation of a spatial concentration of clothing firms. Thanks to the development of the clothing sector, the province of Teramo registered in the decade 1971–81 an increase greater than

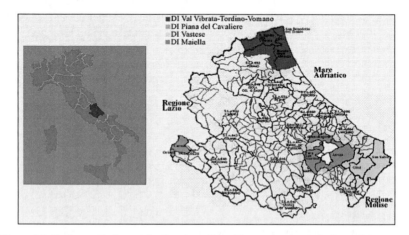

Figure 6.1 Dark grey indicates the location of the Abruzzo region in Italy, and the location of the Vibrata Valley district in the Abruzzo region.

40 per cent in the number of firms and 80 per cent in the number of employees compared to the previous decade (Felice 2001). The triggering factors of district development were the increase on the demand side, market expansion, and the existence of governmental and European incentives.

This development process has continued in the 1980s mainly driven by the outsourcing strategy pursued by external firms based in the northern regions of Italy, which has favoured the birth of local firms in the role of subcontractors – the so called *façon producers* – especially in the manufacturing of shirts and casual clothing (namely jeans). Therefore, district development was strictly associated with a subcontracting vocation. During this phase, the competitiveness of the VV clothing district was mostly based on price and labour cost comparative advantages. During this development phase, a small core of local final firms successfully emerged and grew. This small group of local medium-sized firms has succeeded in producing directly for the market and in introducing their own brands.

This group includes enterprises such as Gruppo Produzione Moda (the former F.I.T.), Casucci, and Gran Sasso. The growth of these local firms has facilitated the creation of new small enterprises as a consequence of their strategy of decentralization of production phases. Indeed, in this period, new small and very small firms were created through spin-off processes by former employees which recognized a potentially profitable business opportunity and decided to exploit it by becoming entrepreneurs themselves.

The downturn in the district's growth started in the early 1990s. The elimination of economic incentives along with increased international competition significantly contributed to eroding the competitive advantages of the VV cluster. In 1996, the Abruzzo Regional Government undertook a policy initiative which led to the legal recognition and subsequent funding of four regional industrial districts, including the VV clothing district (D.G.R. 742/C March 1996). In 1997, the District Committee was established. However, notwithstanding this policy initiative, the district crisis has continued. Some local firms have tried to face this difficult situation by improving the quality of products or by increasing productivity through relocation.

The economic crisis has led to a severe reduction in local firms, which were, in the most part, still dependent on external and internal commissioning firms. The most penalized enterprises have been the many suppliers and façon producers specialized in the manufacturing of low–medium-quality products, whose number has significantly decreased in recent years.

6.4 The district structure: economic, cognitive and institutional features

6.4.1 Economic features

The economic texture of the district shows a high degree of homogeneity (Table 6.2). The cluster is composed of a large number of micro and small firms. Medium-sized and large firms are extremely few. The prevailing governance structure is based on the family business model. There are neither very large enterprises nor foreign owned companies within the district.

Being a district recently formed, most firms are at the first entrepreneurial generation. Twenty-seven per cent of founders in the sample do not have previous experience as entrepreneurs or workers in other firms. Sixty-seven per cent were previously employed in other local firms. Only 6 per cent of the entrepreneurs interviewed were formerly employed in firms located in other Italian regions, while none of them had international work experience.

Within the district there are no subsidiaries of MNCs. Nevertheless, with the exception of a few local final firms, the district is highly dependent from external strategic centres. Indeed, most local firms produce exclusively or partially for clients based outside the district and, thus, lack of any market autonomy.

With regard to the various roles played in the clothing filière, three main types of firms can be identified. The first group is composed of final firms, those producing exclusively or mainly end-products directly for the market with their own brands. These firms are economically and strategically autonomous since they are completely free to choose their productive and commercial strategies. In the whole clothing district, this first group comprises fewer than 20 firms, including the district's oldest and most famous companies. In terms of product specialization,

Table 6.2 Economic features of the sample (N=30)

Sample firms by size (employees)			
≤ 9	10%		
10–49	50%		
50–249	37%		
≥ 250	3%		
Sample firms by ownership			
Independent	90%		
National subsidiary	10%		
Foreign subsidiary	0%		
Sample firms by the entrepreneurial background			
No previous experience	27%		
Former employees of other district firms	67%		
Former employees of external national firms	6%		
Former employees of foreign firms	0%		
Sample firms by type			
	Firms	*Employees*	*Turnover*
Subcontractors of intermediate products/services	37%	36%	8%
Subcontractors of final products	27%	16%	17%
Final firms	37%	48%	75%

these firms represent all the most important product specializations of the district: jeans and casual clothing (e.g. Casucci, Gruppo Produzione Moda); shirts (e.g. NewMen); children's clothing (Gi.Effe Moda); knitwear (Gran Sasso). Final firms usually have several subcontractors. The majority of those interviewed declared they worked with more than 10 subcontractors. Their vertical relationships are typically long-term oriented.

The second group, which comprises the large majority of district firms, includes the so-called façon producers, which manufacture mainly or exclusively a final product for the few indigenous final firms and for other externally based commissioning firms. Among façon producers, it is important to distinguish those working on a very high quality level, which are subcontractors of top fashion companies such as Gucci, Prada, Max Mara etc., and façon producers working for commissioning firms specialized in low to medium-quality segments of the clothing market. By pursuing product upgrading, the former have been able to avoid international competition while the latter are more exposed to the threat of being substituted through relocalization and subcontracting abroad by local and external commissioning firms. Indeed, the economic crisis that originated in the 1990s has triggered a severe reduction of district firms which has penalized especially this second group of façon producers, reluctant to follow a quality improvement strategy. In most cases, façon producers receive from the commissioning firms the clothing parts already cut, along with all the clothing accessories (zip, buttons, tags, threads) ready to be sown. All the value-adding activities (product design and cutting) are performed directly by the commissioning firms while the façon producers execute the most labour-intensive phase (assembly). Consequently, vertical relationships do not include any interaction concerning the product's design or technical content. Façon producers' market position is often quite difficult given their lack of strategic and market autonomy and their strong dependence on the commissioning firms. Finally, it is also worth noticing that façon producers themselves subcontract some work to smaller firms in the district depending on the clients' needs and requests.

The third group includes the specialized suppliers, which carry out specific phases of the clothing manufacturing process such as dyeing, ironing and embroidering. These production phases may add significant value to the final product. For instance, dyeing is extremely important for the aesthetic properties of denim clothes (e.g. jeans). During interviews with final firms, some commissioning firms have explicitly recognized the relevance of these specialized tasks. Indeed, it sometimes occurs that these specialized suppliers provide feedback and suggestions to the commissioning firms on the technical content of working processes to be performed on the product. Interestingly enough, these specialized activities of the production process are those less affected by relocalization and international subcontracting strategies. In the same way the local suppliers specialized in these activities have not been affected in the reduction process as much as those focused on clothing assembly.

Subcontractors are quite dependent and controlled by their clients. As shown in Table 6.3, the most important areas of influence of commissioning firms on subcontractors' decisions concern: the price to charge; product creation and development; production scheduling and planning; and quality control procedures. According to subcontractors, the most important advantage they receive from their associations with principal clients is improved financial stability (Table 6.3).

With respect to *relational patterns*, although vertical relationships are typically stable, inter-firm vertical relationships are quite hierarchical since local subcontractors and façon producers are strongly dependent on commissioning firms. Indeed they execute the most labour intensive phases of the clothing manufacturing processes on the basis of clients' strict technical specifications. The VV clothing district is also characterized by very weak horizontal relationships. Local firms are not engaged in cooperative agreements or strategies.

In contrast with many other well-known Italian industrial districts, specialization in the clothing sector has not triggered the emergence of ancillary and complementary industries. Within the district, there are no firms specialized in complementary technologies, machinery and services.

6.4.1.1 Knowledge base and innovativeness

Data gathered from fieldwork give a picture of the district as a static system, characterized by a weak knowledge base and underdeveloped internal mechanisms of

Table 6.3 Subcontractors' evaluation on the relationship with principal clients (N=19)

Areas of influence of client firms on subcontractors' decisions	Median	Advantages from association with principal clients	Median
The region in which to sell	1	Accessing new markets	2
The customers to whom to sell	1	Accessing new customers	3
The price to charge	5	Provision of tools/machinery	2
The sourcing of capital equipment (e.g. tools, machinery)	3	Accessing new product and process technology	3
Product creation/development	5	Provision of blueprints/ specification/prototypes	2
Quality control procedures (e.g. inspection)	3	Transfer of management/ organization techniques	3
Quality standards adopted (e.g. ISO-9000)*	1	Improved financial stability	4
Delivery system (e.g. JIT)	1	Higher levels of efficiency/ productivity	2
Order scheduling/production planning	5	Improved relationships with your own suppliers	1

Note
Evaluations could vary from 1 (not relevant) to 5 (most relevant).

knowledge generation. This consideration emerges from several aspects. First, the educational profile of both entrepreneurs and workers shows a poor level of formal education and training. District firms show a very weak commitment towards innovation and research and development. The sampled firms do not have internal R&D laboratories, nor employees or financial resources specifically employed in innovation activities. Further, they did not register any patents both nationally and internationally, which are direct indicators of firms' commitment and investments in innovation activities.

Local firms show a low propensity towards innovation: the rate of innovation adoption is quite limited and mostly focused on product adaptation and incremental improvements of the production process (Table 6.4). The most important innovations

Table 6.4 Innovativeness of sample firms in 1999–2001 by employment size classes (N=30)

Type of innovation	<19	20–49	≥ 250	Total
Adoption of product innovation				
No innovation	5	5	0	10
Generated within the firm		7	1	8
Generated within the district	1	0	0	1
Generated in the country	4	6	0	10
Generated abroad	0	0	0	0
Adoption of process innovation				
No innovation	2	1	0	3
Generated within the firm	0	1	0	1
Generated within the district	0	0	0	0
Generated in the country	8	16	1	25
Generated abroad	0	0	0	0
Adoption of innovation in the organization of production				
No innovation	8	9	0	17
Generated within the firm	0	5	1	6
Generated within the district	0	0	0	0
Generated in the country	2	4	0	6
Generated abroad	0	0	0	0
Adoption of innovation in the organization of sales and distribution				
No innovation	10	15	0	25
Generated within the firm	0	3	0	3
Generated within the district	0	0	0	0
Generated in the country	0	0	0	0
Generated abroad	0	0	0	0

are acquired from outside, mostly mediated through interaction with external suppliers, clients and service providers. The innovation propensity decreases dramatically when the organizational aspects are considered: only three firms – all medium-sized enterprises – innovated the organization of sales and distribution in the years 1999–2001, while 12 firms declared they had introduced innovations in the organization of production, half generated internally and half in the country.

Overall, the most striking result is the extremely low endogenous innovation capacity of the district: across the four types of innovation considered in the survey only one firm reported having introduced innovations generated within the district (product innovation).

The most important internal source of technical knowledge for the firms in the sample is the continuous improvement of production processes. As expected, given the lack of a formalized and explicit commitment towards research and development, this result shows that for the respondent firms incremental innovations and practical knowledge generated through the internal and informal/tacit mechanism of learning by doing is still the most important source of knowledge generation. As regards the external sources of technical knowledge, the respondent firms reported that the most important one is the interactions with local and national clients and suppliers. Since vertical relationships have been qualified by the respondent firms as unidirectional interactions based on the strict technical specifications of the commissioning firms, this result must be understood as a tacit form of learning by interacting, which is not based on explicit and formalized cooperative agreements between clients and subcontractors aimed at improving the exchange of codified knowledge and/or the innovation capacity of the network of firms engaged in vertical relationships.

The most important internal sources of organizational knowledge for the firms in the sample are: (1) the skills learnt from continuous improvement of production processes; and (2) the organizational competencies of the entrepreneurs/founders. Again these results show that the internal generation of organizational knowledge is primarily based on the informal/tacit mechanism of learning by doing. It is also worthy noting that, for the firms belonging to the size classes 250–499, another important internal source of organizational knowledge is the skills of the professional managers employed in the company. As the external sources of organizational knowledge is concerned, another interesting point is that all the local sources received a very low score independent of the size of the respondent firm. This result can be explained by two distinct (although potentially complementary) considerations. First, this result may indicate that, compared to the technical knowledge, the organizational one may be more difficult to be diffused and acquired across local firms through involuntary and informal/tacit mechanisms of knowledge generation (learning by interacting or learning by imitating). Second, this result may indicate the absence in the VV district of local actors (competing firms, clients/suppliers, business services, consulting companies, local institutions) able to transfer voluntarily or involuntarily (e.g. through imitation) advanced organizational models and/or procedures to other district firms. Among the external sources of organizational knowledge, the respondent firms have recognized the interaction with national clients and suppliers as a significant source, although the greatest relevance of this factor is especially recognized by the medium-sized firms of the sample (size classes 250–499). This result is explained by the fact that it is especially this group of medium-sized firms that is the one having the resources and incentives to turn to suppliers and consultants based outside the district and, notably, in other Italian regions.

These findings put into question the widely shared, but probably idealized, view that clustering enhances the formation and diffusion of knowledge and the rapid flow of information thanks to substantial 'spillovers in the air' (Maskell 2001; Maskell and Malmberg 1999). The example of the VV clothing district as well as those of other declining clusters shows that the endogenous mechanisms of building innovative capabilities are not equally effective in all districts or clusters (Belussi and Pilotti 2002; Bell and Albu 1999; Sammarra and Belussi 2006) nor are they equally available to all firms within the cluster (Giuliani 2006).

Traditional district advantages such as proximity and socio-economic relational embeddedness favour the diffusion of knowledge through imitative processes. However, the empirical evidence of knowledge flows in the VV clothing district clearly demonstrates that upgrading the cluster's existing capabilities requires more sophisticated mechanisms. In this regard, it is necessary to distinguish between 'knowledge-using-and-replicating mechanisms' which favour the transmission of existing knowledge and 'knowledge-changing mechanisms' which expand the district knowledge base (Bell and Albu 1999). While the former mechanisms can be easily found in most industrial districts, knowledge-changing mechanisms are not simply a by-product of 'spillover in the air' but require proactive strategies of innovation enacted by the local firms endowed with specific skills and capabilities.

6.4.1.2 Institutional aspects

The policies which have favoured the formation of the district are primarily related to the European and national incentives aimed at supporting investments and economic development in the underdeveloped regions of Europe and Italy.[4] After the elimination of these incentives, the VV clothing district has not benefited from any public support. The local and regional governments did not implement any specific policy for supporting the district until 1996, when the Regional Government, in line with national standards (L. 317/91 and L.140/99), has 'legally' defined the VV district along with the other regional industrial districts.

On one hand, local institutions did not articulate any specific policies for the provision of real services to firms, as opposed to the successful district model of Emilia Romagna and Tuscany. On the other, the local culture did not support the emergence from the bottom of a 'communitarian model' (Dei Ottati 1995) based on entrepreneurial networking and spontaneous 'associationism' capable of making up for the local institutions' lack of initiative, in contrast to Veneto's successful district model.

These institutional and cultural limitations have strongly penalized the VV district. Even today, the local system of real services is quite underdeveloped and inadequate. District firms consider that the local consulting and business services sector is not professionalized enough, thus limiting their demand of services at local level to the most traditional, such as accounting, transport and insurances.

The VVD is strongly dependent on the local banking system: as much as 65 per cent of district firms rely on a bank with an agency in the district area (Fabbrini and Olivieri 1999).

The VV clothing district has very weak linkages with the local education system. In the town of S. Egidio alla Vibrata – the heart of the clothing ID – there is one vocational school with textile specialization (the technical industrial institute Giuseppe Peano) specifically focused on training workers specializing in the clothing industry. However, during interviews with both entrepreneurs and local actors we found that there is no direct relationship, exchange or coordination be-tween the activities of the institute and the needs and demand of the local clothing firms. By the same token, very poor relationships exist between the district and the University of Teramo and the other regional universities in the province of L'Aquila and Pescara. Recently local institutions have tried to solve this problem by launching a Masters course in Economics and Management of the Fashion Industry. The Masters programme was established in February 2003 and is aimed at training managers for the fashion and clothing firms. However, at present, the Masters course is not well known among the district firms, although some of them have been directly involved in the initiative.

In recent years a few consortia have settled in the district area. Among the most significant, the consortium ABC includes important firms of the clothing/ leathering sector (over 100) and 'Termomoda', solely for the clothing sector, has seven firms involved.

Among the local institutions special note should be made of the district commit-tee that is the governance structure established by the Regional Government after the identification of the regional industrial districts. The committee is composed by representatives of local actors and institutions (unions, firms' associations, local chambers of commerce, etc.) and it is in charge of selecting the development plan for the district, and choosing the actors in charge of the plan implementation and finding the necessary resources. Up to now, the projects selected and implemented by the district committee have been negatively evaluated by a large number of local actors (e.g. firms' associations) because they were not tailored to the real needs of the firms. Many district firms were not even aware of or informed about the projects that had already been undertaken. Up to now, the concrete implementation of this initiative has failed to fulfil its original aims. Originally (in the mind of the national legislator) the institutionalization of regional districts was intended to produce a change in the local policy style in favour of industrial policies specifically designed and tailored to local needs and socio-economic specificities within each region. However, the concrete implementation in the Abruzzo region has given much more emphasis to the process of identification of the regional districts while little attention has been given to the strategic phase of designing and implementing the development plans in each of the districts identified.

Finally, to complete the description of the local community, a few words must be devoted to the 'intangible institutions' which are traditionally considered the most important for the development of industrial districts (at least in the Italian experience): social norms, culture, trust, identity and 'citizenship behaviours' (Sammarra and Biggiero 2001; Biggiero and Sammarra 2003). In the VV district, these intangible institutions are still very weakly developed. The community of people and firms are not so intertwined and integrated to develop strong and civic relationships and to support inter-firm trust and cooperation. During interviews with local actors, respondents have reported that the local entrepreneurial culture is very individualistic. Firms are not proactive in the expansion of horizontal strategies aimed at establishing inter-firm cooperation and agreements. Likewise, local actors have not been able so far to compensate for the lack of cooperative attitude of local entrepreneurs through the creation of specific policies and initiatives aimed at supporting horizontal strategies and inter-firm cooperation.

6.5 Internationalization and relocation

The VV district shows a moderate and selective degree of internationalization. The survey results indicate a clear polarization among district firms with respect to their degree of commercial internationalization. Only the final firms have achieved a good exporting capacity, with a foreign sales share about 60 per cent of their total turnover, while the many micro and small firms which carry out façon productions or intermediate manufacturing phases do not have access to foreign markets. The most import foreign market for the district's exports is the EU, which absorbs about 75 per cent of the sample total export, while the rest of the world covers another 22 per cent. In terms of entry modes in foreign markets, across all the export-oriented firms in the sample, the most important route of export is traders and intermediaries. This result indicates that most of the exporting district firms still have an indirect relationship with foreign markets. Obviously, this commercial strategy is less risky for local final firms because it involves the investment of a lower amount of resources and competencies (financial and organizational). For this same reason, it is the most frequent among SMEs which do not have a long experience in exporting and a deep knowledge of foreign markets' characteristics and constraints. On the other hand, this indirect route of exporting does not allow local exporting firms to have full control of their product positioning abroad or to acquire a direct knowledge of foreign markets' opportunities and threats.

In recent years, increased competition and international differentials in labour cost have pushed most local final firms and a few subcontractors to undertake a strategy of relocation and subcontracting abroad, mostly targeted towards Romania, Tunisia and Morocco.

Among the sampled firms, five enterprises have carried out greenfield investments in Eastern European countries, one firm has signed an agreement with a Romanian clothing enterprise and one firm has established a joint equity venture in North Africa (Table 6.5). Local firms involved in FDI abroad do not seem to follow the typical district model based on decentralization and inter-firm division of labour in the foreign country. Indeed, their Eastern European affiliates are typically large and integrated firms.

In many cases, when the parent company is a final firm with more than one brand, the foreign subsidiary carries out the manufacturing of the lower cost line of products. This choice is justified by the necessity of moving into lower labour cost countries the production of medium-quality products which cannot be conveniently produced within the district any longer. Interestingly enough, the interviewed companies that had CEEC subsidiaries have declared that their foreign affiliate does not work exclusively nor primarily for the parent companies, but also has other foreign clients, mostly other Italian clothing firms. This strategy is justified by the large scale of the foreign affiliates. However, the parent company keeps control of the decision of to which customers they sell.

The process of relocation has involved not only the medium-sized firms producing a final product with their own brand, but also some small firms focused on a specific phase of the clothing production process. This group of relocating firms has often decided to invest in a foreign country to follow the decision already taken by their principal client.

Among the interviewed firms, seven final firms and two district subcontractors declared using international subcontracting. With respect to geographical distribution of foreign subcontractors (Table 6.6), most (7 out of 11) are located in Romania, two in other Eastern European countries and two in North Africa (Tunisia and Morocco). Interestingly, foreign subcontractors are all medium-sized and large firms: four out of nine fall in the employment size classes 50–249 while five have more than 250 employees (Table 6.7).

Especially for the firms producing intermediate products, the decision to subcontract abroad seems to follow the relocation process already undertaken by their national clients. Quality control on the subcontracted products is based on random visits to the subcontractors' establishment and control checks on products' reception.

Based on field results, the leading reason for FDI and international subcontracting is clear and unequivocal: the most important motivation lies in the possibility

Table 6.5 Firms with FDI abroad by type of investment and country

| Types of FDI | North Africa | *Eastern European Countries* | | | | | |
		Hungary	Romania	Czech Rep.	Slovenia	Poland	Other
Greenfield	0	0	4	0	0	0	1
Acquisition	0	0	0	0	0	0	0
Joint equity venture	1	0	0	0	0	0	0
Other	0	0	1	0	0	0	0
Total	1	0	5	0	0	0	1

Table 6.6 Number of foreign subcontractors by country of location

Country of location		Number of subcontractors	
		absolute value	percentage value
CEECs	Hungary	0	0
	Romania	7	64
	Czech Republic	0	0
	Slovenia	0	0
	Poland	0	0
	Other CEECs	2	18
North Africa		2	18
Total		11	100

Table 6.7 Distribution of CEEC subcontractors by employment size classes

Employment size classes	Number of subcontractors	
	absolute value	percentage value
Less than 10	0	0
10–49	0	0
50–249	4	44
250 and more	5	56
Total	9	100

to exploit labour wage differentials. Therefore, district firms' internationalization strategy is based on efficiency seeking investments (Dunning 1993). Further, respondents declared that the internationalization of production has become a necessity because of the progressive reduction of profit margins in the home country. These results suggest that district firms have reacted to the increased competition in the clothing industry by trying to maintain price competitiveness through FDI and international subcontracting rather than trying to build new factors of success. Indeed, their internal competencies and value chains have not evolved significantly as a consequence of this strategic choice. In contrast to what occurred in other Italian districts specialized in fashion industries, the leading relocating firms have not compensated their foreign investments by shifting their strategic focus on the most value-added and intangible activities of the clothing production chain, such as marketing, logistics and distribution. This means that the type of activities still kept within the district are not intrinsically different from those relocated abroad. In some cases, the relocating firms continue to be focused on the manufacturing process, simply deciding to produce locally the higher quality products lines and to relocate abroad the lower quality brands.

All the interviewed entrepreneurs who have undertaken FDI or international sub-contracting declared that their foreign affiliates/subcontractors register a significant lower productivity compared to the parent company, although they recognize that the labour cost differential is still big enough to overcompensate for the foreign affiliates' lower productivity.

Overall, the net effect of the relocation process for the district was an increase in the competitive pressure on local subcontractors and façon producers. All relocating firms reported that their investments abroad had led to a reduction of the employment levels in the establishments located within the district and a reduction in the amount of work subcontracted locally.

6.6 Facing global challenges: evolutionary pattern, upgrading and relocation

From the formation phase to maturity, the VV clothing district has moved from rapid growth to stabilization without being able to change its original features and limitations. Up to now, the evolution of the district has followed a path-dependent process, strongly constrained by the original imprinting of the formation phase (Belussi, *et al.* 2008).

The emergence of the district has been mainly driven by external forces (the demand for clothing manufacturing of external commissioning firms). The most important triggering factors which pushed the 'proto-district' from the formation phase to development were twofold: (1) the possibility to exploit cost advantages thanks to the existence of fiscal and economic incentives; and (2) the increasing demand for clothing subcontracting due to the outsourcing strategy pursued by externally based commissioning firms. The exogenous nature of the triggering factors has contributed to mould the internal structure and processes of the district and its subsequent evolution. The local production system has developed as a 'satellite district' (Markusen 1996; Sammarra 2003) with a strong subcontracting vocation and dependence from external national commissioning firms. This imprinting was maintained over time and still represents the main structural and cultural weakness of the district.

The increased competition in the clothing industry from a large number of low-labour-cost countries (especially from Asia) along with the persistence of the structural and cultural weaknesses of the VV district have accentuated the economic decline that started in the 1990s. Despite their different roles in the production filière, most district companies have tried to face the new competitive challenge by maintaining the same strategic perspective followed in the past; that is, focusing on low-cost advantages and price competitiveness. Internal homoge-neity and the low level of structural differentiation favoured the formation and maintenance of an inward-looking and 'conservative' perspective, which has in turn exacerbated firms' strategic myopia and district crisis.

Only a small number of local firms were able to pursue product upgrading by improving quality and moving into more sophisticated product lines. Most firms have kept focusing on low-cost competitiveness. International differentials in labour cost have pushed most local final firms and a few subcontractors to undertake an efficiency-seeking strategy of internationalization through relocation and subcontracting abroad, mostly targeted towards Romania, Tunisia and Morocco. Most local companies reacted to the increased competition by trying to lower prices and production costs. This strategy has produced a real 'price war' among district firms which has reduced profit margins for local subcontractors, leading to a severe reduction in district firms. The overall effect for the district was a higher rate of mortality among the many subcontractors specialized in low to medium productions. Indeed, only the few façon producers which succeed in following a quality-improvement strategy have been able to avoid international competition and the threat of being substituted through relocation and subcontracting abroad by local and external commissioning firms.

This pattern, frequently observed in the competitive behaviour of firms from developing countries, which often compete by squeezing wages and profit margins (Giuliani, *et al.* 2005), has been defined as the 'low road' to competitiveness, in contrast to the 'high road' based on functional and intersectoral upgrading (Humphrey and Schmitz 2002). The difficulties encountered by the VV firms in finding new bases for competitiveness show that 'satellite districts' in advanced as well as in developing countries do not offer favourable conditions for the acquisition and maintenance of long-term competitiveness (Sammarra and Belussi 2006). Indeed, as noted by Humphrey and Schmitz (2002), the insertion of district firms in a quasi-hierarchical chain (in which lead firms maintain strong power over other firms in the chain) can provide favourable conditions for process and product upgrading, but generally hinders functional and intersectoral upgrading.

The investigation of the VV clothing district offers important insights into the role played by external linkages for district upgrading. Recent research has stressed the idea that geographical openness is a precondition for district firms to survive (Bathelt, *et al.* 2004; Boschma and ter Wal 2007; Vang and Chaminade 2007). External knowledge linkages reduce the danger of cognitive 'lock-in' and 'over-embeddedness' (Grabher 1993), which may become important obstacles to local learning and innovation. However, the empirical evidence presented in this study clearly shows that local learning mechanisms and the way in which local firms establish and manage external relationships determine the amount and quality of knowledge that local firms are able to absorb from external sources. Indeed, the analysis of knowledge flows in the VV clothing district demonstrated that the local firms' weak commitment to innovation and learning not only hinders an effective process of endogenous knowledge generation and diffusion but also limits the local firms' capability to absorb knowledge and innovation from the outside and creatively use and adapt the acquired knowledge to foster innovation. As Bell and Albu (1999: 1724) noticed, 'knowledge may be acquired from external sources, either relatively passively as a by-product from various kinds of interactions with the outside world or from a range of more deliberate and active search efforts'. The external connections established by the VV clothing firms seem to belong to the former category, emphasizing the lack of entrepreneurial effort of making up for the inadequacy of internal resources devoted to innovation with a proactive and deliberate strategy of external search.

In order to maintain international competitiveness, the most active district firms have recently started a restructuring process which has mostly involved the outsourcing of more labour-intensive operations (assembly) to countries such as the Eastern European countries (in particular Romania) and those on the Mediterranean Rim (in particular Tunisia and Morocco). Although the process of relocation and subcontracting abroad is still moderate, it is worth noting that all the local leading firms except one are already actively engaged in such a process through FDI or international subcontracting. However, the leading relocating firms have not compensated for their foreign investments by shifting their strategic focus on the most value-added and intangible activities of the apparel global value chain. In this respect, we could say that the VV district has followed a model of 'replicative relocation' (Sammarra and Belussi 2006), meaning that the type of activities still kept within the district are not intrinsically different from those relocated abroad. In some cases, the relocating firms keep focusing on the manufacturing process, simply deciding to produce the higher quality product lines locally and to relocate the lower quality brands abroad.

While this process of relocation will eventually allow local leading firms to keep being competitive, the survival of the overall district is put into question in the medium to long term. Indeed, the relocation process obviously involves not only the few local final firms but also the external commissioning firms, especially those targeted on the low to medium market segment, from which the district is still quite dependent.

6.7 Conclusions

This study was aimed at contributing to the literature on the evolution of industrial districts facing global challenges, offering an in-depth analysis of the phenomenon of industrial districts' crisis. This topic has been widely overlooked in literature and demands further empirical evidence and conceptual insights (Alberti 2006).

According to the global commodity chain approach (Gereffi, *et al.* 2005; Gereffi and Korzeniewicz 1994; Gereffi 1999; Bair and Gereffi 2001) the extent to which clusters in global industry can achieve and/or maintain growth and competitiveness will depend on the way in which firms in these clusters becomes incorporated into global chains. Our analysis has shown that the VV clothing district has failed to make the transition from a low-tech, labour-intensive manufacturing and externally dependent district to an advanced local system where the future is in the professional skills of design, IT-based technology, marketing and logistics. Overall, very little progress has been done in terms of logistics, branding (marketing) and design capabilities.

With the exception of the very few medium-sized firms producing directly for the market, local enterprises do not have any control and capabilities on the most added-value activities of the clothing value chain. These important limitations dramatically expose the VVD to international competition from a large number of low-labour-cost countries (especially from Asia) for which the textile-clothing sector constitutes one of the most important sources of income and employment.

The transformation of the whole textile-clothing sector clearly indicates that the district's productive structure is not adequate any more, and needs a profound re-shaping of the local value chain. In order to survive and adapt to the transformation of the textile-clothing sector, the VVD is faced with a number of challenges. Local institutions should support this process of strategic and organizational change by promoting specific actions aimed at informing local entrepreneurs about the new trends emerging in the whole textile-clothing industry at national and international levels. Policy makers could play an important role to make up for the strategic myopia shown by many local firms by designing policy initiatives which take into account the major trends of change occurring in the clothing industry. The policy implication of this work would call for support of district firms in their upgrading efforts.

In the area of innovation, branding and quality improvement, policies aimed at supporting the provision of advanced services to local firms are highly desirable. Local institutions should also provide effective incentives for the adoption of information and communication technologies by local firms. In the area of investment in human capital, training policies are crucially important in creating new professional competencies in the most value-added activities of the clothing value chain, and notably design, cutting, marketing and distribution. Indeed, those professional competencies are not sufficiently developed within the district. Training programmes aimed at supporting local firms in managing the process of generational turnover are also needed.

Notes

1 The empirical research was part of a larger investigation on the evolutionary and relocation patterns of Western and Eastern European industrial districts undertaken in a research project entitled *Industrial Districts' Re-location Processes: Identifying Policies in the Perspective of EU Enlargement*. The project was funded by the European Commission under the 5th Framework Programme (1998–2002) Key Action 'Improving the Socio-economic Knowledge Base'.

2 Alba Adriatica, Ancarano, Bellante, Campli, Castellalto, Civitella del Tronto, Colonnella, Controguerra, Corropoli, Giulianova, Martinsicuro, Morro D'Oro, Mosciano Sant'Angelo, Nereto, Notaresco, Roseto degli Abruzzi, Sant'Egidio, Sant'Omero, Torano Nuovo, Tortoreto.

3 The geographical borders shown in Fig. 6.1 correspond to the administrative definition of the VVD given in the regional Council resolution n. 34/3 (23 July 1996).

4 Abruzzo was included in the 'objective 1' EEC areas for the support to the European developing regions' structural adjustment. At national level, the public incentives were related to the regulation 488/92 for supporting investments in underdeveloped areas); regulation 64/86 (the special intervention for Southern Italy, the so called 'Mezzogiorno'); the Sabatini law of 1965 and note 317/91.

References

Alberti F. G. (2006), 'The decline of the industrial district of Como: recession, relocation or reconversion?', *Entrepreneurship and Regional Development*, 18: 473–501.

Bair J. and Gereffi G. (2001), 'Local clusters in global chains: the causes and consequences of export dynamism in Torreon's blue jeans industry', *World Development*, 29 (11): 1885–1903.

Bathelt H., Malmberg A. and Maskell P. (2004), 'Clusters and knowledge: local buzz, global pipelines and the process of knowledge creation', *Progress in Human Geography*, 28: 31–56.

Bell M. and Albu M. (1999),' Knowledge systems and technological dynamics in industrial clusters in developing countries', *World Development*, 27 (9): 1715–34.

Belussi F. and Pilotti L. (2002), 'Knowledge creation, learning and innovation in Italian industrial districts', *Geografiska Annaler*, 84 B (2): 19–33.

Belussi F., Sammarra A. and Sedita S. R. (2008), 'Industrial districts evolutionary trajectories: localized learning diversity and external growth', paper presented at the Druid 25th Celebration Conference (www.druid.dk).

Biggiero L. and Sammarra A. (2003), 'Social identity and identification processes: enriching theoretical tools to study industrial districts', in F. Belussi, G. Gottardi and E. Rullani (eds.), *The Technological Evolution of Industrial Districts*, Boston MA: Kluwer Academic Publishers, pp. 205–31.

Boschma R. A. and ter Wal A. L. J. (2007), 'Knowledge networks and innovative performance in an industrial district: the case of a footwear district in the South of Italy', *Industry and Innovation*, 14: 177–99.

Dei Ottati G. (1995), *Tra mercato e comunità: aspetti concettuali e ricerche empiriche sul distretto industriale*, Milano: FrancoAngeli.

Dunning J. H. (1993), *Multinational Enterprises and the Global Economy*, Workingham: Addison-Wesley.

Fabbrini A. and Olivieri R. (1999), 'Il distretto industriale di Ascoli Piceno', *Economia Marche*, a. 18(2): 113–29.

Felice C. (2001), *Il modello abruzzese. Un caso virtuoso di sviluppo regionale*, Roma: Meridiana Libri.

Gereffi G. (1999), 'International trade and industrial upgrading in the apparel commodity chain', *Journal of International Economics*, 48: 37–70.

Gereffi G. and Korzeniewicz M. (eds.) (1994), *Commodity Chains and Global Capitalism*, Westport: Praeger.

Gereffi G., Humphrey J. and Sturgeon T. (2005), 'The governance of global value chains', *Review of International Political Economy*, 12: 78–104.

Giuliani, E. (2006). 'The selective nature of knowledge networks in clusters: evidence from the wine industry'. *Journal of Economic Geography*, 7: 139–68.

Giuliani E., Pietrobelli C. and Rabellotti R. (2005), 'Upgrading in global value chains: Lessons from Latin American Clusters', *World Development*, 33(4): 549–73.

Grabher G. (1993), 'The weakness of strong ties: the lock-in of regional development in the Ruhr area', in G. Grabher (ed.), *The Embedded Firm: on the Socioeconomics of Industrial Networks*, London and New York: Routledge, pp. 255–77.

Hanzl-Weiß D. (2004), 'Enlargement and the Textiles, Clothing and Footwear Industry', *The World Economy*, 27(6): 923–45.

Humphrey J. and Schmitz H. (2002), 'How does insertions in global value chains affect upgrading industrial clusters?', *Regional Studies*, 36(9): 1017–27.

ISTAT (1996), *Rapporto annuale. La situazione del Paese nel 1995*, Roma: Istituto Poligrafico e Zecca dello Stato.

Markusen A. (1996), 'Sticky places in slippery space: a typology of industrial districts', *Economic Geography*, 72: 293–313.

Maskell P. (2001), 'Towards a knowledge-based theory of the geographical cluster', *Industrial and Corporate Change*, 10(4): 919–41.

Maskell P. and Malmberg A. (1999), 'Localised learning and industrial competitiveness', *Cambridge Journal of Economics*, 23: 167–85.

Paniccia I. (2002), *Industrial Districts: Evolution and Competitiveness in Italian Firms*, Cheltenham, UK and Northampton, MA, USA.: Edward Elgar.

Sammarra A. (2003), *Lo sviluppo dei distretti industriali. Percorsi evolutivi fra globalizzazione e localizzazione*, Roma: Carocci.

Sammarra A. and Belussi F. (2006), 'Evolution and relocation in fashion-led Italian districts: evidence from two case-studies', *Entrepreneurship and Regional Development*, forthcoming.

Sammarra A. and Biggiero L. (2001), 'Identity and identification in industrial districts', *Journal of Management and Governance*, 4: 61–82.

Stengg W. (2001), 'The textile and clothing industry in the EU: A survey', Enterprise Papers 2 – 2001, Enterprise Directorate-General of the European Commission.

Vang J. and Chaminade C. (2007), 'Cultural clusters, global-local linkages and spillovers: theoretical and empirical insights from an exploratory study of Toronto's film cluster', *Industry and Innovation*, 14: 401–20.

Viesti G. (2000), 'I numeri del made in Italy meridionale', in G. Viesti (ed.), *I distretti industriali nel Mezzogiorno*, Roma: Donzelli Editore, pp. 25–331.

Yin R. K. (1989), *Case Study Research. Design and Methods*, Newbury Park: Sage.

7 Moving immigrants into Western industrial districts

The 'inverse' delocalization of the leather tanning district of Arzignano

Fiorenza Belussi (Padua University) and Silvia Rita Sedita (Padua University)

7.1 Introduction

This chapter looks at an alternative way to approach the delocalization issue, that of labour flexibility as opposed to production transfer to low-labour-cost countries. The resulting new configuration of the organization of production is here called 'inverse' delocalization. The research question addressed is: Do the industrial district (ID) entrepreneurs prefer to move the production, or to move immigrants into the Western IDs? The case of Arzignano is presented, as an interesting second-best solution to the alternative of moving capital to reach lower labour costs abroad, considered here the standard approach chosen by Italian industrial districts facing the opening of the economy and entering a globalized world. In our contribution, it is argued that this second-best solution offers some answers to the problem of district social and economic embeddedness. The chapter is structured as follows: Section 7.2 describes briefly the characteristics of the leather tanning industry. Section 7.3 presents the case of the Arzignano leather tanning industry, involved in a process of 'inverse' delocalization, which is commented on in Section 7.4. Section 7.5 concludes the chapter.

7.2 The leather tanning district of Arzignano

The area delimited by Arzignano[1] – Valle del Chiampo[2] and Montebello (the so-called 'leather triangle' – 130 sq km), represents today the enclave of the Vicenza leather tanning industry and has held, for several years, the world record in the sector, for volume of production and quality of items manufactured. The Italian industry is composed of around 2000 firms and 30,000 employees. It accounts for 65 per cent of European production, and about 16 per cent of international production (Banca Intesa 2006). About one third of the Italian production is localized in the Arzignano district. The district specializes in the production of bovine leather and calfskin, for the footwear, furnishing and automotive industries.

The territory where the district lies has the features of a diffuse industrialization system, characterized by the presence of small and medium enterprises, which employ, respectively, 53 per cent and 22 per cent of the total number of employees in the tanning sector. Considering only leather preparation and tanning activities, and excluding complementary activities, the district, in the year 2002 (Table 7.1), consisted of 658 local units, with a sales turnover of about 4 billion euro, of which nearly half was exported (Table 7.2). The number of direct employees exceeds 8000 and is more than 10,000 if we consider all phases of the *filière*, including the production of chemical ingredients and the machinery producers.

The specific characteristics of the process of leather manufacturing, which is very fragmented, lead to a high level of division of labour. The proliferation of many small firms in the district is the fruit of spin-off processes that occurred particularly during the 1970s. Despite the strong presence of small firms, recently, about one third of the employees are occupied in medium–large firms with more that 100 employees (Table 7.3). During the 1990s, like several other Italian districts, Arzignano has been characterized by many evolutionary changes (Belussi, *et al.* 2003) and by a hierarchization process (Lazerson and Lorenzoni 1999) that has implied the growth in size of some leading local firms and a process of grouping (Iacobucci 2006), related also to an intensification of firm-specific innovative activity (Cainelli and De Liso 2005). Large groups have emerged, such as the Mastrotto Group, Rino Mastrotto Group, the Conceria Cristina and the Conceria Sabrina (Table 7.4). In contrast to the typical Italian district, Arzignano has not activated (on a large scale) a process of relocation or delocalization of activities that were previously commissioned to local subcontractors (Guerrieri and Iammarino 2001; Zucchella 2006). In fact, local firms have absorbed immigrant workers (Table 7.5).

Table 7.1 The Arzignano district: historical evolution

Years	Tanning sector		Other linked manufacturing activities (chemical and machinery producers)	
	# Local units	# Employees	# Local units	# Employees
1951	19	361	63	2068
1961	100	1929	91	2765
1971	161	3209	191	3228
1981	602	6358	230	2606
1991	615	8017	227	2590
2001	649	7988	222	2514
2002	658	8105	218	2567

Source: Our interpretation of ISTAT data (for the years 1951–81) and CCIAA of Vicenza (for the years 1991–2002).

Table 7.2 Performance indicators of the Arzignano district (000 euro)

	Firms	Employees	Sales	Import	Export
2001	760	11,900	4,500,000		1,685,000
2002	736	12,154	4,479,000		1,670,000
2003	720	11,644	4,223,000	757,959	1,461,337
2004	721	11,504	4,257,000	714,713	1,391,400

Source: Our interpretation of the Entrepreneurial Local Association data.

Table 7.3 The Arzignano district: size distribution of firms (2004)

District	Size distribution				
	1–20 employees	21–50 employees	51–100 employees	>100 employees	Total
Firms	71.9	17.5	8.2	2.4	100.0
Employees	29.9	21.2	21.9	27.0	100.0

Source: Our interpretation of Poster (2005) on one group of 482 firms and 12,526 employees.

Table 7.4 Local leading firms in the Arzignano district (2000)

	Sales (euro)	%
Gruppo Mastrotto*	266,000,000	40.5
Rino Mastrotto Group	182,000,000	27.8
Conceria Cristina	105,000,000	16.0
Conceria Sabrina	102,000,000	15.7
Totale	655,000,000	100.0

Source: Our interpretation of Partnership Equal G-local (2004) and Furlan and Plechero (2007).
* from 2003 includes Duma and Conceria Mastrotto.

Today, it is estimated that one out of three workers employed in the sector is a foreign immigrant (explaining the high non-European immigration phenomenon in the area). This district still requires a large number of non-qualified jobs (Table 7.6), which cannot be supplied solely by the Italian workforce.

7.3 Historical development of the Arzignano district

The first documented evidence regarding the tannery business in the Vicenza area dates back to 1300 (Patto per lo Sviluppo del Distretto Vicentino della Concia

Table 7. 5 Immigrant employees in the Arzignano district (2004)

Country	Absolute Value	%
Asia	2,065	44.5
Central Africa	1,294	27.9
East Europe	906	19.5
North Africa	322	6.9
South America	57	1.2
Total	4,644	100.0

Source: Our elaboration of Poster (2005).

Table 7.6 Employees by qualification in the Arzignano district (2004)

	AV	%
Generic blue-collar workers	6895	57.3
Specialized blue-collar workers	2613	21.7
Clerks	1398	11.6
Technicians	678	5.6
Managers	442	3.7
Total	12,026	100.0

Source: Our elaboration of Fonte: Poster (2005).

2004). The first catalogue of the Vicenza tanning products was published in 1855; at the time there were about 20 firms, generally located in the area of Bassano del Grappa, where leathers coming from Milan, Vienna and France were tanned. References to the Valle del Chiampo tanning activity, also lead back to the four-teenth century, even if a consistent emergence of the sector can be placed around the year 1500, together with the development of the wool and silk sectors.

The beginning of a more sophisticated manufacturing of tanned products is ascribed to the period of the domination of the Serenissima Republic of Venice: its marine traffic and the imports of varied manufactured products, coming from the East, had an extremely positive effect on the local leather production, which could count on the contribution of the best techniques existing at the time (see Figure 7.1). This beneficial influence not only gave an advantage to the Venetian producers, but also to those of the hinterland, and in particular to the areas of Vicenza and of the Valle del Chiampo. These areas were particularly suited for this type of production, because they could count on a remarkable supply of fresh water, and trees from which to extract the tannin; two indispensable elements for the leather manufacturing process.

The first signs of organizational progress were manifested in the 1920s, when new firms used the inherited equipment and machinery of the silk factories, which have been active since the first decades of 1900 to produce leather goods. Silk production, in fact, faced an ongoing crisis, caused by a strong reduction in demand, partly due to the two world wars and partly to the strong Japanese competition. The last establishment closed in 1968; in the meantime the leather sector began to boom in the 1950s. If the census of 1951 includes Arzignano, 19 local units and 361 employees were in the sector, and the numbers rose to 100 local units and 1929 employees in 1961 (see Table 7.1).

Employees that were working in the so-called historical tanneries began to start up new activities in new units, building a spin-off process, which in turn

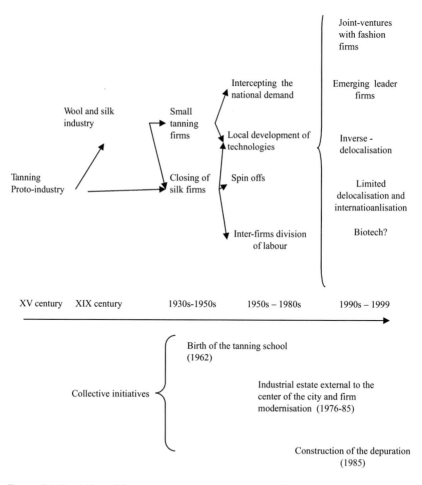

Figure 7.1 Evolution of firm population in the Arzignano district and co-evolution of local institutions.
Source: Our interpretation.

led to the birth of the Arzignano industrial district. The patrimony of technical acquaintances, the overabundance of water, the availability of a pool of specialized labour, were all conditions that favoured the proliferation of new firms, mostly subcontractors who were very dependent on the final-product-controlling complete-cycle firms.

The new establishments, which took advantage of the labour mostly of former workers from the silk sector and former farmers, initially were generally dedicated to the manufacturing of low-quality leathers, such as equine or bovine leathers, for use as lining materials. During this time, product qualification increased remarkably, because some local producers of tanning machinery were founded, initially imitating German firms' technology, and later producing original innovations in 'bottali' technology. This formed the solid basis of the development of the tanning sector: a close technological integration between the most dynamic firms and the producers of the new technology.

The growth of the district called for the creation of some support institutions. In 1965, a technical high school devoted to tanning chemistry, the Istituto Tecnico Industriale per la Chimica Conciaria 'Galileo Galilei', was born, together with an analytical laboratory. Over the years, other specialized training institutions arose, covering all the aspects of the tanning production process, from the quality of the leather to environmental issues and marketing activities. A new Masters course in 'Tecnico di Processo e della Qualità dell'Industria Conciaria' (IFTS) – for tanning processes and quality technicians – has been recently promoted by Agenfor and Padua University, to meet the need for advanced skills.

The growing attention paid to environmental issues, and thus the need to improve the environmental quality of the production process, brought about the foundation of the CO.VI.AM (Concerie Vicentine per l'Ambiente), a consortium of entrepreneurs belonging to the Associazione Industriali of Vicenza – an industry association which pursues the objective of experimenting with all possible technological innovations, uses of alternative products, and anything that can reduce the environmental impact of the tanning production process.

Also noteworthy is the progressive informatization of the districtual firms, and the capacity of the district to develop several initiatives related to this, such as an e-procurement system, a districtual e-commerce system, an extranet – developed horizontally and vertically, and an integrated database system (Rur – Census 2002). In 1985, a collective plant for the treatment of water and industrial residues was built, thanks to the financial support of the local administration, and the generous contribution of the Veneto region. These collective investments were the result of a process of co-evolution of the local firms with the district institutions.

7.4 The 'inverse' delocalization

Normally, the structure of a delocalization process is as follows: the value-added activities stay in the country where the firm was born, while the other, less knowledge intensive ones are farmed out to low-labour or low-energy-cost countries. The results of a process of this type are truly enhanced by the presence of a high-level information and communication technology infrastructure, which fuels the coordination of distance activities.

Some of the manufacturing activities carried out by the Italian industrial districts are characterized by a disparity between the capital intensive activities (difficult to be transferred) and the labour intensive ones (easily transferred), where the former occupy the largest part of the production.

This is the case in the Arzignano district, where the two types of activities can hardly be separated, and this works as an obstacle to operating a delocalization process. The leather tanning industry is a low-tech sector, and plants operating in the district are not only simple places of production, but also 'research labs', where continuous experimentation, feed-back mechanisms and learning by doing take place daily. Transferring some of the plants, or worse, the totality, to a foreign country, is viewed by the entrepreneurs as a loss of value creation.[3]

The worldwide success of the Arzignano district seems to be rooted in a process that we call 'inverse' delocalization, where the plants are not moved from their original place, but, on the contrary, workers from foreign countries increasingly populate the local pool of available labour. This choice is justified by the necessity to keep the production process under strict control, which is a value-added activity, and at the same time, to find a workforce that is happy to spend their time working hard in the plants. It is well known that most of the blue-collar activities in advanced countries and regions, including Italy – and the North-East region – suffer from a lack of internal human resources, since the average level of education of the workforce is high, and the majority of graduates tend to seek white-collar jobs.

The immigrants constitute a valid alternative to the closure or delocalization of productive plants. The massive involvement of immigrants in the specialized leather tanning firms is one explanation for the positive trend of immigration registered in Vicenza province (Anastasia and Bragato 2004). Their nationalities, illustrated in Table 7.5 are predominantly Asian, African (from Ghana, Senegal and Morocco) and Eastern European (from Romania and Slovenia, with far fewer from Albania).

A study of the Fondazione Nord Est on the Arzignano district, conducted in the year 2000, shows that 80 per cent of the entrepreneurs in the sample recognize the lack of human resources as a crucial problem for firm survival, and 90 per cent of them refer to a specialized workforce (Bordignon and Marini 2000); these results are confirmed by our survey, where 13 out of 15 firms interviewed declared a lack of human resources.

If the first stages of the tanning process do not require specific training and a qualified workforce, and can be easily carried out by immigrants without previous experience and with limited knowledge of the Italian language, the last ones, which entail sophisticated machinery, ask for skilled, or trained workers, and can be performed only by Italians or experienced immigrants. This is one of the main reasons why the 'inverse' delocalization can be observed here and not in the Montebelluna sport-system district, where the raw material to be worked is plastic, which is far more easily treated than the process of tanning leather, a material that is difficult to select, cut and treat uniformly for all the output products, and which often requires last minute decisions during the most crucial phases of its manufacturing.

The depth of experience needed for these specific stages of the production is normally found in older workers, mainly those over 50. They have their family in Arzignano and feel a strong tie to the territory where they were born and grew up. This means that they are not really in favour of leaving the country, and living and working abroad, in a low-labour-cost country, if the firm eventually decided to re-localize its manufacturing activities. Similarly, it must be observed that the majority of firms in Arzignano are family businesses. Family firms are less inclined to move production to foreign countries, and thus to transfer the members of the family there. In addition, there are now some localized external economies in Arzignano (e.g. the collective depuration plant) that firms can make use of for their leather tanning activities. If firms were to locate abroad they would have to support the cost of building new infrastructure. This clearly could not be economically viable for a single small unit that has decided to move its production to a foreign country. Only a massive movement involving a collective relocation, made by a significant number of firms willing to share the costs of this environmental infrastructure, could offer an alternative solution. But this would involve a very complicated relationship among firms, which is in contrast with the individualistic tendencies of the local entrepreneurial culture. In the end, only four large firms in the district have experimented with some forms of internationalization (Rino Mastrotto, Gruppo Mastrotto, Dal Maso and Beschin).

7.5 Conclusions

'Inverse delocalization' may be considered a second best option in comparison with the relocation activity of firms in Western countries. Instead of moving, capital firms have decided to attract new labour flows. They clearly bear higher labour costs, but they can take advantage of the district's externalities (good local suppliers, favourable institutions, and the accumulated capabilities of the district). In Arzignano, the 'industrial district atmosphere' is apparent, and is created by the best tanning machinery project engineers, the high expertise of firms specialized in chemical products, the existence of a school, such as the Istituto Conciario Galileo Galilei, and the localization of the most efficient worldwide depuration plant for processing tanning waste. This builds an integrated system that is not easy to replicate everywhere. Thus, at the moment, the option of delocalization does not seem to be a viable strategy for the district, and for the small local firms.

The 'inverse delocalization' solves three types of problems: first, the embeddedness (Grabher 1993) of the know-how localized in local entrepreneurs and technicians; the difficulty in codifying this knowledge makes risky any foreign investment in greenfield activities; second, the presence of non-transferable Marshallian economies, such as the inter-firm division of labour and the collective depuration plant; third, the social embeddedness of local entrepreneurs (Sorenson 2005), who suffer greatly for the costs of foreignness (Zaheer 1995).

Flexible laws for facilitating the entry and integration of immigrants willing to work in this sector could consolidate the inward flows of labour mobility coming from other countries. This model works as a substitute for the model of delocalization that is low-labour-costs-driven, as is shown in the case of Montebelluna (see Chapter 5).

More careful attention given to the absorption of high-tech skills, required by the capital intensive activities, could enlarge the pool of existing professionals, functioning as a substitute for a worldwide capability gathering through knowledge offshoring.

This case fosters some reflections. The 'inverse delocalization' represents an alternative way of territorial development, which avoids the de-industrialization mechanism, and pushes local firms to invest much more in the local area. A final note relates to a consideration of the relationship between inverse delocalization and the market competitiveness of firms. To keep production at home does not mean excluding the possibility of conquering new markets. At the moment, for example, the entrepreneurs of the Arzignano district are constantly involved in the Chinese market, where they supply intermediate components (wet blue, tanned leather or chemical materials) for the production of finished goods.

Notes

1 The leather tanning industry in Italy is composed of three main districts: the Valle del Chiampo in Vicenza province (Veneto), the Santa Croce sull'Arno district in the Valdarno Inferiore in Tuscany, near Pisa, and the Solofra district in the Avellino province (Campania), specializing in bovine leather and kidskin.
2 The municipalities belonging to the Arzignano leather tanning district are: Altissimo, Arzignano, Brendola, Chiampo, Crespadoro, Gambellara, Montebello Vicentino, Montecchio Maggiore, Montorso Vicentino, Nogarole Vicentino, San Pietro Mussolino, and Zermeghedo.
3 This consideration and the following are the result of a survey addressed to 15 firms in the Arzignano district, mainly conducted by E. Molina in the year 2003 (face-to-face and/or phone semi-structured interviews to the entrepreneur for small sized firms, or a member of the top management for larger firms), whose findings are collected in Molina (2003).

References

AA.VV (1977), *Valle del Chiampo. Antologia 1977*, ind. Tip. Dal Molin & Figli.

Anastasia B. (1995), 'Flussi di esportazioni e processi di internazionalizzazione: il contributo dei distretti industriali veneti', *Oltre il Ponte*, 50.

Anastasia B. and Bragato S. (2004), L'immigrazione nella provincia di Vicenza: l'impatto della 'grande regolarizzazione', in, AA.VV, *Osservatorio di Veneto lavoro*, Milano: Franco Angeli.

Banca Intesa (2006), Il distretto della concia di Arzignano, aggiornamento 2006, pubblicazione interna.

Belussi F., Gottardi G., Rullani E. (eds.) (2003), *The Technological Evolution of Industrial Districts*, Boston: Kluwer.

Bordignon F. and Marini D. (2000), *I fattori che frenano lo sviluppo economico del Nord Est* in Quaderni FNE, collana Panel, n.1, Venezia: Fondazione Nord Est.

Cainelli G. and De Liso N. (2005), 'Innovation in industrial districts: evidence from Italy', *Industry and Innovation*, 12: 3: 383–98.

Furlan A. and Plechero M. (2007) 'Three case studies', in G. Corò and R. Grandinetti (eds.), *Le strategie di crescita delle medie imprese: dimensioni, relazioni e competenze*, Milan: Il Sole 24 Ore Libri.

Grabher G. (1993), *The Embedded Firm: On the Socio-economics of Industrial Networks*, London: Routledge.

Guerrieri P. and Iammarino, S. (2001), 'The dynamics of Italian industrial districts: towards a renewal of competitiveness', in P. Guerrieri, S. Iammarino and C. Pietrobelli (eds.) *The Global Challenge to Industrial Districts: Small and Medium-sized Enterprises in Italy and Taiwan*, Cheltenham: Edward Elgar.

Iacobucci D. (2006), 'Capabilities dinamiche e sviluppo per gruppo nelle imprese di piccola e media dimensione', in G. Cainelli, N. De Liso (eds.), *Organizzazioni, Conoscenze e Sistemi Locali*, Milano: Angeli.

Lazerson M. and Lorenzoni, G. (1999), 'The firms that feed industrial districts: a return to the Italian source', *Industrial and Corporate Change*, 8: 36–47.

Marini D. (ed.) (2002), *Il lavoro come itegrazione possibile: gli imprenditori, i lavoratori immigrati e alcune storie di lavoratori autonomi immigrati in provincial di Vicenza*, Quaderni FNE – Collana Ricerche, .6 – maggio 2002.

Molina E. (2003), *La 'globalizzazione inversa': i lavoratori immigrati nel distretto industriale della concia di Arzignano*, unpublished Masters thesis, Faculty of Political Science A.A. 2002–2003, Padua University.

Nascimben M. (1998), *Reti di imprese e sistemi industriali locali. Il caso del distretto conciario vicentino*, unpublished thesis work, Faculty of Statistics, A.A. 1997–1998, Padua University.

Partnership Equal G-local (2004), *Imprese e migrazioni nella società vicentina*, Milano: Franco Angeli.

Patto per lo Sviluppo del Distretto Vicentino della Concia (2004), Regione Veneto, documento presentato in riferimento alla legge regionale 4 aprile 2003.

Poster (2005), Osservatorio del distretto vicentino della concia, report non pubblicato, Vicenza.

RUR – Census (2002), *36° Rapporto sulla situazione sociale del paese*, Fondazione Censis.

Sorenson O. (2005), 'Social networks and industrial geography', in, U. Cantner, E. Dinopoulos and R. F. Lanzillotti (eds.), *Entrepreneurships, the New Economy and Public Policy. Schumpeterian Perspectives*, Berlin-Heidelberg: Springer.

Zaheer S. (1995), 'Overcoming the liability of foreignness', *Academy Management Journal*, 38: 341–63.

Zampiva F. (1997), *L'arte della concia: Ad Arzignano, nel Vicentino, nel Veneto e in Italia: dalle origini ai giorni nostri*, Vicenza: Egida.

Zucchella A. (2006), 'Local cluster dynamics: trajectories of mature industrial districts between decline and multiple embeddedness', *Journal of Institutional Economics*, 2: 21–44.

8 The evolution of external linkages and relational density in the Tuscan leather industry

Lorenzo Bacci (Irpet Florence), Mauro Lombardi (Florence University) and Sandrine Labory (Ferrara University)

8.1. Introduction

The internationalization of SMEs has been the subject of many studies in recent years. The exporting propensity and intensity of SMEs has been analyzed (for instance, Audretsch 2003; Westhead, *et al.* 2004), generally showing that although exporting trends of SMEs have been growing, few SMEs export. The internationalization strategies of SMEs have been shown to depend on their competencies (Gomes-Casseses 1997).

Many SMEs do not work independently but rather in clusters of various forms, and this characteristic has to be taken into account in the analysis of SME internationalization. Thus a number of studies examine the issue of clusters inserting in global chain networks, both in developed (Rabellotti 2004) and developing countries (Nadvi and Halder 2005).

The issue of the difference between isolated SMEs and SMEs inserted in clusters is a relevant one, especially for a country like Italy where a significant part of production is realized in industrial districts (ID). Overall, it appears that Italian ID follow either of two internationalization strategies (Carbonara 2002; Brioschi, *et al.* 2002; Mariotti and Mutinelli 2003; Cainelli and Zoboli 2004): a district firm affirms as a leader and specializes in the functions of marketing and distribution to international markets; or the ID establishes relationships with one or more large firms that have worldwide distribution channels.

The latter case does not appear to have been extensively analyzed yet, although the start of a relationship with a leader is likely to have profound effects on the ID. Garofoli (2003) argues that the relationship between a large firm and an industrial district is likely to have negative effects on the district, in terms of its autonomous capacity to develop, because the large firm tends to dominate the relationships.

Bellandi (2001) provides a classification of the potential links between large firms and local economies. He argues that the effects of the relationship on the local economy depend on the degree of embeddedness of the large firm. He puts forward the hypothesis that involvement in knowledge exchange and institutional building (developmental embeddedness) is more probable when the local factors are neither too weak nor too strong.

A vast literature exists on the relationships between firms, both within successful industrial districts and within geographical clusters (Johannisson, *et al.* 1994, 2002; Steinle and Schiele 2002; Belussi and Sammarra 2005). Numerous studies have shown in particular how social relationships are essential to the performance of an economic and territorial cluster (Becattini 1990; Garofoli 1992, 2003; Audrestch and Feldman 1996) and to entrepreneurship in general (Johannisson 2003). Other studies have centred attention on the role of trust (Nooteboom 1999, 2002, 2004; Dei Ottati 2003; Bathelt, *et al.* 2004; Mistri 2003), while theoretical analyses have examined the dynamics of industrial districts and of local production systems in terms of knowledge creation and exchange (Maskell and Malmberg 1999; Lombardi 2003; Sammarra and Belussi 2006).

This paper focuses on the evolutionary processes that have affected local productions systems composed of many small economic units gravitating around numerous leading firms. Recently, the changing competitive context has implied changes in existing relationships; in addition, new leaders have arrived and local firms have established new types of relationships.

Evolutionary processes are thus interesting to study in the cases we have chosen, and this is what this chapter does, at both a theoretical and an empirical level.

Regarding the theoretical level, we examine the nature, content, scope and structure of relationships (the topology of networks) between units operating in a production system of small firms. Section 8.3 examines a more general theoretical framework, based on the concepts of relational topology, connective geometry and modularity.

Regarding the empirical level of our research, we analyze the case of three local production systems in a particular Italian region, Tuscany, and a particular sector, the 'fashion' sector, in order to provide empirical insights on the effects of the development of business relationships between SME clusters and large firms. The production systems we examine represent interesting cases because they include various types of SMEs and of relationships: some SMEs have been working independently, directly selling on the final market, some SMEs have had relationships with leading firms for a long time and some have only recently started relationships with them. As shown below, the survey allows us to analyze the evolution of the relationships between firms since it contains questions about the changes in recent years and the changes since the start of a relationship with leading firms.

Leading firms can be characterized on the basis of three elements: (1) medium to large dimension, coupled to holding a large share of the final market; (2) the origin (local area or outside); and (3) length of local presence. Firms possessing the three properties are the main focus of our analysis and we call them 'local leaders'. The leading firms that only recently started activity within the local production systems are grouped into the heading of 'other leaders'.

The study of the structuring and evolving process of topology of networks among different firms is based on a survey of SMEs and leaders in three territories in Tuscany, namely the area of Florence and that of Arezzo and the leather production district of Santa Croce. We consider the entire leather 'filière', meaning the production process from leather production (SMEs in the Santa Croce district) to the production of leather products (bags, belts, etc.) and footwear in the SME systems of Florence and Arezzo (that operate in the luxury segment of the market).

The chapter is organized as follows. Section 8.2 presents the theoretical framework, centred on the concepts of connective geometry and relational topology. A general schema is proposed for the analysis of the production cycle. The data set and methodology are described in Section 8.3, while the empirical evidence regarding the industrial district producing leather is presented in Section 8.4 and that regarding the two SME systems producing leather goods and footwear is presented in Section 8.5, together with the morphology of the networks led by leaders with their first and second-tier suppliers (Section 8.6). Section 8.7 provides a conclusion.

8.2. The theoretical framework

The first part of our research is a theoretical analysis that allows us to clarify basic concepts and analytical devices, such as relational topology, connective geometry, modularity and other factors (such as social capital) affecting the evolution of relationships within the local production systems.

We examine the structure of SME networks organized around leaders that use stable relationships with productive entities localized in geographically limited areas. We analyze both physical (supply of components or whole product) and intangible (information, trust) aspects of relationships.

The theoretical background of our analysis comprises different dimensions. The economic space that we examine is composed of interactions between agents which operate within a given production cycle, the output of which is a given good. The action space of agents and their interactions define a field of inquiry, within which a primary role is assigned to the typology of the connections linking operative units. The *geometry of connections* is the theoretical and analytical framework of our research aimed at reconstructing and representing the set of relationships and associations between agents.[1] This means raising questions such as: what types of links exist between firms? What are their determinants? How do they change? What are the variables influencing their evolution?

Within this general framework, we identify the nature and the temporal and spatial distribution of the links between economic units. The temporal stability or variability of relationships and the proximity of interacting agents, together with the modes of development of the links allow us to determine the *relational topology* (Lomi 1991) or *topology of the world* under study (Kephart 1994). We use the concept of '*world of production*' defined by Salais and Storper (1992), i.e. the combination of a particular type of product with particular demand and technological conditions.[2] The 'world' of specialized and dedicated products, which are typical of local production systems, meets the requirements of consumers in markets where demand is 'volatile, variable and based on a wide spectrum of product quality'.

The networks we examine are production networks. The production cycle[3] can be conceived as a sequence of states or phases that inputs must go through in order to match the features of final products with market requirements. Thus any set of phases can be defined as a 'state space'. Each phase parameter (i.e. a feature of a product component) is a point within this multi-dimensional space, within which a trajectory develops between the initial idea and the final realization.

By drawing upon the literature on the modularity theory of the firm (Langlois and Robertson 1995; Baldwin and Clark 1997; Langlois 2002) we conceive a phase as a combination of tasks generating components or partial outputs which must be adapted in order to correspond to other partial outputs and lead to the final product. In this way production phases are viewed as modules of competencies; that is, sets of encapsulated information and knowledge, which in turn develop on the basis of incoming information flows.[4] Different degrees of tacit and codified knowledge characterize the evolution of phases, while their interactions vary according to the behaviour of knowledge and organizational coordinators (also called 'system integrators') (Brusoni and Prencipe 2001). Beyond that, we can enrich the framework by further decomposing each module into sub-modules, i.e. sets of elementary tasks.

In reality possible trajectories are numerous, depending on the possibilities for interactions between phases, for duplications (in parallel or in network) and for physical and information exchange. It is therefore possible to design a linear trajectory, or more or less complex trajectories, depending on the feasible combinations. Feedback loops which do not modify the linear sequence can also be introduced. Other loops could emerge, for example by introducing non-linearities in the global transformation process.

Generally speaking, the production cycle can be organized either as a compact and one-way system or as a set of modules which are distributed in the territory and interact in various ways.

The patterns which have been analyzed, in the literature, range from the 'Chandlerian' models (unitary and multidivisional firm) to the 'Marshallian' ones (industrial districts) and to the more general 'modular network form' (Sturgeon 2002). Within the third form, four cases are distinguished: (1) the Japanese model defined as hierarchical and 'captive', because the suppliers are involved through medium and long-term contracts and cross shareholding; (2) the German network whereby firms of different sizes interact thanks to dense contracting relationships, based on 'self-reliance', within a context of complex economic and financial relationships between banks and firms; (3) the Italian model of 'egalitarian, cooperative' network; and (4) the new American model whereby distinct and decentralized firms share the productive capacity provided by autonomous suppliers able to produce goods using specific competencies and resources.

A production cycle therefore has a range of possible organizational architectures, each of which is based on relationships and interactions between phases and modules as defined above and realized by more or less distinct operative units.[5] In other words, a vertically integrated cycle has zero modularity while modularity is maximum in completely distributed cycles.

The analysis of relationships should include the consideration of an important element, namely the social capital. The concept was first used by Jacobs (1961) and

Loury (1977) and does not have a consensual and universal definition (Anderson and Jack 2002; Sobel 2002; Adler and Kwon 2002; Durlauf and Fafchamps 2003). For our purpose we use the description by Sobel (2002: 139): 'social capital describes circumstances in which individuals can use membership in groups and network to secure benefits'. The social capital exists in a context in which 'understood, socially shared and observed, self-sustaining rules of behaviour' (Sobel 2002: 148) emerge. This means that fundamental ingredients are trust, cooperative norms of behaviour and association between entities, information symmetries and repeated interactions (Knack and Keefer 1997). Existing studies tend to reduce the concept to only some of its dimensions. Thus Knack and Keefer (1997) and Dakhli and De Clercq (2004) measure trust and 'civic norms' in various countries and show that there exists a positive correlation between social capital and economic performance. Within the framework of game theory, Annen (2003) builds a model which demonstrates that cooperative networks have a higher capacity to communicate thanks to their 'inclusiveness'. Information flows and the types of interactions play an important role in both approaches.

Adler and Kwon (2002) review the literature on social capital from different perspectives (sociology, management studies and economics) and distinguish two sets of definitions: one set defines social capital as deriving essentially from the structure of relationships between actors, while the other set defines social capital as mainly resulting from the type of relationships (nature, content, scope). In this paper, we analyze both aspects of relationship, namely structure and type. For the case of the two production systems in Florence and Arezzo, that produce leather goods and footwear, i.e. final goods, we compute an indicator of the social capital in order to assess the effects of the relationship with the leaders on this variable; local SMEs had many of the characteristics of industrial districts before the arrival of leaders (dense relationships, high social capital) and the survey data allow us to assess the changes induced by the presence of the leaders. The case of the Santa Croce ID producing leather, hence raw material to the other two systems, is very different, as we shall see below.

8.3 Data and methodology

Before showing the results of our empirical analysis, we explain data and methodology in more detail in this section.

The empirical analysis aims at tackling three particular questions: (1) whether and how different structures of relationships among firms arise on the basis of information flows and other factors such as social capital; (2) what types of information (technical, financial, market) are exchanged at the local level and what is the intensity of the relationships; and (3) what type of morphology, if any, characterizes the networks and how have they evolved during the period under study.

We use a database built at IRPET (Regional Institute for economic planning of Tuscany), a regional research centre located in Florence, Italy, on the basis of several surveys of the firms in the sector we are concerned with.[6] Regarding the two systems producing final products, a survey of both SMEs and leaders in the fashion sector was conducted in 2002 and 2003. Firm managers were asked questions about both firm characteristics (how production is organized, the skill level of the workforce, company status, age of the firm, and so on) and what type of relationships they develop with other firms in the local area and outside.[7] Questions regarded both actual situation and changes (in the last three years; since the start of a relationship with a leader; etc.). The local production systems have been chosen because of their high degree of specialization in leather goods and footwear: the firms in the two areas represent about 11 per cent of the firms operating in the footwear sector in the region (Tuscany) and 77 per cent of firms operating in the regional leather goods sector; the two areas represent 15 per cent of the employees in the footwear sector and 79 per cent of the employees of the leather goods sector in the region.

The questionnaire was submitted to all members of the local industrial association, of which about 28 per cent responded. The final sample thus contains 155 SMEs that declare to work for 55 leaders. These SMEs are small or very small: the average dimension is 16 employees, with two-thirds of the sample of size 1–15 employees. These firms are essentially in the leather good sector (80 per cent of the firms are in this sector) and in the Florence area (78 per cent).

The leaders have worldwide recognized brands. Some of them have a local origin and have been present in the region for a long time (for instance, Gucci, Ferragamo, The Bridge); some are of local origin but have built or rebuilt relationships rather recently (for instance, Prada in the Arezzo area) and some originate in the rest of Italy (such as Fendi and Dolce and Gabbana) or abroad (for example, Dior or Chanel) and have set up relationships with local SMEs recently.

We have decided to focus attention on three local leaders (Gucci, Prada and Ferragamo) and compare them with leaders originating either from outside the region or abroad, that we group into the category 'other leaders'. The main reason for this choice is that these leaders were interviewed so that we have extensive information on their networks, from both their point of view and that of their suppliers.

A taxonomy of the SMEs was performed (Labory and Zanni 2004), grouping the firms in various categories: 'independent' firms directly sell on the final market and represent 5 per cent of the SMEs; all other firms are suppliers, differently classified as: (1) 'simple suppliers' that do not develop products on their own and only execute orders from the buyer (34 per cent of the total sample); (2) 'phase suppliers' that do not develop products, but tend to execute orders from the buyer with a certain degree of autonomy in deciding how to organize and perform the work (37 per cent of the sample); (3) 'partner suppliers' that develop products and generally have closer relationships with their buyers, in the sense of more intense collaboration and exchange of ideas, but not necessarily co-design (10 per cent); and (4) 'mixed suppliers', which are partners that also directly sell on the final market, thereby developing marketing capabilities (14 per cent).

We examine the links between SMEs and leaders on the basis of SMEs' answers regarding whether and which leaders they work for and whether they are direct suppliers of leaders. We know how many suppliers SMEs have but we do not know their name. Thus we know which firm indirectly works with each leader, but we do not know who is the direct supplier they work with. Hence we derive network information from the data we have but we do not have a good network data set that would have required carrying out the survey with this purpose in mind. However, we think we are able to recover a good set of information on the relationships and the networks, which we classify according to social network analysis parameters. In addition, the information obtained from the direct interviews of the leaders allows us to be confident that our results represent the true leaders' networks well.

We perform basic descriptive statistical analysis and build indicators of the various characteristics of relationships: nature, content and scope. Indicators lose information but have the advantage of measuring the phenomena using different dimensions: for instance, social capital is assessed using six dimensions (each corresponding to a different question; see the Appendix) instead of single proxies as in the literature (as mentioned above). Another advantage derives from the fact that answers to surveys are often biased because of the respondents' subjectivity (exaggeration of positive aspects of business) and interpretation; using different questions allows controlling for such subjectivity or error of interpretation.

We stress that since we do not have a random sample of SMEs, we do not try to make inferences on the population of SMEs of the two areas chosen. We only aim at describing what the data say on the leaders' networks, using in addition the information provided by the leaders' interviews.

Using this methodology, we are thus able to address the following research questions: do most of the SMEs work for leaders, or are they mainly independent? Has this pattern changed recently; that is, in particular, have they become more dependent on leaders in recent years? What type of relationships do the leaders develop with their suppliers? Do the suppliers maintain autonomy of decision, especially regarding design, or do they simply execute orders from the leaders? Are the relationships exclusive, in the sense that SMEs work for one leader and not more?

A particular point must be emphasized: the three territories significantly differ as to both the configurations of relationships between firms and the connections with the markets (local, national and international). Exactly these conclusions can be derived from the study of the Santa Croce ID, where a sample of 23 SMEs was interviewed with a similar questionnaire, allowing us to get insights on the relationships within and outside the district. The next section contains the specific results of the analysis developed by going upstream in the 'filière'.

8.4 The 'first step' of the leather filière: results on the Santa Croce ID

The 23 SMEs interviewed in the Santa Croce district have an average dimension of 36 employees and present an employment structure typical of labour-intensive firms: 71 per cent of the total number of employees on average are blue collar. These firms are the members of the local business association that agreed to answer the questionnaire. They usually are among the best performing firms of the district.

The frontiers of the firms are relatively extended, since a large part of the firm develops productive and commercial relations with other firms located in the district and beyond, often with formalized links (Table 8.1). All the 23 interviewed firms hold shares of at least one other firm. These groups of firms extend essentially within the ID (only one firm holds shares in a firm located outside the ID). Hence the firms in this leather district appear to be related by links that differ from the traditional ID links, whereby firms are legally and economically independent. Regarding commercial relations, the Santa Croce firms in the sample commercialize about 58 per cent of revenue in Italy (Table 8.2).

The degree of internationalization is relatively low. The market of the Santa Croce firms is quite captive and consists in firms located in various Italian regions with sustained demand. Hence the push for internationalization is not as high as for the firms located downstream in the leather filière. The Santa Croce ID results are linked to the SMEs of the Florence and Arezzo systems that we analyze subsequently, but it does not depend on them, since it also sells to the rest of Italy.

In the rest of Italy, the Santa Croce firms predominantly sell in the regions where the leather goods and footwear production is concentrated, namely Marche, Veneto and Lombardy (Table 8.3). Among the firms selling abroad, the main markets appear to be China, Germany and France, followed by Korea. Hence the Santa Croce ID appears to have become a supplier of Asian producers of leather goods and footwear.

In terms of type of clients, the leather producing firms that have stable relationships with leaders represent about 74 per cent of the sample. Hence a number of leaders buy directly in the Santa Croce district to provide raw materials to their suppliers producing the bag, shoes, or other leather goods. However, they represent on average 15 per cent of the total revenue of the Santa Croce firms.

In fact, leather producing firms are quite independent from the buyers because they hold specific tacit (or codified and secret) knowledge of the various means of working leather in order to obtain a particular quality for making a bag or a shoe. That knowledge is specific not to the firm but to the district, since relations between firms imply that this type of knowledge is diffuse within the district. Some leaders

Table 8.1 Relationships in the leather ID (shares)

Number of firms in the sample	Number of firms where they have shares	Localization of the firms where they have shares	
		In the district	Outside the ID
9	1	100%	0%
3	2	100%	0%
5	3	100%	0%
4	4	94%	6%
1	5	100%	0%
1	11	100%	0%

Table 8.2 Revenue according to geographical market

	average	*St. Dev*
Local Market (S. Croce-Valdarno Inferiore)	11.2	22.1
Regional non local market	17.0	19.9
National non Tuscan market	30.5	21.4
International market	41.3	25.8
Total	100%	

Table 8.3 Main markets (percentage of firms citing the region/country as among the first three markets)

Italian regions	*% firms*	*Countries*	*%firms*
Marche	61%	China	52%
Veneto	39%	Germany	35%
Lombardy	26%	France	35%
Campania	22%	Korea	30%
Emilia Romagna	17%	USA	26%
Trentino	4%	Spain	26%
Piemonte	4%	Japan	22%

have acquired leather producing firms in order to acquire that specific knowledge, but they could not impede knowledge flowing throughout the district.

In conclusion, suppliers of raw materials (leather) tend to diversify their markets and are not exclusively linked to particular buyers. The results are different in the subsequent stages of the filière, namely the production and commercialization of leather products that we analyze in more details in the subsequent sections. The subsequent phases of the leather filière present in Tuscany are much more inter-related and this is the reason we analyze them together in the next section.

8.5 Network relationships in the final stages of the leather filière: nature, content, scope and morphology

8.5.1 Nature of the relationships

The relationships between firms are essentially transactions made between formally independent firms. The cross-shareholding between the firms in the sample is not significant: on average less than 20 per cent of the SMEs hold shares of other firms, and about 3 per cent are partially owned by other firms. Hence they do not constitute groups as defined in Iacobucci (2002).

In addition, relationships between firms mainly relate to the production field. Firms were asked whether they have stable agreements with other firms in the local area and outside. Generally, few firms declared having such agreements: 4.5 per cent have agreements for the commercialization of products; 2.6 per cent for research or development. However, 44.5 per cent have productive agreements and only 2.6 per cent of the SMEs have informal relationships on issues of general interests (meetings organized by the Chamber of Commerce or by local institutions, etc.). The major aim of relationships therefore seems to be the improvement of production.

Regarding the stages of the production process, information is provided by the survey on which of the following phases firms cover: design and planning; paper models; sampling and prototypes; preparation, assembly; trimming; control; and packaging. Table 8.4 shows the phases covered as a function of the type of firm.

All independent firms cover the whole production process, except for one that externalizes some phases (assembly and trimming). Some partner firms declare they do not cover the design phase, but they externalize this phase either partly or

Table 8.4 Phases of the production process covered by the SMEs (percentage of total; n=155)

Category of suppliers:	Simple	Phase supplier	Partner	Mixed	Indep.	Total
Phases covered:	(n=53)	(n=57)	(n=16)	(n=22)	(n=7)	(n=155)
Only assembly or only preparation	29	5	19	0		14
Trimming + assembly (or other two phases which are not among the first three)	25	7		4,5		12
Preparation + trimming + assembly (or other three phases which are not among the first three)	13	19		4,5		12
Preparation + trimming + assembly + control or packaging	17	30	19			19
Sampling and prototypes + other phases (assembly to packaging)	6	16		9		9
Paper models + sampling and prototypes + other phases (assembly to packaging)	6	18	19	14	14	13
All the eight phases	4	5	43	68	86	21
Total	100	100	100	100	100	100

completely. Some simple and phase suppliers declare covering the design phase, although these categories are defined as firms which do not develop products. This is due to their particular situation. For instance, one of these firms declares to be operating in the leather goods sector and supplies wallets to a leader that imposes its specifications, while it also produces parts of shoes that it may partly design. We checked for consistency and found that in most cases these firms mistakenly answered that they covered the design phase. Generally, however, the more the supplier simply executes orders, the less numerous the phases it covers. In addition, and as expected, partners and mixed suppliers are more likely to cover all the phases of the production cycle.

8.5.2 Content of the relationships

We analyze the type of information exchanged, dividing it into: (1) technical and productive information; (2) market information; and (3) financial information. An indicator was computed for each of these aspects, indicating whether the exchange of information is low, medium or high. The first indicator was computed using data on the degree to which the buyer provides equipment and technology, controls quality and provides raw material (see Appendix for details). The other two indicators were computed using one question only (due to a lack of other relevant questions): the indicator of market information exchange is based on whether the volume of market information exchanged between the firm and the leader has risen in the last three years,[8] while the financial information indicator is based on firms' indication of whether they receive financial help from their buyer (we chose questions which all sample firms answered).

Table 8.5 reports the results. The first six columns distinguish direct suppliers according to their network, while the last two columns distinguish between direct (first-tier) and indirect (second-tier) suppliers. The exchange of technical and productive information is more intense for first-tier suppliers than for the other tier: the intensity is medium or high for 73 per cent of first-tier suppliers and for 29 per cent of the other tier. Comparing the various networks, intensity appears higher in the networks of the 'local' leaders, relative to the other leaders and to independent firms. Among the local leaders, intensity is highest in the network of Gucci (91 per cent medium-high), followed by Prada (76 per cent) and Ferragamo (75 per cent). Local leaders have been present in the area for a long time and are therefore more locally embedded than other leaders.

Embeddedness is here taken as referring to the fact that 'economic action is affected by actors' dyadic relationships and by the structure of the overall network of relations' (Granovetter 1992: 33): hence embedded means here being inserted in the socio-economic context. It seems therefore that:

1 the larger the buyer, the more intense the exchange of technical and productive information;
2 the more locally embedded the leader, the more intense the exchange of technical and productive information.

Market information appears quite intensively exchanged since the percentage of firms receiving a lot of such information is generally higher than for the previous type of information; as shown in Table 8.5, this is true especially in other leaders' networks. However, this indicator has to be interpreted with care given that it is based on one question only and measures whether information on markets provided by the leader has increased in the last three years. One can expect that firms working for other leaders answer positively to this question, given that they have established relationships recently. Interviews with leaders confirm that exchange of market information only concern partners. Regarding financial information, information exchange is never intense, since only a few leaders provide financial help to their suppliers: mainly Gucci and Prada. Hence we conclude that information exchanged mainly relate to productive and technical aspects.[9]

Table 8.5 shows that stability is also generally high since the average number

Table 8.5 Characteristics of relationships: indicators of intensity of information flows by type (technical and productive, market and financial information), of frequency and of stability of relationships (percentage of firms)

	Gucci	*Prada*	*Ferrag*	*Other Leaders*	*Indep.*	*Direct suppliers*	*Indirect Suppliers*
	(n=49)	*(n=40)*	*(n=24)*	*(n=72)*	*(n=7)*	*(n=90)*	*(n=62)*
Information:							
Technical and productive							
– Low intensity	9	24	25	36	73	27	71
– Medium intensity	74	71	62	59	27	65	24
– High intensity	17	5	13	5	0	8	5
Total	100	100	100	100	100	100	100
Market (percentage of firms with high intensity)	50	42	25	54	40	41	12
Financial (percentage of firms with high intensity)	13	20	0	5	0	9	3
Frequency of relations (percentage of firms with high frequency)	48	62	25	32	37	39	15
*Stability**	14	11	12	11	10	11	8

* Average number of years of the relationships with the leader.

of years for which firms have been working with the leader is 11 years for direct suppliers and eight years for indirect ones. Stability of the relationships between the SMEs and their suppliers is also high, because 98 and 100 per cent have always or almost always the same suppliers of raw material and components respectively. Prada is the only leader that connects to its suppliers via intranet, and therefore the frequency of information flows is higher in this network (given that other means of information exchange are also intensively used): high frequency characterizes 62 per cent of its suppliers. The frequency is higher for direct than for indirect suppliers.

Other parameters used in the analysis of the nature of relationships include specificity and strength. Regarding the former, the specificity of relationships is not high since many SMEs are related to various leaders. Regarding strength, one indicator used is the extent of interpersonal relationships in the area, which does not appear significant in the areas we examine. Another indicator is social capital (see below).

8.5.3 Scope of the relationships

The degree to which firms are involved in the relationships with their buyer can be used to estimate the degree of reciprocity of flows. In our case, the more the buyer imposes requirements or constraints on the supplier, in terms of product specification and some managerial aspects, the more the information flow is unidirectional, i.e. less reciprocal. At the same time a low reciprocity reflects authority in the relationship. Using the answers of the questions relating to the way in which the firm works with its buyer, we constructed an indicator of reciprocity, with the usual three levels (low, medium, high) (see Appendix).

The results are presented in Table 8.6. Reciprocity is generally low since relationships are unidirectional for 57 per cent of SMEs. The categories of suppliers where low reciprocity prevails are those of simple and phase suppliers, in which respectively 75 per cent and 65 per cent of firms have unidirectional relations. Partners and mixed suppliers have more reciprocal relationships with their buyer, since reciprocity is medium or high for respectively 82 and 77 per cent of these categories.

The difference in the reciprocity of relationships between direct and indirect suppliers is not significant: reciprocity is high for about 10 per cent of firms in both cases. This suggests that suppliers have the same type of relationship with their suppliers as they have with the leaders. In fact, 81 per cent of the suppliers of the first tier (direct suppliers to leaders) in turn impose the products and the productive specifications on their own suppliers.

Table 8.6 shows the existence of a sequence of production phases centred around a central unit from which dynamic stimuli (in terms of orders) emerge. The central unit often transmits a 'complete package': model of output; translation into operative parameters that must be met, without much possibility for the operative units to interact; provision of necessary material flows; ex-post control of the assigned parameters.

Table 8.6 Reciprocity of information flows (percentage of all suppliers; n=148)

	Simple (n=53)	Phase (n=57)	Partner (n=16)	Mixed (n=22)	**Total (n=148)**	Direct (n=90)	Indirect (n=58)
Unidirectional (low reciprocity)	75	65	18	23	57	51	63
Unidirectional but with some collaboration (medium reciprocity)	19	32	69	50	34	41	26
Multidirectional (high reciprocity)	6	3	13	27	9	8	11
Total	100	100	100	100	100	100	100

Notes
Low reciprocity indicates a situation where information essentially flows from the leader to the SME, the leader having large authority in the relationship. Reciprocal flows indicate co-decision.

In this way the networks are centred on the leaders that play the role of engines, in the sense that they feed the activities of the supplying firms with their orders. Leaders have authority in the relationships, imposing their requirements.[10] Interestingly, this low reciprocity reproduces in the relationships between the SMEs and their suppliers, since the relationship between first-tier and second-tier suppliers is unidirectional in 75 per cent of cases.

The local production systems can therefore be viewed as sets of hierarchical network machines, whose engines are leaders that distribute selected techno-productive information. In other words, information packages spread according to a cascade model, within which technical constraints on activities become more and more stringent. The degree of freedom reduces as the production cycle is further decomposed into modules and sub-modules.

A last point on reciprocity regards the difference across networks. Table 8.7 presents the degree of reciprocity of relationships according to the network and the suppliers' tier. The first result is that the reproduction of the unidirectionality of relations between leaders and their suppliers to the relations between first-tier and second-tier suppliers is confirmed: apart from networks of independent firms, networks of leaders are characterized by a much lower reciprocity between the first and the second tiers than between the leader and the first tier. The networks with highest reciprocity are those of other leaders and of independent firms, where respectively 64 and 82 per cent of firms have relationships with medium or high reciprocity.

As lower values of reciprocity characterize networks centred on leaders, while more 'egalitarian' relationships are typical of the other networks, it appears that hierarchical networks centred on the leading firms show higher degrees of unidirectionality compared with the networks organized around independent firms.

Table 8.7 Reciprocity of relations in the various networks (n=148)

	Gucci (n=49)	Prada (n=40)	Ferrag (n=24)	Other (n=72)	Suppliers of independent firms (n=18)
Direct suppliers					
Low reciprocity	61	48	50	36	18
Medium reciprocity	35	42	38	50	55
High reciprocity	4	10	12	14	27
Total	100	100	100	100	100
Indirect suppliers					
Low reciprocity	73	67	75	64	43
Medium reciprocity	19	11	25	25	28.5
High reciprocity	8	22	0	11	28.5
Total	100	100	100	100	100

Notes
Low reciprocity indicates a situation where information essentially flows from the leader to the SME, the leader having large authority in the relationship. Reciprocal flows indicate co-decision.

The last parameter of the nature of relationships is trust. We examine this aspect by computing an indicator of the social capital used and built (or embedded according to Uzzi 1997 and Larson 1992) in relationships (see the Appendix for details on the indicator). We measure social capital by its effects (trust, cooperative relations) rather than its source.

We may underestimate social capital since we rely on respondents' awareness of the importance of knowledge and of trust in local operators.

For instance, we used the question: 'do you consider the knowledge of local operators as a strength for your business?'; some respondents may answer negatively although they have extensive knowledge of local operators and (unintentionally) derive benefits from these relationships.

Table 8.8 shows that the level of social capital is generally quite low, since 86 per cent of the firms use a low or medium level of social capital. The difference between leaders is also very interesting. The highest percentage of suppliers with low level of social capital is that of Ferragamo. The suppliers of independent firms develop a social capital in line with the average of the sample. The lowest percentage of suppliers with high levels of social capital is that of other leaders, followed by suppliers of independent firms. Concerning sectors, the level of social capital is medium or high for 58 per cent of the firms in footwear and 45 per cent of those in the leather goods sector. Useful insights can be drawn from the analysis of the criteria of firms' choice of suppliers (Table 8.9). The main criteria mentioned by

Table 8.8 Social capital (percentage of firms)

	Low	*Medium*	*High*	*Total*
All suppliers (n=148)	52	34	14	100
Suppliers of Gucci (n=49)	53	31	16	100
Suppliers of Prada (n=40)	50	33	17	100
Suppliers of Ferragamo (n=24)	58	25	17	100
Suppliers of other leaders (n=72)	43	47	10	100
Suppliers of independent firms (n=18)	50	39	11	100

the SMEs are technical competencies followed by trust and reputation, while price and productive capacity are not primary choice criteria.

We can therefore conclude that technical and social factors prevail over economic variables. A limited set of firms appear to have embedded relationships, while for the majority of firms connections are arm's length ties (Uzzi 1997). The 'world of production' under study is therefore characterized by the existence of networks where the selection of partners and suppliers is not based on random choice; stable partnerships are systematically pursued thanks to the search for qualitative and technical standards. Trust factors and informal links are built by means of repeated interactions. We now turn to the analysis of the morphology of these networks.

8.6. Network morphology

At a broad glance the local 'world of production' appears to be a very dense and highly entangled knot of links. The linkages among economic units are spread in

Table 8.9 Percentage of SMEs in the various leaders' networks that consider the criterion as one of the three most important criteria in choosing the suppliers

	Gucci	*Prada*	*Ferrag*	*Other*	*Indep.*
	(n=49)	*(n=40)*	*(n=24)*	*(n=72)*	*(n=18)*
Technical competencies	83	81	100	84	64
Trust – reputation	52	48	44	48	36
Adaptation to changes	65	33	56	45	36
Price	22	29	37	39	18
Proximity	30	19	31	18	9
Productive capacity	22	24	19	30	18

many directions with extremely diversified strength, depending on the role each firm plays. However, denser architectures can be singled out (see Figure 8.1), that are centred on the leaders, especially Gucci, Prada and Ferragamo which we have chosen to analyze in more detail.

It is important to stress that results have to be interpreted with care since we do not have all the firms belonging to each leader's network.

The network representation we propose does not necessarily reflect the real networks of the leaders, as the inquiry covers a large, but not exhaustive subset of suppliers belonging to different networks. However, we have complementary information from the interviews that were conducted with the three leaders we focus on, which confirm the main characteristics we outline below. So information collected from different sources converges and allow us to point out important differences in the network topology of the three leaders. The structure of the Gucci network is represented in Figure 8.1. Gucci's architecture is highly concentrated. Gucci imposes the model and the details of the work that its suppliers execute. Apart from partners, Gucci's suppliers are not involved in product development or in strategic decision making. The network has a star form and is not a total network, where all actors are related to one another. The Prada network is illustrated in Figure 8.2.

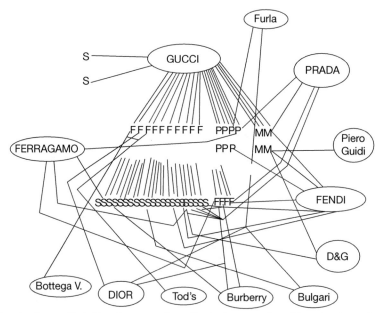

S = simple suppliers; F = phase suppliers; P = partner suppliers; M = mixed suppliers

Figure 8.1 Gucci's network.
    Source: IRPET Survey (Bacci 2004).

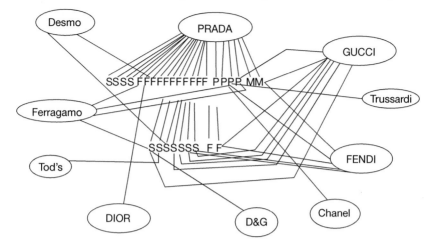

S = simple suppliers; F = phase suppliers; P = partner suppliers; M = mixed suppliers

Figure 8.2 Prada's network.
   Source: IRPET Survey (Bacci 2004).

Prada's network is less hierarchical than that of Gucci in that Prada appears to prefer connecting directly with suppliers rather than having more tiers of suppliers. The Ferragamo network is represented in Figure 8.3. The partners of Ferragamo never work exclusively for this leader. This network differs from the previous two in essentially two respects. First, Ferragamo's suppliers have more links with other leaders; second, these links regard all tiers of suppliers, while in the first two cases the second tier has more additional links with other leaders than the first one.

Table 8.10 provides additional information on the structure of networks. The Gucci network appears as more hierarchical than the other two in that 42.9 per cent of its suppliers are direct suppliers, against more than 70 per cent of the suppliers of both Prada and Ferragamo. The second tier is therefore relatively less significant for the other two leaders, which seem to prefer direct relationships. Gucci also appears as more exclusive in that the links of its suppliers with other leaders are less numerous. The number of links set up by the suppliers of Gucci with other leaders in proportion to the total number of suppliers is lower than those set up by suppliers of Prada and Ferragamo: 22.4 per cent for Gucci, against 30 and 45.8 per cent respectively for Prada and Ferragamo.

The above analysis together with the in-depth interviews of the three leaders imply that the network of Gucci has a hierarchical star form, while the other networks are also hierarchical but with a differentiated relational intensity. The local 'world of production' is therefore characterized by the simultaneous presence of network systems with overlaps between modular configurations, implying a significant degree of redundancy, which allows the production systems to flexibly

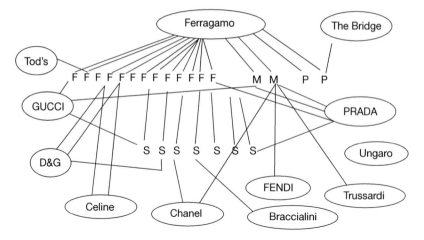

S = simple suppliers; F = phase suppliers; P = partner suppliers; M = mixed suppliers

Figure 8.3 Ferragamo's network.
Source: IRPET Survey (Bacci 2004).

Table 8.10 Some comparison of Gucci, Prada and Ferragamo networks

	Gucci	*Prada*	*Ferragamo*
	(n=49)	*(n=40)*	*(n=24)*
Ratio number of links of suppliers with other leaders and number of suppliers	57.1	80.0	83.3
Ratio number of other leaders the network has links with and number of suppliers	22.4	30.0	45.8
Percentage of direct suppliers relative to total number of suppliers	42.9	70.0	70.8

use technical and operative modules. Strategies appear to be defined centrally and to generate impulses in the local context that are transmitted to various but compatible and complementary architectures. The local production system of SMEs appears to represent a knowledge base, a kind of 'substratum', composed of a set of competencies, on which the leaders draw by setting up links with the various firms.

If the relationship with a leader implies an increasing dependency on an authoritative buyer, why do SMEs maintain such relationships across time? A survey question on what happens after the start of a relationship with a leader allows us to provide insights on this point. The SMEs declare that, after the start of the relationship with a leader:

- profits have increased (especially for suppliers of Gucci and Prada);
- the firm has grown (the number of employees has increased in more than half of the suppliers working for the local leaders, while it has tended to reduce after the beginning of a relationship with leaders originating outside the region);
- the range of products has increased, especially for suppliers of Gucci and Prada (about 64 per cent of suppliers see their product range increase after the start of the relationship, and this percentage rises to 71.4 per cent for suppliers of Gucci and 82.5 per cent for suppliers of Prada, while the percentage is respectively 52.9 and 58.6 for suppliers of Ferragamo and other leaders);
- the skill level of the workforce has increased in more than 80 per cent of the SMEs working for leaders;
- the number of spin-offs from former employees is generally stable and reduces for some suppliers only in the network of Gucci;
- about 17.4 per cent of suppliers working for leaders abandon their own brand after the start of the relationship, and this percentage is higher for suppliers of local leaders than for suppliers of foreign leaders;
- about 12 per cent abandon product research and development, but this percentage is lower in the networks of Gucci and other leaders;
- about a third introduce new technologies;
- about a quarter introduce new materials after the start of the relationship with a leader.

Hence it appears that working with a leader guarantees performance (profit and firm growth) and increases innovation (acquisition of new material, new products and new technologies), although some reduction in autonomous capacity of product development and marketing occurs. This is especially true for suppliers of Gucci, which is the leader with longer local presence. SMEs therefore appear to prefer relationships with leaders rather than directly selling on markets in order to guarantee performance.

Leaders also derive benefits from such relationships, and increasingly so as a result of the changes in the competitive environment of the last 20 years or so. The arrival of new leaders has occurred during the 1990s, when local leaders (Gucci, Prada, Ferragamo) were changing competitive strategies. Changes in the competition required the capacity to strategically anticipate events, for example by 'endogenising' demand rather than reacting to it. Therefore, the increasing need to coordinate multiple flows (of information and physical resources) has led to the design of more 'conscious' forms of coordination among sparse techno-productive modules. It is indeed increasingly important to simultaneously acquire flexibility and planning capacity in order to compete in the globalized and turbulent markets of the fashion industry.

8.7 Conclusions

In this chapter we have analyzed the relationships existing within specific production systems characterized by the presence of leaders of different origin and different dates of arrival in the local systems. We have assessed the nature, content, scope and structure of relationships between SMEs and leaders. The main conclusions of our study can be synthesized in three propositions:

1 leading firms have different network morphologies;
2 hierarchical and overlapping networks with precise dynamic properties are the drivers of evolutionary pathways;
3 leading firms draw upon a widespread 'substratum' of technical and productive competencies supplied by the local SMEs in order to complete their competitive strategies.

While relationships with suppliers of raw material, namely leather, are bidirectional, in that leather producers have specific knowledge about how to obtain particular characteristics of the leather that leaders do not have, relationships of leaders with producers of leather products (parts or complete products) tend to be unidirectional, in that the leader imposes product specification and generally also production techniques that the supplier executes.

These results are particularly significant in order to single out the evolutionary trajectories looming in the near future of the analyzed local production systems.

Following the logical sequence described in Section 8.1, we show that multilayered and partially overlapping networks exist. These networks draw upon a locally distributed 'substratum' of competencies which were initially accumulated within handicraft units. Exchanged information is mainly of the technical and productive type and is organized in such a way that hierarchical networks are able to control multiple flows of input and phase parameters in order to match the features of the product with the previously elaborated design. These networks are characterized by a 'central unit' able to process general information (concerning markets, type of products, technology, etc.) and a sequence of distributed layers of suppliers, among which information diffuses according to a 'cascade model' with stronger constraints down the production cycle. At the bottom lies a local substratum of craftsmanship and at the vertex lie units which realize successful 'aggressive' marketing strategies. This systemic configuration of local production systems is far from the traditional 'Italian model' and also quite different from the Japanese Model identified and explained by Sturgeon (2002). Hierarchical and overlapping networks have the following two main dynamic properties: (1) dominant leading firms coordinate tiers of suppliers on the basis of stable and informal relationships; (2) layers overlap. This is especially true in the last tiers, where it is very common to use some competencies belonging to different connective structures in the production cycle. In this way intense and informal flows of techno-productive information spread.

We therefore claim that an evolutionary dynamic has developed from local systems composed of dense 'dust' of small units, towards structured networks, within which a cascade model of information flows prevail. Networks of independent firms are more reciprocal than the networks centred on leaders. Therefore, it appears that as firms consolidate their links with leaders, their relationships become less and less reciprocal, not only with leaders but also with their own suppliers. Within networks centred on leaders, technical and social variables such as competencies and trust continue playing a more important role than economic factors such as cost and price, especially when the leader is more embedded locally. Social capital does not appear to reach high levels, but our measure might underestimate it for two major reasons. First, it is based on the effects of social capital rather than its source; second, it requires that firms' entrepreneurs be aware of the social capital they use.

While leaders benefit from the SME's high productive know-how, the main advantage SMEs derive from these relationships appears to be an improvement in performance (profits and growth).

These relationships also involve risks for the SMEs. First, a high dependence on leaders from whom they receive technical and productive specifications may induce them to lose autonomous capacities to develop. Second, the leaders (central units) may change localization to draw upon the substratum of competences in foreign areas. It seems that this depends on many factors: prices to a certain extent but above all on the quality of production, resulting from the accumulation of fundamental and locally embedded competencies. The differing knowledge bases and competencies of the small firms allow leaders to rapidly change product, without incurring training and time costs. This would not otherwise be possible in a sector (fashion) where products change several times during the year.

Notes

1 The theoretical framework we choose has an evolutionary root and puts at the centre of attention the cognitive dynamics of agents. See Potts (2000, 2001), Loasby (2000, 2001), Simon (1962, 2002).

2 Salais and Storper (1992), Storper (1996) distinguish between products on the basis of two dimensions: standardized versus specialized goods and generic versus dedicated goods. The first dimension refers to the technology, information and the skills necessary to produce the goods. The second dimension is based on the characteristics of demand, i.e. 'the level of anonymity and uniformity of customers'.

3 Production cycle here means the transformation process from initial ideas to product characteristics that have to match demand parameters.

4 A more general approach to the modularity theory of the firm and of productive process is developed in Lombardi (2007).

5 '*Modularity*' is a general systems concept: it is a continuum describing the degree to which a system's components can be separated and recombined, and it refers both to the tightness of coupling between components and to the degree to which the 'rules' of the architecture enable (or prohibit) the mixing and the matching of components' (Schilling 2000: 312).

6 The project was coordinated by Lorenzo Bacci (see Bacci 2004).

7 The questionnaire is available on request. .

8 If the volume has risen (decreased or remained constant), the level of the indicator is high (low or medium).

9 The questionnaire contained a question on whether SMEs receive information on market trends from the leaders. The response rate was so low (very few said yes) that we did not use this question in the construction of the indicator. Hence our market information indicator only indicates whether the volume of market information exchanged has

increased over the last three years. It has generally increased, but it remains very low in general as compared with technical and productive information.

10 Buyers impose the models and their specification without any collaboration to 63 per cent of the firms in the sample. In addition, the influence of buyers on productive and managerial decisions has increased in the last three years in 57 per cent of firms.

References

Adler P. S. and Kwon S-W. (2002), 'Social capital: prospects for a new concept', *Academy of Management Review*, 27(1): 17–40.

Anderson A. R. and Jack S. L. (2002), 'The articulation of social capital in entrepreneurial networks: a glue or a lubricant?', *Entrepreneurship and Regional Development*, 14: 193–210.

Annen K. (2003), 'Social capital, inclusive networks, and economic performance', *Journal of Economic Behavior and Organisation*, 50: 449–63.

Audretsch D. B. (2003), Introduction in D. B. Audretsch (ed.), *SMEs in the Age of Globalisation*, Cheltenham: Edward Elgar.

Audretsch D. B. and Feldman M.P. (1996), 'R&D "spillovers" and the geography of innovation and production', *American Economic Review*, 3: 630–40.

Bacci L. (ed.) (2004), *Distretti e Imprese Leader nel Sistema Moda della Toscana*, Milano: Franco Angeli.

Baldwin C. Y. and Clark K .B. (1997), 'Managing in an age of modularity', *Harvard Business Review*, September–October: 84–93.

Bathelt H., Malmberg A. and Maskell, P. (2004), 'Clusters and knowledge: local buzz, global pipelines and the process of knowledge creation', *Progress in Human Geography*, 28: 31–56.

Becattini, G. (1990), 'The Marshallian industrial district as a socio-economic notion', in F. Pyke, G. Becattini and W. Segenberger (eds.), *Industrial Districts and Inter-firm Cooperation in Italy*, Geneva: International Institute for Labour Studies, pp. 123–35.

Bellandi M. (2001), 'Local development and embedded large firms', *Entrepreneurship and Regional Development*, 13(3).

Belussi F. and Samarra A. (eds.) (2005), *Industrial Districts, Relocation, and the Governance of the Global Value Chain*, Padova: Cleup.

Brioschi F., Brioschi M. S. and Cainelli G. (2002), 'From the industrial district to the district group: an insight into the evolution of local capitalism in Italy', *Regional Studies*, 36: 1037–52.

Brusoni S. and Prencipe A. (2001) 'Unpacking the black box of modularity: technologies, products and organizations', *Industrial and Corporate Change*, 20(1): 179–205.

Cainelli G. and Zoboli R. (eds.) (2004), *The Evolution of Industrial Districts*, Heidelberg: Physica Verlag.

Carbonara N. (2002), 'New models of inter-firm networks within industrial districts', *Entrepreneurship and Regional Development*, 14: 229–46.

Dakhli M. and De Clercq D. (2004), 'Human capital, social capital, and innovation: a multi-country study', *Entrepreneurship and Regional Development*, 16: 107–28.

Dei Ottati, G. (2003), 'Exit, "voice" and the evolution of industrial districts: the case of the post-World War II economic development of Prato', *Cambridge Journal of Economics*, 27(4): 501–22.

Durlauf, S. N. and Fafchamps, M. (2003), *Empirical Studies of Social Capital: A Critical Survey*, manuscript.

Ferrucci, L. (1999), 'Il distretto industriale pratese: processi evolutivi, path-dependence e logiche di cambiamento', in F. Amatori (ed.), *Annali di storia d'impresa*, Bologna: Fondazione Assi, Il Mulino.

Garofoli G. (1992), *Endogenous Development and Southern Europe*, Aldershot: Avebury.

——. (2003), Introduzione, in G. Garofoli (ed.) *Impresa e Territorio*, Bologna: Il Mulino, pp. 9–39.

Gomes-Casseres B. (1997), 'Alliance strategies of small firms', *Small Business Economics*, 9(1): 33–44.

Granovetter M. (1992), 'Problems of explanation in economic sociology', in N. Nohria and R. Eccles (eds.), *Networks and Organisation: Structure, Form and Action*, Boston: Harvard Business School Press, pp. 25–56.

Iacobucci D. (2002), 'Explaining business groups started by habitual entrepreneurs in the Italian manufacturing sector', *Entrepreneurship and Regional Development*, 14: 31–47.

Jacobs J. (1961), *The Death and Life of Great American Cities*, New York: Random House.

Johannisson B. (2003), 'Networking e crescita imprenditoriale' in G. Garofoli (ed.) *Impresa e Territorio*, Bologna: Il Mulino, pp. 131–68.

Johannisson B., Alexanderson O., Nowicki K. and Senneseth K. (1994), 'Beyond anarchy and organization: entrepreneurs in contextual networks', *Entrepreneurship and Regional Development*, 6: 329–56.

Johannisson B., Ramirez-Pasillas M. and Karlsson G. (2002), 'The institutional embeddedness of local inter-firm networks: a leverage for business creation', *Entrepreneurship and Regional Development*, 14: 297–315.

Kephart J. O. (1994), 'How topology affects population dynamics', in C. G. Langton, *Artificial Life III. A Proceedings Volume in the Santa Fe Institute Studies in the Science of Complexity*, Reading, MA: Addison-Wesley Publishing Company.

Knack S. and Keefer, P. (1997) 'Does social capital have an economic payoff? A cross-country investigation', *Quarterly Journal of Economics*, 112: 1251–88.

Labory S. and Zanni L. (2004), 'Le formule imprenditoriali nel settore moda: caratteri strutturali e strategie competitive delle imprese protagoniste', in L. Bacci (ed.), *Distretti e imprese leader nel sistema Moda della Toscana*, Milano: Franco Angeli, pp. 33–89.

Langlois R. N. (2002), 'Modularity in technology and organization', *Journal of Economic Behavior and Organization*, 49: 19–37.

Langlois R. N. and Robertson P. L. (1995), *Firms, Markets, and Economic Change*, New York: Routledge.

Larson A. (1992), 'Network dyads in entrepreneurial settings: a study of the governance of exchange relationships', *Administrative Science Quarterly*, 37: 76–104.

Loasby B. (2000), 'Market institutions and economic system', *Journal of Evolutionary Economics*, 10: 297–309.

——. (2001), 'Time, knowledge and evolutionary dynamics: why connections matter', *Journal of Evolutionary Economics*, 11: 393–412.

Lombardi M. (2003), 'The evolution of local production systems: the emergence of the invisible mind and the evolutionary pressures towards more visible minds', *Research Policy*, 32: 1443–62.

——. (2007), 'A morphogenetic approach to the evolution of technological capabilities', in R. Leoncini and A. Montresor (eds.), *Dynamic Capabilities Between Firm Organisation and Local Systems of Production*, London: Routledge.

Lomi A. (1991), *Reti Organizzative*, Bologna: Il Mulino.

Loury G. (1977), 'A dynamic theory of racial income differences', in P. Fallace and A. LeMund (eds.), *Women, Minorities, and Employment Discrimination*, Maryland: Lexington Books.

MacKinnon D., Chapman K. and Cumbers A. (2004), 'Networking, trust and embeddedness among SMEs in the Aberdeen oil complex', *Entrepreneurship and Regional Development*, 16: 87–106.

Mariotti S. and Mutinelli M. (2003), 'L'Internazionalizzazione Passiva dei Distretti Italiani', *Economia e Politica Industriale*, 119: 139–54.

Maskel P. and Malmberg A. (1999), 'Localised learning and industrial competitiveness', *Cambridge Journal of Economics*, 23(2): 167–85.

Mistri M. (2003), 'The emergence of cooperation and the case of the Italian industrial district as a socio-economic habitat', *Human Systems Management*, 22: 147–56.

Nadvi K. and Halder G. (2005), 'Local clusters in global value chains: exploring dynamic linkages between Germany and Pakistan', *Entrepreneurship and Regional Development*, 17: 339–63.

Nooteboom B. (1999), 'Innovation, learning and industrial organisation', *Cambridge Journal of Economics* 23(2): 127–50.

——. (2002), *Trust: Forms, Foundations, Functions, Failures and Figures*, Cheltenham: Edward Elgar.

——. (2004), 'Governance and competence: how can they be combined?', *Cambridge Journal of Economics*, 28: 505–25.

Potts, J. (2000), *The New Evolutionary Microeconomics*, Cheltenham: Edward Elgar.

——. (2001), 'Knowledge and markets', *Journal of Evolutionary Economics*, 11: 413–31.

Rabellotti R. (2004), 'How globalisation affects Italian industrial districts: the case of Brenta', in H. Schmitz (ed.), *Local Enterprises in the Global Economy: Issues of Governance and Upgrading*, Cheltenham: Edward Elgar.

Salais R. and Storper M. (1992), 'The four worlds of contemporary industry', *Cambridge Journal of Economics*, 16: 169–93.

Sammarra A. and F. Belussi (2006), 'Evolution and relocation in fashion-led industrial districts: evidence from two case studies', *Entrepreneurship and Regional Development*, 18: 543–62.

Schilling M. A. (2000), 'Toward a general modular systems theory and its application to inter-firm product modularity', *Academy of Management Review*, 25(2): 312–14.

Simon H. A. (1962), The architecture of complexity, *Proceedings of the American Philosophical Society*, 196(6): 467–82.

——. (2002), 'Near-decomposability and the speed of evolution', *Industrial Corporate and Change*, 3: 587–99.

Sobel J. (2002) 'Can we trust social capital?', *Journal of Economic Literature*, March: 139–54.

Steinle C. and Schiel H. (2002), 'When do industries cluster? A proposal on how to assess an industry propensity to concentrate at a single region or nation', *Research Policy*, 31: 849–58.

Storper M. (1996), 'Innovation as collective action: conventions, products and technologies', *Industrial and Corporate Change*, 5(3): 761–90.

Sturgeon, T. J. (2002), 'Modular production networks: a new American model of industrial organization', *Industrial Corporate and Change*, 11(3): 451–96.

Uzz B. (1997), 'Social structure and competition in interfirm networks: the paradox of embeddedness', *Administrative Science Quarterly*, 42: 35–67.

Westead P., Wright M. and Ucbasaran D. (2004), 'Internationalisation of private firms:

environmental turbulence and organisational strategies and resources', *Entrepreneurship and Regional Development*, 16: 501–22.

Appendix: Construction of indicators

All indicators were constructed using questions that all firms answered (for reliability), transforming the variables that resulted from the codification of answers into binary dummies (1 or 0), summing them and defining three levels (low, medium, high) according to the levels of the sum variables.

- Indicator on exchange of technical and productive information: the SME indicates that the leader to which it supplies provides equipment and technology; controls quality; provides material; the SME indicates that it has introduced new technology since the beginning of its relationship with the leader, as well as introducing new materials; in the last three years technology transfers from the leader has increased.
- Indicator on frequency of information exchange: firms indicated whether they use frequently or not various communication means; since all firms responded frequently regarding phone calls and faxes, the indicator of frequency was computed using three dimensions: frequent direct visits, frequent exchanges via intranet and internet (thus also denoting the use of IT in the relationship).
- Indicator of reciprocity of relationships: the variables used are as follows:

1 joint definition of work and active collaboration;
2 no imposition of specifications of the work with or without collaboration;
3 no imposition of supplier(s) and provision of raw materials;
4 way in which the buyer participates in the activities of the supplier;
5 influence of the buyer in the productive and management decisions has not increased in the last three years.

Indicator of social capital: variables used:

1 criterion of trust in the choice of suppliers;
2 criterion of proximity in the choice of suppliers;
3 direct relations via spin-offs;
4 participation to the activities of business associations as a learning channel;
5 the knowledge of local operators as a strength;
6 a cooperative attitude of local operators as a strength;

The level of social capital is low when the resulting sum variable is equal to 0 or 1; medium when the sum is 2 or 3, and high otherwise.

9 Transferring entrepreneurship

The making of the cluster of Timişoara

Fiorenza Belussi (Padua University)

9.1 Introduction

In this chapter[1] we will present the so-called footwear cluster of Timişoara, which is, in fact, localised over an extended area of three Romanian western counties: Arad, Timis and Bihor. In Bihor and in Timis there has been a long tradition of shoe production since the postwar period; the county of Arad is more peripheral, and has a more recent industrialization in footwear production. The cluster took off after 1989, thanks to the entry of foreign investors, which acquired many state companies on the brink of economic collapse, or by using the modality of green-field FDI. They came to Romania mainly to explore the cost opportunity offered by local labour costs,[2] which in comparison with Western costs are very low. Today, an important share of the region's gross product is realized through shoe production. The cluster of Timişoara is not particularly specialized; the main products cover footwear items for men, women, teenagers and children. It produces shoes, sandals, boots and high boots, and some semi-finished components: soles, faces ('tomaie'), and accessories. The footwear sector does not represent the only sectoral specialization of the area because there is also a strong presence of clothing and textile firms. The cluster of Timişoara is now a satellite cluster/district (Markusen 1996) more than a Marshallian cluster, on the basis of the following indicators: it has a very low share of endogenous entrepreneurs; there is not much incremental innovation activity going on in local firms; the cluster communities' practices are still in a latent phase of development.

9.2 Historical development of the cluster

9.2.1 The socio-economic context

The cluster of Timişoara is a cluster located in the western part of Romania, which is a low-income economy.[3] In 2004, the National Gross Domestic Product was about 150.3 billion euro,[4] with 9,660,000 active workers in the country (and an official rate of unemployment of 6.3 per cent).[5] At the end of the 1990s the inflation rate was about 30 per cent. In 2001 it decreased to 17.8 per cent, in 2002 to 14.1 per cent, and in 2004 it was estimated at below 10 per cent.

Due to the cluster's location on the border with Hungary, Serbia and Austria, and due to direct cultural, historical and social links with those nations, the people living in the cluster are used to relations with foreigners and they are used to travelling abroad.

During the 1990s, the cluster attracted a lot of international business partners, in a considerably higher proportion than other Romanian regions. New industries developed following an obvious general trend to respond to the requirements of an open market economy. The economic development of the area was accompanied by a slight increase in the cost of labour, a higher cost for tangible assets, real estate assets, and financial assets. New quality standards needed to be set by local firms for marketing their own local brands (especially for the clothing IDs), in order to consolidate their national market and to ship their products into the EU markets. The cluster covers an area of 23,995 sq km which extends between Timişoara and Oradea (a distance of about 150–200 km), as shown in Figure 9.1, and has about 1,700,000 inhabitants. Three universities are established there: UAV Arad, the University of Oradea, the West University of Timişoara, and many other schools. The area has about 64,000 firms, employing local workers (estimated in 2003 as 445,888 units).[6] The area is densely industrialized (37 firms for each 1000 inhabitants), but not as much as in Italian districts, such as Montebelluna, for instance, where the density reaches 111 establishments for each 1000 inhabitants (see Chapter 5). Additionally, we have to take into account that in Italian districts the average size of firms is much smaller. In the Timişoara cluster, the local rate of unemployment is much lower than the national level, and it is officially around 3.7 per cent of the total workforce.

The number of footwear firms in the cluster is about 300 (308 in 2001), and they employ about 33,000 workers (32,588 in 2001). The Timişoara cluster represents about 12 per cent of the footwear sector in Romania (which accounts at national level for 1732 firms and 108,177 employees, 2001).[7] Sales produced by the local firms have been estimated to be around 189,000,000 euro (2001).[8] But the entire value of the Romanian production in shoes (1,517,156,000 euro, 2001) is equivalent to the sales generated by just one big Italian district – such as Montebelluna. The average sales per employee in the sector have been calculated for the year 2001 to be 14,025, on average, for the entire sector, but much lower for the cluster (5810), and even lower for our sampled firms (4215), which are mainly subcontractors of Western companies. This signifies that a kind of immiserizing growth still exists (Kaplinsky, *et al.* 2002), if after 10 years of striking expansion of firms and employment, the social mechanism of the cluster has not created diffuse wealth, as occurred in the experience of the Italian districts in the postwar period growth. The most recent figures published for the sector at national level show, for 2002, 1,726,866,000 euro of sales, 299,598,000 euro of imports, and 1,223,570,000 euro of exports (export flows are about 70 per cent of sales).[9]

In the cluster there are 20 branches of different foreign banks, which provide finance especially to foreign entrepreneurs, and support the growing businesses, mainly in their import-export operations.[10] Located in the cluster there are also three large former Romanian banks, where the major shareholders have become foreign banks, that are able to provide services for import-export operations: BRD Société Générale (French and Romanian capital), BCR (Romanian, BERD and IMF capital), and BANCPOST (Greek and Romanian capital). Venture capital is represented in the ID by the Financial Investment Company Banat-Crisana (located in Arad with branches in Timişoara and Oradea), but the opportunities to finance unquoted (unlisted and untraded) businesses[11] are small because of the restrictions imposed by the National Securities Commission on the investment companies investing in this type of company.

Another restriction is imposed by the NSC, which limits the access to capital for small and medium businesses, which operate through mutual funds. In the cluster there are problems in financing a new firm, and from our interviews it emerged that this is one of the main factors which depresses local entrepreneurship and new

Figure 9.1 Geographical map of Romania.

start-ups. Another problem is that generally the loans directed to finance capital investments are, at best, medium term. Few banks are ready to accept long-term financing contracts.

9.2.2 The cluster history

The cluster of Timişoara developed at an incredible rate of growth during the 1990s, both in terms of the number of new businesses created and volume of business generated, up to point of having the lowest unemployment rate in the country, and the highest number of private firms in the Romanian regions. Due to political reasons, after 1989, when the fall of socialist production systems was complete, there was a real boom in the privatization of the main state companies, and new entrepreneurial initiatives begun, especially in Timis County. As a result, a great number of SMEs emerged, especially in the footwear sector. According to the 'Romanian Centre for Promoting Foreign Trade', over 83 per cent of the production units existing in the cluster are SMEs, with fewer than 50 employees. This shows the lack of impediments to market entry. Even so, the industry is highly concentrated, and companies with more than 250 employees, while representing 5.3 per cent of the total enterprises, account for almost 61 per cent of total employment and sales. The origin of the cluster is rooted in a mass of state owned companies, localized in the cluster, and particularly Guban, Filty and Banatim in Timişoara, Libertatea in Arad and Solidaritatea in Oradea.

Banatim was founded in 1900 by an Austrian entrepreneur (Frankel Alfred) in Timişoara as a joint stock company, and started its operations in 1901, employing more than 500 workers. In 1928 the factory changed its name in 'Turul' and it became the largest Romanian shoe factory in Romania. In 1930 the company merged with a tanned-leather factory from Cluj. In 1948 the company was taken over by the State and its name was changed first to 'Nikos Beloiannis' and then to 'Banatul'. This company produces men's, teenager's and children's footwear (sandals, shoes, boots and high boots), shoe nails, and impregnated linen for toe caps. Today, renamed 'Banatim', it has a private local ownership, and has imposed its own brands on the Romanian market. However, it works largely as a subcontractor for Italian and German clients.

Filty was founded in 1921 on the initiative of a group of stockholders as a joint-stock company named Filty–Luxury Shoes Company of Timişoara. The aim of the company was to manufacture and market luxury leather shoes for women and men. In 1948 the company was taken over by the State and at the same time the name of the company was changed to Shoe Factory 'Stefan Plavat'. In 1959 a large design department was set up which produced about 450–500 new designs a year, used to launch into production approximately 100 new models. This firm was very successful at that time, and a large part of its production was exported to other Eastern European countries and Russia. A new plant was set up in 1974, in Recas, a commune 25 km east of Timişoara devoted to the production of sports shoes, using plastic moulding technology, and during 1976 an agreement with Adidas Company France was launched for the manufacture of sports shoes. In the 1980s production capacity reached 3.6 million shoe pairs per year, and over 275,000 sandals per year. Today, the company has retained its original name of 'Filty'. Initially, ownership was transferred to the former owners, but subsequently, through a management buyout organized by some technicians, it became a cooperative under a joint-stock company modality. It works mainly with Italian clients.

Guban S.A. originated in 1937 in Timişoara as a small chemical factory. In 1954 it began production of artificial leather, based on PVC. In 1959 it started a vertical downstream diversification creating a department for the production of ladies footwear, and, in 1961, a horizontal diversification, opening a plant for leather footwear. During that time it became the most famous Romanian brand in luxury ladies footwear.

From these three founders some spin-off firms were created, after the change of 1989, and these newly set up firms started their activity with 'lohn contracts' commissioned by foreign producers (mainly Italian from the Veneto and Marche regions) and distributors (German). But the process of ID expansion was sustained by the avalanche of foreign FDI linked to the Veneto district firms of Verona and Montebelluna, which opened up new firms in the Timişoara area. So, the transfer of entrepreneurship into the global value chain helped the Romanian cluster to become a growing area.

9.3 Some methodological notes

During 2003, 30 interviews with local firms were organized, and nine with local actors. All interviews were performed face to face and the average time for an interview was between two and two and a half hours. Out of the entire cluster, a sample of 30 firms (establishments) was selected.[12]

9.4 Firms' characteristics

In comparison with the whole cluster, our sample comprises larger firms (Table 9.1). The 30 footwear firms interviewed employ 7138 employees, and have an average dimension of 238 working units per plant, which is much higher than the typical firm (establishment) size of the Italian district firms.

Intermediate producers tend to have a smaller dimension on average (106 employees) than final producers (314). We interviewed five very small firms (1–19 employees), six small firms (20–49 employees), 12 mid-sized firms (50–249 employees), four medium–large-sized firms (249–499 employees), and three very large firms (more than 500 employees).

The rate of growth of the district, and of the firms interviewed, is impressive. Between 1999 and 2001 in the sample firms employment increased by about 32 per cent (sales of 50 per cent), and in the whole district footwear occupation levels jumped to more than 40 per cent (sales to more than 145 per cent). Given this rapid expansion, our sample accounted for 25 per cent of the whole at the starting year and in 2002 was reduced to only 15 per cent of the entire cluster. In the sampled companies the indicator sales/per employee shifted from 3743 euro to 4214 euro.

Table 9.1 Overall picture of the firms in the sample compared to the whole cluster

	Sample			Cluster			
	1999	2000	2001	1999*	2000*	2001*	
Number of establishments	30	30	30	185	234	308	
Number of persons employed	5399	6780	7138	23,282	28,162	32,588	
Sales (euro)	20,212,371	22,965,695	30,085,854	77,019,572	109,541,679	189,349,939	
Total value of investment in capital goods (euro)	17,432,551	3,097,824	4,498,141	N/A	N/A	N/A	
Average size of firms (number of employees)	180	226	238	126	120	106	

Notes
* Data Source: Romanian Ministry of Finance, www.mfinante.ro; N/A = not available.

In the cluster companies this indicator moved from 3308 euro per employed person to 5810 euro.

It is not the case that sampled firms are performing worse than the cluster companies; the lower level of productivity is simply related to the fact that they are pure 'assemblers' in the low-value segment of the global chain of subcontracting.

Nineteen companies (Table 9.2) out of the sample are final producers (14 being owned by foreign investors). Eleven companies are subcontractors (10 being owned by foreign investors). The overwhelming importance of external entrepreneurs and external capital is clear (24 firms with 4966 employees). This means that 70 per cent of the local workforce is dependent on the strategic decisions of foreign firms.

We divide firms into two categories: final producers and intermediate producers (phase firms and producers of components). Final producers are the most significant segment in our sample (19 firms with 5963 employees; average size 313 employees), in comparison with intermediate producers (11 firms with 1175 employees; average size 107 employees). Firms were mainly created after the political shock of 1989 (28), but we also interviewed two large firms' cluster founders: Banatin and Filty, which both employ more than 1000 employees. They were found to be the less dynamic firms in the cluster: they did not increase their market share or their export flows. As shown in Table 9.3, two firms out of 30 are family business companies. This differentiates the Timişoara cluster from the typical Italian districts. Twenty-seven firms (of which 24 are foreign) are private limited companies and one is a cooperative. This distribution fits perfectly with the distribution at the county and national level. The private limited company is the dominant legal form in Romania, in terms of number of companies.

Most of the foreign companies are wholly owned subsidiaries (21 with owners from Italy), and three are joint equity ventures (two with Italian owners, and one with extra-European owners).

A great number of firms activate their production cycle on the basis of the commissioning firms' specifications, and nearly all intermediate firms do not manufacture their product/tasks according to their design. This reveals the presence of a top-down hierarchical supply chain.

Table 9.2 Overall picture of the firms in the sample by criterion of selection

	Sample	
	Number of firms	*Number of persons employed*
Final producers	19	5963
(of which foreign owned)	(14)	(3796)
Subcontractors	11	1175
(of which foreign owned)	(10)	(1170)

Table 9.3 Distribution of firms (establishments) and employees by type of ownership

	Number of firms	Number of persons employed
Family or entrepreneurial company	2	15
Managerial company	4	2157
State or public body-owned company	0	
Foreign company	24	4966
Total	30	7138

Relationships with suppliers located in the cluster, but owned by Romanian firms, tend to last less on average (one to three years) than relations with cluster firms owned by European firms (more than three years), or with firms outside the cluster. These firms only sometimes build interactive transactions with commissioning firms on design and technical content. They do not rely much on the reputation of their subcontractors, but organize random visits to their workshops.

In our sample, the typology of the subcontracting firm is dominant: 28 firms fall into this category. The group is split into two groups: the group (18 firms) with few client relationships, and the group (10 firms) with many client relationships.

Most of the clients are based in Europe or in other foreign countries, and in a significant part of the sample these firms also interact with foreign-owned firms based in the area. Also, the relationship with clients seems based more on the short term than on long term, and lasts typically for two to three years. These firms only sometimes build interactive transactions with their commissioning firm on design and technical content. Local firms are not able to benefit greatly from the association with their principal clients. The positive aspect is that they obtain quick access to new product and process technology, but they are not able to absorb new management techniques.

9.5 Innovation activity

In the cluster of Timişoara, firms are generally incapable of organizing innovation activities. Out of 30 firms interviewed, only in three cases did we find the presence of the same R&D activity. The district employees in 2001 involved numbered just six persons. Only one firm in our sample recorded a patent at international level. This is correlated to the general absence of innovation activity in firms (Table 9.4).

Firms perceive that factors limiting their innovation activity are the shortage of financial resources, and the rapid imitation by neighbouring firms. But what we discovered, during the interviews, is that the small foreign multinationals located in the area did not have many knowledge linkages with other local firms. Thus, in the cluster model, the generation of spillovers is not obvious. The degrees of technology transfer depend on the absorptive capabilities of local companies, which in

Table 9.4 Innovativeness of the firms by employment size classes in the years 1999–2001

	Employment size-classes					
	1–19	*20–49*	*50–249*	*250–449*	*500+*	*Total*
Adoption of product innovation						
No innovation	3	6	8	4	2	23
Generated by the firm	2		1			3
Generated within the cluster						
Generated in the country			1			1
Generated abroad					1	1
Adoption of process innovation						
No innovation	3	6	6	4	1	20
Generated by the firm	2		2			4
Generated within the cluster			1			1
Generated in the country						
Generated abroad			1		2	3
Adoption of innovation in the organization of production						
No innovation	4	6	9	4	2	25
Generated within the firm	1					1
Generated within the cluster						
Generated in the country			1		2	1
Generated abroad						1

this case are very low, and by the existence of many subcontracting relationships, which, again, are quite infrequent in the analyzed sample. The relationships of our interviewed firms were mainly non-local.

In this cluster the spillover effects tend to be weak because firms deal in a vertical supply chain with external MNCs which work mainly on standard orders. The aim of the external MNC is primarily to use cheap labour and to quickly re-export the goods, without making any effort to upgrade the labour force (UNCTAD 1999). Our results are in line with the existing literature, which did not find much evidence of knowledge spillovers resulting from FDI investment (Chowdhury and Mavrotas 2005; Markusen and Venables 1999; Blomströ, Globerman and Kokko 1999; Blomströ and Sjoholm 1999).

Technology transfer is not just a one-way flow of knowledge (Lall 1993) from home to host country. MNCs, by contrast, can be downstream distributors of technology as much as upstream hunters of technology (Lan and Young 1996). Conversely for the host-country firms, knowledge acquisition becomes intertwined

Table 9.5 Ranking of the most relevant sources of technical knowledge (average values*)

Sources of knowledge	Rank (average values)			
	Internal	Local	National	International
Knowledge gained through in-house R&D	2.2			
Knowledge gained from continuous improvement of production processes	4.0	–	–	–
Knowledge derived from parent or subsidiary companies	3.4	–	–	–
Knowledge developed through company's internal education and training programmes	2.1	–	–	–
Knowledge embedded in experts hired on the labour market		1.9	1.5	1.9
Knowledge derived from interactions with clients and/or suppliers		2.6	2.8	3.5
Knowledge derived from cooperation with other companies		2.3	2.3	2.7
Knowledge derived from imitation of products		1.6	1.6	1.8
Knowledge embedded in technologies, licences, components, etc. acquired from outside (technological innovation)		1.6	1.4	1.5
Knowledge gained from interactions with public institutions (e.g. universities; public research centres; local government; etc.)		1.8	1.8	1.9
Knowledge gained from interactions with semi-public institutions (e.g. chambers of commerce; industry associations, trade unions, etc.)		2.0	2.0	1.9
Knowledge provided by consultants and private research centres		2.1	1.4	1.6
Knowledge gained from publicly available information (e.g. trade fairs, publications)		2.1	2.1	2.3

Note
* Evaluations could vary from 1 (not relevant) to 5 (most relevant).

with upstream and downstream activities. The question relevant for our purposes is whether these innovation-network models hold empirically also for East European clusters (Lorentzen, Mollgard and Rojec 2003). The firms in the sample are mostly followers in terms of design and innovation, and their technological competence is imported by the parent companies (Table 9.5), and slowly upgraded continuously by internal improvements.

Among the external to the firm knowledge sources, relatively high importance is placed on the item 'knowledge gained from the interaction with clients and/or suppliers'.

9.6 The globalization of the cluster

9.6.1 Commercial ID flows

Internationalization is considered one of the key factors for development in IDs. A higher circulation of products, materials and knowledge often characterizes firms concentrated in a cluster or in a district. Let us focus now on the issue of commercial flows (export and import of goods). Import and export flows to/from the cluster are active mainly with two countries: Germany and, above all, Italy.

9.6.2 International subcontracting relationships with foreign firms

In the 1999–2001 period, a rather greater part of the production is shifted to foreign countries (mainly Italy) through inward processing. As regards the sample investigated, more then 90 per cent of the production is exported with this modality, being related to international subcontracting chains. Data show a relative stability of this process during the period analyzed.

Twenty-four firms out of the 30 cluster firms analyzed represent the activities of a foreign investor. In fact, the model that emerges from the analysis of the Timişoara district is not just a simple construction of a global supply chain, but a model of internationalization of the Italian districts, which have generated a 'twin' cluster, where more labour-intensive phases of production are realized. Because Romania lacked endogenous entrepreneurship, technological know-how, and organizational capabilities of efficient shoe assembly, small entrepreneurs from the Veneto region (and in some cases from the Marche region) went directly to this area where they could find two necessary conditions: low labour costs, and a previously existing manufacturing socialization in the footwear industry with the availability of workers possessing the necessary skills. The resulting FDI is typically a greenfield investment, set up usually between 1996 and 2002. In our sample we found only one acquisition and one joint venture.

Almost all the activities of the local firms are influenced by the parent companies: the choice of the products, the type of customers served, and the suppliers, which provided intermediate parts or raw materials.

9.7 Some main conclusions on the evolutionary pattern of the cluster

The most crucial event in the evolution of the cluster was a historical accident: the Revolution of December 1989, which opened the way for the entry of foreign firms. The cluster has benefited in these years from a striking growth, but with the only result that the unemployment rate is now the lowest in the country. We cannot observe the growth dynamic which characterized the classical canonical Marshallian districts in Italy. The are no initial signs of an endogenous development, and thus of the typical mechanism of wealth distribution, which in Italy was an important social characteristic of the district model. Ten years is not a long time, but many indicators are negative, even for the local population. The cost of land is continuously increasing, and the price of utilities is increasingly closer to the EU level; the same could be said for the cost of transportation. Basically, we could argue that the wages are still reflective of an underdeveloped country (the minimum wages are below 100 euro per month, and even in the foreign companies they do not exceed, on average, 200 euro per month) but the cost of living has started to rise closer to the EU level.

The transport infrastructure is very old and poorly maintained; new investments have not supported the business environment.

The main sources of knowledge creation in the cluster are the foreign companies, but we did not find evidence of knowledge spillovers among the Romanian firms. External knowledge in Italian industrial districts has been absorbed, because firms have built international networks (an active process), not just because of the entry of multinationals (a passive mechanism). The dominant pattern of technology transfer in Timişoara is based on continuous incremental marginal improvements in assembly techniques. In the area it is still very difficult to find and hire a good and experienced shoe designer. This is because upstream activities are still organized in the older Italian districts (of the Veneto or Marche regions).

What are the real chances of local firms entering rapidly into the mechanism of local learning and upgrading?

Even large firms, here, like Filty, with more than 1000 employees, are not able to reach the international markets autonomously, and recently they have been acquired by an Italian firm.

Minute costs in Timişoara are about 0.10 euro, while in Italy they have reached 0.50 euro. So the cluster still shows a competitive advantage in terms of labour prices. But competing exclusively on costs is dangerous. China can do better, and also Korea, and Thailand too: some local firms (and some local distributors, like Exprit),[13] are now relocalizing their subcontracting chains in Asia, and Geox, the biggest Italian firm in the area, is ready to leave with its large factory to move to China.

A satellite cluster such as Timişoara is less embedded, and local firms are more volatile. In the near future, the evolution towards a Marshallian development could be possible, but we hesitate to say it is likely.

Notes

1 This work is mainly based on an empirical study in which I have participated; see the analyses of Istituto Tagliacarne (2004), Western shoes industrial district, case study, partner: Uav Arad, Roma, mimeo.

2 The net average wage is around 90–100 euro per month – FEPAIUS, Mioara Tudor, Ex-Chairman.
3 The estimated income per capita is 63.2 euro per month (see note 4).
4 The payments balance still suffers from a huge deficit. In 2004, the total export of goods and services was 19.2 billion euro, and the total import of goods and services 23.3 billion euro.
5 Romanian Statistical Yearbook (2002) and www.Economy of Romania.
6 Romanian Statistical Yearbook (2004).
7 See note 4.
8 Data source – Romanian Ministry of Finance, www.mfinante.ro.
9 Source of information: National Institute of Statistics.
10 The most important are: San Paolo IMI Bank (Italian capital), Unicredit Bank (Italian capital), Italo-Romena Bank (Italian and Romanian capital), Reiffaisen Bank (Austrian capital, Alpha Bank (Greek capital), ABN Amro Bank (Dutch capital), and HVB (Austrian capital).
11 Companies that are not listed and not traded on a regular capital market such as BVB or RASDAQ.
12 In the sample selected there is a representative mix of the composite nature of the cluster firms: large and small producers, footwear final producers and subcontractors, producers of middle and low market segments, and local and multinational firms.
13 Source: firm interview.

References

Blomströ M and Sjoholm F. (1999) 'Technology transfer and spillovers: does local participation with multinationals matter?', *European Economic Review*, 43: 915–23.
Blomströ M, Globerman S. and Kokko A. (1999) 'The determinants of host country spillovers from foreign direct investment: review and synthesis of the literature', paper presented at conference on 'Inward Investment, Technological Change and Growth', London.
Challenge of Development, Geneva: United Nations Publication.
Chowdhury A. and Mavrotas G. (2005), 'FDI and growth: a causal relationship', Research Paper UNIDO, 25.
Economy of Romania, www.Economy of Romania.
FEPAIUS, Mioara Tudor, Ex-Chairman, mimeo.
Istituto Tagliacarne (2004), 'Western shoes industrial district', case study, partner: Uav Arad, Roma, mimeo.
Kaplinsky R., Morris R. and Readman J. (2002), 'The globalisation of product markets and immiserising growth: lesson from the South African furniture industry', *World Development*, 30: 7: 1159–77.
Lall S. (1993), 'Promoting technology development: the role of technology transfer and indigenous effort', *Third World Quarterly*, 14(1): 95–108.
Lan R and Young S. (1996), 'Foreign direct investment and technology transfer: a case study of foreign direct investment in north-east China', *Transnational Corporations*, 5(1): 57–83.
Lorentzen J, Mollgard P. and Rojec M. (2003), 'Host-country absorption of technology: evidence from automotive supply networks in Eastern Europe', *Industry and Innovation*, 3: 5–20.
Markusen A. (1996), 'Sticky places in slippery space: a typology of industrial districts', *Economic Geography*, 72: 293–313.

Markusen J. and Venables A. (1999), 'Foreign direct investment as a catalyst for industrial development', *European Economic Review*, 43: 335–56.
NIESR, September, London.
Romanian Ministry of Finance, www.mfinante.ro
Romanian National Institute of Statistics, Bucharest.
Romanian Statistical Yearbook (2002).
Romanian Statistical Yearbook (2004).
UNCTAD (1999), 'World Investment Report', 'Foreign Direct Investment', New York.

10 The internationalization of the 'footwear agglomeration' of Timişoara

How deeply embedded are local firms?

Simona Montagnana (University of Varese)

10.1 Introduction

Since 1990 Romania together with other Central and Eastern European countries (CEECs) began the process of international economic integration as a consequence of trade liberalization and of new modalities of productive organization at an international level. The processes of productive delocalization and production's international decentralization initiated by developed countries' enterprises favoured the formation of industrial agglomerations or industrial clusters.

Romania in particular specialized in traditional sectors such as footwear and textiles-clothing. In this context, the internationalization of Italian district enterprises played an important role within the processes of formation and transformation of some industrial agglomerations. It is interesting to analyze the role of district enterprises in clustering processes. Still under debate is the question whether is possible to replicate the Italian district model in developing countries. Similarly the issue of sustainability of industrial clusters (characterized by the presence of foreign enterprises and by the insertion of these clusters in the new international division of labour (NIDL) (Fröbel, *et al.* 1980)) remains unanswered. There are few empirical cases that contribute to this debate. The present work is a case study research, inspired by this debate, and its objective is to offer an empirical contribution to the analysis of spatial agglomeration in Eastern European countries.

I have chosen Timişoara as empirical focus of my paper because it is one of the most important footwear production clusters in Romania and because this cluster is characterized by a conspicuous presence of Italian district enterprises. Through the story of the growth of the footwear cluster in Timişoara, the present research aims at verifying whether the Italian district enterprises are embedded in this territory and whether they replicate the district model.

The analysis of a cluster starts from the identification of its actors and its functional mechanisms. It means to study the production organization and thus the existence of local relationships. From the study of labour division at a local level (Garofoli 1983, Maillat, *et al.* 2003) and of relationships among enterprises and among enterprises and other local economic agents (institutions, trade unions, banks, etc.), it is possible to understand the level of embeddedness of the territory's enterprises (Bellandi 2001; Grabher 1993a; Granovetter 1989).

The chapter is divided in 10 sections. In Section 10.2 I lay out the theoretical debates involving two main paradigms in developing studies: the clusters and the global commodity chains (GCC) perspectives. The next section (10.3) offers a description of the footwear cluster's history. Section 10.4 discusses the methodology. These two paradigms offer a theoretical frame for this case study. Sections 10.5 and 10.6 briefly describe the cluster's structure and the main characteristics of the interviewed enterprises. Section 10.7 analyzes the cluster's actors based on their different origins and characteristics. Section 10.8 analyzes the relations between enterprises, focusing on subcontracting and supplying relationships. Finally, Section 10.9 offers a social network analysis. The chapter ends with a conclusive analysis (Section 10.10).

10.2 Theoretical background

Cluster theory is founded on the idea that the geographical and sectorial concentration of enterprises determine several positive external effects leading to a higher efficiency (Arthur 1990). This enhances the potential development of territories where the clusters are located. The strong interest in clustering processes depends greatly on the recent economic growth of some developing countries combined with successful export performance of labour-intensive, light manufacturing goods, such as footwear and apparel. This economic growth would be favoured both by an international economic integration and by the birth of industrial clusters in these territories.

Re-reading Alfred Marshall's *Principles of Economics* and looking at the theoretical foundation of the clustering process, new interpretative models are developed, which can explain the economic development of some territories. Throughout the 1980s and 1990s the so-called Italian school (Becattini 1989; Bellandi 2001; Brusco 1992; Garofoli 1991) drew attention to the organizational dimension of production at a local level. The experiences of Third Italy were translated into a model of the industrial district.

> The crucial characteristic of industrial districts is the existence of strong networks of (largely) small firms which through specialization and subcontracting divide amongst themselves the labour required for the manufacture of particular good: specialization induces efficiency, both individually and at the level of the district; specialization combined with subcontracting promotes collective capabilities. Economies of both scale and scope are the result
>
> (Sengenberger and Pyke 1991: 1).

The increase in efficiency is also promoted by a mix of competition and cooperation between local actors. The so-called *social embeddedness* of actors within the industrial district reduces the opportunistic behaviour and also transaction costs. In this sense the degree of embeddedness of an industrial district is inevitably tied to the relationships of its firms and institutions (Bellandi 2001). Innovation and change are fundamental aspects in the evolution of an industrial district. The productive internalization – through international subcontracting and delocalization – is one strategy that industrial district firms have adopted to compete in the global market.

Starting with the debate of the Italian school and with the many successful European and American cases, other interesting contributions around clustering phenomena developed. For instance Storper and Harrison (1991) suggested a renewed interpretive vision about industrial agglomerations. Using both a functional approach and a territorial approach they proposed a classification of economic development exploiting three different dimension: labour division, (input–output analysis), governance of relationships and territory.

In the same way Markusen (1996) offered a new nomenclature of *industrial spatial types*, in which big enterprises or multinational enterprises played a fundamental role for the socio-economic sustainability of some territories. In particular she introduced the *hub-and-spoke district and the satellite industrial platform.* The former is characterized by a *regional structure* that *revolves around one or several major corporations in one or a few industries.* The latter is 'comprised chiefly of branch plants of absent multinational corporations – this type of district may either be comprised of high-tech branch plants or consist chiefly of low-wage, low-tax, publicly subsidized establishment' (Markusen 1996: 296).

Different contributions came from other academic schools. For instance Camagni (1991) introduced the concept of *milieu innovateur.* Boschma and Frenken (2003) proposed an evolutionary perspective of industrial districts.

The literature that is focused on local dimension can be framed into more general studies that address more general and global aspects of the economy. Empirical evidence has shown indeed how often the birth and development of clusters in developing countries are connected to processes of international production's fragmentation and consequently to the global value chain (GVC). In the 1990s Gereffi and others developed a framework, called '*global commodity chains*' that tied the concept of the value-added chain directly to the global organization of industries. The global commodity chains emphasize the importance of coordination across firms, but also the growing importance of new global buyers as key drivers in the formation of global dispersed and organizationally fragmented production and distribution networks (Gereffi, *et al.* 2005). Gereffi (1994, 1999) suggests that in general one should distinguish between producer-driven and buyers-driven types of commodity chain. The former type is found in large-firm manufacturing sectors such as the car or aircraft industries. The latter type is more commonly associated with small-firm sectors such as the footwear and apparel industries. These firms are dependent on big buyers that govern the global value chain.

Starting from the study of clustering phenomena in developing countries and from the global commodity chain, Altenburg and Meyer-Stamer (1999) have suggested a new classification of clusters framed in global chain. They have 'identified, for Latin America, three ideal types of clusters, each having a different genesis, firm structure, organization principles, development trajectory, opportunities, and bottlenecks' (Altenburg and Meyer-Stamer 1999: 1694).

(a) Most frequent are survival clusters of micro and small-scale enterprises which produce low-quality consumer goods for local markets, mainly in activities where barriers to entry are low. (b) Some clusters are made up of more advanced and differentiated mass producers which for the most part prospered in the import substitution period and mainly produce for the domestic market. They typically comprise a heterogeneous mix of enterprises ranging from petty producers to large Fordist industries. Trade liberalization forced these clusters to face international competition and induced far-reaching structural change. (c) Clusters of transnational corporations (TNCs) exist in technologically more complex activities, such as the electronics and auto industries. These clusters are dominated by large branch plants of world-class manufacturers and usually serve both national and international markets. They typically have few linkages with domestic SMEs and institutions. They comply with the criteria of a cluster because – in contrast to simple assembly plants (e.g. in the clothing industry) – they include several stages of the value chain and derive competitive advantages from local external economies.

The commodity chain framework is a useful tool in the study of a cluster because it analyzes the external linkages, which generally have a limited attention in the literature on local models. The external linkages and the positioning of clusters into a commodity chain can produce positive effects as well as FDI (Humphrey 1995; Dunning 1993, Potter, *et al.* 2003). Nevertheless it is true what Humphrey (1995) asserted, writing about clustering and commodity chains:

Whether or not insertions into a commodity chain will create development potential for a cluster will depend on both cluster position in the chain and the capacity of firms and institutions to make use of or create sources of competitive advantage and opportunities for upgrading (p. 158).

It is widely recognized that linkages with multinational enterprises can have positive effects on clusters' firms (Castellani and Zanfei 2006). For instance, multinational enterprises can diffuse managerial and organizational competencies in the host countries and can introduce more advanced technologies (leading to an improvement in labour quality and therefore to an increase in productivity). Consequently, local enterprises can upgrade and start using innovative raw materials and innovative semi-finished goods through interaction with foreign enterprises. In general the upgrading and diffusion of this kind of innovation are not automatic processes, but rely on a series of factors. First of all upgrading depends on the degree of native enterprises' absorptive capacity. Second, it depends on the typology of value chain governance between native and foreign enterprises, that can be either a market-based relationship among firms or a vertical integration relationship (with hierarchies), or even a mixture of these two types; that is, modular, relational and captive relationship (Gereffi, *et al.* 2005).

10.3 The cluster's history

The footwear cluster in Timişoara is characterized by a peculiar development path and represents an interesting case study. It is, in fact, a cluster born from the old organizational model of planned economy, typical of CEECs. This model consisted of large state-owned enterprises, vertically integrated, that produced goods for the national market and for Eastern European markets.

At the end of the eighties, with the end of the Soviet block, Romania, like other CEECs, opened to international trade and foreign investments. Romania, and in particular some Romanian provinces including Timişoara, benefited from Italian investments. This province indeed, located in Romania's most western region, represents a preferential location for enterprises coming from Italy. Timişoara is the closest city to Western Europe: it is 170 km from Belgrade and 300 km from Budapest. In addition, during the Communist regime the region of Timis was characterized by the presence of several state-owned footwear enterprises.

In the 1990s the privatization process of state-owned enterprises began, together with the reorganization of economic activities. The reorganization of state-owned enterprises determined the end of a vertically integrated productive cycle on one hand and on the other hand the dismissal of many workers. The new entrepreneurs were managers and employees of the old state-owned enterprises. At first the managers could buy such state-owned enterprises. Next, fired employees started up small artisan ateliers (*spin-offs*) to satisfy the local market's demand. In this first stage of transformation (1990–93) a process of international decentralization of production by Italian buyers also occurred.

Some of the old state-owned enterprises were integrated into global commodity chains (e.g. shoes for the Sistema Moda Italia). In this phase the decentralization determined also an outsourcing of less strategic and more labour intensive stages of production to ex-state-owned enterprises. In a later period (1993–96) several Italian enterprises working as subcontractors relocated to Timişoara in order to take advantage of lower labour costs. Only later (1996–2000) foreign footwear enterprises delocalized a part of their production there.

The triggering factors for the development of this cluster were an increase on the demand side and the intense delocalization of production phases by Italian firms based in the Veneto and Marche industrial districts. Between 2000 and 2005 the cluster progressively became more complex: the process of delocalization also involved enterprises supplying specific components (soles, thread, laces, etc.).

Despite the cluster's increased complexity, the last five years have shown a reduction in footwear employment in the Timis region. Although in 2005 Timis Province was the western region with the largest number of footwear workers (9679 employees), it was also the only province to cut back on employment (Figure 10.1). This is mainly because Timis Province became less and less attractive (due to higher labour and settlement costs) compared to eastern provinces.

As a consequence several enterprises left Timis, while the number of enterprises located in other provinces increased.

10.4 Methodology

My on-site research in Timişoara was conducted during two trips, each of about three weeks in duration, in November 2003 and June 2004. Supplemental field-work before these trips consisted of interviews with footwear manufacturers in Italy that provided me with information about their international strategies. These companies are located in Veneto, the most important region of North East Italy for production of footwear.

Regarding the on-site research in Timişoara, the primary method of data collection consisted of two types of face-to-face interviews. In order to investigate the economic and social peculiarities of the area of Timişoara, in the first visit I carried out open-ended interviews with key informants and officials representing local authorities, such as associations of entrepreneurs (Chamber of Commerce, Industry and Agriculture of Timişoara), representatives of trade unions, and local offices of Italian institutions (such as Antenna Veneto and Unimpresa). In the second visit I interviewed a heterogeneous group of firms on the basis of a semi-structured questionnaire. An effort was made to obtain a picture that could be the most representative of the footwear firms in Timişoara. Interviewed enterprises included final firms and subcontractors, native and foreign firms. The interviews were usually followed by a tour of production facilities. Out of the approximately 110 enterprises active in the footwear manufacturing industry in the County of Timiş,[1] 48 firms were interviewed. I also used secondary sources of information,

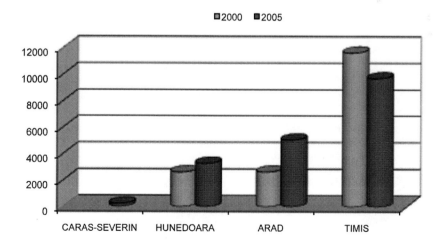

Figure 10.1 Distribution of the number of employees in the fashion industry.
Source: personal analysis of INSSE data.

including national and trade data, articles and local newspapers, to monitor dynamics of change over the period.

The main research questions concern the possibility of reproducing the industrial district model in a developing country. As it has emerged in the analysis carried out by the literature on industrial districts, the so-called social embeddedness is quite high and the network of firms is quite strong. For this reason I tried to analyze the degree of embeddedness of the footwear cluster in Timişoara and the network of firms. For this purpose in the interviews I asked questions on the relationships with customers, subcontractors, suppliers and local or public institutions. I also investigated the possibility of Italian firms staying in this territory: some questions asked directly about the reasons for delocalization or decentralization of Italian firms and about the evolution of attractive factors in Timişoara.

10.5 The agglomeration's structure

Timişoara counted over 100 active enterprises in the footwear sector in 2001 and employed about 15,000 workers. In 2001 the cluster was characterized by medium and large-sized enterprises. Fifty-five per cent of the enterprises had fewer than 50 employees, employing about 6 per cent of the entire workforce; while 14 per cent of the enterprises had more than 250 employees, with over 65 per cent of the sector's total workforce (Table 10.1). There are three enterprises that have almost 1000 employees. One is Geox's productive unit and the other two are ex-state-owned enterprises, privatized respectively in 1990 and 1996 and bought by an important Italian company based in the Marche region.

As shown in Table 10.2, the cluster specializes in the productive cycle's final phases. In 2001 almost all the cluster's enterprises produced footwear and footwear uppers.

As it is often the case with footwear specialized areas, this cluster is characterized by a lack of tannery firms (the only company listed as a tannery actually works as a commercial enterprise).

In fact, branches of international leading foreign enterprises coexist with subcontractors that produce finished goods or semi-finished goods for important 'Made in Italy' brands and with artisan enterprises that serve the local and national market. In the Timişoara area, leading enterprises such as Geox, AlpineStars and Cesare Paciotti have opened productive units. Similarly, subcontractors working for brands such as Armani, Ferragamo, Prada, Pollini and Salomon have decentralized their productive activity to this territory.

10.6 The characteristics of the interviewed enterprises

The empirical investigation involved 48 enterprises, both Romanian (31 per cent) and Italian (69 per cent). In particular among the Italian capital enterprises, almost one half came from Marche and the other half from Veneto. It is interesting to observe that 60 per cent of the enterprises are part of a group or the entrepreneur is related to other enterprises within the same sector in Italy. More than half of the

Table 10.1 Distribution by dimensional class of the number of active enterprises and employees (2001)

Class	Enterprises		Employees	
1–10	31	28%	145	1%
11–50	30	27%	849	5%
51–100	18	16%	1312	8%
101–250	17	15%	2810	18%
251–500	7	6%	2283	14%
501–1000	6	5%	4102	26%
Over 1000	3	3%	4276	27%
Total	112	100%	15777	100%

Source: analysis of Register of Companies data.

Table 10.2 Product distribution with regard to the number of enterprises and employees in the Timis region (2001)

Caen	Product category	Enterprises	Those active	Employees	Average employees
1910	Tannery	5	1	11	11
1920	Bags and leather accessories	14	13	547	42
1930	Shoes	115	98	15,219	155
	Total	134	112	15,777	141

Source: analysis of Register of Companies data.

enterprises were formed or privatized before 1999 (see Table 10.3). The average size in terms of workforce of the interviewed enterprises is 168 employees. The smallest enterprise has six employees, the largest 910. As shown in Table 10.3, about 41 per cent of the enterprises are to be considered 'micro' or small, 39 per cent are medium-sized and 19 per cent are large. Among these the foreign enterprises tend to be larger than local ones.

All the sample firms are engaged in manufacturing activities. Ninety-six per cent are essentially productive units, while the others mainly perform commercial activities. As shown in Table 10.4, 83 per cent of the interviewed enterprises are specialized in final phases of production. In particular, 42 per cent of the enterprises are footwear factories, while 29 per cent are uppers factories.

Table 10.3 Characteristics of the enterprises

		Enterprises		Employees	
		No.	%	No.	%
Size	Micro (1–9 employees)	2	4%	13	0.2%
	Small (10–49 employees)	17	35%	459	6%
	Medium (50–249 employees)	19	40%	2883	36%
	Large (+ 250)	10	21%	4695	58%
	Total	48	100%	8050	100%
Year of foundation or constitution	Before 1994	8	17%	2234	28%
	1994–1999	19	40%	3265	41%
	After 2000	19	40%	1801	22%
	(Not availible)	2	4%	750	9%
	Total	48	100%	8050	100%
Group participation	independent enterprise	19	40%	1428	18%
	Branch (informal)	4	8%	1207	15%
	Branch	23	48%	4915	61%
	group leader	2	4%	500	6%
	Total	48	100,0	8050	100%
Capital ownership	Foreign	33	69%	6083	76%
	Romanian	15	31%	1957	24%
	Total	48	100%	8050	100%
Entrepreneur's origin	Romania	15	100%	1957	100%
	Italy, other region	3	12%	236	2,5%
	Italia, Marche region	15	45%	3037	38%
	Italia, Veneto region	14	42%	2820	35%
	Total	48	100%	8050	100%

10.7 The cluster's actors

The footwear cluster in Timişoara seems to be actually heterogeneous as it contains small, medium and large-sized enterprises, both national and foreign, final goods enterprises, subcontractors, independent enterprises and branches of foreign enterprises. The cluster's complexity has gradually increased in the last few years thanks to the entry of other important economic actors such as banks, associations and local institutions.

Table 10.4 Distribution of the number of interviewed enterprises with regard to goods produced or manufacturing phases

Footwear production phases	Firms
Footwear factories	26
Uppers factories*	14
Component-making enterprises	8
Punches	1
Models*	2
Soles, etc	1
Polyurethane	1
Glues, adhesives, etc	3
Machinery and equipment	1
Total	48

* An ex-state-owned enterprise worked both as subcontractor of capacity (producing uppers) and as a speciality subcontractor (producing models).

In the previous section the cluster's formation process was explained. Here, based on the owner's characteristics and considering the origin of the enterprise, four categories are delineated (Table 10.5).

1 Ex-state-owned enterprises: they are generally enterprises with Romanian capital taken over by the former executive class. Only a quarter of the state-owned enterprises were bought by Italian enterprises.
2 Enterprises originated from spin-off processes: generally they are start-ups created by workers from ex-state-owned enterprises or foreign enterprises.
3 Foreign enterprises originated from some sort of relocation processes: this is the case of entrepreneurs that closed their own economic activity in their original country and relocated to this territory. In this case the entrepreneur may form a new enterprise or buy an existing one (Table 10.5).

Table 10.5 Classification according to enterprise origin – distribution by nationality

	Romanian		Italian		Total	
Ex-state enterprise	5	33.3%	2	6.1%	7	14.6%
Spin-off enterprise	10	66.7%	2	6.1%	12	25%
Complete relocation	0	0%	8	24.2%	8	16.7%
Partial delocalization	0	0%	21	63.6%	21	43.7%
Total	15	100%	33	100%	48	100%

4   Foreign enterprises resulting from international delocalization processes: they are (formally or informally) subsidiaries of enterprises located abroad.

As shown in Table 10.5, foreign enterprises dominate the panel. Despite a limited dimension, the cluster is characterized by different types of enterprises, with a different role played in the footwear filière and with specific competencies (Belussi 1992). Therefore the firms of this sample can be grouped in three main categories (Table 10.6):

1   Romanian final firms;
2   subcontractors
    •   horizontal or capacity subcontractors
    •   vertical or speciality subcontractors;
3   foreign enterprises' productive units.

Obviously these three types of firms may have been originated in different ways. They can be ex state-owned enterprises, spin-off firms, relocated or delocalized firms.

10.7.1 Romanian final firms

Out of the interviewed enterprises 14 per cent are included in this category. These are small enterprises with an average of 25 employees and produce exclusively or mainly hand-made goods for the national end market with their own brands. They are exclusively Romanian enterprises, mostly originating from spin-off processes initiated by employees (usually designers and model makers) from ex-state-owned enterprises. Only in one case has the spin-off process originated from foreign enterprises located in Timişoara. Such enterprises that are economically and strategically autonomous are usually characterized by a light structure. The entrepreneur often carries out all corporate functions, from sales to production. Concerning the type of products offered, these enterprises are able to produce personalized goods,

Table 10.6 Classification according to enterprise type and distribution by nationality

	Romanian		Italian		Total	
Productive unit of Italian firm	0	0%	16	55%	16	36%
Subcontractor of capacity	9	60%	9	31%	18	40%
Subcontractor of speciality	(1)	–	4	14%	4	10%
Romanian final firm	6	40%	0	0%	6	14%
Total	15	100%	29	100%	44	100%

Notes
Four foreign enterprises belonging to the footwear filière are not included in any of the previous definitions; these are enterprises that focus mainly on commercial activities.

even though their specificity consists mainly in producing limited series goods. The quality of their products is medium or low; this is due more to the use of raw materials and semi-finished goods of low quality than to productive capacity.

10.7.2 Subcontractors

Subcontracting activities in Timişoara's cluster are of two types: horizontal or capacity subcontracting and vertical or speciality subcontracting (Lorenzoni 1990, 1992, 1997; Tracogna 1999). The use of a horizontal subcontractor occurs when an enterprise cannot reach internally some desired level of production and therefore acquires a supplementary work capacity from another firm. In general, a subcontractor of capacity originates from the need to reach advantages in terms of costs and productive flexibility and to rapidly respond to possible increases in demand. The use of vertical subcontractors originates instead from the need to incorporate knowledge and competencies that are not present within the enterprise or reflects 'non-core' phases in the externalization processes within the enterprise (Nassimbeni, *et al.* 1993).

Within the sample 50 per cent of the interviewees are subcontractors, and are medium-sized, both foreign (originated from processes of international relocation of production through *greenfield* and *brownfield* investments), and Romanian (ex-state-owned enterprises and firms originating from spin-offs) (Table 10.7).

Among the subcontractors, the most common (and also the oldest) sub-category consists of subcontractor of capacity (82 per cent). This type of subcontracting is almost exclusively related to the elaboration of some specific phases such as hemming and sewing phases and only rarely cutting. Almost all the value-adding activities (design, cutting and assembly) are performed directly by the commissioning enterprises. Obviously, this relationship creates a high level of dependence and subordination of the subcontractors towards the commissioning enterprises (Gereffi, *et al.* 2005). The commissioning enterprises are always Italian and are located both in Timişoara or generally the western region of Romania and in Italy. Generally, these subcontractors have no more than two or three clients, even if sometimes they serve just one client.

The second subcontractor category (subcontractor of speciality) is less diffuse (18 per cent) and concerns manufacturing components or some particular productive phases, for instance moulds and soles. These subcontractors arose quite recently (after 2000). Their commissioning enterprises are not only local and regional firms (although these are the most important ones) but also firms located in other parts of Romania and Italian firms. Unlike the subcontractors of capacity, subcontractors of speciality have a large choice of clients, thanks to their high level of competencies.

10.7.3 Productive unit of Italian enterprise

This category of firms builds on the partial delocalization of production through the opening of a new productive factory (*greenfield* investments) or through the acquisition of ex-state-owned enterprises or foreign enterprises (*brownfield* investments). These enterprises, having generally a medium or large size, represent formal or informal subsidiaries of Italian enterprises. As such, they carry out only the productive function and usually almost all phases of the productive cycle of the product, including the packaging phase. But they usually lack any other function: administrative activities, R&D, sales and logistic functions are handled by the headquarters. The headquarters indeed autonomously decides on the suppliers, the technology to be used, the raw materials and generally all the techno-productive characteristics of the goods to be produced, as well as the strategy to follow. They also send almost all input for production to the productive unit, thus blocking all relations with other enterprises (Gereffi, *et al.* 2005).

Because of the frequent use of outsourcing the productive units are able to change quickly the models in production and also to produce goods in small series and/or in large quantities. Some interviewed enterprises produce sports footwear (snowboard shoes, trekking and climbing shoes, hunting shoes and motorcycle shoes) with high technological quality.[2] Some of these firms, although representing affiliates of other enterprises, play the role of *leader enterprises*, as is the case of Geox and Cesare Paciotti (Viesti 2000; Garofoli 2002). In other cases the interviewed enterprises do not work exclusively for the parent company, but also have other Italian clients.

10.7.4 The other actors

In recent years, Timişoara's cluster has been enriched by other categories of enterprises. Besides the above-mentioned types there are now many Italian enterprises and only a few Romanian enterprises that sell and in some cases produce components and specific tools[3] for the footwear sector. Generally, the goods offered by these companies do not have a strategic role for the cluster's enterprises: they are goods of secondary importance such as adhesives, mastics, soles, etc. The enterprises that produce capital goods only moved their commercial branches here, maintaining the production in Italy.

Apart from large and small enterprises, subcontracting and final firms, and apart from enterprises that can be defined as independent or subsidiary of other enterprises, there are also other actors that have a direct or an indirect role in the cluster. Among these are business associations, institutions, banks (both local and foreign), universities and professional training centres. Timişoara hosts an important university pole. There are four public and six private universities as well as a training school for the footwear sector.

At the institutional and associative level an important operator for enterprises is the representative office of the Chamber of Commerce, Industry and Agriculture. Other Romanian institutions have been created only recently. Among the most relevant are the Agency for the Development of the Western Region and the associations of private enterprises representing small and medium-sized Romanian enterprises. These institutions offer several different (though highly valued) services to their associates.[4] More recently two Italian institutions were created: *Antenna*

Veneto Romania and *Unimpresa Romania*. The former is the first stable structure established by the Italian institutional system in the western part of Romania. It was founded in 2002 with an agreement between the Chamber of Commerce of Veneto[5] and the Chamber of Commerce of Timişoara. Antenna Veneto Romania should act as a window for entrepreneurs from Veneto that would like to arrive and consolidate economic relations with Romania. The objective of this initiative is that of stimulating economic relations between Veneto and Romania, offering general informational services, operative assistance, personalized consultancy and services for economic promotion. It must be noted that this structure is not fully operative at present. Another initiative is Unimpresa Romania[6], an association created in 2003 in response to a request for representation expressed by Italian entrepreneurs located in Romania and by many Romanian authorities that, for their developmental projects, were looking for a single and representative referent for Italy. The main service offered by Unimpresa to its associates is representation with Romanian institutions. Among its functions is also that of acting as a liaison with Romanian authorities' offices for single enterprises and upon request assisting with business affairs in both Italian and Romanian official institutions. Like Antenna Veneto Romania, Unimpresa Romania is not yet fully operational and has only 100 associated enterprises.

The Italian presence in Timişoara was further enriched by financial credit institutes and institutional investors. On a financial level Timişoara is characterized by a large number of international banks.

10.8 Relationships between the cluster's enterprises

In order to understand the degree of enterprises' embeddedness in the territory in which they are located I also analyze the local relations (Bellandi 2001) and therefore the organizational scheme at a territorial level.

The interviewed enterprises can be divided in two groups: the ones adopting an organizational model characterized by the division of labour and the enterprises with a vertical semi-integration model. The enterprises that do not adopt an outsourcing strategy mainly belong to subcontractors of speciality and Romanian final firms.

One of the important issues in the study of Timişoara's footwear cluster is the role of outward processing trade (OPT). This instrument consists of temporary exportations and re-importations under a special customs regime, and represents the main way of international subcontracting. Moreover OPT is an instrument of production processes' international fragmentation (Corò and Volpe 2003; Feenstra 1998; Graziani 2001; Schiattarella 1999). This system of productive organization strongly influences the relations between enterprises and their clients as well as between other economic operators (suppliers and subcontractors). In particular this organizational system directly involves Italian productive units and subcontractors whose clients are located in Italy (or in one of the EU countries) and the subcontractors that have indirect relationship with Italian firms.

The international fragmentation of productive processes and their insertion in the global value chain represented a big development opportunity for the cluster of Timişoara, arising from productive processes' modernization, qualitative upgrading of products and the transfer of entrepreneurial and managerial skills, as was the case for instance of the Sialkot cluster in Pakistan (Nadvi and Halder 2005).

10.8.1 Subcontracting relationships

The sample's enterprises recognize in Timişoara's cluster a modest but increasing variety of subcontractors, not only in terms of number of firms, but also in specialization and competencies. In the last five years this cluster has been enriched by enterprises specializing in component production and in more valued-added manufacture stages. This larger variety has favoured an increase of outsourcing. When interviewed, slightly more than half of the enterprises were adopting a productive decentralization strategy; in particular the productive units of the Italian enterprises are those that mainly resorted to outsourcing (Table 10.7).

With externalization the enterprise gains not only a superior productive flexibility but also a reduction in production costs. Obviously, when evaluating the possibility to make or to buy, an enterprise must take into account both the reduction of production costs and the increase in risks related to such an externalization, to which selection and coordination costs correspond (Raffa 1993).

The geographical proximity with subcontractors and in some cases the same origin of Italian enterprises have favoured the creation of specific advantages. These are known in literature as *agglomerative economies* and are also acknowledged in the enterprises themselves. Apart from such advantages, the clustering of subcontractors has caused advantages in terms of timing and in particular it has determined a reduction in transportation times of semi-finished goods.

The reduction of selection costs, and especially coordination costs and delivery times, are important aspects according to many of the Italian enterprises interviewed. Most of them are heavily affected by short production and delivery times, because they often work for *pronto moda* (quick production runs) and sometimes indirectly for *prêt-à-porter* (ready to wear) firms. Working for highly demanding markets, the enterprises have small margins of error; the choice of suitable subcontractors that can coordinate efficiently is therefore crucial. Nevertheless

Table 10.7 Do you outsource?

	Yes	No
Productive unit of Italian firm	87.5%	12.5%
Subcontractor of capacity	44.4%	55.6%
Subcontractor of speciality	0%	100%
Romanian final firm	16.7%	83.3%
Total	52.3%	47.7%

geographical proximity's advantages are often hindered by the lack of trust between native and Italian firms, which can make their relations difficult.

In the cluster of Timişoara there are many reasons why enterprises externalize some of the productive stages. The main ones concern the need to rapidly respond to increasing demand, leaving unchanged the enterprise's productive capacity. Outsourcing can also involve manufactures that the enterprise is not able to carry out by itself. The preference for this type of subcontracting has many reasons: in some cases it depends on the lack of specific competence or productive processes; in other cases decentralized manufacture requires a productive scale that is superior to the enterprise's needs.

The subcontracting relations have changed through the years. The first Italian enterprises that entered this territory initially adopted a discriminatory behaviour regarding the choice of subcontractors. At that time the productive relations with local enterprises were the delegation of less strategic and simpler manufacturing phases. More complex manufacturing activities were assigned to Italian subcontractors, located in Timişoara but originating from the same territories. This approach has slowly changed over time, thanks to the upgrading of Romanian enterprises and the higher level of trust. Today most of the interviewed Italian enterprises have started to decentralize even the more complex productive phases to the native enterprises, and consider irrelevant the nationality of the subcontractors in the cluster. The need for lower production costs has urged some of the interviewees to decentralize to a bigger number of subcontractors and to decentralize less valuable productive phases to enterprises located in other territories, such as Moldavia and Ukraine.

The empirical investigation has shown a quasi hierarchy and captive value chain governance regarding the subcontracting relationships (Table 10.9):

- all subcontractors of capacity have an executive role and none of them is involved in R&D activities;
- the buyers continuously operate a high degree of monitoring and quality control;
- the specialized Romanian subcontractors tend to work almost exclusively for one or two Italian enterprises;
- commercial orders are managed on a seasonal base and relationships are not always continuous and regular;
- Italian buyers and Italian productive units acquired the subcontractor with which they had established a relationship before.

The monitoring and quality control of subcontractors depend on their lack of specific technical abilities. By contrast, subcontractors of speciality, thanks to the enterprises' technical know-how, tend to be more involved in the prototype creation phase and therefore do not undergo quality control by the buyers' technicians.

So far, from what has emerged, I can affirm that in the cluster of Timişoara most subcontractors follow a dependent subcontracting model. Relations are based on a heavy cost reduction plan, this being the main reason many enterprises in

Timişoara began using subcontractors located in territories with lower order costs. Next to these relationships there is another type of relationship, less dependent and more evolved, that only concerns a small number of the interviewees. These are relations with subcontractors of speciality. In this case the cost factor, although important, is less important, while firm specialization and know-how assume a fundamental role.

10.8.2 Supply relationships

One critical weakness of Timişoara's footwear cluster is the scarcity of local supply for most of the goods necessary for production. Machines and production plants always come from abroad, as well as raw materials and many of the strategic components. This is due to the fact that, at an international level, the production of most raw materials is concentrated in a small number of large enterprises situated in Western countries. Similarly, the production of machinery for the footwear industry is concentrated mainly in Italy. Moreover OPT has acquired a strong role in this territory during the 1990s, inhibiting the localization of typical footwear products' distributors. It is only in the last five years that the cluster has been enriched by distributors of marginal goods (mastics, adhesives, labels, etc.), foreign branches that sell capital goods and raw materials and enterprises that offer services such as accounting, legal and fiscal consultancy, data processing, etc.

The lack of raw materials and capital goods producers is the main reason why all the Italian enterprises located in Timişoara have maintained, directly or indirectly, their own supply network in Italy or abroad. The use of local suppliers for Italian enterprises is limited to marginal and standardized goods bought by catalogue, for which geographical proximity to headquarters or to commissioning enterprises is not a strong requirement. Geographic considerations are instead an issue for the Italian affiliate or for the subcontractor that can obtain small objects such as needles, adhesives, glues, utensils, etc. Indeed an important advantage deriving from the increased concentration of supply concerns the logistic process and in particular the delivery time optimization from the time when the need arises to that of the product's delivery. The high standardization level of the goods offered by the suppliers located in the cluster facilitates their substitution.

The Romanian final firms are the type of enterprise that use the largest number and variety of suppliers and this makes sense considering that these enterprises must purchase all the input necessary for their own production (Table 10.8). The scarce capacity to operate in international markets has forced these enterprises to maintain commercial relationships with Romanian suppliers, even though these enterprises recognize the existence of a higher product quality in the Italian supplier and in the foreigner supplier in general. It is with the recent arrival of Italian distributors in this territory, and generally in Romania, that this type of firm has started to establish business relationships with foreign suppliers and to use new materials and new production processes.

Regarding the subcontractors, it is necessary to distinguish between subcontractors of speciality and subcontractors of capacity. The former usually have

Table 10.8 Goods purchased – distribution according to typology of enterprise

	Romanian final firm	Subcontractor of capacity	Subcontractor of speciality	Productive unit of Italian firm
Raw material	+	–	+	–
Strategic Component	+	–	+	–
Marginal component	+	+	+	+
Machinery and equipment	+	+	Only equipment	Only equipment

+: goods purchased directly by the firm
–: goods purchased by headquarters or by the buyers and dispatched to the firm.

decisional autonomy regarding purchases. Suppliers in this typology are often large enterprises located outside the cluster, both in Romania or Western countries. By contrast, the subcontractors of capacity have very little decisional autonomy regarding the input goods. These subcontractors always receive all necessary inputs (raw material and semi-finished goods) from commissioning enterprises. The supplying activity delegated to these enterprises mainly involves the acquisition of marginal goods purchased through a catalogue (such as needles, glue, adhesives, labels, etc.). Generally, subcontractors of capacity purchase these goods from Italian enterprises located in the cluster.

As in the case of subcontractors of capacity, Italian productive units purchase only small amounts of marginal goods from Italian firms localized in the cluster. Other empirical researches (Turok 1993; Steward 1976; Nadvi 1999) underline the scarcity and lack of strength in the relationship that the foreign enterprises' branches have established with the agglomeration enterprises in which they are located. However, in recent years more than two-thirds of the companies have increased the number of suppliers (there was no case of a decrease in this number).

Generally, at local level the supply relationships are based on a high degree of standardization of product that determines a value chain governed by market-based relationships between firms (Table 10.9).

10.8.3 Relations with other local actors

The relationships with local institutions are another element contributing to the embeddedness of an enterprise in the territory where it is located (Bellandi 2001). Such institutions do not only offer specific services but should also help disseminate information.

For this reason the interviewees showed an apparently lukewarm interest towards the institutions within the territory. Slightly more than half of interviewed enterprises are registered with the Chamber of Commerce, Industry and Agriculture

Table 10.9 Value chain governance for different types of firms

Suppliers	Subcontractors	Types of firms	Customers
Markets	Markets	Romanian final firm	Markets, Quasi-hierarchy*
Markets	Quasi-hierarchy	Subcontractor of capacity	Quasi-hierarchy
Markets	-	Subcontractor of speciality	Captive
Markets	Quasi-hierarchy	Productive unit of Italian firm	Hierarchy, quasi-hierarchy

* The value chain is a quasi-hierarchy when the customers of Romanian final firms are other firms that operate in the Italian value chain.

of Timişoara; several Italian enterprises are associated with Unimpresa Romania while none are registered with Antenna Veneto.

Although a relevant number are associated with the Chamber of Commerce, more than half of the enterprises state that no information is exchanged with this operator, while one enterprise out of three confirms sporadic relations. The choice to belong to the Chamber of Commerce or to any other association has been based on the need to gather information.

The territory apparently offers many financial opportunities in terms of Romanian banks as well as foreign banks; however, none of the Romanian banks is present as a local bank (Signorini 2003).

The enterprises generally complain about difficult relations with such operators. The main problems involve access to credit and the enormous guarantees requested to obtain financing. Credit institutes located within the territory do not operate as local banks.

Training and formative activity is scarce. Apart from several ex-state-owned enterprises that offer a long traineeship within their productive structures, the other interviewed enterprises are not involved in training programmes.

Table 10.10 A summary of the main behaviours about local relationships

Nature of local linkages	Unequal trading relationships, opportunistic behaviours, conventional subcontracting and emphasis on cost-saving
Duration of linkages	Short-term contracts
Quality of job at local level	Many low skilled, low paid, temporary and casual
Benefits for native firms	Markets for native firms to buy standards, high-quality components, subcontracting means restricted independent growth capacity
Italian investors' ties to the locality	Branch plants or firms restricted to productive activity and to labour-intensive phases, no or very weak relationships with local institutions
Prospects for local economy	Vulnerable to external decisions

Regarding the trade unions, only 15 per cent of the enterprises confirm that their employees are associated with national unions and these are ex-state-owned enterprises that have continued to adhere to the trade union after their privatization. The other enterprises openly state their opposition to any kind of employee aggregation.

10.9 Social network analysis

In this section the results of a social network analysis (Wasserman and Faust 1994) applied to the interviewed enterprises will be presented. Information presented in graphs, although not exhaustive, will constitute a complementary analysis. This type of analysis represents a simplification of the relationships between enterprises as it could ignore important aspects such as the dynamics of the network, the intensity of connections and their duration. Moreover the analysis is necessarily reduced to a sample of firms, and not to the entire population; consequently some important information regarding strategic actors can be omitted. Through a *roster recall method* I investigated the relationships between sample firms: each firm was presented with a complete list (roster) of the other firms in the cluster, and they were asked the following question: Could you mark, among the actors included in the roster, those that have established productive relationships, and those that have transferred relevant information and technical knowledge to this firm? A first result is that almost all the relations involve subcontracting relationships (see Figure 10.2). No collaborative linkages with only exchange of information or knowledge are created between firms. Almost always interviewed enterprises affirmed that they have flows of knowledge to aid problem solving only with their commissioning enterprises or headquarters and with their suppliers. Generally, there is a very weak connection between firms operating in the same position in the chain and the connection (if any) only concerns the subcontracting activities. As one can see in Figure 10.2 and Table 10.11, the density[7] of productive relationships within each type of firm is generally low. On the whole sample firms are characterized by a density index equal to 10,11. This means that 11 per cent of the possible relations have been formed (Table 10.11). It is a rather low value, considering that the index varies from 0 to 1 and considering that both past and actual relations have been examined. From the computation of the so-called centrality index[8] and from the average number of formed relationships the prominent role that the subcontractors of speciality assume within the cluster is confirmed (see Figure 10.3). These enterprises act as connectors for the other typologies of enterprises. Moreover, it has emerged from the interviews that subcontractors of speciality together with supply enterprises represent a channel for the diffusion of innovation within the cluster. More generally, as far as the productive relationships are concerned, the productive units of Italian firms appear to be the leading firms. In Figure 10.3 it is clear how the productive units of Italian firms correspond to the type of firms that mainly govern the linkages with other firms. Often productive units of Italian firms put in contact different subcontractors, organizing and coordinating the productive phases that each subcontractor is required to carry out.

Table 10.11 Density, centrality and average relationship, distribution by type of firm

	Density index	Development standard (density)	Centrality index	Average relationship
Productive unit of Italian firm	0.08	0.27	0.28	4.1
Subcontractor of capacity	0.05	0.22	0.07	4.8
Subcontractor of speciality	0.50	0.50	0.33	10.8
Romanian final firm	0.27	0.44	0.20	4.5
Cluster	0.11	0.31	0.35	–

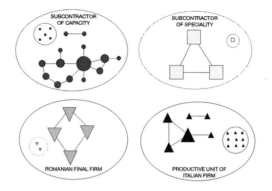

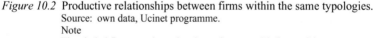

Figure 10.2 Productive relationships between firms within the same typologies.
Source: own data, Ucinet programme.
Note
The circled firms are those that do not interact with firms of the same type.

10.10 Conclusions

The appearance of Italian enterprises promoted the birth and development of a footwear cluster in Timişoara. During the 1990s the role of the Timişoara cluster in the footwear commodity chain evolved: from a cluster of phase subcontractors to a cluster of final subcontractors. Although the complexity of the cluster has increased in the past few years, its weaknesses still remain and this fact is one of the main messages of this paper. A small upgrading is clearly occurring at the industry level in Timişoara and at firm level as an outcome of the evolution of relationships among native firms and Italian firms. New activities in the chain gradually have begun to take place in this territory, for instance the production of shoe-stretchers, shoe-sock, shoelaces, etc. Native firms have started to utilize new capital goods and new raw materials and accessories. Nevertheless these firms are characterized by a backwardness that hinders the upgrading of their capabilities.

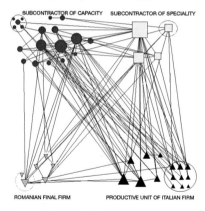

Figure 10.3 Productive relationships of different typologies between firms.
   Source: own data, Ucinet program.
   Note
   *   the circle firms are those that do not interact with firms of the same type;
   **   larger node corresponds to firms that have more linkages with other firms;
   *** the arrows describe the direction of ties between firms.

The cluster of Timişoara seems to follow two different models of organization
of production. There is a small group of firms formed by Romanian final firms
that usually act as island firms and do not decentralize any activity to other firms.
Conversely, the majority of firms play the role of dependent subcontractors: they
follow a hierarchical organization model and operate within the Italian value chain.
This group of firms works as a buyer-driven cluster for different Italian industrial
districts. This hierarchical organization strongly influences firms' activity. First,
the Italian buyers do not create linkages with local firms that are able to promote the
territory. The knowledge diffusion is limited by the type of relationships between
firms that are characterized by a short duration and are almost never based on trust.
The ties between local and Italian firms do not follow a collaborative approach.
The emphasis on labour costs saving is stronger than the productive increment,
since costs reduction is the prime reason to delocalize. The most recent salary
increases have pushed some firms to outsource in other territories where they can
achieve lower labour costs. In this sense it is possible to affirm that the subcontracted network has lengthened outside the cluster. Consequently, the firms of this
buyer-driven cluster are forced to reduce their production costs in order to offer
a competitive price. Second, this hierarchical organization gives place to forms
of value chain governance that constrict the autonomy of enterprises in terms of
decision making. This inhibits the possibility of firms to link and to cooperate with
the suppliers and limits the capacity of firms to create networks and therefore the
possibility of a self-sustaining system.
   To conclude, the firms of the sample do not form a solid network that can sustain
the development of the district, as usually always happens in an industrial district.
In particular the district seems to act more like a labour cost saving centre than

as a solid social and productive cluster. Italian firms are weakly embedded in this area and they have not reproduced the same atmosphere of the Italian industrial district.

Some policy interventions could be necessary to strengthen the linkages between firms. In particular policy action should address a qualitative upgrading of sub-contracting in order to promote the division of labour among the firms and also to enhance the exchange of information.

There are several dimensions of future research. First of all, a deeper analysis of technological *spillovers* within the cluster would be of primary interest. This analysis would consist in a first stage of the role of change and innovation within the cluster, in order to see whether some innovative technology has been introduced and how its diffusion has affected the production. A second stage could address the absorptive capacity of firms and their possible upgrading patterns.

A second line of research is the comparative analysis of a different industrial cluster in the same area: the textile industry in Timişoara shares many common features with the footwear cluster, not least its role in the delocalization and decentralization of Italian firms. Within the study of this cluster the same research questions can be made as for the footwear cluster and similarities and differences could be seen.

Notes

1 Timisoara is the most important town within Timis County that together with Arad, Huneduara and Caras Severin constitutes the region called West (also named region 5).
2 These are subsidiary of enterprises localized in the technological district of Montebelluna.
3 These enterprises represent 4.4 per cent of the sample.
4 Based on the personal opinion of interviewed firms' representatives.
5 Apart from the Veneto region's sponsorship, its realization was made possible by the collaboration of regional entrepreneurs' associations and by important financial credit institutes interested in the Romanian market that offered some financial support.
6 Unimpresa is the product of a common internalization project of some of the main Italian organizations such as Confindustria, Confartigianato and Ance (National Association of Building Contractors) that together have created a foundation for Romanian legislation called 'Fundatia Sistema Italia Romania'.
7 The density index is calculated as follows:

$$\Delta = \frac{2L}{g\,(g-1)}, \; 0 < \Delta < 1$$

where L indicates the number of lines or actual relations, while g is the number of ac-tors present in the network. The density of a network starts from 0, if no relations are present, and reaches 1 if all possible relations are active. For further information see Wasserman and Faust (1994).
8 The network's centrality index is calculated as follows:

$$C_d = \frac{\sum_{i=1}^{g} [C_d\,(n^*) - C_d\,(n_i)]}{\max \sum_{i=1}^{g} [C_d\,(n^*) - C_d\,(n_i)]}, \; 0 < C_d < 1$$

where C(n) indicates the degree of centrality of each actor; the index ranges from a minimum value equal to 0 (all the actors have the same centrality) up to a maximum of 1 (when an actor perceives himself in a central role). For more information see Wasserman and Faust (1994).

References

Altenburg T. and Meyer-Stamer J. (1999), 'How to promote clusters: policy experiences from Latin America', *World Development*, 27: 9.

Arthur W. B. (1990), 'Positive feeedbacks in the economy', in W. B. Arthur (ed.), *Increasing Returns and Path Dependence in the Economy*, Michigan: Michigan University Press.

Becattini G. (1987), *Mercato e forze locali: il distretto industriale*, Il Mulino.

———. (1989), *Modelli locali di sviluppo*, Bologna: Il Mulino.

Bellandi M. (2001), 'Local development and embedded large firms', *Entrepreneurship and regional development*, 13.

Belussi, F. (ed.) (1992), *Nuovi modelli di impresa, gerarchie organizzative ed imprese rete*, Angeli, Milano.

Boschma R. A. and Frenken K. (2003), 'Evolutionary economics and industry location', *International Review for Regional Research*, 23.

Brand S., Hill S. and Munday M., (2000), 'Assessing the impacts of foreign manufacturing on regional economies: the case of Wales, Scotland and the West Midlands', *Regional Studies*, 34: 4.

Brusco S. (1992), 'The idea of the industrial district: its genesis', in F. Pyke, G. Becattini and W. Sengenberger (eds.), *Industrial Districts and Inter-firm Cooperation in Italy*, Geneva: International Institute For Labour Studies, ILO.

Camagni R. (1991), 'Local milieu, uncertainly and innovation networks: towards a new dynamic theory of economic space', in R. Camagni (ed.), *Innovation Networks: Spatial Perspectives*, London: Belhaven Press.

Castellani D. and Zanfei A. (2006), *Multinational Firms, Innovation and Productivity*, Cheltenham: Edward Elgar.

Corò G. and Volpe M. (2003), 'Frammentazione produttiva e integrazione internazionale nei sistemi di piccola e media impresa', *Economia e Società Regionale*, 1.

Dunning J. H. (1993), *Multinational Enterprises and the Global Economy*, Reading: Addison-Wesley.

Feenstra R. C. (1998), 'Integration of trade and disintegration of production in the global economy', *Journal of Economic Perspective*, 12: 4.

Fröbel F., Heinrichs J. and Kreye O. (1980), *The New International Division of Labour: Structural Unemployment in Industrialized Countries and Industrialization in Developing Countries*, Cambridge: Cambridge University Press.

Garofoli G. (1983), *Industrializzazione diffusa in Lombardia*, Milano: Franco Angeli.

———. (1991), *Modelli locali di sviluppo*, Milano: Franco Angeli.

———. (2002), 'Piccole imprese e distretti industriali: lo sviluppo endogeno nel Mezzogiorno', *La Questione Agraria*, 3.

———. (ed.) (2003), *Impresa e Territorio*, Il Mulino.

Gereffi G. (1994), 'The organizations of buyer-driven global commodity chains: how U.S. retailers shape overseas production networks', in G. Gereffi and M. Korzeniewicz (eds), *Commodity Chains and Global Capitalism*; Westport: Praeger.

———. (1999), 'International trade and industrial upgrading in the apparel commodity chain', *Journal of International Economics*, 48: 1.

Gereffi G., Humphrey J. and Sturgeon T. (2005), 'The governance of global value chains', *Review of International Political Economy*, 12: 1.

Gorg H. and Strobl E. (2002), 'Multinational companies and indigenous development: an empirical analysis', *European Economic Review*, 46: 7.

Grabher G. (1993), 'Rediscovering the social in the economics of inter-firm relations', in G. Grabher (ed.) *The Embedded Firm: on the Socioeconomics of Industrial Networks*, London: Routledge.

Granovetter M. (1989), 'Economic action and social structure: the problem of embeddedness', *American Journal of Sociology*, 91.

Graziani G. (2001), 'International subcontracting in the textile and clothing industry: fragmentation, new production patterns, in S. W. Arndt and H. Kierzkowsky (eds.), *The World Economy*, Oxford: Oxford University Press.

Humphrey J., (1995), 'Industrial reorganization in developing countries', *World Development*, 23: 1.

Lorenzoni G. (1990), *L'architettura di sviluppo delle imprese minori. Costellazioni e piccoli gruppi*, Bologna: Il Mulino.

——. (ed.) (1992), *Accordi, reti e vantaggio competitivo. Le innovazioni nell'economia d'impresa e negli assetti organizzativi*, Milano: Etaslibri.

——. (ed.) (1997), *Architetture reticolari e processi di internazionalizzazione*, Bulogna: Il Mulino.

Maillat D, Kebir L. and Bailly A. S. (2003), 'Sistemi produttivi territoriali e sviluppo endogeno', in G. Garofoli (ed.) *Impresa e Territorio*, Il Mulino, Bologna.

Markusen A. (1996), 'Sticky places in slippery space: a typology of industrial districts', *Economic Geography*, 72: 293–312.

Nassimbeni G., De Toni A. and Tonchia S. (1993), 'L'evoluzione dei rapporti di subfornitura', *Sviluppo & Organizzazione*, 137.

Nadvi K. (1999), 'Shifting ties: social networks in the surgical instrument cluster of Sialkot, Pakistan', *Development and Change*, 30: 1.

Nadvi K. and Halder G. (2005), 'Local clusters in global value chain: exploring dynamic linkages between Germany and Pakistan', *Entrepreneurship and Regional Development*, 17.

Potter J., Moore B. and Spires R. (2003), 'Foreign manufacturing investment in the United Kingdom and the upgrading of supplier practices', *Regional Studies*, 37.

Raffa M. (1993), 'Un modello di valutazione del grado di dipendenza tra le grandi e le piccole imprese', *Piccola Impresa/Small Business*, 1.

Schiattarella R. (1999), 'La delocalizzazione internazionale: problemi di definizione e di misurazione. Un'analisi per il settore "Made in Italy"', *Economia e politica industriale*, 103.

Sengenberger W.and Pyke F. (1991), 'Small firms, industrial districts and local economic regeneration', *Labour and Society*, 16: 1.

Signorini F. (2003), Intervista a Federico Signorini, Newsletter Area Studi, Maggio 2003.

Steward J. C. (1976), 'Linkages and foreign direct investment', *Regional Studies*, 10.

Storper M. and Harrison B. (1991), 'Flexibility, hierarchy and regional development: the changing structure of industrial production systems and their forms of governance in the 1980s', *Research Policy*, 20.

Tracogna A. (1999), *Le problematiche di sviluppo e i percorsi evolutivi delle imprese subfornitrici*, Milano: Franco Angeli.

Turok I. (1993), 'Inward investment and local linkages: how deeply embedded is "Silicon Glen"', *Regional Studies*, 27.

Viesti G. (2000), *Come nascono I distretti industriali*, Editori Laterza, Bari.
Wasserman S. and Faust K. (1994), *Social Network Analysis: Methods and Applications*, Cambridge: Cambridge University Press.

Part III

Industrial districts and clusters in the global value chains

11 Local systems playing globally

Heterogeneous districts in the ornamental horticulture global value chain

*Fiorenza Belussi (Padua University)
and Silvia Rita Sedita (Padua
University)*

11.1 Introduction

The aim of this work is to describe the significant variety occurring among the horticultural districts in the Netherlands and in Italy. Our empirical analysis allows us to apply the two largely used concepts of industrial districts and clusters, pinpointing their different meaning. A symbiotic division of labour has been discovered among the three districts considered: Boskoop, Pistoia, and Saonara, which dates back to the international fragmentation of the value chain. Our work shows that the application of science in horticultural districts has transformed them in knowledge-intensive districts. This process is more visible in the case of the Dutch cluster than in the Italian districts. Several theoretical concepts regarding agglomeration, and the main characteristics of the ornamental horticulture industry, will be discussed in this chapter, with a special focus on three case studies regarding the Boskoop, Pistoia, and Saonara districts.

The principal idea discussed here is to understand the internal dynamics of the three districts, and their external relationships, along the value chain, which overcomes the boundaries of the single area or even of the single country. Section 11.2 provides the theoretical background of our research. Section 11.3 briefly outlines some important characteristics of the ornamental horticulture industry in the larger horticulture-agriculture context. Section 11.4 describes the evolutionary pattern of the three horticultural districts, and outlines a comparison. Section 11.5 provides a brief comparison of the three cases. Some conclusions are set out in Section 11.6.

11.2 Districts' heterogeneity and global supply chains

The concepts of 'industrial district' and 'cluster' have entered the language of our economic daily life. However, there is a semantic ambiguity in the use of the two terms, because under the umbrella terms of 'district' and 'cluster', extensively used in economics, business, regional economics, industrial economics, economic geography, and sociology, different models of (local) development, and inter-firm arrangements, can be recognised. As a result, today, we have a large number of contributions that unfortunately denote with the same term a wide variety of phenomena. This chapter offers an empirical application of the use of these two terms which highlights how it is possible to make a precise distinction between these 'chaotic concepts'[1] (Martin and Sunley 2003), on the basis of an empirical study, developed after a systematic analysis of the literature (Belussi 2005). Let us start with Marshall's concept of the industrial district (Marshall 1920), based on the importance of external economies to understanding the development of an agglomeration of small and medium-sized firms. The industrial district is an organizational model of interconnected firms, a hybrid model between market and hierarchy, and a territorial model (a specific localized system characterized by a high sectoral specialization). Since the work of Marshall, economists have stressed that the characteristics of an industrial district are related to the benefits of external economies emerging from the close proximity of firms working together in the same industrial town, or in a decentralized 'industrial district'. Other important elements of the model are: (1) the concentration of many small factories specializing in different phases of the same production processes; (2) the gradual accumulation in the area of a skilled labour force; and (3) the creation of subsidiary industries and specialized suppliers. External economies, depending on 'the aggregate volume of production of the kind of neighbourhood' (Marshall 1920: 265), can be juxtaposed to the internal economies related to the coordination of activities under the vertically integrated factory. Marshall advocated that, *at least for certain types of production*, two (equally efficient) manufacturing systems could be employed: the large vertically integrated firm, and the industrial district.

We can, thus, arrive at the following definition:

1 the Marshallian industrial district describes a specific system of firms closely localized where there is a certain type of common productive specialization, which allows inter-firm division of labour and positive external economies;
2 the district is characterized by a high density (prevalence, but not absolute dominance) of small–medium-sized firms;
3 firms cooperate along the supply chain, at least because there is an extended inter-firm division of labour;
4 typically, the district derives leadership in a special industry (Marshall 1919: 287) from the 'industrial atmosphere' if, as Marshall underlined, obstinacy or inertia of firm behaviours, in changing times, will not 'ruin it';
5 we have an industrial district if in the same area there is a wide variety of similar producers, because this stimulates a highly creative faculty and, sometimes, intercommunication of ideas between machine makers and machine users (Marshall 1919: 603).

Using the Marshallian approach we can derive several analytical consequences. First, the industrial district is not a universalistic model of firm clustering. Second, the industrial district is a specific organizational model, *ceteris paribus*, equally efficient – in the condition of technical or economic divisibility of activities – to that of the large firm (from this we cannot always imply that a bunch of similar small firms, specialized in a particular activity, and clustered in one area, are *per se* efficient: for instance, they could adopt inferior technologies to those in use by large organizations). This is equivalent to saying that a local agglomeration of small firms may (but not must) resort to an entrepreneurial positive model, without setting a deterministic causal law, as it was implied *ad nauseam* by the international literature of the 1980s, shaped in the vein of Krugman's contributions (agglomeration of firms is always connected to dynamic firm growth or positive externalities, as he called them, if the cost of urbanization and congestion are not too high). Third, a single firm network cannot form a district: the same definition of industrial district recalls the concept of a large population of firms, and introduces the concept of a sizeable 'threshold' of local firms. Fourth, in the industrial district we can clearly find a mechanism of increasing return embedded in the territory, but there is also the possibility of contemporary increasing returns bound to the individual organization, and even some large firms and plants located in industrial districts. In districts there is still room for increasing organizational efficiency depending on individual firms' strategies. Thus, from the Marshallian theory we assume that external efficiency in industrial districts is related to the volume of activities (scale efficiency), but there are also other forms of efficiency related to increasing returns and to innovation dynamics (dynamic efficiency): they are conditioned by the stage of evolution of each industrial district.

To summarize, most of the social features of this ideal type of organization are related to:

1 extended inter-firm division of labour with no asymmetries of power among the clustered enterprises (Sforzi 2003);
2 equilibrium between cooperation and competition among rival firms (You and Wilkinson, 1994; Asheim 1996);
3 social integration (Brusco 1982, 1990);
4 existence of trust, which enforces cooperation, economizes on transaction costs and fosters flexibility and innovation (Dei Ottati 1996);
5 moderate or strong forms of learning (Belussi and Pilotti 2002).

A cluster is defined in the *Concise Oxford Dictionary* as – *'a group of similar things growing together'*. This definition implies either a spatial proximity or a functional relatedness of the same, or of closely related, things, which may be involved in a dynamic process. This ambiguity, or double meaning, is intrinsically related to the use of the term cluster in the work of Porter. For Porter:

A cluster is a geographically proximate group of interconnected companies and associated institutions in a particular field, linked by commonalities and complementarities (1998: 199).

Porter never defines the spatial boundaries of his territorial system under analysis. For him a cluster is not just a small portion of a territory, a piece of identifiable 'localized industry'. Porter (1998: cap. 7) extensively mentions the existence of 'regional clusters', mapping them in the US (for instance the Californian wine cluster), Portugal, Sweden and Italy, but in his book he also presents 'national clusters' such as the *Italian* (our italics) clusters of the fashion and shoes industries. In his work Porter also specifies that tracing the boundaries of a cluster is often a matter of degrees, and that this is a creative process, related to the understanding of links and complementarities existing among industries and institutions. In fact, he argues, the 'external effects', significantly related with competitiveness and productivity, determine the very boundaries of a cluster.

But if we study the 'economic interrelatedness' of a cluster, we can shift easily from spatial interconnections, which are defined by the geographical proximity, to virtual connections (Gallaut and Torre 2005), which are related to the many external linkages that each local organization activates with the external world: in other words, by doing so, we put at risk the same possibility of defining a 'given system', and we lose the limiting boundary conditions between what is inside and outside our model.

Clearly, there is nothing wrong in using the term cluster. But we must acknowledge that we refer to a class of economic systems that: (1) are not spatially defined; (2) do not have a minimum threshold of agglomeration (three firms are not a district in a Marshallian sense, but they can belong to a cluster); (3) do not have a history-based identity (its definition depends strongly on the research assumptions); (4) do not have a close relationship with the local community; and strictly speaking (5) do not have a local evolutionary pattern of growth.

Thus, the term cluster can accommodate a very general class of phenomena, while the term district is a more specific subset. To shift from the cluster concept to the industrial district notion we need three necessary conditions:

1   agglomeration (density of similar, or sectoral interrelated, firms in a restricted area);
2   interaction with the local institutions and among the individual firms; and
3   social embeddedness (a certain level of identity, trust and cooperation which is historically formed during the process of 'districtualization' or 'clustering', as discussed for instance by Hu, Lin and Chang 2005). The third necessary condition is linked with the Marshallian approach: a communitarian view of the economic and social system under examination, which is represented as a unique and historically dependent territorial system (Belussi, Gottardi and Rullani 2003; Sforzi and Lorenzoni 2002; Paniccia 1998 and 2002).

Conditions 1 and 2 suffice for the identification of a local cluster with possible different geographical borders. Condition 3 introduces the idea of a socio-economic embeddedness, locally bounded because of face-to-face social interactions. This is a necessary condition for the definition of an industrial district.

In the international literature, unfortunately, this distinction does not always hold. Various means and methodologies have been used to identify and measure the type and characteristics of industrial districts and clusters, in a type of interchangeable meaning.[2] For instance, in the Nordic European countries there is a common usage of the term cluster as a close substitute for the term industrial district (Cooke and Huggins 2003; Maskell 2001; Maskell and Lorenzen 2004), but the local systems under analysis satisfy the three conditions presented above. In our view a mix of quantitative and qualitative analyses is required for the identification of an industrial district (Belussi and Gottardi 2000; Belussi, Gottardi and Rullani 2003).

Well-known quantitative and systematic approaches, based on regional input-output analysis, location quotient analysis, and systematic benchmarking exercises, widely used for cluster analysis and for identification of clusters (for example, European Commission 2001; OECD 1999a and b and 2001a and b; DTI 2001; and Harvard Business School 2002) can be considered only as a first step in the identification of an industrial district.

A possible four-stage system for measuring linkages within industrial districts/clusters is here proposed (see also Belussi 2006).

1 Identification of industrial districts' geographical *boundaries* using either quantitative measures (e.g. concentration indexes, input-output and innovation interaction matrices) or historical sources.
2 Mapping of firm networks using *social network analysis* to identify and measure types of relationships occurring in industrial districts, in relation to the type of analysis conducted.
3 In-depth analysis to measure the stage of *evolution* of industrial districts.
4 Qualitative case studies to explore the rich details of the *firm characteristics and linkages* in the industrial district.

The heterogeneity that characterizes industrial districts has been well emphasized by the international literature and recently also by Sammarra (2003), where for instance a synthetic taxonomy of the Italian industrial districts is proposed. The essential parameters used to discriminate between different typologies are the following: (1) the socio-economic structure (including the relational structure and the type of governance); (2) the prevalent strategy of district firms (including the degree of openness); (3) the learning mechanism (and the attitude towards innovation); and, finally, (4) the institutional environment.

The classification suggested does not take into account the product specificity, and the variety of processes of production, which can be viewed as additional distinctive elements of a possible taxonomy.

Still, the official classification of products in high tech, medium-high tech, medium-low tech, and low tech, put forward by the OECD (2001) is not truly representative of the peculiar knowledge intensity of each sector, as has been discussed by Sedita (2005). Accordingly, investments in a plurality of learning activities also affect industries not properly considered at the edge of economic growth, such as in the case of the ornamental horticulture industry analyzed below.

These learning activities are internally (to the district) supported by firms' strategies, and by their proactive efforts (R&D, engineering departments, focused working groups), but also they are the result of firm interactions, both locally and globally developed.

We are referring to firm networks, which include local suppliers, customers, and global supply chains (Gereffi, *et al.* 2005, Bair and Gereffi 2001). Networks access can potentially upgrade firms belonging to the district. Sometimes the global connections do not carry on any transferable knowledge or organizational routines, but they work as powerful governance structures whose leaders are the commercial actors. This is the case of the Netherlands and in particular of the Boskoop district, and of its intense and distributed business networks spread throughout the world.

Richardson (1972), in his seminal article, highlighted the motivations for firms to enter business networks: in order to obtain complementary but dissimilar competencies they lack, and that need to fit the specific organizational productive demand, and which cannot be bought on the market ready-made. In the industrial districts, this has implied the continuous search for specialized producers, and for critical competences, but it has also called for cheaper producers, either geographically co-located or more and more dispersed in low-wage countries. This is why, in a period of fragmented but integrated global production processes, the construction of global supply chains (Gereffi, *et al.* 2005) has gained ground, both as buyer-driven chains (ruled by retailers and large commercial buyers) or producer-driven chains (MNCs).[3]

The differing ability to interpret and take the opportunities offered by the network characterizes the three districts illustrated in this chapter. They are ranked in a sort of hierarchical order, with first place taken by the Boskoop district (where there are the most powerful international retailers), second is occupied by the Pistoia district (which plays in part the role of international producers of several final goods which are sold by Dutch wholesalers on the international market), and the last district considered in this ranking is the Saonara district (where local firms cover the Italian market and are specialized in the service of landscaping, being low exporters). The relations among firms in these three districts are often regulated not by long-term subcontracting but by spot transactions. Our analysis has shown that the three districts are not autonomous. Instead they are linked by a symbiotic relationship, where the entire value chain is characterized by a strong inter-firm division of labour (being research and development activities and commercial distribution carried out in the Boskoop district and in the Netherlands cluster).

11.3 The ornamental horticulture industry

The ornamental horticulture industry exhibits clearly how the globalization of the markets can affect a product – the flower or a plant – that is easily transportable so that production can be moved to lower energy costs countries, or countries with better climates, or finally, countries with lower labour costs.

One way to avoid the negative effect of increasing local costs in nursery garden districts, as argued by Cresti (1991), is for firms (and public institutions) to invest in research and product/process innovation, as well as to increase collaborations with universities and research centres, with the purpose of keeping 'in house' the most profitable activities, and to outsource the lowest value added ones.

The Netherlands is presently at the forefront of this industry, and contains a whole cluster of related activities and a specialized district (Boskoop), because, even with the highest labour costs and the most unfavourable climate, it has been able, over time, to develop a strong expertise in horticulture production, and in related R&D activities. This attitude towards product and process innovation places the Netherlands in a leading position, allowing it to exert its power as a strong supplier of cut flowers and young potted plants to be sold throughout all of Europe.

The Italian producers, mainly organized in industrial districts, despite their ancient tradition, their territorial embeddedness, and the excellent climate, became strongly dependent on the Netherlands, which is now the 'head' of a global value chain.

The ornamental horticulture industry is composed of the floriculture and nursery sectors. The floriculture sector covers firms specialized in production of cut flowers and cut foliage, whereas the nursery sector comprises the cultivation of a wide variety of plants and gardening products, as shown in Figure 11.1. Both are involved in production and sales.

The ornamental horticulture industry in Europe is dominated by the Netherlands, but Italy holds second place, producing 23 per cent of the entire European market. According to the 2000 census of the agricultural industry,[4] the Italian sector is composed of almost 19,000 firms, which cultivate an area larger than 12,600 ha (7200 ha in the open air), producing more than 25,500 types of flowers and plants. If we include all the firms in the *filière* (business services and induced activities) the number of firms rises to 30,000 units, with 130,000 employees (Ferretti 2004).

Even though the ornamental horticulture industry is far from being high-tech, it has firmly and extensively adopted ICT technologies for the commercialization, conception and production of new products.

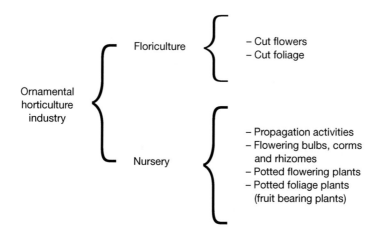

Figure 11.1 An abridged classification of the ornamental horticulture industry.
Source: Dutch Floricultural Wholesale Board.

Concerning the commercialization stage, we refer mainly to the applications of business-to-business (B2B) technologies, and to the construction of e-marketplaces, which use the 'reverse' (to lowest price) auction mechanism.[5]

The emergence of B2B and e-marketplaces, spanning both vertical and horizontal markets, has restructured the competitive field of this industry, by aggregating scale in the final selling phase, increasing market and value chain transparency. The use of automated transactions has rendered the de-verticalization of the value chain possible, and, as a consequence, it has created a high level of dis-intermediation.

The Dutch cooperative enterprise Bloemenveiling Aalsmeer (VBA), the most prominent floricultural products auction in the world, involves about 7000 cultivators from all over the world and some 55,000 transactions daily. The VBA works as a virtual marketplace, where buyers can purchase flowers and plants from the clocks[6] (that run from the highest to the lowest price) using the Remote Purchasing service (KOA), simply via the Internet. This is a window-shopping mechanism. Wholesalers and consumers, by viewing the un-priced supply of product, can ascertain in advance what they need to buy, mark the batches that interest them, and they will be informed in good time if the product is about to be auctioned, so that they can switch to the correct clock for one-shot buying. There is also freedom to purchase outside the auction room, which has significant advantages for repetitive shots. For example, it allows an organization to buy items from the same producer, and it creates more cooperative interactions, and thereby integrates data from the auction with internal firms' data systems.

Concerning the conception of new products, we refer basically to new varieties of flowers and plants. The creation of new varieties takes place within advanced laboratories (located in universities or large MNCs). The Praktijkonderzoek Plant & Omgeving (PPO – Applied Plant Research) in Boskoop, for instance, is a research lab that was formed by a merger of the experimental station for crop research and other regional research centres in the Netherlands, in the year 2000. The PPO researchers actively collaborate with Wageningen University, and the research centre Wageningen-UR, and this enables the industry to update knowledge and to meet changing research requirements of firms.

New technologies in plant cell and tissue culture are applied both to cell culture for propagation (through asexual reproduction methods), and to plant transformation with recombinant DNA (Cocking 1989). Sometimes, genetically engineered plants do not transfer the new embedded characteristics to subsequent generations. Thus, they have to be reproduced only through cell propagation.

PPO is active both in plant propagation and in recombinant DNA engineering. It aims also to create sustainable management systems, supporting quality management in the chain, cultivation management, plant health, and efficient utilization of resources and structuring of rural areas. It configures itself as a link between practice and science, conducting research not only on modern greenhouse practices – conditioned storage and treatment rooms, experimental fields, laboratories and climate chambers – but also on commercial issues.

Similar to PPO, in Pistoia there is Ce.Spe.Vi., an s.r.l. (limited liability) company, founded in 1981, by the Chamber of Commerce and the Cassa di Risparmio of Pistoia and Pescia (a local bank), for the creation of a centre of nursery plant experimentation and propagation, and for promoting the use of the company's capital to other nursery agencies or associations. In Pistoia there is little plant DNA recombination research activity. The centre accommodates warehouses, offices, a meeting room, two fixed experimental greenhouses in steel and glass, and an area equipped for plant breeding in containers. Ce.Spe.Vi. has also developed a system of mother-plants, organized in collaboration with the CNR (National Research Centre) Institute of Florence for the propagation of trees (mainly conifers), flowers, and hedge shrubs. This initiative has recently merged with the National Germplasm[7] Bank, a joint project of the Ce.Spe.Vi. together with the Department of Florence University 'Ortoflorifrutticoltura' (horticulture plus floriculture plus fruit-growing).

Process technologies are also significant for the industry. In regard to automation technologies, it is evident that they can streamline the process, sustain cost cutting, and help reach scale economies. Process technologies are applied to irrigation systems and fertirrigation, farm tractors, trailers, power cultivators, ploughs, clod busters, extraction machineries, motor mowers, and elevating trucks. Dutch firms are at the front line in these technologies, followed by mechanical firms specializing in agricultural machinery, which are mainly based in Emilia Romagna (within the district of Reggio Emilia) and in the Veneto region.

The evolution of the Dutch global value chain is illustrated in Table 11.1 and in Figure 11.2, where the power of the Netherlands is evidenced. The Netherlands plays the role of a monopolist supplier of cut flowers distributed throughout

Table 11.1 Dutch exports of horticultural products

Sales turnover (million euro)

	2002	2003	2004	% 04/03
Germany	1.512	1.585	1.71	–0.9%
UK	729	741	797	7.5%
France	606	649	654	0.7%
Italy	281	317	333	5.1%
Belgium	164	184	190	3.0%
Denmark	107	123	138	12.4%
Austria	127	133	135	1.4%
Switzerland	141	134	126	–6.0%
USA	143	115	101	–12.4%
Spain	72	85	97	14.1%
Other countries	671	678	729	5.0%
Total	4.553	4.744	4.869	2.2%

Source: Dutch Floricultural Wholesale Board.

Table 11.2 Structure and performance indicators of the three districts (2003)

District	Number of firms	Area covered (ha)	Number of employees	Sales (million euro)	Export (%)
Boskoop*	1000	2200	2500	350	90
Pistoia**	1767	4403	5000	300	45
Saonara*	151	1000	800	15.5	10

Source: *Our survey;**Regione Toscana – Settore Statistica.

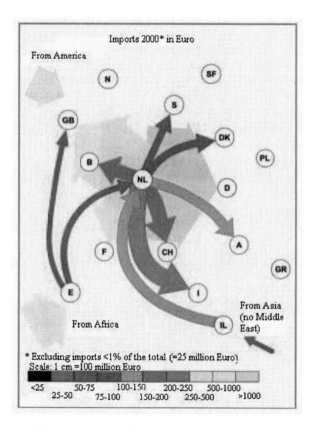

Figure 11.2 Intra EU exchange of cut flowers.
Source: International Association of Horticultural Producers (AIPH)/Union Fleurs,
International Statistics Flowers and Plants, 2001.

Europe. In particular, Italy has consistently increased its imports of horticultural products. This process was accelerated by the constitution of the 'Mercato Unico Europeo' (Economic European Area – EEA), which occurred on 1 January 1993. In 2004, exports to Italy contributed to a sales turnover of 333 million euro for the Netherlands, an amount that increased 5.1 per cent between 2003 and 2004.

11.4 Three case studies[8]

Few studies have been conducted on the international ornamental horticulture industry, which is neither well known, nor examined in its economic, social and territorial aspects. The Italian productive industry likewise has not been studied to any extent. In Italy there is a vast assortment of horticultural products, from cut flowers to potted plants for apartments, and plants for gardens and large parks. Some typical national products are ornamental citrus in terracotta pots, olive trees of all the varieties and shapes, and the special Mediterranean plants. This makes Italy one of the most heterogeneous and commercially interesting countries in the horticultural sphere.

Some ornamental horticulture production takes place in territorially circumscribed areas, and its organization assumes the appearance and characteristics of the classical industrial districts, such as in the case of Pistoia, in Tuscany, and Saonara (in the province of Padua), which will be further analyzed.

However, the Italian production is strictly dependent on several Dutch activities, as the Netherlands is the leading country in this industry, as noted earlier. In this chapter we have chosen to focus on three ornamental horticulture districts, two located in Italy, and one in the Netherlands: in Boskoop. In Table 11.2 structural features and performance indicators of the three districts are presented.

11.4.1 The Boskoop ornamental horticulture district

The most important production centre in the Netherlands is Boskoop. Boskoop can be considered a horticulture district belonging to a very specialized and dense area (called here a cluster) of activities related to the same sector (the region/country of the Netherlands). The horticultural sector is indeed responsible for 41 per cent of the entire agricultural production in the Netherlands, and the ornamental plants sector accounts for two-thirds of the latter. The ornamental plants sector also accounts for about 25 per cent of the Dutch trade surplus (Maijers, *et al.* 2005). In Boskoop (Table 11.3), hundreds of firms are producing ornamental plants and conifers (in greenhouses and in the open air).

The origin of the district dates back to the Renaissance period, when local farmers learned from the Rijnsburg Coventry the art of fructiferous grafting.[9] For a long time they applied the new techniques only to fructiferous plants, but during the seventeenth century they started production of ornamental plants, using the same methodologies. Interestingly, as in the Italian case, in the nineteenth century local production was mainly concentrated in a few large firms. Subsequently, the process of spin-off of qualified manual workers, thoroughly studied in the district theory,

Table 11.3 Structure and performance indicators of Boskoop district (2003)

	Number of horticultural firms	Area covered (ha)	Number of employees	Sales (million euro)
Boskoop	1000*	2200	2500	350
The Netherlands	4000	12,000	4170	445
Percentage weight of the district	25.0	16.7	60.0	78.7

Note
* of which 100 firms are wholesalers.

Source: interviews conducted during the survey.

gave rise to a multitude of small specialized firms. However, the district firms[10], until the Second World War, were still quite undeveloped, and commercial circuits were mainly local, with few exports. The real business started during 1970s, as a result of the growth of international demand, and development of economies (horticultural plants are a luxury good sold in affluent societies).

Why is horticultural production so specialized in Boskoop? Boskoop bears some unique characteristics, including a fertile and moist soil type, and high humidity, ideal for plant cultivation. Thus the district is specialized in the production of young plants, which are cultivated only up to low–medium height. Boskoop producers are able to develop all types of plants (such as *Fagus, Magnolia, Buxus, Acer,* etc.), except of course tropical species. Production is mainly in the open air.

The 'savoir fair' is passed from father to son, and by the sharing of knowledge with on-the-job training for newly employed people. In the past, there was a local vocational training school based on horticulture, but now it is closed, because firms deal directly with more advanced centres and universities. During the analysis we found that these firms share a sense of identity from being part of a district, and younger entrepreneurs are more directly involved in cooperation with public institutions, and with rival firms within the collective associations.

Firms are mainly family businesses, often comprising two or three employees plus the owner. Greenhouse producers and open air growers no longer sow plants by themselves. Sowing and cultivation of young plants has become the work of highly specialized nurseries, using advanced computer techniques, and robots. The whole production process is a prime example of advanced technology applied to horticulture. Family firms do not deal with the market directly, and work on behalf of the wholesalers. It is a type of subcontracting arrangement existing among manufacturing sectors, such as footwear or clothing. Wholesalers annually stipulate contracts for buying a clearly defined set of products, which they will sell at the international level.

These contracts are regulated by external institutions, and are limited by strict obligations, on both sides. So, foreign clients cannot simply override the wholesale structure, buying directly from the producers. They can have access only to redundant production, and in any event, they must pay by cash in advance.

The largest firms in the district are wholesalers; typically they are private, limited companies with five to 20 employees, and with a range of sales varying between 2.5 million and 5 million euro. These firms, and generally local entrepreneurs, belong to the third or fourth generation of growers. Local wholesalers sell mainly in the EU, and in Canada, the US and Japan. They import adult plants from Italy, France and Germany. The feature of Boskoop is that, using advanced logistic techniques, in 24 hours, clients receive their orders in all parts of Europe, and also in other parts of the globe. In Boskoop there is an incredible variety of plants that can be bought. Variation is the typical resource of industrial districts, where production is decentralized, and many specialist firms co-exist.

Wholesalers sell primarily to garden centres (60 per cent), or to other wholesalers (30 per cent), or to public institutions (10 per cent).

Plants are small, so money is saved in packaging and transportation costs. There are mainly six international horticultural exhibitions, and two are organized in the districts studied here: Plantarium in Boskoop, IPM in Essen, Glee in the UK, Four Oaks in the UK, Iberflora in Spain, and Flormart/Miflor in Padua. Local district firms are connected to Boskoop's entrepreneurial associations (see Figure 11.3) as well as to national associations.[11]

Many public/private bodies (see Figure 11.3) assist firms (both producers and commercial firms) in their daily activities, and are responsible for the provision of 'real services', such as marketing the district on an international level (PPH—Plant Publicity Holland), and R&D activity (PT – Product Board for Ornamental Horticulture). This latter organization invests about 4.5 million euro each year in research.

NBvB (National Horticulture Firms Association) has signed a general agreement with LTO-Nederland, the association that represents all the Dutch agricultural sectors. In addition, it takes part in numerous other committees and executives councils, such as PT.

Firms directly support their specialized associations, for advertising and marketing, and for relevant R&D, but many governmental agencies are also involved in related R&D activities.

Many projects on logistics have been launched by the associations, with the use of public funds. For example, recently they have supported the introduction of a single, uniform type of trolley throughout the Netherlands, and the standardization of packaging, such as the chrysanthemum box. These projects show that the higher the level of standardization in logistics, the more efficiently the logistic processes can proceed. The general association of entrepreneurs, VBN, plays a central part in creating and maintaining that standardization. All the VBN-approved forms of packaging, for example, have a unique VBN code. Suppliers, auctions and the buyers all use those codes. Indeed, they would be unable to communicate with one another without them. The VBN is responsible for distributing and issuing the codes. The management of the standardized VBN packaging units is the responsibility of the ornamental plant sector's packaging pool, SiVePo.

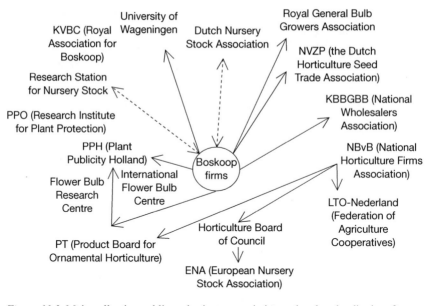

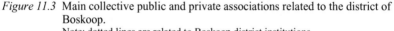

Figure 11.3 Main collective public and private associations related to the district of Boskoop.

Note: dotted lines are related to Boskoop district institutions.

Local associations are active in setting rules and fair business practices, which are now standardized and codified (see: *Trade Rules for Flower Bulb Trading* and *The Dutch Terms and Conditions of Trade for Nursery Stock*). One of the essential associations is the Council for Nursery Stock, where KBGBB and NBvB are represented. The Council for Nursery Stock sets policy for environmental issues, trade rules, and participates in EU consultation in the European Nursery Stock Association (ENA).

The local association of Boskoop (KVBC) has collections of Dutch heritage plants in reserved areas of Boskoop private producer's farms, and this is a kind of genetic living museum. The members of KVBC can ask for small quantities of these plants from the firm that manages the reserve, so they can reproduce on a large scale old forgotten species. The association publishes specialist manuals and a yearly book called *Dendroflora*.

PT is financed through the small revenue obtained from each sale. The money collected is used to finance innovation projects, and all activity that sustains the sector.

PPH was created in 1952 for the collective marketing of horticulture of the Dutch cluster, and it is financed by PT.

PPO is the research centre, which represents the intersection between horticultural practical and science, and runs experimental stations.

NVZP, the Dutch Seed Trade Association, represents firms working in breeding, production and trade of plant propagating material. It offers its members a platform for exchange of knowledge and information, provides information and advice, coordinates joint research projects, and acts as an employers' organization for collective labour agreements.

Then there is the General Dutch Service for the Quality Control that certifies all agricultural and horticultural products, and monitors that the level of pesticides is sufficiently low, as prescribed by EU norms.

As regards the public institutions, the renowned University of Wageningen (Wageningen UR) must be mentioned as it produces researchers and has contributed to the success of the district and the horticulture sector.

Additionally, we must acknowledge the software producers that worked with the Beurshal organization in the first years of the 1980s to build an automated system for selling and buying horticultural products (VARB), which is now one of the most advanced systems of electronic commerce.

VARB works together with the site www.plantscope.nl which provides users with scientific data, correct nomenclature with all synonyms, commercial information, product codes, data on patents and copyrights, and regulations on their potential use.[12]

Governmental agencies are very much involved in the sector.[13]

There is also a special tribunal for horticulture commerce, which deals immediately with all litigation (*Boskoops Scheidsgerecht voor de Boomkwekerij*). Members of Dutch associations are pay less for their use of this service. Finally, all payments not executed are registered in a special archive, and local firms are assisted with specialist legal advice. International hearings are initiated, if issues are not resolved promptly. There is also an archive on delinquent clients, based on the historical file of defaulted payments, to which local firms can have access, and they can make special inquires, in order to ascertain clients' credit status.[14]

Thus, the Boskoop district, which contains breeding firms, firms raising plants, growers, and trade distributors, has developed some specific institutions (associations, research, and training institutions), but is also immersed in a larger national agriculture and horticulture cluster,[15] which has developed supplying sectors, process and packaging industries, and transportation and logistics sectors (see Figure 11.4).

Recently a Dutch Innovation platform was set up by the government to stimulate innovation in Dutch knowledge-intensive industries, including the flower and food sectors. The idea is to reinforce the connections between knowledge institutions, innovative suppliers, leader entrepreneurs, and buyers.

The Boskoop district is a clear-cut open innovation system. Innovation did not take place within a vertically integrated company, with everything in-house, but was instead the result of open cooperation between firms, research centres and universities.

The concept of 'open innovation system' means that networks of organizations (private and public) are involved in innovation (Chesbrough 2003).

Dutch horticulture is an advanced cluster that produces sophisticated items (Figure 11.4). The long-standing division of labour among firms, and the use of

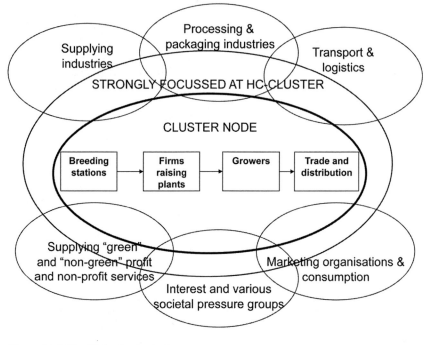

Figure 11.4 The Netherlands cluster.
Source: den Hertog (2003).

scientific methods applied to the reproduction of plants (and to manufacturing and transportation techniques), has created a large and professional supply industry: (1) propagating material; (2), plant breeding suppliers of vegetable seed and young plants; (3) greenhouse construction and installation companies,[16] (4) suppliers of harvesting and sorting machines; (5) innovative machines for logistical improvement of the production process; and (6) suppliers of other horticultural goods (equipment, accessories) such as pots, trays, covers and sheeting. There are also, of course, many specialized consultants that work in the horticultural sector.[17]

The horticultural suppliers are not only active in the Netherlands. They operate increasingly on the world market. Almost a quarter of the production value of this sector is obtained abroad nowadays (den Hertog 2003).

The breeding of horticultural crop plants has a long history in the Netherlands. Traditionally, seed companies were located in the north-west, around Enkhuizen. But subsequently, many plant breeders moved, or were created also in (or near) Westland, a municipality in the western Netherlands. Because of the importance of the Dutch market, many plant breeders from the United States, Japan, France, and other countries are present here. Due to the highly specialized nature of plant breeding, and the high costs involved, firms tend to collaborate also with foreign firms located in the area.

In spite of the internationalization of the plant breeding sector, much of the scientific research into new varieties has remained in the Netherlands. This gives a high competitive advantage to seed firms, which export a significant proportion of their seed products. Netherlands is now the home of plant breeding, and the innovator of new plant and flower varieties (Maijers, *et al.* 2005). A close look at the national innovation system is reported in Table 11.4.

11.4.2 Pistoia ornamental horticulture district

Pistoia is the 'greenest province' of Italy, with over 50 per cent of its territory covered in conifer forests, hardwood forests and typical coastal vegetation. The hills are carpeted with rows of grape vines and olive trees that produce high quality wines and extra virgin olive oils. The plains are adorned with splendid cultivations of ornamental plants and flowers, which are a dominant feature of Pistoia's economy and make it famous all over Europe. The ornamental horticulture industry is the most important agricultural activity; it contributes 25 per cent of the gross product of Tuscany's agriculture, and represents 5 per cent of the overall European ornamental horticulture industry, making Pistoia one of the most important productive districts of the continent.[18]

Three categories of firms can be identified in the Pistoia district, according to their size: (1) small firms: small producers, specialized in the production of one only variety of plant, upon request of one large company, with which they subscribe to yearly contracts that guarantees them the job, but with small profit margins; (2) medium-sized firms: producers that both produce and commercialize their products. They tend not to be dependent on larger companies, and they aim to grow at the national and international levels. Therefore they are part of international networks with which they interact occasionally; (3) large firms (about 20 firms): they concentrate their activity on the wholesale trade of their productions, destined mostly for foreign markets (in the EU); they invest much of their revenues in R&D activities, often carried out in-house in advanced laboratories. As a result, they have been able over a period to create five new varieties of plants (one *Magnolia grandiflora* variety, two *Quercus robur*, two *Robinia*). The assortment of plants cultivated in the district is very large in terms of species, but the specialization is in evergreens, deciduous plants, and conifers. In the Pistoia industrial district the enterprises and the public system have been able to meld an entrepreneurial culture with scientific knowledge, creating, as a result, modern ornamental horticulture enterprises, and advanced structures of training and technical-scientific support, such as the bachelor course in Nursery Techniques and Landscape Architecture.

In the district, there is a strong firm specialization, and the division of labour between companies has been extended so much that it can be easily stated that a plant raised in Pistoia can be object of the attention of two, three or even four different enterprises before being ready to reach the market. The experience that some of the firms have accumulated is so valuable that they have become significant at the national level – this is the case with companies that develop gardens and parks,

Table 11.4 The Netherlands innovation system

Period	Characterization	Productivity boosters	Knowledge architecture
1945–1965	Reconstruction and food safety	Soil productivity Crop protection Variety improvement	Research and information as trouble-shooters. Auctions increase sharply.
1965–1980	Mechanization	Heating Climate control Plant material Mechanization of labour Large scale export through liberalization of EU market	Close cooperation between government and industry. Development of the agricultural knowledge system (OVO/Research, Information, education triptych).
1980–1993	Computerization	Introduction of computer boosts hydroponic cultivation, trickle irrigation, carbon dioxide fertilization, assimilation-clarification	The knowledge systems support the introduction of new technology. Study groups for growers. Development of management information systems. Auctions develop data-processing, as well as guidelines for environmentally aware cultivation.
1993–2000	Chain reversal	Great changes in sales structure and knowledge systems Market changes from supply-driven to demand-driven Privatization of information and research	Emergence of chain-thinking, growers associations and brand strategy. Social concerns play a greater role (e.g. environment). Licence to produce. Knowledge system breaks up into individual parties.
2000–	Mobilization and integration	Multidisciplinary approach Combination of various types of knowledge From 'formula to concept' Demand-and supply-articulation Chains and chain management	Knowledge circulation instead of knowledge development. Networks, communication of practices, knowledge circles. Socio-technical networks, knowledge groups. Horticultural academy. Globalization of market and production. Certification and quality assurance systems. Supply chain management. Licence to deliver.

Source: Our elaboration of Buurma (2001).

means of production (containers, fertile soil, greenhouses and plant engineering, etc.), or which supply services (and associated materials goods).

Moreover, the district is characterized by products that originate from the tradition of the small Tuscan farms of the Renaissance era, namely the cultivation in pots of citrus and other exotic species, or topiary for furnishing classic gardens.

But today many firms in the district buy young plants from the Netherlands, which they then cultivate in their nurseries. However, the largest firms are able to sell their cultivated plants back to the Dutch garden centres. The Netherlands lacks the right soil and sun for the maturation of the plants, and production costs are much higher than in Italy. So, we can observe an interesting division of labour that takes place between the two districts: scientific activities and propagation tasks (which are also related to the application of biotech techniques to the propagation phase) are more developed in the Netherlands, where local firms benefit from the existing well developed 'national innovation system', while the 'manufacturing' process of plants' development, from the small to the adult plant, is organized by the Italian district.

We see that horticultural districts are no longer low-tech activities, but science is applied differently in the two districts, and districts have an integrated flow of knowledge exchanged in goods and services. Some districts have specialized in knowledge-intensive activities, while others are less knowledge-intensively specialized.

In the former, biotech activities are behind the development of knowledge in plant reproduction and in product innovation (the generation of new varieties), and in ICT applied to logistics, selling and marketing techniques.

In the latter – which can not benefit from a national advanced system in plant reproduction and in biotech science – we see interesting new applications of mechanical labour saving techniques for irrigation, transport automation, and so on, which are more related to medium–low value added phases of the value chain, and some limited progress in new propagation techniques related to typical endogenous niche products, which the Dutch have not developed greatly (such as Mediterranean plants). It is a process very similar to the one that takes place in clothing and footwear districts, described in other chapters of the book, with the difference that in those industries more advanced Italian districts, specialized in design, production techniques and marketing activities, govern the entire global supply chain (and often own the foreign firms that in the manufacturing districts operate in 'manufacturing' phase).

In this context, it is interesting to observe that Pistoia firms are also involved in commercial activities with Saonara firms, to which they sell plants and some mechanical equipment for the nursery sector. In the Pistoia district there are some specialist firms that have developed new machinery (in collaboration with the advanced Italian mechanical sector/cluster in agricultural machinery of Reggio Emilia, in Emilia Romagna, and of Padua, in the Veneto region). They now are among the largest Italian suppliers of these products.

11.4.2.1 Historical development of the Pistoia district

The birth of the ornamental horticulture district in Pistoia dates back to 1849, with the work of a young gardener of Villa Bozzi: Antonio Bartolini. The garden of Villa Bozzi, and those of its surroundings, very soon became too small to contain all the plants produced, so Bartolini convinced his father to rent a narrow piece of land on the 'Lucchese' Provincial road. Here he built up his first small nursery, and it was also the first in Pistoia; soon his brothers started to work with him, making it a small family firm.

In 1851 the rooms of the former 'Convento del Carmine', a monastery, accommodated the first Pistoia horticulture exhibition. Between 1870 and 1900 several important fairs dedicated to horticulture took place, since the Bartolini Brothers company was no longer the only one in the Pistoia horticulture industry. Among the 15 firms operating at the end of the 1800s, we can mention the Bianco Bianchi, the Raffaello Fedi and the Massimiliano Capecchi companies (all founded during the 1880s), the Martino Bianchi Company (1888), and the Chiari Company. In 1895, Ernesto Tonelli built an important nursery in the garden of the 'Madonna del Soccorso', and he was the first one to 'export' his own production to the Livorno market.

The growth phase of the Pistoia horticulture industry began during the first two decades of the 1900s. The agricultural companies grew in dimension and number, and the activities that previously were carried out within the walls of the city began to cover pieces of land outside them (in eastern and southern directions).

In the course of only two decades the area expanded quickly to cover 200 ha under cultivation, much larger than the average of that time. Furthermore, between 1909 and 1923 a significant number of agricultural institutions, researching, experimenting, and diffusing knowledge, began to support the horticulture industry production in Pistoia.

In 1911 the AOPI (Italian Professional Horticultural Association) was created, involving horticulturists, floriculturists, nursery professionals, garden constructors, seed traders and florists. It was the first association in Italy dedicated to scientific, technical or practical knowledge transfer among professionals in the industry.

In 1923 the 'Regal Practical and Theoretical Observatory of Fruit-growing' was founded in Italy, for research and experimentation in the field of fruit-bearing plants. The Observatory had two main objectives: (1) maintaining the plant varieties and treating diseases afflicting the various cultivations; and (2) organizing fruit growing courses, conferences, and working as a consultant to enhance the development of the industry.

As a result of such initiatives, a formal education system, focused on the arts of agriculture, was initiated in the city, through the institution of regular courses of pruning, grafting and diverse agrarian techniques. These initiatives were at the foundation of the future Agricultural College 'De Franceschi'.

In the 1920s, after having overcome the crises due to 'fillossera' (phylloxera)[19] and to the First World War, the Pistoia horticulture enterprises were ready to reassert themselves in Italy and in foreign countries.

Between the 1920s and the 1940s new firms were established, as a result of spin-off from the larger nurseries, giving rise to a quick development of the district. Unfortunately, the district suffered another crisis due to the Second World War. Several firms closed down and this left a large vacuum in the district.

As in the Netherlands, the 1950s were characterized by a phase of strong expansion; the number of firms and employees increased dramatically, the area under cultivation increased from 500 ha in 1956 to more than 3000 ha at the end of the 1960s. New institutions and specialist schools were created to serve the Pistoia firms. From 1965 entrepreneurs began to participate in international fairs such as the Flormart (in Padua) and the Miflor (in Milan).

During the 1970s the Pistoia companies introduced innovative improvements such as large scale cultivation of plants in pots.

In the 1980s topiary plants assumed great importance in the market. Following the demand, Pistoia firms introduced cultivation of shrubby creepers not only in pots, but also with particular shapes, using trellises to obtain a completely original product. The innovative activity of the firms of the district found a new supporter in the Ce.Spe.Vi, the experimental nursery centre founded in 1981, whose purpose and work has been discussed already in Section 11.3.

The experience of the terrible frost of 1985 prompted the creation of a new university course in nursery techniques and management, which was active from 1992.

During the 1990s a product innovation was a feature of the district: the cultivation of large trees in containers. Olive trees, strawberry-trees, palms, carob trees, oaks and other species were dug up and transported to Pistoia, unloaded, placed in large pots with the appropriate soil, pruned, and placed in fields to grow. In this way, they could be sold to enrich 'instant' gardens, a new trend in the sector, as confirmed by Hodgson (2004).

As a result of advances in horticulture production, and the continuous growing of new species, during the twentieth century the area under cultivation increased to 5000 ha. The district now is composed of roughly 2000 firms with 5000 employees, and the value of its production in recent years has reached about 300 million euro in sales.

11.4.3 The Saonara ornamental horticulture district

The industrial district of Saonara is located in the province of Padua. Along with Pistoia, it is one of the most ancient horticultural districts in Italy. In the district more than 40 per cent of the 2000 ha are used for nursery cultivation. About 1000 firms form the district.[20]

The majority of firms in the district are family companies (30 per cent), with a very small land area (around 1 ha): mostly one-man companies (the entrepreneur himself). Some of them employ extra-family employees (from three to eight persons), and only two or three firms have more than 20 employees. Moreover, employees are often linked to the firm by a seasonal contract.

The district is specialized in rose bushes and fruit-bearing trees. Production also includes ornamental plants for gardens, trees, and plants for landscaping and forestry. Firms are also limited exporters. Recently some firms have begun to specialize in gardening, and private and public garden maintenance. The revenues of those producers depending on wholesalers' purchases tend to be low. Being active in the gardening service sector provides a good way to escape the price mechanism provided by marketplace technologies, which place producers in global competition, following a pure neoclassical mechanism. Prices are no longer dependent on 'local' costs but are fixed in a global context.

All the firms operating in the district have some relationships with Pistoia, in order to buy plants, materials and equipment at lower prices than sold by local Padua suppliers. For this purpose firms have developed an effective logistical system, which is organized in two ways (with plants and materials bought in Pistoia) and sold to Pistoia (mainly rose bushes). Some of the firms are connected to the Netherlands, from where they buy rootstocks and young plants. Thus, Pistoia is more specialized in cut foliage and 'instant garden' plants, and Saonara in roses. Saonara is also involved in the service sector of garden and public flowerbed maintenance, for which they are able to put together 'bunches' of different plants: some bought and some cultivated by them.

Despite their relationships with Pistoia and Boskoop, the Saonara firms are backward: they are not adopting advanced techniques in product development, and they are neither innovators nor followers. This is probably due to a lack of intrinsic motivation and cultural embeddedness, which make the entrepreneurs very resistant to novelties and self-upgrading.

Saonara is a typical case of a district suffering from inward-looking behaviour.

The district lacks experimentation centres, which are judged as indispensable by entrepreneurs. In Legnaro there is Agripolis, a university pole of the Faculty of Agrarian and Veterinarian Medicine, incorporating also the Veneto Centre for Agricultural Studies, and in Padua there is a secondary school specialized in agriculture studies, the Istituto Tecnico Agrario 'Duca degli Abruzzi'. However, there are not many close and productive connections. The Faculty of Agriculture has recently proposed two courses specific for the sector that is a bachelor course in Nursery Techniques and a bachelor course in Landscaping, Parks and Gardens. But the local entrepreneurs are reluctant to employ graduate students in their small firms, and to provide internships for the university students.

Despite the existence of specific education programmes, a poor network of internal relationships, which involve institutions, universities and firms, contributes to creating a relational vacuum, where knowledge circulation and collaborative projects are not easily pursued.

The absence of effective meta-organizers, which operate as district boundary spanners (i.e. a training institution or a district museum) constitutes a strong limit to the evolution of the Saonara district, and keep it qualitatively and technologically distant from both the Boskoop and the Pistoia districts.

Similarly, there is the presence in Padua of an important international fair, Flormart/Miflor, which hosts, twice yearly, the leading operators in the ornamental horticulture industry.[21] Surprisingly, and paradoxically, this fair does not contribute considerably to the Saonara district firms' performance.

Again, the Saonara case shows that the development of a single firm depends strongly on its geographical localization.

The conditions related to the presence of communities of practice and advanced firms networks with science institutions is not only an individual characteristic, but it depends on the 'atmosphere' in which relations with the local environment are maintained.

This appears to be a fundamental prerequisite to the diffusion and adoption of novelties. Distant relationships with extra-district operators are not a sufficient condition for the innovative development of internal products and processes. The district assists firms with knowledge 'interpretation', and district institutions provide the necessary knowledge circulation on the basis of which external relations can be fruitful. As a result, Saonara district configures itself as a weak component of a global value chain, where the Netherlands is the innovator that sells its new products (in the shape of young plants) to Saonara, which does not have the capabilities to develop technological improvements, and to experiment *in loco* the creation of new flower and plant varieties.

11.4.3.1 Historical development of the Saonara district

The historical origins of the ornamental horticulture industry go back to the city of Venice, which, between the fifteenth and eighteenth centuries, assumed the role of creative centre for the local development of botanic science. The Venetian aristocracy has consistently maintained a passion for the cultivation of rare plants, creating beautiful gardens in the lagoon city, and on 'terra firma'. The nobleman Gabriele Farsetti, in the eighteenth century, built, around his historic house in Santa Maria di Sala near Padua, a large enterprise dedicated to the cultivation of ancient plants (botanic gardens, meditation gardens, fruit-bearing fields, and so on), and published twice, in 1793 and 1796, catalogues detailing all his plant varieties.

Following this first attempt to codify ornamental horticulture knowledge, some more popular oriented publications were distributed, aimed at a wider audience than just the scientific and academic circles. From 1763 a public institution for the cultivation of fruit and garden plants was active in Padua, founded by decree of the 'Veneto Dominio' (the Venice Republic).

This phenomenon of popularization of sector-specific knowledge is also evidenced in the fact that in the first half of the nineteenth century the participation in flower exhibitions was not only a privilege of the aristocracy, and the wealthy classes, but also as simply a passion for average people (Bussadori 1990).

The association 'Società Promotrice del Giardinaggio', active in Padua between 1846 and 1868, was at the basis of a widespread dissemination of horticultural practices. This association started to sponsor numerous flower exhibitions in Padua, and to promote flower expositions in private villas. So, in the area, we find a slow growth of these activities, whose expansion was intensified in the first decades of the twentieth century. By the 1930s the district firms were specialized in the cultivation of roses, lilies, dahlias, carnations and gladioli.

During the 1940s, local horticultural businesses began to employ new technologies developed in Europe: greenhouses, heating systems, pumps, washing boxes, bathtubs etc.

Pioneer firms included the following companies: Fassina, Croff, Gribaldo, Rizzi, Sgaravatti, Zorzi and Van Den Borre. At that time these were substantial firms, but for one reason or another they closed down or decreased in size.

Particularly important, in this historical context, is the story of the Sgaravatti family firm, which made the name of Saonara known throughout Europe.

Angelo Sgaravatti, born in 1798, became in 1815 an expert gardener for Count Morosini. In 1820 he bought a small piece of land from the Count (1 ha) – whose economic fortunes went into decline as happened to many Venetian nobles – on which he built a small ornamental horticulture production.

In 1936 the 'Fratelli Sgaravatti Piante' firm bought a firm in Pistoia: the 'Stabilimento d'orticoltura Bianco Bianchi', where more favourable climatic conditions allowed for the cultivation of conifers. In 1946, the firm acquired some land in Rome. The family firm was very dynamic during the King of Italy's reign. The firm closed down during the 1960s and passed into the hands of its workers, under the name Cooperativa Co.Vi.Sa, which no longer exists.

In Padua there are many activities related to horticulture production organized by the provincial agriculture association (Unione Provinciale Agricoltori, and Coltivatori Diretti, and CIA – Confederazione Nazionale dell'Industria e dell'Agricoltura).

A specific association for horticulture was set up only in 1985 (Associazione Vivaisti Padovani), but it is not very active in organizing conferences, R&D agreements with the university, firms' cooperation, and training activities. Thus, another institution was founded in 2000 (Consorzio Florovivaisti Padovani). It specializes in quality certification (ISO 9001), organizing the participation of members in exhibitions, and publication of a technical manual for the production of ornamental horticultural plants for members.

11.5 A brief comparison of the three cases

In Table 11.5 we can find some illuminating comparisons based on our qualitative interviews with the firms. The three districts are very old, and are now mainly composed of small firms. In all three cases during the 1930s and the 1940s, large firms were dominant in the districts, but a strong process of decentralization occurred in the postwar period.

However, the exploitation of scientific methods has greatly contributed to globalizing the Dutch district, and to make this district a very particular combination of scientific activity and practical knowledge embedded in manufacturing tasks. It is clear, from our interpretation, that local and national institutions played a very different role.

A global division of labour is now linking the three districts along the value chain: Pistoia and Saonara must buy nearly all the small plants they need in the Netherlands, where propagation activities are more developed, and then grow the small plants in Italy. In some cases, adult plants are re-exported to the Netherlands, and sold in global markets, through the advanced commercial structures of the Dutch distributive sector.

Table 11.5 A comparison of the three districts (Saonara, Pistoia and Boskoop)

	Saonara district	*Pistoia district*	*Boskoop district*
Natural resources	Friable soil	Friable soil and Mediterranean climate	Fertile and moist soil
Climatic conditions	Medium	Very good	Unfavourable
History	Founder firm: Sgaravatti in 1820	Founder firm: Bartolini in 1849	Horticultural specialization emerged during the sixteenth century Numerous firms emerged during the nineteenth century Take off post Second World War
District specialization	Fructiferous plants, and rose bushes Maintenance of public gardens and green areas	Cultivation of ornamental plants ready for 'instant gardens'	Small plants, seeds, and propagation (R&D-intensive production)
Quality of the product	Very good	Very good	Very good and certified on the basis of numerous criteria by the Central Dutch Service for Quality (Naktuinbouw)
Labour market	Specialized	Specialized	Specialized
Co-operation	Very low	Medium level	Very high (both among firms and institutions)
Infrastructure	Medium	Medium	Advanced through the existence of Rotterdam port (diversity and volume of cargos)
Entrepreneurial organizational capabilities	Very low for SMEs, medium for larger firms	Very low for SMEs, medium for larger firms	Very high for all firm sizes
Diffusion of new technology	Limited	Higher	Very high Logistics and e-commerce retail; presence of VBA, the most prominent floricultural products auction in the world

(continued)

	Saonara district	Pistoia district	Boskoop district
R&D	None	Few links with Italian universities	High R&D flows provided by public expenditure and by firms' associations
Promotion	None	None	PPH – Plant Publicity Holland

Source: Our interpretation from interviews with firms.

11.6 Concluding remarks

This chapter started with a question about the differences between the notions of industrial district and cluster. We argued that the main differences between these two concepts are related: (1) to the definition of the geographical border (which in the case of an industrial district is strictly linked to the possibility of the emergence of a historical-dependent system, where social relations influence the economic dynamics); and (2) to the presence of a social embeddedness provided by the sense of identity of the local community, the building of local institutions, and the presence of some forms of cooperation. The heterogeneity of industrial districts is appreciated only through a type of analysis which uses qualitative sources, and *ad hoc* investigations. In fact, as we have discussed at length, even in a circumscribed industry such as ornamental horticulture, the three districts are remarkably different, in research capabilities, types of products, adoption of technology, market share, business models, and relations with local institutions. The influence of globalization has not reduced the diversity but it has contributed to increase specialization and to enforce the symbiotic division of labour among them. In this chapter we have presented the evolution of three horticultural districts, two of them, the less advanced, in Italy, the other (Boskoop) part of the larger horticultural Dutch cluster.

The development of the ornamental horticulture industry exhibits clearly how the globalization of markets can affect the localization of the industry. A product – the flower or a plant – is easily transportable. Thus, we would expect that production would be moved to lower energy cost countries, or to countries with better climates, or with lower labour costs. However, the Netherlands is presently at the forefront of this industry, and contains a whole cluster of related activities and a specialized district (Boskoop), because, even with the highest labour costs and the most unfavourable climate, it has been able, over time, to develop a strong expertise in horticulture production, and in related R&D activities.

A large number of specific institutions have sustained this trend, developing several collaborations with universities and research centres, with the purpose of keeping 'in house' the most profitable activities (in science application: plant propagation, new plants engineering, seeds production, and in distribution: logistics, auction, marketing, and retailing), and to outsource the lowest value added ones, such as plant growing.

This attitude towards product and process innovation places the Netherlands in a leading position, allowing it to exert its power as a strong supplier of cut flowers and young potted plants to be sold throughout Europe.

Notes

1 It is also true that the terms industrial district and cluster are used synonymously. In some cases this depends on the national origin of the researchers: Italian researchers (Garofoli 1989; Belussi 1996) often use the terms industrial districts or local production systems; the term cluster or industrial cluster reflects Anglo-Saxon research, and the strong influence of Porter's work.

2 The Italian Institute of Statistics, ISTAT, with the contribution of Fabio Sforzi, based on the analysis of the daily commuting of the local working population, divided Italy into different geographical areas of local labour systems (LLS). In 199 cases, these areas were considered, with a good approximation, as areas characterized by the presence of industrial districts (Sforzi 1989, Brusco and Paba 1997). However, this is a classic case of semantic ambiguity. The 199 Italian systems selected are in fact a geographical aggregation and not districts. In a complex cartographic elaboration recently the IPI Institute (2002) has published a series of maps incorporating the various qualitative and quantitative methodologies used in various researches and in official regional documents for the identification of industrial districts in Italy. In each map a different geography of the industrial districts is displayed. The confusion is widespread in cartography.

3 The international trade has been strongly influenced by intra-industry trade and PPT (passive perfectioning traffic), giving rise to enormous flows of outsourcing. Within IDs, the first wave of outsourcing began in traditional sectors during the 1970s, in clothing, textile, footwear, and cheap electronics, and in the 1990s it developed greatly due to the fall of the Berlin Wall, and the integration of Eastern European countries into the European Community, and of the integration of the large economies of developing countries such as China, India and the Far East into the global market created by WTO.

4 ISTAT (2000).

5 A reverse auction is an on-line procurement method used to obtain quotations for commodities and services. In a reverse auction, something is purchased from the lowest quote (which is the 'reverse' of a normal auction, typically organized for unique artistic items sold to the highest quote to discerning bidders). A reverse auction is typically organized via the Internet, where in the same market there are hundreds of (and not just one) suppliers and hundreds of wholesalers, whereby bidders anonymously bid against each other for a specific quantity of given items. Bidding takes place at a specified date and time, and continues for a specified amount of time or until no more bids are received. Producers first list their products, and then wholesalers will begin to express interest. The Netherlands invention has transformed a traditional 'art auction' market mechanism into a typical district 'market' model for phase firms (subcontracting), where producers are strongly induced to cut their prices, and the market is very transparent, as described by the Italian researchers (Becattini 2003).

6 This auction method uses a clock: the clock hand starts at a high price and drops until a buyer, by pressing a button, stops the clock to bid and accept (part of) the lot. A Dutch cauliflower grower invented the clock in the 1870s to reduce the time spent by growers at markets.

7 The germplasm is the genetic material, especially its specific molecular and chemical constitution, that compromises the inherited qualities of an organism. Germplasm banks are collections of genetic material, principally in the form of seeds, conserved

in temperature and humidity conditions that enable the material to be used over long periods of time. The bank serves to keep species in a dormant state, always ready for germination whenever fresh material is needed, whether for new research studies or to obtain plants for their reintroduction into their natural habitat.

8 This work is based on secondary data collections and face-to-face interviews with 30 local entrepreneurs (in small and large firms) in the three districts analyzed (10 firms per district), on the basis of a qualitative questionnaire developed conjointly by the authors of this chapter and by our assistant Zoccarato. Zoccarato conducted the interviews. In addition we have explored a long list of web pages of horticultural institutions, as explained in Belussi and Sedita (2005). Considering the theoretical framework proposed in Section 11.2 we have fulfilled steps 1, 3, and 4.

9 Sources: information provided during interviews with Dutch horticultural firms.

10 The term 'district' is not clearly used in the Netherlands, where they, on the contrary, frequently use the Porterian term 'Dutch Horticulture Cluster'. Often these studies refer to a national dimension, and the term 'cluster' is used to underline the synergic relations between firms and the public actors.

11 Within national associations 'plant groups' are created, which deal with specific species. They organise training activity, business trips, etc.

12 In order to finance the high cost of plant breeding it is important that the breeders are paid for their efforts through plant breeders' rights and licences. It is now possible for breeders to claim rights for new varieties in about 30 countries.

13 A good example of partnership between government and the horticulture industry is the tendency to pursue common policy goals; the Ministry of Agriculture and the associations have agreed jointly to fund research aimed at enabling growers to reduce carbon dioxide emissions by 15 per cent over 10 years, in line with the Dutch Government's commitments under the Kyoto Accord. The government has adopted a similar partnership approach to a four-year plant-breeding programme for the ornamental sector (1.5 million euro of investment each year). The aims are to address problems in the supply chain, shelf life resistance to pests and disease, quality improvements, and product innovation.

14 The organization of information on client reputation is not unique to Boskoop. To our knowledge there is something similar also in another Italian district: the footwear district of the Riviera del Brenta (Belussi 2000).

15 Zundert, west of Brabant, is the centre of parks and garden plants producers. Also in the north there is significant tree production. Many producers now are shifting to ornamental plants production. Lottum, situated in Limburg province, is redeveloping for roses and grafting box production. The latter are produced on a large scale also in Gronighen, in the east. There are three big centres for large trees: Haaren and Oudenbosch, in North Brabant, and Opheusden, in Gheldria province. Fructiferous plants are produced in Flevoland, Limburgo, North Brabante and Zelanda. North provinces, on the coast, are famous for tulips and perennial plants. Water plant producers are more widespread in the country.

16 There are about 40 firms in the greenhouse construction business, including system suppliers and fitters of glasshouse technology. AVAG is the Dutch Association of Contractors and Fitters in Glasshouse Horticulture.

17 The total production value of this sector amounted in 1996 to 1.7 thousand million euro (den Hertog 2003).

18 The district covers five municipalities in the Pistoia province: Pistoia, Serravalle Pistoiese, Agliana, Quarrata and Montale.

19 The fillossera (*Phylloxera vastatrix* or *Viteus vitifoliae*) is a sap-sucking aphid parasite, which feeds on the roots of grapevines, Originally from North America, it reached Europe during the end of the nineteenth century.

20 The district covers 10 municipalities of the Padua province: Saonara, Campagna Lupia, Campolongo Maggiore, Vigonovo, Piove di Sacco, Ponte San Nicolò, Polverara, Legnaro, S.Angelo di Piove, and Strà.

21 The fair covers about 30,000 sq m, hosting yearly more than 1000 exhibiting firms and 35,000 visitors. Source of this data is the Flormart/Miflor website, years 2000–03.

References

Aiph/union Fleurs (2001), *International Statistics. Flowers and Plants*, 49, edited by Florian Heinrichs, Institut für Gartenbauökonomie der Universität Hannover.

Asheim, B. (1996), 'Industrial districts as "learning regions": a condition for prosperity', *European Planning Studies*, 4: 379–400.

Bardelli, F. (1999), *Storia del vivaismo a Pistoia*, Pistoia: Etruria Editrice.

Bair J. and Gereffi G. (2001), 'Local clusters in global chains: the causes and consequences of export dynamism in Torreon's blue jeans industry', *World Development*, 29 (11): 1885–1903.

Becattini, G. (2003), 'From the industrial district to the districtualization of production activity: some considerations', in F. Belussi, G. Gottardi and E. Rullani (eds.), *The Technological Evolution of Industrial Districts*, Boston: Kluwer.

Belussi F. (1996), 'Local systems, industrial districts and institutional networks: towards a new evolutionary paradigm of industrial economies', *European Planning Studies*, 4: 1–15.

——. (2000), *Tacchi a spillo*, Padova: Cleup.

——. (2005), 'On the theory of spatial clustering: the emergence of various forms of agglomeration', in: F. Belussi and A. Sammarra (eds.), *Industrial Districts, Relocation and the Governance of the Global Supply Chains*, Padua: Cleup, pp. 3–59.

——. (2006), 'In search of a theory of industrial districts and clusters', in B. Asheim, P. Cooke, and R. Martin (eds.), *Cluster in Regional Development*, London: Routledge.

Belussi F. and Gottardi G. (2000), *Evolutionary Patterns of Local Industrial Systems: Towards a Cognitive Approach to the Industrial District*, Aldershot: Ashgate.

Belussi F. and Pilotti L. (2002), 'The development of an explorative analytical model of knowledge creation, learning and innovation within the Italian industrial districts', *Geografiska Annaler*, 84: 19–33.

Belussi, F. and Sedita, S. R. (2005), 'The global value chain and the symbiotic division of labour between Dutch and Italian ornamental horticulture districts: the cases of Saonara, Pistoia, and Boskoop', in F. Belussi and A. Sammarra (eds.), *Industrial Districts, Relocation and the Governance of the Global Supply Chains*, Padua: Cleup, pp. 87–107.

Belussi F., Gottardi G. and Rullani E. (eds.) (2003), *The Technological Evolution of Industrial Districts*, Boston: Kluwer.

Brusco S. (1982), 'The Emilian Model: productive decentralisation and social integration', *Cambridge Journal of Economics*, 6: 167–84.

——. (1990) .The idea of the industrial district: its genesis', in F. Pyke, G. Becattini, and W. Sengenberger (eds.) *Industrial Districts and Inter-firm Co-operation in Italy*, Geneva: International Institute for Labour Studies.

Buurma J. S. (2001), *Dutch Agricultural Development and its Importance to China. Case-study: the Evolution of Dutch Greenhouse Horticulture*. The Hague: LEI.

Chesbrough H. (2003), *Open Innovation: The New Imperative for Creating and Profiting from Technology*, Boston: Harvard Business School Press.

Cocking E. (1989), 'Plant cell and tissue culture', in J .J. Marx (ed.) *Revolution in Biotechnology*, Cambridge: Cambridge University.

Cooke P and Huggins, R. (2003), 'High technology clustering in Cambridge', in F. Sforzi (ed.) *The Institutions of Local Development*, Aldershot: Ashgate.

Cresti B. (1991), *Il vivaismo ornamentale. Innovazione e crescita di un settore tradizionale*, Studi e Informazioni, Quaderni 35, Firenze: Banca Toscana.

Dei Ottati G. (1996), 'Trust, interlinking transactions and credit in industrial districts', *Cambridge Journal of Economics*, 18: 529–46.

Den Hertog P. (2003), 'The role of cluster policies in economic growth and competitiveness', paper presented at the European Seminar on Cluster Policy, 10 June, Copenhagen.

DTI (2001), *Business Clusters in the UK – A First Assessment*, London: DTI.

ECP.NL (2005) *Amsterdam: EbXML for managers*.

Elshof P. (1998), 'The Dutch flower sector: structure, trends and employment', SAP 2.68/WP.122, ILO working paper, Geneva: International Labour Office.

European Commission (2001), *Methodology for Regional and Transnational Technology Clusters: Learning with European Best Practices*, Brussels: Enterprise Directorate General.

Ferretti R. (2004), 'L'andamento del florovivaismo in Europa nel 2004', *Linea Verde*, Ottobre 2004.

Galaut J. and Torre A. (2005), 'Geographical proximity and circulation of knowledge through interfirm relationships', *Scienze Regionali*, 1: 5–25.

Garofoli G. (1989b), 'Industrial districts: structure and transformation', *Economic Notes*, 19 (1): 37–54.

Gereffi G., Humprey J. and Sturgeon T. (2005), 'The governance of global value chain', *Review of International Political Economy*, 12(1): 78–104.

Harvard Business School (2002), *Cluster Mapping Project*, Institute for Strategy and Competitiveness, Cambridge, MA: Harvard Business School.

Hodgson I. (2004) 'Italian plants with designer appeal', *The Garden*, March 2004, 129(3): 194–99.

Hu T., Lin C. and Chang S. (2005), 'Role of interaction between technological communities and industrial clustering in innovative activity: the case of the Hsinchu district, Taiwan', *Urban Studies*, 42(7): 1139–60.

IPI (2002), *L'esperienza italiana dei distretti industriali*, Rome: Ministero delle attività Produttive.

ISTAT (2000), *Quinto Censimento Generale dell'Agricoltura*, URL: http://www.istat.it/

Maijers W., Vokurka L., Van Uffelen R. and Ravensbergen P. (2005), 'Open innovation: symbiotic network. Knowledge circulation and competencies for the benefit of innovation in the Horticulture delta', paper presented at the IAMA Chicago conference, 19 April.

Marshall A. (1919), *Industry and Trade*, London: Macmillan.

——. (1920), *Principles of Economics*, 8th edn., London: Macmillan, First edition [1891] (London: Macmillan).

Matthews R. (1986), 'The economics of institutions and sources of growth', *Economic Journal*, 96: 903–18.

Martin R. and Sunley P. (2003), 'Deconstructing clusters: chaotic concept or policy panacea?', *Journal of Economic Geography*, 1: 5–35.

Maskell P. (2001), 'Towards a knowledge based theory of the geographical cluster', *Industrial and Corporate Change*, 10(4): 921–43.

Maskell P. and Lorenzen M. (2004), 'The cluster as market organisation', *Urban Studies*, 41(5/6): 991–1009.

OECD (1999a), *Boosting Innovation: The Cluster Approach*, Paris: OECD.

——. (1999b), *Economic and Cultural Transitions towards a Learning City: The case of Jena*, Paris: OECD.

——. (2001), *Science, Technology and Industry Scoreboard 2001 – Towards a Knowledge-Based Economy*, Paris: OECD

——. (2001a), *World Congress on Local Clusters*, Paris: OECD.

——. (2001b), *Innovative Clusters: Drivers of National Innovation Systems*, Paris: OECD.

Paniccia I. (1998), 'One, a hundred, thousands of industrial districts: organizational variety in local networks of small and medium-sized enterprises', *Organizational Studies*, 19: 667–99.

——. (2002), 'A critical review of the literature on industrial districts: in search of a theory', in I. Paniccia, *Industrial Districts: Evolution and Competitiveness in Italian Firms*, Cheltenham: Edward Elgar.

Porter M. (1998), *On Competition*, Boston: Harvard Business School Press.

Rallet A. and Torre A. (2004), 'Proximité et localisation', *Economie Rurale*, 280: 25–41.

Richardson G. (1972), 'The organization of industry', *Economic Journal*, 82: 883–96.

Sammarra, A. (2003), *Lo sviluppo dei distretti industriali*, Roma: Carocci.

Sedita S. R. (2005), 'Knowledge vs. technology: investigating the relationship between R&D and knowledge intensity in the Danish manufacturing industry', paper presented at the 5th Triple Helix Conference, 18–21 May 2005, Turin (Italy).

Sforzi F. (1989), 'The geography of industrial districts in Italy', in E. Goodman and J. Bamford (eds.), *Small Firms and Industrial Districts in Italy*, London: Routledge.

——. (2003), 'The industrial district and the new Italian economic geography', in, *The Technological Evolution of Industrial Districts*, Boston: Kluwer.

Sforzi F. and Lorenzoni F. (2002), 'I distretti industriali', in IPI (ed.) *L'esperienza italiana dei distretti industriali*, Roma: Ministero delle attività Produttive.

Van Klink A. and Visser E. J. (2004), 'Innovation in Dutch horticulture: fresh ideas in fresh logistics', *Journal of Social and Economic Geography*, 95(3): 340–46.

VBN (2005), Annual report, Leiden.

You J. and Wilkinson F. (1994), 'Competition and cooperation: towards understanding industrial districts', *Review of Political Economy*, 6: 259–78.

12 Industrial districts and globalization

Learning and innovation in local and global production systems

Fiorenza Belussi (University of Padua, Italy) and Bjorn T. Asheim (Lund University and CIRCLE, Sweden)

12.1 Introduction

Industrial districts (Becattini, *et al.* 2003; Belussi, Gottardi and Rullani 2003) in the Third Italy, which has been the paradigmatic example of localized learning and endogenous growth, used to be characterized by the whole value chain (Porter 2000) being carried out locally in the districts. This is no longer the normal case, as specific phases of the value chain, typically the most labour intensive and/or the most polluting phases, are increasingly being located outside the districts in previous East European countries and/or countries in the Third World, as a result of an industrial restructuring caused by increased global competition as well as stricter environmental regulations (Belussi and Macdonald 2003; Belussi, Gottardi and Rullani 2001; Rullani 2002). This results in a transformation of the industrial structure in the districts as well as a territorial fragmentation (Bonomi 1997) of the previous local value chain (Sammarra 2003). The outsourcing goes either to locally owned and existing factories in the Eastern and Southern European countries, or to subsidiaries of the outsourcing firms or to both. Many empirical works have documented the strategies of delocalization of Italian districtual firms (Carminucci and Casucci 1997; Cavalieri 1995; Scarso 1996; Corò and Grandinetti 1999a and 1999b; Caroli and Lipparini 2002; Belussi 2003a).

This has resulted in a concentration of only the most knowledge and/or capital intensive phases of the industrial activity (R&D, design, product development, marketing etc.) in the original industrial districts, often taking place in more or less formally integrated larger groups of district firms (Cainelli 2002). Other SMEs in the districts adapt to this local fragmentation process by changing status from being subcontractors in local production systems to assume the same role in global production systems.

Another important tendency, which has speeded up the territorial fragmentation of the local systems, has been the transition from an 'internal to the district governance' of knowledge to a more open 'globally integrated governance' (Belussi and Pilotti 2002). This has happened both in specific high-tech districts (i.e. biotech sectors) and in industrial agglomerations (e.g. traditional industrial districts specialized in textile-clothing, footwear, leather, and furniture, Schiattarella 1999). As a consequence, in these production systems a general increase in firms' knowledge intensity has occurred. But this implies also that the relevant perspective for the analysis of the knowledge base of firms is neither the individual firm nor always the local system of firms, but often extra-local production or learning systems (Becattini and Rullani 1996; Malmberg and Maskell 1999; Maskell and Malmberg 1999; Maskel, *et al.* 1998; Maskell 1999a; Biggiero 1999).

A third tendency, which is clearly observable, is an increased number of FDIs in industrial district types of clusters (Porter 1998). Typically, the most innovative and competitive medium-sized firms were being bought up (Sanguigni 2002). This new development gave rise to a potential conflict between the local innovation network or system in the districts and the newly entered corporations, due to integration of the acquired district firms into the strategic business systems of the MNCs (Caves 1982; Dunning 1993). Incoming FDIs, carrying 'foreign' institutional incentives and constraints (e.g. corporate governance system characteristics through their internal capital allocation and monitoring system are not necessarily compatible with, or complementary to, the local and regional innovation systems) (Whitley 1993 and 1999; Rugman and Verbeke 2003). In other words, this poses the question of to what extent foreign direct investments are value creating or value exploiting when they interact with the cluster or district firms (Lorenzen and Mahnke 2002). The governance of knowledge production is central to the theory of MNCs (Dunning 1997; Dunning and Narula 2004; Feenstra 1998; Ernst and Kim 2002).

FDI dominates in all sectors where there are important firm-specific factors (Hymer 1976; Buckley and Casson 1976; Dunning 1993; Cantwell 1998; Cantwell and Janne 1999), including the advantages deriving from the utilization of in-house produced technology or from possessed brands, when activities may be separated from the headquarters and exploited at international level, better still if combined with other location-based advantages (Kogut 1985). However, MNCs increasingly internationalize their knowledge development activities by plugging into existing pools of knowledge, setting up new plants or facilities, in particular locations. The internationalization process thus appears to be supported, not just by the intention of using the existing in-house knowledge, but by the desire to acquire and absorb external strategic knowledge (Lorenzen and Mahnke 2002), setting up explorative R&D in foreign countries (Kuemmerle 1998). However, can we evaluate the entry of multinationals in the district analyzed? Why did MNCs arrive in these districts? Which model of entry did they use? How did the entry of multinationals change the model of knowledge governance within the districts, and the flows of knowledge spillovers that typically characterized the model of the IDs?

The impact of these processes is clearly ambiguous and difficult to judge. Depending on the specific conditions in which they emerge, these processes could be looked upon in two ways. On the one hand, as the negative side of globalization, which reduces the competitiveness of some industries and localities, characterized by high costs (and high wages) or, on the other hand, they could be considered a necessary adjustment and adaptation to the globalization process itself. In the first case, these tendencies could be seen also as a potential threat to local learning (Pla-Barber, Puig and Camps 2007) and, thus, to the locally 'embedded' competitive advantages of districts (Porter 1990), which base their development on endogenous forces (Asheim and Cooke 1999). Instead of blaming the MNCs for the erosion of the district model – overwhelmed by the superior performance of 'global nodes', thus MNCs or transnational firms, in terms of productivity, profitability, and power (Amin 1993; Amin and Robins 1990) – in the second case, the process of delocalization (or partial territorial relocation of industrial district) is understood within a slow but inevitable path of 'district disclosure', which is organized by local agents in order to avoid 'lock-in' tendencies in the local economy. Thus, delocalization is a necessity for districts to be able to stay innovative and competitive also in the future.

In any event, these processes will have consequences for the relative importance of local versus non-local conditions (Isaksen 2005) and relations for future regional development (Bathelt, *et al.* 2004, MacKinnon, *et al.* 2002). In what follows we shall look closer into these tendencies, which will undoubtedly be reinforced by the ongoing process of globalization, and especially we will pay attention to the consequences of the entry of FDIs into local economies, in order to assess the capacity of selected industrial districts to keep on with disclosure process, and to continue to upgrade the knowledge bases of local-district firms in order to retain their competitive advantage.

This paper will present a theoretical framework for investigating these tendencies and will use case studies from the Third Italy and Scandinavia as empirical illustrations. Our contribution will especially focus on what has recently been called local 'buzz' (Storper and Venables 2003); that is, local creativity deriving from a process of agglomeration of knowledge and information. It is here argued that relations of proximity are still necessary for industrial districts (and other forms of local clusters) in order to stay innovative and retain their competitive advantage, but global 'pipelines', access to external knowledge and information, are becoming a key factor (Bathelt, *et al.* 2004) for supporting and strengthening such local 'buzz'.

12.2 The Scandinavian case

Jæren[1] is a regional cluster of specialized production with a traditionally high degree of inter-firm cooperation. This cooperation was until recently institutionalized through TESA (technical cooperation), a competence network that was established by local firms in 1957, with the aim of promoting technological development among member firms, which were mostly small and medium-sized, export-oriented firms producing mainly farm machinery. This has, among other things, resulted in the district today being the centre of industrial robot technology in Norway with skills in industrial electronics and microelectronics far above the general level in Norway. The main characteristics of the original cluster include a high degree of local ownership and thus local strategic control and a labour market characterized by high union density, low external mobility, cooperative industrial relations, and of course a high degree of inter-firm cooperation, based on the presence of social capital. Thus, this cluster has traditionally represented a local institutional structure characterized by positive complementarities (i.e. incentives towards long-term investment strategies in human capital arising out of ownership, participative industrial relations and inter-firm cooperative relationships).

The regional cluster, which still is very competitive and export oriented, has undergone considerable changes during the last 10 years due to globalization. During this period many companies have been bought up and transformed into subsidiaries of multinational corporations. Thus information gaps between strategic decision makers (foreign systems of corporate governance) and local firms have been created. On the other hand, some medium-sized firms have grown to reach the *status* of multinational corporations themselves. They have thus created a link between a local corporate innovation system and the structure of subsidiaries located worldwide.

ABB's acquisition of Trallfa Robot in 1988, now called ABB Flexible Automation, which is Europe's leading producer of painting robots for the auto-motive industry, was the first major example of FDIs, while Kverneland, one of the world's largest producers of agricultural equipment, is the main example of a local firm becoming a MNC. Today the company has production facilities in 14 countries, and has during the last 15 years bought firms in Italy, Denmark, Germany, the Netherlands, France and Australia. Other examples of FDIs entry are the Swedish Monark take-over of Øglænd DBS in 1989, and subsequent integration into Grimaldis' Cycleurope in 1995, and the British company Williams Plc, now Kidde Plc, which bought up the NOHA group in 1998. The first and the last cases, i.e. ABB and NOHA, will serve as the main empirical illustrations of the diverging trends observed in the district analyzed.

All of the companies in TESA have thus been more or less affected by the constant drive towards globalization and 'corporatization'. External firms have shown little focus on regional and local issues. The 'corporatization' was a challenge for the TESA network. As the member companies become less independent, focusing on their multinational corporation, the centrifugal forces in the network become increasingly stronger.

As a result of these tensions, all the firms belonging to, or in alliances with, large corporations, independent of national or foreign ownership, are no longer members of TESA. This means that the TESA network is in danger of being closed down, with potentially negative consequences for the local area. The individual firms belonging to international corporations have substituted (or attempted to substitute) the local innovation system with a clear in-house mechanism of innovation generation. External contacts have been developed with the national and international innovation system (Lundvall 1992 and 1996; Nelson 1993).

The entry of MNCs could not represent in principle such a problematic issue. Global firms may make available to local organizations everyday resources such as logistics, sales and marketing: competencies that often organizations are able to develop only if they reach a certain size. So, MNCs may act as a connector between the local firm and other external knowledge sources, which the local innovation system at Jæren is not capable of supporting. A positive example is represented by the ABB case.

The most internationally well-known firm at Jæren is ABB Flexible Automation. At the time Trallfa Robot was bought by ABB, it supplied around 50 per cent of the European market for painting robots to the automotive industry. If ABB had applied their normal restructuring strategy, the robot production at Jæren would have been closed down, and moved to Västerås in Sweden, where production of handling robots takes place on a much larger scale. Instead, Trallfa was assisted technologically in the transition from hydraulic to electrical robots, the production capacity at Jæren was increased considerably, and markets expanded to include both the US and Asia. This means that ABB Flexible Automation today covers 70 per cent of the demand for painting robots in the European automotive industry, and 30 per cent in the USA. Generally, it is described as the most profitable ABB-unit in Norway. The factory at Jæren has been upgraded to a so-called 'supplying unit' in the ABB system, and the production of other types of painting robots has in part been transferred from ABB factories in Germany to Jæren. The success story of ABB Flexible Automation is partly to do with locally embedded resources, notably the informal, tacit knowledge and practical skills of the workforce, as well as the stock of accumulated codified knowledge possessed about painting robots at the factory at Jæren. It has, however, also to do with the ways in which R&D projects, skills, and scientific knowledge have been created and renewed (Nonaka and Takeuchi 1995; Nooteboom 2001 and 2002). ABB has supplied the enduring[2] capital to the firm needs.

Knowledge of robot technology contained within the TESA network initially represented strong local specific capabilities or 'untraded interdependencies'. They were recognized by ABB as being extremely important (Asheim 1999a and 1999b), thus explaining the decision not to relocate it. The complex synthetic nature (Laestadius 1998) of the activities of ABB Flexible Automation requires the integration of knowledge from such different sources as mechanics, information technology, chemistry and physics. Further, the degree of market pressure with respect to improving the product in a cost-efficient way is high, which in turn implies that generating and mobilizing knowledge held collectively by the workforce is extremely important. Evidence from the company suggests that its knowledge base now has strong elements of tacit knowledge accumulated collectively and on a broad basis in the whole firm workforce. The company has developed multi-functionality, cross-disciplinarity and company-specific training in a context of long-term employment as a prerequisite for its competitive strength. The development of these organizational characteristics, to a large extent based on the existence of a well-functioning organizational 'community model' (Soskice 1999; Wenger 1998) of the local labour market, and high levels of decentralization and informal coordination among highly skilled workers, seem critical to the competitive strength of the company. This model is embedded in the regional institutional framework, notably in the participative industrial relations (Asheim 2001; Asheim and Isaksen 2002).

Learning interfaces in interaction with other organizations are limited

– cooperation with ABB Västeraas as well as a few local spin-offs, high-precision/ low volume component producers being the only exceptions. The firm, however, is connected to external sources of knowledge related to different component areas, such as chemistry and physics.

Thus, knowledge held in embedded firms is extremely sticky in that 'learners need to become insiders of the social community in order to acquire its particular viewpoint' (Brown and Duguid 1991; Lam 1998a and 1998b), implying an organizational stickiness. Hence, as long as the knowledge produced remains specialized and non-substitutable, the organization, which represents a place with a high degree of specific learning, will endogenously resist relocation. Knowledge flows are visible between the local ABB unit and its corporate headquarters. They demonstrate the importance of the strategic integration. As long as the local unit can show satisfactory long-term results, it operates under few operational restrictions with a high degree of responsibility decentralized to local management, thus reducing the information gap between strategic decision makers and the learning processes where resources are allocated. This in turn implies that strategic decision making is based on first-hand knowledge of the organization and its learning processes, rather than the latter being structured by a top-down process.

A different case is that of the NOHA group. This firm is now specialized in high-volume production of relatively non-complex (and standardized) products, which through extensive automation projects in the late 1980s and early 90s managed to attain superior cost advantages over the competitors localized in low-cost countries. In this process the willingness of the original owner to allocate resources continuously to learning and technological upgrading, also through the use of the competence existing in the TESA network, played an important role, which resulted in a vital accumulation of specialized, sticky knowledge concerning process development and automation. As the product in question is durable and replacement demand is therefore low, a broader market access and a deeper market penetration were considered the right firm strategy needed to exploit economies of scale and scope. This was, originally, successfully achieved through specific cooperation with external distributors in Europe, Asia and the Middle East.

The producer was early involved in a limited internationalization process, by being owned by a holding company that expanded with similar or complementary activities to other places in Norway as well as to the rest of Scandinavia. However, during the 1990s the firm's distribution system was increasingly integrated with those of its competitors. This created a loss of competitiveness, resulting in escalating distributive costs and reduced market penetration. Thus, the company had to look for a new corporate partner. But, later on, this new partner was in turn acquired by a global corporation.

The firm was subjected to an international restructuring with the injection of everyday and general resources. However, the implications for the future development of the company remain unclear, as there seems to be substantial tension between two distinct business systems of the home and the host country. Our data show that the local company, after the take-over, has no financial leverage to internally develop new processes and new products.

Thus, the future development of the firm will be determined exogenously by the parent company: now the local firm has no more linkages to access external sources of knowledge. This indicates the presence of a hierarchical governance structure, illustrating what Lazonick and O'Sullivan (1994) call 'value extracting strategies' through prohibiting investments in autonomous process and product innovations. The MNC which has acquired the local firm has moved substantial volumes of production to Jæren, but this seems to be more the result of trying to obtain scale economies than a strategy for new knowledge creation at the Jæren plant. The firm governance is obtained on the basis of an arm's-length financial system. So, short-term profitability is pursued at the expense of strategic learning, innovations and long-term investments in capital equipment and human capital.

This contrast between two quite distinct business systems – the Norwegian, here influenced by the Jæren industrial culture, and the UK mode of firm coordination, typically framed within a pure liberal market economy – might explain why key personnel has chosen to leave the company after the take-over. Differences in management styles, innovation strategies and industrial relations have isolated this firm from the local innovation system. This may also produce in future the disintegration of the specialized knowledge held locally by the firm and, possibly, a future local endogenous development through spin-off and new firm formation by the firm's dissatisfied blue-collar workers and technicians.

Considering the pattern of evolution of this Scandinavian specialized cluster in mechanical engineering, several critical points can be identified.

First, the 'cluster disclosure' to external knowledge through the internationalization of the corporate governance can often be seen more as a means of access to increasingly critical everyday resources (such as logistics and sales services), rather than as a result of reduced local 'embeddedness'. Some strategic aspects of the firm 'knowledge governance' still remain based on a localized process of knowledge accumulation and exploitation and renewal of its specialized capabilities.

Clearly, as in the above-mentioned ABB Flexible Automation case, inter-organizational innovative synergies among the various MNC units have occurred, among the firm's R&D laboratories, and this has increased the R&D strength of the local unit. Knowledge transfer among MNC units is a much more complicated matter than is often perceived (Foss and Pedersen 2002). Again the 'embeddedness' might be concealed by the fact that there is now a reduced dependence of the companies on local suppliers and subcontractors.

Thanks to its relation with the MNC headquarters, the local company is now able to utilize specialized capabilities located outside the Jæren cluster. ABB has now developed an extensive European network based on long-term relations with component producers. But this does not mean, by itself, that 'local specialized knowledge' in the Jæren cluster has become 'ubiquitous' or that intra-MNC knowledge trade has substituted it, nor that the local firms analyzed are becoming less embedded in the territorial system.

Second, in the understanding of the type of relationships created by the entry of MNCs and the district, the most relevant variable seems to concern the characteristic of the corporate governance in the home region of the parent company. In turn, this invites us to dwell upon the interfaces between the entry of FDIs and the existing 'local' business, financial, institutional and learning systems.

Third, the entry of MNCs in local districts should be used to enrich our understanding of the role of MNCs as knowledge infrastructures. MNCs constitute a possible learning interface between potentially divergent 'knowledge architectures' of different foreign and local companies.

But, knowledge creation and accumulation can also be linked to societal differences in industrial relations, finance and education (Amable 1999).

In particular it can be hypothesized that, with regard to the structure of industrial relations and education systems, there exist structural barriers to knowledge transfer that cannot be overcome by formal structures of ownership (Lam 1998a; Wenger 1998).

12.3 The Northeast Italian case

In order to analyze the impact of globalization processes on the industrial district model in Italy, we have selected one, to our knowledge, of the most advanced cases of the Northeast area: the Montebelluna district.[3] Montebelluna is a district specialized in sport-system shoes, and the entry of multinationals during the 1990s has been quite significant.

This district is localized at the heart of the Veneto region, north of Treviso, in the foothills of the Dolomites, and it is placed within an industrial economy strongly characterized by the presence of the ID model, whatever criteria we utilize to identify it.[4] The Montebelluna district[5] is considered one the most innovative districts in Italy, because it is formed by dynamic evolutionary firms, which have introduced important radical innovations in the past. This has given rise to the international dominance of the district in the technologies for the production of ski boots, and, in relation to that, the district has enjoyed widespread success in international market outlets (Belussi and Pilotti 2002).

The Montebelluna district is formed by about 400 firms – 300 producers of footwear and 100 producers of clothing – employing about 8000 workers (6000 units in footwear and 2000 in clothing).

Since the end of the 1970s, Montebelluna has been recognized worldwide as the world centre for sport shoes, and even the review *Newsweek*, in February 1979, dedicated an article to it, defining Montebelluna as the capital of the 'snow industry'.

This district is no longer a canonical (Marshallian) industrial district, where production is fractionated into a myriad small and medium-sized firms, and where activities are organized on the basis of a districtual division of labour.[6]

This district is now a technological district, and Montebelluna is an area of extraordinary international concentration of competencies and production capabilities: a globally specialized area which directly or indirectly produces a large share of the total worldwide output of a distinct range of products. As reported by local sources (Osem 2001), at present 80 per cent of motorcycle shoes produced in the world, 75 per cent of all ski boots, 65 per cent of after-ski boots, 50 per cent of technical mountain shoes, and 25 per cent of in-line skates are manufactured in Montebelluna.

The process of globalization began in the mid 1980s, with the intensification of export flows and the entry of MNCs. In the mid 1990s the Montebelluna district was already very open to international markets: about 70–80 per cent of ski boots production was exported, and at the end of the 1990s, half of its production of a diversified range of products. So, 1100 billion lire[7] of goods were exported to EU countries, such as Germany, France, Spain and the UK, and to the US and Japan. Many large local companies opened commercial offices abroad and an intense exchange of external relationships, commercial and productive contacts character-ized the daily work of local firms (Aage 2002).

After the important date of 1989, the East European countries provided a unique opportunity to develop international supply chains, based on the manufacturing of simple phases such as shoe assembly. It is difficult to evaluate directly the impact of the delocalization processes on the district. Official data of export trends in the province of Treviso show that in 2001 local firms exported about 430,292,000 euro of goods to Romania (ISTAT 2002). These operations are related to the shoe and sport clothing segments' supplying of intermediate components for Romanian subcontracting firms or Romanian FDIs. Interestingly, they correspond to about 35 per cent of the total output produced in the Montebelluna district.

The construction of international supply chains, mainly organized through Romanian firms, has clearly exerted a big impact on local subcontracting and on the firm population of the district. Between 1979 and 2000 the number of shoe producers declined from 511 to 304. Final firms in the district are now less than 170, but the number of local subcontracting firms is still significant, and the decline of activity has been mainly concentrated in the so-called 'tomaifici' (producers of uppers). In the meantime, large groups emerged in the district, and in 1989 the multinational Benetton group entered with the acquisition of Nordica, one of the largest leading local firms. The statistical trend of local employment shows only a relatively small decline. For instance from 1997 to 2001 local employment in the sport system moved from 9830 to 8782 units.

The district is still rich in manufacturing activities, specialized suppliers, design-ers and other activities connected with the filière of the sport-system, and has not become a 'hollow district', which only governs externally delocalized production activities. However, it must be noted that for 8782 employees that are working in Montebelluna, in the external belt of subcontracting activities, decentralized mainly in Eastern European countries, there are about 60,000 workers (estimation based on the Montebelluna 'boot museum' calculation). It is in fact striking that last year the local association of entrepreneurs defined Timisoara as the eighth province of the Veneto region. In addition we have to consider that this district is located within an area of full employment, with the lowest unemployment rate in Italy (about 1.8–2.0 per cent of the active population).

So, the process of district restructuring has not resulted in long-term and un-employable manpower. Globalization has enriched the district with the necessary market labour flexibility, without taking into account the fact that many small local owners of subcontracting firms, which suddenly lost their 'outsourced' orders, have opened up new workshops in Romania, or work in the district as super-controllers of the quality of Romanian subcontractors (our interviews).

An obvious indicator of the performance of the district is the total output realized in Montebelluna. Despite the declining number of local firms and employment, data on production and output are still positive, showing a general trend of expansion. Including clothing (but not the multinational Benetton), the output of the district of Montebelluna has grown from 1992 billion lire in 1999 to 2834 billion lire in 2001 (Osem 2001).

In the Montebelluna district we can find traces of the first outward processes of internationalization already occurring in the mid 1970s. At that time, two local firms (Lotto and Diadora), producing tennis and jogging shoes, a production far from the typical injection-plastic ski boot product, started to outsource the entire production to Far East subcontractors. They were following a competitive strategy that was a pure imitation of the path of the large multinationals such as Puma, Adidas and Nike, which were occupying the market niche of technologically simple sport shoes for tennis and jogging. This strategy was perceived as obliged by the fact the technologies used were quite stabilized, based on standardized machinery, and on a type of production that did not require particularly high competency from the local labour force. So, the only relevant strategic factor was the cost of labour, which in Montebelluna was clearly much higher than in any developing countries in the Far East.

These two firms, however, were strongly rooted in the local context: Lotto was founded by the former owner of Caber, which was sold to new entrepreneurs, and Diadora was a firm producing ski boots that did not adopt the new plastic technology, and that focused on its production of mountain boots. Local entrepreneurs speak of 'equilibrated globalization', to explain that the process of disclosure of Montebelluna is not at all antagonistic with the existence of the district and with the local 'knowledge governance' of the most knowledge-intensive phases: design, innovation in components, prototyping of new models, and new technologies of cycle coordination (Gann and Salter 2000). This knowledge will never tend to become 'ubiquitous', and in fact all R&D laboratories of MNCs entering the district are still in Montebelluna. When Salomon tried to move its research laboratory to Paris it encountered a decisive opposition from the local technicians who were from Montebelluna. Human capital in the district is still less mobile than is thought.

With the sale of Caber in 1974, we also find the first inward process of multinational entry in the district. Caber was bought by the American Spalding, which then transferred it to the Canadian Warrington, and in 1987 it was acquired by the French multinational Rossignol (owner also of the Lange firm at Mollaro, near Trento, founded by Bob Lange, the first conceiver of the plastic ski boot). One notes that, in turn, the Rossignol-Lange group has recently been acquired by Adidas (1997). In 1990 the Austrian group HTM, owner of the Head brand (ski boots and skis), acquired Brixia, a firm that in the past had bought the historical local brands of Munari and San Marco. In 1993 San Giorgio (ski and mountain boots) entered the Salomon group. In 1994, Icaro Olivieri, owner of Canstar Italia, a firm specialized in moulding and metal components for ski boots, snowboards, hockey rackets, and in-line skates, which also owned Canstar Canada in North America, sold his firm to the giant multinational Nike. In 1995 the Meran firm, which owns the Risport brand, was acquired by the Rossignol-Lange group.

External acquisitions went on, during the 1990s, exactly when many local firms started to abandon the district. So 'entry' and 'exits' processes coexisted, but with different motivations. External multinationals were attracted by the existence of local competence and technological capabilities and tapped into the local district to absorb the relevant accumulated tacit and codified knowledge of the district. Local firms used the international division of labour to produce cheaper items. They outsourced outside the district the more standardized phases of upper assembling and shoe montage, searching for cheap labour (in Eastern European countries, such as Romania, Hungary and Poland).

However, some movements in firm governance were activated also from inside the district, or from other national firms. In 1993 Tecnica acquired one of the most prestigious German firms, Lowa, and this is a case of outward internalization. In 1998 Diadora was acquired by Invicta, a large Italian (small multinational) firm from Turin. In 1997 two historical firms for winter production – Dolomite and Tecnica – merged. In 1998 Lotto was acquired by a group of Montebelluna entrepreneurs, with the support of a merchant bank from Luxemburg. In 2003 Nordica – which was part of the Benetton sport-system group – was sold to Tecnica, which has now become the biggest firm in the district for the production of winter sport items. The access to everyday resources such as logistics, marketing and sale distributors explains the continuous growth of firm size in the district.

However, this is not determining simply a shift of the competitive advantage of the district towards MNCs.

The acquisition of Nordica from Benetton resembles the case of the NOHA group discussed above. Benetton tried to integrate within its retailing systems the 'sport products' of the district, but it did not work. Benetton could not understand the sophisticated market for sport items, nor the consumer preferences and attitudes (so the exclusive retail chain for sport items never took off – sportspeople like to be exposed to the new products of all producers, and they do not go to one shop that possesses only one brand). But also the knowledge governance failed, and quality went down in Nordica. As a result, after losing a great deal of money, Benetton sold Nordica to a district entrepreneur (Tecnica).

Another important aspect of the globalization process is linked to the inward processes that are represented by the activity of subcontracting by foreign multinationals that are coming to Montebelluna to exploit the know-how in the production of sport shoes that has been accumulated here. As has been noted by Durante (1996), many international brands provide orders for some specific projects (or highly skilled tasks) to the Montebelluna firms for the production of mountain-ski-winter-trekking shoes: Cabelas, Decathlon, Intersport (McKinley), LL Bean, Eindl, Mephisto, Merrl, Raiche, Rockpor (Reebok), Timberland, Fila, Ambro, Mizuno, Asics, Mitre, Umbro, and Vasque.

All these large groups utilize the core competencies of the district. This process has been called by Cafferata (1993) and Grandinetti and Rullani (1992) 'diffused globalization', to contrast it with the 'elitarian mondialisation', based exclusively on the actions of large multinationals.

This long list of the main events in Montebelluna history allows us to focus our attention particularly on two aspects.

First, a typical Italian district has been penetrated by some of the most important multinationals of the sector without disappearing. This is clearly in contrast with what occurred in the past in Manchester and Birmingham. The decline of districts is not irreversible.

Second, is there then a theoretical contraposition between the district form and the multinational model of firm? We witness here a curious merging between global a-spatial networks (Castells and Henderson 1987; Castells 1996), thus, multinational firms, and localized networks of producers; that is; districts. On one hand, economies of proximity seem to be still relevant. Local systems based on knowledge and on the reproduction of scarce competencies and capabilities are able to maintain their specificity, and to accumulate with time their competitive advantages. On the other hand, the model of multinationals, and the connected scale and scope economies, appear to be still relevant and endowed with penetrating power. In one sense the two models in the Montebelluna case are still co-evolving. Multinational firms that entered the district needed a territorial connection, and, in contrast, local firms left the district to multiply the advantages of non-district, long-distance, local connections (Bell, *et al.* 2001; Belussi 2003a).

In our research (Belussi 2003b) we analyzed the cases of the MNCs entering the Montebelluna district through qualitative in-depth interviews with MNCs actors and to district agents. We will base our conjecture on the analysis of the cases of Nike, Htm, Invicta, Rossignol-Lange and Salomon, which represent MNCs' entry in the Montebelluna district through FDI. This allows us to dwell upon some critical aspects.

Firstly, all managers interviewed[8] explained the entry of their multinational firm in Montebelluna with the aim of acquiring local competencies related to the technology of ski boots production (very innovative specialized suppliers and subcontractors are located in this district). Two out of the five multinationals came to Montebelluna with the idea of enlarging their production range. They wanted to diversify their production, but they lacked the necessary competencies. So, multinationals used the Montebelluna competencies for achieving only a few tasks: design and engineering, research on new materials, technologies, production techniques, creation of prototypes, and high-quality production.

Second, all five multinationals have acquired the entire ownership of the districtual firm that they have bought, and make use of the plant acquired without destroying the competencies located there. They maintained and increased the role of the local firms and their R&D offices. They did not move the manufacture of their products to Montebelluna. They used the local plant as an engineering office for the conceptualization of new products.

Third, the tapping into the district has not worried greatly the actors of the local district (firms and institutions). In the local environment we still find a high diversity of opinions on the matter, ranging from scepticism and fear to optimism on the role that multinationals may play for the 'modernization' and the further development of the district.

Fourth, the multinationals attribute some shortcomings to the district: the absence of managerial capability by local firms (they are still very traditionally organized along the lines of a type of family business), the weakness of logistical infrastructures, the lack of some professional figures, the inefficiency of the local transport infrastructure, etc. However, they give a positive evaluation of their experience: the localization in Montebelluna has not given rise to a too high informative spillover, and they do not feel they are at a risk of being imitated by local firms (no more than would be the case if they were located elsewhere).

Fifth, the entry of multinationals has contributed to elevating the level of competitiveness among local firms, accelerating an exit process among the less competitive. The entry of multinationals has also accelerated a local reaction from the largest leading firms. Now many firms have merged and 'small Italian multinationals' have been created (Madsen and Servais 1997). In Montebelluna the entry of MNCs has also stimulated local entrepreneurs to adopt new models of firm governance. Let us quote here the cases of Geox and Stonefly: two high-growth organizations, recently founded. They created a high-tech niche for outdoor shoes, they have a strong recourse to patenting activity, advertising, dominance of distributive channels, etc. Clearly the presence in Montebelluna of firms like Nike, that with its headquarters in Oregon at Beaverton organizes an international supply chain of about 500,000 workers, cannot allow Montebelluna entrepreneurs to rest on their laurels. Anyway, this is nothing more than the stuff of competition.

12.4 Conclusions

From our analysis three main issues emerged. The first question concerns the relationship between the endogenous development and the territorial specificity of competitive advantage, and, on the other hand, the existence of potential forces of territorial fragmentation, acting upon this structure. District disclosure is the striking aspect connected to the presence of globalization forces which decentralize both the production of goods and of knowledge, within a productive frame where specialization functions as an attractor for building comparative advantages. Hence, is globalization a necessary prerequisite for local learning, or does it contribute to disembeddedness or to the ubiquitification (Maskell 1999b) of the specialized knowledge possessed by local firms in districts or clusters? Our analyses clearly indicate that specialized knowledge and its related learning processes can still remain locally embedded, even if in some cases we have a change and a hybridization with external sources. Local system embeddedness matters but organizational embeddedness does too (Granovetter 1985). So, firms in local systems evolve following different patterns, and competitive districts still maintain a cohesive shape.

Second, the relative importance of local versus non-local learning is still a question related to the way in which 'core learning processes' are activated and to the dynamism of local actors, and not a question of non-local learning being substituted for local learning.

Third, the presence of foreign ownership in the form of MNCs' entry in the district is *per se* problematic, but not a strong destructive force. When foreign ownership creates abundant supplies of enduring capital, and the actual use of this capital is determined by local strategic management, as in the case of ABB, foreign ownership can vastly improve the competitiveness of local firms by enhancing and supporting local learning. Or, alternatively, as in the case of Montebelluna, MNCs can tap into the knowledge circuit of the district without dismantling its structure. Clearly, centrifugal forces are at work, and the existence of long-distance supply chains represents not only a 'district disclosure' but a contrasting force to agglomeration and to the district 'density'. The experiences of MNCs in the two districts analyzed illustrate how the availability of everyday resources such as logistics, sales and marketing etc. are of vital importance to the local development. In this perspective, foreign ownership emerges as a prerequisite for sustained localized learning because MNCs are rich in those resources that typically industrial districts do not possess with abundance: managerial skills, marketing and communication capabilities, coordination capabilities, high ability to protect innovation, etc. Some 'synergies' emerge rather than opposition between local learning processes and the global exploration and exploitation of knowledge. MNCs can feed the local units with the transfer of knowledge. Similarly, non-local learning interfaces are essential as firms increasingly find themselves in need of specialized knowledge. These learning interfaces complement rather than substitute whatever goes on locally – such as inter-firm learning or in-house learning. Leaving firm level implications aside, there is, however, no doubt that there are negative implications for the local cluster when delocalization occurs. Established local inter-firm networks are broken as firms substitute them with non-local ones, reducing the growth ability of the area, but there are also other developmental business opportunities related to the use of the international division of labour.

Notes

1 This part is partially based on the empirical work of Herstad Severre J., whom we thank.
2 This firm represents a paradigmatic development of the Scandinavian model (Archibugi and Lunvall 2001): i.e. the lack of exposure to financial short-termism and transparency of corporate control (Ruigrok and van Tulder 1995).
3 This work is partially based on an EU project 'West-East industrial districts relocation', coordinated by F. Belussi and internationally organised by the institute Guglielmo Tagliacarne in Rome.
4 See for instance Anastasia and Corò (1993), and Anastasia, Corò, and Crestanello (1995).
5 The district is composed of many adjacent municipalities, which include both the 'historical part of the district' (Caerano, Cornuda, Crocetta, Pederobba, Montebelluna, Maser, Nervesa, Trevignano, Volpago, and Giavera,) and a 'fringe area'.
6 The district firm population is based on *final firms* (branded and non-branded final producers), *specialised suppliers* (machinery producers, model makers, designers, upper

producers, die makers, sole producers, injection specialists, mould firms, producers of levers, shoe laces, etc.), and devoted to labour-intensive phases *subcontracting* (leather cutting firms, boots assembly firms, upper sole sewing, partial shoes assembly, etc.).
7 Data provided by the Chamber of Commerce of Treviso.
8 The interviews were organized in the period between January 2001 and March 2002. Most of the interviews carried out with the local managers of MNCs were personally carried out by Claudio Piva, who used a semi-structured questionnaire crafted jointly. I would like here to thank him for his assistance. Some further reflections are in Piva (2002). By agreement with the interviewees the results will be reported in an anonymous form.

References

Aage T. (2002), 'Absorptive capacity of firms in industrial district', paper presented at Eape Conference, Siena, 8–11 November.

Alderman, N. (forthcoming), 'Mobility versus embeddedness: the role of proximity in major capital projects', in A. Lagendijk and P. Oinas (eds.), *Proximity, Distance and Diversity: Issues on Economic Interaction and Local Development*. Aldershot: Ashgate.

Amable, B. (1999), 'Institutional complementarity and diversity of social systems of innovation and production'. *Working Paper*, CEPREMAP.

Amin A. (1993), 'The globalisation of the economy: an erosion of regional network?', in, G. Grabher (ed.), *The Embedded Firm. On the Socioeconomic of Industrial Networks*, London: Routledge.

Amin A. and Robins K. (1990), 'Industrial districts and regional development: limits and possibilities', in F. Pyke, G. Becattini and W. Sengenberger (eds.), *Industrial Districts and Inter-firm Co-operation in Italy*, Geneva: ILO.

Anastasia B. and Corò G. (1993), *I distretti industriali in Veneto*, Nuova dimensione, Ediciclo, Portogruaro.

Anastasia B., Corò G., and Crestanello P. (1995), 'Problemi di individuazione dei distretti industriali: esperienze regionali e rapporti con le politiche', *Oltre il Ponte*, 52.

Archibugi D. and Lunvall B. (eds.) (2001), *The Globalising Learning Economy*, Oxford: Oxford University Press.

Asheim B. T. (1996), 'Industrial districts as learning regions. Conditions for prosperity', *European Planning Studies*, 4: 379–400.

——. (1999a), 'Interactive learning and localised knowledge in globalising learning economies.' *GeoJournal*, 49(4): 345–52.

——. (1999b), 'TESA bedrifter på Jæren – fra et territorielt innovasjonsnettverk til funksjonelle konserndannelser?', in A. Isaksen (ed.), Regionale innovasjonssystemer. Innovasjon og læring i 10 regionale næringsmiljøer. *STEP-report* R-02, The STEP-group, Oslo, pp. 131–52.

——. (2000), 'Industrial districts: the contributions of Marshall and beyond', in G. Clark, M. Feldman and M. Gertler (eds.), *The Oxford Handbook of Economic Geography*, Oxford: Oxford University Press, pp. 413–31.

——. (2001), 'Learning regions as development coalitions: partnership as governance in European workfare states?' *Concepts and Transformation. International Journal of Action Research and Organizational Renewal*, 6(1): 73–101.

——. (2002), 'Temporary organisations and spatial embeddedness of learning and knowledge creation', *Geografiska Annaler, Series B, Human Geography*, 84B(2): 111–24.

Asheim B. T. and Cooke P. (1999), 'Local learning and interactive innovation networks in a global economy', in E. Malecki and P. Oinas (eds.), *Making Connections: Technological Learning and Regional Economic Change*, Aldershot: Ashgate, pp. 145–78.

Asheim B. T. and Herstad S. (2002), 'Regional clusters under international duress: between local institutions and global corporations', paper, Centre for Technology, Innovation and Culture, University of Oslo.

Asheim B. T. and Isaksen A. (1997), 'Location, agglomeration and innovation: towards regional innovation systems in Norway?' *European Planning Studies*, 5(3) 299–330.

——. (2002), 'Regional innovation systems: the integration of local "sticky" and global "ubiquitous" knowledge', *Journal of Technology Transfer*, 27: 77–86.

Baccarani C. and Golinelli G. (1993), 'Tratti del divenire dei distretti industriali', *Quaderno dell'Istituto Tagliacarne*, 8: 15–46.

Badie B. (1995), *Le fin des territoires*, Paris: Fayard.

Bathelt H., Malmberg A. and Maskell P. (2004), 'Clusters and knowledge: local buzz, global pipelines and the process of knowledge creation', *Prog. Hum. Geog.* 28(1): 31–56.

Becattini G. and Rullani E. (1996), 'Global systems and local systems', in F. Cossentino, F. Pyke and W. Sengenberger (eds.), *Local and Regional Response to Global Pressure: the Case of Italy and its Industrial Districts*, Geneva: Research Series ILO.

Becattini G., Bellandi M., Dei Ottati G. and Sforzi G. (2003), *From Industrial Districts to Local Development: An Itinerary of Research*, Cheltenham: Edward Elgar.

Becchetti L. (2002), La competitività delle piccole e medie imprese italianrispetto ai concorrenti internazionali: capacità di export e forme di internazionalizzazione intermedia, in Galli G. and Paganetto L. (a cura di), *La competitività dell'Italia*, II, Le Imprese, Ricerca del Centro Studi Confindustria, Il Sole 24 Ore, Milan.

Bell J., McNaughton, R. and Young, S. (2001), 'Born-again global firms: an extension to the born global phenomenon', *Journal of International Management*, 7(3): 173–90.

Belussi F. (2003a), 'Processi di internazionalizzazione e delocalizzazione delle PMI e dei distretti industriali', in Unioncamere-Le PMI nell'economia italiana. Rapporto 2002, Milano: Franco Angeli.

——. (2003b), 'The changing governance of IDS: the entry of multinationals in local nets. The case of Montebelluna', paper presented at the Druid Conference, Copenhagen, 12–14 June.

Belussi F. and Macdonald F. (2002), *The evolution of industrial districts and policies towards them: developing policies to help enlargement of the European Union by using the experiences of Western European countries, State of the Art Report on 'Industrial Districts' Relocation Processes: Identifying Policies in the Perspective of the European Union Enlargement'*, Tagliacarne, mimeo.

Belussi F. and Pilotti L. (2002), 'Knowledge creation, learning and innovation in Italian industrial districts', *Geografiska Annaler*, 84: 19–33.

Belussi F., Gottardi G. and Rullani E. (2000), 'Il futuro dei distretti', *Piccola Impresa/Small Business*, 2: 3–22.

Belussi F., Gottardi G. and Rullani E. (eds.) (2003), *The Technological Evolution of Industrial Districts*, Boston: Kluwer.

Biggiero L. (1999), 'Markets, hierarchies, networks, districts: a cybernetic approach', *Human System Management*, 18: 71–86.

Bonomi A. (1997), *Il capitalismo molecolare*, Torino: Einaudi.

Brown, J. S. and Duguid P. (1991), 'Organisational learning and communities-of-practice – towards a unified theory of working, learning and innovation', *Organization Science*, 2(1): 40–57.

Buckley P. and Casson M. (1976), *The Future of Multinational Enterprise*, London: Holmes & Meier.

Buckley P., Clegg, J. and Forsans, N. (1997), *International Technology Transfer by Small and Medium Sized Enterprises*, London: Macmillan.

Cafferata A. (1993), 'La transizione dell'impresa multinazionale', *Sinergie*, 32.

Cainelli G. (2002), 'L'evoluzione dei distretti industriali in Italia', *Quaderni IDSE*, 5 December.

Cantwell J. (1998), 'The globalisation of technology: what remains of the product-cycle model?', in A. Chandler Jr, P. Hagström and O. Sölvell (eds.), *The Dynamic Firm*, New York: Oxford University Press.

Cantwell, J. and Iammarino, S (1998) 'MNCs, technological innovation and regional systems in the EU: some evidence in the Italian case', *International Journal of the Economics of Business*, 5: 383–408.

Cantwell J. and Janne O. (1999), 'Technological globalisation and innovative centres: the role of corporate technological leadership and locational hierarchy', *Research Policy*, 28: 119–44.

Carminucci C. and Casucci S. (1997), 'Il ciclo di vita dei distretti industriali', *L'industria*, 2.

Caroli M. and Lipparini A (eds.) (2002), *Piccole imprese oltre il confine. Competenze e processi di internazionalizzazione*, Roma: Carocci.

Castells M. (1996), *The Rise of the Network Society*, Oxford: Blackwell.

Castells M. and Henderson J. (1987), *Global Restructuring and Territorial Development*, London: Sage.

Cavalieri A. (ed.) (1995), *L'internazionalizzazione del processo produttivo nei sistemi locali di piccola impresa in Toscana*, Milano: Angeli

Caves R. (1982), *Multinational Enterprise and Economic Analysis*, Cambridge: Cambridge University Press.

Cooke, P. (1992), 'Regional innovation systems: competitive regulation in the New Europe', *Geoforum*, 23: 365–82.

——. (1998), 'Introduction: origins of the concept', in H. Braczyk, P. Cooke and M. Heidenreich (eds.), *Regional Innovation Systems*, London: UCL Press, pp. 2–25.

——. (2001a), 'Regional innovation systems, clusters, and the knowledge economy'. *Industrial and Corporate Change*, 10(4): 945–74.

——. (2001b), 'Industrial innovation and learning systems: sector strategies for value chain linkage'. Chapter 6 in UNIDO, *World Industrial Development Report* (WIDR), Vienna.

Cooke, P., Boekholt P. and Tödtling F. (2000), *The Governance of Innovation in Europe. Regional Perspectives on Global Competitiveness*, London: Pinter.

Corò G. (2000), 'La delocalizzazione: minaccia, necessità o opportunità?', in I. Diamanti and D. Marini (eds.), *Nord Est 2000, Rapporto sulla società e l'economia, Fondazione Nord Est*, Venice.

Corò G. and Grandineti R. (1999a), 'Strategie di delocalizzazione e processi evolutiv nei distretti industriali italiani', *L'Industria*, a. 10(4): 897–924.

——. (1999b), 'Evolutionary patterns of Italian industrial districts', *Human Systems Management*, 2.

Di Bernardo B. (1997), 'Reti: un nuovo paradigma?', in E. Benedetti, M. Mistri and S. Solari (eds.), *Teorie evolutive e trasformazioni economiche*, Padova: Cedam.

Dosi, G. (1988), 'The nature of the innovative process', in G. Dosi, C. Freeman, R. Nelson, G. Silverberg and L. Soete (eds.), *Technical Change and Economic Theory*. London: Pinter Publishers, pp. 221–38.

Dunning J. (1997), *Alliance Capitalism and Global Business*, London: Routledge.

——. (ed.) (1993), *The Globalisation of Business*, London and New York: Routledge.

Dunning J. and Narula R. (2004), 'Industrial development, globalisation and multinational enterprises: new realities for developing countries', in J. Dunning and R. Narula (eds.), *Multinationals and Industrial Competitiveness*, Cheltenham: Edward Elgar.

Ernst D. and Kim L. (2002), 'Global production networks, information technology and knowledge diffusion', *Research Policy*, 31(8–9): 1417–29.

Feenstra R. C. (1998), 'Integration of trade and disintegration of production in the global economy', *The Journal of Economic Perspective*, 12(4): 31–50.

Foss N. and Pedersen T. (2002), 'Transferring knowledge in MNCs: the role of sources of subsidiary knowledge and organisational context', *Journal of International Management*, 8: 49–67.

Freeman, C. (1987), *Technology Policy and Economic Performance: Lessons from Japan.* London: Pinter.

——. (2002), 'Continental, national and sub-national innovation systems – complementarity and economic growth.' *Research Policy*, 31: 191–211.

Gann, D. M. and Salter A. J. (2000), 'Innovation in project-based, service enhanced firms: the construction of complex products and systems', *Research Policy*, 29: 955–72.

Grandinetti R. (1993), 'L'internazionalizzzione "sommersa" delle piccole imprese', *Rivista Italian di Economia e Statistica*, 47(3–4): 119–42.

Grandinetti R. and Rullani E. (1992), 'Internazionalizzazione e piccole imprese: elogio della varietà', *Piccola Impresa/Small Business*, 3.

——. (1996), *Impresa transnazionale ed economia globale*, Roma: Nis.

Granovetter, M. (1985), 'Economic action and social structure: the problem of embeddedness', *American Journal of Sociology*, 91: 481–510.

Guerrieri P., Iammarino S. and Pietrobelli C. (eds.) (2001), *The Global Challenge to Industrial Districts: Small and Medium-sized Enterprises in Italy and Taiwan*, Cheltenham: Edward Elgar.

Hymer S. (1976), *The International Operations of National Firms: a Study of Direct Foreign Investment*, Cambridge, MA: The Mit Press.

Isaksen, A. (2005), 'Regional clusters between local and non-local relations: A comparative European study', in A. Lagendijk and P. Oinas (eds.), *Proximity, Distance and Diversity: Issues on Economic Interaction and Local Development*, Aldershot: Ashgate.

Kogut B. (1985), 'Designing global strategies: profiting from operational flexibility', *Sloan Management Review*, 26: 27–38.

Kuemmerle W. (1998), 'Foreign direct investment in industrial research in the pharmaceutical and electronics industries: results from a survey of multinational firms', *Research Policy*, 28: 179–93.

Laestadius S. (1998), 'Technology level, knowledge formation and industrial competence in paper manufacturing', in G. Eliasson and C. Green (eds.) *Microfoundations of Economic Growth. A Schumpeterian Perspective*, Ann Arbor: The University of Michigan Press, pp. 212–16.

Lam A. (1998a), 'The social embeddedness of knowledge: problems of knowledge sharing and organisational learning in international high-technology ventures.' *DRUID Working Paper* 98–7, Aalborg.

——. (1998b), 'Tacit knowledge, organisational learning and innovation: A societal perspective.' *DRUID Working Paper* 98–22, Aalborg.

Lazonick W. and O'Sullivan M. (1994), 'Skill formation in wealthy nations: organizational evolution and economic consequences.' *STEP-report* R-23, Oslo.

Litvak I. (1990), 'Instant international: strategic reality for small high technology firms in Canada', *Multinational Business*, Summer, 2: 1–12.

Lorenzen M. and Mahnke V. (2002), 'Global strategies and acquisition of local knowledge: how MNCs enter regional clusters', *DRUID Working Paper* 8: 1–24.

Lorenzoni G. (1997), *Architetture reticolari e processi di internazionalizzazione*, Bologna: Il Mulino.

Lundvall, B.-Å (1996), 'The social dimension of the learning economy', *DRUID Working Papers*, 96–1, Aalborg: Aalborg University.

——. (ed.) (1992), *National Innovation Systems: Towards a Theory of Innovation and Interactive Learning*. London: Pinter.

MacKinnon, D., Cumbers A. and Chapman K. (2002), 'Learning, innovation and regional development: a critical appraisal of recent debates', *Progress in Human Geography*, 26(3): 293–311.

Madsen T. and Servais P. (1997), 'The internationalisation of born global: an evolutionary process?' *International Business Review*, 6(6): 561–83.

Malmberg A. and Maskell P. (1999), 'Guest editorial: localized learning and regional economic development', *European Urban and Regional Studies*, 6(1): 5–8.

Maskell P. (1999a), 'Globalisation and industrial competitiveness: the process and consequences of ubiquitification', in E. Malecki and P. Oinas (eds.), *Making Connections: Technological Learning and Regional Economic Change*, Aldershot: Ashgate, pp. 35–59.

——. (1999b), *Knowledge Creation and Diffusion in Geographic Clusters*, Copenhagen: Druid, mimeo.

Maskell P. and Malmberg A. (1999), 'Localised learning and industrial competitiveness', *Cambridge Journal of Economics*, 23: 167–85.

Maskell, P., Eskelinen H., Hannibalsson I., Malmberg A. and Vatne E. (1998), *Competitiveness, Localised Learning and Regional Development*. London: Routledge.

Nelson R. (ed.) (1993), *National Innovation Systems: A Comparative Analysis.* Oxford: Oxford University Press.

Nonaka I. and Takeuchi H. (1995), *The Knowledge Company*, Oxford: Oxford University Press.

Nooteboom B. (2001), 'Problems and solutions in knowledge transfer', paper presented at Max Planck Institute Conference, Jena, February 2001.

——. (2002), 'A cognitive theory of the firm', paper presented at workshop on theories of the firm, Paris, November 2002.

Osem (2001), *Rapporto Osem 2001*, Treviso: Veneto Banca.

Oviatt B. and McDougall P. P. (1994), 'Toward a theory of international new ventures', *Journal of International Business Studies*, 25(1): 45–64.

Piore M. J. and Sable C. F. (1984), *The Second Industrial Divide: Possibilities for Prosperities*, New York: Basic Books.

Piva C. (2002), I processi di globalizzazione dei distretti industriali, il caso di Montebelluna, unpublished thesis, Padua University.

Pla-Barber J., Puig F. and Camps J. (2007), 'Is the influence of industrial district on internationalisation strategies eroding after globalisation? Evidence from a traditional manufacturing industry', paper presented at the 33rd EIBA workshop, 13–15 December, Catania.

Porter, M. (1990), *The Competitive Advantage of Nations*, London: Macmillan.

——. (1994), *Capital Choices – Changing the Way America Invests in Industry*, Boston: Council on Competitiveness/Harvard Business School.

——. (1998), 'Clusters and the new economics of competition', *Harvard Business Review*, November–December: 77–90.

——. (2000), 'Location, clusters and company strategy', in G. Clark, M. Feldman and M. Gertler (eds.), *The Oxford University Handbook of Geography*, Oxford: Oxford University Press.

Quadrio Curzio A. and Fortis M. (2000), *Il made in Italy oltre il 2000*, Bologna: Il Mulino.

Rugman A. and Verbeke A. (2003), 'Multinational enterprises and clusters', *Management International Review*, 43(Special Issue 3): 151–69.

Ruigrok, W. and van Tulder R. (1995), *The Logic of International Restructuring*, London: Routledge.

Rullani E. (1998), 'Internazionalizzatine e nuovi sistemi di governance nei sistemi produttivi locali', in G. Corò and E. Rullani (eds.), *Percorsi locali di internazionalizzazione*, Milan: Angeli.

——. (2001), 'New/Net/Knowledge economy: le molte facce del postfordismo', *Economia e Politica Industriale*, 110.

——. (2002), 'Dallo sviluppo per accumulazione allo sviluppo per propagazione: piccole imprese, clusters e capitale sociale nella nuova Europa in formazione', East West Cluster conference, Udine, 28–31 October.

Sammarra A. (2003), *Lo sviluppo dei distretti industriali. Percorsi evolutivi tra globalizzazione e localizzazione*, Roma: Carocci.

Sanguigni V. (2002), 'Inward and outward processing trade as ways of internalisation of Italian SMEs production activities', paper presented at the international conference 'Business policies and strategies in a global market. A framework for SMEs: case studies', Turin, 14 November.

Scarso E. (1996), 'La rilocalizzazione internazionale del processo produttivo e i sistemi locali del veneto: videnze dai settori moda', *Economia e Società Regionale*, 4.

Schiattarella R. (1999), 'La delocalizzzione internazionale: problemi di definizione e delimitazione. Un'analisi per il settore del Made in Italy', *Economia e Politica Industriale*, 103.

Soskice D. (1999) 'Divergent production regimes: coordinated and uncoordinated market economies in the 1980s and 1990s', in H. Kitschelt, P. Lange, G. Marks, J. Stephens (eds.), *Continuity and change in contemporary capitalism*, Cambridge: Cambridge University Press.

Storper, M. (1997), *The Regional World – Territorial Development in a Global Economy*. London/New York: The Guilford Press.

Storper M. and Venables A. (2003), 'Buzz: face to face contact and the urban economy', paper presented at the Druid Conference, Copenhagen, 12–14 June.

Wenger, E. (1998), *Communities of Practice: Learning, Meaning and Identity*. Cambridge: Cambridge University Press.

Whitley, R. (1993), 'The internationalisation of firms and markets: its significance and institutional structuring', *Working paper* 251, Manchester Business School.

——. (1999), *Divergent Capitalisms – the Social Structuring and Change of Business Systems*. Oxford: Oxford University Press.

13 Industrial clusters in the Brazilian ceramic tile industry and the new challenges of the competition in the global value chain

Renato Garcia (Polytechnic School of the University of São Paulo, Brazil) and Gabriela Scur (FEI University, Brazil)

13.1 Introduction

This chapter investigates the impact of the new challenges in the international scenario of competition on the ceramic tile industry in Brazil and, specifically, on the dynamics of its two main local production systems, located in the regions of Criciúma, in the state of Santa Catarina, and the Santa Gertrudes region in the state of São Paulo.

These new characteristics of international competition have reshaped the organization of the global value chains, mainly because of the sharp growth of exports from China, which has become the major world manufacturer of ceramic tiles, the dynamism and innovation of the Spanish industry, and decreased participation by the Italian industry.

Despite increased international competition, Brazilian industry went through a period of expansion, with a simultaneous growth in domestic sales and exports. This growth was reflected in the high dynamism of the Brazilian industry, which relied both on the expansion of the supply of ceramic tiles and on marked changes in the techno-productive parameters of the firms. Some factors in this process that played a fundamental role in the creation and dissemination of new knowledge and in fostering innovative activities by producers should be stressed; these are the glazing materials suppliers, the manufacturers of capital goods and the local service-rendering institutions. It should also be emphasized that the organization of the industry into local production systems played an important role, since it facilitated the dissemination and circulation of new knowledge among the actors.

The next section demonstrates this by presenting the main characteristics of the global chain of the ceramic tile industry. Following that, a brief panorama of the Brazilian industry and of its two main local production systems, the regions of Criciúma and Santa Gertrudes, is presented. Later, we present some considerations about the dynamics of the Brazilian ceramic tile industry and its insertion in this new competitive international scenario, with a special focus on the mechanisms that create and disseminate knowledge among local producers.

13.2 The global value chain in the ceramic tile industry

In the last few years, standards for the global ceramic tile industry have been undergoing important transformations, which is also true for other industries. The main characteristics of these transformations shape the new challenges of global competition, with changing positions and market shares for the main players. It may seem paradoxical, but the changing international competition in the ceramic tile industry occurred simultaneously with strong growth in consumption of ceramic tiles worldwide; around 5.6 per cent per year in the first half of the 2000s.[1] With reference to global production, China consolidated itself as the main manufacturer of ceramic tiles, responsible for almost one-third of global physical production in 2004 (Table 13.1 and Figure 13.1).

Spain occupied second place with 9.5 per cent of the world's production in 2004, surpassing third-place Italy's 8.7 per cent. The fourth largest producer was Brazil, responsible for 8.4 per cent of global production. In this context, among the four largest ceramic tile manufacturers in the world, only the Italian industry did not present positive growth rates, and domestic production decreased by almost 7 per cent in the first half of the 2000s decade. The negative growth of the Italian industry is basically associated with its diminished participation in the international market (Table 13.2).

As we can see in Table 13.2, the Italian industry was still the main world exporter

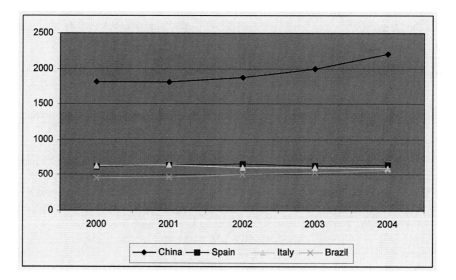

Figure 13.1 Top manufacturing countries.
Source: ASCER (2006).

Table 13.1 World production of ceramic tiles (millions of sq. metres)

Countries	2000	2001	2002	2003	2004	2005
China	1807	1810	1868	2000	2200	3100
Spain	621	638	651	627	640	648
Italy	632	638	606	603	589	572
Brazil	453	473	508	534	566	594
India	97	109	215	240	270	320
Indonesia	200	220	230	260	260	N/A
Turkey	175	155	163	189	216	N/A
Mexico	138	167	159	171	177	N/A
Vietnam	55	95	105	110	165	N/A
Thailand	56	63	100	135	157	N/A
Other countries	1216	1245	1337	1454	1531	N/A
TOTAL	5450	5614	5942	6323	6771	N/A

Source: ASCER (2006).

Table 13.2 World exports of ceramic tiles (millions of sq. metres)

Countries	2000	2001	2002	2003	2004	2005
Italy	436.3	440.7	437.7	417.6	412.5	392.0
Spain	311.5	339	356.5	335.7	340.5	342.0
China	24.3	53.1	124.8	206.4	270.0	310.0
Brazil	56.8	59.5	73.9	103.6	125.8	114.4
Turkey	61.5	56.4	72.2	84.1	85.5	88.0
Others	263.4	261.7	271.8	320.4	324.9	N/A
TOTAL	1153.8	1210.4	1336.9	1467.8	1607.4	N/A

Source: ASCER (2006).

of ceramic tiles in 2004, responsible for more than 25 per cent of the total world trade.[2] However, during the 2000–04 period, we witnessed significant growth by Spain, which consolidated itself as the second largest world supplier with 21 per cent of the total trade; by China, which reached very significant growth rates and attained a nearly 20 per cent share of world trade; and by Brazil, whose exports more than doubled during the same period.

In contrast to the situation of Italy and Spain, where domestic production is strongly directed to the external market, in both Brazil and China local production had historically been directed to serving their respective huge domestic markets.

As can be seen, these countries are both large consumers of ceramic tiles, with China in the lead.

However, despite their large domestic markets, both countries have reported growth in the international market, especially China, whose growth rate during the last few years has been particularly high.

To a large extent, the growth of these countries in the international market has been associated with the growing markets for ceramic tiles, particularly the US, which is now the largest purchaser of this product in the world. One special difficulty in the ceramic tile trade should be noted: their heavy weight, which means very high transportation costs due to a reduced value-weight relationship.

One important characteristic of the industry is that its production is organized into industrial clusters, common throughout the sector and to all the major international producers.

In China, production is concentrated around the city of Foshan, in the province of Guangdong, where there are about 3000 companies which manufacture about 60 per cent of the country's total production and 25 per cent of world ceramic tile production.

In Italy, the manufacture of ceramic tiles is concentrated in the region around the city of Sassuolo, where there are about 315 companies, responsible for around 80 per cent of Italy's production (Galbadon-Estevan, *et al.* 2007). In addition to the manufacturers of ceramic tiles, the local system of Sassuolo stands out due to the presence of capital goods manufacturers for the ceramic industry (Russo 1985, 2004), who can take advantage of their geographic proximity as an important source for innovations.

As indicated earlier, the Italian ceramic tile industry has been facing marked difficulties from increased international competition, as shown by its decreasing share of the international market. However, in response, several Italian companies have tried to invest in establishing manufacturing units in other countries. According to Gambuli (2001), 16 Italian firms were operating abroad in many countries, some with more than one plant: for example, three in the US, six in France, two in Spain, one in Portugal, one in Germany, one in Sweden, one in Finland and one in the Czech Republic.

This is one of the reasons that Italy's global market share has decreased, since part of the market which should have been supplied by Italian firms is now served by local units operated by Italian companies. On the one hand, this strategy strengthens the competitiveness of Italian firms, but, as a secondary effect, it has weakened the local system in Sassuolo, as evidenced by declines in local production and employment. The firms that decided to establish manufacturing units abroad lost the benefits which derive from the clustering of firms in Sassuolo, and try to compensate for this by greater proximity to their consumer market.

In Spain, we can also perceive the existence of an important local system of ceramic tile production in the region around the city of Castellón. There are 294 companies in the region, predominantly of small and medium size, which are responsible for 90 per cent of Spanish production (Alegre-Vidal, *et al.* 2004; Galbadon-Estevan, *et al.* 2007).

As in the Italian experience, the local system of Castellón stands out due to its concentration of ceramic tile manufacturers, as well as the presence of glazing materials suppliers. They specialize in manufacturing chemical products used in the ceramic industry, such as frits and ceramic colourants. Also in this case, the development of glazing materials production is related to the intense user-producer interactions, stemming from their geographic proximity. It should be pointed out that the presence of glazing materials suppliers is particularly important for the ceramic tile industry, since the manufacture of this material is an increasingly important source of innovation.

Since the early 1990s, the local system of Castellón has shown strong dynamism based, above all, on technological advances, expressed by heavy investments in machinery and equipment and, mainly, in the development of an important glazing materials industry. In contrast to the Italian experience, the companies of Castellón are more specialized, which has contributed to intensifying the interactive relationship with their suppliers. In terms of capital goods supply, the huge interactions between Castellón ceramic tile producers and the Italian machinery suppliers are noteworthy.

Developing local manufacturers of frits and ceramic colourants is also important. According to Meyer-Stamer, *et al.* (2004), towards the end of the 1990s there were 24 local frit and ceramic colourant companies, many of them with production units abroad. This fact is particularly important for local producers, and represents a special competitive advantage for the Spanish local system, since glazing materials have become an important source of innovation in the ceramic tile industry. Over recent decades, activities related to product development and designs have been transferred from tile manufacturers to the suppliers of frits and ceramic colourants, who started to undertake a larger number of these activities. As evidence of this, Meyer-Stamer, *et al.* (2004) point to the fact that the product development departments of the glazing material suppliers were far larger than those of the ceramic tile firms.

The growth of the Spanish industry on the world market is strongly related to these factors, since a high share of domestic production is concentrated in the local system of Castellón. The high level of knowledge in ceramic tile manufacturing, especially of tacit knowledge, has strengthened the innovative performance of local firms, with positive effects on their share in the global market. This pattern of response by Spanish firms to the new challenges of international competition has been very successful, and the firms have grown, despite the strong increase of Chinese exports.

13.3 The ceramic tile industry in Brazil

Brazil is the second largest world consumer of ceramic tiles, just behind China, and ranks as the fourth largest producer. The development of ceramic tile manufacturing in Brazil was due to many factors, such as: its large domestic market; the abundance of natural raw materials, especially clay; the availability of energy and access to the manufacturing technologies incorporated in capital goods. During the

1990s, the Brazilian ceramic tile industry displayed high rates of growth, associated mainly to the growth of the domestic market (see Table 13.3).

The growth of the domestic market for ceramic tiles in Brazil was due, mainly, to the increase in domestic income in this period. However, it is important to stress the falling price for ceramic tiles on the domestic market, as a result of stronger competition in this market, with a restructuring of the manufacturing process in the firms, cost reductions, and important increases in productivity. Differently from most international experiences, a large part of the manufacturing process in the Brazilian ceramic tile industry uses the 'dry process'. This process involves lower costs and quality standards compatible with international requirements.[3] The production system of the ceramic tile industry in Brazil includes 94 companies and 117 industrial plants distributed throughout all the regions of the country. It has about 25,000 employees (data from the national firm's association – ANFACER). Ceramic tile manufacturers are spread throughout Brazil, but are strongly concentrated in four main regions (as shown on the map in Figure 13.2): the region of Criciúma, in the state of Santa Catarina in southern Brazil; the metropolitan

Figure 13.2 Main agglomerations of ceramic tile manufacturers located in Brazil.

Table 13.3 Production, exports, domestic consumption and installed capacity of the Brazilian tile industry

| | Millions of sq. metres | | | | | Percentage | | |
Year	Production	Exports	Domestic Consumption*	Domestic Market Sales	Production Capacity	Export/ Production	Production/ Capacity
1990	172.8	12.7	160.1	n.d.	300.0	7.3	57.6
1991	166.0	13.9	152.1	149.9	312.0	8.4	53.2
1992	202.7	21.1	181.6	179.1	312.0	10.4	65.0
1993	242.9	25.6	217.3	214.1	320.0	10.5	75.9
1994	283.5	29.7	253.8	259.9	353.0	10.5	80.3
1995	295.0	29.4	265.6	261.6	362.0	10.0	81.5
1996	336.4	27.9	308.5	309.1	385.0	8.3	87.4
1997	383.3	29.6	353.7	339.8	385.0	7.7	99.6
1998	400.7	34.6	366.1	358.7	455.0	8.6	88.1
1999	428.5	42.6	385.9	383.3	492.0	9.9	87.1
2000	452.7	56.7	396.0	393.3	536.7	12.5	84.3
2001	473.4	59.5	413.9	416.3	556.9	12.6	85.0
2002	508.3	73.9	434.4	456.3	564.4	14.5	90.1
2003	534.0	103.5	430.5	421.0	571.4	19.4	93.5
2004	565.6	125.8	439.8	448.4	621.6	22.2	91.0
2005	568.1	113.8	454.3	442.2	650.7	20.0	87.3
2006	594.2	114.4	479.8	485.7	672.4	19.3	88.4

* Production minus Exports; because of the low imports.

Source: Authors (based on ANFACER, and Ferraz 2002).

region of São Paulo, the most industrialized region of the country, with the largest consumer market; the region of Mogi Guaçu, located in the interior of the state of São Paulo; and the region of Santa Gertrudes, also in the interior of the state of São Paulo. Together, these regions are responsible for about 90 per cent of domestic output.

Among these regions, there are two industrial agglomerations which comprise local production systems: Criciúma and Santa Gertrudes. These two experiences will be analyzed in the following sections.

13.4 Some methodology notes

The Criciuma district was composed of about 15 ceramic tile companies, 14 suppliers of raw materials (among producers and distributors, all of them providing services to the tile companies) and five manufacturers/distributors of machinery goods and replacement parts. The Santa Gertrudes district has 36 ceramic tile producers, 30 glaze suppliers and 35 manufacturers/distributors of capital goods and replacement parts (data from 2005).

The sample was built by using the database of the local firm's association (ASPACER – Ceramic Tile Producers Association of São Paulo State; and ASULCER – the South Brazilian Association) and was defined from the secondary data about such firms. The biggest firms were selected, that have made more important innovative moves, which includes productive processes and industrial organization, management of intangible assets (trade marks, distribution and commercialization channels), product development and presence in the foreign market. The companies and local players interviewed are shown in the Appendix.

The information presented in this chapter comes from 11 in-depth interviews with managers of ceramic tile firms and three glazing material suppliers, and from four qualitative interviews with local actors. Data were collected in the period of August–December 2005. The main agents in the face-to-face interviews were top-ranking managers and the person responsible for the local institution. For the completion of information collection, follow-up telephone interviews were often necessary.

In the Crisciúma district, five tile producers were interviewed; one of them works with the dry process. In addition, one firm that produces special tiles (for decoration) and two glaze suppliers were interviewed. Four were founded at the end of the 1980s and 90s. The others were founded in the 1950s, 60s and 70s. Two firms have around 100 employees, two approximately 300, and, finally, two big firms are composed of around 2000 employees. However, in terms of turnover, besides these two big firms, one more firm has a turnover above 60 million Brazilian Reais (around US$35 million in 2005), and for this reason it was considered large. Three firms can be characterized as medium-sized, and the special tiles producer is the newest one and is small.

In general, firms are managed by families and capital is closed for external investors. But three local firms have joint stock market shares and are managed by professional executives. The big firms' production capacity is around 3.3 million square metres, two are around 300,000, one produces 600,000 and the special tiles producer has a capacity of 60,000 square metres.

The product mix is diversified and the manufacturing units produce all kinds of tiles, for instance porcelain tiles, enamelled, not enamelled, wall tiles and floor tiles. Another firm acts in the special pieces market. It is important to note that the major firms in Criciuma operate through the water process (atomized) but there is one in the sample which uses the dry process.

In the Santa Gertrudes district, five ceramic tile manufacturers and one glazing material supplier were interviewed. Two tile producers work through the water process. Four were founded in the 1990s and two are from the 1930s and 40s. Most of the firms are composed of around 200 employees, and only two have 500 employees. Two ceramic tile manufacturers have a turnover above 60 million Brazilian Reais and are classified as large. The others are medium sized.

Almost all local firms are managed by the entrepreneur and his family, and only one firm is in a process of professionalizing the board. The biggest manufacturer in terms of production capacity operates with 2.5 million square metres per month, two around 800,000 square metres and the other two are capable of producing 500,000 square metres per month.

Only the firm which has the water process offers a full product mix since they produce special pieces, floor and door tiles and porcelain tiles. It is important to note that this porcelain was imported from China and the firm just labels it in Brazil – this tendency has increased in Brazil.

13.5 The Brazilian industrial districts in the ceramic tile industry

The two main agglomerations of ceramic tile producers in Brazil are both in the regions of Criciúma and Santa Gertrudes, which concentrate about three-quarters of the total domestic output.

Table 13.4 Overall picture of the sample compared to the whole Criciuma district in 2004

Variables	Sample	District
Number of firms	6	15
Number of employees	4535	4847
Production capacity (sq. m/month)	6,210,000	7,270,000
Sellers' internal market (sq. m/year)	66,621,280*	45,115,179
Sellers' external market (sq. m/year)	14,860,720*	29,876,715
Turnover (US$)	1,067,269,100*	333,865,260

Source: author's own elaboration; *This amount takes into account establishments located outside the district.

Table 13.5 Overall picture of the sample compared to the whole Santa Gertrudes district in 2004

Variables	Sample	District
Number of firms	5	36
Number of employees	1594	8000
Production capacity (sq. m/month)	5,130,000	28,000,000
Sellers' internal market (sq. m/year)	49,829,000	228,000,000
Sellers' external market (sq. m/year)	4,927,000	28,000,000
Turnover (US$)	216,918,650	395,730,585

Source: author's own elaboration.

The region of Criciúma, in the state of Santa Catarina, is the most traditional industrial cluster of ceramic tile firms in Brazil. Some local producers started their operations in the 1950s, motivated by the existence of coal in the region, which was used to fuel the ovens. In the 2000s, the local system has been responsible for around one-third of the Brazilian total output of ceramic tiles, and about two-thirds of exports. It has become the main centre for product innovation and design. In general, local firms do make greater efforts in product development and design and thus they define the fashion trends and product design on the domestic market.[4]

The Santa Gertrudes region, in the state of São Paulo, is a much younger industrial cluster. The origins of the local system were related to the existence of a great clay pit, well suited for use as raw material for ceramic tile manufacturing. In fact, the local production of bricks and roof tiles started at the beginning of the twentieth century. But in the 1990s, ceramic tile production gained a strong dynamism, and about 45 local firms came into existence, which are now responsible for about 50 per cent of Brazilian output and 15 per cent of exports.

13.5.1 The industrial district of Criciúma

The ceramic tile industry of Criciúma is the most traditional production centre in Brazil. Some of the still-active local firms started operating in the 1950s, but the period of greatest dynamism occurred during the 1970s and 80s, linked to the growth of the domestic market for ceramic tiles. This period of high activity ended in the 1990s, when local manufacturers faced a severe crisis from strong domestic competition, as a result of the growth in the manufacture of ceramic products, especially from the local system of Santa Gertrudes.

This crisis provoked significant restructuring movements by local firms, especially among the larger ones. This restructuring involved such factors as: de-activating old manufacturing lines and opening new ones; expansion, construction and acquisition of manufacturing plants; modernization of equipment, in addition to changes in organizational and managerial structures. This process resulted in substantial growth in production, due to the modernization of manufacturing plants, of production rationalization processes, in addition to a greater concentration of production in larger industrial plants.

However, this process of restructuring and technological modernization did not prevent a reduction in the share of local producers in the domestic market. The main vector of the decreasing share of local firms was the growth of Santa Gertrudes' producers, who began to occupy the position formerly held by the old main manufacturing centre. With the increased competition in the domestic market, the firms of Criciúma tried to find solutions to their reduced output by increasing their efforts at innovation, both by modernizing the manufacturing process and by reinforcing their product development and design activities.

During the restructuring process, several local firms outsourced some activities, particularly the production of glazing material and enamelling, that had been done inside their borders. That means that local firms used to maintain activities related to the chemical industry. From the 1990s onwards, this strategy became problematic, as the ceramic tile firms were no longer able to follow the faster dissemination of innovations by the specialized glazing materials suppliers.

It is worth remembering that one of the most important changes in competition in this industry during the 1990s was the increased importance of glazing material firms in defining the characteristics of the final product. This obliged companies to internalize the important capabilities on innovation and product development and design.[5]

For this reason, firms which had been carrying out glazing and enamelling activities internally were compelled to abandon them.[6] For the glazing material companies born from this change, it was possible to centralize and intensify product development and design efforts. Coincident with the outsourcing of glazing and enamelling activities, new players came into the glazing material supply industry. Several companies, many of them, although not all, Spanish, built manufacturing units in the region, which permitted local firms to intensify interactions with their suppliers. This had positive effects on innovation and product development.

The glazing material suppliers started to sell their products to ceramic tile producers, and also to offer a combination of related products and services, among them product conceptualization and drawing, and manufacturing process assistance, especially in adapting new products and processes and applying them to local raw materials and other local conditions. The Brazilian affiliates of Spanish glazing material suppliers, for instance, often use the know-how from their head offices and research and development centres, in Spain, to solve problems for their Brazilian clients. In the area of product design, they maintain close interactions with important international centres and their design centres and transfer this knowledge to local producers, not just by acquiring products, but also through a series of correlated services of high economic value.

Some authors, such as Ferraz (2002), have pointed out a negative side of this strategy for the local firms, since the presence of foreign glazing material suppliers in Brazil causes difficulties, and does not stimulate the creation and diffusion of capabilities in areas such as product development and design among the local firms.

Meanwhile, the new organizational structure of the ceramic tile industry and its supply chain demonstrates that the presence of specialized glazing materials suppliers is almost a requirement in order to be much quicker in generating, adopting and disseminating innovations in the ceramic tile industry. So, this does not stimulate, but practically hinders, the tile producers from carrying out these activities. The experience of the Spanish ceramic tile industry in the region of Castellón is particularly illustrative of this phenomenon (Galbadon-Estevan, *et al.* 2007).

Another important factor in the ceramic tile industry restructuring process in the region of Criciúma was the modernization of local manufacturing plants, through new investments in capital goods. This resulted in a high volume of machinery imports, mainly from Italy, the world's main supplier of capital goods for the ceramic industry, and the establishment of branch offices of those companies in Brazil. Normally, local units are not manufacturers of capital goods, but they do play an important role for the company, both in providing replacement parts and in functioning to bring suppliers and their products closer to users in Brazil.[7]

As a result of these technological and organizational restructuring efforts, the ceramic tile producers began to focus their activities on the manufacturing of ceramic tiles. At the same time, this permitted the opening and the growth of new companies in correlated activities, as in the case of the glazing material industry, which stimulated an increase in the complexity of the local system. In the middle of the 2000 decade, the local system was then composed of about 13 ceramic tile companies, 14 suppliers of raw materials (among producers and distributors, all of them providing services to the tile companies) and five manufacturers of machinery, equipment and replacement parts.

In addition, this increased complexity of the local system of Criciúma created new spaces for the action of local institutions, closely linked to a more qualified demand from local ceramic tile producers. In fact, the transformations which reached the local system of Criciúma throughout the 1990s induced the emergence of new institutions to support innovating initiatives.

A clear example of this was the creation of the Centre for Ceramic Technology (CTC), in 1995, by joint action among the local association of manufacturers, the local SENAI, and the Federal University of Santa Catarina.[8]

The main goal of the Technological Centre was to create an organization capable of rendering technical and technological services to local firms, such as analysis of materials, experiments and laboratory tests, certification of products and production processes, technological information, as well as research and development projects that interact with local firms.

Among the most important services, a specialized structure was created to carry out tests for product quality certification. Nevertheless, the laboratory at the Technological Centre was accredited by the Brazilian institute of metrology (INMETRO – National Institute of Metrology, Standardization and Industrial Quality), to provide ISO 9001 certifications for firms, in addition to issuing internationally recognized certification for final goods. The Technological Centre also has an experimental manufacturing line, a pilot plant, which is capable of simulating the entire ceramic manufacturing process to develop raw materials, enamels and ceramic products on a semi-industrial scale. Among the outstanding research projects it has developed are a study of the applicability of raw materials; the development of ceramic raw bodies as well as vitreous and vitro-ceramic glazing materials; ceramic colourants; analysis and characterization of defects in ceramic products, and the study of reutilization of industrial residues.

Another institution which was created at the height of the restructuring of the local system during the 1990s was the Upper Level Course for Ceramic Technology, created in 1996; the result of a joint action between the local manufacturers' association and a local university (UNESC).

This teaching institution joined two other apprenticeship institutions for technical training of labour. The first one is the Maximiliano Gaidzinski School, founded by the president of the largest local firm, which is dedicated to the teaching of technical apprenticeships. Its goal is to supply qualified professionals and to undertake a social project for the region at the same time. This school became the most important institution for obtaining technical apprenticeships in the whole country, supplying technicians to firms throughout Brazil. The other technical programme in the region is administered by the local unit of SENAI.

Finally, the existence of the Interdisciplinary Laboratory of Materials of the Federal University of Santa Catarina (LabMat-UFSC) should be noted. Despite its location in Florianopolis, capital of the state of Santa Catarina, 200 km away from Criciúma, the laboratory has several lines of research geared towards the development of new ceramic materials from raw materials, production processes, and traditional ceramic products, including vitreous and vitro-ceramic materials.

As can be seen, in this context, there is a huge institutional framework to support the activities of local firms, both in training labour and qualifying technicians as well as in providing technical and technological services and developing research projects linked to the activities of local manufacturers. However, as several authors point out (Meyer-Stamer, *et al.* 2004; Ferraz 2002), there are difficulties in the relationships between firms and local institutions, which have prevented the establishment of more numerous and longer lasting joint projects among those involved. As an example, there have been few joint projects between local producers and the Technological Centre, and its participation has been largely restricted to providing technical and technological services such as experiments and laboratory tests. The same phenomenon has occurred with the university-enterprise interactions.

Thus, although the answer for local firms to new challenges of competition in the domestic market meant increased efforts at innovative activities, they are not taking full advantage of the institutional framework available in the local system. The result is that they cannot benefit from all the positive externalization opportunities generated by the clustering of firms.

13.5.2 The industrial district of Santa Gertrudes

The local production system of ceramic tiles in Santa Gertrudes and its environs is located in the interior of the state of São Paulo, a state which is responsible for around 45 per cent of the country's GDP and in which is concentrated the main consumer market for several products, including ceramic tiles. There are about 45 tile companies in the region, which are responsible for about half of the country's physical production of ceramic tiles. The origin of the local system was strongly associated with the availability of clay which was used by small firms to produce bricks and roof tiles. From the 1980s onwards, however, the local firms invested in manufacturing ceramic tiles, using the locally available raw material to manufacture tiles intended for medium and low-income consumers.

With these investments, local firms experienced huge growth in the 1990s, by taking great advantage of the increasing demand for ceramic tiles in Brazil. Two main factors played important roles in this growth process.

The first was the importance of the availability of low-cost raw materials in the region, which allowed local firms to manufacture ceramic tiles by using the dry process. This manufacturing process presents slightly inferior technical characteristics to the water process but, on the other hand, substantially lower costs.[9] These lower costs are related to the ease of extracting and obtaining clay from nature and to lower production costs, as a result of the shorter time needed for the production process, meaning great economy. However, problems caused by the uncontrolled extraction of clay in the region and the low technical standards in this activity, especially the lack of techniques for geology, mineral engineering and environmental legislation should be pointed out. The absence of mineral research has deleterious effects on the activities of the quarried mixture and on the homogenization of the mineral lots, causing variations in the quality of the lots which, in many cases, are only detected in the manufacturing phase of ceramic tiles. This leads to significant losses. There are also environmental problems created by the extraction of clay.

The second important factor in the fast growth of the local system of Santa Gertrudes was the substantial investments of firms in modernizing their manufacturing process, especially the acquisition of up-to-date technological capital goods. In addition to acquiring modern ovens used in the firing process, the firms bought new systems for raw body preparation to attain lower grain size which allowed significant improvements in the process of granulation and humidification.

It is worth stressing the importance of the capital goods suppliers, especially the Italians, to the local producers, since they permitted the accelerated modernization of local companies, in particular by adapting equipment to the characteristics of the local production process.

In this way, the growth of the ceramic tile producers of Santa Gertrudes involved the creation and the diffusion of capabilities in the area of manufacturing, as can be seen by the modernization of the manufacturing process. It should be stressed that the Italian suppliers of capital goods played an essential role in the development of these capabilities by transferring knowledge to the local producers.

However, we must also point out the importance of two other factors which contributed to the growth process: the suppliers of glazing materials and the local service-rendering institutions, especially the CITEC – Centre of Technological Innovation.

The role of the glazing material suppliers was particularly important due to the new features of competition in the ceramic tile industry. Product development and design were done by the suppliers and, to a great extent, transferred to the local producers. Since the ceramic tile producers of Santa Gertrudes did not possess internal product development departments, they could rely on services from their suppliers, which relieved them of the responsibility of establishing their own structures for development.

It is worth recalling that, in general, the local manufacturers serve medium and low-income consumers, for whom product requirements are less important. Thus, local manufacturers of ceramic tiles did not need to establish internal product development areas, since they relied on products designed by their suppliers of frits and ceramic colourants. This accelerated growth for local producers, who did not need to develop capabilities of their own, and it also took advantage of external capabilities, by strengthening their linkages.

The role of the Technological Centre (CITEC) was also very important. It was created in Santa Gertrudes in 2002, through a partnership between the producers' association and the local public administration, with the support of the Ceramic Centre of Brazil (CCB), the main Brazilian institution providing services to companies in the industry. As designed, the Technological Centre was conceived to carry out tests and laboratory analyses for product certification in accordance with Brazilian and international norms.[10]

However, the role of the Technological Centre of Santa Gertrudes far surpassed the tasks of product certification, since its activities also began to include those related to the manufacturing process and to technical and technological assistance. As an example, the post-sales technical assistance services of the Technological Centre involved dealing with claims from final consumers, both with reference to judicial disputes between producers and final consumers, as well as the supply of services to consumers, including the issuance of technical certificates attesting to the characteristics of the ceramic products. The Technological Centre also has an Innovation Centre for Products and Design, which has a physical structure and human resources qualified to create decorative projects, develop and disseminate innovative project management methodologies, carry out iconographic research, especially attempts to stimulate the creation of self-identity in products for the local systems. In addition, the Technological Centre carries out research and development projects on new raw materials and products, some of them in cooperation with local universities.

In this sense, the role of the Technological Centre in fostering the development of local capabilities was very important. Despite the fact that its activities were initially linked to product certification, the Technological Centre played a much larger role, above all with reference to the upgrading which could be seen in terms of manufacturing activities. This occurred because in order to reach the technical requirements necessary in their products and reach the levels demanded by the certification systems, local firms were forced to upgrade their manufacturing processes. They were assisted in this by the Technological Centre, which provided some important services to the local producers.

It should be observed, however, that despite the existence of a product and design innovation area within the Technological Centre, the most important activity of the institution became limited to the function of manufacturing, with few advances in innovation activities and product development. The main reason for this is that the manufacturers of ceramic tiles of Santa Gertrudes did not accumulate larger capabilities in product development and design, an activity which remained under the responsibility of their glazing material suppliers. It is interesting to note that, perhaps due to the technical simplicity of products manufactured by the local firms, they did not even integrate the innovative capabilities which had improved the interchange with their chemical raw material suppliers, which would have allowed them to take better advantage of the possibilities opened up by the user-producer interactions.

It is important to emphasize that the growth of local firms has been associated with the strong growth of the domestic market, mainly in the 1990s and in the early 2000s. Nevertheless, the fast growth of local producers was accompanied by a significant upgrading process, mainly of manufacturing activities. This upgrading was a result of the articulation of several agents such as machinery suppliers, glazing material companies and the local institutions, in addition to the local firms.

13.6 Some conclusions: the Brazilian industrial districts and the global value chain

In the face of the new competitive challenges in the global value chain of the ceramic tile industry, this section analyzes the main factors which impact the Brazilian ceramic tile industry, and more specifically, its two major local production systems, Criciúma and Santa Gertrudes.

It is worth remembering that the main movements which characterized the global competitive scenario in the recent period were: the huge growth of China in the global market, which became the major global manufacturer of ceramic tiles; the growth of the Spanish industry, strongly associated with the interaction with the glazing material suppliers in the local system of Castellón; and the decreased share of the Italian industry, despite a strong concentration of its capital goods industry in the region of Sassuolo.

Brazil has a small share in the global market. Particularly due to its huge domestic market, the production of ceramic tiles is driven mainly by Brazilian consumers. However, there has been a substantial increase in exports in the last few years.[11] It seems contradictory, but the huge growth of the Brazilian ceramic tile industry over the last few decades was strongly associated with the increase of the domestic market. Nevertheless, the local production systems of ceramic tiles of Santa Gertrudes showed higher growth rates in comparison to the Brazilian average, which meant that local producers increased their share in the domestic market and pushed other firms to look for new markets abroad. This is one of the main reasons for the growth of Brazilian exports, since firms, mainly from outside the local system of Santa Gertrudes, were looking for new markets overseas.

This is one of the main differences between the experience of the ceramic tile industry in Brazil and other countries, such as Italy and Spain, which also have an industrial structure moulded on local production systems. Compare, for example, the Italian industry. Despite significant growth in Brazilian exports of ceramic tiles in recent years, the export rate in Brazil reached slightly over 20 per cent of the total domestic output in 2004. The Italian industry had a rate of around 70 per cent for the same year, which clearly shows its huge share in the global chain and the importance of the international market to domestic output.[12]

On the other hand, Brazilian imports of ceramic tiles are very small. This shows that despite the huge Brazilian domestic market, which is the second largest in the world, and the strong global competition, foreign firms do not participate in the Brazilian market. Further, Brazilian firms which have strong commercial assets, such as brand names and trade channels, do not subcontract foreign suppliers to manufacture goods to be sold in the Brazilian domestic market, which is a common occurrence in other industries, such as clothing and footwear. The reason for this strategy is the physical characteristics of ceramic tiles, which have a very low value-weight relationship, as pointed out earlier. In addition, the Brazilian industry showed strong growth in supply and manufacturing capacity, as well as in the upgrading of its productivity.

Thus, China's growth in the global market did not strongly affect the Brazilian ceramic tile industry, since there was small growth in imports. In the global market, where the Chinese industry became the greatest global supplier, with important effects on the competitive standards of the global chain, the Brazilian industry was little affected. Despite this adverse international scenario, we can verify a significant growth of Brazilian exports of ceramic tiles, which nearly doubled in the 2000–04 period (as shown in Table 13.2).

In this way, the Brazilian ceramic tiles industry is not strongly inserted in the global value chain of the ceramic tiles market, such as other industries like textiles, clothing, footwear and furniture. The majority of sales of the Brazilian ceramic tiles firms came from the domestic market, and imports are very small. Even with the huge growth of some international players and the strong international competition, the Brazilian firms are able not only to attend to the domestic market, but also to increase external sales.

To do that, however, the Brazilian firms are strongly connected in another kind of value chain, the knowledge value chain. Recently, the Brazilian firms were able to catch a lot of knowledge flows that came from abroad and learn from them. Let us take a look at each one of the main factors that contribute to the process of knowledge accumulation and learning among local firms. Some deficiencies of the local knowledge and in the firms' capabilities, especially in the two main important local systems, were solved by getting new knowledge from external and global sources. This process is very similar to that which was presented by Belussi, *et al.* (2006), since local agglomerated firms were able to augment their capabilities by learning from the global knowledge flows that came from international sources.[13]

The growth of the Brazilian ceramic tile industry in the last few years has been accompanied by important quality changes, with reference to the creation and accumulation of technical production capabilities. This process was particularly important in the local system of Santa Gertrudes, which shows higher dynamism. It could be stressed that this is a typical case in which the linkages between the production systems and the knowledge system, as pointed out by Bell and Abu (1999), occurs in a way that allows local firms to accumulate new capabilities.

There are several important factors that show the importance of the process of creating and diffusion of knowledge and accumulating capabilities. The first was the capital goods suppliers to the industry, mainly from Italy. They constituted a great source of knowledge and innovation, since the acquisition of new machinery and intensive interactions with them provided important upgrading to the manufacturing systems for the Brazilian firms, both in Criciúma and in Santa Gertrudes, including strong increases in productivity.

The second factor was the interaction with glazing material suppliers, especially of the frits and ceramic colourants utilized in ceramic tiles. In the case of the firms of Criciúma, these interactions created conditions for manufacturers to incorporate new attributes and added value into their tiles. In the case of the Santa Gertrudes producers, the interactions with the glazing material firms made rapid growth possible, since it was not necessary for small firms to internalize product development capabilities; a task assumed by the glazing material suppliers.

Third, local institutions provided real services to producers. Thus, they played an important role. This could be verified in a particular way in the case of the local system of Santa Gertrudes, where the local Technological Centre played an important role in creating and disseminating new knowledge among the local firms. Despite its initial role as a provider of analytical services and laboratory tests for product certification, the Technological Centre became an important channel for disseminating technical and technological knowledge among the local firms.

Finally, it is worth mentioning that the geographical proximity of the firms, and the local production systems, also played a very important role in creating and spreading new technical and technological knowledge among firms. Geographical proximity, common to these localized productive structures, stimulated the circulation of knowledge, and the set of benefits originating from the agglomeration of players and making them available to manufacturers. This allowed firms to improve their capabilities by the upgrade of the knowledge system, by using the terms of Bell and Abu (1999), with very good results to the production system.

Notes

1 The data presented in this section were compiled from information collected from ASCER – The Spanish Association of Manufacturers of Ceramic Tiles. However, the data are expressed in physical volume, i.e. production in millions of square metres and not in financial values, as would have been more adequate.

2 It is worth pointing out, once more, that the data presented refer to the physical production of ceramic tiles and not the financial value of the production. This is particularly important for the analysis of the Italian industry, since its industry is the more innovative in terms of fashion trends in the industry, and therefore manufactures and exports products of higher added value. In this context, analysis of foreign trade based on information of physical production certainly underestimates the participation of the Italian industry.

3 The process of producing ceramic tiles through the 'dry process' uses clay extracted from nature, dried and ground, resulting in a raw body, suitable for pressing. Through

the 'water process', the clay is watered, pulverized and atomized so that the water can be removed to obtain the raw body. The main difference, in this case, is not using water to obtain the raw body. As will be pointed out in the next section, this manufacturing method is most utilized in the local system of Santa Gertrudes.

4 Meyer-Stamer, *et al.* (2004) named the local system in Criciúma 'the local system of Santa Catarina', a reference to the state in which it is located and to include some tile manufacturers who are not exactly located in the region of Criciúma.

5 As shown earlier, this modification in the standards of competitive edge in the industry is at the core of the dynamism of the Spanish ceramic tile industry (Albors 2002).

6 An important example of a local company which abandoned its enamelling activities was Cecrisa; this activity generated a spin-off, Colorminas, which in 2000 started to act as an independent glazing material supplier rendering services to several other ceramic tile companies located in the Criciúma cluster and in other regions of the country.

7 This was the case of Sacmi, an Italian company which designs and manufactures capital goods for the ceramic industry, such as atomizers, presses, ovens, casting moulds and silk screens. The company established its own branch office in Brazil in order to serve its clients, especially in the supplying of replacement parts.

8 SENAI – National Service of Industrial Apprenticeship, is an institution of national scope and its local units provide services in two main areas: (1) the training and obtaining of apprenticeships through the offering of intermediate level (technical courses and high level technology); and (2) providing technical and technological services such as laboratory tests, experiments and product certification. Normally, the local SENAI units establish their services in accordance with the industrial activities of the regions and the local demands of the production system.

9 The appearance of lower technical characteristics in the dry process takes place due to the non-atomization of the raw body, which prevents the necessary mould distribution, generating greater waste.

10 The Technological Centre was contained within the structure of the Ceramic Centre of Brazil, which has been accredited since 1998 to issue certification of ceramic products.

11 It is important to point out that ceramic tiles have a low value-weight relationship, which makes this product poorly tradeable internationally. For this reason, the development of national industries of ceramic tiles is always associated with the existence of a significant internal demand; which is to say that all the main producing countries are, at the same time, great consumers.

12 In Spain, the coefficient of exports was slightly above 50 per cent of internal production in 2004, while in China, due to its vast domestic market, this index only reached 14 per cent in the same year.

13 Belussi (2008) shows in her research on Montebelluna sportswear district (in this volume, Chapter 5) that in the evolutionary pattern of local firms they were able to get some important knowledge flows that came from abroad.

14 This firm has more than five establishments, three located in Santa Catarina, one in Goias and one in Minas Gerais.

15 This firm has more than six establishments, four located in Santa Catarina, one in Bahia and one in Minas Gerais.

References

Albors J. (2002). 'Networking and technology transfer in the Spanish ceramic tiles cluster: its role in the sector competitiveness', *Journal of Technology Transfer*, 27: 263–73.

Alegre-Vidal J., Lapiedra-Alcamí R. and Chiva-Gómez, R. (2004), 'Linking operations strategy and product innovation: an empirical study of Spanish ceramic tile producers', *Research Policy*, 33(5), July.

Bell M. and Abu M. (1999),' Knowledge systems and technological dynamism in industrial clusters in developing countries', *World Development*, 27(9).

Belussi F., Pilotti L. and Sedita, S. (2006), 'Learning at the boundaries for industrial districts between exploitation of local resources and the exploration of global knowledge flows', Working Paper no. 2006–40. University of Milan.

Ferraz G. (2002) 'Nota Técnica Final da Cadeia Cerâmica', in L. Coutinho, *et al.* (eds.) *Estudo da Competitividade de Cadeias Integradas no Brasil: impactos das zonas de livre comércio*. São Paulo: IE/NEIT/UNICAMP. Contrato MDIC/MCT/FINEP.

Galbadon-Estevan D., Lucio I. and Esparza E. (2007), 'Appropriability, proximity, routines and innovation', proceedings of DRUID Summer Conference, Copenhagen, Denmark, 18–20 June.

Gambuli P. (2001), 'Tendências mundiais da produção de revestimentos cerâmicos', *Cerâmica Industrial*, 6(6), November–December.

Meyer-Stamer J., Maggi C., Siebel S. (2004), 'Upgrading in the tile industry of Italy, Spain and Brazil: insights from cluster and value chain analysis', in H. Schmitz (ed.) *Local Enterprises in the Global Economy: Issues of Governance and Upgrading*, Cheltenham: Edward Elgar.

Russo M. (1985) 'Technical change and the industrial district: the role of interfirm relations in the growth and transformation of ceramic tile production in Italy', *Research Policy*, 14(3): 329–43.

——. (2004), 'Processi di innovazione nei distretti e globalizzazione: il caso di Sassuolo', *Economia e Societá Regionale*, no. 3, Milan: Franco Angeli.

Appendix

Interviewed firms

FIRM	SECTOR	LOCATION
Esmaltec	Glaze material	Santa Gertrudes
Batistella	Tile Producer	Santa Gertrudes
Unigres	Tile Producer	Santa Gertrudes
Villagres	Tile Producer	Santa Gertrudes
Delta	Tile Producer	Santa Gertrudes
Buschinelli	Tile Producer	Santa Gertrudes
Cecrisa[14]	Tile Producer	Criciuma
Ceusa	Tile Producer	Criciuma
Eliane[15]	Tile Producer	Criciuma
De Lucca	Tile Producer	Criciuma
Vidres	Glaze material	Criciuma
Colorminas	Glaze material	Criciuma
Gabriella	Tile Producer – mosaics	Criciuma
Moliza	Tile Producer	Criciuma

Local actors interviewed

ORGANIZATION	TYPE	LOCATION
CCB-Brazilian Ceramic Centre	Research centre	Santa Gertrudes
ASPACER – Ceramic Tile Producers Association of São Paulo	Trade union	Santa Gertrudes
CTC/MAT	Research centre	Criciuma
SINDICERAM	Trade union	Criciuma

14 Local development and innovation policies in China

The experience of Guangdong specialized towns

Annalisa Caloffi (Florence University)

14.1 Introduction

The complex web of global productive relations that characterizes the economic scenario generates radical changes in the dimension of local competitiveness. This raises new questions about the dynamics of change and upgrading in the industrial clusters and districts, and the governance of the same.

In particular, as stressed by several theoretical and empirical contributions, the insertion of enterprises, clusters and localities of industry within global-scale industrial organizations can enhance or limit their possibilities of development, thereby modifying their patterns of growth or decline (Arndt and Kierzkowski 2001). These possibilities are strongly influenced, though not determined, by the dynamics of power distribution along the global value chains (GVCs) in which enterprises and clusters are inserted (Gereffi, *et al.* 2005; Humphrey and Schmitz 2002), and they may be enhanced by a strategic supportive action implemented by local or supra-local agents. This brings us back to the cluster level, its business and governance structure, its systemic properties, the role played by the different local stakeholders, and the networks of business and institutional links that connect them (Altenburg and Meyer-Stamer 1999). Therefore, the analysis of global and local forces in action needs to be suitably integrated in order to identify the most appropriate policy levers and levels of intervention for promoting cluster upgrading.

An interesting laboratory for an understanding of the meshing between local and external forces in the growth of industrial clusters is represented by the Chinese case. The principal findings of a long-term fieldwork study on industrial clusters and *specialized towns* in Guangdong (China) have offered us deeper insight into this rich variety of forces. The study has highlighted the role played by both foreign enterprises and local reserves of entrepreneurship and competence, as well as the influence of regional policies supporting the development of industrial clusters (Bellandi and Di Tommaso 2005; Caloffi and Hirsch 2005; Bellandi and Caloffi 2008). Building on this base, our analysis of some selected Chinese industrial clusters localized in Guangdong Province aims to shed light on the role played by local policies on cluster upgrading within different business and institutional contexts.

The chapter develops as follows. Drawing on the extensive literature on models of local development (Becattini, *et al.* 2003), and on contributions on the insertion of industrial clusters within global value chains (Humphrey and Schmitz 2002), Section 14.2 addresses the role of local governance and policies in affecting cluster upgrading. The great variety of industrial clusters in China is briefly outlined in Section 14.3, together with the main policy interventions aimed at supporting their development. This description is enriched in Section 14.4 with the analysis of a select number of clusters inserted within GVCs. Drawing on the selected examples, Section 14.5 attempts to focus on the different policy levers for cluster upgrading and to discuss their relevance within the different business and institutional settings. Finally, the chapter closes with a number of concluding remarks.

14.2. Local governance and innovation policies for cluster upgrading

Recent contributions have stressed the impact of global-scale industrial organizations on the development of enterprises attempting to explain how the insertion within global value chains (GVCs) may modify their patterns of growth or decline. These patterns are influenced, though not determined, by the governance structure of the GVCs in which the enterprises are inserted. However, they may be modified by strategies aimed at leveraging the variables which shape the power distribution along the GVCs: complexity and codification of transactions, and capabilities in the supply-base (Gereffi, *et al.* 2005). These strategies are mainly developed at firm level, but they may be influenced by the socio-economic environment in which the latter are inserted. Innovation policies in particular can play a significant role, by promoting the development of the firms' knowledge base and competencies or the adoption of international product and process standards.

What happens when *a cluster* is inserted within a GVC? The shift to a meso-level perspective introduces some complications, mainly related to the definition of the concept of upgrading and to the local governance mechanisms.

Considering the upgrading, as proposed by Humphrey and Schmitz (2002), this can be identified with the result of the development into a cluster of product, process, functional and intersectorial innovation. A cluster upgrades when it acquires a higher added value by creating new and better products, by producing more efficiently, by moving into higher value-added activities, by acquiring new functions or by entering into new productive activities. Within a cluster showing systemic properties – and within industrial districts in particular – the successful implementation of innovation processes is closely linked to the maintenance of a lively innovative ecosystem (Lazzeretti and Storai 2003; Albino, *et al.* 2007) in which the clustered firms feed on knowledge flows produced by the other local (and also external) agents. This ecosystem is grounded on a socio-institutional base (including local customs and habits providing a guide for the agents' behaviour) which enables the achievement of an architecture of specific public goods, fostering the realization of collective processes of innovation (Bellandi 2006).[1] Therefore, cluster upgrading is strictly linked to the evolution of the related socio-institutional fabric (Dei Ottati 2002; Crouch, *et al.* 2001; Mehrotra and Biggeri 2007).[2]

Let us now take a look at the (local) governance mechanisms. The production and reproduction of the local institutions that drive agents' behaviour is embedded in a strategic action carried out by the local actors (Schmitz 1995; Bellandi 2006). However, local institutions evolve along with the cluster and the locality of industry, and hence may change over time, with direct and indirect effects on local governance mechanisms. The organization of action to support the local system is therefore more difficult (although more necessary) in the presence of internal or external shocks which engender radical changes in the local rules of thumb, as it may happen with the cluster insertion within external-driven GVCs. Let us take the case of clusters situated in developing countries. Here, in particular, the insertion of the cluster within GVCs may facilitate inclusion in new markets and quality upgrading of product and process in the short term, but the effects on local governance and local development can be questionable. Some case studies discussed in literature show how the activity of global buyers can gradually modify both the industrial and the governance structure of a cluster, by reshaping the local division of labour or by altering the distribution of power among the local agents (Gereffi 1994; Humphrey and Schmitz 2002; Bair and Gereffi 2001). Such changes may undermine the importance of 'old' productive and cognitive linkages and the activity of a part of local enterprises and agents (those not included within the GVC), alter the composition of the local stakeholder groups, and gradually modify the local rules of thumb. In the medium term, the strategies of (functional) upgrading of the cluster may be prevented not only by global players wishing to preserve their core competencies, who may limit the development of the enterprises inserted within the chain, but also by the loss of old productive, cognitive and strategic linkages at local level. Therefore, the organization of a supportive action at cluster level may be hampered by the loss of a local stakeholders group, thus by a weaker local governance.[3] Here endogenous solutions may be aimed at mobilizing new governance levers, by promoting the creation of a (new) community of interests, and providing new incentives and new rules that permit the agents' coordination (Meyer-Stamer 2003). However, endogenous solutions based on the mobilization of the local stakeholders alone generally appear to be inadequate and there is scope for policy support coming from different levels (Cammett 2007).

Let us consider the policies for promoting cluster upgrading. The majority of cluster innovation policies are aimed at supporting the knowledge base and competencies of the local ecosystem. Therefore, they are not confined to a more or less limited range of actions aimed at leveraging the complexity, codification and specialization of clustered firms, nor to policies promoting innovation in a narrow sense, but extend to a wide range of different types of intervention (1) supporting collective processes of learning and innovation (Belussi 1999; Mytelka 2000) and (2) featuring the marked involvement of local governance mechanisms (Crouch, *et al.* 2001).[4]

However, as stressed by the literature on industrial districts and local development, both local and higher level policies are required to support the development of systemic conditions which, furthermore, cannot be provided solely by regulation and planning but ought – at least partly – to be already in existence. This is not the case of generic geographical agglomerations of enterprises, which may be generated and strongly driven by external forces, and where upgrading strategies may be aimed at promoting the embedding of the external enterprises by fostering the creation of forward and backward linkages between local and external enterprises (Bellandi 2001). Here a new local governance structure has to be built through the identification and mobilization of local stakeholder groups, along with targeted action geared to the creation of new rules of the game (Sabel 1994). This action calls for intensive collaboration between local and higher level authorities (Raines 2002; Meyer-Stamer 2003).

If the cluster insertion within GVCs is considered, the possibilities of upgrading and the correct identification of policy levers and levels of intervention demands a profound analysis of the industrial and governance structure of the cluster, comprising the identification of the local stakeholders and their networks of business and institutional links. As suggested by several contributions, there are no comprehensive recipes or standard solutions. However, the identification of different models or types of cluster – their different business and institutional structure, organization and performance – may help in defining their growth potential and the policy levers to be implemented (Altenburg and Meyer-Stamer 1999). This can assist in the formulation of an interactive policy, designed to act on the relations between local and external actors (Rodrik 2004) and thus to alter the distribution of power among them.

14.3. Policies promoting industrial clusters in China

The experience of Chinese industrial clusters may help us to understand the meshing of global and local forces in the development of different kinds of cluster and localities of industry, and the role played by innovation policies in promoting cluster upgrading. As highlighted by several theoretical and empirical contributions, the growth of Chinese industrial clusters has been largely fostered both by the activity of transnational enterprises, which have established their productive bases in China, and by the emergence of nuclei of endogenous competencies and entrepreneurship that have developed in some areas in particular (Ma and Lin 1993; Christerson and Lever Tracy 1997; Eng 1997; Bellandi and Di Tommaso 2005; Enright, et al. 2005).[5]

Focusing on the conditions that have favoured the birth and the initial development of the Chinese clusters, we can roughly identify 'exogenous' and 'endogenous' clusters (Leung 1996; Eng 1997; Sonobe, et al. 2002). The development of the first type of cluster is clearly connected with policies attracting foreign investors to specific zones (initially the Special Economic Zones, but subsequently a larger range of areas including industrial parks or similar infrastructures; Li (2003),[6] thus creating geographical agglomerations of enterprises which do not necessarily reveal systemic conditions. The second type – the various cases of clusters of Chinese-owned enterprises – is strictly linked to a wide range of policies aimed at promoting local development.

This simple distinction yields a great variety of forms of local development.

Pursuing the conditions that promoted the birth and initial development of the clusters, several contributions help us to identify the presence of 'endogenous' industrial clusters that have evolved from a productive base of handcraft traditions – and have emerged as a consequence of the dissolution of state-owned enterprises (SOEs) and township and village enterprises (TVEs) (Biggeri, *et al.* 1999; Sonobe, *et al.* 2002; Long 2005) – and of market-driven industrial clusters (Ding 2006) that have developed on the basis of local tradition of either craft production or long-distance peddling.[7] These types of industrial cluster are characterized by Chinese family-owned (private) SMEs often operating within traditional low-tech sectors, and their business and institutional structures often reveal a certain similarity with those of industrial clusters (Bellandi and Caloffi 2008). Local policies have greatly supported the growth of these clusters (Lu and Wei 2007), partly as a result of a major process of decentralization launched at the beginning of the 1980s.[8] The actions have been directed towards specific sectors (the clusters' sector of specialization) and their design and implementation has extensively involved both local governments and local stakeholders (enterprises, business associations etc.) (Qiu and Xu 2004). Among the most important of such actions, we would mention the creation of innovation centres offering innovative services to the clustered enterprises (quality testing, marketing, legal and business consultancy etc.), exhibition malls and trade markets.

Obviously, such intervention has been directly or indirectly aimed at promoting product, process, functional and inter-sectoral innovation. The creation of trade markets, for instance, was intended to promote the functional upgrading of the clustered firms by providing the local enterprises with an alternative to the foreign client channel for reaching the market (Lombardi 2007; Bellandi and Caloffi 2008). But, most important, these policies have been aimed at fostering collective processes of learning and innovation.

Recalling the definition of policies promoting collective processes of learning and innovation provided by Belussi (1999), Table 14.1 offers some examples of intervention – designed and implemented by various forms of public-private partnerships – activated within the Chinese clusters.

Most of these involve activities implemented by collective infrastructures, such as the innovation centres (ICs), inspired by an international model of business development service centres, and by the Italian model of 'real services centres' in particular (Brusco 1994; Bellini 2003).

We will explore some of these policies in greater detail in the following sections, with the help of a few selected examples.

14.4. The case of the specialized towns of Guangdong

We should now like to focus on the analysis of a group of six specialized towns located within Guangdong Province, and in particular on the industrial clusters that constitute their core.[9] Specialized towns (STs) are localities of industry characterized by a significant agglomeration of industrial activities, where a high proportion of the same are concentrated in a sectoral-defined specialized industry. An official

Table 14.1 Examples of Chinese policies promoting collective processes of learning and innovation

Policy goals	Examples of policy intervention carried out in Chinese clusters
Fostering processes of mobilization of the existing local knowledge	Promotion of the activity of the specialized business associations in fixing rules and communication standards (based on past traditions) and in promoting benchmarking activities. Promotion of specific training activity based on the traditional productive specialization.
Sustaining processes of cross-fertilization with external knowledge	Introduction of new technologies within the individual enterprises of the cluster (national and local funds for equipment renewal) and within the local IC (laboratory for applied research). Promotion of agreements with external consultants (on design, specific technologies etc.). Support for the dissemination of international standards (ICs offering quality testing services). Creation of trade markets. Promotion for participation at national and international fairs.
Coordination and circulation of information	Creation of a network of local information offices. Creation of databases on fashion trends, products and technologies. Creation of websites hosting information on local enterprises.
Creation of specific identities	Creation and promotion of the label 'one product one town' to identify towns hosting industrial clusters.
Storage of knowledge in the collective memory	Creation of specific cultural 'deposits' hosting the history of the productive specialization. Promotion of studies on local development.

Source: our elaboration of Belussi (1999).

definition of ST is provided by the Guangdong provincial government and is applied to policies promoting cluster upgrading. More specifically, the Guangdong Department of Science and Technology (DST) has launched a special programme aimed at supporting the creation of specialized centres for innovation and technological development. The application of the programme entails verification of the status of 'specialized town' and, where the outcome is affirmative, leads to an official designation.[10]

The STs considered here are located in the Foshan and Dongguan prefectures, respectively east and west of the Pearl River Delta (PRD). The STs located in the Foshan prefecture host industrial clusters specialized in traditional low-tech sectors (textiles, clothing and footwear) while the western area of the PRD hosts clusters specialized in electronics and PC components (Table 14.2). All the clusters observed are inserted within GVCs. However, while the STs of the Dongguan area are mainly inserted in hierarchical chains, the STs situated on the other side of the PRD are comprised within captive or modular chains, or develop market relations with their national or foreign clients (Gereffi, *et al.* 2005).

The STs located within Dongguan Prefecture are more distinctly characterized by the presence and the role played by foreign investors, and can be considered as typical 'exogenous' clusters. However, while in Qingxi there is a diffuse foreign presence, the Shijie business structure is largely based on the presence of a small set of Taiwan-based MNEs.[11] Both clusters are characterized by a high incidence of migrant population (used here as a proxy for migrant workers)[12] that fuels the productive capacities of the foreign enterprises. On the other hand, the STs located in Foshan Prefecture are closer to an 'endogenous' model (of producer-driven clusters), featuring a strong(er) role of local competencies and entrepreneurship.

The definition of cluster structure is based on Markusen (1996). The definition of the GVC governance structure is based on Gereffi, *et al.* (2005).[13]

However, the origins of the clusters are only part of the story, which needs to be completed by an analysis of the business and institutional structure of the cluster. We can begin with two of the STs under consideration – Shijie and Qingxi – which can be labelled 'satellite platforms' (Markusen 1996). The ST clusters host multinational platforms (mainly Taiwan-based MNEs) that have established their productive bases within the area.[14] Here, foreign investors manage the low-tech productive phases of PC and electronics production: high-tech components are sourced from other branches of the MNEs[15] and assembled with the low-tech components produced within the locality. The majority of the local workforce employed by the MNE platforms consists of migrants (Caloffi and Hirsch 2005). In both clusters a small group of Chinese-owned enterprises work as subcontractors for the foreign enterprises localized within the clusters. These are micro to small enterprises, mostly engaged in activities of assembly, or the manufacture of low added-value products. Entry barriers are low, since equipment, machinery and materials (as well as design) are usually supplied by the foreign client, on which they depend. Consequently, these areas are characterized by a high turnover in the number of Chinese-owned enterprises.[16] These clusters are fully inserted within hierarchical GVCs, which are managed by the foreign headquarters of the MNEs. A small and volatile subset of the clusters – involving the Chinese-owned enterprises and outworkers – is linked by captive relations to the global clients located within the clusters.

To move on to the 'hub and spoke' clusters, the business structure of Yanbu and Pingzhou is dominated by a small group of foreign (Taiwanese) and Chinese-owned firms, vertically integrated. These clusters are mostly inserted within captive global value chains, in which the leading enterprises manufacture for foreign clients. Here, the leaders are surrounded by a large constellation of Chinese suppliers, generally in subordinate relations to the former. These are micro to small enterprises producing medium–low quality components or products or performing assembly activities for the leading enterprises of the clusters, which supply them with materials, equipment and design. Beyond the client-supplier relationship, there are generally

Table 14.2 Principal features of the specialized towns (2005)

ST	Xiqiao	Huanshi	Yanbu	Pingzhou	Shijie	Qingxi
Location (Prefecture)	Foshan	Foshan	Foshan	Foshan	Dongguan	Dongguan
Productive specialization	Textiles	Clothing	Clothing	Footwear	Electronics	Electronics
Cluster structure	Proto-district	Proto-district	Hub and spoke	Hub and spoke	Satellite platform	Satellite platform
Productive traditions	Very long	Long	Long	1960s	Recent (1980s)	Recent (1980s)
Total population	33,185	2,522	35,775	46,023	81,552	66,548
Migrant population (% of TP)	27.2%	73.6%	47.2%	20.4%	79.5%	89.9%
Specialized enterprises	1330 (51% of TE)	720 (36% of TE)	100	600	1200 (16% of TE)	>500
Specialized employees	60,000 (43% of TEM)	–	20,000	60,000	>20,000	55,000 (18% of TEM)
Specialization index	42.6%	31%	25.3%	37.6%	71.8%	63.1 %
Foreign enterprises (% of TE)	3.8%	25%	20%	33.2%	28%	70%
GVC governance	Market	Market/ Modular	Captive	Captive	Hierarchy	Hierarchy

Key: TP = total population; SE = specialized enterprises (sectorial specialization); TE = total
   enterprises of the town; TEM = total employees of the town.

few connections between the local enterprises, and the intra-cluster relationships between suppliers appear to be predominantly based on price competition.

The 'proto-district' definition refers to a subset of clusters which share some basic similarities with the industrial district model (business structure dominated by locally owned SMEs, intra-district trade between buyers and suppliers, key investment decisions made locally, cooperation between firms in the creation of specialized public goods etc.). The business structure of the clusters consists largely of Chinese-owned enterprises, most of them operating as ODM, although an increasing number of enterprises have developed their own brands. Many enterprises in the 'proto-district' clusters are vertically integrated, but vertical and horizontal infra-cluster linkages are on the increase. In recent years in particular, there has been a sharp increase in the number of independent enterprises working in a particular segment of the productive process or in services (mainly logistics and transport). Moreover, there are also fairly long-standing horizontal links between the local enterprises (local pools or consortia for procurement of materials, setting of standards etc.). Most of the enterprises of these clusters have direct access (at low cost) to the external market, thanks to the trade markets set up through local government initiatives since the end of the 1990s. These infrastructures have made a significant contribution to upgrading the local enterprises, providing them with a market channel – for purchasing input or selling goods – that is an alternative to those of the major clients or providers. Although quantitative data are lacking, our interviews with local entrepreneurs localized within the trade markets confirm that the availability of this kind of infrastructure has helped the enterprises to broaden the number and diversify the type of their clients. Following our fieldwork study, the local industry that was entirely bound up in captive relations with a small set of buyers from Hong Kong has gradually evolved towards modular or market relations developed with a broader set of foreign and national buyers.

14.5. Policies promoting upgrading and innovation in Guangdong industrial clusters

We now move on to an appraisal of the policies designed to promote the upgrading of the observed clusters. We will examine both success stories and cases of failure.[17] It should be noted that both are ascribable to the presence/lack of one of the following elements:

- *Policy tools and levers*: the identification of cluster-specific policy levers and the adoption of tools that are consistent with the specific business and institutional features of the clusters.
- *The policy process*: the identification of the most relevant local stakeholders and their involvement in the design and implementation of the policies.

Let us start with the *satellite platforms inserted within hierarchical GVCs*: The example of Shijie is fairly emblematic of the failure of the application of cluster-upgrade policies in a cluster which does not show any systemic character. In order to promote the growth of the small and volatile number of Chinese enterprises, local government funded the creation of an Innovation Centre (IC) specialized in electronics. The idea was that the IC would provide the Chinese-owned enterprises with various kinds of innovative services at low or no cost (e.g. quality testing, laboratory for applied research activities), to encourage their stable presence within the MNE networks of subproviders. Although the centre is still young (it was set up in 2004), it has already experienced many difficulties due to the *dirigiste* (centralized) style of management and the major discrepancy between the services it offers and the activities performed by the local enterprises. Effectively, there is no demand for the services offered by the IC, neither from the MNEs, which source these services from their headquarters, nor from the Chinese-owned enterprises, which are highly volatile and rely on the materials, equipment and services provided by the MNEs. Moreover, the creation of the IC has not been associated with any other actions aimed at supporting the development of local enterprises or outworkers.[18]

Policies to stimulate the upgrading of the Qingxi cluster have been mainly aimed at promoting the embeddedness of the foreign investors within the area, by means of continuous interaction and specific agreements between the local government and the Taiwanese and the Hong Kong business associations.[19] The local policies have been focused in two main directions. On the one hand, to face the growing competition from other areas (wide diffusion of industrial parks targeting the activity of foreign investors; Li 2003), the local increase in the cost of labour and the emergence of diseconomies of agglomeration (pollution and overcrowding), local government has implemented a number of actions aimed at improving the local natural and social environment (creation of infrastructures reducing air and water pollution, development of a segment of services – e.g. hotels – targeted at foreign investors' needs) and at creating a logistics platform. On the other hand, the local government has promoted the integration of young local students or graduates in the MNE plants. Thanks to a continuous interaction with the foreign investors, supported by the collaboration of the provincial government, the local government has tried to promote a better matching between the activities of the foreign enterprises and the development of the local workforce.[20] A number of agreements have been stipulated with local vocational schools or with technical universities located in the nearby Shenzhen Specialized Economic Zones. Some of these actions are beginning to yield fruit. A number of students have been recruited for training sessions in the MNE and some local graduates have been employed by the foreign managers (approximately 30, according to our interviewees).[21]

We now move on to the policies implemented in clusters that are also more clearly driven by local forces, starting with *hub and spoke clusters inserted within captive GVCs*. The example of Pingzhou to an extent mirrors the case of Shijie discussed above. Here, too, the local IC was set up on the basis of planning devoid of any prior market research and without any attempt to consult or involve the local enterprises: the local government selected the managers, the employees and the kind of services to be offered. After two years the centre was closed, since it had failed to achieve the set objectives. It was then reopened in 2005, and is now managed by a Chinese-owned enterprise localized within the area, and boasting a large network of subproviders. Thus, it could become an instrument for promoting the upgrading of a relatively small set of local enterprises.[22] More difficult to predict at present is the possible impact in terms of the development of the cluster as a whole. The creation of a trade market in Yanbu ST, promoted by the local government together with a group of local enterprises, has proved more successful. Here planning activities have gone together with market research and involvement of local stakeholders. The local government has created a specialized trade market where both the leading enterprises, producing as ODM or OEM for foreign buyers, and their Chinese subproviders may rent or buy shops at low cost and sell their products and components.[23] According to our fieldwork, this has allowed the leading enterprises of the cluster in particular to expand the number of their clients.[24] In addition, local government has promoted the creation of a local business association, bringing together the local leaders and their local networks of subproviders. The association will be in charge of the design of actions aimed at supporting marketing activities. Special funds are available for local enterprises taking part in national or international trade fairs, and for entrepreneurs who wish to create and promote their own brands.[25]

Finally, we come to the *proto-district* clusters, inserted within modular or market GVCs. In the STs of Xiqiao and Huanshi, local policies have been oriented to the support of product, process and functional upgrading, but, more importantly, they have been aimed at fostering collective processes of learning and innovation (Section 14.3). As previously noted, these policies have progressively allowed the local enterprises to shift from captive relations with Hong Kong buyers to modular or market relations with a larger range of national and foreign buyers.

The case of Xiqiao is particularly significant. The development of the cluster has benefited from the major support of a series of policies that have enabled the local enterprises to enter the market autonomously, and have boosted collective processes of growth and innovation. More specifically, local government fosters processes of mobilization of the existing local knowledge by creating a set of specialized infrastructures related to the development of the local industry. In addition to the trade market mentioned above, local government, in collaboration with the local branch of the Textile Association, has promoted the creation of an innovation centre specialized in providing services to the textile enterprises of the cluster.[26] Specific actions have been aimed at sustaining processes of cross-fertilization with external knowledge. This has resulted in support for the renewal of machinery and for sourcing external consultants (in design in particular). In detail, between 1994 and 2004 the local government has made an investment of 400 million RMB and has provided loans at low or no interest to help the enterprises to purchase new equipment (Zhongshan University 2003).[27] Another important intervention – implemented in 1997 by the Xiqiao district government and the China Textile Information Institution – was the creation of a non-profit public service department specialized in developing new textile products. This department was initially devoted to the analysis of the technical characteristics of medium and high-quality clothing originating from Hong Kong and other countries. At present, instead, it provides technical support to the small and medium enterprises in the performance of design activities using CAD technology and equipment made in Korea.[28] The dissemination of information on fashion trends was achieved through the 'Southern Textile Information Web', created in 1998 in collaboration with Donghua University. The web platform also supports activities of e-commerce and trading on the net. In both clusters, public policies have been designed to stimulate the creation of specific identities and the storage of knowledge in the collective memory. The governments of both Xiqiao and Huanshi have promoted the local productive tradition through the creation of ST labels: 'Xiqiao famous home of textile'; 'Huanshi the home of childwear'. In Xiqiao, this has been linked to the rediscovery of the historical craft traditions (dating back to the Ming dynasty) in textile (silk) production and of the first modern entrepreneurs who pioneered new techniques and developed new machinery by gradually modifying the old looms used for silk production. These labels are used as levers for advertising the products of the local enterprises taking part in trade fairs and exhibitions.

14.6. Concluding remarks

The Chinese case can be considered an interesting laboratory for the analysis of policies designed to promote the upgrading of clusters inserted within different business and institutional contexts. Drawing on the small number of cases taken into account here, and on the literature on the insertion of clusters within GVCs and industrial clusters and local development, some general observations can be sketched out.

An initial and fairly simple observation focuses on the need to achieve a balance between the analysis of external and endogenous forces affecting cluster upgrading. Whereas the analysis of the GVCs has a significant capacity for explaining the system of power that exists across the chains, and the possibilities of upgrading for the enterprises inserted within them, its transposition to cluster level needs to be carefully calibrated. It is advisable that the analysis of the GVC governance structure should first be combined with that of the power distribution at local level. Second, it should be accompanied by an analysis of the local processes of learning and innovation, and their dynamics. Third, it should be borne in mind that the analyses are made more complex by the interrelations between external and local forces, on one side, and between governance and learning and innovation processes on the other, relations which need to be opened up. Moreover, a cluster may comprise different global and local VCs, with complex direct and indirect effects on the development of the cluster and the locality of industry as a whole. Though simple in its formulation, the combination of the analysis of external and endogenous forces for the promotion of cluster upgrading needs to be further investigated and delineated.

A second observation touches upon policy levers and tools. The promotion of cluster upgrading – not only in the Chinese clusters observed – is often reduced to the use of particular policy instruments, and more specifically to the creation of systemic infrastructures (e.g. the creation of ICs) supporting innovation and quality improvement in agglomerations of SMEs. This is inspired by a very partial understanding of the experience of successful industrial clusters. Literature on policies promoting local development stresses how cluster upgrading may be facilitated, not simply by the use of a particular policy tool, but much more effectively by a supportive action aimed at fostering the emergence of a local community of interests in which private incentives are consistently oriented towards the achievement of processes of local development. Incentives and rules of thumb may change, as for instance in the integration of teams of local enterprises within captive (buyer-driven) GVCs. Thus, the key to success for policies promoting cluster upgrading lies in their capacity to react to changes by modifying the incentives (as in the case of Qingxi) and to favour the emergence of new communities of interests (as in the case of Yanbu). In any case, the policy action should focus on specific goals to be achieved and tools to be implemented. This demands the development of strategic capacities which the governments may not necessarily possess (nor the private sector *per se*), but that can emerge from the interaction between the two, and from the experiments they implement. The solution – and this may be considered as a third relevant lesson on governance mechanisms – lies in monitoring and supporting the progressive involvement of local stakeholders (the adoption of a *confrontational style*; Messner and Meyer-Stamer 2000) and in the experimentation of intervention (Rodrik 2004). Windows of opportunities may also arise in the case of externallydriven clusters such as satellite platforms. Here supra-local governments may play a specific role in strengthening the bargaining power of local governments and in contributing to the formulation of a framework of rules.

Notes

1 As stressed by Belussi (1999: 742), 'The process of accumulation and transmission of knowledge can be viewed as collective not only because it is dispersed amongst many individuals. It is collective in the sense that the storage of knowledge and experience is made largely by collective entities (...) and in the productive cultural traditions of each local system (tacit skills, customs and habits developed locally).

2 Clearly, without wishing to underestimate the importance of the strategies implemented by the individual enterprises, which are the principal actors in the local governance mechanisms (Belussi 1999; Humphrey and Schmitz 2002; Giuliani, *et al.* 2005).

3 As discussed by Humphrey and Schmitz (2002) for the case of the Sinos Valley, the growth of large producers inserted within quasi-hierarchical GVCs has gradually changed the network of business relations and the distribution of power at local level. The gradual misalignment between the incentives of the large enterprises producing for foreign clients and those of the small local enterprises has gradually weakened the representativeness of traditional collective organisation, such as the local business associations, and has thus hampered the realization of a collective strategy of upgrading driven by the latter.

4 According to Metcalfe and Ramloagan (2007: 5) we refer to a broad concept of innovation, which is rooted within a continuous learning process in which firms and other agents '*master and implement the design, production and marketing of goods and services that are new to them, although not necessarily new to their competitors – domestic or foreign*'. Moreover, as the authors recognize '*the manner in which knowledge is acquired depends greatly on social processes of interaction and communication and thus on organization. The consequence is that the development of knowledge, and thereby innovation, depends on these same social processes by which flows of information are organised*' (ibid, p. 5).

5 Even though official statistics on this phenomenon are still lacking, Li & Fung (2006) report over 800 clusters scattered throughout Zhejiang Province, with approximately 237,000 enterprises employing over 600,000 workers and more than 100 industrial clusters within Guangdong Province. Drawing on data provided by the Guangdong Department of Science and Technology, Di Tommaso and Rubini (2005) report data on around 70 specialized towns in 2004. A large and growing body of contributions provides detailed information on other provinces.

6 Although foreign investors are no longer obliged to locate within specific zones (thus creating 'artificial' clusters), most of the foreign enterprises tend to be attracted to locations in the various types of industrial park, in view of the availability of tax breaks or other incentives offered by the local governments.

7   High-tech industrial clusters, that we do not explicitly address here, may be considered as a third specific variant of the 'endogenous' industrial cluster.

8   As a consequence of the policy of (fiscal) decentralization, launched in 1980, the local governments acquired the autonomy to pursue a variety of development policies plus the incentives to do so (Shirk 1993). Central government has maintained control over key regulatory aspects of the industry, but local governments are free to experiment with alternative means of organizing and promoting local firms and local clusters (Thun 2004).

9   The analysis is based on the main findings of a fieldwork investigation carried out with the support of the Zhongshan University and the South China University of Technology (Guangzhou, China). The fieldwork study was carried out during the period 2004–2005, within the programme 'The China and Italy Research and Learning Project', promoted by c-Met '05 and a network of Italian and Chinese institutions. It was based on interviews with key informants (entrepreneurs, local governments, business and trade unions and innovation centre representatives) and on questionnaires submitted to the enterprises of the towns. For each ST, the survey was structured around 30 questionnaires to the enterprises and 10 direct interviews with key informants (including five entrepreneurs). Statistical data are mainly taken from local government archives. Where possible, these were compared with data provided by the DST and with official statistics (NBS 2005).

10   In line with the criteria defined by the DST, the towns have to satisfy three requirements: (1) from an administrative aspect they must be 'towns', 'counties' or 'urban districts'; (2) in terms of sectorial specialisation, at least 30 per cent of the manufacturing output (and/or employment) must be generated by one particular industry (defined on the basis of the equivalent of our 3 digit classes), which is defined as a 'specialized industry'; (3) the value of the annual industrial output of the town must be more than 2 billion Yuan (Di Tommaso and Rubini 2005).

11   The leading Taiwanese plant of the cluster employs about 20,000 people. According to our fieldwork research, this figure accounts for over two-thirds of the total specialized workforce of the town.

12   Even though the former population does not necessarily coincide precisely with the latter, the majority of migrants are workers compelled to migrate from poor rural areas (usually from internal Chinese provinces) to richer coastal regions (Ma and Lin 1993; Yao 2001).

13   The identification of the different local development models (hub and spoke clusters; satellite platforms) has been made on the basis of a fieldwork investigation (see note 10) that helped us to verify the presence of the features assigned by Markusen (1996) to the different models. When the most relevant of these features are present in our observed clusters, the Markusen term is applied. The label 'proto-district' refers to the fact that only some of the features outlined by Markusen (and only some of the most relevant features identified by the extensive literature on Italian industrial districts) are present (in particular, the local division of labour is less extended than in the industrial district model).

The definition of the GVC governance mechanism is based on that outlined by Gereffi, *et al.* (2005). The definition is applied in a loose sense: the specific governance structure of the GVC in which the clusters and enterprises under study are inserted is identified on the basis of the information collected during the fieldwork (on clients, providers and the other crucial elements identified by Gereffi, *et al.*, ibid) and – where available – that of other studies. Therefore, these labels are intended to describe the structure of a specific stage of the chain, that linking the cluster with the foreign clients or buyers. Since the cluster may be involved in several GVC, we have identified the structure of the GVC involving the largest part of the cluster.

14   In addition to the world brand MNEs, the clusters host MNE plants (ODM – original design manufacturers; or OEM – original equipment manufacturers) producing electronics

components, often together with their foreign subproviders. The variety of enterprise is greater in Quingxi, while in Shijie, as well as the principal enterprise (ODM), there is also a small group of ODM/OEM MNE plants.

15 The R&D department and the export department are generally located in the foreign headquarters, with which the enterprises maintain continuous and intense connections. In only a few cases have Taiwanese enterprises established their R&D departments within the STs under study, and only one large enterprise located in Qingxi has its export department inside the town. However, a number of multinationals localized in Qingxi have set up their R&D departments in Beijing and Shanghai, close to the major universities and educational infrastructures.

16 As emerged from our interviews with local government officials, these micro enterprises are often family-run, highly volatile firms which are not recorded in the official statistics.

17 The judgement is expressed on the basis of the reflections on cluster upgrading that have been developed in Section 14.2 (hence it is expressed on the basis of product, process, functional or intersectorial innovation or collective learning processes). Given the lack of an activity aimed at evaluating the impact of the specific actions implemented by local government, and the lack of official statistics providing data on the specialized industry at local (town or township) level, the positive or negative judgement is based on the results of the fieldwork investigation.

18 Information derived from direct interviews with IC managers and local government representatives (see note 10). For a general reflection on IC Centres in Guangdong Province, see Qiu and Xu (2004).

19 The local branch of the Taiwanese business association was founded in 1990 and brings together around 50 enterprises specialized in electronics. The Hong Kong business association was founded in 1998 and groups 109 enterprises. They provide a wide range of services to their members: legal and business consultancy, support for export activities, funding. These are private associations, legally recognized by the local government (data referred to 2004). A specific public department is in charge of dialogue with the foreign investors. The personnel of this department consists of young Chinese graduates in Business Management from foreign universities.

20 Although the MNE platforms located within the area generally perform low added-value activities (production of standardized components with low added-value or performance of assembly activities), there is a general tendency for the MNE plants to progressively move to Guangdong (or to China) increasingly large sections of their productive processes. As illustrated by Enright, *et al.* (2005), in order to satisfy both quality and cost control demands, several MNEs initially offshored to Guangdong the production of more sophisticated components, followed by a number of services (e.g. quality testing, logistics).

21 Data referred to 2005 (see note 10).

22 According to our fieldwork, the leader enterprise will use the centre (employing its own staff) to provide services to its subproviders (quality testing in particular). The agreement with the local government states that the enterprise will benefit from the revenues generated by the sale of the services.

23 At present, half of the local enterprises have a shop within the trade market.

24 At present, the effect appears to be weaker for the small Chinese subproviders. Although some of the local component-manufacturing enterprises have autonomously entered the market (a small number if compared to the producers of final products), the results of our fieldwork investigation show that they have not significantly expanded the number of their local (or extra-local) clients. Moreover, the effect in terms of expansion of the local division of labour appears to be weak.

25 Although the policy is inspired by the generic principle of 'supporting the best and the brightest', the funds are not provided on the basis of formalized selective criteria.

26 The strong involvement of the local branch of the Textile Association, and hence of the

local entrepreneurs (combined with the support provided by the national association), in both the design and the management of the centre has been a crucial factor of success in its development.

27 The renewal of the machinery has been a gradual process. It started with the involvement of the state-owned enterprises (with the introduction of expensive looms from Belgium, as well as computerized looms) and only at a later stage – encountering certain and difficulties – reached the entrepreneurs. The entrepreneurs were reluctant basically because they were afraid of not finding adequate maintenance services for the new machinery *in loco*. Moreover, the utility of the innovation was not clearly perceived, seeing that the entrepreneurs were mainly producing medium–low quality products for the internal market. However, considering that at present approximately half of the machinery in the cluster is of a new type, and that the renewal of the equipment has boosted productivity (+20–30 per cent) and improved the quality of the products, the local government intervention can be considered a successful experience.

28 The new models created are sold to the local private enterprises at a low price, after which the department provides technical support to the enterprises in setting up the machinery for the manufacturing process. It is interesting to note that each new model can be sold to only one or a few enterprises, so as to maintain its exclusivity.

References

Albino V., Carbonara N. and Giannoccaro I. (2007), 'Why proximity matters for industrial district competitiveness: a complexity science-based view', paper presented at the Regional Studies Association International Conference, Regions In Focus?, Lisbon, 2–5 April 2007.

Altenburg T. and Meyer-Stamer J. (1999), 'How to promote clusters: policy experiences from Latin America', *World Development*, 27(9): 1693–1713.

Arndt S. W. and Kierzkowsky, H. (eds.) (2001), *Fragmentation: New Production Patterns in the World Economy*, Oxford: Oxford University Press.

Bair J. and Gereffi G. (2001), 'Local clusters in global chains: the causes and consequences of export dynamism in Torreon's blue jeans industry', *World Development*, 29(11): 1885–1903.

Becattini G., Bellandi M., Dei Ottat, G. and Sforzi F. (2003), *From Industrial Districts to Local Development: An Itinerary of Research*, Cheltenham: Edward Elgar.

Bellandi M. (2001), 'Local development and embedded large firms', *Entrepreneurship and Regional Development*, 13(3): 189–210.

——. (2006), 'A perspective on clusters, localities, and specific public goods', in C. Pitelis, R. Sugden and J. R. Wilson (eds.), *Clusters and Globalisation. The Development of Urban and Regional Economies*. Cheltenham: Edward Elgar, pp. 96–113.

Bellandi M. and Caloffi A. (2008), 'Forms of industrial development in Chinese specialized towns: an Italian perspective', in B. Andreosso, H. Lenihan and D. Kan (eds.), *EU SMEs in a Globalised World: Lessons from the Edge*. Cheltenham: Edward Elgar.

Bellandi M. and Di Tommaso M. (2005), 'The case of specialized towns in Guangdong, China', *European Planning Studies*, 13(5): 707–29.

Bellini N. (2003), *Business Support Services: Marketing and the Practice of Regional Innovation Policy*, Cork: Oaktreepress.

Belussi F. (1999) 'Policies for the development of knowledge-intensive local production systems', *Cambridge Journal of Economics*, 23: 729–47.

Biggeri M., Gambelli D. and Phillips C. (1999), 'Small and medium enterprise theory: evidence for Chinese TVEs, *Journal of International Development*, 2(2): 197–219.

Brusco S. (1994), 'Servizi reali, formazione professionale e competenze: una prospettiva', in M. Bellandi and M. Russo (eds.), *Distretti industriali e cambiamento economico locale*, Torino: Rosenberg e Sellier, pp. 223–30.

Caloffi A. and Hirsch, G. (2005), 'Sistemi produttivi locali e città specializzate nell'industria della moda del Guangdong', in M. Bellandi and M. Biggeri (eds.), *La sfida industriale cinese vista dalla Toscana distrettuale*, Firenze: Toscana Promozione.

Cammett M. (2007), 'Business–government relations and industrial change: the politics of upgrading in Morocco and Tunisia', *World Development*, 35(11): 1889–1903.

Christerson B. and Lever Tracy C. (1997), 'The Third China? Emerging industrial districts in rural China', *International Journal of Urban and Regional Research*, 21(4): 569–88.

Crouch C., Le Galès P., Trigilia C. and Voelzkow H. (2001), *Local Production Systems in Europe: Rise or Demise?*, Oxford: Oxford University Press.

Dei Ottati G. (2002) 'Social concertation and local development: the case of industrial districts', *European Planning Studies*, 10(4): 449–66.

——. (2003), 'Exit, voice and the evolution of industrial districts: the case of the post-World War II economic development of Prato', *Cambridge Journal of Economics*, 27(4): 501–22.

Di Tommaso M. and Rubini L. (2005), 'La geografia della produzione in Guangdong: agglomerazioni di imprese e città specializzate' in M. Bellandi and M. Biggeri (eds.), *La sfida industriale cinese vista dalla Toscana distrettuale*, Firenze: Toscana Promozione, pp. 39–80.

Ding K. (2006), 'Distribution system of China's industrial clusters: the case study of Yiwu China Commodity City', *Institute of Developing Economies Working Paper*, 75.

Eng I. (1997), 'The rise of manufacturing towns: externally driven industrialization and urban development in the Pearl River Delta of China', *International Journal of Urban and Regional Research*, 21(4): 554–68.

Enright M. J., Scott E. E. and Chang K. (2005), *The Greater Pearl River Delta and The Rise of China*, Singapore: Wiley and Sons.

Gereffi G. (1994), 'The organization of buyer-driven global commodity chains: how US retailers shape overseas production networks', in G. Gereffi and M. Korzeniewicz (eds.), *Commodity Chains and Global Capitalism*, Westport: Praeger, pp. 95–122.

Gereffi G., Humphrey J. and Sturgeon T. (2005), 'The governance of global value chains', *Review of International Political Economy*, 12(1): 78–104.

Giuliani E., Pietrobelli C., Rabellotti R. (2005), 'Upgrading in global value chains: lessons from Latin American clusters', *World Development*, 33(4): 549–73.

Humphrey J. and Schmitz H. (2002), 'How does insertion in global value chains affect upgrading in industrial clusters?, *Regional Studies*, 36(9): 1017–27.

Lazzeretti L. and Storai D. (2003), 'An ecology based interpretation of district "complexification": the Prato district evolution from 1946 to 1993', in F. Belussi, G. Gottardi and E. Rullani (eds.), *The Technological Evolution of Industrial Districts*. Boston and Dordrecht: Kluwer, pp. 409–34.

Leung C. K. (1996), 'Foreign manufacturing investment and regional industrial growth in Guangdong Province, China', *Environment and Planning A*, 28: 513–36.

Li C. L. (2003), 'Guangdong playing the "foreign card": politics and economics across territorial boundaries', in G. Drover, G. Johnson and J. T. Lai Po-wah (eds.), *Regionalism and Subregionalism in East Asia: The Dynamics of China*, Huntington, New York: Nova Science Publishers, pp. 151–67.

Li & Fung Research Centre (ed.) (2006), 'Overview of the industrial clusters in China', *Industrial Clusters Working Paper Series*, 1. http://www.idsgroup.com/profile/pdf/industry_series/LFIndustrial1.pdf

Lombardi S. (2007), 'Specialized markets in local productive systems: theoretical and empirical results from the Chinese experience in Zhejiang province', paper presented to the 10th International EUNIP Conference, Prato, 12–14 September 2007.

Long Z. (2005), 'A study on the industrial clusters in Guangdong', paper presented to the Conference *Enter the Dragon: China's Emergence and International Competitiveness*, Hong Kong (China), 7–11 November 2005.

Lu L. and Wei Y. D. (2007), 'Domesticating globalisation, new economic spaces and regional polarisation in Guangdong Province, China', *Tijdschrift voor Economische en Sociale Geografie*, 98(2): 225–44.

Ma L. J. and Lin C. (1993), 'Development of towns in China: a case study of Guangdong Province', *Population and Development Review*, 19(3): 583–606.

Markusen A. (1996), 'Sticky places in slippery space: a typology of industrial districts, *Economic Geography*, 72(3): 293–313.

Mehrotra S. and Biggeri M. (eds.) (2007), *Asian Informal Workers: Global Risks Local Protection*, London: Routledge.

Messner D. and Meyer-Stamer J. (2000), 'Governance and networks. Tools to study the dynamics of clusters and global value chains', paper prepared for the IDS/INEF Project *The Impact of Global and Local Governance on Industrial Upgrading*; http://www.meyer-stamer.de/2000/govtools.pdf

Metcalfe S. and Ramlogan R. (2007), 'Innovation systems and the competitive process in developing economies', *The Quarterly Review of Economics and Finance*, doi:10.1016/j.qref.2006.12.021.

Meyer-Stamer J. (2003), 'Participatory appraisal of competitive advantage (PACA): launching local economic development initiatives', *Mesopartner Working Paper* 01/2003.

Mytelka L. (2000), 'Local systems of innovation in a globalized world economy', *Industry and Innovation*, 7(1): 15–32.

NBS (National Bureau of Statistics) (2005), *China Township and Village Statistics*, (Beijing: China Statistics Press) (in Chinese).

Qiu H. and Xu J. (2004), 'The actions of local governments in the technological innovation of industrial clusters', paper presented to the conference: *Regional Innovation Systems and Science and Technology Policies in Emerging Economies: Experiences from China and the World*, Guangzhou, Zhongshan University, 19–21 April 2004.

Raines P. (ed.) (2002), *Cluster Development and Policy*, Aldershot: Ashgate.

Rodrik D. (2004), 'Industrial policy for the twenty-first century', paper prepared for UNIDO; http://ksghome.harvard.edu/drodrik/publications.html

Sabel C. F. (1994), 'Learning by monitoring: the institutions of economic development', in N. J. Smelser and R. Swedberg (eds.), *The Handbook of Economic Sociology*, Princeton, NJ: Princeton University Press, pp. 137–65.

Schmitz H. (1995), 'Collective efficiency: growth path for small-scale industry', *The Journal of Development Studies*, 31(4): 529–66.

Shirk S. L. (1993), *The Political Logic of Economic Reform in China*, Berkeley: University of California Press.

Sit V. F. S. and Yang C. (1997), 'Foreign-investment induced exo-urbanisation in the Pearl River Delta, China', *Urban Studies*, 34: 647–77.

Sonobe T., Hu D. and Otsuka K. (2002), 'Process of cluster formation in China: a case study of a garment town', *Journal of Development Studies*, 1: 118–39.

Thun E. (2004), 'Keeping up with the Jones': decentralization, policy imitation, and industrial development in China', *World Development*, 32: 1289–1308.

Unger J. and Chan A. (1999), 'Inheritors of the boom: private enterprise and the role of local government in a rural South China township', *The China Journal*, 42: 45–74.

Yao Y. (2001), 'Social exclusion and economic discrimination: the status of migrants in China's coastal rural areas', China Centre for Economic Research (CCER) Working Paper, n.E2001005.

Zhongshan University (2003), 'A case study of the textile cluster of Xi Qiao, Nan Hai – an analysis of the Technological Innovations, *mimeo*.

Part IV

High-tech industrial districts and clusters in the global value chains

15 The institutional design of clusters in the Greater Paris Region

Najoua Boufaden (ADIS, Université Paris Sud), Sofiène Lourimi (ADIS, Université Paris Sud) and André Torre (UMR SAD-APT, INRA INA PG Paris)

15.1 Introduction

The cluster-based approach, first proposed by Porter, has had undeniable success. Initially developed as a tool of entrepreneurial growth, it is now the basis of many industrial and local systems policies and is used as a development tool by the OECD (2005) and the World Bank (2002). The amount of literature devoted to this subject is enormous and has given rise to much debate about good practices, policies of technology transfer, of development of both human and natural local resources (see for example Karlsson, *et al.* 2005, or Dunning 2000). Clusters are everywhere.

Whether clusters serve as objects of analytical studies or of public policies, two points are commonly made with regard to this approach (Hakanson 2005; Giuliani and Bell 2005).

The first concerns the knowledge (or innovation) exchange interactions between actors, whether they are non-commercial, informal, knowledge transfer or creation interactions, or, more rarely, commercial exchanges related to intellectual property rights for example; the second is related to clusters' input-output structure. It is acknowledged that exchange relations between local actors, between suppliers and clients for example, can have synergetic and spillover effects at local level, whether on the goods or on the labour markets.

Both approaches, though very interesting, fail to take into account one variable, which we believe is essential. It is the institutional dimension, which plays an important role in the functioning and organization of clusters. By institutions we mean the *visible* institutions – that is incubators, venture capital, intermediation organizations or regional innovation centres for example – which play an essential role at local level in the processes of development of clusters. They are at the origin of many undertakings, promote the creation and growth of firms and facilitate communication and exchange within the clusters through their action at network level.

The one and only objective of this article is to shed light on the role played by institutions in the implementation and functioning of clusters. For this purpose, we base our analysis on the observations of two clusters of the Greater Paris Region, one dedicated to biotechnologies, the other to optics-photonics. In the next section (15.2) of this paper we shall discuss the institutional roots of clusters, by, first examining their relations with institutions and then by presenting the institutions present in the Greater Paris Region. In Section 15.3, we describe firms' strategic approaches and the nature of their interactions with institutions using the example provided by the biotechnology and optics-photonics clusters of the Paris Region.

15.2 The institutional roots of clusters

A century after Alfred Marshall developed the concept of industrial district, Michael Porter has given new life to the concept of local system with his cluster-based approach in which clusters are defined as *'A geographically proximate group of interconnected companies and associated institutions in a particular field, linked by commonalities and complementarities. The geographic scope of a cluster can range from a single city or state to a country or even a group of neighbouring countries'*. The success of this concept and of the local systems of production associated with it is generally attributed to the existence of internal interactions, of knowledge relations and of the building of mutual trust between the members of the clusters. We wish to show here that, in certain situations, the institutional dimension also plays a determinant role; for this purpose we shall first perform a critical examination of the interactionist approach and of local innovation systems and will then present the institutions that are present in the above-mentioned clusters.

15.2.1 Clusters and institutions

According to Porter, the significance of clusters lies in the fact that they provide firms with a favourable environment in terms of competition, specialized input and institutional support. These factors reinforce cooperation between the members of the cluster and facilitate the diffusion of knowledge, and in doing so improve strategic positioning processes and enable firms to identify the 'best practices'; in short they improve the competitive advantage of the firms located within the cluster. Porter sees a cluster as a self-reinforcing system that stimulates the competitive strategies of the firms in the cluster and hence the competitiveness of its members. This process depends in part on personal relationships and face-to-face communication and networks, and puts the stress on the relation between the social network and firms competitiveness theories (Martin and Sunley 2003).

The success of these clusters can be explained by going back to the very foundations of the interactionist approach, i.e. the input-output relations between the actors of the local systems, particularly between firms. It is the growth pole approach – proposed by Perroux or Myrdal – that prevails here, with the idea that local systems of production rest on the agglomeration of firms with complementary activities. Buyer-seller relations develop between firms located in the same cluster and create positive synergies in terms of local or territorial development. Indeed, an increase in the production volume of one of the firms – particularly if it is a large organization – results in increased purchase volumes and therefore in an increase, upstream, in the production volumes of the firms that sell intermediate goods to the former. Gradually, the effect spreads throughout the whole productive structure, among suppliers or subcontractors, and leads to an increase in the local system's total production volume. We see here that this approach has limitations in that it is only valid when the local production system is constituted of complementary, rather than isolated, industries, which is not the case of all clusters. Further, it is based on the hypothesis that the effects spread mechanically throughout the production structure, which is far from being validated; indeed some local firms might quite possibly prefer to buy all or part of their supplies from suppliers located outside the cluster.

The second explanation, interactionist in nature, is far more widespread. It is related to the idea that clusters are places, which by nature facilitate the diffusion of knowledge between the local productive units. The hypothesis is that knowledge transfer is more effective when it takes place within a geographically restricted area – clusters in this instance – or, in other words, when it occurs between actors that are located in proximity to one another. This geographical proximity is supposed to be advantageous because it is thought to make the transfer of knowledge between the members of a local system easier and faster than it is between partners that are geographically distant from one another. It also facilitates the implementation of cooperation or partnership projects between firms, laboratories or universities located within a cluster.

This approach rests on two founding principles, principles that also explain the existence and the success of clusters. The first principle concerns the cooperation or collaboration opportunities provided by the presence, within the same geographical area, of different productive organizations. Thus, geographical proximity is thought to facilitate contacts. Not only does it enable the different actors to meet more easily – without having to spend time and money on long and expensive trips – but it also enables them to interact as often as necessary and thus to develop tighter relations with one another. Thus, geographical proximity reduces transport costs as well as the transaction costs related to distance, by enabling actors to conduct inexpensive face-to-face interactions. But, from a more dynamic point of view, it also facilitates the implementation of common projects through the development of learning relationships: the different actors learn to know and understand one another, to work and collaborate together. Network type relationships based on trust can grow through the development of closer interpersonal relations that sometimes grow into friendships outside work.

The second principle concerns the characteristics of the knowledge exchanged by the actors; knowledge the transfer of which requires geographical proximity, which clustering provides. This principle can be summed up as follows. Innovation activities are believed to be related to the possibility of producing or acquiring knowledge and in particular scientific knowledge emerging from public or private research. But this knowledge is characterized by its imperfect appropriability, in other words by the fact that it does not easily remain the sole property of its creator: it can be reproduced or imitated. The imperfect appropriability of knowledge results in the existence of many spillover effects generated by innovating firms and benefiting other firms in the same sector, or that link together researchers belonging to different organizations. These effects are known as knowledge spillovers, effects that only occur among firms that are located in proximity to one another because of the particular nature of the knowledge exchanged. According to Polanyi (1962), this knowledge can be divided into two distinct but sometimes complementary categories: tacit knowledge and codified knowledge. The latter, which includes all written sources, or those that are easily communicated through manuals or books, can be transferred over long distances, and can therefore be reproduced or copied by people who took no part in the initial process of creation or innovation. But the other type of knowledge, tacit knowledge, is incompatible with distance. It can only be imitated through observation, practice, and learning; it resides within human beings and within their daily behaviour and can only be communicated through face-to-face interaction. The advantages of the co-location of research activities and of innovating firms are clear here. Thus, organizing innovation activities at local level, promoting spatial proximity or the development of clusters appears necessary.

These two interactive approaches are based on 'naturalist' or 'mechanical' assumptions, and although they are centred on the relations that exist between the different economic actors, they only attribute a limited role to these actors. In the case of input-output relations, these processes are above all mechanical and rest on the belief that there exists a perfect knowledge transfer between industries, and do not take into account the strategies of the actors, the different production costs, or the respective competencies of the local and external suppliers. As for the approach in terms of local transfer of tacit knowledge, it is based above all on a naturalist hypothesis: it is the very characteristics of knowledge that explain the co-localization of research and innovation actors, and not the latter's strategies. In comparison, the approach in terms of cooperation or collaboration focuses more on the actors' strategies. But it is still based on the hypothesis that these actors – whether they are firms or research laboratories – are driven together by their respective interests and are pushed naturally to interact with one another. The example of technology transfer organizations is often mentioned in this context, but little attention is paid to their role and position within local production systems or clusters.

Yet, a large number of institutions and organizations play an essential role in the creation and development of clusters. Need we remind the reader that most technopoles, scientific parks and clusters were created as a result of decisions made by local public authorities, the state or by the decentralized departments of the latter; and that many organizations exist for the purpose of helping entrepreneurs start and develop new ventures, of helping the latter develop relations with other organizations or facilitating their interactions with the milieu. Not to mention the fact that, in the field of innovation, knowledge creation and transfer, these activities are performed under the aegis of, or thanks to, organizations such as centres for knowledge exchange, or agencies for the promotion and support of innovation. Clearly, clusters cannot only be described in terms of inter-firm relations. Indeed, local institutions play an essential role in the functioning and development of clusters at two levels at least: firstly, these institutions, through global and local development policies, determine the structure and organization of the cluster; secondly, they play a crucial role in the creation and development of relations between local firms.

The role of institutions in technological change has been emphasized in many studies about innovation systems (Lundvall 1992; Nelson 1993). Indeed, the complexity and uncertainty that characterize technological innovation processes make it necessary to mobilize a variety of actors and competencies, but also an institutional body comprising institutions or organizations capable of supporting innovation, of providing an organizational framework of rules and standards (Coriat and Weinstein 2002). The mission of the institutions is to coordinate interactions between the different organizations and actors of the system, as well as knowledge utilization. They do so by promoting fundamental research, technological transfer and the creation of firms, or by providing financial or organizational support. But what role do they play at spatial level, particularly in clusters?

15.2.2 The institutional structures of the biotech and optics-photonics clusters of the Greater Paris Region

The research studies we have conducted in the biotech (Bellon, Plunket and Boufaden 2005) and optics-photonics industries (Lourimi and Torre 2007) of the Greater Paris Region have enabled us to identify, within these two clusters, four main categories of institutions. The latter are grouped according to their main objective, that is the provision of financial support, of infrastructures, of access to networks of actors in the economic and the research arenas.

15.2.2.1 Financial institutions

The main mission of financial support institutions is to promote innovation in firms and laboratories by financing the innovative projects the actors of the cluster wish to undertake. Four categories of financial support institutions have been identified in the Paris Region:

The institutions specialized in providing financial support to young innovative businesses, by offering venture capital and start-up funds. Because the needs for financial support of small innovative firms change according to their stage of development, several types of institutions, such as venture-capital companies, traditional banks or the capital market, come into play in a successive or complementary manner. Generally, when entrepreneurs create a new business, part of the initial capital comes from their own savings or from friends and family ('love money') and another part comes from 'traditional' local financial institutions. They sometimes also obtain support from *business angels* when the latter are convinced of the technological potential of the project. This initial capital contribution is used to start the business, gain access to technology (licence negotiation), employ consulting experts to help them create and develop a business plan they need to attract financial support from private investors.

The institutions that help finance the innovation projects undertaken by firms. This category of financial support includes subsidies and loans granted to firms to help them develop innovation projects (OSEO [a public organization that provides support to SMEs], CRITT [Centre for Innovation and Technology Transfer], and various types of financial support from the public authorities).

The institutions that provide support (in the form of subsidies or loans) for cooperative innovation projects ('poles de compétitivité' ['competitiveness clusters'], RRIT [Research and Technological Innovation Networks]).

15.2.2.2 Institutions that provide facilities and infrastructure

The first mission of these institutions is to support firms (young innovative firms or high-tech SMEs) by offering them access to facilities and infrastructure that match their needs. Among them are:

Incubators (e.g. Incuballiance or Genopole). These organizations provide guidance and support to individuals with projects to create innovative firms; their support consists of providing training-related assistance, advice, financial aid, and industrial premises within the incubator. Incubators are located within or in close proximity to scientific centres, so as to maintain close relationships with research laboratories (researchers, young doctorate holders); Individuals with this type of projects are for the most part former students or employees of these research laboratories and have access to the scientific and technological resources available in the centre. Incubators also offer financing solutions for the pre-start-up phases of projects, including equity investment, loans, etc. Through these different modes of intervention, incubators help young entrepreneurs and assist them to cover the marketing, tax-related and legal administrative tasks expenses and offer coaching or training services adapted to the project's needs.

Specialized incubators (International Partnership for the Hydrogen Economy at the Ecole Polytechnique of Paris, or Innov'Valley in Marcoussis). These organizations provide premises to high-tech SMEs that need access to specialized, broadband network infrastructure etc.

Traditional incubators, comprising institutions that provide non-specialized premises to entrepreneurs that wish to start or develop a business in the Paris region (business parks).

15.2.2.3 Institutions promoting the transfer and application of scientific knowledge

These organizations play a more or less important role in firms' processes of development depending on the maturity of the industry (emerging or mature industry) and on the origin and nature of the technologies involved (technologies developed from the knowledge produced by public research organizations, or from the knowledge accumulated by the industry over decades of activity).

The industrial biotech sector, for example, cannot operate coherently without the implementation of tools promoting the transfer and application of the scientific knowledge created through academic research. Since the 1999 law on innovation was adopted, several organizations have been founded to promote the development of research activities. Among them, let us mention the Curie Institution for Medical and Clinical Cancer Research Applications, Pasteur BioTop, the DRITT-SAIC (Industrial Relations and Technology Transfer/Industrial and Contract Activities) of the Paris IV University, etc). A certain number of private organizations of this type have also emerged: the FIST (France Scientific Innovation and Transfer, subsidiary of the CNRS and of OSEO) and Inserm Transfert (a limited company and private subsidiary of the Inserm). Finally, incubators such as Paris Biotech, Pasteur Bio-Top and Agoranov also strive to transform scientific and technological inventions into viable and innovative businesses.

These institutions intervene in different ways depending on the sectors. Thus, in the biotech sector they are a crucial component in the process of creation of new businesses, whereas in the optics-photonics sector they do not always come into play. In this more mature industry, this process of creation does not merely consist of the transformation of the knowledge generated by public research into technologies. The process is often initiated by actors of the industry itself (joint ventures, large groups selling factories, or selling off parts of their operations to other entrepreneurs, creation of new businesses by engineers from universities or engineering schools).

15.2.2.4 Networking institutions

A cluster is run on the basis of two strategic priorities consisting of developing competencies and reinforcing the network to which the various firms belong. The first priority is related to the organization of training programmes, conferences, seminars and symposiums which help improve and consolidate researchers, technicians and engineers' knowledge in particular fields of application. It can also consist in organizing meetings on specific topics between firms and regional research laboratories. The second priority is to reinforce the interactions between the different actors of the network and to generate synergy effects, by promoting the implementation of cooperative research and innovation projects, facilitating a better and more efficient utilization of the knowledge generated by public research and helping SMEs develop relations with large national or international corporations. Several institutions make it their mission to centralize relevant information – on which innovation is based – so as to help firms gain quicker and cheaper access to the resources and services they need, such as advice or information about partners, platforms or national/international requests for proposals, etc. This category of institutions includes organizations such as the Local Productive Systems that specialize in specific industries (optics, electronics and software in the case of Opticsvalley). It also includes clusters that specialize in one specific field, such as the Evry Genopole, specialized in genomics and bioinformatics.

15.2.2.5 'Hybrid' institutions operating at various levels

These four categories of institutions are not alone in performing the functions described above. Other types of institutions, such as 'pôles de compétitivité' for example, operate at various levels by helping firms finance their innovation projects on the condition that the latter cooperate with different actors of the cluster (large groups, SMEs, public research laboratories). Thus, this category of institutions plays the double role of financer and network facilitator. In the case of the optics-photonics and biotech sectors of the Paris Region, the 'pôles de compétitivité' that play this role are the Medicen Paris Region cluster (in the fields of life sciences and healthcare technologies) and the Paris Region (in the fields of complex systems).

A study of the strategic approaches adopted by firms in the optics-photonics and biotech sectors of the Greater Paris Region shows that the various types of institutions (those providing finance, those promoting knowledge transfer, and those reinforcing networking) are used differently by firms depending on the phase in the production cycle and on their positioning on the value chain. This is what we shall analyze in the next section of this paper.

15.3 Strategic models of firms and interactions with the institutional environment: the case of the biotech and optics-photonics firms in the Paris Region

Research on the innovation and development strategies implemented by biotech and optics-photonics firms in the Paris Region shows that firms often make use of the services provided by the different types of institutions so as to obtain the type of support they need to achieve their goals. Beyond this general observation, the diversity of the possible interventions reveals that the nature of the support provided depends on the characteristics of the industry and on the phase of development the firms have reached. In the case of biotechnologies, the primary role of institutions seems to provide the necessary (financial and material) conditions for the creation of new firms: the cluster can be likened to a gigantic incubator. On the other hand, the institutional optics-photonics cluster seems to both provide financial support to businesses for (collaborative or individual) innovation projects and to facilitate networking between the different organizations.

15.3.1 The case of the biotech cluster

The slow development of the French biotechnology industry is often attributed to the 'cultural resistance' of researchers, who only recently became aware of the benefits of transforming the knowledge they produce into technologies and business opportunities. Yet, mentalities have changed since the 1999 law on innovation and research was implemented. The law provides a legal framework that promotes and facilitates the creation of innovative technology businesses, particularly by young researchers, students or employees of the public sector. The latter are authorized to participate, as members or directors, and for a certain period of time, in the creation of a new company. At the end of this period they must choose between returning to the public sector or leaving it to stay in the company. For a maximum period of six years, they are seconded and therefore retain their civil servant status.

The measures and programmes implemented, since the 1999 law was adopted, to promote knowledge and technological transfer have had remarkable results in terms of business creation. In our sample,[2] half the firms created since the early 1990s are either spin-offs from research laboratories (CNRS, CEA, INRA, Pasteur Institute, INSERM) or firms created, independently, by researchers. The contribution of research to the creation of firms has increased dramatically since 1999, with a peak in 2001. Since then economic growth has slowed down and funding has become scarcer. Furthermore, a succession of governmental measures have been introduced to improve the legal and tax framework under which young innovative firms are created (financial contribution to the creation of new innovative enterprises by the French Research Ministry, public subsidies and start-up funds, the Common Funds for Investment in Innovation, research and development tax credit, etc). These elements underlie the analysis of strategic groups of firms and of the interactions between businesses and institutions within the Paris biotech cluster.

15.3.1.1 The different strategic groups in the Paris biotech cluster

The biotech cluster comprises four strategic groups of firms with very different modes of development. Four 'business models' have been identified, on the basis of the factors that define the nature of a firm's activities and explain the origin of its turnover, its results and of their evolution (Plunket and Boufaden 2007). Four strategic dimensions are taken into account: knowledge transfer, financing, collaborations and markets.

A. THE 'PRODUCT-ORIENTED' STRATEGY GROUP

This model is mostly used by research-based firms under five years of age, and developing technologies that have applications almost exclusively in the healthcare sector. They are often spin-offs from public research organizations; they pursue a long-term development strategy and do not seek to sell their technologies but rather to develop them further. The activities are based on internal and collaborative research. Less than a quarter of these firms have (commercial and productive) partnership agreements with organizations outside the Region, and one firm out of three has products in the clinical or evaluation stage of development. These firms' development potential is real but their strategies are very risky, for two reasons: (1) their activities do not enable them to be financially self-sufficient in the short term since only 8 per cent of them have sold property rights and only 8 per cent have commercialized products; (2) investors are reluctant to finance companies whose strategy is based almost exclusively on the expectation of profitability in the long term.

B. THE 'DUAL, PRODUCT-ORIENTED' STRATEGY GROUP

This group comprises firms that engage in the long-term development of products while performing service activities that can generate profit in the short term. Their technologies have applications in the healthcare sector primarily, but 30 per cent of these firms develop technologies that have applications in bio-informatics. They are all involved in collaborative R&D projects with partners in and outside the Paris Region. Their approach to product development is characterized by a high level of R&D activities, and products in the clinical or evaluation stage of development. They commercialize their technologies in various ways, in the form of services provided to other organizations, subcontracting or platform leasing. These firms' medium-term approach seems less risky than that of the previously mentioned group because they have developed strategies of service provision and subcontracting based on the research they perform. Thus, they derive sufficient income from their activities to operate. Their challenge consists of finding the right balance between short and medium-term exploitation (the production and com-mercialization of an existing technology) and long-term exploitation (development of new technologies).

C. THE 'DUAL, SERVICE-ORIENTED' STRATEGY GROUP

Most of the companies in this group are less than five years old and have an above-average number of employees. Their activities are based on research and they derive their income from trading or licensing property rights. They all have (commercial and productive) partnership agreements with organizations outside the Paris Region and most of them collaborate with organizations within the Region. These firms enjoy a high level of financial autonomy because their research ac-tivities are oriented towards the sale of patent rights and because they get most of their total turnover from royalties. Just like the firms in the above-mentioned group, their situation is stable enough to ensure their medium-term development but their long-term future depends on their achieving a healthy balance between the production and the marketing of technologies.

D. THE STRATEGIC GROUP ORIENTED TOWARDS 'NON-HEALTHCARE-RELATED PRODUCTS'

This group comprises firms whose technologies are used in the fields of agricul-ture, bio-informatics, environment and food-related biotechnology. They pursue a long-term development strategy centred on the marketing of their products, and thanks to which they enjoy relative financial autonomy. This marketing strategy rests on agreements with a network of commercial and productive partners, outside and in the Paris Region. Their activities are based on internal and collaborative re-search performed with partners both in and outside the Region. Furthermore, 25 per cent of these firms are spin-offs of large industrial groups that are liable to provide them with financial support. Given the areas in which these firms specialize, their production does not involve long and costly clinical trials; however, we observe some reluctance on the part of venture capitalists, which might be due to the difficulty of identifying the potential of value creation of their activities.

This typology implies different development prospects and different needs. Some of these needs are material needs (access to premises, to technology platforms), some are service related (for the elaboration of a business plan, forging relationships with other organizations, for gaining access to knowledge) or financial needs (obtaining financial support, gaining easier access to venture capital). Because biotechnology companies are dependent, for their development, on these resources, they turn (sometimes very reluctantly) to existing institutional organizations for support. However, relations with these institutions often fail to have the expected results. This is due to the fact that their performance also depends on the nature and on the stage of development of the activities conducted by the firms.

15.3.1.2 Interactions between firms and institutions in the biotech cluster

In order to analyze the interactions between firms and institutions in the biotech cluster, it is necessary to thoroughly examine the kind of relations these firms develop with each category of institutions (as described in Section 15.2.).

THE RELATIONSHIPS BETWEEN BIOTECH FIRMS AND FINANCIAL INSTITUTIONS

Biotech companies interact with different types of financial institutions during their lifetime. One of the most remarkable facts is the prevalence of regional financing arrangements such as the allocation of start-up funds or of public subsidies. Besides these funds, *business angels* and *love money* generally serve to finance the creation stages and the launch of the firms' activities. Together, these different actors finance almost 65 per cent of the needs of biotech firms in the Paris Region (Bellon, *et al.* 2005).

Three to five-year-old companies have easier access to venture capital. Half of the financing of these firms comes from the Region, 25 per cent from national institutions and another 25 per cent from international institutions. Biotech firms in the 'product-oriented' strategy group have these characteristics, which is probably due to the fact that 44 per cent of these firms have products in the clinical stage of development and 24 per cent have products in the evaluation stage. The same applies to firms with a 'dual, service-oriented' strategy. The financial stability (achieved thanks to the royalties earned through licensing) of these firms and the R&D activities they perform play in their favour and increase their chances of obtaining venture capital. However, things are different for firms with a 'dual, product-oriented' strategy and for those oriented towards 'non-healthcare related products'. Among the former, only 7 per cent have had access to venture capital, because they dedicate a good part of their resources to the provision of services whose profitability is not significant. For different reasons, firms specializing in technologies related to agriculture, bio-informatics, food-related biotechnology and the environment are also unattractive for venture capitalists (only 8 per cent of these firms have access to venture capital). Venture capitalists find it difficulty to identify the potential value creation of their activities.

Once biotech firms have been in operation for at least six years, they obtain venture capital more easily. Approximately 70 per cent of the venture capital comes from financial organizations located outside the Paris Region. Thus, these firms seem to turn towards investors outside Paris for support but they are not necessarily successful in obtaining sufficient funds to ensure their development. Indeed, although the percentage of venture capital in the overall financing of firms increases, the latter remains insufficient to cover the high costs of product development and of clinical trials, in the case of firms specialized in healthcare technology.

THE RELATIONS BETWEEN BIOTECH FIRMS AND INSTITUTIONS THAT PROVIDE INFRASTRUCTURE

The support provided by the various types of institutions can also be material. Several organizations provide premises to young researchers/entrepreneurs to enable them to develop their projects. Furthermore, many young entrepreneurs, particularly those who previously worked in public research laboratories, do not have the managerial skills that are necessary to run a business. They need support and guidance concerning the legal and administrative aspects of the creation of the firm and those related to intellectual property rights. This is the role played by incubators to which the government has decided to allocate 23 million euro, through the launch of the 'incubation – start-up capital of technological firms' call for project proposals.

Chambers of commerce are the most appreciated partners of firms that are starting up and that need support in terms of management (legal aspects, accounting, etc.). These firms turn to chambers of commerce – rather than to consulting firms – for support in drafting business plans or in performing a market survey. Knowledge transfer institutions, on the other hand, are hardly mentioned, which is all the more surprising as over one third of the firms in our sample are spin-offs from knowledge transfer units of research organizations such as Pasteur Bio-Top, INRIA, Inserm Transfert, etc. Apart from providing premises to young researchers, these knowledge transfer centres fail to deliver the very services they were created to provide. Actions that would actually promote the transfer of knowledge are limited and in some cases non-existent.

Initially, a biotech spin-off is a very small organization that is heavily dependent on financial support and on assistance in the skills required to perform knowledge transfer in the field of biomedical research, and in particular in human health biotechs. Environmental or food biotech companies are generally spin-offs from larger organizations that provide them with the support they need for their development.

THE RELATIONS BETWEEN BIOTECH FIRMS AND 'NETWORKING' INSTITUTIONS

Although it is generally acknowledged that the support provided by the various institutions contributes significantly to the success of incubation, creation and start-up stages, their role in helping start-ups forge relationships with other strategic actors and in the diffusion of strategic information is considered less significant by entrepreneurs. For a biotech company, collaboration in R&D and/or production and marketing are essential stages. The complexity of the technological process of innovation requires that firms gain access to a wide range of skills. Collaboration with public research organizations or other firms can give a start-up company access to the complementary skills that are necessary to the success of its projects.

For biotech companies that adopt a product-oriented strategy or a 'dual, product-oriented' strategy, collaboration in R&D is essential. Ninety-two per cent of the firms in the first group (and 100 per cent of those in the second group) have R&D collaboration agreements with partners in the Paris Region. Because one third of the firms in this sector are spin-offs from public research laboratories, and because in another third at least one of the founders is an academic researcher, public universities and laboratories are considered to be their natural business partners. Networking institutions play a relatively insignificant role in helping these firms develop R&D partnerships with other firms.

When a firm plans to develop or market a particular product, finding partners and having access to new networks of actors becomes essential to its survival and development. This is the case for firms whose main activities are centred on research and development of new technologies and on the sale of patent rights or on technology transfer agreements. One hundred per cent of these firms have agreements with commercial and productive partners located outside the Paris Region. Given the narrowness of the local market, several institutions, such as Evry Génopole or the chamber of commerce, play the role of intermediaries and organize events to enable firms to meet potential partners. But the survey shows that the contributions of associations such as France Biotechnologie or the Club Alpha, in helping firms finding commercial, financial or research partners are the most valuable.

In the context of technology watch strategies, access to information concerning new scientific opportunities, technological possibilities and market evolutions are crucial questions. Biotech firms seek information concerning the market structure, their competitors, new technological niches, scientific discoveries, new alliances formed by competing firms, mergers and bankruptcies, and they do not rely on the services of any particular institutions to gain access to this type of information. The informal relationships these firms develop with clients, suppliers, consultants or other entrepreneurs – often outside the Paris Region – represent one of their main sources of information.

15.3.2 The case of optics-photonics cluster

Most firms with optics-photonics know-how have developed in the framework of the 'Great Technological Programmes' implemented by the French governments between the Second World War and the 1970s. These programmes were aimed at boosting not only the defence industry, but also the sectors considered strategic by the state (nuclear, space, aeronautic technologies, telecommunications, etc.). Their objective was to equip France with key technologies, in order, particularly, to strengthen the country's independence vis-à-vis the other superpowers (Mustar and Laredo 2002).

The creation of the CEA,[3] which took place in the context of these programmes, largely benefited the Greater Paris Region by initiating the emergence, and during the 1950s, the development of the optics-photonics industry in various districts of the Region. Several phases of development of the optics-photonics industry can be distinguished (Decoster, Matteaccioli and Tabariés 2004). The first phase, between 1950 and 1960, saw the development of subcontracting firms created by former employees (qualified workers and supervisors) of the CEA. In the 1970s and 80s, a second phase saw the emergence and development of a new type of SMEs with greater technical know-how and involved in more complex subcontracting relations consisting of rich and intense knowledge exchange. In the 1990s, after years of development, the optics industry of the Paris Region faced an important workforce reduction (of approximately 30 per cent). These elements underlie the analysis of strategic groups of firms and of the interactions between businesses and institutions within the Paris optics-photonics cluster.

15.3.2.1 The strategic categories of firms in the optics-photonics cluster of the Paris Region

The optics-photonics cluster comprises four strategic categories of firms that differ significantly in terms of how they innovate and position themselves on the market, in terms of their capacity of negotiation with suppliers and clients and of competitive pressure. These differences have an impact on the way in which each group interacts with its environment to meet its specific needs.

A. THE 'RADICAL TECHNOLOGICAL BREAKTHROUGH' STRATEGIC GROUP

What characterizes 'technological breakthrough' start-ups is the fact that their goal is to introduce, on the market, competitive products based on an entirely new technology. The solutions developed on the basis of recent knowledge do not necessarily have a pre-identified market and were not developed in order to respond to a specific need of the market. This is the *techno-push* approach.[4] Their ability to impose themselves on the market depends, among other things, on the cost/performance ratio of their new technology and on their being able to set new standards on the market. For these reasons, the 'breakthrough' start-ups of the Paris Region develop strategic relations with public research laboratories (access to infrastructures, to expertise, etc.) but also with 'early users' (operationalization phase/processes resulting from new knowledge). Our studies show that the laboratories these start-ups interact with are, for the most part, located in the Paris Region. And even though proximity seems to count in their relations with research laboratories, it does not seem to be central to their interactions with 'early users'. These key characteristics determine how 'breakthrough' start-ups interact with the local institutions that support innovation.

B. THE 'HIGH-TECH SME' STRATEGIC GROUP

The 'high-tech' SMEs are characterized by a high level of internal R&D that enables them to develop and market many innovations on a regular basis. They tend to specialize in one generic technology (infrared, laser technology, etc.) on the basis of which they develop a wide range of products for use in one or two sectors (healthcare, automobiles, aeronautics, environment, defence, telecommunication, etc.). Hindered by constant competition from substitute products (electronics, electro mechanics, etc.), these SMEs have little negotiating power vis-à-vis their clients (generally large firms). As a result of these characteristics 'high-tech' SMEs mostly develop relations with other firms in the framework of projects of development/adaptation of existing products to the needs of the market, for example, and also, to a lesser extent, with research laboratories so as to gain access to expensive infrastructure and specific skills.

C. THE 'HIGH-TECHNICALITY SMES' STRATEGIC GROUP

The 'high-technicality' SMEs are characterized by a high level of technical specialization, and by the production of limited series of products and customized goods for use in precisely defined market niches. The firms in this strategic group have little negotiating power with their clients (large firms, large research laboratories) because they supply small quantities of non-strategic goods; but they enjoy strong negotiation power with their suppliers. There is no identified, immediate threat from substitute products, which is due, among other things, to the weakness of the markets, which do not attract the interest of firms that target mass markets (large firms with many facilities in low cost countries). But they are likely sooner or later to face competition from new substitute technologies with more favourable cost/performance ratios, and which might then endanger the very existence of the firms that have adopted this strategy. Because of these characteristics, these SMEs mostly develop subcontractor relations with large corporation or research laboratories. They seldom interact with these large firms or research laboratories as partners, nor do they participate in the co-development of products.

D. THE 'LARGE LEADING FIRMS' STRATEGIC GROUP

One of the characteristics of these large 'leading' firms is the internationalization of their R&D and production operations. Their activities have spillover effects on the local economy in that they purchase products from suppliers, develop technologies with SMEs or research laboratories and determine current and future consumer preferences in terms of products and services. Their negotiating power with clients (the state or private market) is balanced and they enjoy strong negotiating power with their suppliers. Finally, the short and medium-term threat of competition from substitute products is rather weak. The latter is all the weaker as the large corporations have the financial capacity to buy the firms that develop products and processes based on radically innovative technologies.

15.3.2.2 The different kinds of firm–institution interactions within the optics-photonics cluster

The existence of different strategic groups of firms in the optics-photonics cluster is related to that of different behaviours in terms of interactions with external actors. An examination of the different types of interactions shows that each group of firms develops specific types of relational networks so as to strengthen its innovation and production capacities and therefore be competitive on the market.

A. THE RELATIONS BETWEEN OPTICS-PHOTONICS FIRMS AND FINANCIAL INSTITUTIONS

The initial stage in the development of 'technological breakthrough' start-ups necessitates close and frequent interactions with financial institutions. The times has not yet come to market, or even develop, a product: in the initial stage they must focus on ensuring that the project they are undertaking is viable from a technical, market and industrial property viewpoint. This stage cannot therefore be financed by investors who demand profitability, and necessitates the intervention of public (or para-governmental) institutions that propose pre-start-up funds. Three sources of pre-start-up funds are available in the Paris Region: the public research organizations at the origin of the innovative idea, the French Research Ministry via the programme of financial contribution to the creation of new innovative firms, and, finally, 'local initiative platforms' (Scientipole Initiative). In the second (creation) and third (initial development) stages, the financing question becomes even more crucial; indeed start-ups depend on the financial support of the different institutions in order to be able to launch their activities, develop products and test them on the market. The conventional financial market and venture capitalists are relatively absent during these early stages, but this absence is compensated by start-up funds often provided by the state or by institutional investors (CDC, OSEO, Region, IdF, CG, etc.). During the fourth and fifth stages of development (take-off and growth) the sales of the start-up increase, its products get adopted by the market, and the firm needs financial support in order to be able to pursue its commercial development and to continue innovating on an already existing product. This is when venture capitalists and banks come into play.

High-tech SMEs forge close relations with financial institutions, in the context of individual or cooperative innovation projects undertaken with large corporations or public research laboratories. This second category of financial support enables them to gain access to a network of firms (large corporations, particularly) and to share the risks and costs associated with R&D projects. Thus, 'pôles de compétitivité', which have gained momentum in the last few years, have attracted this category of firms. 'High-technicality' SMEs also seek public funding to help them develop innovations internally, but they have fewer relations with financial institutions, because their activities are less centred on innovation and their financial situation is more precarious.

Finally, the large firms interact mostly with institutions that provide funds to help finance R&D projects or large-scale industrial development projects. Thus, the large 'leading' firms develop close relations with local institutions ('pôles de compétitivité' in particular), but also national (ANR, AII) and European institutions (through the Research and Development Framework Programme or of European programs outside the EU).

THE RELATIONS BETWEEN OPTICS-PHOTONICS FIRMS AND 'KNOWLEDGE TRANSFER' AND 'INFRASTRUCTURE SUPPORT' INSTITUTIONS

The relations between 'technological breakthrough' start-ups and 'infrastructure support' institutions such as incubators are central in the first stages of the creation of a new firm. Once the project has matured and the technological concept is validated, premises must be found, and this is where relations with institutions such as incubators come into play. Thus, the relations between 'infrastructure support' institutions and start-ups are vital for the latter, for they involve much more that the mere provision of premises to firms. Indeed, incubators not only offer premises at preferential rates, but they also provide coaching services to new firms. Specialized incubators also help start-ups connect with other institutions that provide support to firms.

'High-tech' and 'high-technicality' SMEs and the large 'leading' firms interact less than other types of firms with the institutions that provide infrastructure, because they have no difficulties in finding appropriate premises in the Paris Region.

THE RELATIONS BETWEEN OPTICS-PHOTONICS FIRMS AND 'NETWORKING' INSTITUTIONS

When 'technological breakthrough' technologies reach the stage when they can launch a product on the market, their goal is to reinforce their position in the industrial world. Thus, the start-ups that spin off from public research organizations switch from a research-oriented to an industrial-oriented network. At this stage of development, production and commercialization of new products firms are confronted with problems related to human resources management, to the growth of their market (increase of production capacity, commercial strategy, recruitment of new production staff) and to its pursuit of R&D activities. At this stage, firms need to position themselves strongly within innovation networks (SPL, CCI, 'pôles de compétitivité') so as to be able to develop relations with new partners.

High-tech SMEs also interact with institutions that help them establish links with thematic networks (SPL, 'pôles de compétitivité') so as to expand their relations with local organizations, increase market and R&D partnership opportunities, and gain access to information concerning the activities of other local organizations (competitors, clients, suppliers, public research etc.). 'High-technicality' SMEs use networking institutions differently to the way they are used by the previous two strategic groups. Their primary goal is to increase their market shares rather than to develop technological partnerships. Thus, this group of SMEs uses networking institutions as a way to gain access to new prime contractors.

Large firms also interact with institutions that develop innovation networks, in order to establish links with all the actors in the local clusters (start-ups, SMEs, laboratories). Large firms use these networks as a complementary channel of access to locally produced knowledge. And so, in this case, it is the networks that seek to mobilize large firms, so that they can benefit from the latter's expertise and innovation and business capacities.

15.4 Discussion

This analysis has enabled us to reveal the similarities and differences between the two clusters (see Table 15.1 below). These results seem to confirm the importance of the role played by local institutions in the creation and the short and long-term development of clusters of high-tech firms. However, beyond the institutional framework put in place in order to provide support to high-tech firms, there exist significant differences according to the various high-tech sectors observed. We note, for example, that an important number of 'knowledge transfer' institutions such as incubators are present in the biotech cluster, which tends to indicate that these institutions play an essential role in the creation of new enterprises and in the transfer of academic knowledge. Most firms present in the cluster were created and developed in an incubator, which is hardly surprising in that the biotech sector in France is relatively young.

The first generation of biotech firms, which developed and manufactured products of traditional biotechnology, emerged in the 1980s. But the biotech sector only got truly organized in the late 1990s with the emergence of the second generation of firms, which concentrated on molecular biology. As for the optics-photonics industry, it is more mature as it started in the 1960s–70s. This is the reason why organizations such 'network facilitators' play an essential role in the organization of the optics-photonics cluster. Firms that belong to industries that have reached a high level of technological maturity turn to institutions that can help them develop links with new partners, find new clients, and more generally that can help them reinitiate the process of innovation, which is essential to their ability to maintain a competitive advantage in the face of increasing global competition.

Table. 15.1 The specificities of the relations between the biotech and the optics-photonics clusters and their institutional environment, in the Greater Paris Region

Firm /institution interactions	Financial institutions	Infrastructure and knowledge transfer institutions	Networking institutions
Biotech cluster	Public funds for new firms' start-up and creation stages. Firms struggle to finance the more advanced stages of production and commercialization. Shortage of venture capital.	Incubators and organizations that promote the transfer of technological and academic knowledge play an essential role in the generation of new biotech firms. The support offered by these institutions is often limited to the provision of premises and of access to internal databases.	Local marketing policies aimed at attracting potential partners for local firms. The firms perceive these policies as having little impact. They conduct a permanent information watch so as to establish links with new networks.
Electro-optics cluster	Start-ups, high-tech SMEs and large firms have close and frequent interactions with financial institutions. Goal: develop projects elaborated internally or reduce the costs of (individual or collaborative) innovation projects.	All categories of firms develop relations with institutions that provide technological infrastructure. But these interactions are only vital for the development of 'technological breakthrough' start-ups; start-ups which are particularly dependent on these institutions' support during the first stages of their development.	All categories of firms develop relations with networking institutions: start-ups seek to strengthen their position in the industrial world, by finding 'early users' for example. High-tech SMEs look for partners to develop their R&D or industrial projects. High-technicality SMEs seek access to new markets.

15.5 Key conclusions

The aim of this article has been to contribute to the debate on the institutional dimensions of clusters, by analyzing the various tools that are available to local actors and how they are used by entrepreneurs. The studies conducted on the biotech and optics-photonics clusters of the Greater Paris Region have enabled us firstly to distinguish four main categories of local institutions: financial institutions, institutions that provide infrastructure, knowledge transfer institutions and, finally, networking institutions. Secondly, we have shown that the relations between firms and their institutional environment vary according to the category the firms fall into (and according to) their level of development, in terms of production and innovation.

Notes

1 See 'Data and method of analysis of the biotech cluster' in the Appendix.
2 Commissariat à l'Energie Atomique (the French Atomic Energy Commission), formerly called the Centre for Nuclear Research.
3 The source of the new knowledge is the research conducted by large public laboratories, which are at the forefront of their respective technological fields, and have the ability to convert the results of their research into products.

References

Aharonson S. B., Baum J. A. C. and Feldman, M. P. (2004), *Industrial Clustering and the Returns to Inventive Activity: Canadian Biotechnology Firms, 1991–2000*, Danish research Unit of Industrial Dynamics (DRUID) Working Paper, 04–3.
——. (2007), 'Desperately seeking spillover? Increasing returns, social cohesion and the location of new entrants in geographic and technological space', *Industrial and Corporate Change*, 16(1): 89–130.
Bellon B., Plunket A. and Boufaden N. (2005), *Etude sur les Biotechnologies en Ile de France*, http://www.adislab.net/docs/RAPPORT_CDC.pdf .
BIPE (2003), 'Data and method of analysis of the electro-optics cluster', Study provided for the Paris Region Opticsvalley Cluster Organization, Paris: Mimeo.
Coriat B. and Weinstein O. (2002), 'Organizations, firms and institutions in the generation of innovation', *Research Policy*, 31: 273–90.
Decoster E., Matteaccioli A. and Tabariés M. (2004), 'Les étapes d'une dynamique de territorialisation: le pôle optique en Ile-de-France', *Géographie, Economie, Société*, 6(4): 383–413.
Dunning J., (2000), *Regions, Globalization and the Knowledge-Based Economy*, Oxford: Oxford University Press.
Giuliani E. and Bell M., (2005), 'The micro-determinants of meso-level learning and innovation: evidence from a Chilean wine cluster', *Research Policy*, February, 34(1): 47–68.
Hakanson L. (2005), 'Epistemic communities and cluster dynamics: on the role of knowledge in industrial districts', *Industry and Innovation*, 4, December: 433–63.
Karlsson C., Johansson B. and Stough R. (eds.) (2005), *Industrial Clusters and Inter-Firm Networks*, London: Edward Elgar.
Lourimi S. and Torre A. (2007), 'Le secteur de l'Optique en Ile de France Sud. Un cluster?' *Territoires du Futur*, May, 6: 57–68.

Lundvall B. A. (1992), *National Systems of Innovation: Towards a Theory of Innovation and Interactive Learning.* London: Pinter.

Martin R. and Sunley P. (2003), 'Deconstructing clusters: chaotic concept or political panacea?' *Journal of Economic Geography*, 3(1): 5–35.

Mustar P. and Larédo P. (2002), 'Innovation and research policy in France (1980–2000) or the disappearance of the Colbertist State', *Research Policy*, 31(1): 55–72.

Nelson R. R. (1993), *National Systems of Innovation: A Comparative Study.* Oxford: Oxford University Press.

OECD (2005), *Business Clusters, Promoting Enterprise in Central and Eastern Europe*, Paris: OECD.

OST (2006), *Indicateurs de Sciences et de Technologies*, sous la direction de Ghislaine Filliateau, Paris: Economica.

Plunket A. and Boufaden N. (2007), *Quels Business Modèles pour les Entreprises de Biotechnologie de l'Ile-de-France?* Working paper ADUS, University Paris South.

Polanyi M. (1962) 'Tacit knowing: it's bearing on some problems of philosophy', *Review of Modern Physics*, October 34(4): 601–16.

Swann, P. and Prevezer, M. (1996), 'A comparison of the dynamics of industrial clustering in computing and biotechnology', *Research Policy*, 25(7): 1139–57.

Traoré, N. (2004), 'Canadian Biotech firms' creative capacity: on the role of absorptive capacity, relational capital, learning, and firm characteristics', *International Journal of Biotechnology*, 6(1): 1–19.

World Bank (2002), http:/www.worldbank.org/poverty/scapital/whatso.htm

Appendix

Data and method of analysis of the biotech cluster

The Greater Paris Region is home to the largest number of French biotech firms (approximately 40 per cent). The share of the region in the national scientific and technological production – estimated by the number of European patents applied for or granted in the fields of biotechnologies and pharmaceutical technologies – is 57.1 per cent. These firms are located across the whole of the region but there are a few agglomerations of firms in the region (Paris, Evry Genopole, Saclay). The Paris Region benefits from the presence of a world-renowned fundamental research infrastructure. It is the national leader in the fields of medical research, fundamental biology and applied biology/ecology, in terms of publications. This situation contrasts with that of other European countries such as the United Kingdom or Germany, where the regional distribution is more uniform. We find that the Paris Region is more specialized in medical research than in fundamental biology and applied biology/ecology and that it ranks third behind the PACA and Rhone Alpes regions in these two scientific fields (OST 2006).

Biotechnologies are more and more defined as a set of generic technologies that are applied to several domains such as human healthcare, agriculture, the environment, agri-food and bio-informatics (Swann and Prevezer 1996; Traoré 2004; Aharonson, *et al.* 2007). For this reason it is difficult to identify biotech firms and evaluate their R&D activities on the sole basis of the nomenclature of

French activities (the NAF code). In order to study the characteristics of the biotech firms located in the Paris Region, it is necessary to identify the firms by using the main public directories available. The study is based on a sample of 61 enterprises selected following several data collection stages and after cross-referencing the data from different directories:

- The 'Biotechnologies France' directory (managed by the Research Ministry).
- The Genopole directory (Evry industrial cluster).
- The directory of the Association for the Development of biotechnologies and bio-industries.
- The 'France biotechnologies' directory (professional association of French biotech companies and their partners).

Synthesizing these directories made it possible to establish a list of 458 private law companies located in the Paris Region and participating in biotechnology activities (headquarters, R&D, production, commercialization, service provision, consulting agencies, and venture capital). These firms we contacted telephonically so as to identify those which perform R&D in the field of biotechnologies and fulfil the following criteria: (1) perform R&D in the Paris Region; (2) use and/or produce biotechnologies in the R&D process; this exercise reduced the list to 244 companies. Among them, 107 agreed to answer a questionnaire, between June 2004 and June 2005; 61 of the answered questionnaires could be used.

This survey has been conducted in the framework of a research project implemented by the ADIS (Paris XI University) and received the support of the Research Institute of the Deposit and Consignment Office CDC. Once the survey was completed, a report presenting the main results and an analysis of the structure of the biotech industry in the Paris Region was written (Bellon, Plunket and Boufaden 2005).

Data and method of analysis of the electro-optics cluster

The Paris Region is home to over 550 firms with activities in the field of optics-photonics and employing over 16,700 people; that is about half of the country's potential workforce in this field. Within this industrial network, 123 companies employing 6400 people have been identified as conducting activities of production and development of goods and services based on optics-photonics technologies. Most of the companies are concentrated in the south-west of the Paris Region and more specifically in the Essonne and the Yvelines *Départements*, in which is concentrated approximately one quarter of the total workforce of the electro-optics industry of the Paris Region, and over one third of the total public research workforce (BIPE 2003). The main markets of optics-photonics companies are those of information and communication technologies (optics-photonics components), the spatial and defence industry (infrared imagery, missile guidance systems, laser rangefinders, etc.), healthcare and life sciences (lasers in the field of biotechnologies, digital radiology), scientific instrumentation (microscopy and lithography making use of far-ultraviolet radiation), industrial production (laser prototyping, optical sensors, laser marking, etc.) and other markets (e.g. light emitting diodes that have higher luminous efficiency than traditional incandescent bulbs).

The study is based on a sample of 44 economic actors in the optics-photonics cluster of the Paris Region. These actors were identified using the databases developed by Opticsvalley. We conducted interviews with representatives of 21 industrial entrepreneurs (the Greater Paris Region is home to 123 industrial firms specialized in optics-photonics), nine public research laboratories, six organizations providing support to enterprises (organizations for economic development, local chambers, CRITT), five public departments (e.g. Regional Council, General Councils, agglomeration communities) and three financial institutions. The questions were related to the organization of the firms' activities, their innovation strategies, to how they network and to the role of geographical proximity. This study has been conducted in the framework of a research project implemented by INRA (UMR SAD-APT) and the ADIS (Paris XI University) and received the support of 6th Framework programme of the EEC.

16 The development of local-global linkages in the biotech districts in Germany

Local embeddedness or distance learning?

Dirk Fornahl (BAW Institute for Regional Economic Research and Chung Anh Tran (Universität Karlsruhe, Institute for Economic Policy Research – IWW)

16.1 Introduction

Empirical observations reveal that in a wide range of industries' firms tend to cluster in geographic space – biotechnology is no exception. In the United States, one finds biotechnology concentrations in San Diego, South San Francisco, the Research Triangle Park in North Carolina, and the region off Route 128, just north of Boston (for a more detailed mapping, see Stuart and Sorenson 2003). In Germany, biotechnology clusters are located for example in Bavaria and in the Rhineland (Zeller 2001).[1]

Hence, the biotechnology sector is located in specific clusters (Dohse 2001), but the question is why such clustering occurs? Since biotechnology as a science-driven and knowledge-intensive industry draws most critically on knowledge as a resource, which is relatively mobile, traditional explanations based on transportation cost arguments do not hold.

Explanations in biotechnology have focused mainly on Marshall's (1890) ideas on agglomeration externalities (Marshall 1890). Under these accounts, co-location of specialized firms allows these firms to operate more efficiently by sharing some critical resource, such as knowledge or information (Muscio 2006), the output of some critical supplier (e.g. of reagents; Feldman and Francis 2003) or the supply for some nearby pharmaceutical or agro-chemical firms (Feldman 2003). Biotechnology firms may also jointly profit from their proximity to universities, medical schools or research hospitals which provide employees, innovative research and the potential for clinical trials. Others, however, have suggested that geographic concentrations are based on positive externalities generated by diversity, where knowledge spillovers occur between organizations with different background (Jacobs 1969), and not on specialization as in Marshall's approach. On the contrary, a too narrow specialization can hamper future development (Grabher 1993).

No matter whether externalities of the Marshall or Jacobs's type prevail, the core question is how the firms in the region can access the knowledge and therefore profit from the co-location. In this paper we concentrate on one type of transfer channel, namely cooperation or networks. Although (informal) social networks play an important role in accessing a critical resources such as knowledge (Sorenson and Audia 2000), we especially focus on formal knowledge interactions represented by co-patenting activities in the following.[2] As pointed out, firms can profit from being co-located to other firms from which they can source knowledge in order to produce new products or introduce new processes. Studies of declining clusters illustrate that such economic advantages are not everlasting and that the decline of clusters even seems to be caused by its very advantages in the past (Martin and Sunley 2006; Grabher 1993). The reason for a decline not only lies in an exhausted regional technological trajectory, but also in the long-existing, closed and homogeneous local networks, which are unable to renew the cluster by integrating new and often external knowledge. Thus, the same local networks which generated the regional advantage can lead to a decline when their rigidity results in losing the ability to adjust to a changing environment. In order to sustain a regional competitive advantage, local interactions and outside linkages must be balanced in order to generate synergies and to introduce new knowledge at the same time (Albino, *et al.* 1999; Bathelt, *et al.* 2004).

This paper addresses the balance between local and external linkages and cooperative knowledge generation in general. The remainder of this paper presents this idea in greater detail by proceeding as follows: Section 16.2 provides a detailed background for the interaction of local and external knowledge interaction. The empirical part of the paper starts with a short overview of the activities in four German biotechnology regions (Section 16.3). In Section 16.4 we analyze the knowledge interaction of agents coming from these regions operating in biotechnology. In Section 16.5 we discuss the core findings of the empirical study and give an outlook.

16.2 Theoretical background

Biotechnology is a knowledge-based industry and, hence, the most important resource required for the success of a biotech firm is knowledge and intellectual capital. A firm must have access to the most recent scientific and technical knowledge in order to successfully develop and market a product. In general there are two external possessors of knowledge that a biotechnology firm needs. These are university and research organizations in biotechnology and other closely related fields (Zucker and Darby 1996). The other sources are other existing biotechnology and pharmaceutical companies (Haug 1995). In the following we analyze which type of organization is central for the knowledge sourcing of the firms in the regions under investigation.

Two aspects hinder the acquisition of external knowledge related to biotechnology: although many research results are published in scientific papers which are publicly available, knowledge in biotechnology is not only complex, but also often tacit, which both increase the difficulty and costs of knowledge transfer. The transfer of complex knowledge – where the results depend on the steps involved in getting there – or tacit knowledge typically requires that the sender helps the recipient to identify and correct mistakes in transmission (Sorenson, Rivkin and Fleming 2006) or intensive face-to-face interaction between the recipient and the possessor of the knowledge is necessary (Polyani 1966). Hence, knowledge in biotechnology is generated by close contact with experts in the field or from being an expert oneself (Owen-Smith and Powell 2004; Stuart, Ozdemir and Ding 2007). In this paper we focus on the former by examining how biotechnology firms can source external knowledge by being in close contact with other agents and organization. We concentrate on direct interaction in which firms can collaborate and in doing so learn from each other, leaving aside other ways to acquire external knowledge such as social contacts to employees of other firms or labour mobility.

Inside a region unintended and intended information (Muscio 2006) and knowledge spillovers take place. Local spillovers represent all the unintended knowledge and information exchange between organizations. On the other hand, intended transfer occurs based on mutual exchange relations (Malmberg and Maskell 2002) in the local setting as well and is at least partly spatially focused. This spatial focus is caused by the fact that by and large individuals as well as firms are embedded in a social and geographic context. A number of factors contribute to the local character of social networks. First and foremost, the formation and maintenance of a relationship requires that two individuals meet and lasting relationships emerge through repeated interactions (Blau 1964). This is more likely in close geographic proximity because geographic as well as social proximity affect the costs of interaction, and consequently the odds that relationships emerge and persist over time. Distance imposes two types of costs. First, distance raises the direct costs of interaction because travel requires both time and money (Zipf 1949). Second, as the distance between two actors lengthens, the likelihood of an intervening opportunity – an equally preferred but closer contact – increases as well (Stouffer 1940).

Since these regional social networks structure the interaction of agents and provide a framework for knowledge exchange and cooperation, knowledge spreads more easily inside a region. Due to the manifold exchange processes within a specific location, the transaction costs are lower and the efficiency of knowledge transfer is higher for local interactions. Furthermore, a larger diversity of organizations is perceived within than outside this location. Using the biotechnology industry in the US as an example Phene, *et al.* (2006) find out that technological distances are easier bridged between firms in the US than with partners abroad. Especially if a frequent exchange of knowledge and quick feedback processes are necessary, as in the case of complex biotechnology knowledge, the locality of interactions assists knowledge transfer. Though social relationships can and do span geographic and social spaces, these 'distant' ties remain the exception rather than the rule. Therefore, the ability to secure resources from other regions, which depends on these relationships, tends to decrease with geographic distance.

Although these local interactions support the innovativeness and growth of the local firms, disadvantages might arise as well because the firms in the regions become too narrowly specialized and internally focused, losing their ability for renewal and adaptation to changing external conditions (Tichy 2000; Grabher 1993). The region can become negatively locked in to its previously successful development path with too little heterogeneity and diversity to generate new ideas (Jacobs 1969). The reason for a lock-in lies in the long-existing, closed and homogeneous networks, which are unable to renew the cluster by integrating new and often external knowledge. Furthermore, most biotechnology firms compete on a world market and accordingly also have to access knowledge their competitors from regions or nations outside their home region have access to. The connections between the firms within the cluster and firms respectively organizations outside the cluster integrate such necessary new knowledge into the region and keep the networks open (Albino, *et al.* 1999; Bathelt, *et al.* 2004). This leads to a situation in which the internal (with a focus on exploitation) and external linkages (with a focus on exploration) must be balanced. This means that in order to profit from local synergies and the advantages of local interactions as described above there also has to be access to knowledge by external linkages at the same time. The firms in a region have to sustain the balance between the internal convergence and divergence by the external knowledge. As pointed out before, such external linkages are costly and they require information on potential partners as well as reputation to persuade these partners to form a link. Hence, not all firms of a region will be able to establish external linkages.

Cohen and Levinthal (1990) argue that the utilization of external knowledge depends on the absorptive capacity of the firms. Beside this firm-specific capability, the utilization of knowledge also depends on the regional characteristics that make knowledge accessible. There is a firm- and a region-specific dimension to the ability and necessity to access external knowledge which are discussed briefly below.

While small and especially young firms rely on the regional social networks for resource access, older and larger firms have other possibilities to access such resources. The importance of proximity to these resources and the relevance of local social networks decline as the industry matures and firms grow or become older (Stuart and Sorenson 2003). First they might already have the resources inside their own firm because they generated them on their own (e.g. the firm accumulated tacit knowledge through learning-by-doing) or merged with larger (pharmaceutical) firms. Second, they have established new (more far reaching) channels to access resources in other locations. Hence, the impact of geographic proximity is reduced when firms grow larger and older. Based on these findings in our analysis we focus on the type of firms sourcing knowledge in order to examine whether different types of organizations show different types of behaviour concerning their external linkages.

Additionally, the diversity of clusters must refer to their size (Menzel and Fornahl 2007). Large clusters like the Silicon Valley consist of many firms with a great diversity of technologies and knowledge. And also the industrial districts of the Third Italy represent clusters, albeit smaller and in a very specific form. The size and the technological diversity of clusters must correspond to each other:

large clusters can contain a larger diversity than small clusters and nevertheless generate sufficient synergies between firms because of their size. Accordingly, smaller clusters must be strongly focused in order to be able to utilize synergies. This also increases the likelihood that smaller cluster have relatively more local linkages or very few and very specific external linkages to other organizations holding knowledge necessary for their innovative activities. We examine whether clusters of different size show a different pattern regarding their (external) linkages and interactions.

From the discussion above it can be summarized that knowledge is one of the core resources necessary to generate product and process innovation in the biotechnology industry. In this they are at least partly dependent on external knowledge sourcing to keep up with new scientific research and processing skills. Important channels for such external knowledge sourcing processes are local and external linkages. As is presented in the next section, the analysis focuses on formal linkages represented by co-patenting activities. Since the type of exchange partners (knowledge source and recipient) plays a role in the necessity and possibility of knowledge exchange, the paper discusses the characteristics of these partners (e.g. size or age of organization). Furthermore, the location of the external partners and the characteristics of the regions, especially the size of the regional cluster, are examined. The empirical study concentrates on four specific regions in Germany which are briefly presented in the following.

16.3 Unit of analysis: sketching the BioRegio regions

In 1995 the German Federal Ministry of Education and Research (BMBF) announced a competition to strengthen the German biotechnology industry. Policy makers realized that the biotechnology sector became a cornerstone of economic growth in knowledge-based economies. Cooke (2001) argues that in this regard Germany lags 20 years behind the US in respect to the commercialization of the biotechnology industry and even 10 years behind the UK. Therefore, the federal government recognized that they had to intensify their endeavours to wipe out the deficiencies of the German biotechnology sector which was caused by the late start of this emerging industry in Germany. The BMBF designed a contest at regional level. With regional cooperation between private and public organizations, e.g. private enterprises, universities, research institutions etc., in 17 regions organizations were asked to present concepts for biotechnology research and commercialization. Some of the regions consist of just one city, such as Freiburg, Jena etc. The majority, however, are compositions of bigger cities which lie close to each other such as Braunschweig-Göttingen-Hannover or involve cooperation of whole federal states such as Berlin-Brandenburg. The contest was not only meant to boost research and development activities; the government also wanted to stimulate the patent activities of German researchers. The proclaimed goal was to promote Germany to become the leading player in Europe in the biotechnology sector. In November 1996 an independent jury selected the three winner regions: Munich, Rhineland (Cologne, Düsseldorf, Wuppertal and Aachen) and the Rhine-Neckar Triangle

(Heidelberg, Mannheim and Ludwigshafen). Jena convinced the jury to give them a 'special vote'. The sum of 90 million euro was divided into 25 million euro for each of the winning regions and 15 million euro for Jena.

The underlying criteria by which the regions where chosen contain nine points (BMBF 1996). The jury did not only count the scale and numbers of existing companies, research facilities and universities with an affinity towards biotechnology. They also considered the surrounding infrastructure for new biotechnology ventures such as supporting facilities, e.g. patent offices, consulting firms etc., cooperation between biotechnology research facilities and hospitals, and credible strategies for the future.

16.3.1 A brief summary of the BioRegio regions

In the case of the BioRegio Munich decisive facts such as the scientific environment consisting of research organizations and universities generating a large amount of qualified employees and high-quality research, the existing cooperation between hospitals and biotechnology enterprises and the short distance to the European Patent Office (EPO) convinced the jury. Regarding the existing enterprise-hospital cooperation it is not surprising that the biotechnology enterprises in the BioRegio Munich have a focus on drugs and medications.

BioRegio Rhine-Neckar Triangle excels with the number of multinational firms, e.g. BASF, Roche, Abbot, Merck etc. Located between the universities of Heidelberg and Mannheim, these firms have traditionally fostered interaction between science and industry. The access to a qualified labour force, not only for the biotechnology sector but also for the IT sector, is an advantage of this region.

Multinational firms such as Bayer, Henkel, Cognis etc., characterize the BioRegio Rhineland. Beside the global firm linkages, the biggest German urban area presents a number of technology parks situated near the universities and research facilities of the bigger cities in this region. Attracting labour forces from all over the world with a multinational environment, e.g. the cities of Cologne and Düsseldorf, the BioRegio Rhineland offers a fruitful ground for an emerging knowledge-based industry.

The 'special vote' for the BioRegio Jena is a result of new orientation in the biotechnology sector. Strongly supported by the state Thuringia Jena focuses on the creation and production of instruments and devices for the biotechnology industry. BioRegio Jena is, in contrast to the winners of the BioRegio contest, a more rural area; with a population of less than 100,000 inhabitants the human resource pool lags far behind the other regions. On the other hand, over 30 per cent of the Jena workforce holds a higher education degree. Jena is also the most important centre for optical technology and precision mechanics in Germany, which was thought to affect the potential to develop bio-instruments successfully.

All in all one can say that the three winners of the BioRegio contest resemble each other in some aspects, but also have large differences in other aspects. Similarities can be found in the existence of well-known universities and research facilities and hence a great pool of qualified employees and scientific knowledge.

Apart from the BioRegio Munich, the other two BioRegio regions, Rhineland and Rhine-Neckar, are characterized by the existence of multinational firms in the area of pharmaceuticals. The difference in the specialization of the BioRegio regions in large parts can be traced back to these multinational firms. Thus, Rhineland and Rhine-Neckar focus on chemical and pharmaceutical biotechnology. In contrast to the other two regions, Munich concentrates more on the development of medical biotechnology. BioRegio Jena can be seen as an exception in all aspects. With the small number of inhabitants and the focus on bio-instruments this region differs strongly from the other three regions.

We chose these four regions for the following reasons: obviously these regions planned to become the centres of biotechnology in Germany. That means we already have a cluster or, respectively, they were meant to become clusters. Jena was chosen to analyze whether size matters for the internal and external knowledge linkages. We did not consider Berlin or the BioRegio region Berlin-Brandenburg, because it was not selected during the BioRegio contest as recipient of any public funding.

16.4 Empirical analysis

16.4.1 Data background

For our analysis we refer to the so-called *PATSTAT April 2007* database. The *EPO*[3] *Worldwide Statistical Patent Database* was created by the Patent Statistics Task Force.[4] To isolate the necessary data we used four criteria.

First, we isolated all patents filed at the European Patent Organization (EPO) and the World Intellectual Property Organization (WIPO). Therefore we assumed that all patents which are important or which are mentioned to be important for the global market are filed at the EPO or went through the filing process of the WIPO.

Next we identified all patents which occurred in the technology field 'bio-technology'. According to the OST/INPI/ISI concordance in the version of 2000 which links the IPC codes on the patents to 30 technology fields, we identified the biotechnology patents by their IPC codes.

For the analysis of the origin of the patents we searched the address for all persons in Germany (persons with country code 'DE') in the PATSTAT database. Therefore we built a list of zip codes related to the BioRegio regions. To take the commuters into account we did not just add all 'Kreise' (districts) of the mentioned cities, but also considered the hinterland of those cities. The separation of core and periphery was kept throughout the whole analysis. By merging the list of persons' location with the patent list it was possible to identify all patents with at least one applicant or at least one inventor from the BioRegio regions.

For the definition of the time frame we decided to take two periods in order to be able to analyze changes over time and to especially examine whether BioRegio might have affected the degree of external linkages. Period one includes the six years from 1993 to 1998. Even though the decision of the BioRegio contest was in November 1996 we took into account that effects which can be measured by patent activities only take effect after around 18 months (time of publication). Period two includes the eight years after the BioRegio contest from 1999 to 2006. The second period is longer because the number of patents decreased for the last two years due to the delay between application for a patent and the publication.

After generating this list of patent applications and their information on applicants, inventors etc., it was possible to perform the subsequent analysis. The final table included 7329 biotechnology patents for Germany as a whole and 3730 patents which have at least one applicant or inventor from the BioRegio regions. The latter list is the basis for our analysis.

Altogether we detected 11,001 applicants and 36,733 inventors. The maximum numbers were 10 applicants for one patent and even 40 inventors for one patent. On average there was one applicant and four inventors per patent.

16.4.2 Patenting activities in the BioRegio regions

Patent activities in emerging markets have always been dynamic. The patent activity in the German biotechnology sector is no exception (see Figure 16.1). After a slow start in 1993 and 1994 the number of patent applications began to rise rapidly to their height in 2001. The decreasing number of patent applications likely refers to the burst of the New-Economy-Bubble.

The recession stopped the source of venture capital and, hence, the necessary financial resources for further explorations. Our analysis shows that this process can be measured for Germany and the BioRegio regions as well.

Due to the different sizes of the BioRegio regions the patent activity has different characteristics. Jena has a small number of patent applications compared to the other regions. Taking the number of inhabitants into consideration Munich,

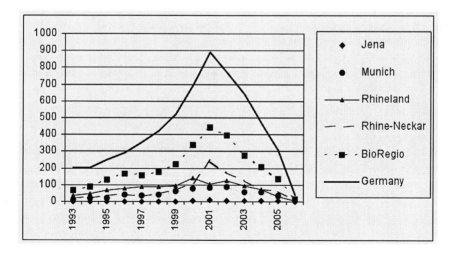

Figure 16.1 Weighted[5] biotechnology patent activity in Germany (DE).

Rhineland and Rhine-Neckar show figures of comparable size, with Rhine-Neckar being the strongest region in total and relative counts. Jena, however, still lags behind the three winners of the BioRegio contest. The strong decrease in 2005 and 2006 should not be overestimated. One should keep in mind that figures for patent statistics always have a delay of at least 18 months.

A closer look at Figure 16.1 shows that the German overall patent activities decrease much faster than the BioRegio regions with the exception of the Rhine-Neckar. The reason for the relatively constant patent activities in the BioRegio regions are probably based on the impact of public funding and the support by the government even though the big players of the BioRegio regions are firms. This support made some firms more independent of private venture capital money, but still the bursting of the bubble had a significant impact.

Table 16.1 lists the top players of the BioRegio regions. As can be seen, the dominant type of organization responsible for most of the patents in the regions is the private firm. In Jena they cover around 61 per cent of the players patenting in the biotechnology sector and firms in Rhineland cover as much as 87.5 per cent. The large pharmaceutical firms like Roche, BASF, Bayer and Degussa especially dominate the patenting activities in the two regions. Munich seems to have three strong institutes in the top three positions of the list.

One should know that the Fraunhofer-Society and the Max-Planck-Society in most cases apply centrally for a patent in Munich, even if the invention was made in one of their affiliates in other parts of Germany.

16.4.3 Knowledge sourcing by BioRegio regions

16.4.3.1 Open or closed knowledge generation

The first step in the analysis of the linkages used for knowledge generation and acquisition is to examine which tendencies exist to engage in cooperative arrangements in general. This tendency manifests itself in the number of patents for which not a single but multiple applicants applied.[6] These applicants have very likely cooperated in the knowledge generation because they also share the legal rights granted by the patent. Hence, the share of multiple applicant patents in a region indicates whether the organizations in the region tend to engage in cooperation for knowledge generation external to the single organization or whether they develop their new inventions on their own and have an internal knowledge generation approach.

The results of this analysis are presented in Table 16.2. In Jena 86 per cent of the patents are applied for by a single applicant in the first time period and this percentage increased to 90 per cent in the second time period. In Munich and the Rhineland this percentage is around 90 per cent for both periods of time as well. Only the Rhine-Neckar Triangle shows a different pattern with a decrease of the single-applicant patents from 97 per cent in the first period to 81 per cent in the second period. Thus, in three of the four regions the share of single-applicant patents remains stable on a high level, while in one region the share decreased but

Table16.1 Top applicants in the BioRegio regions

Jena	1999–2006*	#**	1993–98	#	Type
Clondiag Chip Technologies GmbH	1	9	1	4	Firm
SIRS-Lab GmbH	2	7			Firm
Hans-Knöll-Institute for Natural Prod. Res. and Infection Biology	3	5	2	1	Institute
HaemoSys GmbH	4	3			Firm
Institute of Photonic Technology (former Institute for Physical High Tech.)	5	3	4	1	Institute
Carl Zeiss Jena GmbH	6	2			Firm
Glatt Ingenieurtechnik GmbH	7	2			Firm
Friedrich Schiller University of Jena	8	2			University
Jenpolymers Ltd	9	1			Firm
Depuy Biotech Jena GmbH	10	1			Firm
Presselt, Norbert	11	1			Person
Claussen, Uwe, Prof. Dr Med.	12	1			Person
Jena Bioscience GmbH	13	1			Firm
Bockmeyer, Clemens	14	1			Person
Biomedical Apherese Systeme GmbH	15	1			Firm
Analytik Jena AG	16	1			Firm
Id Pharma GmbH	17	1			Firm
Zipfel, Peter, F., Prof. Dr.	18	1			Person

(continued)

Munich	1999–2006	#	1993–98	#	Type
Max-Planck-Society	1	87	1	57	Institute
Fraunhofer-Society	2	59	3	18	Institute
GSF National Research Centre for Environment and Health	3	42	2	42	Institute
Icon Genetics GmbH	4	26			Firm
Consortium f. elektrochemische Industrie GmbH	5	23	4	11	Firm
MediGene AG	6	16	6	6	Firm
Infineon Technologies AG	7	16			Firm
Siemens AG	8	14	7	6	Firm
Micromet AG	9	14	10	2	Firm
Vermicon AG	10	12			Firm
Bacher, Adelbert	11	10			Person
Xerion Pharmaceuticals AG	12	8			Firm
Technische Universität Munich	13	6			University
Wilex AG	14	6			Firm
Holm, Per Sonne	15	6			Person
MorphoSys AG	16	6	5	6	Firm
GPC Biotech AG	17	5			Firm
Avontec GmbH	18	5			Firm
Icon Genetics AG	19	5			Firm
Procorde GmbH	20	5			Firm

Rhine-Neckar	1999–2006	#	1993–98	#	Type
BASF	1	279	2	85	Firm
BASF AG		*200*		*80*	*Firm*
BASF Plant Science GmbH		*79*		*5*	*Firm*
Roche Diagnostics GmbH	2	240	1	224	Firm
German Cancer Research Centre	3	85	3	50	Institute
European Molecular Biology Laboratory (EMBL)	4	22	8	5	Institute
LION bioscience AG	5	15			Firm
MTM Laboratories AG	6	14			Firm
Axaron Bioscience AG	7	13	10	2	Firm
Febit Biotech GmbH	8	9			Firm
Heart BioSystems GmbH	9	9			Firm
Südzucker AG	10	8	5	7	Firm
Cellzome AG	11	7			Firm
University of Heidelberg	12	6	9	4	University
Affimed Therapeutics AG	13	6			Firm
febit AG	14	5			Firm
Biopharm Gesell. zur biotech. Entw. von Pharmaka mbH	15	5	4	9	Firm

(continued)

Rhineland	1999–2006	#	1993–98	#	Type
Degussa GmbH	1	255	4	14	Firm
Bayer	2	239	1	73	Firm
Bayer HealthCare AG		179		11	Firm
Bayer CropScience AG		40		8	Firm
Bayer Technology Services GmbH		14			Firm
Bayer AG		9		54	Firm
Forschungszentrum Jülich GmbH	3	64	2	27	Institute
Qiagen GmbH	4	55	5	13	Firm
Henkel	5	42	3	20	Firm
Cognis IP Management GmbH	6	33	6	5	Firm
Artemis Pharmaceuticals GmbH	7	23			Firm
Coley Pharmaceutical GmbH	8	16			Firm
Amaxa GmbH	9	13			Firm
Direvo Biotech AG	10	13			Firm
Evotec Technologies GmbH	11	12			Firm
DSM Biotech GmbH	12	10			Firm
Grünenthal GmbH	13	10	8	3	Firm
Rhein Biotech GmbH	14	10			Firm
Dahl, Edgar, Dr.	15	9			Person
Biofrontera Pharmaceuticals AG	16	7			Firm

Notes
* Rank in time period 1999–2006
** Number of patents in time period 1999–2006 the applicants were listed on.

Table 16.2 Comparison of single and multiple applicant patents in the BioRegio regions

Region	Single applicant	Single applicant	Multiple applicant	Multiple applicant	Total	Total
	1993–98	*1999–2006*	*1993–98*	*1999–2006*	*1993–98*	*1999–2006*
JE	5.0 (86%)	31 (90%)	0.8 (14%)	3.5 (10%)	5.8	34.5
JE-P	0.0	2.0 (86%)	0.0 (0%)	0.3 (14%)	0.0	2.3
MU	93 (91%)	302 (90%)	9 (9%)	33.8 (10%)	102.0	335.8
MU-P	60 (89%)	123 (89%)	7.3 (11%)	15.6 (11%)	67.3	138.6
RN	392 (97%)	528 (81%)	11.83 (3%)	121.9 (19%)	403.8	649.9
RN-P	6.0 (72%)	14 (85%)	2.3 (28%)	2.5 (15%)	8.3	16.5
RL	63 (94%)	419 (93%)	4.3 (6%)	34 (7%)	67.3	453.0
RL-P	125 (93%)	371 (91%)	9.0 (7%)	38.8 (9%)	134.0	409.8
Total	744 (94%)	1790 (88%)	45 (6%)	250 (12%)	789.0	2040.0

Key: JE = Jena; P = Periphery; MU = Munich; RN = Rhine-Neckar Triangle; RL = Rhineland.

still a very large number of patents were made by single applicants. The reason for this is mainly that most organizations applying for a patent also want the legal rights linked to the granted patent for themselves without sharing the rights and potential surplus with other organizations. The opposite picture emerges for the analysis of patents with multiple inventors (Table 16.3). Most of the patents have multiple inventors and this does not change strongly over time. Although it is not clear whether these inventors belong to the core firm or to different firms, this indicates a tendency towards a broad knowledge base necessary to develop a biotechnology patent, which is due to the complexity of biotechnology. Two core results emerge from this analysis: (1) the number of multiple applicant patents is relatively low while the number of multiple inventor patents is relatively high; (2) no difference concerning the share of multiple applicants or multiple inventors between the regions and no real change over time can be detected. A firm-level analysis indicates that one single applicant was responsible for most of the multiple applicant patents in the Rhine-Neckar Triangle in the second period of time: Roche Diagnostics filed 80 per cent of its patents together with another applicant in this period. Thus, it is not really a regional difference generating the observation for this region, but a deviating behaviour by a single multinational firm which is cooperating or co-applying for patents together with its mother firm F. Hoffman-La Roche in Switzerland. Boehringer/Mannheim was bought in 1998 by F. Hoffman-La Roche: before 1998 the firm patented locally on its own (named Boehringer/Mannheim, but in the patent data appearing as Roche Diagnostics) and afterwards together with the mother firm in Switzerland. We extend the analysis for multi-inventor and multi-applicant patents in the following sections.

Table 16.3 Comparison of single and multiple inventor patents in the BioRegio regions

Region	Single inventor 1993–98	Multiple inventor 1999–2006	Total 1993–98	1999–2006	1993–98	1999–2006
JE	0.0 (0%)	2.0 (7%)	9.5 (100%)	27.5 (93%)	9.5	29.5
JE-P	1.0 (26%)	2.0 (13%)	2.9 (74%)	14 (87%)	3.9	16.0
MU	15.0 (15%)	38 (16%)	86.1 (85%)	205.7 (84%)	101.1	243.7
MU-P	2.0 (4%)	23 (19%)	42.6 (96%)	98.5 (81%)	44.6	121.5
RN	3.0 (5%)	20 (11%)	52.2 (95%)	158.9 (89%)	55.2	178.9
RN-P	9.0 (10%)	15.0 (8%)	77.4 (90%)	173.1 (92%)	86.4	188.1
RL	9.0 (11%)	31.0 (12%)	73.0 (89%)	218.2 (88%)	82.0	249.2
RL-P	12.0 (14%)	13.0 (7%)	76.0 (86%)	186.04 (93%)	88.0	199.0
Total	51.0 (11%)	144.0 (12%)	419.7 (89%)	1081.8 (88%)	470.7	1225.8

Key: JE = Jena; P = Periphery; MU = Munich; RN = Rhine-Neckar Triangle; RL = Rhineland.

16.4.3.2 Geographical reach of knowledge sourcing

In this section we focus on the geographical location of inventors and applicants of patents in order to figure out how important local, national and international links are. Tables 16.4 and 16.5 illustrate the geographic distribution of inventors which have developed patents for which the applicant is located in one of the BioRegio regions.[7]

Concerning their local linkages, organizations from Jena especially rely very strongly on inventors from the same location (or its surroundings), with 84 per cent of inventors coming from geographically proximate locations.[8] The other three regions show different tendencies. For the core region of Munich and the Rhine-Neckar Triangle 29 per cent and 26 per cent of inventors are from the core region or its periphery. Their surroundings instead are more locally focused (with 65 per cent and 55 per cent of local linkages) with the Munich periphery strongly oriented towards the Munich core (with 46 per cent of inventors) and the Rhine-Neckar periphery concentrating on their own area (with 41 per cent of inventors from this region). The Rhineland and its periphery are in between Jena and Munich/Rhine-Neckar with around 58 per cent or 64 per cent of linkages to local inventors. A similar picture results for the national and international linkages. Munich and the Rhine-Neckar region have relatively strong national linkages to inventors from Germany, while this share is much lower for the Rhineland and even negligible for Jena. The international perspective looks different. The Rhineland and the Rhine-Neckar Triangle have the strongest international connections, followed by Munich and again with Jena in the last position. A disaggregation shows that most of the international linkages are with inventors in the US, with Switzerland,

Austria, United Kingdom and France in the next ranked positions. Linkages to inventors from the US are nearly as important as all the linkages to other countries taken together. For all regions it can be concluded that such international linkages to inventors represent only a small share of their linkages. Another aspect must be noted: linkages from one BioRegio region to another BioRegio region do only show up in the data very rarely. Hence, other regions in Germany seem to play a much larger role for a BioRegio region than another BioRegio region.

The relevance of local linkages changed from period 1 to period 2: Jena and the periphery of the Rhine-Neckar Triangle became more delocalized with a higher share of inventors from the national or international level. For Munich the share of local linkages increased while the national share decreased and the international one nearly stayed constant. The same holds for the core Rhine-Neckar Triangle with a slight increase in the number of international linkages. Both Rhineland areas exhibited a decrease of local linkages, but while the core increased the national linkages and decreased the international ones, the periphery decreased the national linkages and increased the international ones. Although the importance of linkages to the US decreases, they still accounted for a considerable amount of the international linkages, followed by Switzerland, the Netherlands, France and the United Kingdom.

Summing up the findings from this section we can observe that all regions have a mixture of local, national and international linkages, but the balance between the different types changes over time. Linkages between different BioRegios are very few. Although it is difficult to draw a final conclusion from the results, there seems to be an underlying pattern of development. Very small or new regions like Jena or the Rhine-Neckar Triangle periphery have a very high amount of local linkages in the beginning which decreases over time, giving way to a higher number of national or international linkages. The other regions interestingly show very different development strategies: the core Rhineland focusing on national linkages, its periphery on international ones, the core of the Rhine-Neckar Triangle on local and international ones at the same time and Munich on local linkages. If the definition of a long-term sustainable cluster is based on the existence of dense local linkages to use local synergies and of external international linkages to adopt new knowledge and scientific methods, the core of the Rhine-Neckar Triangle and the periphery of the Rhineland with 41 per cent to 22 per cent and 52 per cent to 32 per cent especially meet this criterion. It is amazing that Munich as the key player (Cooke 2001) in German biotechnology has such a low degree of international connectivity. A problem in the evaluation arises from the fact that currently there is no information on the quality of the generated patents or of the knowledge that is sourced by these linkages. Few, but well selected, linkages might have a strong positive effect. Nevertheless, we can conclude that the international knowledge linkages are relatively weak, at least if measured by the international inventors linked to BioRegio patent applicants. There exists no common pattern of activities, but the links are based on the local structure of organizations with a strong dependence on the existence of large (pharmaceutical) companies.

In order to shed some more light on the mechanisms we analyze how different types of applicants from the BioRegio regions are externally linked to other organizations.

16.4.3.3 Analyzing applicants' geographical and organizational linkages

In order to find the relevance of different types of applicants for the establishment of linkages, in the last step of our analysis we focus on the linkages of certain groups or applicants as well as top applicants in the BioRegio regions: First we view the linkages between top applicants from the BioRegio regions and the regions or nations of the linked inventors and the linked applicants. Next we examine the type of applicants which tend to build linkages. Finally, we analyze the co-applicant partners of some top BioRegio applicants.

Applicants from the core of the BioRegio Munich show strong linkages to non-BioRegio Germany. While local linkages are dominated by applicants from companies, the most important applicants for links to national inventors are the Fraunhofer-Gesellschaft and the Max-Planck-Society. As already mentioned, most of the linkages of these two applicants are those to affiliates of the institutes. Compared to the two institutes, the 'Consortium für elektrochemische Industrie' has a stronger connection to local knowledge sources.

In the periphery of Munich the GSF-National Research Centre is the strongest player. It has many inventor connections with local as well as national inventors. In all cases international knowledge sources seem not to be important for applicants in Munich and it is more likely that the institutes try to cooperate with partners in Germany or Munich. This partly contrasts the findings by Kaiser and Liecke (2006) which found that Munich biotechnology companies cooperate locally or with international partners. 'High-flying' biotechnology firms such as MorphoSys AG or MediGene AG do not play an important role with regard to local, national or international linkages; only Micromet has some significant linkages to local inventors.

Rhine-Neckar shows different characteristics in the linkage patterns. Again firms dominate the national and international linkages, while local linkages are affected this time by research organizations (e.g. the German Cancer Research Centre or the European Molecular Biology Laboratory) and universities. In the national domain the local firms are cooperating with inventors from Munich and in the international domain links to Japan, Sweden, Switzerland and the US dominate. The big multinationals BASF and Roche dominate this region. The connections of BASF show a strong heterogeneity. The company is not only linked to local inventors and applicants, but also has national and international connections. At the international level strong partners are located in the US and Sweden. Roche Diagnostics has similar tendencies: strong local and national (especially to Munich) linkages coincide with international links to the US and at the international level Roche is strongly linked to Switzerland due to it being the home of the mother company. It is obvious that in Rhine-Neckar firms tend to have built up connections

Table 16.4 Linking BioRegio applicants with inventors (1993–98)

1993–98	Germany	JE	JE-P	MU	MU-P	RN	RN-P	RL	RL-P	Worldwide
JE	0.9 (15%)	2.4 (41%)	2.5 (43%)	0 (0%)	0 (0%)	0 (0%)	0 (0%)	0 (0%)	0.1 (1%)	0 (0%)
JE-P	0 (0%)	0 (0%)	0 (0%)	0 (0%)	0 (0%)	0 (0%)	0 (0%)	0 (0%)	0 (0%)	0 (0%)
MU	56.5 (57%)	1.5 (2%)	0.3 (0%)	22.9 (23%)	5.8 (6%)	0.9 (1%)	0.4 (0%)	5 (5%)	1.1 (1%)	5.6 (6%)
MU-P	15 (22%)	0 (0%)	0 (0%)	31 (46%)	13.1 (19%)	0.2 (0%)	0.3 (0%)	0.8 (1%)	0.5 (1%)	6.6 (10%)
RN	180.3 (45%)	0 (0%)	0 (0%)	23.5 (6%)	15.9 (4%)	40.9 (10%)	64.6 (16%)	5.1 (1%)	1.9 (0%)	65.7 (17%)
RN-P	2.1 (25%)	0 (0%)	0 (0%)	0 (0%)	0 (0%)	1.2 (14%)	3.4 (41%)	0 (0%)	1 (12%)	0.7 (8%)
RL	16.2 (24%)	0 (0%)	0 (0%)	0.3 (0%)	0 (0%)	0.2 (0%)	0.3 (0%)	23.2 (34%)	16.4 (24%)	10.9 (16%)
RL-P	34.8 (26%)	0.1 (0%)	0 (0%)	1.1 (1%)	0.9 (1%)	0.6 (0%)	1.2 (1%)	34.4 (26%)	51.3 (38%)	9.2 (7%)

Table 16.5 Linking BioRegio applicants with inventors (1999–2006)

1999–2006	Germany	JE	JE-P	MU	MU-P	RN	RN-P	RL	RL-P	WW
JE	7.7 (22%)	17.7 (51%)	5.8 (17%)	0.1 (0%)	0 (0%)	0 (0%)	1.9 (5%)	0 (0%)	0 (0%)	1.4 (4%)
JE-P	0 (0%)	0.3 (11%)	1.7 (74%)	0 (0%)	0 (0%)	0 (0%)	0 (0%)	0 (0%)	0 (0%)	0.3 (14%)
MU	149.3 (45%)	1.8 (1%)	1.7 (0%)	111 (33%)	32.3 (10%)	3.1 (1%)	2.2 (1%)	8.9 (3%)	3.2 (1%)	20.3 (6%)
MU-P	33.2 (24%)	0.8 (1%)	0 (0%)	49.1 (35%)	42.4 (31%)	3.9 (3%)	0.4 (0%)	1.1 (1%)	0.2 (0%)	7.6 (5%)
RN	209.7 (33%)	0.1 (0%)	0 (0%)	10.1 (2%)	5.7 (1%)	135.7 (21%)	129.5 (20%)	4.2 (1%)	1.9 (0%)	143.9 (22%)
RN-P	6.9 (42%)	0 (0%)	0 (0%)	0 (0%)	0 (0%)	0.2 (1%)	7.7 (46%)	0.3 (2%)	0 (0%)	1.5 (9%)
RL	248.1 (55%)	1.2 (0%)	0 (0%)	1.6 (0%)	0.1 (0%)	0.4 (0%)	3.3 (1%)	102.6 (23%)	50.5 (11%)	44.2 (10%)
RL-P	62.5 (15%)	0.1 (0%)	0 (0%)	4.1 (1%)	0.8 (0%)	0.5 (0%)	1.9 (0%)	92.4 (23%)	116.8 (29%)	129.6 (32%)

with partners external to the region or Germany. This is strongly affected by the local multinational companies, while smaller biotechnology firms such as Lion Bioscience have some local linkages to inventors but only very few international ones.

The analysis of the Rhineland provides similar results as for the BioRegio Rhine-Neckar. Drivers of the linkages are the big multinational firms. In contrast to Rhine-Neckar the firms show different patterns of connection. Degussa, Henkel and the Forschungszentrum Jülich are more likely to cooperate with local and national partners. Bayer (and all its affiliates) and Qiagen not only have local and national connections, but also many international links (especially to the US). On the international level Bayer Healthcare is responsible for most of the linkages to the US and works together with many inventors there. Other strongly linked countries are Switzerland and the Netherlands. In the case of Cognis IP Management there exist just a few local and national partners but an interestingly high rate of linkages with inventors from the US.

For the BioRegio Jena, our analysis shows that the linkages in this region are negligible. In respect to the small number of patent applications applicants in Jena have no appreciable cooperation with partners.

The deeper examination of the applicants leads to six crucial findings.

First: companies are part of most linkages between applicants, while there are nearly no linkages between public organizations without any firm involved. Hence, companies are the core players for the development of biotechnological patents. Second, universities and research centres in particular that are patenting in biotechnology are linking to local and national inventors, while multinational pharmaceutical companies are responsible for most linkages to inventors or co-applicants in other countries. Third, we find that the knowledge cooperation strategies of small to medium-sized biotechnology firms strongly differ: for example, MediGene focuses on cooperation with research facilities while MorphoSys, Micromet or Vermicon tend to cooperate with firms and Qiagen has a strategy in between. Fourth, we find that most of the international linkages of Roche Diagnostics are linkages with the mother company in Switzerland. The same holds for Icon Genetics which has all linkages into the US to Icon Genetics itself. Hence, this points to a strategy in which local knowledge clusters are linked by multinational companies based on foreign subsidiaries. Fifth, large organization such as Bayer and the three research facilities in Munich do not have any peculiar focus in selecting their co-patenting partners. Their cooperation can be characterized by a strong heterogeneity. Only one long-lasting co-patenting partnership can be identified: Degussa built fruitfully on cooperation with the Forschungszentrum Jülich, generating more than 20 patents together. Sixth, it is difficult to identify a functioning biotechnological cluster in Germany because the local strategies strongly differ from one another. Munich is very locally focused, while the Rhineland and the Rhine-Neckar Triangle have external linkages to other countries (including the US) built by mostly multinational enterprises and having at the same time local linkages to universities and research organizations. The latter two regions serve as an example of a cluster, but they are lagging small to medium-sized biotechnology companies. Although firms such as Qiagen or Lion Biosciences are active, this basis might not be sufficient in the future.

16.5 Conclusions and outlook

Knowledge is the key resource for biotechnology. Companies in biotechnology have to balance their strategies between protecting their core knowledge and even more importantly generating 'new' knowledge. At the same time these companies aim at gaining from local synergies and to utilize knowledge sources external to the locality. In our paper we have analyzed how companies access these knowledge sources for biotechnology by examining formal linkages represented by co-application and co-invention activities of players in the German biotechnology sector. We focused on four clusters in Germany, namely the three winners of the BioRegio contest and the BioRegio region Jena, and analyzed two time periods to consider not only the impact of regional size but also potential changes over time.

First of all, we identified that the number of biotechnology patents in Germany rose from 1993 to 2001 and decreased afterwards due to the burst of the New-Economy-Bubble. In the next steps of the analysis we concentrated on the linkages between actors in the patenting activities. Particularly we looked at the origin of applicant–applicant cooperation, the location of inventors and proceeded to a closer examination of the cooperation of some specific applicants.

In case of applicant–applicant cooperation our analysis leads to similar results for all four regions. All regions have a high quota of about 80–90 per cent of single-applicant patents and apart from the Rhine-Neckar all regions have increasing rates for single-applicant patents. Connections between applicants are dominated by cooperation between multinational affiliates and their mother companies or subsidiaries. The opposite picture arises for multi-inventor patents. Most patents are generated by several inventors working together. The former finding is caused by the aim of the patent applicants to have the right to use the patent on their own without sharing potential gains with other applicants. The latter results from the complexity of the knowledge base necessary to generate patents. Different bits of knowledge represented by different inventors have to be combined.

For the applicant–inventor linkages we discover that all of the four regions have a mixture of local, national and international linkages, but the consistency differs over time and place. Jena and Rhine-Neckar start with a high share of local linkages which decreased over time, giving place to national and international linkages, while the Rhineland has more national linkages and its periphery already started with more international linkages. Munich, however, shows a surprisingly small number of international connections. The multinational companies play an important role in the bridging of geographic space with many linkages, for example, to the US based on these types of firms. Since Munich has no such firms (in the biotechnological, chemical or pharmaceutical) field, this is probably the reason for the low degree of international connectivity.

For the examination on the applicant level we identified that companies are involved in most of the linkages between applicants. Universities and research centres tend to work together with local or national inventors while large pharmaceutical companies have knowledge sources all over the world, although we have to consider that most of those linkages refer to intra-firm linkages such as with Roche Diagnostics and Icon Genetics. Besides a strong heterogeneity in the cooperation pattern of most of the organizations such as Bayer, Fraunhofer Society, Max-Planck-Society and GSF, there is one outstanding local co-patenting activity which was detected between Degussa and the Forschungszentrum Jülich, which very actively cooperate.

Finally, we can detect that the BioRegio regions of the Rhineland and the Rhine-Neckar Triangle show signs of biotechnology clustering. Munich, however, has an unexpected local focus whereas Jena lags behind the three winner regions in many aspects.

Regarding the differences of the four regions our findings show that regions containing a mixture of companies operating on the national and international level as well as public organization have an advantage concerning their connectivity. This is in line with Cooke (2005) who argues that direct state involvement or the size of a company as such does not positively affect the likelihood of becoming a successful biotech region in Europe. Our findings especially point to the fact that regions which intend to use international knowledge sourcing also have to attract multinational enterprises; not for the sake of their size but to utilize their international connectivity and, hence, their access to knowledge sources.

One shortcoming of our study is that we can identify applicant–applicant linkages as well as linkages between applicants and inventors (including their location), but we are unable to link inventors to organizations. We do not know whether an inventor works for the core firm, a university or a different firm. This restricts the evaluation because, for example, even if we find that there exist only a few firm–university linkages, it might be the case that all the inventors of a patent work at a university, but the core firm is the only applicant.

Nevertheless, we can conclude that the density and geographic extent of the linkages relevant for knowledge sourcing strongly depend on the different local peculiarities and especially the mixture of local actors ranging from research centres and new dedicated biotechnology firms to multinational companies. The result that regions differ with regard to their interaction patterns is in opposition to the assumption of Kaiser and Liecke (2006), who analyze the cooperation activities in Munich and claim that these results should be applicable to other regions as well. The currently unanswered question is which type of interaction leads to the best long-term performance. The examination of the connection between performance and different types of linkages offers opportunities for future research.

Notes

1 For geographic concentration in biotechnology in other countries, see for example Niosi and Bas (2001), on Canada; Lemarié, Mangematin and Torre (2001), on France.
2 Note that these formal interactions can build upon other transfer channels such as labour mobility or informal networks (Zellner and Fornahl 2002) and that such formal

interactions can generate new informal interactions in the future as well.
3 European Patent Organization.
4 Members of the Task Force: European Commission (EC), the European Patent Office (EPO), the Japanese Patent Office (JPO), the US National Science Foundation (NSF), the US Patent and Trademark Office (USPTO) and the World Intellectual Property Organization (WIPO).
5 Numbers are weighted by the number of applicants per patent.
6 The patents are not weighted for Tables 16.2 and 16.3. All patents are included on which at least one applicant or one inventor from the BioRegio regions is named.
7 The patents are weighted by the number of linkages between applicants as well as by the number of linkages between inventors.
8 Note that the number of observations is very low for Jena in the first period of time.

References

Albino V., Garavelli A. C. and Schiuma G. (1999), 'Knowledge transfer and inter-firm relationships in industrial districts: the role of the leader firm', *Technovation*, 19: 53–63.

Bathelt H., Malmberg A. and Maskell P. (2004), 'Clusters and knowledge: local buzz, global pipelines and the process of knowledge creation', *Progress in Human Geography*, 28: 31–56.

Blau P. M. (1964), *Exchange and Power in Social Life*, New York: Wiley.

BMBF (1996), *Biotechnology in Germany*, Bonn.

Cohen W. M. and Levinthal, D. A. (1990), 'Absorptive capacity: a new perspective on learning and innovation', *Administrative Science Quarterly*, 35: 128–52.

Cooke P. (2001), 'New economy innovation systems – biotechnology in Europe and the USA', *Industry and Innovation*, 8: 267–89.

——. (2005), 'Regionally asymmetric knowledge capabilities and open innovation – exploring 'Globalisation 2' – a new industry organisation', *Research Policy* 34(2005): 1128–49.

Dohse D. (2001), 'Technology policy and the regions: the case of the BioRegio Contest, *Research Policy*, 29: 1111–33.

——. (2007), 'Cluster-based technology policy – the German experience, *Industry and Innovation*, 14: 69–94.

Feldman M. P. (2003), 'The locational dynamics of the US biotech industry: knowledge externalities and the anchor hypothesis', *Industry and Innovation*, 10(3): 311–28.

Feldman M. P. and Francis, J. L. (2003), 'Fortune favours the prepared region: the case of entrepreneurship and the Capital Region biotechnology cluster', *European Planning Studies*, 11: 765–88.

Grabher G. (1993), 'The weakness of strong ties. The lock-in of regional development in the Ruhr area', in G. Grabher (ed.), *The Embedded Firm*, London: Routledge, pp. 255–77.

Haug P. (1995), 'Formation of biotechnology firms in the greater Seattle region: an empirical investigation of entrepreneurial, financial and educational perspectives, *Environment and Planning*, A27: 249–67.

Jacobs J. (1969), *The Economy of Cities*, New York: Random House.

Kaiser R. and Liecke M. (2006), 'Sector review of the European biotechnology sector, deliverable report for the EURODITE project', reference number D3b.

Lemarié S., Mangematin V. and Torre A. (2001), 'Is the creation and development of biotech SMEs localized? Conclusions drawn from the French case', *Small Business Economics*, 17: 61–76.

Malmberg A. and Maskell P. (2002), 'The elusive concept of localization economies: towards a knowledge-based theory of spatial clustering', *Environment and Planning, A* 34: 429–9.

Marshall A. (1890), *Principles of Economics*, London: Maxmillan.

Martin R. and Sunley P. (2006), 'Path dependence and regional economic evolution', *Journal of Economic Geography*, 6: 395–437.

Menzel M. P. and Fornahl D. (2007), *Cluster Life Cycles – Dimensions and Rationales of Cluster Development*, Mimeo.

Muscio A. (2006), 'Patterns of innovation in industrial districts: an empirical analysis', *Industry and Innovation*, 13: 291–312.

Niosi J. and Bas T. G. (2001), 'The competencies of regions – Canada's clusters in biotechnology', *Small Business Economics*, 17: 31–42.

Owen-Smith J. and Powell W. W. (2004), 'Knowledge networks as channels and conduits: the effects of spillovers in the Boston biotechnology community', *Organization Science*, 15: 5–21.

Phene A., Fladmoe-Lindquist K. and Marsh L. (2006), 'Breakthrough innovations in the US biotechnology industry: the effects of technological space and geographic origin', *Strategic Management Journal*, 27: 369–88.

Polyani M. (1966), *The Tacit Dimension*, Garden City, New York: Doubleday.

Sorenson O. and Audia P. G. (2000), 'The social structure of entrepreneurial activity: geographic concentration of footwear production in the United States, 1940–1989', *American Journal of Sociology*, 106: 424–62.

Sorenson O., Rivkin J. and Fleming L. (2006), 'Complexity, networks and knowledge flow', *Research Policy*, 35: 994–1017.

Stouffer S. A. (1940), 'Intervening opportunities: a theory relating mobility and distance', *American Journal of Sociology*, 99: 614–39.

Stuart T. E. and Sorensen O. (2003), 'The geography of opportunity: spatial heterogeneity in founding rates and the performance of biotechnology firms', *Research Policy*, 32: 229–53.

Stuart T. E., Ozdemir S. Z. and Ding W. W. (2007), 'Vertical alliance networks: the case of u niversity-biotechnology-pharmaceutical alliance chains', *Research Policy*, 36: 477–98.

Tappi D. (2005), 'Clusters, adaptation and extroversion – a cognitive and entrepreneurial analysis of the Marche music cluster', *European Urban and Regional Studies*, 12: 289–307.

Tichy G. (2001), 'Regionale Kompetenzzyklen – Zur Bedeutung von Produktlebenszyklus und Clusteransätzen im regionalen Kontext', *Zeitschrift für Wirtschaftsgeographie*, 45: 181–201.

Zeller C. (2001), 'Clustering biotech: a recipe for success? Spatial patterns of growth of biotechnology in Munich, Rhineland and Hamburg', *Small Business Economics*, 17: 123–41.

Zellner C. and Fornahl D. (2002), 'Scientific knowledge and implications for its diffusion', *Journal of Knowledge Management*, 6(2): 190–98.

Zipf G. K. (1949), *Human Behavior and the Principle of Least Effort*, Reading, MA: Addison-Wesley.

Zucker L. G. and Darby M. R. (1996), 'Star scientists and institutional transformation: patterns of invention and innovation in the formation of the biotechnology industry', *Proceedings of the National Academy of Sciences*, 93: 12709–16.

17 Two sides of the same coin? Local and global knowledge flows in Medicon Valley

Jerker Moodysson, Lars Coenen and Bjørn T. Asheim (Lund University, Sweden)

17.1 Introduction

When conceptualizing modern biotechnology, Brink, *et al.* (2004) suggest that a distinction should be made between 'core' biotechnology and associated sectors such as pharmaceuticals, medical technologies, agriculture and food. Dedicated biotechnology firms (DBFs) are generally seen as the main actors that represent the 'core' of modern biotechnology. A DBF is defined as a firm whose predominant activity involves the application of biotechnology techniques to produce goods or services and/or the performance of biotechnology research and development (OECD 2005). Over the past 20 years DBFs have become increasingly important for the establishment and growth of biotechnology clusters. At its genesis in the 1970s, however, biotechnology, and in particular drug development based on biotechnology, was primarily the domain of academic research and, to a limited extent, large pharmaceutical companies. Through subsequent processes of creative destruction, shifts in basic science from chemistry to modern biology based drug design created strong incentives for new entrants (DBFs) and reduced the earlier dominance of pharmaceutical companies that were locked into the traditional, chemical technological paradigm (Casper and Matraves 2003; Cooke 2007).

Innovation processes carried out by DBFs are highly complex. They draw not only on heavily specialized and advanced knowledge but are also dependent on broad, complementary knowledge and skill sets to evolve the initial idea into a marketable product that can be launched commercially. As a result, the set of knowledge and skills that is needed is rarely found within the boundaries of one single firm (Moodysson and Jonsson 2007). Instead, DBFs provide paradigmatic examples of firms employing an open innovation model based on interactive learning and highly distributed knowledge networks (Chesbrough 2003; Smith 2005). As a result of this, the spatial organization of biotechnology innovation is characterized by agglomeration and interaction in local clusters while at the same time being connected to global networks (Moodysson 2007). This dual geography poses interesting challenges to the received wisdom of clusters and industrial districts which has put a premium on the importance of localized learning processes (Gertler and Wolfe 2006). However, when analyzing biotechnology clusters, localized learning tells only one part of the story while neglecting the long-distance ties and relationships. In order to shed light on the geography of innovation for a biotechnology cluster, this chapter studies different forms of knowledge flows among actors in the Medicon Valley cluster. Two complementary methods are used: (1) data on co-authorships, co-inventions and formal partnerships are used for a mapping of knowledge flows; and (2) a number of innovation processes are decomposed into concrete activities and analyzed with regard to the spatial distribution of collaborators involved. While the first method is used primarily for descriptive purposes, explanations are sought through the second.

The biotechnology cluster Medicon Valley is located in the cross-national Øresund region which spans the greater Copenhagen area in Denmark and the Lund-Malmö area in the province of Scania in southern Sweden. It hosts the full, complementary array of related actors that constitute a biotechnology cluster: DBFs, universities and other leading public research organizations (PROs) and large pharmaceutical and medical technology (medtech) firms.

The remainder of the chapter looks as follows. Section 17.2 outlines the theoretical framework, mainly drawing on the regional innovation systems framework, complemented by insights on distributed knowledge networks and learning in interpersonal communities. In doing so, we combine a micro- and meso-perspective on knowledge creation. To analyze local *and* global knowledge flows we explore the existence of communities of practice and epistemic communities in the cluster. Prior to this we provide a general cluster analysis of Medicon Valley. The chapter concludes with a discussion of the main findings.

17.2 Theoretical framework

17.2.1 Regional innovation systems

Recent work on innovation systems indicates that the region is a key level at which innovative capacity is shaped and economic processes coordinated and governed (Cooke, *et al.* 2004; Doloreux and Parto 2005; Fritsch and Stephan 2005). This has among other things led to the development and widespread use of the regional innovation system (RIS) concept (Autio 1998; Braczyk, *et al.* 1998; Cooke, *et al.* 2000; Asheim and Gertler 2005). While other territorial innovation concepts found in the literature often have a broader concern, addressing the organization of production systems (industrial districts, new industrial spaces) and corporate organization broadly defined (clusters), the RIS approach targets innovation directly as its primary object of study. However, the choice for this approach suggests by no means that it is analytically superior to other territorial innovation models. Rather it should be seen as an amalgam concept synthesizing the ideas and lessons from other territorial innovation models (Doloreux 2002).

A RIS is defined as a set of interacting knowledge exploration and exploitation subsystems at the regional level which are linked to global, national and other regional systems (Cooke 2004). These subsystems are embedded in a common regional socio-economic setting. The regional exploitation subsystem is understood as the regional production structure made up by firms, in particular where these exhibit clustering tendencies. This provides an important link to the cluster concept, defined as geographically proximate groups of interconnected firms in the same or adjacent industrial sectors that create competitive advantage based on the exploitation of unique resources and competencies, which have to be reproduced and developed through continuous innovation (Porter 1990, 2000). This underlines the dynamic character of competitive advantage as a result of innovation, which represents the high road to economic development, in contrast to the low road based on cost competition. However, as argued elsewhere (Asheim and Coenen 2005; Tödtling and Trippl 2005) it is important not to conflate the RIS and cluster concepts. As implied in the definition above, clusters are sector-specific while the RIS approach can reach across various industries in the region. Moreover, the latter allows for greater scope to take multi-level analysis into account (Cooke 2005).[1]

The regional exploration subsystem refers to the organizational infrastructure that supports innovation in the regional industry. It refers to a variety of organizations whose primary purpose is to produce, maintain, distribute, manage and protect knowledge for the society and economy in which it is embedded (Smith 1997). Universities and other institutes of higher education, research institutes and public laboratories are all involved in the production and coordination of scientific and technological knowledge and are thus an important part of this subsystem. It would, however, be misleading to take a linear view on the knowledge flows between the knowledge infrastructure (at the generative end) and firms (at the receptive) or to assume a one-to-one relation between the knowledge that is explored and exploited. By referring to processes of 'interactive learning' the associative and reciprocal character of the knowledge exchange and diffusion process is emphasized (Cooke 1998). Moreover, these interactive learning processes are understood as social processes that cannot be understood independently of its institutional and cultural contexts (Asheim 2000; Lundvall 1992).

17.2.2 Localized learning

Studies on localized learning have addressed the relationship between firms and the locality in which they are located (Maskell, *et al.* 1998; Maskell and Malmberg 1999; Malmberg and Maskell 2002). A central argument in this strand of research is that firms build their competitive advantage in interaction with localized capabilities. It builds on the fairly self-evident assumption that no firm is in complete control of all the resources it needs. Therefore it is dependent on its regional environment. Arguably, globalization renders more and more traditional localized inputs or resources, such as natural resource endowments, infrastructure and built environment, ubiquitous. This means they become available everywhere at more or less the same cost. Being less sensitive to this ubiquification process, it is therefore 'more likely today that it is the available knowledge base and institutional set-up that matter' (Malmberg and Maskell 2006: 4). Moreover these authors argue that through processes of cumulative causation the existing knowledge bases and institutional set-ups are reproduced, generating stable patterns of industrial specialization and territorial differentiation. This takes shape through the development of regional clusters (Rosenfeld 1997). They form the basis of a local milieu facilitative to knowledge spillovers and other forms of 'learning by being there' (Gertler 2004). On the horizontal dimension, competition between local firms may induce experimentation and differentiation with new products and processes, which, in turn, diffuse relatively easily throughout the cluster (Porter 2000). Examples of specific mechanisms for these knowledge flows are inter-firm mobility of skilled personnel and local monitoring and demonstration effects (Malmberg 2003). On the vertical dimension, intense user-producer learning is favoured through networks of supplier, service and customer relations. Also knowledge collaboration between firms and support organizations is considered to benefit from proximate relations. The rationale for knowledge being easily diffused throughout the cluster builds on the observation that its people and firms share similar or complementary interests in their work; that is, by working within the same industry (Giuliani 2005).

What exactly is meant with 'local' in the context of localized learning and clusters remains elusive, however. According to Malmberg and Maskell (2002), localized learning is probably best viewed as a combined result of close and distance interactions (see also Bathelt, *et al.* 2004; Oinas 1999). It should therefore be noted that the advantages of spatial proximity in localized learning primarily follow from a common or at least commensurate cognitive, institutional, social and cultural setting or context rather than geographical proximity *per se*. A potentially useful approach to capture all interactions and to avoid a myopic, scalar trap is to follow the network wherever it takes us. The notions of distributed knowledge networks, communities of practice and epistemic communities prove to be very helpful in this respect.

17.2.3 Modes of knowledge creation and distributed knowledge networks

While Asheim and Gertler (2005) and Asheim, *et al.* (2007) have introduced and used the distinction between different knowledge bases (analytical, synthetic and symbolic) on a macro- and meso-level to explain different geographies and types of innovation processes of firms belonging to various industries, it has also been developed further to unpacking learning processes *within* firms in an industry – e.g. biotechnology – by referring to the different acts of 'analysis' and 'synthesis' in specific innovation projects (Simon 1969), and, thus, take more explicit account of the knowledge content of the actual interactions that take place in networks of innovators (Archibugi, *et al.* 1999). However, both these *modes of knowledge creation* appear in different mixes in most firms and industries with different intensity in different phases of product and process innovation processes, and with different spatial outcomes (Moodysson, *et al.* 2008).

As a result of the growing complexity and diversity of contemporary knowledge creation and innovation processes, firms being part of such network-organized innovation projects increasingly need to acquire new knowledge to supplement their internal, core knowledge base(s) – either by attracting human capital possessing competencies based on a different knowledge base or by acquiring new external knowledge base(s) by collaborating with external firms through R&D cooperation, outsourcing or offshoring of R&D, and/or with research institutes or universities, which underline the importance of firms' absorptive capacity. The strategy of acquiring and integrating external knowledge base(s), therefore, implies that more and more a shift is taking place from firms' internal knowledge base to increasingly globally 'distributed knowledge network' and 'open innovation' (Chesbrough 2003). A globally distributed knowledge network is 'a systemically coherent set of knowledge, maintained across an economically and/or socially integrated set of agents and institutions' (Smith 2000: 19). This is manifested by the increased importance of and attention to clusters, innovation systems (regional, national and sectoral), global production networks and value chains for firms' knowledge creation and innovation processes, demonstrating that 'the relevant knowledge base for many industries is not internal to the industry, but is distributed across a range of technologies, actors and industries' (Smith 2000: 19).

17.2.4 Localized and distributed knowledge communities

Research on the actual knowledge flows and linkages between actors in an innovation system or cluster seems to be relatively sparse (Giuliani and Bell 2005). It calls for a shift from a static analysis of innovation networks and actors as repositories of knowledge to a more dynamic position that stresses the (social) practice of knowledge creation 'in action' (Amin and Cohendet 2004; Brown and Duguid 2000; Ibert 2007). The literature on 'communities of practice' provides an important source of inspiration by identifying key entities driving the firm's knowledge-processing activities (Asheim and Gertler 2005). Communities of practice are defined by the communal (shared) practice of its members, who undertake or engage in a task, job or profession while communicating regularly with one another about their respective activities (Brown and Duguid 2000). Typical examples are networks of field service staff at large companies or business coalitions. The members are informally bound together by shared experience, expertise and commitment to a joint enterprise (Gertler 2004). They are able to produce and internalize shared understandings through collaborative problem solving. Communities of practice appear to accommodate the situated, pragmatic and interactive nature of learning processes 'in action' within and across organizations in a better way than individual-centred or classical organization-centred approaches (Amin and Cohendet 2004).

Coenen, *et al.* (2004, 2006) distinguish between communities of practice that are linked to synthetic (i.e. engineering-oriented) modes of knowledge creation and epistemic communities (Knorr Cetina 1999; Cowan, *et al.* 2000) that are linked to analytical (i.e. scientific research-oriented) modes of knowledge creation. The latter are bound together by the members' commitment to enhance a particular set of knowledge without being concerned about the application of such knowledge. Typical examples are (informal and latent) networks of academic researchers specialized in similar or related scientific fields, sharing an 'epistemic culture' (Knorr Cetina 1999). Knowledge dynamics in epistemic communities can more easily involve distanced ties and relationships supported by increased mobility offered through cheap and extensive air travel, the Internet, and specialized literature (Amin and Cohendet 2004).

Characteristically, epistemic communities accept some collectively accredited procedural authority (e.g. peer review) and a set of conventions to facilitate their common goal of pursuing knowledge. Such a set of conventions allow scientists to speak the same universal, scientific 'tongue', facilitating transnational communication. Kuhn (1970) refers to these community-specific conventions as the 'disciplinary matrix' (p. 182) consisting of formal components or representations (e.g. $E = mc^2$), commitment to beliefs in particular models (e.g. that molecules of a gas behave like tiny elastic billiard balls in random motion), subscription to certain values (e.g. the accuracy of predictions) and, finally, of the well-known Kuhnian paradigms or problem-solving exemplars. Communities of practice, on the other hand, are often concentrated around a concrete problem-solving practice or task (typical for synthetic modes of knowledge creation) that requires frequent and specialized communication and 'co-action', which in turn is facilitated by co-location.

Based on this we hypothesize that knowledge collaborations in epistemic communities tend to be less sensitive to distance which, in turn, facilitates global networks. Being based on synthetic modes of knowledge creation, communities of practice, on the other hand, have a tendency to be more sensitive to proximity between the actors involved, thus favouring local collaboration. The following section first provides a descriptive account of the Medicon Valley cluster's development over time in which a local outlook has gradually been complemented by a global outlook. Subsequently it provides an overview of the main actors and finally an analysis of their patterns of collaboration and the nature of the knowledge linkages as an attempt to assess if our hypothesis on the main distinction between local and global interaction are supported by the empirics.

17.3 The origin and development of the Medicon Valley cluster, its main actors, and their knowledge linkages

17.3.1 Evolution of the cluster

The life science sector in Scania (the Swedish part of Medicon Valley) has long traditions through the presence of Astra (subsequently merged with Zeneca to become AstraZeneca) and Pharmacia (subsequently merged with Upjohn to become Pharmacia & Upjohn, and eventually acquired by Pfizer). Both these companies historically located important parts of their research activities in Lund. AstraZeneca are still present with a major research unit employing 1200 persons. After the Pharmacia merger the research on cancer and immunology was spun out to form the Lund based Active Biotech AB in 1997, while the rest of the company's activities disappeared from Sweden. Active Biotech AB is today, with 90 employees, the second largest and second oldest healthcare related DBF in the region, after BioInvent International AB which today employs a staff of around 100 persons. BioInvent was created in the mid 1980s and reshaped into its current form in 1995 by researchers at Lund University that wanted to commercialize their research. Besides these two medium-sized firms, the Swedish part of the region hosts about 35 other DBFs of varying size and age. A large share of the companies are university spin-offs (e.g. Camurus, Cellavision, Genovis and Wieslab) while others are local sub-units of global biotechnology companies (e.g. Acadia with headquarters in San Diego and research unit in Malmö). Also the Danish part of the region has been a strong milieu for life science for a long time. Large anchor firms like Novo Nordisk and Lundbeck are still among the major players in the world, but local spin-off companies like Novozymes (one research part of Novo Nordisk), local but world leading diagnostics companies like Dako (founded in Copenhagen 1966, today with sub-units in Colorado and California), and strongly associated pairs of complementary companies like Neurosearch (a biopharmaceuticals spin-off from Novo Nordisk) and NsGene (cell technology research spin-off from Neurosearch), have contributed to a renewal of the bioregion meeting new requirements on the global market. In total the Danish part of the region hosts about 90 DBFs.

The name Medicon Valley was first introduced in 1994 by the Øresund Comittee. This is a forum of public agencies from the Danish and Swedish part of the region with the mission to stimulate binational regional development. Feeding into one of the existing industrial specializations of the region, pharmaceuticals and medical technologies, it decided to focus specifically on the emerging field of life science. Besides the historical localization of large pharmaceutical industries (in fact, 60 per cent of Scandinavian pharmaceutical companies are located in Medicon Valley) an enormous potential for life sciences exists within the region as it hosts 11 universities and 26 hospitals. However, the potential of becoming a global bioregion or 'megacentre' (Cooke 2007) is conditioned by the ability to further integrate the two national counterparts of the region (Coenen, *et al.* 2004). This has been a recurring challenge for the Medicon Valley cluster. Efforts to promote actual integration took off in earnest with the formation of Medicon Valley Academy (MVA) in 1997 (in 2007 the organization changed its name to Medicon Valley *Alliance*). MVA was initiated by Lund and Copenhagen Universities as an EU Interreg II project. The rationale behind the initiative was to stimulate the formation of a cross-border life science region, by promoting local integration and cross-fertilization between industry and academia. The MVA initiative has contributed to the development of the cluster, not the least because of its power of attraction on venture capital, research funds and human capital. This, together with the general transformation of the biotechnology knowledge field towards increased variety and complexity, has led to a shift in dominance from large pharmaceutical or medtech companies taking care of the entire value chain to small DBFs mainly focusing on basic research and early stages of development (Cooke 2005). Sixty-five new DBFs have been established in the region since 1998, and if R&D based service firms are included, the number of start-ups exceeds 100. Today there are approximately 130 DBFs in the region (MVA 2006).

The shift in dominance from single actors spanning the entire value chain to actors mainly active in the early stages of the value chain has also affected the integration of the cluster and the need to link up with actors in other bioregions.

Actors in life science are today by necessity part of global research networks rather than purely regional ones. Due to their extreme specialization they are forced to seek collaboration among the few potential partners available worldwide, and these are often located in the small set of biotechnology 'megacentres' in the US or the rest of Europe (Moodysson and Jonsson 2007). For reasons like this, the initial enthusiasm over MVA as an initiative with the aim to strengthen local and cross-border integration has partly diminished. Several of the firms gradually realized that 'network promoting' activities without substantial output in terms of new formal collaboration were hard to justify, and academic actors felt a growing alienation against what they felt was more 'the business of the local business' than something for them to engage in (Benneworth, *et al.* 2007). As a result, MVA has adapted its strategy to meet the requirements from its members of a more dedicated focus on promoting global visibility of world class research. In its present 'vision and mission' statement the focus has thus been broadened, not only to promote regional integration but also: 'initiate synergetic collaboration with other bio-regions and organizations and, together with others, promote and brand Medicon Valley, as well as the entire Øresund region, locally and globally' (MVA 2006).

A recent example of this strive to link up with other global biotech 'megacentres' is the UK-Medicon Valley Challenge Programme initiated in 2005. The aim is to develop world class biotechnology research and products by promoting research exchange and interaction between organizations in the Medicon Valley cluster and the biotechnology clusters in Cambridge, London, Liverpool-Manchester and Edinburgh. Examples of concrete activities within the programme are seminars, exchange of experiences between MVA board members and their UK counterparts, a joint EU 6th Framework Programme including MVA and the Scottish Enterprise, and a UK-Medicon Valley Post Doc Programme (MVA 2006). The long-term vision of this collaboration is, according to the MVA chairman Per Belfrage, to create: 'an air bridge from Medicon Valley to London and Cambridge, giving young scientists from Copenhagen and Lund the opportunity to experience these hot spots without having to move families and without having to worry about exorbitant housing prices'.

17.3.2 Main actors of the cluster

Firms are key actors in the cluster as main drivers for innovation and industrial dynamics. Using a RIS terminology the firms represent the knowledge exploitation subsystem. According to MVA (2006) there are, in addition to the 130 DBFs, 70 pharmaceutical companies and 130 medtech companies located in the region. However, not all of these firms are engaged in or affected by research and development related to life science. When omitting those that only have sales or service departments in the region, or for other reasons cannot be classified as knowledge intensive firms, the number of firms representing the knowledge exploitation subsystem of the Medicon Valley RIS is reduced to approximately 150 companies. Of these 150 firms, 130 can be classified as DBFs while the remaining 20 are either large pharmaceuticals or medtech firms. Universities are obviously also important actors representing the knowledge exploration subsystem of the RIS. Their role can be described according to three tasks. First, they provide training and education to create and sustain a skilled pool of local researchers and scientists. Second, universities conduct publicly funded scientific research which can serve as knowledge input for DBFs. Finally, there is the so-called 'third task' of universities which refers to direct collaboration between university and industry in the form of contract research as well as commercializing scientific research through licences and start-ups of knowledge-intensive firms by university researchers. The most important universities in the region are the universities of Lund and Copenhagen due to their long history of scientific excellence in medicine, biology and chemistry.

Lund University was founded in 1666 and hosts eight faculties and a multitude of research centres and specialized institutes. It is today the largest unit for research and higher education in Sweden covering more or less all academic disciplines. The university has approximately 40,000 students and 6000 employees. More than 3000 postgraduate students work at Lund University. Most doctorates are awarded in the medical sciences, followed closely by technology and the natural sciences. In 2006 the university had 581 professors. The most important research units for the Medicon Valley cluster are the Faculty of Medicine, the Biomedical Centre (BMC), the Faculty of Science and Lund Institute of Technology. The BMC assembles all the university's life science research under one roof, located adjacent to Lund University Hospital. This was primarily an attempt to rationalize the university research and strengthen the brand name of Lund University as a centre of excellence in biomedical research. Hence, this initiative was mainly geared at strengthening the knowledge exploration subsystem of the regional innovation system, while at the same time it contributed to promoting the integration of knowledge exploration and early stages of knowledge exploitation. The concentration of related activities in one unit is completely in line with Lund University's building centres of excellence as part of a general development towards a more entrepreneurial university (Melander 2006). The 'flagship' of BMC is without doubt the Lund Strategic Research Centre for Stem Cell Biology and Cell Therapy (Stem Cell Centre), established in 2003. Since the autumn 2006 BMC also houses a Bioincubator unit, which draws both on the concept of IDEON Incubation, and the services at the immediately adjacent IDEON Science Park, which was the first science park to be established in the Nordic countries in 1985, and on the university hospital hybrid BMC as a source of new businesses, to extend the scope of commercialization undertaken by the university to the active formation of biotechnology firms.

The University of Copenhagen was founded in 1479 and is the first university of Denmark. Spread over eight faculties from January 2007 after the integration of Danish University of Pharmaceutical Science and Royal Veterinary and Agricultural University as two new faculties, there are approximately 37,000 students and more than 7000 employees. Except for management and engineering faculties, the University of Copenhagen qualifies as a broad, comprehensive university. Most relevant for Medicon Valley are the Faculties of Health Sciences (Medicine) and Science (as well as parts of the two new faculties). The University of Copenhagen selected four Research Priority Areas for the years 2003 to 2007.

The Research Priority Areas were set up to promote cross-faculty cooperation, encourage interdisciplinary research and education and strengthen the communication of research results and dialogue with society. One of these research areas is 'Biocampus', targeting core biotechnological research.

In addition to firms and universities, research institutes play an important role for basic research and discovery. The most important institutes in Medicon Valley are the Carlsberg Research Centre, The Hagedorn Research Institute, AstraZeneca's respiratory research unit in Lund, the Swedish Institute for Health Economics, the Swedish Institute for Food and Biotechnology, Statens Serum Institut, The Danish Cancer Society and healthcare institutions such as Copenhagen Hospital Corporation, Copenhagen County Hospital, Lund University Hospital and Malmö University Hospital.

Network organizations aim to be key venues and meeting grounds that provide the social platforms to exploit the opportunities of co-location in a cluster. Medicon Valley Alliance (MVA), which was referred to in the previous section on cluster evolution, is the largest and probably most important network organization for Medicon Valley with 280 members (counted January 2008). If anything, MVA should be considered as the cluster organization. As a member financed network organization it works to promote the necessary interaction for network formation and knowledge transfer between academia, public health, and biotechnology related industries. Important tools in this are seminars and conferences, as well as initiating and coordinating projects associated with educational, scientific and business activities in the region. MVA also sets up and manages comprehensive knowledge databases and has initiated a range of working groups to analyze regional competencies within specific subject areas. In addition, MVA contributes to the regional and international marketing of Medicon Valley by visiting and presenting the cluster at conferences and other events. In 2007 MVA established an 'embassy' unit in Kobe and there are concrete plans for establishing similar units in Vancouver, Seoul, Hong Kong and Beijing.

Another important network organization is the Øresund University, a consortium of 14 universities and university colleges in the region with the objective to increase quality and efficiency among the participating institutions by opening up all courses, libraries and other facilities to all students, teachers and researchers. Øresund University is, similar to MVA, part of Øresund Science Region, an umbrella organization which joins the forces of six regional research and innovation platforms and a number of regional coordination bodies in an attempt to strengthen regional cooperation and integration between universities, industry and the public sector. The six ØSR platforms are Medicon Valley Academy, Øresund IT Academy, Øresund Food Network, Øresund Environment Academy, Øresund Logistics and Øresund Design. The activities of the platforms include establishing partnerships, benchmarking, enhancing research and education, innovation, technology transfer and marketing.

The remainder of this chapter presents the result of our analysis of the actual knowledge interaction among the core actors of the cluster (DBFs and university research groups) which thereby represents an indirect assessment of the impact of actions carried out by network organizations like those described above or, alternatively, the challenges that they face.

17.3.3 Collaboration within and beyond the cluster boundaries

The patterns of collaboration between DBFs and related actors observed through the extensive research (the 'mapping') display strong similarities with other global life science nodes in Europe as well as in North America (Gertler and Levitte 2005; McKelvey, *et al.* 2003; Zeller 2004) which illustrate the importance of local as well as non-local linkages. Local partners seem to be most frequent in collaboration that results in patents (78 per cent) whereas half of all collaborations in scientific publications built on non-local partnerships (52 per cent). The spread of formalized partnerships shows that both localization and globalization effects are at hand; however, with a clear dominance of the latter. The findings presented in Table 17.1 roughly map the patterns of collaboration, but on a substantial level they give no explanation. To address this question, in-depth studies of specific innovation processes that allow for an unpacking and analysis of the knowledge interplay between actors, the role of their competence profile, and the spatial implications of this, are applied. As opposed to the extensive mapping, which merely covers formal knowledge collaboration between DBFs and related actors, the in-depth analysis of a selection of cases also covers informal collaborations which are not documented through patents, publications or any other secondary sources of information.

In all, the in-depth analysis covers 20 innovation processes, 10 from the commercial sphere (projects owned by DBFs) and 10 from academia (projects owned by university research groups). The degree of commercial awareness, as well as the commercial success, varies between the cases. The potential innovations are in many of the cases still in the making. However, since the main interest is focused on the innovation processes and the patterns of collaboration between actors involved rather than the outcome of these processes, the cases are all referred to as innovation processes even though some of them may end up as inventions

Table 17.1 Relative share (percentage of partners by location) involved in knowledge collaboration with the 109 DBFs located in Medicon Valley for 2004

Type of collaboration	MV	North America	Rest of EU	UK	Other SE	Other DK	Asia	Other	Total	Absolute numbers
Formal partnerships	28	33	21	10	4	1	1	3	100	218
Scientific publications	48	10	18	6	8	7	1	3	100	1397
Granted patents	78	3	10	1	3	1	1	3	100	977

Source: our elaboration.[2]

without commercial success. The rationale for the selection of cases was to include a number of typical cases of healthcare related DBFs and research groups (which represent the vast majority of the actors in Medicon Valley) and a number of non-typical cases of functional foods, bioinformatics and environmental biotechnology (which represent growing but still fairly limited niches of biotechnology in the region). An overview of the cases is provided in the Appendix.

With regard to modes of knowledge creation, all the cases studied in depth include elements of both scientific research oriented (analytical) and more applied (synthetic). The patterns of collaboration with external partners are shaped both by the individual actors' engagement and embeddedness in various interpersonal networks (communities), and by more formalized alliances in which the organizations (i.e. DBFs and university research departments) are embedded. This (individual and organizational) embeddedness can be characterized as a combined local-global phenomenon. Therefore, it has not been possible to classify the projects as purely, or even primarily, analytical or synthetic, nor as predominantly local or global. Instead the cases analyzed represent complex combinations of both these dichotomies. This makes them highly relevant for a study like the one presented in this chapter.

All except one of the organizations studied (i.e. the project owners) are members of MVA, but their active engagement varies. None of them has established any formal relations with other actors in the region as a result of their engagement in MVA, but it has helped them to get information about what is going on in the region, and their interpersonal relations with other participants in MVA activities have in some cases helped them to identify interesting candidates for new staff recruitment. It is also the case that most staff working at the DBFs received their education from a local university, and a fairly large share are recruited directly from the university or from any of the large pharmaceutical or medtech companies in the region. Both Pharmacia and Astra Zeneca are described as important suppliers of human capital by many of the Lund based DBFs. In the late 1990s when Pharmacia downsized heavily, sold out their research activities, and eventually left the region completely, a number of new firms were founded by former Pharmacia staff, the most successful example in the Medicon Valley region being Active Biotech. In this new situation, in many ways indicating an emerging crisis for pharmaceuticals in the region, Active Biotech and other firms could benefit from a large pool of qualified labour that suddenly became available. This obviously resulted in indirect knowledge spillovers within the region and is today described not as much as a crisis but as an important triggering event in the further development of the biotechnology cluster. A similar situation occurred in 2004 when the Pharmacia spin-off company Active Biotech downsized their research activities heavily. Within one year the staff was reduced by 50 per cent, which resulted in more than 100 highly qualified employees becoming available for other firms in the region.

However, direct knowledge inputs relevant for the innovation processes analyzed in this study, whether they are received through formal or informal collaborations, are in most of the cases sought from other sources than from local firms and universities. Typical ways of searching for knowledge inputs are to use the personal network of fellow researchers and ask for recommendations of competent persons or, in case the knowledge required that cannot be found through the pre-established personal networks, through scanning the scientific literature, patent databases or other official sources. There are also examples of linkages established at international trade fairs and conferences but these are not as common as linkages established through activation of latent interpersonal relations in the scientific community. The often referred examples of joint initiatives and knowledge spillovers occurring as results of spontaneous informal meetings in the canteen of a science park or local pub, sometimes referred to as 'local buzz' (Bathelt, *et al.* 2004; Asheim, *et al.* 2007), seem, however, to be somewhat of a myth. No such examples are identified in the present study.

Even though a large and increasing share of the direct knowledge linkages between DBFs and university research groups are globally oriented, both in the total population and among the cases selected for in-depth studies, there are indeed examples of joint knowledge creation within the cluster. Two of the companies selected for in-depth studies have a history of strong ties between them, and two of the companies have been, and to a certain extent still are, closely related to two of the research groups. When discussing the nature of these local linkages, their degree of formalization and the story behind their establishment and evolution, it became clear that key individuals play a crucial role here. The two companies involved in joint knowledge creation were founded by the same entrepreneur who also had a career as professor at the local university. He held the position as CEO and CSO (chief service officer) in the start-up phase of both these companies and he brought with him staff from his university department when starting up the companies. As a result of this there were tight linkages between the companies and his department in an initial phase. Over the years, however, the linkages between these companies, as well as between the companies and the university department, have partly diminished. Today, the companies share the same technology platform, but there is no direct knowledge interaction going on between them. Also the linkages to the local university have been replaced by linkages to research groups in other parts of the world. A similar story can be told about the third company with linkages to one of the university research groups. These linkages are a result of the fact that the CSO of the company maintains a part time position as professor at the local university.

Also in more general discussions of the nature and emergence of knowledge linkages within the region and on a global scale it became clear that key individuals' personal networks are very important for local as well as global linkages. Most of the local linkages between DBFs and the local universities are results of labour mobility. Either the founder of a spin-off company has kept linkages to his/her old university department or staff has been recruited directly from the university. Researchers at several of the DBFs are also part-time affiliated with the local universities and supervise students that later are recruited by their companies. When following up on the results of the partnerships, patents and publications surveys (presented in Table 17.1) with the DBFs selected for in-depth case studies, it became evident that a large share of the intra-regional co-publications, which indeed reflects formal knowledge collaboration, were related to individual researchers' own, more or less firm-independent, collaboration rather than being representative examples of knowledge collaboration between the firms as such and the local universities. In this way local linkages and indirect knowledge transfers between individuals are continuously reproduced, but the direct knowledge collaboration in terms of joint project engagement is quite limited. Such direct knowledge interactions are instead to a growing extent established with partners on a global scale, in many cases through formalization of latent networks in the researchers' epistemic communities. Many of the mechanisms representing what the literature refers to as 'localized learning' (e.g. Malmberg 2003) are hence in this specific type of activity more globally distributed phenomena than exclusively attached to the local milieu of the actors.

As regards the content of knowledge exchange and modes of knowledge creation the hypothesis raised in the introductory part of this chapter was largely confirmed. Analytical knowledge creation, drawing on formal models and scientific protocols, seems to be less sensitive to distance decay, while synthetic knowledge creation, drawing heavier on practical experimentation and trial and error exercises, is more sensitive to proximity between the interacting actors. Much of the joint analytical knowledge creation can be handled over long distances using ICT-based communication tools, while the synthetic knowledge creation in many of the cases requires direct face-to-face interaction and simultaneous access to the material (e.g. the living organisms and/or drug candidates) on which trials are conducted. However, since most of the innovation activities identified in this study involve elements of both analytical and synthetic knowledge creation, and since the activities are organized in a reiterative and partly overlapping manner, definite conclusions on how the specific character of the innovation processes can contribute to explain the aggregated pattern of local and global knowledge flows in Medicon Valley would require further research.

17.4 Conclusions

In the theoretical section on localized learning a number of stylized cluster dynamics were specified. By way of concluding this chapter we shall return to these to see whether local and global knowledge flows in the Medicon Valley cluster should be considered as 'two sides of the same coin' or if they represent totally different dimensions of knowledge dynamics.

The first dynamic, mobility of skilled personnel, is predominantly, if not exclusively, a local phenomenon. Despite the process of globalization and the following trend towards 'ubiquitification' of knowledge, the human capital (i.e. the carriers of knowledge) is still very much a localized resource. There is certainly some degree of brain circulation; researchers go abroad and come back with new influences and experiences. However, the vast majority of the researchers in the firms and research groups analyzed in this study are rooted in the region and most of them receive their education from the local university. The majority of firms are spin-offs from the university or any of the large pharmaceutical companies in the region, and most new staff are recruited from these sources. The second dynamic, monitoring and demonstration effects, are on the other hand predominantly a global phenomenon. There are very few examples of knowledge spillovers through observation and informal social gatherings among actors in the cluster (Asheim, *et al.* 2007). Such knowledge exchanges, which sometimes lead to formalization of joint initiatives, are typically handled within interpersonal communities of key researchers, and these communities are increasingly globally oriented. The third dynamic, user-producer learning, is also predominantly globally configured, not the least because of the strong specialization of actors in the field of life science. There are a very limited number of potential users (e.g. customers) available worldwide, and the likelihood that any of these should be located in the same region as the DBF or research group is very low. Rather, they are typically found in other strong bioregions in the US or the rest of Europe (Moodysson 2007). The fourth dynamic, collaboration between firms and support organizations, is both a local and a global phenomenon. The DBFs in Medicon Valley can benefit from activities organized by support organizations like the MVA and other regional agencies, as well as from activities by the local universities and technology transfer organizations, but they are also interlinked with support organizations outside the region, not the least in the context of the EU.

Finally, the sharing of the same or complementary interests in their work by firms and people primarily seems to be a global phenomenon in biotechnology. Globally distributed communities fill the role of latent networks in which individuals are embedded, as opposed to many cases of traditional industries where this is territorially confined (e.g. in industrial districts).

Notes

1 Despite substantial overlap, it is important to acknowledge two key differences between these concepts. The boundaries of a cluster are primarily defined on the basis of an industrial sector while a regional innovation system is limited by the jurisdictional borders of the region. This also means that a regional innovation system, normally, is larger in size and support several clusters.

2 Information about formal partnerships was extracted from company websites and annual reports. This means that all partnerships revealed by the firms in those documents are included in the material. The partners were then classified with regard to location, grouped as specified in the table and, finally, an aggregated pattern of collaborations were revealed. Knowledge collaborations involving patents and scientific publications were identified through screenings of the on-line databases provided by the Science Citation Index (ISI Web of Knowledge) and the United States Patent and Trademark Office (USPTO). First, all patents, patent applications and scientific publications produced by the 109 DBFs that were located in Medicon Valley by 2004 were identified. Second, all inventors and authors involved in these patents/patent applications and publications were identified through a manual screening of patent and publication abstracts. Third, these co-inventors and co-authors were classified with regard to location, grouped as specified in the table and, finally, an aggregated pattern of knowledge collaboration was revealed. In this way, the patents and publications were used as documentation of previous knowledge collaboration, while the content of these documents, as well as the characteristics of the knowledge exchanged between the collaborators, were not further analyzed.

References

Amin A. and Cohendet P. (2004), *Architectures of Knowledge: Firms, Capabilities and Communities,* Oxford: Oxford University Press.

Archibugi D. and Lundvall B. Å. (eds.) (2001), *The Globalizing Learning Economy,* Oxford: Oxford University Press.

Archibugi D., Howells, J. and Michie J. (1999), 'Innovation systems in a global economy', *Technology Analysis & Strategic Management,* 11(4): 527–39.

Asheim B. (2000), 'Industrial districts: the contributions of Marshall and beyond', in G. L. Clark, M. P. Feldman and M. S. Gertler (eds), *The Oxford Handbook of Innovation,* Oxford: Oxford University Press, pp. 413–31.

Asheim B. T. and Coenen L. (2005), 'Knowledge bases and regional innovation systems: comparing Nordic clusters', *Research Policy,* 34: 1173–90.

Asheim B. T. and Gertler M. (2005), 'The geography of innovation: regional innovation systems', in J. Fagerberg, D. Mowery and R. Nelson (eds.), *The Oxford Handbook of Innovation,* Oxford: Oxford University Press pp. 291–317.

Asheim B. T., Coenen L. and Vang, J. (2007), 'Face-to-face, buzz, and knowledge bases: sociospatial implications for learning, innovation, and innovation policy', *Environment and Planning C: Government and Policy,* 25(5): 655–70.

Asheim B., Coenen L., Moodysson J. and Vang J. (2007), 'Constructing knowledge-based regional advantage: implications for regional innovation policy', *Int. J. Entrepreneurship and Innovation Management,* 7(2/3/4/5): 140–55.

Autio E. (1998), 'Evaluation of RTD in regional innovation systems', *European Planning Studies,* 6(2): 131–40.

Bathelt H., Malmberg A. and Maskell P. (2004), 'Clusters and knowledge: local buzz, global pipelines and the process of knowledge creation', *Progress in Human Geography,* 28: 31–56.

Benneworth P., Coenen L., Moodysson J. and Asheim B. (2007), 'Exploring the multiple roles of Lund University in strengthening the Scania Regional Innovation System: towards institutional learning?' Working paper, CIRCLE, Lund University.

Braczyk H. J., Cooke P. and Heidenreich M. (eds.) (1998), *Regional Innovation Systems: the Role of Governance in a Globalized World,* London: UCL Press.

Brink J., McKelvey M. and Smith K. (2004), 'Conceptualizing and measuring modern biotechnology', in M. McKelvey, A. Rickne and J. Laage-Hellman (eds.), *The Economic Dynamics of Modern Biotechnology,* Cheltenham: Edward Elgar, pp. 20–42.

Brown J. S. and Duguid P. (2000), *The Social Life of Information,* Boston: Harvard Business School Press.

Casper S. and Matraves C. (2003), 'Institutional frameworks and innovation in the German and UK pharmaceutical industry', *Research Policy,* 32(10): 1865–79.

Chesbrough H. (2003), *Open Innovation,* Boston: Harvard Business School Press.

Coenen L., Moodysson J. and Asheim B. T. (2004), 'The role of proximities for knowledge dynamics in a cross-border region: biotechnology in Øresund', *European Planning Studies,* 12(7): 1003–18.

Coenen L., Moodysson J., Ryan C., Asheim B. and Phillips, P. (2006), 'Comparing a pharmaceutical and an agro-food bioregion: on the importance of knowledge bases for socio-spatial patterns of innovation', *Industry and Innovation* 13(4): 393–414.

Cooke P. (1998), 'Introduction: origins of the concept', in H. J. Braczyk, P. Cooke, and M. Heidenreich (eds.), *Regional Innovation Systems,* Oxford: Oxford University Press, pp. 2–25.

——. (2004), 'Introduction: regional innovation systems – an evolutionary approach', in P. Cooke, M. Heidenreich, and H. J. Braczyk (eds.), *Regional innovation systems: The role of governance in a globalized world*, London and New York: Routledge, pp. 1–19.

——. (2005), 'Rational drug design, the knowledge value chain and bioscience megacentres', *Cambridge Journal of Economics, 29:* 325–41.

——. (2007), *Growth Cultures: the Global Bioeconomy and its Bioregions*, London: Routledge.

Cooke P., Boekholt P. and Tödtling F. (2000), *The Governance of Innovation in Europe: Regional Perspectives on Global Competitiveness*, London: Pinter.

Cooke P., Heidenreich M. and Braczyk H. J. (eds.) (2004), *Regional Innovation Systems: The Role of Governance in a Globalized World*, London and New York: Routledge.

Cowan R., David P. and Foray D. (2000), 'The explicit economics of knowledge codification and tacitness', *Industrial and Corporate Change*, 9(2): 212–53.

Doloreux D. (2002), 'What we should know about regional innovation systems', *Technology in Society*, 24: 243–63.

Doloreux D. and Parto S. (2005), 'Regional innovation systems: current discourse and unresolved issues', *Technology in Society*, 27: 133–53.

Fritsc M. and Stephan A. (2005), 'Regionalization of innovation policy: introduction to the special issue', *Research Policy*, 34(8): 1123–27.

Gertler M. (2004), *Manufacturing Culture: The Institutional Geography of Industrial Practices*, Oxford: Oxford University Press.

Gertler M. and Levitte Y. (2005), 'Local nodes in global networks: the geography of knowledge flows in biotechnology innovation', *Industry and Innovation*, 12(4): 487–507.

Gertler M. and Wolfe D. (2006), 'Spaces of knowledge flows: clusters in a global context', in B. Asheim, P. Cooke, and R. Martin (eds.), *Clusters and Regional Development: Critical Reflections and Explorations*. London and New York: Routledge, pp. 218–35.

Giuliani E. (2005), 'Cluster absorptive capacity: why do some clusters forge ahead and others lag behind?', *European Urban and Regional Studies, 12(3):* 269–88.

Giuliani E. and Bell M. (2005), 'The micro-determinants of meso-level learning and innovation: evidence from a Chilean wine cluster', *Research Policy*, 34(1): 47–68.

Ibert O. (2007), 'Towards a geography of knowledge creation: the ambivalences between "knowledge as an object" and "knowing in practice"', *Regional Studies*, 41(1): 103–14.

Knorr Cetina K. (1999), *Epistemic Cultures: How the Sciences Make Knowledge.* Cambridge MA: Harvard University Press.

Kuhn T. S. (1970), *The Structure of Scientific Revolutions.* Chicago: University of Chicago Press.

Lundvall B. Å. (1992), *National Systems of Innovation: Towards a Theory of Innovation and Interactive Learning*, London: Pinter.

Lundvall B. and Borras S. (1998), *The Globalising Learning Economy: Implications for Innovation Policy*, Luxembourg: Commission of the European Communities.

McKelvey M., Alm H. and Riccaboni M. (2003), 'Does co-location matter for formal knowledge collaboration in the Swedish biotechnology-pharmaceutical sector?', *Research Policy*, 32: 483–501.

Malmberg A. (2003), 'Beyond the cluster: local milieus and global connections', in J. Peck, and H. Yeung (eds.), *Remaking the Global Economy*, London: Sage, pp. 145–62.

Malmberg A. and Maskell P. (2002), 'The elusive concept of localization economies: towards a knowledge-based theory of spatial clustering'. *Environment and Planning*, A 34(3): 429–9.

——. (2006), 'Localized learning revisited', *Growth & Change,* 37(1): 1–19.

Maskell P. and Malmberg A. (1999), 'The competitiveness of firms and regions: "ubiq-uitification" and the importance of localized learning', *European Urban and Regional Studies* 6(1): 9–26.

Maskell P., Eskelinen H., Hannibalsson I., Malmberg A. and Vatne E. (1998), *Competitiveness, Localized Learning and Regional Development: Specialization and Prosperity in Small Open Economies*, London: Routledge.

Melander F. (2006), *Lokal Forskningspolitik: Institutionell dynamik och organisatorisk omvandling vid Lunds Universitet 1980–2005*, Lund University: Lund Political Studies 145, Department of Political Science.

Moodysson J. (2007), *Sites and Modes of Knowledge Creation: On the Spatial Organization of Biotechnology Innovation*, Lund University: Meddelanden från Lunds Universitets Geografiska Institution, Avhandlingar CLXXIV, Department of Social and Economic Geography.

Moodysson J. and Jonsson O. (2007), 'Knowledge collaboration and proximity: the spatial organisation of biotech innovation projects', *European Urban and Regional Studies*, 14(2): 115–31.

Moodysson J., Coenen L. and Asheim B. (2008), 'Explaining spatial patterns of innovation: analytical and synthetic modes of knowledge creation in the Medicon Valley Life Science Cluster', in *Environment and Planning A*, 40(5): 1040–56.

MVA (2006), *Medicon Valley Academy Annual Report 2006*, Lund and Copenhagen: Medicon Valley Academy.

Nonaka I. and Takeuchi H. (1995), *The Knowledge Creating Company*, Oxford and New York: Oxford University Press.

OECD (2005), *A Framework For Biotechnology Statistics*, Paris: Organization for Economic Cooperation and Development.

Oinas P. (1999), 'Activity-specificity in organizational learning: implications for analysing the role of proximity', *Geojournal*, 49(4): 363–72.

Porter M. E. (1990), *The Competitive Advantage of Nations*, London: Macmillan.

——. (2000), 'Locations, clusters, and company strategy', in G. L. Clark, M. P. Feldman and M. S. Gertler (eds.), *The Oxford Handbook of Economic Geography,* Oxford: Oxford University Press, pp. 253–74.

Rosenfeld S. A. (1997), 'Bringing business clusters into the mainstream of economic development', *European Planning Studies*, 5(1): 3–23.

Simon H. (1969), *The Sciences of the Artificial*, Cambridge: MIT Press.

Smith K. (1997), 'Economic infrastructures and innovation systems', in C. Edquist (ed.), *Systems of Innovation: Technology, Institutions and Organisations*, London: Pinter.

——. (2000), 'What is 'the knowledge economy'? Knowledge intensive industries and distributed knowledge bases', paper presented at the DRUID Summer Conference, Aalborg, Denmark, June 2000.

——. (2005), 'Measuring innovation', in J. Fagerberg, D. C. Mowery and R. R. Nelson (eds.), *The Oxford Handbook of Innovation*, Oxford: Oxford University Press pp. 148–77.

Tödtling F. and Trippl M. (2005), 'One size fits all? Towards a differentiated regional innovation policy research?' *Research Policy*, 34(8): 1203–19.

Zeller C. (2004), 'North Atlantic innovative relations of Swiss pharmaceuticals and the proximities with regional biotech arenas', *Economic Geography*, 80(1): 83–111.

Appendix: Overview of cases

Area of focus	*Owner of project and type of actors involved*	*Main challenge*	*Expected outcome*
Biophysical chemistry	*University research group* and other university research groups	Revealing structures and mechanisms of biomolecules	New scientific insights and potentially new methods for drug development
Molecular biophysics	*University research group* and other university research groups and DBF	Revealing structures and mechanisms of biomolecules	New scientific insights and potentially new methods for drug development
Microbiology	*University research group* and other university research groups	Revealing mechanisms of biogenesis of heme-containing proteins	New scientific insights and potentially new knowledge for application by DBFs and the pharmaceutical industry
Neurobiology	*University research group* and other university research groups	Revealing mechanisms of cellular differentiation	New scientific insights and new strategies for cell transplantation
Restorative Neurology	*University research group* and other university research groups, clinical doctors and clinical laboratory	Revealing mechanisms for regulation of neurogenesis	New strategies for recovery after stroke and treatment of neurological diseases
Environmental biotechnology	*University research group* and industry	Revealing mechanisms of biodegradation	New methods for production of biodegradable goods
Computational biology and biological physics	*University research group* and other university research groups and clinical laboratory	Revealing mechanisms of genomics signal processing	New strategies for prediction and treatment of breast cancer
Immunology	*University research group* and other university research groups and DBF	Revealing mechanisms of immunomodulation	New scientific insights and new knowledge for input in strategies for treatment of autoimmune diseases

Area of focus	**Owner** of project and type of actors involved	Main challenge	Expected outcome
Immunotechnology	*University research group* and other university research groups and DBF	Revealing mechanisms of human antibodies	New scientific insights and new knowledge for input in strategies for treatment of autoimmune diseases
Clinical biochemistry	*University research group* and clinical doctors and clinical laboratory	Revealing molecular mechanisms that regulate blood coagulation	New scientific insights and new strategies for prediction and prevention of thrombosis
Biopharmaceuticals	*DBF* and university research group and contract research organization	Identifying, selecting and reproducing human antibodies	New antibody based drug candidate for treatment of HIV
Biopharmaceuticals	*DBF* and university research group and pharmaceutical companies	Developing new and optimizing existing therapeutic and diagnostic proteins	Improved protein based drug candidates
Biopharmaceuticals	*DBF* and contract research organizations, clinical doctors, pharmaceutical company	Exploring and optimizing bioavailability and therapeutic performance of peptides, proteins, and insoluble small molecules	New and improved drug formulation
Biopharmaceuticals	*DBF* and university research group, contract research organization and pharmaceutical company	Identifying and controlling immunomodulatory properties that affect the communication between cells	New immunomodulatory drug candidate for treatment of multiple sclerosis
Biotechnology diagnostics	*DBF* and university research group and clinical laboratories	Specifying structures and mechanisms of antigens	New methods for analyzing autoimmune diseases
Biotechnology diagnostics	*DBF* and clinical doctors and clinical laboratories	Monitoring cell morphology	More efficient and reliable cell morphology analyses

(continued)

Area of focus	**Owner** of project and type of actors involved	Main challenge	Expected outcome
Biotech supplier/ manufacturer	*DBF* and university research groups and other DBFs	Revealing and controlling mechanisms of bioseparation and gene transfer	New tools and methods for gene transfer
Bioinformatics	*DBF* and university research group and engineers	Predicting and controlling liquid conductivity	New methods for monitoring a supply chain over time
Health and nutrition	*DBF* and clinical doctors, food producer and contract research organization	Exploring the workings of a specific bacterial strain on the intestine	New functional foods
Biomaterials and implants	*DBF* and clinical doctors, university research group, contract research organization and medical technology company	Exploring and controlling periodontal regeneration	New method for periodontal therapy/ implants

18 Local innovation systems, upgrading and innovation policy

Lessons from the Bangalore cluster, India

Jan Vang (Copenhagen Institute of Technology, Aalborg University) and Cristina Chaminade (CIRCLE, Lund University)

18.1 Introduction[1]

Upgrading and catching up are and have long been central themes in economics and development studies (Belussi 1996; Schmitz 2006; Kaplinsky 2006; Pietrobelli and Rabellotti 2006). The field is, however, currently being challenged by the rapid growth of certain Asian countries, clusters and regions[2] which are not only catching up but becoming technology leaders in certain fields.[3] The phenomenon is so new that little is known about the factors underpinning this rapid growth. Little attention has been paid to how the challenges in moving from competing on costs to competing on knowledge creation are affected by the firms' embeddedness in local innovation systems and clusters and how the relationship between the firm strategy and the local innovation system evolves over time.

This paper is concerned with unpacking the importance of local innovation systems for the transition of firms in developing countries that strive towards moving from competing on costs to competing on innovations and to discuss the related policy consequences.

Innovation is considered a crucial factor in generating economic growth and development (Lundvall 1992; von Hippel 1988). Most recent work on innovation suggests that the region, cluster or district is a key level at which innovative capacity is shaped and economic processes coordinated and governed (Gu and Lundvall 2006; Vang and Asheim 2006) and, as a consequence, strong focus has been made on the endogenous-led growth of the cluster. That is how the local support system (i.e. universities) is crucial for the local firms – especially the SMEs – attempts at competing as innovators. If the local support system cannot finance and undertake experimentation which can then be commercialized by the private firms the private firms themselves have to carry the high risks and costs (i.e. in-house research as opposed to mainly development) associated with pursuing an innovation-based strategy hence will often not engage in such an endeavour.

Initially, clusters were conceptualized as self-organizing and self-containing systems and firms were most often treated as black boxes responding to or reflecting the support system. The consequence for the policy sphere was a strong focus on constructing or building self-containing local innovation systems. However, developing countries' experiences with so-called self-contained systems (albeit on a national level) represented by import substitutions industrialization strategies (ISI) have shown that self-contained systems have seldom been delivered the expected or desired results in a developing country context (i.e. non-productive rent seeking), thus alluded to a need for strategies combining internal and external sources of capital technology and knowledge. This refers to a multi-scalar approach emphasizing the connectivity between different spatial levels; being between individual actors across national borders, between clusters from different parts of the word, etc. (Belussi, *et al.* 2006).

Thus local innovation systems (LIS) and clusters in developing countries are increasingly being conceptualized as specialized hubs in a globalized innovation and production network (Asheim, *et al.* 2006; Chaminade and Vang forthcoming). The different nodes (i.e. firms, agencies, organizations) have linkages to nodes in other regions or countries. In global innovation and production networks, LIS in developing countries – represented by their firms – have then been traditionally allocated the lowest activities in the value chain.[4] However, a few local innovation systems in developing countries are beginning to challenge this conceptualization by hosting and supporting indigenous firms moving up the value chain (traditional upgrading), innovating for socio-cultural neighbouring markets (niche strategy) and/or using the competences built in the initial phases of development for shifting into related industries (diversified upgrading). Yet, there is still only a poorly developed understanding of how the local system of innovation evolves to support this transition process and what the role of public policy is in building the local conditions to support the needs of the indigenous firms – and especially the SMEs – in this transition process. This paper aims at reducing this omission by looking at how the local system of innovation in Bangalore has made (is making) a transition from low-cost provider to innovator. Where the literature on innovation systems in the developed world assumes the existence of a developed innovation system, this chapter looks at to which extent an innovation system is needed for supporting the transformations process. LIS in this paper refers to both immature and fragmented innovation systems and to fully integrated innovation systems.[5] For doing so, we focus on the transition of Bangalore's software innovation system and cluster.[6] Bangalore's local innovation system is among the most notable successes in attaining the goal of moving up the value chain (albeit still far from having succeeded in this upgrading process as we will argue in this chapter). Recent research has documented that Bangalore has become one of the most important IT clusters outside the OECD countries (though Japan, Germany and Ireland's software exports are larger than India's (Arora and Gambardella 2004). Bangalore is also interesting as a case since it grew basically from scratch without localized lead users pulling the demand of technologies and has managed to sustain the world's highest growth rates within the industry (Arora and Gambardella 2004). It is argued that a combination of easy access to qualified and relatively cheap technical human capital has attracted a number of transnational corporations (TNCs) during the 1980s and 90s (e.g. IBM, Motorola, Hewlett-Packard, Siemens, 3M, Texas) (Vang and Overby 2006). The TNCs have stimulated a tremendous development of the IT software industry either through outsourcing of routine activities or though establishing offshore subsidiaries (there is some dispute as to whether the preceding ISI-phase was a prerequisite for these processes to unfold). This literature, however, has not yet paid much attention to how these TNCs contributed to building competences in the district, how these competences are being used by the SMEs (and other larger indigenous firms) to upgrade and what are the policies needed for supporting the indigenous firms' attempts to move further up the value chain. This chapter attempts to answer some of these questions. The paper is based on fieldwork conducted in Bangalore in October 2006 as well as on a literature review.

The structure of the remainder of the paper is as follows. First, the theoretical framework – local innovation systems – is introduced; special attention is paid to the importance of decentralization, social capital and collective learning as well as to establishing the link between the LIS and the cluster concepts. The importance of these dimensions of LIS and cluster is examined in the context of Bangalore and the implications for LIS literature discussed. This is followed by a section which attempts to tease out some case-specific policy lessons on building LIS in developing countries. Then we highlight central conclusions.

18.2 LIS, SMEs, TNCs and the transition process

The main argument of the chapter is that upgrading to highest value activities is only possible when there is an environment that supports interactive learning and innovation. This is referred to as a local innovation system (LIS). Activities in the higher end of the value chain involve a high degree of innovation and interaction with the customer and other firms and organizations. In the case of SMEs, this interaction takes place at best at local level, with other firms and organizations located in the same geographical area. For this reason, the chapter applies and adapts the so-called LIS[7] approach to developing countries.

Local innovation systems can be seen as a 'constellation of industrial clusters surrounded by innovation supporting organizations' (Asheim and Coenen 2005). Thereby, the local innovation system is made up of two main types of actors and the interactions between them. The first type of actors concerns the companies in the main industrial cluster, including their support industries (e.g. customers and suppliers). In this sense, industrial clusters represent the production component of the local innovation system. In the LIS approach, industrial clusters are defined as the geographic concentration of firms in the same or related industries (Porter 1998; Pietrobelli and Rabelotti 2004, 2006; for a critique, see Martin and Sunley 2003). The second type of actors, supporting the innovative performance of the first type of actors, includes research and higher education institutes (universities, technical colleges, and R&D institutes), technology transfer agencies, vocational training organizations, business associations, finance institutions, etc. They can be created and governed by the central, regional or local government – or private organizations. The importance in a LIS perspective is their physical presence in the area. The underlying idea behind the role attributed to the public sector is that innovations rest on uncertainty (as opposed to risk) and hence make it to 'risky' for firms to carry the costs of the research component of innovations; especially for the SMEs. Firms are more inclined to finance and be risk-taking in respect to commercialization of research; that is development. Innovative activities are also seen as increasingly complex and require the existence of competences beyond the scope of the individual firm. This does not imply that private firms can never take on activities normally attributed to the public section in the IS literature, rather that they are less inclined to do so because of the associated uncertainty and complexity. Hence, as we will show below the lack of a well-functioning (i.e. mature) LIS forces indigenous firms to carry greater research costs and risks than their competitors in the developed world.

In well-functioning LIS (see Figure 18.1), proximity facilitates the knowledge and information circulation needed in the particular industry in a particular context. In the context of LIS, it is important to underline that (Chaminade and Vang 2006) supporting indigenous firms and especially the SMEs in their innovation-oriented upgrading process is a matter of not only facilitating the access to technology, but also providing what we have referred to before as *soft infrastructure* (increasing the qualifications of the human resources, facilitating organizational change, support-ing social capital). This is a prerequisite for taking advantage of knowledge created by the support system (when it exists) – or developing an absorptive capacity. The LIS approach puts the emphasis on the systemic dimension of the innovation process. In innovation systems research, innovation is the result of an interactive learning process most often stretching across firm borders (Lundvall 1992). LIS are especially relevant for SMEs as their interaction takes place mainly at the local level (Asheim, *et al.* 2003; Cooke and Morgan 1998; Cooke and Wills 1999; Schmitz 1992). Moreover, this literature explicitly finds that mostly SMEs extra/firm rela-tions are more confined to the cluster than those of large firms (Cooke and Morgan 1998; Asheim, *et al.* 2003) due to their higher dependence on tacit knowledge. This forces them to rely more on personal ways of transferring (tacit) knowledge and on learning-by-doing and interacting. LIS underscores the importance of several nodes in the knowledge and innovation process, especially the knowledge created by universities as direct input to development processes or through education of a competent labour force. In short, four related system-elements can be identified (Doloreux 2002, Vang, *et al.* forthcoming):

- Firms within a cluster (constituting the knowledge exploitation subsystem).
- Knowledge infrastructure (constituting the knowledge exploration subsystem) in which universities are included.
- Institutions (the 'rules' regulating the behaviour of the actors in the LIS and their interaction).
- Policy (intended to improve the overall innovative performance of the LIS).

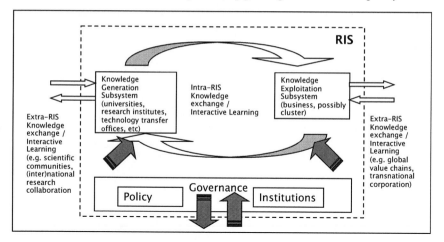

Figure 18.1 Nodes and interactions in a LIS.
Source: Vang, *et al.* forthcoming, based on Coenen (2006).

The soft infrastructure of the LIS (human capital and social capital) is considered crucial to explain innovation in the indigenous firms, especially the SMEs localized in the local arena as we have argued before (Chaminade and Vang 2006). The extent to which they can learn through the interaction with the local environment is a function of their absorptive capacity (Cohen and Levinthal 1990), i.e. the ability to utilize available information and the information and knowledge that comes from the interaction with users or with knowledge providers (i.e. research institutions). Central to building absorptive capacity is the accumulation of human capital and other forms of knowledge. Firms need to have the necessary human capital to identify, acquire and transform the knowledge required for innovation. This is traditionally created by the public education system and by research universities. Large indigenous firms can occasionally compensate for the local gaps in the innovation systems by searching more globally for knowledge and competences. Yet, as Kaufmann and Tödtling (2002) point out, SMEs need to use the human resources more intensively than large firms in their innovation process. However, in general terms SMEs face difficulties in attracting and retaining qualified human resources, especially when they are competing with TNCs as in developing countries.

Interactive learning, especially among indigenous firms might be facilitated by social networks or (inclusive) social capital. The World Bank defines social capital as the institutions, relationships, and norms that shape the quality and quantity of a society's social interactions (World Bank 1998). Unless there is a high degree of social capital cooperation, communication and thus interactive learning is limited (Nooteboom 2000).

In developing countries there is an extensive stream of literature discussing the role of TNCs in the provision of competences (human and organizational) to the indigenous firms (including the SMEs). It is argued that the impact of the TNCs on the local economic development is dependent on the strategic coupling between the local assets and the TNC's assets (Coe, *et al.* 2004 cf. Vang and Asheim 2006). However, this coupling is problematic when the TNC is only approaching the developing cluster to access their cheap labour force. The result is that the developing countries enter the race to the bottom competing only on the basis of low cost labour, low taxes, poor environmental and labour market regulations and so forth. But, when clusters offer some knowledge-based competitive advantage (such as qualified human resources) TNCs can function as an important source of capital and knowledge, leading to competence building and the generation of positive externalities in the local innovation system. As we will discuss later, attracting and retaining TNCs is a matter of (among other issues) being able to reduce the institutional differences between the two countries (home and host). Transnational communities might play an important role in facilitating the interaction between the TNC and the local SMEs (Vang and Overby 2006; Saxenian 1994, 2001).

Interactive learning and thus innovation (stimulated by TNCs or not) only takes place when both human capital and social capital (or networks) are present in the system of innovation, but how these two components are built over time and what the impact is in the firms located in the cluster remain questions to be answered.[8] To understand how this transformation takes place we will now turn to the local innovation system in Bangalore, India.[9] We will pay special attention to how competences are accumulated in the LIS (in particular, we will investigate the role of the external linkages of the cluster, that is, the role of TNCs and transnational corporations in building competences in the indigenous firms). In that respect, we will stress the importance of institutional distances between local innovation systems, which is a dimension not normally touched upon in the LIS literature for understanding the transnational interaction across LIS boundaries. This is central to understand the globalization of innovation processes.

18.3 Bangalore: India's leading software cluster

Situated in Karnataka State, Bangalore has become one of the most important IT clusters outside the US to the extent that it is known as 'India's Silicon Valley' (Nadvi 1995) and certainly the most important in India. Bangalore city, home to around six million inhabitants, is the centre of the city-region spread out around Bangalore. Bangalore is not only the hub for IT-related industries but also houses several high-tech clusters (defence, aeronautics) and is considered to be the scientific and engineering centre of India in terms of research, training and manufacturing. India's best research university, the Indian Institute of Science, is based in Bangalore. Despite the weight of TNCs in the Bangalore IT sector, the large majority of firms are small and medium-sized enterprises (NASSCOM 2005).

Bangalore is well known for its impressive software growth export rates, superior to those of competing IT hubs such as Ireland, Israel, Brazil or China (Arora and Gambardella 2004, 2005; Athreye 2005). The value of exports, for example, typically have grown more than 30 per cent annually while revenues have risen

30–40 per cent. Bangalore is also still highly attractive to TNCs. According to the NASSCOM-McKinsey Study of 2005 India has an estimated share of 65 per cent within the global IT services offshoring segment and around 46 per cent of the global business process outsourcing (BPO) market. The main reason for choosing India is to be found in the gradual accumulation of high quality of the human capital, growth in the number of officially certified firms and possible herd behaviour among TNCs.

A closer look at the statistics shows that most of the exports are due to software services in the low end of the value chain. The process of developing software starts with the identification of the needs of the end user (requirements analysis) and high-level design of the application for the end user. These two activities are considered the software R&D part. They require deep knowledge of the customer's business, close interaction with the customer as well as high-level design skills. These activities are in the higher end of the value chain. Once the product specifications are designed, it follows a series of routine activities of coding, low-level design and maintenance. These are typically the activities that have traditionally been outsourced to other countries such as India. The value added of those activities is low and contact with the end user is not necessary. The routine activities basically draw on codified programming skills while the sophisticated tasks draw on a combination of codified programming competences, and firm-specific – tacit and quasi-codified – competences developed through creating customized programs (in the best cases through interaction with users).

However, a handful of firms in Bangalore seem to be rapidly moving up the value chain, being able to perform both high-level design and requirement analysis. In order to discuss the scope and implications of this move, the large majority of researchers have focused on the strategy of the firms and their competitive advantage in terms of qualification of the human resources and costs. However, little attention has been paid to the role of the local system of innovation in supplying the resources (hard and soft) needed to sustain the growth of the industry and support the transformation of the cluster.

Roughly speaking, we can talk about two different phases in the development of the IT cluster in Bangalore (Chaminade and Vang forthcoming): an initial phase of accumulation of competences and move from body-shopping to more advanced forms of outsourcing and an emerging phase that seems to be relying on interactive learning and innovation as a means to upgrade in the value chain. Both phases will be described with more detail next.

18.3.1 The competence-building phase

18.3.1.1 Industry and learning dynamics during this first phase

The software industry has since its emergence been dominated by US firms as it was driven by interaction between national US security institutions and universities. Until the 1980s, production of IT services was still predominantly a US phenomenon (subsequently an OECD country phenomenon) and outsourcing of

IT services mainly occurred in Silicon Valley, while the east coast IT firms were vertically integrated.

From the late 1980s and onwards, the industry has gradually globalized. In the developing world the vast majority of the IT-based business was located in India. The main reasons for choosing India was cost reduction, the existence of excess capacity of engineers, time zone difference, and widespread English skills. The local Indian innovative capacity within the field was limited as few Indian firms at that time had significant IT competences. Rather, the majority of firms were situated in the low end of the IT service industry. At the same time, most US firms had only limited experience with outsourcing to developing countries. To phrase it differently, this combination of few high-skilled Indian firms and little experience in transacting within developing countries generated a high degree of uncertainty for the US firms around issues such as which subcontractors had the appropriate competences, which subcontractors were trustworthy and which bureaucratic and cultural obstacles they would face (Vang and Overby 2006).

The institutional differences between the US and India were noticeable[10] as Box 18.1 summarizes.

Due to the high institutional distance the US firms experienced a high degree of uncertainty which created costs and difficulties in transacting. The institutional differences initially constrained US firms' propensity to outsource to and establish subsidiaries in India.

The multinationals appreciating the opportunities in India arguably tried to lower these transaction costs. Two critical issues explain the final decision of the US firms to locate in Bangalore: First, the approach to the Indian firms was made gradually to test the reliability of the Indian subcontractor, before any significant task was finally outsourced (learning between TNCs and SMEs). Second, the transnational community played a significant role in reducing the institutional difference between the two countries.

18.3.1.2 Interactive learning between TNCs and indigenous SMEs

Initially, the US firms only moved rather simple and minor activities to India such as maintenance of existing code or reengineering code from one programming language. US firms recognized three reasons for Indian firms not to engage in opportunistic behaviour during these initial contacts: first, the value of future collaboration might exceed the value of reneging on current contracts; second, the need for reaching minimum efficient scale; and, finally, the importance of reputation in the industry. The activities that were initially moved did not involve any high degree of asset specificity, and hence they did not expose the firms to great risk.

Moreover, in the initial phase many small new firms specialized at that time in providing body-shopping services[11] – that is sending software programmers to the (US) client to provide maintenance services – (Arora, *et al.* 1999, 2001). Despite the critics that this strategy has received over time, it seems clear that it helped to reduce the institutional distance between the two countries. The indigenous firms

Box 18.1 Institutional distance between US and India

The differences between Western economies and India are well established in the sociological literature. Weber pointed to the radical differences between Hinduism and Christianity. Some of the concrete challenges firms offshoring to India face are related to the caste system (whom to hire, what it means if you hire a low caste in a higher position), language (Indians speak English fast and their body language is significantly different from Westerners' body language), clarity of arguments (Indians tend not to give straight answers in meetings with bosses), that the US is a low-context culture (i.e. low degree of specifications) and India is a high-context culture (i.e. requiring a high degree of specifications), among others things. The business psychologist Geert Hofstede has tried to systematize cultural differences and measured the difference between India and the US. He divides culture into five dimensions: Power Distance, Individualism, Uncertainty Avoidance, Masculinity and Long term orientation.

Cultural Differences between India and the US

	PD	I	U	M	LT
India	77	48	40	56	61
USA	40	91	46	62	29

Source: www.spectrum.troyst.edu/~vorism/hofstede.htm

According to Hofstede the major differences between India and the US are in the degree of power distance, where India is a society characterized by a high degree of power distance, which is only moderate in the US. The US is a very individualistic country, which is not the case for India. Finally, Indians tend to favour long-term commitments as opposed to short-term commitments in the US. Together these findings indicate a large institutional distance.

became more familiar with the work organization and requirements of the US firms (delivery times, quality, reliability) while the US firm started to gradually outsource tasks to be performed entirely in Bangalore. In a sense, this build-up of trust between the partners was the result of the interaction and mutual learning between the TNC and the indigenous firm providing the software service. As acknowledged by Parthasarathy and Aoyama (2007) the TNCs induced both process and functional upgrading in the indigenous SMEs.

Yet this is not enough to explain the initial uptake in outsourcing and foreign subsidiary establishment in India. As co-founder of Infosys, one of India's leading technology firms, explains:

In the early 90s, when we went to the United States to sell our services, most chief information officers didn't believe that an Indian company could build the large applications they needed. ... We realized that there was a huge gap between, on the one hand, how prospective Western clients perceived Indian companies and, on the other, our own perception of our strengths.

To adequately explain the increase in outsourcing and offshoring from the US to India it is necessary to understand the role of members of the Indian transnational community in the US.

18.3.1.3 The role of the transnational community

The importance of the Indian community is indicated by the stylized fact that in Silicon Valley alone more than 750 IT firms have a CEO with Indian background (2001 numbers), Indians received around half of the H1-B visas (special visas for experts) and half of them (135,000 in 2001) work in the IT industry (www.north-south.org). Moreover, members of transnational communities are also returning to India. Several members of this community held important positions in US firms. These members played a significant role in shaping the outsourcing and offshoring decisions in the US firms as the following examples illustrate. Large institutional distance and significant uncertainty prevented US-based Motorola from utilizing the advantages of India. In 1991, Motorola established MIEL, a software subsidiary in Bangalore. Despite the obvious cost advantages no product sector within Motorola was willing to risk sourcing its software needs from MIEL. Ramachandran and Dikshit (2002) explain: 'The first breakthrough came when Arun Sobti, an Indian who was a senior manager in Motorola's Land Mobile Product Sector in Florida, USA, decided to give MIEL a chance.' They also did some internal marketing with other divisions in their companies even though this was not part of their formal roles. According to Ramachandran and Dikshit, although the first project from Sobti was successful, Sobti was unable to give any more projects to MIEL, because he faced budgetary cuts in his division. However, Sobti continued to help: He put Shrikant Inamdar, the then General Manager (Operations) in MIEL on to the Cellular sector, and he personally lobbied with the sector's management and helped MIEL get its second contract for a Motorola product called CT2. Since the work was in the cellular domain, it afforded MIEL an opportunity to learn about the wireless technology that Motorola was famous for.

International social capital (in the structural sense) was also important when Texas Instruments (TI) set up its first international IT-subsidiary in Bangalore, India in 1985. The establishment was made possible because the Indian TI vice president Mohan Rao utilized his professional position in the US and his knowledge of the Indian political bureaucratic system to facilitate TI's entrance into India. Rao used this combination to get access to top-level people in the Indian government, which in turn allowed him to push the ideas of building an Indian IT industry and to establish a TI plant in India. In other words, his knowledge of the Indian political culture allowed him to reduce the bureaucratic uncertainties and deal directly with top-level politicians in the Indian government. The bureaucracy also ran more smoothly because TI bought the most modern IT equipment and gave it to the Indian government.

Hence, in line with Saxenian, we argue that 'As they [Indians in the US] gained seniority in US companies in the 1990s, many non-resident Indians (NRIs) were instrumental in convincing senior management to source software or establish operations in India to take advantage of the substantial wage differentials for software skill'. Hereby the Indian transnational community in the US played a crucial role in the development phase of the Indian software industry.

18.3.1.4 What it takes from the LIS to support this strategy

The most important role of the local innovation system during this first phase was the supply of highly qualified yet very cheap labour force for the provision of software services to the TNCs. In other words, Bangalore became the dominant location for the outsourced and offshored TNC activities because of the concentration of highly skilled labour in Bangalore. This attracted the indigenous firms and TNCs. The attractiveness of Bangalore was determined by its dominant position within the educational and research systems in India where Bangalore had a privileged position in comparison with other Indian clusters. Today Karnataka State, hosting the Bangalore cluster, has a total of more than 65 engineering colleges (albeit of varied quality).

Bangalore benefited from central government choice of locating some of the best educational institutions in the region such as the world renowned Indian Institute of Science and other research centres such as the Indian Institute of Information Technology, Raman Research Institute, National Institute of Mental Health and Neuro-Sciences, Central Food Technological Research Institute, Indian Space Research Organization, National Aeronautical Laboratory, and others. Additionally, as a result of military research strategies Bangalore has been the centre for advanced science and military research. Bangalore was mainly chosen for physical geographical reasons such as dust-free air which was a requirement for military testing.

The co-location of educational and research institutions created the conditions behind a cumulative causation process allowing Bangalore to become the dominant centre of IT. However, the supply-side aspects only became efficient when combined with an export-oriented development strategy which 'put the resources to work'. The provision of highly qualified human resources together with the co-location of a great number of educational and research institutions set the grounds for the emergence of the local system of innovation.[12] The local advantages provided by Bangalore could explain the initial interest of the US firms in locating their outsourcing activities in the cluster. But, what has been the role of the government in creating the local conditions that facilitate the emergence of the Bangalore LIS?

18.3.1.5 The role of the government in the accumulation of competences

After the initial policy failures the central state's policies did play an important role of creating the conditions making India an attractive location; the initial support from the central government was dismantling the rather counterproductive ISI strategy.[13] This resulted in the development of a more pro-export 'hands-off' policy where the central state reduced the import duties and created incentives for exporting.

Second, the Indian central government has been most successful in providing the required human capital in the cluster and in sustaining the educational effort over time. As Arora and Gambardella (2004) acknowledge, the:

> Accredited engineering capacity in India increased from around 60,000 in 1987–88 to around 340,000 in 2003, and IT capacity has increased from around 25,000 to nearly 250,000. NASSCOM figures indicate that in India the number of IT graduates increased from 42,800 in 1997 to 71,000 in 2001. By comparison, the number of IT graduates in the U.S. increased from 37,000 in 1998 to 52,900 in 2000. During this period the IT workforce (which does not directly correspond to IT degree holders) in the U.S. was probably eight to tenfold larger than the IT workforce in India.

But with the exception of these two major policies and the provision of research institutes in the area (Parthasarathy and Aoyama 2007), the role of the government in building the industrial and innovation capacity of the cluster has been very limited (Van Dijk 2003). 'Until 1991–92, there was virtually no policy support at all for the software sector. Even the term "benign neglect" would be a too positive phrase to use in this connection', writes the former head of Department of Electronics, Dr Sen (quoted from Parthasarathy 2004a).

One could argue that the fact that Bangalore firms have to some extent been capable of moving up the global value chain is more the result of a deliberate strategy of the transnational firms to locate in Bangalore and of the indigenous firms for building up their absorptive capacity than a consequence of strong policy intervention (beyond investments in education). Moreover, an important albeit not statistically documented dynamic in this phase was cluster growth by spin-offs created by Indians that previously worked for a large TNC as derived from the interviews conducted by the authors.

The change in the strategy away from 'body-shopping' – used in the initial phase – to distance work was also facilitated partly by the advances of ICT technologies as well as deliberate strategies among the TNCs to modularize and standardize some of their IT processes.

This provided the background for the distance work which in turn allowed the Bangalore firms to maintain a broader knowledge base at home (Parthasarathy 2004a, 2004b) and improve the career opportunities (and subsequently reduce the turnover rate with its negative implications for the firms' ability to build firm-specific knowledge), hence secure better absorptive capacity.

The question now is how these accumulated competences in the firm and in the cluster can be used to move further on in the global value chain.

18.3.2 Towards an innovation phase?

Very recently we have been witnessing an upsurge of literature claiming that there is a move towards higher added value activities in software production in Bangalore and an increasing number of foreign companies have established or are in the process of setting software centres in India from where they export to other countries (Arora, *et al.* 1999, 2001).[14]

As indicated earlier, higher activities involve the design and prototyping of new products or systems, which is considered as R&D software services (Barr and Tessler 1996). Although we acknowledge that most of the firms are still operating in the low end of the value chain, we want to investigate what the implications are of such an upgrading strategy for the local innovation systems of Bangalore, as well as the policy implications.

It should be noted that what will be described next should be interpreted as an emerging trend rather than a consolidated tendency or general move in the LIS.[15]

It is, however, important to discuss the implications of such an emerging trend in the very early stages, as policy makers could play a very significant role supporting this transition to higher added value activities through innovation and interactive learning embedded in an effective local system of innovation.

For doing so, we will take as an example the provision of R&D services in embedded software (Parthasarathy and Aoyama 2007) which is summarized in Box 18.2. Furthermore, it seems that the 'low-cost' road (i.e. competing on the basis of low costs) can not endure too long as the salaries of the Indian engineers are rapidly increasing (Saxenian 2001; Parthasarathy and Aoyama 2007), with growth rates far superior to those of the US.

18.3.2.1 Industry and learning dynamics during the second phase

Bangalore has maintained its position as the dominant software cluster in India well ahead other clusters in the country, as Figure 18.2 shows.

Bangalore is probably the cluster now capable of providing the most advanced IT services, and indigenous firms have started to outsource to other cheaper emerging clusters.

As the industry has matured both Bangalore and US firms have improved their competences in handling offshore outsourcing to build up cultural competences and create their own local networks.

Employee attrition and wage increases has forced the firms to introduce human capital management and other advanced management techniques in their firms (Arora, *et al.* 1999; Athreye 2003, 2005).

This, together with a tendency to codify procedures and improve the transfer of knowledge, has increased the organizational capital of the firm (hence their absorptive capacity).

Box 18.2 Upgrading to the provision of software services in the embedded software industry in Bangalore

Embedded software is a particular branch of the industry which combines hardware and software. It is designed to perform tasks without human intervention. The best example is the chip. In the embedded software industry there is an increasing number of firms that have started to provide intellectual property blocks (R&D) that are integrated in various embedded systems. Upgrading in this segment of the software industry is possible because the firms have acquired new capabilities, comply with international standards and have gained a reputation internationally. According to the CEO of Sasken Communication Technologies, 'companies go to Bangalore for complete solutions, based on the expertise, knowledge base and credibility of the local firms, and no longer for cost reasons'. Innovation has been stimulated by a growing number of start-ups that specialized exclusively in R&D services targeting niche markets (combination of upgrading in the value chain and diversification). Interaction with other local firms is also increasing, to be able to assemble IP blocks and sell a complete solution to a TNC, both based on formal and informal networks. Parthasarathy and Aoyama indicate that 'local networks are being developed among domestic firms in Bangalore, in part because of the emergence of local business opportunities and in part because of a greater interest among firms to exploit new opportunities' (p. 23).

Source: Parthasarathy and Aoyama (2007).

They have also invested in development of management competences (Saxenian 2001) which constituted an important constraint for Bangalore firms aiming at moving up the value chain (there is still a tendency in the firms to promote people to managers before they have the appropriate experience; often after only two or three years). The broader knowledge base combined with the existence and gradual building of reputation in the US market plus an aggressive certifying strategy among most Indian firms is allowing some firms to move up the global value chain (to the provision of R&D services for multinational firms) and, even in some cases, to develop their own innovation strategy and enter new niche markets with their own final product.[16]

According to the National Association of Software and Service Companies (NASSCOM), the main industry association, 'R&D service exports accounted for US$1.21 billion, or 15.8% of India's software exports, in 2001–02. The figures

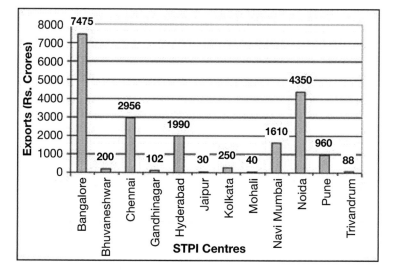

Figure 18.2 Exports of IT related products by region.
Source: www.bangaloreit.in (2006).

grew to US$1.66 billion and 17.4% respectively in 2002–03, and is estimated to grow to US$9.2 billion by 2010' (NASSCOM 2005; PTI 2004, quoted from Parthasarathy and Aoyama 2007).

Offshoring or outsourcing R&D projects to India/Bangalore involve larger challenges than outsourcing/offshoring standardized and routine activities. The former activities are sequential, can be decomposed and codified. This is not the case for the R&D activities (Nelson and Winter 1982) and the literature on innovations – outside the innovation systems literature – has typically associated these activities with in-house activities (near the headquarters). This is because markets for information, knowledge and technology (Arora, *et al.* 2001) are riddled with imperfections derived from the culturally specific, embedded, tacit and firm-specific knowledge associated with R&D activities as these types of activities are normally associated with culturally specific, embedded, tacit and firm-specific knowledge. The evidence suggests that TNCs are increasingly locating high-end R&D activities to Bangalore but they tend to keep the project in-house for secrecy reasons; in-house they are even modularized so employees cannot 'steal' ideas, as some of the interviewees pointed out.

18.3.2.2 What it takes from the LIS to support this strategy

Three central challenges, related to institutional distance, constrain the outsourcing or offshoring of innovative activities (i.e. R&D):

• First, innovative activities do require face-to-face communication as they involve a high degree of tacit knowledge. Tacit knowledge is embedded in the cultural and geographical context and hence difficult to translate from one geographical context to another (even for members of the transnational community). In the context of the US–India it implies a high frequency of meeting between the two parties, thus diminishing the cost advantages that working with Indian firms report to US firms.

- Second, the cost advantages for the US of locating R&D activities in India is considerably lower than with routinized activities as they carry additional transaction costs, communication costs as well as a higher risk (in a context where there is not a lack of supply of competent employees in the US). The higher costs are a function of the need to increase face-to-face interaction (thus involving a lot of travelling), the scarcity of research staff in India, especially those that can think 'out of the box', as the interviews suggest.

- Finally, one needs to add that IP rights for software are virtually non-existent apart from for embedded software which makes it highly risky to outsource or offshore innovative and/or R&D activities. As Barr and Tessler (1996) point out, the outcome of the R&D software services is a finished product that can be easily copied and distributed at no cost. In this sense, offshoring of software R&D is riskier than any other form of R&S outsourcing. IP rights are a crucial element here.

Additionally, one of the crucial factors is that – apart form formal competences which several Indian firms have by how – the activities up the value chain require learning from the end users (and lead users) which in turn demands a close interaction with them; firms need to interact closely with the end user and posses great technical capability and deep knowledge on the business processes of the client (Arora, *et al.* 1999). But those clients are mostly located in the OECD countries.[17] This again places the TNCs in a central role, as they are located in the OECD countries. The transnational community has been an active player in 'pushing' the Indian firms up the value chain, especially as venture capitalists, by reducing the dimensions of institutional distance relevant when talking about R&D projects between the US and India. They typically funded ventures that have a front end (sales and marketing) in the US and a back end (software development) in India. Other members of the Indian transnational community have become intermediaries/salespeople for software companies, either as consultants or employees. A few have also opened companies in India, leveraging their relationships in the US (e.g. Pradeep Singh of Aditi, a former Microsoft employee). Firms such as TiE (The IndUS Entrepreneurs) started spanning both the US and India and creating a global network. This raised the image of India as a source of high technology and indirectly promoted software contracts to Indian firms. Also, managers who have worked for other multinationals in India play a key role. For example, Raman Roy, who set up GE Capital's back-office in Gurgaon (near Delhi), was later persuaded by a leading venture capital firm to set up his own company to provide third-party services. His company, Spectramind, was subsequently acquired by Wipro, a large Indian IT services company.

Additionally, the upgrading strategies of indigenous firms have been constrained by the lack of interactive learning and cooperation between the indigenous firms in Bangalore (Chaminade and Vang, forthcoming); there has continued to be interactive learning along vertical dimensions (between SMEs and TNCs) but horizontal or collective learning has not developed much in the software industry in general. In other words the Indian firms did only to a limited extent engage in interactive learning compared to more bustling IT clusters such as Silicon Valley. The successful case of the embedded software industry (see Box 18.2) is a clear example of the advantages of collective action and learning among groups of SMEs. SMEs have been able to provide final products to the TNC by assembling different modules that were developed by other firms (Parthasarathy and Aoyama 2007). That is, a group of SMEs, each of them specialized in one part of the final product, gained economies of scale and scope by collaborating in the provision of an R&D service. Furthermore, informal social networks are also quite frequent in the embedded software segment.

While the embedded software case is inspirational, this type of interaction is not yet frequent in the software industry in general. The lack of collective learning can partly be explained by formal constraints imposed on the Indian subcontractors (i.e. security concerns and lack of appropriate IP rights) as well as the high degree of competition among the indigenous SMEs. As we have argued before (Chaminade and Vang 2006) social capital in the cluster is very weak and (at most) limited to the networks of alumni associations. The lack of local social capital has prevented collective learning, the transfer of knowledge and best practices among the indigenous SMEs and thus constrained the bargaining power of the indigenous firms – especially the SMEs – vis-à-vis the TNCs.

Additionally, as software production becomes more advanced and the Bangalore firms are trying to diversify into other domains, their ability to act as knowledge creators seems to be hampered by the limitations of the national and local innovation system. In a sense the indigenous firms have to maintain the basic research in-house (and largely paid for by themselves), relying on a 'self-sponsored' corporate innovation systems. In contrast, the firms in the OECD countries can tap into national and local innovation systems by engaging in private-public partnerships concerning R&D. The larger Bangalore firms have tried to reduce these differences by setting up some minor subsidiaries in important research clusters and by buying up of firms. This process is, however, new and the strategy to buy firms is only limited to a handful of firms that have the financial resources (interviews with local experts). Compared with firms in the OECD countries the possibilities for relying on this strategy are also limited. Hence, currently we are witnessing several big problems for the firms in diversifying into new domains (outside their specialization in banking and finance).[18]

Furthermore, the supply of qualified human resources seems to be reaching a limit. If one eliminates the handful of world-class technical institutions, the picture is one of shortages of high-quality staff (Arora and Gambardella 2005; NASSCOM-McKinsey 2005), and under-investment in research facilities (Vang, *et al.* forthcoming). With few exceptions universities are almost exclusively devoted to the provision of (qualified) manpower to the local firms (Basant and Chandra 2006). Research is often more basic research and, as a consequence, universities are not playing a significant role in supporting innovation and generating research results for the local firms.[19]

In contrast with the previous phase where the focus was on the accumulation of competences in the system of innovation and not so much on the interaction between the different elements of the system, innovation is based on interactive learning among firms, and between firms and the final customer. The analysis of the Bangalore LIS shows that none of the two types of interactions is really strong in the system. In this sense, there is a great opportunity for policy makers to put in place the conditions necessary for building Bangalore's future. However, some interesting initiatives seem to be taking place. NASSCOM is quite active in promoting the development of local entrepreneurial networks (Parthasarathy and Aoyama 2007). Entrepreneurial organizations and bridging institutions have been traditionally very good vehicles to stimulate the collaboration between SMEs, even when no prior collaboration existed (Chaminade 2004).

18.3.2.3 The role of the government in supporting innovation and interactive learning

The role of the government supporting interactive learning and innovation, although critical in this phase, is almost absent in the Bangalore case. The idiosyncratic character of the R&D activities as opposed to more routine activities pleads for a more decentralized governmental intervention (i.e. increasing role of the local government). From our perspective, at least two policy instruments could be initially used to stimulate the systemic propensities of the Bangalore LIS.

As we have mentioned, joint action is particularly relevant for SMEs in this phase. By collaborating, and diversifying by combining the acquired competences, firms can experiment with path shifts that might allow them to encroach on the lead firms that dominate every value chain, as the case of embedded software suggests. Thus policies should stimulate collaborations exploiting scale and scope. This has been done traditionally in the developed world by allocating financial support (e.g. via R&D subsidies) only to consortia of SMEs or of SMEs and research institutions. Policies, particularly at local level, can also facilitate associational activities that bring together local producers, researchers, service providers and even the government with the objective of solving collectively a problem that is affecting all the system, such as the need for better communication infrastructures in the cluster (Saxenian 2001).

Additionally, the experiences in Ireland, Israel and China suggest (Breznitz 2005; Sands 2005; Tschang and Xue 2005) that the government might play an important role by using public procurement as an instrument to stimulate experimentation and innovation in the local firms (i.e. the government as lead customers) (Arora and Gambardella 2004). This has been done in India on a very limited scale (Kumar and Joseph 2006). Public procurement might be very important to create local markets and give the right incentives to the indigenous SMEs to use their competences for innovation.[20] However, public procurement might also steer the local innovation towards products or services that have relatively low value in international markets. In this sense, a well-informed government is a prerequisite for the success of public procurement. Additionally, there is a need to level the playing field so that IT products and services sold in the domestic market enjoy the same tax benefits as those currently enjoyed by export goods and services (Saxenian 2001).

18.4 The transition of the system of innovation: some lessons from the Bangalore case

The notion of systems of innovation carries implicitly the idea of interaction and mutual dependency among the different elements of the system. What the Bangalore case clearly shows is that systems in developing countries are developed over time, in close interaction with the strategies of the indigenous firms, the government and the transnational corporations.

The local system of innovation emerges when the cluster starts accumulating competences and organizations: a critical mass of local firms involved in a similar or related activity (i.e. a cluster), qualified human resources and good training institutions, organizational capabilities and research facilities. In the initial phases those competences are hardly connected to each other, that is, the systemicness of the local system is still very low. However, the external linkages of the LIS are fundamental. Local social capital is weak while international social capital (i.e.) links between Diaspora members and entrepreneurs, indigenous incumbents, educational institutions and government officials in their home country is central (see below). Established LIS can to a large extent maintain their position by a continued focus on supply-side factors (i.e. human capital) due to the cumulative causation process. Focus on the supply side allows for maintaining cost advantages in combination with incremental minor movements up the value chain.

The competences accumulated in the LIS and the firms located in the cluster during the first stages (from the interaction with the TNC or the provision of human capital from the cluster) start to be used to upgrade in the value chain. However, this is not sufficient for firms to move further up in the value chain. 'Radical' upgrading can take two forms (Izushi and Aoyama 2007): (1) indigenous firms – including SMEs – can move up to higher value added activities in the value chain; or (2) firms can diversify and enter into higher value market niches. The first of the two strategies might be problematic as the value chain is usually dominated by lead firms with a strong market power. The second strategy might be more feasible, but requires a sound knowledge of the market and the competences to move to a different market segment (diversify).

The systemic propensity of the LIS becomes now a critical factor. Innovation is a socially embedded interactive process (Lundvall 1992). Firms and individuals do not innovate in isolation but in continuous interaction with other individuals and other organizations and with the users.

If, during the first phase, interaction was mainly limited to the relationship between the TNCs and the local SMEs, during this second phase the formal and informal networks among SMEs are of utmost importance in supporting innovation and upgrading. Interaction is not only important as a form of 'pooling resources' that are limited for SMEs but as a vehicle to exchange information, knowledge and practices which are needed for the upgrading. By interacting with each other SMEs learn about new markets, new products, techniques etc. And it is this interactive learning that supports innovation and upgrading.

The type of interaction is different when concerned with low-end activities as innovative and R&D activities involve a high degree of uncertainty, tacit knowledge and – potentially – highly valuable knowledge which is difficult to write complete contracts for, thus a stronger reliance on social capital. Strong local social capital is extremely important in this phase (Chaminade 2004; Chaminade and Vang 2006) as it facilitates trusting relations between subjects within the firm and between different firms (Nielsen 2003). It decreases transaction costs, increases quantity and quality of information, facilitates coordination and diminishes collective action problems and thus facilitates the transfer of knowledge. Knowledge is highly embedded in the context.

Interaction with the customer is also crucial. User-producer interaction is one of the most important forms of innovation (Lundvall 1988) especially for certain sectors such as software (Pavitt 1984). As mentioned earlier, during the first phase of development, the dominant form of interaction is between the SME and the TNC. SMEs do not have direct access to the final customer but provide specific modules of the final product or perform specific tasks for the TNC. However, in this phase direct contact with the lead customers is crucial for the indigenous firms – including SMEs – that aim at upgrading. And when it comes to the R&D strategies of the firms – even concerning basic research – they are likely to have to rely more on a supply strategy than the user-producers interaction strategy increasingly used in OECD countries, which increases the uncertainty and hence the probability of investments failures. The access to the local customer might be more problematic in developing countries as the local market is usually underdeveloped, thus not providing a good testing field for new products or services, especially in high-tech sectors such as IT. The LIS needs to provide the links with the markets (local or international). With few exceptions (Brazil and China) local markets for software in the developing countries are weak. Instead, local firms tend to target the external markets, usually working for a TNC as the Bangalore case illustrates. To some extent the access to final international customers can be facilitated by transnational communities. Transnational communities reduce the institutional distance between the home and the host country. It diminishes the transaction costs derived by the access to external markets, but there are still several aspects that cannot be bridged. The IP system, for example, still needs to be developed and implemented for software. Additionally, the school system increasingly needs to focus on the requirement of innovations (i.e. creativity as opposed to focusing on the transmission of technical knowledge). Managers reported that this was a large obstacle among a large proportion of their employees ('fear of failures', 'fear of mistakes') due to the hierarchical family-oriented culture in India where even crucial decisions of importance for the individual are taken by their parents or their bosses (most IT firms do, however, maintain a rather decentralized organizational firm supporting so-called learning organizations). Additionally, lack of middle managers constrains the possibility for improving the efficiency, reliability and creativity of the firms.

In sum, it is necessary to think about LIS as dynamic entities, especially in developing countries where well functioning LIS are not prevalent. Contrary to what is argued in the LIS literature, it seems that the systemic propensity of the systems is not necessary in the first phases, where the objective is to attract foreign investment and accumulate competences. However, it becomes a crucial factor when the firms attempt to move up the value chain with activities that involve a higher degree of innovation. In this phase, the absence of networks between the different components of the system might seriously hamper the development of the cluster and the local firms.

18.5 Policy implications: local versus central government intervention

From a policy perspective, one of the clearest conclusions is that the role of the local and central government also changes over time (and in parallel with the transformation of the strategies of the firms and the LIS). In the initial phases the local government bodies do not play an important role as the factors for attracting TNCs usually fall within the domain of the central government, apart from ensuring a well functioning infrastructure and bureaucracy (i.e. limited corruption and red tape). The countries compete on the traditional measures associated with comparative advantages (i.e. low costs) in developing countries, thus the ability to attract the standard and routine activities, and so forth. The central state, however, should ensure sound macroeconomic policies (i.e. low inflation), non-discrimination between exports and imports; possibly with selective measures protecting infant industries. Central state policies should focus on the supply side[21], on reducing the transaction costs for TNCs to outsource or offshore to developing countries[22] and on providing reasonable intellectual property controls:

- On the supply side especially important is a need for an integrated approach stressing the provision of highly qualified human capital with practical skills. It is, however, not enough to just stress the importance of creating a well educated workforce (which includes higher education, but also primary and secondary education systems).
- As discussed earlier the main constraints preventing TNCs from taking advantage of the supply of human capital are the transaction costs associated with institutional distances between the home country of the TNC and the host country of the outsourced or offshored activity. In the initial phases, where the objective is to attract TNCs to the cluster and link them to the local SMEs, reducing this institutional distance is an important policy objective. From a

policy perspective, this can be done mainly by reinforcing the national and local institutions (regulations, patent laws, etc.) or training the local firms in the management of inter-cultural differences and targeting the members of the transnational community.

- Finally, the central government needs to develop reliable intellectual property rights that allow the companies outsourcing R&D services to protect their products from copying and other negative spillovers of information. The outcome of an R&D service is a final product, almost ready to be commercialized. In this sense NASSCOM has been crucial in ensuring intellectual property protection for the Indian software firms (Parthasarathy and Aoyama 2007).

From a knowledge perspective the type of activities involved in software are standardized, hence there is not a strong need for decentralizing the decision power structure. But local governments might play a role in creating incentives to attract the educational and research institutions and the TNCs to their clusters. In this sense, there are good reasons to allow the local governments freedom to build education and research institutions (this, however, can result in increased inequality within the country).

The role of the local government is more prominent during the second phase where a sound knowledge of the different actors in the system, their competences and their interaction is needed. The local governments need to stimulate local networks and the local markets. This calls for a decentralized decision making structure as local government – given the developed competences and capacity – possesses the local stock of knowledge, especially the 'emerging' needs. In other words, local governments are likely to play a more conducive role in facilitating the upgrading process as they have incentives for being dedicated to the needs of their particular cluster (though even an area such as Bangalore has it own 'twisted' incentives that lead to occasional discrimination against the software industry). National government bodies might have competing development agendas (growth versus regional equality, for example). Additionally, if local government bodies are directly involved in setting up and managing education and research institutions they can better be tailored to the need of the firms in the cluster. And probably the local government bodies will be more sensitive to the SMEs' particular needs in this context (certainly in democratic states where SMEs constitute a large bulk of voters).

18.6 Conclusions

The case highlights the importance of looking at the dynamics of the system, that is, its emergence and evolution over time. Markets in the initial phase might prove more efficient than assumed by LIS theorists and thus there might be less need for local policies as such (apart from those stressing the supply side); certainly LIS polices without a complementary macro policy will not result in local development. In addition there seems to be lees need for emphasising policies underpinning social capital formation and collective learning in the initial phase;

collective learning mainly becomes relevant at a time where the indigenous firms have built competences until a certain level and diversity (before this there will be diminishing returns for collaboration with other indigenous firms as opposed to TNCs). Decentralization is also less urgently called for than that suggested by LIS theorists. However, in the second phase reliance on markets seems less convincing as the market imperfections constrain distance collaborations – also the incentives for distance collaboration are smaller as cost differences are minor. Thus while there is a need for upgrading the human capital (to maintain focus on the supply side) the government public procurement policies become central for compensating for market imprecations and lack of localized lead customers and for stimulating collective learning. A decentralized decision making structure becomes crucial in the latter phase.

The case clearly highlights the need to adopt a flexible and accommodative policy that takes into account the changes in the needs of the local firms, the endowments of the local innovation system and the international networks going beyond traditional self-contained systems. As Saxenian (2001) suggests, upgrading in the global value chain requires moving away from 'replication' of successful models (i.e. Silicon Valley) to new pathways that respond to the specific conditions of each of the clusters. The LIS approach allows policy makers to foresee the threats and possibilities of the future of the IT Bangalore LIS. We argue that, unless there is a clear investment in the systemic propensities of the LIS, the possibilities of the indigenous SMEs to upgrade are seriously limited.

Finally, to put our findings in perspective, innovation systems and clusters on one hand, and TNCs on the other, are conceived as a binary relation, but future research should pay more attention to the intra-national dynamics of the TNCs' location strategies (as suggested by Chen and Vang 2008). This will allow for rethinking the multiscalar approach in a new dynamic fashion that emphasizes how local nodes are nodes not only in global networks but also in intra-national networks and support systems. This is likely to provide new insights into the importance of local innovation policies, policy specializations etc. Yet, while that is a promising future path, it is beyond the scope of this paper.

Notes

1 We thank Hubert Schmitz, Ralphie Kaplinsky and Parthasarathi Banerjee for their comments and suggestions to earlier versions of this paper. We are also grateful to the comments received by the participants of the Antwerpen workshop on 'The rapid industrialization of China and India' (April 2006) and the ESTO project workshops, particularly Suma Athreye, Nick von Tunzelmann and Marc Bogdanowicz. Finally, we thank Fiorenza Belussi and Silvia Rita Sedita for inviting us. All errors remain ours. The paper draws on the same data as our forthcoming paper in Research Policy – Chaminade and Vang (forthcoming).

2 We will introduce our definitions later in the text. The literature is currently not clear on the differences between the different concepts. Sufficient here should be that the innovation systems refer to the (local) support system while the cluster is the spatial concentration of similar or related industrial activities within the innovation system. Regions tend to carry the connotations of formal regions.

3 The literature is especially focusing on India and China and the insights from Japan's and the so-called tigers development trajectories are included (see *IDS Bulletin* 37(1), 1 January 2006 for an overview).

4 In IT, for example, testing of software, standard programming, and so forth.

5 It should be emphasized that we do not argue for one modernization model only, nor that modernization should follow the same paths or reach the same goals. Fully developed innovation systems do not exist in developing countries yet.

6 To be more precise we focus on Bangalore's software district which is embedded in the weak LIS. Most attention is paid to the firm level analysis.

7 LIS is in many ways is similar to regional innovation systems yet without the same focus on the formal regions.

8 There is an emerging literature alluding to the transition process of systems of innovation, particularly in Asia (Lundvall, *et al.* 2006 compiles several studies of innovation systems in transition in Asia) but very few theoretical works unfolding how this transition takes place (Galli and Teubal 1997 is one of these few attempts).

9 We do not wish to engage in the conceptual discussion on the differences between industrial districts, clusters and regional innovation systems. We merely use the approaches as hermeneutical devices for unpacking and addressing the included themes.

10 Institutions refer to 'the rules of the game in a society or, more formally, are the humanly devised constraints that shape human interaction' (North 1990: 3). Institutional distance refers to the perceived differences in institutional frameworks (often associated with problems) between the firms' home and 'host' country (Vang and Overby 2006). Peng explains that 'no firm can be immune from the institutional frameworks in which it is embedded' and 'that when organizations [TNCs] attempt to expand beyond their national boundaries they implicitly take with them their nation's history of socioeconomic choices' (Peng 2002: 251).

11 Body-shopping was explicitly recognized in the Computer Policy of 1984 (Saxenian 2001).

12 While we cannot provide statistical data on the number of employees that came from these research institutions in the initial phase, our interviews confirm that they played a significant role (technology spillovers, however, were more limited in scope).

13 Though it should be remembered that TATA and other indigenous firms were established during the ISI phase.

14 Saxenian (2001) claims that there is little more than anecdotal evidence of this move towards more sophisticated design and programming projects.

15 The majority of Bangalore and Indian firms – especially SMEs – however, remain in the lower end of the software industry, which indicates that the upgrading strategy is still limitedly successful; an indicator of this is that value of sales/employment is 50 (slightly higher than China and Brazil on respectively 37,6 and 45,5) which is significantly lower than in US (195,3), Japan (159,2) and Germany (132,7) (Arora and Gambardella 2004). This is in line with the NASSCOM-McKinsey Study 2005 that suggests that cost advantages are still the main reason for choosing Bangalore/India (despite that India is slightly more expensive than competing countries).

16 It should be noted that the two strategies are not mutually exclusive but can be found in the same firm. However, the diversification strategy is still very scarce, with just a little anecdotal evidence of a limited amount of firms that have adopted this strategy. For this reason, we will hereon focus mainly on the traditional upgrading strategy (moving up the value chain to the provision of R&D services).

17 It should be mentioned here that most of the production of the software sector in India goes to external markets (according to Arora, *et al.* exports account for 65 per cent or the software revenue) and this number is growing.

18 Even within banking and finance the largest Bangalore firms have hardly any propriety software. Infosys has one important program; mainly used in developing countries.

TATA IT branch has just bought up Australian firms having propriety software within the domain.

19 See Vang, *et al.* forthcoming for a more detailed discussion on the role of universities in the development of Bangalore system of innovation.

20 Many scholars argue that Indian SMEs already have the design capabilities.

21 In contexts where education is within the domain of the regions this changes the division of labour between the central state and the regions.

22 We do not suggest that there is only one way to attain the growth in the initial phase, and research analyzing the contrasting experiences of the home-market centred experiences of China and Brazil is called for (Arora and Gambardella 2004).

References

Albu M. (1997), 'Technological learning and innovation in industrial clusters in the south', SPRU electronic working papers, SPRU, University of Sussex.

Arora A. and Badge S. (2006), 'The Indian software industry: the human capital story', paper presented at the DRUID Conference, Copenhagen, June 2006.

Arora A. and Gambardella A. (2004), 'The globalization of the software industry: perspectives and opportunities for developed and developing countries', NBER Working Paper series. N. 10538.

Arora A. and Gambardella A. (eds.) (2005), *From Underdogs to Tigers. The rise and Growth of the Software Industry in Brazil, China, India, Ireland and Israel*, New York: Oxford University Press, pp. 7–40.

Arora A., Fosfuri A. and Gambardella A. (2002), 'Markets for technology and their implications for corporate strategy', Carnegie Mellon Heinz School Working Papers, www.heinz.cmu.edu/wpapers

Arora A. Arunachalam V. S., Asundi J. and Fernández R. (1999), 'The Indian software industry', Carnegie Mellon Heinz School Working Papers, www.heinz.cmu.edu/wpapers/author.jsp?id=ashish

——. (2001), 'The Indian software services industry: structure and prospects', *Research Policy*, 30(8): 1267–88.

Asheim B. T. and Coenen L. (2005). 'Knowledge bases and regional innovation systems: comparing Nordic clusters', *Research Policy* 34(8): 1173.

Asheim B., Coenen L. and Svensson-Henning M. (2003), 'Nordic SMEs and regional innovation systems – final report', Lund: Lund University: 95.

Asheim B., Coenen L. and Vang-Lauridsen, J. (2006), 'Face-to-face, buzz and knowledge bases: socio-spatial implications for learning, innovation and innovation policy', *Environment and Planning C.*

Athreye S. (2003), 'The Indian software industry', Carnegie Mellon Software Industry Centre. Working paper 03–4, http://www.softwarecenter.cmu.edu/CenterPapers/Indian_Software.pdf

——. (2005), 'The Indian software industry', in A. Arora and A. Gambardella (eds.), *From Underdogs to Tigers*, New York: Oxford University Press, pp. 7–40.

Barr A. and Tessler J.(1996), 'The globalization of software R&D. The search for talent', Standford Computer Software Project, http://www-scip.stanford.edu/scip/

Basant R, and Chandra P. (2006) 'Role of educational and R&D institutions in city clusters: an exploratory study of Bangalore and Pune regions in India', mimeo.

Belussi F (1996), 'Local systems, industrial districts and institutional networks: towards a new evolutionary paradigm of industrial economics?' *European Planning Studies*, 4(1): 5–26.

Belussi F., Pilotti L. and Sedita S. R. (2006)' Learning at the boundaries for industrial districts between exploitation of local resources and the exploration of global knowledge flows', paper provided by Department of Economics University of Milan Italy in its series Departmental Working Papers, no. 2006–40, http://www.economia.unimi.it.

Bitran E. (2004), 'sistema de innovación, consorcios tecnológicos y clusters dinámicos en Chile. En Foco, Santiago de Chile', *Expansiva* 16.

Breznitz D., 2005, 'The Israeli software industry', in A. Arora and A. Gambardella (eds.), *From Underdogs to Tigers*, New York: Oxford University Press, pp. 72–98.

Chaminade C. (2004), 'Social capital and innovation in SMEs: a new model of innovation? Evidence and discussion', paper presented at SPRU/CENTRIM Seminar series, October.

Chaminade C. and Vang J. (2006), 'Innovation policy for SMEs in Asia: an innovation systems perspective', in Henry Wai-Chung Yeung (ed.), *Handbook of Research on Asian Business*, Cheltenham: Edward Elgar.

——. (forthcoming), 'Globalisation of knowledge production and regional innovation policy: supporting specialized hubs in developing countries', *Research Policy*, 37(10).

Chen Y and Vang J. (2008), 'Global innovation networks and MNCs: lessons from Motorola in China', *International Journal of Business and Management Research* 1(1): 11–30.

Coe N., Hess M., Yeung H., Dicken P., Henderson J. (2004), '"Globalizing" regional development: a global production networks perspective', *Transactions of the Institute of British Gepgraphers*, 29(4): 468–84.

Coenen L. (2006), 'Faraway, so close! The changing geographies of regional innovation', PhD dissertation. Lund: Lund University.

Cohen W. and Levinthal D. (1990), 'Absorptive capacity: a new perspective on learning and innovation', *Administrative Science Quarterly*, 35: 128–52.

Cooke P. and Morgan K. (1998), *The Associational Economy: Firms, Regions and Innovation*. Oxford: Oxford University Press.

Cooke, P. and Wills D. (1999), 'Small firms, social capital and the enhancement of business performance through innovation programmes', *Small Business Economics*, 13: 219–34.

Doloreux D. (2002), 'What we should know about regional systems of innovation', *Technology in Society*, 24: 243–63.

Galli R. and Teubal M. (1997), 'Paradigmatic shifts in national innovation systems', http://ifise.unipv.it/Publications/Paradigmatic.pdf

Giuliani E. (2004), 'Laggard clusters as slow learners, emerging clusters as locus of knowledge cohesion (and exclusion): a comparative study in the wine industry', LEM Working Papers. Pisa, Laboratory of Economics and Management – San'Anna School of Advanced Studies: 38.

Giuliani E. and Bell M. (2005), 'When micro shapes the meso: learning networks in a Chilean wine cluster', *Research Policy*, 34(1): 47–68.

Giuliani E., Rabellotti R. and van Dijk M. P. (2005), *Clusters Facing Competition: The Importance of the External Linkages*, Aldershot: Ashgate.

Gu S. and Lundvall L. (2006), 'Policy learning as a key process in the transformation of China's innovation system', in B. Å. Lundvall, P. Intakumnerd P and J. Vang (eds.) *Asian Innovation Systems in Transition*, Cheltenham: Edward Elgar.

Izushi H. and Aoyama Y. (2007), 'Industry evolution and cross-sectoral skill transfers: a comparative analysis of the video game industry in Japan, the United States and the United Kingdom', *Environment and Planning*, A 38(10): 1843–861.

Kaplinsky R. (ed.) (2006), 'Asian drivers: opportunities and threats', IDS Bulletin 37.

Kaufmann A. and Tödtling F. (2002), 'How effective is innovation support for SMEs?: an analysis of the region of Upper Austria', *Technovation*, 22: 147–59.

Kumar N. and Joseph K. J. (2006), 'National innovation systems and India's IT capability: what lessons for ASEAN newcomers?' in B.-Å. Lundvall, I. Patarapong and J. Vang (eds.) *Asian Innovation Systems in Transition*, Cheltenham: Edward Elgar.

Lundvall B.-Å. (1998), 'Innovation as an interactive process: from user-producer interaction to the national system of innovation', in G. Dosi, *et al.* (eds.), *Technical Change and Economic Theory*, London: Pinter.

——. (ed.) (1992), *National Systems of Innovation. Towards a Theory of Innovation and Interactive Learning*, London: Pinter, pp. 296–317.

Lundvall B.-Å., Patarapong I. and Vang J. (eds.) (2006), *Asian Innovation Systems in Transition*, Cheltenham: Edward Elgar.

Martin R. and Sunley P. (2003), 'Deconstructing clusters: chaotic concept or policy panacea?', *Journal of Economic Geography* (3): 5–35.

Nadvi K. (1995), *Industrial Clusters and Networks: Case Studies of SME Growth and Innovation*, Vienna: UNIDO.

NASSCOM (2005), www.nasscom.org. Accessed on 20 September 2005.

NASSCOM-McKinsey (2005), 'The emerging global labor market', http://www.mckinsey.com/mgi/rp/offshoring/

Nooteboom B. (2000), 'Learning by interaction: absorptive capacity, cognitive distance and governance', *Journal of Management and Governance*, 4(1–2): 69–92.

Parthasarathy B. (2004a), 'Globalizating information technology: the domestic policy context for India software production and exports', *Interactions: An Interdisciplinary Journal of the Software Industry*, http://www.cbi.umn.edu/iteractions/parthasarathy

——. (2004b), 'India's Silicon Valley or Silicon Valley's India? Socially embedding the computer software industry in Bangalore', *International Journal of Urban and Regional Research*, 28(3): 664–85.

Parthasarathy B. and Aoyama, Y. (2007), 'From software services to R&D services: local entrepreneurship in the software industry in Bangalore, India', *Environment and Planning A*.

Pavitt K. (1984), 'Sectoral patterns of technical change: towards a taxonomy and a theory', *Research Policy*, 13: 343–73.

Peng M. W. (2002), 'Towards and institution-based view of business strategy', *Asia Pacific Journal o Management*, 19: 251–67.

Pietrobelli C. and Rabellotti R. (2004), 'Upgrading in clusters and value chains in Latin America: the role of policies', Sustainable Department Best Practices Series. New York: Inter-American Development Bank, p. 97.

Pietrobelli C. and Rabellotti R. (eds.), (2006). *Upgrading and Governance in Clusters and Value Chains in Latin America*, Washington: Inter-American Development Bank.

Porter R. (1998), 'Clusters and the new economics of competition', *Harvard Business Review*, 76(6): 77–90.

Ramachandran J. and Dikshit P. (2002), 'Motorola India Electronics Private Ltd. Case study', mimeo, 'Indian Institute of Management Bangalore. Case study', Mimeo, Indian Institute of Management Bangalore.

Sands A. (2005), 'The Irish software industry', in A. Arora and A. Gambardella (eds.), *From Underdogs to Tigers*, New York: Oxford University Press, pp. 41–71.

Saxenian A. (1994), 'Regional advantage: culture and competition in Silicon Valley and Route 128', Cambridge: Harvard University Press.

——. (2001), 'Bangalore: the Silicon Valley of Asia?' Centre for Research on Economic Development and Policy Reform. Working Paper no. 91, http://www.sims.berkeley.edu/~anno/papers/bangalore_svasia.html

Schmitz H. (1992), 'On the clustering of small firms', *IDS Bulletin – Institute of Development Studies*, (23): 64–9.

——. (2006), 'Regional systems and global chains', Paper presented at the Fifth Internationl Conference on Industrial Clustering and Regional Developments. Available online at http://www.oec.pku.edu.cn/icrd/

Tschang T. and Xue L. (2005), 'The Chinese software industry', in A. Arora and A. Gambardella (eds.), *From Underdogs to Tigers*, New York: Oxford University Press, pp. 131–70.

Unido (United Nations Industrial Development Organization) (1997), 'Progress and prospects for industrial development in least developed countries (LDSC) – towards the 21st century', Fourth LDC Ministerial Symposium: Industrial Capacity Building and Entrepreneurship Development in LDCs with particular emphasis on agro-related industries, Vienna.

Unido (United Nations Industrial Development Organization) and UUND Program (2004), *Partnerships for Small Enterprise Development*, New York, United Nations.

Van Dijk M. P. (2003), 'Government policies with respect to an information technology cluster in Bangalore, India', *The European Journal of Development Research*, 15(2): 93–108.

Vang J. and Asheim B. (2006), 'Regions, absorptive capacity and strategic coupling with high-tech TNCs: lessons from India and China', *Society, Science and Technology*, 11(1).

Vang J. and Overby M. (2006), 'Transnational communities, TNCs and development: the case of the Indian IT-services industry', in B.-Å. Lundvall, I. Patarapong and J. Vang (eds.), *Asia's Innovation Systems in Transition*, Cheltenham: Edward Elgar.

Vang J. Chaminade, C. and Coenen L. (forthcoming), 'Learning from the Bangalore experience: the role of universities in an emerging regional innovation system', in A. D'Costa and G. Parayil (eds.), *New Asian Dynamics of Science, Technology and Innovation (ST&I)*, Palgrave Macmillan Series in Technology, Globalization and Development.

Von Hippel E. (1988) *Sources of Innovation*, Oxford: Oxford University Press.

World Bank (1998), *Social Capital in Africa*, Available online at http://www.worldbank.org.

——. (2002), *Understanding and Measuring Social Capital. A Multidisciplinary Tool for Practitioners*, New York: World Bank.

Index

Entries in **bold** denote references to figures and tables.

Industrial Relations in Education
Bargaining for Change in the Education Industry

Bob Carter, *University of Leicester, UK*
Howard Stevenson, *University of Leicester, UK*

All phases of education from pre-school to post-compulsory, in virtually all parts of the world, have experienced unprecedented reform and restructuring in recent years. Restructuring has largely been driven by a global agenda that has promoted the development of human capital as the key to economic competitiveness in the global market.

February 2009: 288pp / HB: 978-0-415-41454-8: £80.00

This book is part of the series:
Routledge Studies in Employment and Work Relations in Context

The aim of the Employment and Work Relations in Context Series is to address questions relating to the evolving patterns and politics of work, employment, management and industrial relations. There is a concern to trace out the ways in which wider policy-making, especially by national governments and transnational corporations, impinges upon specific workplaces, occupations, labour markets, localities and regions. This invites attention to developments at an international level, marking out patterns of globalization, state policy and practices in the context of globalization and the impact of these processes on labour. A particular feature of the series is the consideration of forms of worker and citizen organization and mobilization. The studies address major analytical and policy issues through case study and comparative research.

This book adopts an inter-disciplinary approach drawing not only on education research but also from the fields of industrial sociology, management studies and labour process theory to locate the reform agenda within a wider picture relating to teachers, their professional identities and their experience of work. In doing so the book draws on critical perspectives that seek to challenge orthodox policy discourses relating to remodelling.

Illustrating of how education policy is shaped by discourses within the wider socio-political environment and how unionization and inter-organizational bargaining between unions exerts a decisive, but often ignored, influence on policy development at both a State and institutional level, this book is a must read for anyone researching or studying employment relations.

Routledge
Taylor & Francis Group

For more details, or to request a copy for review, please contact:

Gemma Walker, Marketing Co-ordinator
Gemma.Walker@tandf.co.uk   020 7017 6192

Managing Organizational Change in Public Services
International Issues, Challenges and Cases

Edited by Rune Todnem By, *Queen Margaret University, UK*
Calum Macleod, *Queen Margaret University, UK*

Forming part of the Understanding Organizational Change series, Managing Organizational Change in Public Services focuses on the organizational dimension of change management in public services. Combining aspects of change management theory with 'real life' practice in the form of organizational cases from different regions and sectors, this edited collection identifies and analyzes significant issues regarding the development, implementation and evaluation of public service change initiatives. Featuring contributions from leading authors in the field, this text provides an overview of organizational change management with a focus on leadership, management, and strategies for change.

March 2009: 304pp / HB: 978-0-415-46758-2: £80.00 / PB: 978-0-415-46759-9: £23.99

Looking at cases from Europe and North America, *Managing Organizational Change in Public Services* offers both a global, as well as a cross-sector analysis of this complex and challenging process. Different sectors that are examined include:

- Transport
- Health
- Education

This book offers an excellent introduction to change management and how it works within the public service organizations internationally. It will be vital reading for all those engaged with the study or practice of this dynamic subject.

Routledge
Taylor & Francis Group

For more details, or to request a copy for review, please contact:

Gemma Walker, Marketing Co-ordinator
Gemma.Walker@tandf.co.uk   020 7017 6192

Public Management and Governance

Edited by Tony Bovaird, *University of Birmingham, UK*

Elke Löffler, *Governance International, UK*

The role of government in managing society has once again become a hot topic worldwide. A more diverse society, the internet, and new expectations of citizens are challenging traditional ways of managing governments.

February 2009: 376pp / HB: 978-0-415-43042-5: £85.00 / PB: 978-0-415-43043-2: £25.99

The second edition of *Public Management and Governance* examines key issues in efficient management and good quality service in the public sector. With contributions from leading authors in the field, it goes beyond the first edition, looking at the ways in which the process of governing needs to be altered fundamentally to remain legitimate and to make the most of society's many resources.

Key themes include:

- challenges and pressures facing modern governments worldwide
- the changing role of the public sector in a 'mixed economy' of provision
- governance issues such as ethics, equalities, and citizen engagement

This new edition has an increased international scope and includes new chapters on partnership working, agency and decentralised management, process management, and HRM. Comprehensive and detailed, it is an ideal companion for undergraduate and postgraduate students of public management, public administration, government and public policy.

Routledge
Taylor & Francis Group

For more details, or to request a copy for review, please contact:

Gemma Walker, Marketing Co-ordinator
Gemma.Walker@tandf.co.uk   +44 (0) 207 017 6192

Flagship Marketing
Concepts and places
Edited by **Tony Kent**, University of the Arts, London, UK
Reva Brown, Oxford Brookes University, UK

Flagships are the physical apogee of consumerism, places where brand experiences are most defined and interactions with consumers are highly refined. This book marks the first comprehensive study of the concept of the flagship, bringing together a range of scholarly insights from the field, covering issues such as consumerism, areas of consumption and experimental marketing theory and practise. The ways in which flagship projects communicate brand values, both externally and internally, form an important part of this book, and provide new perspectives on late twentieth century commercial and cultural policy and practice.

April 2009: 224pp / HB: 978-0-415-43602-1: £75.00

Kent and Brown offer a truly interdisciplinary approach to the concept, offering a variety of perspectives on the debates surrounding flagship function and its role as a place of consumption. Chapters focus on the development of prestigious stores, hotels and arts and cultural centres, as showcases for branded experiences and products and as demonstrations of commercial and public policy. Cases and examples include The Eden Project in the UK, automotive showrooms in Germany, hotels in Dubai and Las Vegas, and Vienna's cultural quarter. Theoretical discussion explores the tensions between costs and profitability, conspicuous consumption and the sustainability of iconic forms. The book enables readers to explore the flagship concept from different perspectives, and while a marketing approach predominates, it provides a disciplinary challenge which will open up new ways of understanding the concept.

Routledge
Taylor & Francis Group

For more details, or to request a copy for review, please contact:

Gemma Walker, Marketing Co-ordinator
Gemma.Walker@tandf.co.uk   020 7017 6192